D1105111

SOCIAL ATTITUDES and PSYCHOPHYSICAL MEASUREMENT

Edited by
BERND WEGENER
Zentrum für Umfragen, Methoden und Analysen
Mannheim, West Germany

 LAWRENCE ERLBAUM ASSOCIATES, PUBLISHERS
1982   Hillsdale, New Jersey

Lawrence Erlbaum Associates, Inc., Publishers
365 Broadway
Hillsdale, New Jersey 07642

Library of Congress Cataloging in Publication Data
Main entry under title:

Social attitudes and psychophysical measurement.

   "This volume . . . is the product of a symposium on
'Social psychophysics' that took place in Mannheim,
West Germany, in October 1978''—pref.
   Includes bibliographies and indexes.
   1. Social sciences—Methodology—Congresses.
2. Attitude (Psychology)—Congresses. 3. Psychophysics—
Congresses. 4. Senses and sensation—Measurement.
I. Wegener, Bernd, fl. 1977-   [DNIM: 1. Attitude.
H61.S5896   300'.1'9   81-5421
ISBN 0-89859-083-3   AACR2

Printed in the United States of America

Contents

**PART III: DIFFERENCES AND RATIOS IN SENSORY
AND SOCIAL PSYCHOPHYSICS**

Preface

This volume on *Social Attitudes and Psychophysical Measurement* is the product of a symposium on "Social Psychophysics" that took place in Mannheim, West Germany, in October 1978[1]. The conference was held to enable psychophysicists and social science practitioners to exchange views about the possibilities of adapting psychophysical theories and methods to the measurement of attitudes. Gains, it was hoped, would be mutual.

If attitude researchers are successful in demonstrating that psychophysical ideas can be applied to the measurement of nonphysical stimulus objects, the concepts of psychophysics might become the basis for a comprehensive theory of sensation. On the other hand, the social science researcher who is aspiring to an improved quality of attitude scales could well profit by a confrontation with the standards of measurement characteristic of the research efforts in sensory psychophysics. The contributions to this volume reflect this interdisciplinary spirit and are thus of interest not only to professional psychophysicists but equally to all scholars in the social science disciplines who feel that an operational foundation for the much exploited concept of "attitude" is needed.

The unprepared reader should be cautioned, however, for he or she will be disappointed if looking for that one and embracing psychophysical theory to serve as the guide for the assessment of attitudinal phenomena. Modern psychophysics has ceased to be one monolithic body of theory, which in earlier times could be associated with the fundamental work of Gustav Fechner. Instead,

---

[1]The conference was supported by a grant from the *Deutsche Forschungsgemeinschaft* (DFG) and was hosted by the *Zentrum für Umfragen, Methoden und Analysen* (ZUMA) in Mannheim.

its corporate parts form diverse facets of paradigms, each defining psychophysics from a somewhat different perspective and at a different theoretical level. Consequently, there is not one single strategy for the application of psychophysical ideas to the realm of attitudes. In fact, for some theoretical expositions of psychophysics, applications to nonphysical stimulus situations are not feasible at all.

In spite of the heterogeneity of present-day psychophysics, the common ground for all proposed psychophysical theories is the increasing recognition that psychophysical measurement and the formulation of psychological laws are intertwined inextricably. The importance of formulating psychological laws in terms of measurement requirements might help us to understand why one unifying theory of psychophysics is not available. Psychological representations may be sought at different layers of the organism and may involve environmental mediation to a varying extent. From a formal point of view, the problem of which level to choose is a matter of the way in which formal measurement structures are to be interpreted and where to search for validating empirical regularities. In the process of real research, however, formal structures will have to be expanded in various ways in order to meet the demands of a specific field of application. Most important in this respect is that different realms of applications call for different procedures of measurement. The different techniques used—though they might be compatible with one and the same formal structure—establish different empirical theories that may yield incompatible results because they tap different internal processes or representations. Therefore, the heterogeneity of today's proposed psychophysical theories might be an unadulterated mirror of the complex stratification of sensation.

It is true that, lacking a unifying theory, we are still unable to organize these different strata. Nevertheless, it will be beneficial to abandon the simplistic idea of a single and elementary sensation continuum, which has been the goal of psychophysics. This insight is worth passing on to social science practitioners who measure attitudes by means of psychophysical methodologies. If attitudes—like impressions of the physical environment—have abundant internal representations, research directed toward a comprehensive theory of sensation will have to encompass as many regular relations as possible between these different forms of representations and behavioral variables. Conversely, when making use of current results of psychophysics within substantive research, the social science practitioner should consider the fact that any one-indicator approach may be misleading.

Accordingly, the reader of this volume is given an opportunity not only to discover the richness of conceptual schemes and theories of the advancing psychophysics, but he or she is also supplied with a considerable number of application strategies for the measurement of attitudes. In spite of the growing psychophysical literature and the vast number of publications on attitude measurement, a book that is explicitly dedicated to merging both disciplines is not available. The present volume is an attempt to compensate for this deficiency. No book having this aim can be comprehensive, but the selection of the contributions and the renowned competence of the authors may justify the claim that this volume can serve as an up-to-date introduction to the dominant themes of contemporary psychophysics and their possible applications to attitude research.

The contributions have been organized into three rather independent parts. In the first part, different *theories* of psychophysics and corresponding approaches to subjective magnitude are presented. The five chapters forming Part I—in conjunction with a taxonomical Introduction preceding it—give an outline of the various paradigms of present-day psychophysics. The second part of the volume is devoted to the social *applications* that are based on these different paradigms. Part II consists of seven chapters, some of which report on new empirical studies employing psychophysical methods, and others that treat general problems with regard to the establishment of a social psychophysics. Finally, the five chapters of Part III emphasize *controversies*, especially the ratio-difference controversy, which poses one of the central problems to modern psychophysics. Actually, the problem of whether ''ratio'' or ''difference'' measurement is the appropriate method for assessing subjective magnitude or whether both are justified—and if so, how their results interrelate—may well prove to be a touchstone for making progress toward a general theory of sensation. In this respect, particular attention should be given to the final chapter by Michael H. Birnbaum, written after the Mannheim conference and directed toward an integration of the conflicting views of ''direct'' scaling, which are voiced in this book.

The volume in its present form has a long history of preparatory activities, the conference at Mannheim being only one step along the way to publication. Most noteworthy is that nearly all contributions to the conference have been reworked and extended by the authors in order to incorporate major themes and suggestions raised during the conference. Also, the authors obliged by making cross-references to other chapters of the book wherever appropriate. Thus, this volume presents more than a collection of individual papers. Rather, it reflects the efforts of continuous fruitful exchanges between the authors and the editor, cooperating to produce as cohesive a book as possible. I wish to acknowledge the authors' support and their willingness to cooperate to this end. I am also indebted to Max Kaase, the Executive Director of the *Zentrum für Umfragen, Methoden und Analysen* (ZUMA), for his support in organizing the Mannheim symposium at ZUMA.

Bernd Wegener

INTRODUCTION

Outline of a Structural Taxonomy of Sensory and Social Psychophysics

Bernd Wegener
Zentrum für Umfragen, Methoden und Analysen (ZUMA), Mannheim, West Germany

Can the knowledge we have gained in sensory psychophysics be applied to the realm of social attitude assessment? This question comes to mind only because sensory psychophysics, in comparison with social attitude theory, is so advanced that it is likely to be profitable when ideas of the former are made use of in the latter. However, whereas sensory psychophysics is based on the study of subjective magnitude in relation to physical magnitude, *social* psychophysics is divested of any prior measured physical correlate. Accordingly, turning to sensory psychophysics, the question of where to find a prototype theory not restricted to psychophysical settings and able to incorporate *non-metric* stimulation is promptly raised. What really is desired then is a *comprehensive* theory of sensation. How close has psychophysics come to this goal?

An answer to this question can be attempted along two lines. One method is to collect all unsuperseded psychophysical theories that have been proposed during the course of the discipline and to inspect them one by one to determine whether their claim is appropriate for forming a comprehensive theory, and whether that which they claim is justified. This, however, presupposes a rather firm idea of how this comprehensive theory of sensation ought to look. Obviously, the existence of such a firm idea is equivalent to a comprehensive theory, and thus the effort of searching for possible candidates for that theory is totally beside the point.

Another way of tackling the problem is this: It can be argued that the various approaches of contemporary psychophysics all touch upon important aspects of the object under study, regardless of how narrow their views or how limited their explanatory power. Together they form a considerable body of knowledge, the synopsis of which defines what we know about sensation and sensational pro-

1

cesses. What must be done, however, is to try to relate the various pieces available and join them together to produce the sensation theory conjectured by psychophysics as it now stands. The resulting product will be "comprehensive" inasmuch as it is unifying.

In this introduction to a volume on psychophysics and its "social" applications, I intend to explore the *factual unity* of psychophysics along these lines— that is, by piecing together what psychophysics has to offer in order to obtain a tentative outline of the comprehensive theory of sensation that is expressed as the total number of paradigms psychophysicists today entertain. It should be understood that in doing so no prior distinction need be made between sensation and attitude, except that the former is stimulated by physical events whereas the latter is evoked by events within the realm of *Kulturerscheinungen* (Carnap, 1928), and the only prerequisite for these is that they be nominally distinct.

Seeking unity presupposes that the parts from which unity is to emerge are such as to tolerate their combination or subsumption. In particular, the comparison of theories calls for metatheories, or ultimately for one theory, and this metatheory will be the criterion by which individual theories are accepted as contributing to the unifying theory or not. The metatheory cannot be substantive (psychophysical) in nature because this would merely iterate the demand for a still broader metatheory. Rather, the metatheory should provide a formal scheme by which the structures of the respective individual theories may be analyzed in order to decide whether there are relations of subsumption with regard to pairs of individual theories, or whether two theories may not be related at all, consequently forming two separate "paradigms."

A substantial part of this introduction, therefore, must be devoted to reflections about the choice of the appropriate metatheory. A structural taxonomy of psychophysics based on this metatheory is outlined, and an attempt is made to specify the relations between sensory and social psychophysics within the framework of this taxonomy. The taxonomy is "structural" insofar as only the relations between *formal* properties of the individual psychophysical theories are considered; no attempt is made to evaluate the claims of empirical validity attached to these theories. The other aim of this introduction is to draw attention to the diverse approaches to psychophysics that are dealt with in this volume. It should be noted that this intention restricts the scope of the taxonomic endeavor to the extent that basic psychophysical theories not represented in this book are here treated in a subsidiary way only. However, this is true only with respect to the research centering around signal detectability. As psychophysics is sometimes confused with psychophysiology, it might also be noted that the latter is excluded from all considerations.

I procede first of all (Section 1) by indicating the different "paradigms" of psychophysics with which we concern ourselves. Following that (Section 2), the metatheoretical frame of reference for logically structuring theories of psychophysics is outlined. The underlying concept for this "theory of theories" is that a theory should be perceived as a hierarchy of sets of models for a formal structure, each set having characteristic properties. For each level within this hierarchical scheme, examples are given in the sequel: In Section 3, the most general model for a theory of psychophysics (its *frame*) is outlined; Section 4 adds methods for application to this general model (yielding a *core* for a theory of psychophysics); following that, in Section 5, established empirical laws of psychophysics are incorporated into the hierarchy of sets (giving *expanded cores*); and in Section 6, several strategies of application along with additional laws to which these applications relate are discussed.

1. FOUR PARADIGMS

One hundred and twenty years of psychophysical research have produced at least four distinct paradigms with regard to the problem of measuring sensation and of interrelating sensational and nonsensational variables.

The initial paradigm was established by Gustav Theodor Fechner (1860, 1877), and it dominated psychophysical reasoning for at least three quarters of a century. The main thrust of the *Fechnerian paradigm* comes from the assumption that discriminatory behavior is lawfully related to subjective experience such that, whenever two pairs of stimuli are equidiscriminable to a person, the corresponding pairs of subjective values may be represented by pairs of numbers that have equal differences. Thus, sensation is inferentially defined by judgments about distinctiveness of stimuli. Thereby, consciousness of sensational quanta need not be considered at all. The phenomenological content may in fact be assumed to be something inaccessible and private.

The second paradigm is more common sensual in nature, arguing that people know what they feel and, consequently, can give meaningful reports about subjective states of mind. Quantification of sensation, therefore, can and should employ methods in which subjects themselves give quantifying judgments that may be taken as genuine *Protokollsätze* of real phenomena. Among proponents of this *judgmental approach,* however, there is continuing disagreement about which mode of judgment should be used and which gives the correct representation of the inner map. Followers of S. S. Stevens (1975) are convinced that only direct magnitude estimation with numerals (or extensive reaction modalities) that have all the properties of real numbers will give the correct account, whereas others, being even more strongly committed to everyday judgments, hold that the most natural way we report on strength of sensation is to choose verbal categories from an ordered set.

A third position has been proposed only recently (Krantz, 1972; Shepard, 1978). Its particular characteristic is that sensation is perceived as being basically relational in nature. Stimuli are not mapped into the subjective domain one by one, but by operations of comparison involving two stimuli at a time, thus evoking a sensation "ratio." This theory has been given the name *"relation theory,"* but it is interesting to note that terming it "Plato's theory" would have been equally appropriate. It was Plato's belief that numbers (except primes) are generated by a principle he termed the "underterminate duality" of magnitude (αόριστος δυάς), a point of view opposed by Aristotle (1978, A 987 b) who gave priority to the principle of the ἕν. Modern relation theory is the attempto to logically reconstruct Plato's idea and, accordingly, it has been presented in the form of a completely axiomized theory (Krantz, 1972). As such, it is open to many empirical interpretations but its main concern so far has been "ratio" judgments of pairs of stimuli, primarily in cross-modality matching, the representation of which is empirically constrained by order relations between pairs of responses.

In all three paradigms mentioned thus far, it should be apparent that the word "sensation" is attributed to a scale on the basis of mere conviction. Apart from the philosophical dispute over "realism vs. instrumentalism," a continuing problem in psychophysics is that there are many ways of defining what a sensation is and how it can be measured. We have no evidence for rejecting one suggestion in favor of another, given that each is consistent within itself. Hence, we do not know what a sensation continuum is.

It seems, however, that the most recent developments in psychophysics tacitly tend towards a new position, a forth paradigm in which a definition for a sensation scale is not fixed in advance, but rather in which formal criteria are established to provide guidelines for a decision on such a definition. Several formulations of criteria have been suggested (e.g., Birnbaum, 1978, and Chapter 17 this volume; Birnbaum & Veit, 1974; Falmagne, 1974; Shepard, 1978). All have in common their author's conviction that it would be unfortunate to have several scales of sensation depending on the number of tasks, methods, or paradigms provided. Instead, the appealing feature is the ability to merge all different scales into one scale, which will then gain the status of a valid sensation scale.

Clearly, a primary aspect of this position is economy of explanatory concepts. In this respect it is harmonious with current views in the philosophy of science, according to which the guiding principle in scientific concept formation is richness of empirical content and predictive power. Therefore, a theory of sensation that establishes a task-independent scale will have a "progressive" quality in comparison with others, and may even exert falsifying pressure (Lakatós, 1970).

With the prospect of the development of a framework for merging scales ahead, the real problem is, of course, determining how the convergence of scales is to be accomplished if, indeed, it can be accomplished at all. Obviously, it will not do merely to seek sophisticated transformation schemes by which scales of different types can be related (see, for instance, Chapters 14, 15, and 16, this volume) because interscale transformations do not tell us to which *basic* scales the others should be adapted to. Thus, there is a growing number of studies that are concerned with isolating fundamental *cognitive operations* which must be ascribed to a person when he or she is giving sensational reports with different experimental methods and vis-à-vis one-, two-, or even four-stimulus situations (see Chapters 4, 5, and 17, this volume). Thereby, it is hoped that a subjective scale may be identified to which others are relative. It should be noted that this fourth paradigm adds the study of sensational abilities and processes to the traditional scaling approach of psychophysics (as was demanded by Savage [1970] and is also demanded by Marks, Chapter 1, this volume).

It is claimed that these four approaches to sensation—*Fechner's approach,* the *judgmental approach,* the *relational approach,* and the *cognitive operations approach*—are distinct with regard to basic assumptions made and, because of this distinctiveness, they are called "paradigms" (a term on which some light is shed later). Of course any attempt to compartmentalize a science will attract the reproach of gerrymandering. However, if we are successful in showing that the four paradigms are relatable by some super-paradigmatic standard such that they form a research program of competing theories (Lakatós, 1970), then the taxonomy suggested will have gained systematic rather than merely ad hoc value.

In the next section, I discuss the general framework within which a comparison of psychophysical theories may be pursued. The schemes to be introduced are elaborated on only insofar as their explication is needed for an informal evaluation of the four paradigms. The basic ideas of the metatheory have been formulated by J. N. Sneed (1971), and the reader should turn to his book for a detailed presentation (cf. also Stegmüller, 1973; Wegener, 1977).

2. PARADIGMS AND THE NONSTATEMENT VIEW OF THEORIES

2.1. The Problem of Theoretical Terms

"Sensation" is an entity not directly observable. A priori we know only of its quantity, that is, that it must have a degree. Everything else is left to experience (Kant, 1956, B 218). Because it is unobservable, however, sensation maintains the status of a theoretical term when subjected to empirical investigation.

Carnap (1954) thought that theoretical concepts should be defined within a theoretical language and that terms so defined could be related to empirical phenomena by rules of correspondence connecting the theoretical language with a language of observables. In application, however, this proposal amounts to a circularity. Putnam (1962) writes: "A theoretical term, properly so-called, is one which comes from a *theory* [p. 243]." Thus, identical terms may be theoretical in one context and nontheoretical in another. But defining terms as theoretical implies that the theory in relation to which they are theoretical is known—a circular assumption because this would have to involve the theoretical terms already defined as such.

This logical difficulty is also encountered if Carnap's two-language approach is abandoned. For suppose that a theory is completely formalized and is mathematical in structure, and suppose, further, that S is this formal structure and a is the set of its possible applications such that

$$a \text{ is an S} \tag{1}$$

describes the *empirical claim* of the theory exhaustively. In order to obtain numbers for a theoretical function t of S, we need to validate sentences of the form "t_i is an instance of t." It is, however, uncertain whether any values found are values of t_i described by a_i unless we have at least one other application of S, "a_j is an S," say, the truth of which we are convinced and from which the form of the t-function is known. The same is true, of course, for a_j, demanding an a_k and so on ad infinitum.

A solution to this *problem of theoretical terms* has been proposed by Ramsey (1965) who suggested the elimination of theoretical terms from a theory all together. Suppose $t_1, \ldots, t_n \in \bar{T}$ is the set of the theoretical predicates of a theory, and $o_1, \ldots, o_n \in \bar{O}$ the set of all observable predicates of this theory, such that $\langle \bar{T}, \bar{O} \rangle$ describes the complete empirical claim of the theory. It is possible then to eliminate all t-predicates from the expression by replacing them by variables $v_1, \ldots, v_n \in \bar{V}$ not part of the theoretical claim of the theory before, and to introduce these by n ordered existential quantifiers for predicates. If the theoretical claim of a theory is expressed as $\langle \bar{T}, \bar{O} \rangle$, the t-predicates have meaning within ordinary language (as, for instance, a "sensation value"), and they are "obscure" because this is so. In an empirical claim of a theory expressed as $\langle \bar{V}, \bar{O} \rangle$, however, t-predicates are replaced by predicates $v_1, \ldots, v_n$ which have meaning only within the structural framework of the theory. Thereby "obscure" surplus meanings characteristic for elements of $\bar{T}$ are extinguished. Thus, the problem of theoretical terms disappears because the theoretical terms disappear. The deductive power of the original theory is not infringed on by this manipulation.

The formal treatment Ramsey has given the problem, however, is only valid for theories axiomized in the first-order predicate calculus. Factual expositions of theories generally take the form of informally introduced set-theoretical systems in which formal structures are expressed by set-theoretical predicates in order to apply to classes of individuals and classes of functions. It is possible to generalize Ramsey's idea to these situations if, in addition to the restricting existential quantifiers, the set of predicates to which these existential quantifiers apply are defined *as expansions of other sets of predicates of a theory* (Sneed, 1971, Chap. 3). Thereby a strong connection of the v-predicates to the general relational framework of a theory is established.

Let S be the formal-mathematical structure of a theory and a a set of possible *partial* models for S, that is, models that may be extended in such a way as to become possible models for S. If we regard a as a description of observables, then

$$(\exists x) \ (x \text{ is an } E_a \wedge x \text{ is an } S) \tag{2}$$

may express that the observable facts a can be "filled out" to produce a possible model for S, E_a being short for "an extension for a." Form 2 is another way of writing 1 if one interprets the set of extending predicates as descriptions of theoretical functions of the theory: These t-functions, when combined with a, will yield a possible model for S.

A theory of sensation, then, like any other theory involving nonobservables, has to provide for the distinction between descriptors of observable facts and theoretical functions such that a formal structure is satisfied by the combination of both. With regard to physical theories, 2 is the basic outset for the development of Sneed's "theory of theories." I propose that this concept may be applied to psychophysical theories as well. Before this is attempted, however, let us take a look at the general features of the metatheory.

2.2. The Integral Empirical Claim of a Theory

In order to be appropriate for the ways in which measured values of theoretical functions are used in factual expositions of theories, 2 has to be further specified. Two classes of specifications are proposed here. The first (to be described in this subsection) is relevant when 2 is to apply to different situations and contexts with respect to which a theory is ascribed validity; the second (Subsection 2.3) considers the concept of the dynamic development a theory might undergo when it is applied and tested in real research. With regard to both features only a very brief account is provided here.

The empirical claim of a theory expressed in the form 2 is a very specialized conjecture because it applies only to elements of a. That is, there is just one universal application. Almost all theories, however, are designed for several different intended applications. Classical particle mechanics is an example, because it is to apply not only to stellar bodies but also to tides, or the pendulum. A psychophysical theory designed for magnitude estimation *and* difference measurement would be another example. The implication of this for 2 is that the empirical claim of a theory will have to be formulated for *sets* of partial possible models, involving *sets* of theoretical functions, and also *sets* of different formal structures.

Moreover, inasmuch as there are different intended applications for a theory, all of these have to be "connected" by certain *constraints* (Sneed, 1971, p. 66) such that it will be obvious that the different applications deserve to be subsumed under one and the same theory. These constraints introduce relations that are to hold among the values of theoretical functions employed in different applications of the theory. Thus, constraints may take the form of consistency requirements with regard to different methods and objects of measurement such that the different ways of measuring do not violate specified uniqueness conditions for the functions of the theory.

Finally, it would be advisable to provide for special *laws* with regard to individual sets of intended applications. Each of these laws would define certain restrictions with regard to the formal structure S that is common to all intended applications. If laws are to be accountable to a specific class of applications, there will also be a need for special constraints to insure that individuals of this class all yield the same values with regard to the laws involved.

Th empirical claim of a theory of form 2 then has to be expanded to consider three distinctive criteria: It has to be designed for several different sets of applications; constraints must be provided; and, with regard to different intended applications, there may be additional laws and special constraints with respect to all applications for these laws.

Considering these criteria, the empirical claim of form 2 becomes:

$$\exists\ \bar{x}\ \{\bar{x}E\bar{a} \wedge \bar{x} \subseteq \bar{S} \wedge C(\bar{x},R,\rho)\ \wedge\ \exists\ \bar{x}_1\ [\bar{x}_1 \subseteq \bar{x} \wedge \bar{x}_1 E\bar{a}_1 \wedge \bar{x}_1 \subseteq \bar{S}_1 \wedge C(\bar{x}_1,R_1,\rho_1)]$$

$$\vdots \tag{3}$$

$$\wedge\ \exists\ \bar{x}_n\ [\bar{x}_n \subseteq \bar{x} \wedge \bar{x}_n E\bar{a}_n \wedge \bar{x}_n \subseteq \bar{S}_n \wedge C(\bar{x}_n,R_n,\rho_n)]\}.$$

We call 3 the *integral empirical claim of a theory*. $\bar{x}E\bar{a}$ is supposed to symbolize that $\bar{x}$ is an extension of $\bar{a}$, E being an operator for extending sets. $\bar{x} \subseteq \bar{S}$ expresses that $\bar{x}$ is an instance of the set of formal structures $\bar{S}$, and $C(\bar{x},R,\rho)$ specifies constraints with regard to $\bar{x}$, R being a set of empirical relations and ρ their representation in the numerical relational structure. Intuitively, the integral empirical claim may be expressed as follows: With regard to a theory T having the structure $\bar{S}$ there exist sets of theoretical functions that are constrained by sets of relations $\langle R_i, \rho_i \rangle$ and that can extend elements of sets $\bar{a}_1$ to $\bar{a}_n$ of $\bar{a}$ such that these elements become instances of S_1 to S_n, which represent restrictions of $\bar{S}$ (or of each other). Form 3 thus expresses the complete claim of a theory as *one unique and elementary statement*.

2.3. Frames, Cores, Expanded Cores

The integral empirical claim of a theory is not the theory itself, however. This is so for two reasons. First, 3 can be expressed in many ways—different sets of logically equivalent axioms may be constructed, each of which will yield a predicate "is an $\bar{S}$" of identical extension. The theory T, which subsumes all of the different expressions of 3, is obviously something apart from these expressions. Rather, we are invited to think of theories as being represented by *propositions* for which there are multitudes of linguistic or formal-mathematical expressions. The second reason for distinguishing between a theory and its integral empirical claim is pragmatic in nature. If 3 were to be the theory itself, then every modification of 3 would necessarily exterminate the theory. Modifications of the claim of a theory, in fact, are required all the time. A theory is always confronted with counterevidence, and additional laws have to be introduced in order to account for new facts and additional applications. In these instances, it would be extremely inconvenient to identify a theory with expressions of form 3. Instead, a theory should be conceptualized as something stable even though its empirical conjectures represented by claims of form 3 will vary continuously during the dynamic development of the theory.

If a theory is not identical with its claim, what is a proper explication of a theory? One plausible suggestion is that a theory be identified with the formal-mathematical structure $\bar{S}$, provided that $\bar{S}$ can be made independent of the choice of the logically equivalent axiomatic systems expressing $\bar{S}$. That is, the propositional content of $\bar{S}$ is the definition of a theory. One way of dealing with propositions is to list the set of linguistic inscriptions appropriate to them. With regard to formal structures of theories this amounts to saying that a *formal structure may be expressed by the set or sets of models by which it is satisfied.* This is the fundamental aspect of what Sneed calls the *nonstatement view* of theories. It is opposed to the traditional statement view, because a theory no longer is expressible as a statement but as the enumeration of sets of models for $\bar{S}$[1].

If a theory is expressed as a set of models M (satisfying an $\bar{S}$) it must exhibit a number of distinctions paralleling those we have introduced in 3. First of all, there are, beside M, those models that consist only of possible observables and nontheoretical functions. These models are *partial possible models,* designated as *PP. PP* are partial possible models because they may be extended by theoretical functions such as to form *possible models* of a given formal structure and we represent these by P. For a complete description of both classes of models, some function r is also needed to make possible the distinction between theoretical and nontheoretical functions with regard to a theory. r is a function mapping P into *PP:* For each possible model there is one partial possible model that is generated if the theoretical functions are "left aside."

Using this notation, the *frame* F for a theory may be formulated as $\langle P, PP, r, M \rangle$; $M \subseteq P$ and $PP \subseteq P$ (Sneed, 1971, p. 166). This formulation displays the set-theoretical structure of a frame for a theory; suggestions for further definitions of the explicit nature of the involved sets are omitted here (readers interested in the details should consult Sneed, 1971, pp. 167ff.). Instead, a core for a theory is defined.

---

[1] It should be noted that, within a philosophy of science context, the pitfalls of Platonism need not be considered. The set of appropriate satisfying models for a formal-mathematical structure will be specified by the scientific community and those who propose and try to validate a theory. Therefore the problem of extension with regard to an $\bar{S}$ is settled within the factual process of the development of a science.

Corresponding to the empirical claim of a theory of form 3, we need also to consider constraints on P, which provide that theoretical functions yield identical values within different contexts of application. If we call the set of these constraints C, then considering the potential set of all possible models, C is such that a subset is selected for which the constraints hold and this subset forms P. With this set of constraints added, the frame for a theory is extended and becomes $\langle P, PP, r, M, C \rangle$. This is called a *core* H *for a theory* (Sneed, 1971, p. 171). It is evident, moreover, that the core for a theory is the core for an empirical theory only if it can potentially be applied to empirical instances (or intended applications), the set of which is I. I, of course, should be a subset of PP, and a *theory* is defined then as T = $\langle$H, $I\rangle$ if H is a core for a theory and $I \subseteq PP$. However, characteristics of different intended applications are likely to call for different *laws* within one and the same theory. Taking these into account will yield an *expanded core* E *for a theory* consisting of the core H and sets of laws L. In order to be applicable to different sets of intended applications, special constraints C_L with regard to those partial possible models for which the laws L are to apply must be included in the expanded core along with a specific binary relation α, which assigns members of PP to laws in L. Omitting again the apparatus of formal definitions for L, C_L and α, the expanded core for a theory may be expressed as E=$\langle P, PP, r, M, C, L, C_L, \alpha \rangle$. Accordingly, an *applied core for a theory* can be written as $T_E = \langle$E, $I\rangle$. T_E may also be called an *expanded theory* (Sneed, 1971, pp. 178ff.).

Defining an expanded theory as consisting of a frame, a core, its expansions, and realms of intended applications has three advantages over conceptions within the traditional "statement" view. *First,* a theory formulated as a set-theoretical calculus is independent of contingent linguistic and axiomatic particularities, which do not affect the propositional content of its formal-mathematical structure. *Second,* a theory T_E is not deprived of its identity every time it is applied to new instances because there is possibly a core of T_E that is unaffected by changing applications and revisions of laws. The *third* advantage of a theory formalized in terms of the nonstatement view focuses on the problem of theory comparison and, conversely, on the incommensurability of "paradigms." Why this is so is shown next.

2.4. Reducing Theories

Theories, if they are unique statements as in 3, are systems of sentences. As such they are faced with the *problem of coherence*. As Quine has stressed repeatedly, observational sentences, like theoretical sentences, face the tribunal of observation not singly but in a body (Quine, 1959, p. xii). That is to say, a sentence, be it theoretical or observational, is either logically coherent with respect to the body of sentences available for a scientific community, which implies that the sentence "belongs" to this very system of sentences, or it is contradictory to the system.

In the latter case it is a matter of decision as to whether we tolerate the contradictory sentence as a description of an "anomaly" that is not part of the system, or whether we attempt to "make drastic enough adjustments elsewhere in the system" (Quine, 1953, p. 43) in order to integrate the originally contradictory sentence into a new coherent body. Consequently, a system of sentences subjected to "drastic enough adjustments elsewhere in the system" such that otherwise contradictory elements may be incorporated into the revised system, will not be deducible from the original system of sentences. Both constitute two different worlds with regard to the empirical phenomena they describe. In the terminology preferred by Kuhn (1970), in this situation we are confronted with two different *paradigms* that form incommensurable entities.

This dilemma is characteristic for the statement conception of theories but may be circumvented if theories are reinterpreted as enumerations of sets of models, as in Sneed's nonstatement theory. In a theory reconstructed in nonstatement terminology, coherence need not be given across all elements of that theory: Different sets of laws, for instance, that must not be compatible with each other may be part of two different *expanded* cores, and both expanded cores may nonetheless form elements of one and the same theory if an identical core H is basic to both expanded cores. Thus, two paradigms that are incommensurable from a "statement" perspective could turn out to be two commensurable parts of a common theory T of which they are extensions if a nonstatement-view analysis is supported. For two separate paradigms (of psychophysics, say) to be subsumable under one set-theoretical structure, it is mandatory that both may be traced back or reduced to a *common core*. Only if this reduction is unsuccessful will both paradigms maintain self-reliancy, and no "comprehensive" theory covering both can be established.

It should also be noted that, implicit to the idea of a theory reduction, methodological norms are satisfied. Any expanded theory T_E, which is reducible to another expanded theory $T_{E'}$, is a superseded theory with regard to $T_{E'}$. Lakatós' (1970) notion of a falsifying problem shift within a "progressive" research program is replaced in set-theoretical terms by the idea of the efficiency of a theory with regard to its partial possible models: A theory $T_{E'}$ covering a larger set of partial possible models $PP_{E'}$ than another theory T_E falsifies T_E if $I_E \subseteq I_{E'}$.

At least three disjunctive conditions must be fulfilled if two theories are to be reducible to another; if one or more of these is not satisfied, the two theories form incommensurable paradigms:

1. Both theories should be expansions of the identical core H, and if $E(H)_i$ and $E(H)_j$ are two expanded cores, one must be a restriction of the other or both are of identical extension: $PP_{E_i} \subseteq PP_{E_j} \bigvee PP_{E_j} \subseteq PP_{E_i}$.

2. With regard to two expansions $E(H)_i$ and $E(H)_j$ having different realms of intended applications, the following relation should hold: $I_i \subseteq I_j \bigvee I_j \subseteq I_i$. Note that there is a decision involved with regard to this requirement. Suppose that I_0 is the set of intended applications for which a theory T_E has originally

been designed by some researcher or group of scientists (this is what Kuhn calls the *paradigm examples* for a theory [Kuhn, 1970, pp. 43ff. and 187ff.]). The claim of somebody else that T_E be valid also for $I_0 + I_n$ may be accepted or not: There can be no rational criterion for specifying the extension of a set of appropriate intended applications for a theory. The mere "family resemblence" between the members of I_0 and I_n provides only a vague criterion for inclusion because we have no a priori characterization of I such that I_0, $I_n \in I$ (cf. Wittgenstein, 1953, § 67).

3. If two expanded theories are *not* expansions of one and the same core H such that we have $E(H)_i$ and $E(H')_j$, then both expanded theories may be compared only if one is reducible to the other. This can mean one of two things: (a) reducing two expanded theories to each other such that $E(H)_i \subseteq E(H')_j \bigvee E(H')_j \subseteq E(H)_i$ may be possible because $H \subseteq H' \bigvee H' \subseteq H$. In the case of two different cores, one is included in the other, that is, there is a set of axioms common to both; (b) reducibility may also be assumed with regard to the expanded cores of the two theories involved, regardless of whether or not their respective (nonexpanded) cores are reducible to each other. In this case, all that need be given is $PP_{E(H)_I} \subseteq PP_{E(H')_j} \bigvee PP_{E(H)'_j} \subseteq PP_{E(H)_i}$.

The exact form of the reduction relations for these three kinds of entailment of sets involves a mapping relation between the partial possible models of theories and is not dealt with here (see Sneed, 1971, pp. 221ff.). It should be evident, however, that there are several ways of relating theories from a nonstatement perspective, which might otherwise be thought of as paradigms.

With regard to psychophysics and the question of whether or not it is possible to construct a "comprehensive" theory of sensation from the different theoretical proposals and applications of psychophysical theories, our prime interest must be, first of all, to identify a frame F and a core H for a theory of psychophysics. Both of these should be basic to a set of expanded cores $\{E_1, \ldots, E_n\}$, each member of which, in turn, could be basic to a set of applied cores (or expanded theories), $\{T_{E_i 1}, \ldots, T_{E_i m}\}$ or $\{\langle E_i, I_1 \rangle, \ldots, \langle E_i, I_m \rangle\}$. "Is basic to" is to mean that a relation of reduction is given.

Turning to psychophysics, I now begin by looking for a candidate for a *frame*.

3. A FRAME FOR A THEORY OF PSYCHOPHYSICS

3.1. Four Problems of Theory Construction

From a formal point of view, a theory of psychophysics has to cope with at least four distinct problems:

1. It must provide a homomorphism ψ by which an empirical relational structure can be mapped into the realm of positive real numbers, Re^+, on the premises that specified axioms are satisfied empirically.
2. A theory of psychophysics has to determine a set of numerical procedures for constructing representations that are appropriate for the solution found for problem 1.
3. The theory must include as many special laws, involving ψ, as possible in order that the scale may profitably be called a scale for "sensation."
4. A theory of psychophysics should be able to tolerate different intended applications or interpretations. That is, its formal structure should be general enough to apply to different experimental settings, tasks, and sets of stimuli.

Within the framework of the nonstatement view of theories, the four problems can easily be recognized: Solving the representation problem 1 means finding a *frame* for a theory, $F = \langle PP, P, r, M \rangle$. Adding sets of constraints C to the frame yields a *core* for that theory, $H = \langle PP, P, r, M, C \rangle$; constraints are given by specific scaling procedures for ψ, which are consistent with each other. Thus, defining a core for a theory is to solve problem 2. If special laws, theoretical or nontheoretical, are added to the core we have an *expanded core*, $E_T = \langle H, L, C_L, \alpha \rangle$, and specifying laws (along with special constraints and a mapping function α) is equivalent to solving problem 3. Finally, the expanded theory is applied to different sets of partial possible models, $I \subseteq PP$, and inasmuch as this is possible, problem 4 is solved.

3.2. Requirements for a Frame

The frame for a theory of psychophysics is a measurement structure yielding a representation ψ. The measurement structure must be general enough to allow for restrictions. One of these restrictions will have to distinguish sensory psychophysics from social psychophysics. That is, the frame we are seeking must result in a representation ψ regardless of the nature of stimuli. This requirement excludes candidates for a frame in which a physical continuum S^2 or a class of physical continua are necessary for interpretation.

In order to select a measurement structure of ψ that may account for sensory and nonsensory psychophysics, a fundamental communality of both component disciplines must be emphazised. Sensory psychophysics is concerned with two functional relationships:

---

[2]In order to be comparable to the original presentations of the theories of psychophysics, which are dealt with in the following, the notations used there are also used in this paper. Therefore, unless there is an obvious relationship, the notations have no carry-over meaning from one section to another except when explicitly stated.

$$\psi = f_1(S), \tag{4}$$

$$R = f_2(\psi), \tag{5}$$

R being a scale of externally recordable responses. Empirically, only

$$R = f_3(S) = f_2\{f_1(S)\} \tag{6}$$

is given, and ψ does not explicitly appear in this equation, nor are f_1 and f_2 empirically assessable. The overall relation, f_3, is observable, but only if, for instance, the judgment function f_2 is arbitrarily fixed will we have gained access to ψ.

Stevens assumed f_2 to be a power function, and because the overall relation can be approximated by a power function, the psychophysical relation yielding ψ had to be a power function, too. However, f_2 can be equally well assumed to be, for instance, an exponential function, in which case the psychophysical relation, f_1, is logarithmic. As has been noted by a number of commentators, *both* assumptions are consistent with cross-modality matching theory (e.g., Ekman, 1964; Luce & Galanter, 1963; Shepard, 1978; Treisman, 1963). In a cross-modality experiment, a sensation of one modality, ψ, is "matched" against the sensation of another modality, ψ'; because

$$\psi = f_1(S),$$

$$\psi' = f_1'(S'), \tag{7}$$

the observable relations are

$$S = f(S') = f_1^{-1}\{f_1'(S')\},$$

$$S' = f^{-1}(S) = f_1'^{-1}\{f_1(S)\}. \tag{8}$$

Because f can be approximated by a power function for empirical data, the input functions, f_1 and f_1', can be either *both* power or *both* logarithmic functions (cf. Subsection 5.1). It must be conceded, therefore, that psychophysics has to cope with an indeterminacy concerning the measurement of subjective values (Shepard, 1978). The indeterminacy characteristic for sensory *as well as* social psychophysics is expressed as Eq. 5 because the introduction of input functions (f_1 or f_1') is an *additional restriction* for situations in which stimuli have the structure of Re^+. From this, it follows that the fundamental representation problem of psychophysics is concerned with finding a subjective scale ψ by construction of a *response scale* ρ. The properties of ρ will thus restrict the set of functions $\{f_2\}$ of Eq. 5 to those transformation functions that are permissible with regard to ρ. Specifying a frame for a theory of psychophysics, therefore, involves a decision as to what level of measurement a response scale should have and thus predetermines the possible form of judgment functions.

There is another requirement that may guide us in the selection of an appropriate structure for a frame. In Eqs. 4 through 8 we have distinguished relationships between S, R, and ψ on the basis of the traditional psychophysical supposition that a single stimulus intensity S_i evokes an inner subjective magnitude ψ_i which in turn, via a judgment function, gives rise to a specific response R_i. It is obvious that this "mapping" model is unable to represent the fundamental relativity of sensational experiences as well as the explicit relativity of comparison tasks. It seems appropriate, therefore, to constitute the frame for the psychophysical theory by choosing a representational structure that can account for an ordering on a Cartesian product of responses.

This argument points to the relation-theory paradigm, mentioned in Section 1. Proponents of relation theory have emphasized several advantages that relation theory has in contrast to the traditional mapping theory. The most obvious advantage seems to be that it is difficult to imagine situations in which a stimulus is perceived in total isolation. The term "absolute judgment" is only of historical value and was coined to distinguish judgmental methods from procedures based on variability (Wever & Zener, 1928) but not to exclude the relatedness that is fundamental to all experiences.

3.3. The Structure of the Frame

An axiomatic treatment of relation theory has been proposed by Krantz (1972) and Krantz, Luce, Suppes, and Tversky (1971, pp. 164–167). In its most general form it specifies a binary relation, denoted $\gtrsim$, which may be interpreted as an order relation of pairs according to their "ratio," if the subject is instructed to form "ratios." The representation derived is

$$a_i b_i \gtrsim u_j v_j \ \text{ iff } f_i(a_i)/f_i(b_i) \geq f_j(u_j)/f_j(v_j), \tag{9}$$

where i and j indicate two different response modalities of responses a_i, b_i and u_j, v_j respectively. Thus, 9 is a general representation that may also account for direct or indirect cross-modality matching tasks. If we define $f_i = \exp f_i^-$, for i and j respectively, the ratio representation is converted into a difference representation:

$$a_i b_i \gtrsim u_j v_j \ \text{ iff } f_i^- (a_i) - f_i^- (b_i) \geq f_j^- (u_j) - f_j^- (v_j). \tag{10}$$

The system describing either representation is made up of five axioms that form an *extended algebraic-difference structure* that Krantz et al. (1971) term a cross-modality ordering structure: If $A_1, \ldots, A_m$ are nonempty sets and $\gtrsim$ is a binary relation on $\cup_{i=1}^{m} A_i \times A_i$ the following axioms should hold:

A1. $\gtrsim$ is a *weak order*.
A2. If $a_i b_i \gtrsim u_j v_j$, then $v_j u_j \gtrsim b_i a_i$ (*reversability*).
A3. If $a_i b_i \gtrsim u_j v_j \wedge b_i c_i \gtrsim v_j w_j$, then $a_i c_i \gtrsim u_j w_j$ (*monotonicity*).
A4. *Solvability*.
A5. *Archimedian* axiom.

It is proposed here that this set of axioms is the frame F for a theory of psychophysics and that the concurrent psychophysical "paradigms" are expansions of this frame. In a nonstatement terminology, a_i, b_i, c_i, ... , and $a_i b_i$, $a_i c_i$, ... are partial possible models of the theory for which F is a frame. Those partial possible models satisfying A1–A5 are possible models because functions f_i or f_i^- may be constructed for them, i.e., either $\gtrsim$ is represented by the numerical ordering of ratios of scale values $f_i(a_i)$, or $\gtrsim$ is represented by the numerical ordering of differences of scale values $f_i^-(a_i)$. It has been shown that 9 yields a logarithmic interval scale and 10 an interval scale (cf. Krantz et al., 1971, pp. 152ff.).

4.   A CORE FOR A THEORY
OF PSYCHOPHYSICS

4.1. Pair-Estimation, Magnitude Estimation, and Cross-Modality Matching

If the frame is to be applied within a theory, the first requirement is that its formal structure produces comparable values within different systems of applications. In psychophysics this requirement takes the form of consistency requirements between different psychophysical methods of data assessment. Therefore, in order to derive a *core* H for a theory of psychophysics, constraints with regard to the set of possible models *P* must be introduced to secure consistency between different scaling procedures, all of which are appropriate for the measurement structure of the frame.

Following Krantz's exposition of relation theory we are, first of all, concerned with three methods of scaling; all three are "ratio methods," namely, pair-estimation, magnitude estimation, and cross-modality matching. As is argued in the section to follow, psychophysical methods due to other "paradigms" are in need of additional constraints if their results are to be consistent with the frame A1–A5.

For *pair-estimation,* subjects are instructed to form numerical "ratios" with regard to stimulus pairs and with respect to an attribute defining a certain sensory or nonmetric continuum. Thus, pair-estimation yields responses in the set Re^+ of positive real numbers. Strictly speaking, the responses are not numbers but learned names. However, in data analyses these names for numbers are treated as numbers, and the particular representation problem is solved when a homomorphism is found that maps elements of the set of number responses into elements of Re^+. It has been demonstrated (Krantz, 1972) that this homomorphism exists if, in conjunction with A1–A5, a pair-estimation function P_i is introduced satisfying the following two conditions: (I) $P_i(a_i,b_i) \geq P_j(u_j,v_j)$ iff $a_i b_i \gtrsim u_j v_j$; (II) $P_L(a_L,b_L) \cdot P_L(b_L,c_L) = P_L(a_L,c_L)$. Whereas I is an assumption that is obvious for the ordering $\gtrsim$ on $A_i \times A_i$ if it is to be preserved for P_i in Re^+, condition II needs some explication. In order to combine the pair-estimation function with the ordering $\gtrsim$, we must specify how numbers are used. It seems sensible to assume that they are used according to the properties of real numbers, but it would be contrary to introspection to require that sensations and sensational reports are governed by "silent arithmetics" associating ratios with pairs of stimulus intensities and comparing ratios with ratios. Relation theory, therefore, postulates a mediating sensation continuum exhibiting all the properties of real numbers. As physical length has all the properties of real numbers, it is assumed that comparison of sensation intensities is related to an inner continuum of length, and the relating function is simply the pair-estimation function, P_L, for this length continuum.

The choice of the length continuum for the internal measure is, of course, facilitated by empirical results pointing to the veracity of length perception. It is assumed that input and output functions (f_1 and f_2 of Eq. 6) are identity functions. This assumption, however, makes use of a theoretical law that is not needed when determining the core for a theory of psychophysics. It suffices to postulate that there is some mental, mediating continuum, A_L, having the properties of II. The mediating process by which a sequence of pair-estimations is linked to $\gtrsim$ and P_i is supplied by condition I if $i \neq L$ and $j = L$. If $i = j = L$, the stronger assumption is made that the ordering of physical length pairs by "ratios" is the same as the ordering by mental estimations of length ratios.

The second numerical judgment method constraining the extended algebraic-difference structure of the frame is *magnitude estimation*. In magnitude estimation, the subject is presented stimuli one at a time and must successively assign numbers to them. Standard instructions stress that the numbers assigned should be "proportionate" to the sensations evoked by the stimuli. Often, the experimenter fixes one stimulus-number pair in advance, i.e., he or she assigns a *modulus*. If $a_i, b_i \in A_i$ and $p \in Re^+$, (b_i, p) could specify a modulus, and a magnitude estimation judgment of a_i is $N_i(a_i|b_i, p)$, then by definition, $N_i(b_i|b_i, p) = p$.

Empirically, magnitude-estimation scales with different moduli differ only with respect to similarity transformations. That is, $N_i(a_i|b_i,p)/N_i(c_i|b_i,q) = k_i(p/q)$, where $k_i(p, q)$ is a constant. If $a_i = c_i$, this equation changes to $N_i(a_i|b_i, p)/N_i(a_i|b_i, q) = p/q$.

Assuming the mediating capacity of an internal length continuum, it is easy to establish a link between pair-estimation and magnitude estimation. If, for a magnitude-estimation task, the modulus is (b_i, p), it is assumed that the magnitude estimation response to a_i is made by an internal reference to the mediating continuum A_L such that $a_i b_i \sim a_L b_L$. We then have as a third constraining condition: (III) If $a_i b_i \sim a_L b_L$, then $N_i(a_i|b_i, p) = pP_L(a_L, b_L)$.

Condition III yields a consistency between pair-estimation and magnitude estimation, for if there is a scale f_i on A_i such that

$$P_i(a_i, b_i) = f_i(a_i)/f_i(b_i), \tag{11}$$

the *ratio* of magnitude estimates for the members of the pair-estimate $P_i(a_i, b_i)$ equals the pair-estimate, i.e., $N_i(a_i|c_i, p) = f_i(a_i)$ satisfies Eq. 11.

Finally, in *cross-modality matching*, subjects choose a stimulus in one continuum to match a stimulus in another, either by adjusting a_i to match a_j or by adjusting a_i and a_j to a third (possibly nonmetric) stimulus a_k. Again, the experimenter may advocate a modulus pair (b_i, b_j), and a cross-modality response may be expressed as $C_{ij}(a_i|b_i, b_j)$ if the A_j-modality is matched to A_i. We then have $C_{ij}(b_i|b_i, b_j) = b_j$ by definition.

The concept of "matching" is expressed by a fourth condition: (IV) If $C_{ij}(a_i|b_i, b_j) = a_j$, then $a_ib_i \sim a_jb_j$. That is, if b_i is matched by b_j and a_i is matched by a_j, then the sensation "ratios" a_ib_i and a_jb_j are equivalent.

In IV, a_i, b_i, a_j, b_j are physical values of intensity. Consistency of cross-modality matching with numerical judgments of either P_i or N_i is given by again turning to the mediating internal continuum A_L. If condition IV is satisfied, it is assumed that the subject chooses a pair a_Lb_L such that $a_ib_i \sim a_Lb_L \sim a_jb_j$. By I, it follows that $P_i(a_i, b_i) = P_L(a_L, b_L) = P_j(a_j, b_j)$. Substituting for $P_i(a_i, b_i)$ the equivalent magnitude estimates with modulus (c_i, p), and for $P_j(a_j, b_j)$ the magnitude estimates with modulus (c_j, q), we have

$$\frac{N_j\{C_{ij}(a_i|b_i, b_j)|c_j, q\}}{N_j(b_j|c_j, q)} = \frac{N_i(a_i|c_i, p)}{N_i(b_i|c_i, p)}. \tag{12}$$

Because $C_{ij}(a_i|b_i, b_j) = a_j$, we see that, regardless of the moduli chosen, the ratio of magnitude estimates of a_i and b_j equals the ratio of magnitude estimates of a_i and b_i.

The magnitude-estimation function of Eq. 12 moreover, satisfies theorem 9, i.e., magnitude-estimation scales are numerical respresentations of f_i. We may conclude that the system of scaling procedures that satisfies conditions I through IV is a legitimate constraint for the structural frame of A1–A5. This frame, F, together with conditions I through IV constitute the *core* H for a theory of psychophysics. So far, however, this core is a core only for psychophysical "ratio" measurement.

4.2. Difference, Category, and Discrimination Scales

I now turn to two other groups of psychophysical methods—to "difference" measurement, which forms a branch of the judgmental approach, and to discrimination scaling (Fechner's approach). Both groups of methods exhibit a formal equivalence, and it is possible to incorporate them into our core H.

As noted earlier, the ratio representation of the extended algebraic-difference structure of the frame is structurally equivalent to a difference representation (cf.

Eq. 10). If there is only one response modality, that is, if $i = j$, the representation takes the form of

$$a_i b_i \gtrsim u_i v_i \quad iff f_i^-(a_i) - f_i^-(b_i) \geq f_i^-(u_i) - f_i^-(v_i). \tag{13}$$

It seems plausible to assume that the ordering which yields this representation is an ordering of "differences" rather than of "ratios." This assumption—though it is of interest to proponents of "cognitive operation theory"—does not alter the frame F, if $\gtrsim$ is identical in both cases.

Constraining conditions for the judgment of "differences" may be determined by a pair-difference function D_i, which is characterized by the following two conditions: (I') $D_i(a_i, b_i) \gtrsim D_i(u_i, v_i)$ iff $a_i b_i \gtrsim u_i v_i$; (II') $D_i(a_i, b_i) + D_i(b_i, c_i) = D_i(a_i, c_i)$. If the orderings of I and I' are not distinct, condition II' also holds for $i = L$, and it can be assumed that "differences" like "ratios" are mediated by the internal length continuum A_L. It should be noted, however, that I' and II' are directly deducible from I and II, and the primed and unprimed conditions do not differ as constraints for F because $f_i = \exp f_i^-$.

A substantially new constraint for F with regard to D_i, however, can be introduced if the qualitative order relation $\gtrsim$ is assumed to be different for "ratio" and for "difference" judgments. Let us suppose that there is an ordering $\gtrsim_D$ for a "difference" task and an ordering $\gtrsim_R$ for a "ratio" task, and let us suppose that both orderings satisfy algebraic-difference structures of the form A1–A5 (with $i = j$), $\gtrsim_D$ yielding a difference representation with interval-scale properties, and $\gtrsim_R$ yielding a ratio representation with log-interval properties. It has been shown (Krantz et al., 1971, pp. 153f.) that, if these premises are satisfied, we may construct a representation ϕ_i such that the same scale accounts for "ratio" and "difference" judgments, that is

$$
\begin{aligned}
a_i b_i \gtrsim_D u_i v_i &\quad iff \quad \phi_i(a_i) - \phi_i(b_i) \geq \phi_i(u_i) - \phi_i(v_i); \\
a_i b_i \gtrsim_R u_i v_i &\quad iff \quad \phi_i(a_i)/\phi_i(b_i) \geq \phi_i(u_i)/\phi_i(v_i).
\end{aligned}
\tag{14}
$$

Assuming f_i is a strictly increasing function of f_i^-, the following two conditions with regard to $\gtrsim_D$ and $\gtrsim_R$ are necessary if ϕ_i is to exist:

B1. $a_i b_i \gtrsim_D a_i a_i$ iff $a_i b_i \gtrsim_R a_i a_i$.

B2. If $a_i d_i \sim_R b_i e_i \sim_R c_i f_i$, then $a_i b_i \gtrsim_D b_i c_i$
    iff $d_i e_i \gtrsim_D e_i f_i$.

If B1 and B2 are satisfied by empirical data, ϕ_i is a ratio scale. That is, if ϕ_i' is any other function with the same properties, then $\phi_i' = a\phi_i$, $a > 0$.

This then leads to a constraint for F, if it is enlarged by B1 and B2, which specifies a particular situation for "ratio" and "difference" scaling such that a single set of scales ϕ_i' is available for both. From the scale properties of 14, the interscale relationship to be expected between f_i^- and f_i is also deducible: (V) $\phi_i = f_i^- + \kappa + \alpha f_i^\beta$. Moreover, because it can be shown for certain situations (Orth, Chapter 15, this volume) that a category function K_i exists such that

$$a_i b_i \gtrsim_D u_i v_i \; \textit{iff} \; \mathrm{K}_i(a_i) - \mathrm{K}_i(b_i) \geq \mathrm{K}_i(u_i) - \mathrm{K}_i(v_i), \tag{15}$$

and K_i is an interval scale, the numerical relation between category ratings and "difference" judgments will be $\mathrm{K}_i = a \, f_i^- + b$, if $\gtrsim_D$ fulfills A1–A5 (with $i = j$).

Therefore, as an additional constraint for F in conjunction with the restrictions of B1 and B2, Eqs. 11 and 15 can be formulated:

$$(\mathrm{VI}) \; \frac{\mathrm{K}_i(a_i) + \kappa}{\mathrm{K}_i(b_i) + \kappa} = \frac{\alpha\{\mathrm{N}_i(a_i|c_i, p)\}^\beta}{\alpha\{\mathrm{N}_i(b_i|c_i, p)\}^\beta} = \frac{\phi_i(a_i)}{\phi_i(b_i)} \; .$$

The conclusion to be drawn from the foregoing discussion is that the structural frame F and its representations may apply to "ratio" and "difference" judgment methods. If the "interlocking conditions" of B1 and B2 are satisfied for two distinct orderings $\gtrsim_D$ and $\gtrsim_R$, it will be possible to distinguish "ratio" from "difference" judgments or from category ratings if the latter yield an interval scale. Conditions V and VI represent numerical consistency requirements between scales derived from D_i, N_i, and K_i; pair-estimation and cross-modality functions may easily be incorporated.

Because of the general form of the representation of 13, it is also possible to integrate *discrimination methods* within this framework. Fechner's problem of finding that "smooth" and continuous function between physical and subjective intensities, for which every subjective increment corresponding to a just noticeable difference on the stimulus continuum is constant (Fechner, 1860, pp. 54ff.), may be generalized to a larger class of possible discrimination functions (Falmagne, 1974; Luce, 1959a; Luce & Galanter, 1963). One may ask whether, given an index of discriminability $\mathrm{M}(a, b)$, a scale u can be constructed such that

$$\mathrm{M}(a, b) \leq \mathrm{M}(c, d) \; \textit{iff} \; u(a) - u(b) \leq u(c) - u(d). \tag{16}$$

A discrimination function corresponding to M might be empirically defined by any of the classical psychophysical methods for determining thresholds. For instance, one could use the constant-stimuli method, in which the discrimination index is defined from choice probability, that is, the probability that a is chosen over b. Other discrimination methods are also feasible, but it is obvious that all discrimination methods are sensitive only to certain sets of pairs of stimuli. The constant-stimuli method, for instance, is applicable only for those stimulus pairs whose elements are not "too far apart," otherwise $\mathrm{M}(a, b) = 1$ or $\mathrm{M}(a, b) = 0$. It is primarily because of this selective sensitivity that the representation of 16 is not deducible from the structural frame A1–A5 without certain additions to the axiomatic system.

Falmagne (1974) proposes a more restricted version of the algebraic-difference structure of the frame, in which the discrimination index M is defined on a set D of $A \times A$. When (a, b) is in D, then a is said to be *comparable* to b, or aDb. Comparability of a and b is restricted to $a \geq b$, and $M(a, b)$ is bounded within an interval. It is also obvious that $M(a, b)$ must be strictly increasing in the first and strictly decreasing in the second of the variables. For the constant-stimuli method, the interval for M could be set to $.5 \leq M(a, b) \leq 1$. From this, a weak version of a convexity axiom for discrimination may be inferred: If $.5 \leq M(a, b) \leq 1$, $b \leq d \leq c \leq a$, then it is reasonable to expect $.5 \leq M(c, d) \leq 1$. The key to the discrimination structure, however, is provided by a monotonicity condition resembling A3, which is restricted to comparable stimuli. Counterparts to the technical axioms of A1–A5—solvability and an Archimedian axiom—may also be specified; reversability of D is not required because aDb is defined for $a \geq b$.

Following Falmagne (1974), the particular conditions for discrimination theory (omitting technical axioms) in accordance with the structural frame F may be summarized:

C1. M is continuous on D, strictly increasing in the first variable, strictly decreasing in the second variable.
C2. (i) if aDb, then $a \geq b$;
    (ii) if aDb, and $b \leq d \leq c \leq a$, then cDd.
C3. If $M(a, b) = M(c, d)$, and aDe, cDf, bDe, and dDf, then $M(a, e) = M(c, f)$ *iff* $M(b, e) = M(d, f)$.

If these conditions are satisfied, a scale u in accordance with 16 exists, and u is an interval scale. Moreover, whenever $0 \leq u(c) - u(d) \leq u(a) - u(b)$ and aDb, then also cDd.

Again, constraints can be formulated with regard to this revised structure in order to make its representation compatible with different psychophysical methods. With respect to different *discrimination* methods, we restrict ourselves to those cases in which $D' \subseteq D$. Under what circumstances will the corresponding scales u' and u be linearly related? Given that M' and M both satisfy C1–C3 and that aD'b and cD'd, we demand that M' and M induce the same ordering on D'. Because $M(a, b) \leq M(c, d)$ *iff* $u(a) - u(b) \leq u(c) - u(d)$ and $M'(a, b) \leq M'(c, d)$ *iff* $u(a) - u(b) \leq u(c) - u(d)$, the condition to be satisfied is: (VII) $M(a, b) \leq M(c, d)$ *iff* $M'(a, b) \leq M'(c, d)$. Falmagne (1974) specifies additional restrictions for situations in which D' and D cannot be assumed to overlap.

Can consistency requirements also be established between discrimination and *judgmental methods*? This is possible if, for example, for "difference" measurements the ordering $\gtrsim_D$ on $A \times A$ satisfies an algebraic-difference structure, and a discriminations measurement satisfies C1–C3. As has been shown in a related context (Falmagne, 1974), the discrimination scale linearly relates to f^-, i.e., $u = Af^- + B$, $A > O$, if and only if for all $a, b, c, d \in A$: (VIII) $M(ac, bc) = M(ad, bd)$ *iff* $(ac)D(bc) \wedge (ad)D(bd)$. This condition can be extended to a "ratio" ordering $\gtrsim_R$. If the orderings of $\gtrsim_D$ and $\gtrsim_R$ are identical, the interscale relation will be a logarithmic relation, $u = A \log f + B$. If both orderings are distinct, if both satisfy algebraic-difference structures, and if both satisfy B1 and B2, we expect (because of V) $u = \alpha f^\beta + C$.

This concludes our discussion of the *core* for a theory of psychophysics. We have found that if F is the frame for a theory of psychophysics, it is possible to formulate three subsets of constraints for F, which together can account for scaling procedures of: (1) magnitude theory (P_i, N_i, and C_i); (2) difference theory (D_i and K_i); (3) discrimination theory (M). $\langle F, C \rangle$ is the core H for a theory of psychophysics if conditions I through VIII make up the set C of all constraints for our frame.

Strictly speaking, $H = \langle F, C \rangle$ is an abstract calculus that can be introduced without making reference to any sort of interpretation. In the section to follow, empirical laws that relate to the core are added and thus make possible the definition of expanded cores $E_i = \langle H, I_i \rangle$. It is only then that interpretations of H are mandatory.

5. EXPANDED CORES

5.1. The Power Law

The first empirical law to be introduced is Stevens' power law. The law applies to "ratio" measurement, and one way of expressing it is: (IX) $N_i(a_i|b_i, p) = p(a_i/b_i)^{B_i}$, where $B_i > O$ is a constant. Condition IX is an empirical generalization for (geometrically) averaged responses and "moderate" values of a_i, $b_i \in A_i$. The law is deducible from the specifications of the core if elements of A_i are interpreted as energy values such that A_i has the structure of Re^+, i.e., elements of A_i may be multiplied or divided. Assume, for instance, that $a_ib_i \sim (pa_i)(pb_i)$ for all real numbers p. The ratio representation of 9 will yield $f_i(a_i)/f_i(b_i) = f_i(pa_i)/f_i(pb_i)$, or:

$$f_i(pa_i)/f_i(a_i) = f_i(pb_i)/f_i(b_i). \tag{17}$$

Because a_i, $b_i \in Re^+$, both sides of Eq. 17 depend only on p such that for all a_i $f_i(pa_i)/f_i(a_i) = f(p)$, or:

$$f_i(pa_i) = f(p)f_i(a_i). \tag{18}$$

This functional equation has one and only one continuous solution (Luce, 1959b, p. 87):

$$f_i(a_i) = \alpha_i a_i{}^{\beta_i}$$

$$f(p) = p^{\beta_i}$$

which is the general form of Stevens' power law.

Consistency requirements (C_L in nonstatement terminology) for the law with regard to the scaling procedures defined earlier are easily established. A subject in a magnitude-estimation task, for example, given a stimulus a_i with modulus (b_i, p) will find those internal length sensations such that the "ratios" $a_i b_i$ and $a_L b_L$ are equivalent and the subject will then assign to a_i the value $pP_L(a_L, b_L)$. Because $a_i b_i \sim a_L b_L$ iff $f_i(a_i)/f_i(b_i) = f_L(a_L)/f_L(b_L)$, and $f_i(a_i) = k\, a_i^{\,B_i}$ and $f_i(b_i) = k\, b_i^{\,B_i}$, we replace $(a_i/b_i)^{B_i}$ for $P_L(a_L, b_L)$ in condition III and derive condition IX. From here, other constraints for the power law corresponding to the conditions elaborated on in Section 4 may readily be specified.

The pretention of the power law is that it is a psychophysical law, i.e., a function relating stimuli and internal states. Empirically, of course, only stimulus–response relations are obtained, as in IX, where a_i, b_i are physical energy values and N_i is a function yielding values in the set of positive real numbers. Strictly speaking, therefore, neither the psychophysical function nor the judgment function are known.

Contrary to what has been claimed by Stevens, cross-modality matching does not circumvent this indeterminacy concerning the subjective magnitudes of sensations (Shepard, 1978). In a cross-modality task it is assumed that subjects equate sensation "ratios" of different sensory continua such that $\psi(a_i, b_i) \sim \psi(u_j, v_j)$ iff $f_{1i}(a_i/b_i) = f_{1j}(u_j/v_j)$. The premise of this condition may be written as: $(u_j/v_j) = f\ddagger(a_i/b_i)$ if $f\ddagger = f_1 f_{1j}^{-1}$. Introducing a third stimulus to both continua such that $(w_j/u_j) = f\ddagger(c_i/a_i)$ and $(w_j/v_j) = f\ddagger(c_i/b_i)$, we have, by A3 and because A_i, $A_j \subset \mathrm{Re}^+$, $(w_j/v_j) = (w_j/u_j)(u_j/v_j) = f_1\dagger(c_i/a_i)\, f_1\dagger(a_i/b_i)$ and:

$$f\ddagger(c_i/b_i) = f\ddagger(c_i/a_i)\, f\ddagger(a_i/b_i). \tag{19}$$

Multiplying a_i, b_i, c_i by some n such that $na = 1$ reveals that Eq. 19 is of the form $f\ddagger(xy) = f\ddagger(x)f\ddagger(y)$. Similar to Eq. 18 the general solution to this functional equation is $f\ddagger(z) = z^B$ and thus for all i, j

$$f_{1i}f_{1j}^{-1}(a_i/b_i) = f\ddagger(a_i/b_i) = (a_i/b_i)^{B_i}. \tag{20}$$

It is well-known that the functional composition of Eq. 20 may be satisfied by a set of functions of which the set of power functions and the set of logarithmic functions are subsets. Thus, the indeterminacy with regard to subjective values will not be eliminated by cross-modality matching. Because of the monotonicity assumption of the frame, we know only that the input functions must be the same for all modalities i, j.

In this subsection, I have introduced an expansion of the core H of psychophysics, yielding an *expanded core*, which I call E_1. E_1 is an expansion of H because a set of laws, derivative to Stevens' power law, and constraining conditions were added to the core. The mapping relation α (cf. Subsection 2.3), which assigns partial possible models to laws, is implicitly given by demanding that values of $a_i \in A_i$ are physical energy values and the response methods to be applied are "ratio" methods.

5.2. Fechner's Massformel

I next describe an alternative set of laws for the core H, which if appended to H constitute an expanded core E_2 of H. This expanded core and the previous one, E_1, are not strictly distinct not only because they are based on one and the same core but also because both expanded cores overlap for some versions of the laws for E_2. The expanded core E_2 is best established via discrimination measurement but, by condition (VIII), may be generalized to difference measurement. E_2 is specified if we define the scale u in the representation of 16 as follows:

$$M(a, b) \leqslant M(c, d) \; iff \; \log(a+k) - \log(b+k) \leqslant \log(c+k) - \log(d + k), \quad (21)$$

where a, b, c, d ϵ A are physical energy values and k is a constant. One may ask: What are the properties a discrimination index M must have—except that it satisfies the requirements of the core—that the representation of 21 is feasible for a set of metric stimuli of A?

Let us assume that for some discrimination index M, a Weber function Δ exists such that

$$\Delta(b, p) = a - b \; iff \; M(a, b) = p. \quad (22)$$

$a - b$ is that difference between two stimuli yielding one and the same value of the discrimination index, i.e., for any value of b a stimulus value a is specifiable such that all pairs (a, b) are equidiscriminable, that is, $M(a, b) = p$. Assuming the linear generalization of Weber's law to hold (Luce & Galanter, 1963, p. 212), we have $\Delta(b, p) = h(p)b + C(p)$, where h is a strictly increasing function and $C(p)$ a constant. If $C(p)/h(p)$ is also constant, then

$$\Delta(b,p) = h(p)(b + \gamma), \quad (23)$$

which is referred to as Weber's law (Falmagne, 1971).

Furthermore, Eq. 22 implies that $u \{b + \Delta(b,p)\} - u(b) = g(p)$ or (X) $u\{b + h(p)(b + \gamma)\} - u(b) = g(p)$, when $g(p)$ is constant and independent of b. This equation is solvable for $u(b) = \log (b + \gamma)$ and $g(p) = \log \{h(p) + 1\}$. Therefore, Eq. 21 can be established if $M(a, b)$ is constrained by the Weber law (Falmagne, 1971; Krantz, 1971; Luce & Edwards, 1958).

Unfortunately, Eq. 23 is not the only possible form for the Weber law and, in fact, it is not the only one satisfying the representation of Eq. 16. Fechner asserted only that all subjective just noticeable differences on u be equal. This was a very natural assertion considering the epistemological atomism of his time (Mach, 1886). In seeking the "identity" of the physical and the subjective worlds (1860, Vol. 1, pp. 8ff.) Fechner made no attempt, however, to specify the form of the psychometric function or the discrimination methods used. That is, his *Massformel* and Weber's assumption are independent of each other. If, for instance, Fechner's problem is rephrased in contrast to X as (X') $u \{b + \Delta(b,p)\} - u(b) = g'(p)$, where g' is defined to be *strictly monotonic* and independent of *b,* a variety of solutions for *u* does exist, Weber's law defining only one. Moreover, if Weber's law [Eq. 23] holds, the *u*-scale can be obtained by integrating the reciprocal of the Weber function, which is not possible in general (Krantz, 1971; Luce & Edwards, 1958).

One of the interesting alternatives to Weber's law that differs from Eq. 23 has been shown to be implicit in the following representation of *u*:

$$M(a,\ b) \leqslant M(c,\ d) \ \textit{iff} \ \frac{a^\beta + k}{b^\beta + k} \leqslant \frac{c^\beta + k}{d^\beta + k} \ ,$$

whereby it is supposed that *aDb, cDd,* that is, that *a* and *b* and *c* and *d* are "comparable." If $k \neq O$, it has been demonstrated (Falmagne, 1974, p. 148) that the Weber function Δ for M(*a, b*) is of the form

$$\Delta(b,p) = \{h(p)(b^\beta + k) - k\}^{1/\beta} - b. \tag{24}$$

If $\beta = 1$, Eq. 24 reduces to Eq. 23, that is, to Weber's law. Therefore, we see that a restriction to Weber's law does lead to $u(x) = \log(x^\beta + k)$ as a solution to Fechner's problem and, hence, to a power law.

Concluding this discussion of discrimination measurement, I would like to mention a particular feature of discrimination theory which, if generalized, may yield interscale relationships between different *judgmental* scales. First, suppose that Weber's law holds not only for the stimulus continuum but for a subjective continuum as well (an assumption, incidentally, from which the power law with regard to *physical* intensities may easily be derived; cf. Brentano, 1874, pp. 96ff.). Note, secondly, that the Weber function Δ can be defined as a measure of uncertainty, which is a function of scale values for any continuum for which Weber's law holds. That is, $\sigma_x(x)$ denotes the variability of a probability distribution for discriminating $x_1 + x_{1+n}$ from x_1, if $x_1 D x_{1+n}$.

Eisler has shown (1963, 1965; Eisler, Holm, & Montgomery, 1979) that, between two monotonically related subjective variables *x* and *y,* which are functions of the same (physical) variable, the "general psychophysical differential equation" $dy/dx = \sigma_y(y)/\sigma_x(x)$ holds, which essentially corresponds to Fechner's *Fundamentalformel* (1860, Vol. 2. p. 10). The relationship $y = f(x)$ can be obtained by integration, so this procedure generalizes Fechner's integration method to a subjective scale from which another subjective scale can be constructed. For instance, *x* could be a magnitude-estimation scale for which $\sigma_x(x)$ is known and from which *y,* with an assumed constant Weber function, may be constructed. Several studies have confirmed that category scales closely agree with *y,* therefore it has been concluded that these category scales are discrimination scales (see Montgomery, Chapter 14, this volume).

Summarizing this section on expanded cores, it can be stated that psychophysics utilizes two expanded cores, E_1 and E_2, both of which have an identical *core* H. The family of empirical laws basic to E_1 is contingent on

Stevens' power law. Fechner's *Massformel* constitutes E_2, but it must be acknowledged that Weber functions other than Weber's law may lead to different representations—one such representation even implies the power law. If certain restrictions are imposed, discrimination theory is also compatible with "difference" as well as "ratio" measurement. Therefore, there are potential crosscuts between E_1 and E_2.

6.   STRATEGIES FOR APPLICATIONS OF EXPANDED CORES

6.1. Scales and Operations

Applications of the core and its expansions have a common goal: to construct a subjective scale that satisfies major conditions of either E_1, E_2, or, possibly, of both. However, a scale satisfying E_1 and/or E_2 need not be a *sensation* scale, for the expanded cores define only requirements for numerical representations of responses but not for the transformation functions f_1 and f_2 (cf. Eqs. 5 and 6). Several strategies for application to determine one or both of the transformation functions have been developed, three of which are to be outlined here.

In accordance with the relational conception basic to the core, the fundamental rationale for all three application schemes is

$$R_{ij} = f_2\{f_1(S_i) \oplus f_1(S_j)\}, \tag{25}$$

where $\oplus$ symbolizes a comparison operation with regard to stimuli S_i and S_j. Most simply, this operation is given an algebraic interpretation—it is either additive or multiplicative. The three strategies to be described are part of what has been labeled the *fourth* paradigm in Section 1 because their common goal is to construct sensation scales independent of particular tasks, and it is hoped that the assumption of specific "cognitive operations" will provide insight into which scales are basic if different tasks produce different scales.

A theory contingent on E_1 is the *magnitude-estimation theory* by Rule and Curtis (Chapter 4, this volume). Rule and Curtis assume that, when subjects are instructed to judge "differences," their subjective values for individual stimuli can be recovered by reconstructing their judgments through subtractive operations. The model proposed is

$$M_{ij} = a_D(S_i^k - S_j^k)^m + b_D, \tag{26}$$

that is, both the output function for "differences" and the input function for single stimuli are power functions when M_{ij} are magnitude estimates of "differences." In a considerable number of experiments, Rule and Curtis have estimated m from Eq. 26 and found average values of about $\frac{3}{2}$. Because exponents from magnitude estimations of single stimuli are about 1.5 times larger than exponent values for k derived from Eq. 26, it was concluded that the input function for single stimuli is also about $\frac{3}{2}$, yielding

$$M_i = a\ S_i^\beta + b = a\ S_i^{km} + b.$$

Moreover, Rule and Curtis (like Attneave, 1962 and others) have found that subjective number is a negative accelerated function of objective number; this function approximates a power function with an exponent of roughly the reciprocal of 1.5. Therefore, it is obvious that f_2 in magnitude-estimation experiments approximates the inverse of the psychophysical function for numbers. One of the conclusions to be drawn from this theory is that psychophysical functions of E_1 for all studied modalities have considerably smaller exponents than those that are obtained if linear output functions are assumed. From a practical point of view, the form of these psychophysical functions will lead to predictions almost indiscriminable from those based on logarithmic psychophysical relations (Wagenaar, 1975; see also Chapter 11, this volume).

The Rule and Curtis theory assumes that stimuli are measurable on a physical continuum of energy values in order to be able to apply estimation procedures for the parameters of the model. The theory also proposes that the functional form of f_1 and f_2 is that of power functions. Both restrictions may be dropped when a more general strategy of research is adopted. This strategy of research comes under the heading "functional measurement theory," which is relative to the notion of a "cognitive algebra" governing internal operations of comparison (Anderson, Chapter 5, this volume). Assuming stimulus independence and the linearity of the input function, this approach renders it possible to fit some simple algebraic model to Eq. 25 and thereby validates an assumed judgment function. If different modes of judgment are employed, the goodness of fit to a specific algebraic model may serve as a decision criterion for the appropriateness of a certain judgment method.

The methodology of functional measurement can be illustrated by the treatment of difference measurement for which $D_{ij} = f_{2D}(\psi_j - \psi_i)$ may be assumed to be a plausible cognitive model if D_{ij} is a direct judgment of stimulus differences. In a factorial design in which the two stimulus variables are independently manipulated in a row by column matrix, the factorial plot of the responses will form a set of parallel curves if the subtractive model is valid and if f_{2D} is linear. Given these premises, rows and columns represent independent response vectors such that marginal means are estimates of subjective scale values that are unique up to positive linear transformations. The functional measurement approach allows for testing an algebraic model together with response linearity. Additionally, estimates of linear subjective scale values are feasible. If the judgment function, however, is assumed to be not linear but rather only monotonic, a less restrictive requirement follows—the model in this case predicts that it should be possible to rescale the data to parallelism.

Proofs of the "parallelism theorem" have been repeatedly presented by Anderson (see Chapter 5, this volume), and Krantz and Tversky (1971) have derived qualitative laws regarding composition rules. These qualitative requirements are a prerequisite for any metric evaluation but, if they are satisfied, then functional measurement simultaneously establishes the validity of internal operations and congruent subjective scales on the basis of statistical analyses. It should be noted that for multiplicative combination rules interaction within a factorial plot is predicted to be due entirely to the bilinearity of the row-by-column curves, which together form, in this case, a fan of diverging lines. It can be shown that if scale values are recovered from a multiplicative model, they will be unique up to a power transformation.

Algebraic models have been studied in numerous experiments using physical and social stimuli (e.g., Anderson, 1979, and References to Chapter 5, this volume). Quite often it was found that simple algebraic models were able to explain large proportions of variances of combination tasks. It is noteworthy that functional measurement is indifferent with regard to the judgment methods used. Thus, it is an empirical question whether a specific cognitive model for a judgment task should be regarded as an expansion of E_1 or of E_2.

There is, however, some ambivalence with regard to the "validity" of cognitive models. If a subtractive model, for instance, can be fitted to a set of factorial data, it is also possible to apply an exponential transformation to the data in order to yield a ratio model. In this case, the scale values may also be derived from the new model, and the inverse of the transformation function serves as a judgment function. There are no internal constraints for choosing one model and neglecting the other. Empirically, therefore, if "ratio" judgments and "difference" judgments with regard to the same set of stimulus pairs are monotonically related, it is not possible to decide whether a ratio or a subtractive model is appropriate (Torgerson, 1961) and whether subjects really judge "differences" or "ratios" respectively when told to do so.

A third research strategy has been developed to attack this indeterminacy (see Birnbaum, Chapter 17, this volume). The characteristic feature of this strategy is that judgment tasks are studied that involve not only pairs of stimuli but also pairs of pairs such that comparisons of stimulus *relations* are possible—for instance, "ratios of differences," "ratios of ratios," "differences of ratios," and "differences of differences." With regard to these four-stimulus judgment tasks, different predictions are made depending on whether judges obey the given instructions or not. Birnbaum considers five possible theories of stimulus comparison that may be tested with a four-stimulus design. Three of these theories allow a decision with regard to the fundamental operation of stimulus comparison, and two do not.

The first theory assumes that subjects judge according to instructions—that is, that there are two operations. This *two-operation theory* implies that "difference" and "ratio" judgments of identical stimulus pairs should not be monotonically related, but instead should exhibit different orderings that will satisfy conditions B1 and B2 of Subsection 3.3. The other theories Birnbaum considers assume that subjects do not act according to instructions. In *subtractive theory,* subjects compute differences in the simple pair-comparison tasks regardless of whether "differences" or "ratios" are requested, and either a ratio or a difference operation is applied to these intervals for comparison of relations. Another theory is *ratio theory,* which assumes ratios to be the fundamental operation for two-stimulus comparison, and the subjects compare two ratios by either division or subtraction. Birnbaum calls a fourth theory *indeterminacy theory* because, if this theory is valid, it is impossible to decide whether the fundamental operation for simple comparisons is a ratio or a subtractive operation. Indeterminacy theory assumes only one sort of operation for two-stimulus comparison as well as for comparison of pairs of stimuli. Finally, it is also possible that there are two fundamental operations as well as two subjective scales, one for each operation. This *two-worlds theory* would be appropriate if subjects assigned numbers to each pair of either "ratios" or "differences" and computed on these numbers for comparison of pairs according to instructions.

In an impressive number of experiments, Birnbaum and his co-workers (see Chapter 17, this volume) have tested the differential predictions made by these five theories of stimulus comparison. Their present conclusion is that subtractive theory gives the most coherent account of the data. Moreover, if the judgments of simple differences are assumed to be due to linear judgment functions, scale values for all other tasks may be transformed to fit the scales derived from the "difference" judgments. Particularly, the "ratio" and the "ratio of ratios" judgments exhibit an exponential judgment function, whereas the other tasks are linearly related to the scales derived from "difference" judgments. This scale convergence lends validity to the conjecture that the comparison operation of judgmental tasks is subtraction and that the common scale deserves to be called a sensation scale. Clearly, subtractive theory is an expansion of E_2 for which the specific comparison tasks form a particular set of intended applications.

6.2. Contextual Effects

Sensations are relative to the contexts in which they are made. The expanded theories of psychophysics and their applications discussed so far do not account for any contextual influences. Inasmuch as contextual conditions are incorporated into the expansions, however, their generality will be enlarged and additional applications may emerge.

Confronted with contextual dependencies, there are two principal strategies: The effects may be treated as error variation, the source of which is secondary to the theorist, or, conversely, explicit attention may be paid to the contextual factors as such, and lawful descriptions of their influences on the sensation scale may be sought. It is evident that the second of these approaches concentrates on empirical generalizations with regard to new variables, whereas the first assumes true scores and already established laws. The difference between both approaches is due to the choice between an inductive vs. a deductive strategy of research.

An example of the deductive strategy is given by Cross' treatment of the psychophysical regression error (Chapter 2, this volume). His theory applies to magnitude scaling and assumes Stevens' power law to be valid. Thus, it is an expansion of E_1. Being interested in the underlying unity of sensory reactions, Cross capitalizes on empirical variations and anomalies that arise from factors not inherent in the stimuli or the judgment task per se but that constitute errors whose elimination is desirable. From an analytic point of view, two classes of error variables are possible—those uncorrelated with the stimuli (u) and those covarying with the stimuli (ρ). If it is assumed that the biasing effects operate on the numerical responses N of magnitude estimations, then, on the basis of the strong form of the power law, the responses N are predictable from $N = S^{\beta+\rho} u$.

The pertinent question is how to estimate the true value for β when the empirical exponents always constitute the sum of both β and ρ. A similar equation may be derived for a magnitude-production task in which N is presented as the stimulus and S is to be adjusted such as to match the subjective magnitude of N. Again, splitting error influences (now active on S) into two classes, v and $\tilde{\rho}$, and labelling the production exponent $\tilde{\beta}$, we have an equation relating the two modalities: $S = N^{\tilde{\beta}+\tilde{\rho}} v$.

Usually the biased magnitude exponent ($\beta+\rho$) will be smaller than the biased production exponent $1/(\tilde{\beta}+\tilde{\rho})$ and their (geometric) average has been proposed as an estimation of the true value of β. However, no exact calculation is feasible because—even if it is assumed that the output exponent $\tilde{\beta}$ is the inverse of the input exponent β—there remain three unknowns with regard to the two observational equations.

A solution for this problem had been previously proposed by Cross (1974) and found application within the magnitude scaling of attitudes (see Chapters 6 and 7, this volume). It required that both variables, N and S, be matched to an arbitrary third physical modality. Assuming that the number exponent is unity, the resulting indirect cross-modality matching relation between N and S should be $(\tilde{\beta}+\tilde{\rho})/(1+\rho)$. Thus, if estimation and production functions were also determined, the three unknowns could be estimated from three equations. However, implicit in this procedure is the assumption that biases remain invariant in the two matching continua across different stimulus continua—an assumption in no way testable from the data. In his contribution to the present volume, therefore, Cross suggests an alternative solution that involves multivariate reasoning and appropriate experimental settings. If several response modalities are used, a set of structural equations corresponding to the psychophysical production functions can be deduced, one equation for every response mode expressing variances and one for every pair of modalities expressing covariances. It is demonstrated that such a system of equations is closed for at least three modalities if the variance of the unobservable dependent variable is set to unity. Thus, error components may be calculated from empirically obtained variation measures which are, however, relative to the choice of base for the logarithmic transformation used to linearize the psychophysical relations.

When attacking contextual effects *without* the assumption of true scores, research will be aimed at the proliferation of factors that are relevant for influencing sensations and sensational reports. Regarding this, context research in psychophysics is not restricted to either of the expanded cores or to particular methods. For magnitude estimation, a number of experimental parameters affecting the scale values have been studied. The most impressive results have been obtained in connection with variation of stimulus and response range (Poulton, 1968; Teghtsoonian, 1973; Teghtsoonian & Teghtsoonian, 1978), sequential dependencies (Cross, 1973; Luce & Green, 1974), or with regard to the choice of modulus (Beck & Shaw, 1961). This empirical research, however, is outweighted by the great number of studies concerned with contextual influences on category judgments, that is, with a theorizing relative to E_2. Most prominent in this domain is Parducci's *range-frequency theory* (Chapter 3, this volume). According to Parducci's (1963) range-frequency theory, subjects in a category-rating task act as though they were deliberately making a compromise between two basic tendencies of judgment: ". . . (a) to divide the range of stimuli into proportionate subranges, each category of judgment covering a fixed proportion of the range; and (b) to use the categories of judgment with proportionate frequencies, each category being used for a fixed proportion of the total number of judgments [p. 4]."

In a simple "range" model of category ratings it may be assumed that the range of subjective values s is mapped proportionately into the available range of categories such that

$$\frac{C_i - C_1}{C_n - C_1} = \frac{s_1 - s_{min}}{s_{max} - s_{min}} \, ,$$

when s_i is the value for the judged stimulus, s_{max} and s_{min} are the extreme values of the stimulus set, C_i, C_n, and C_1 are the category ranks assigned to s_i, s_{max}, and s_{min} respectively. Range-frequency theory adds to this proportionality of range the proportionality of stimulus frequency such that every category is chosen an equal number of times. This idea may be expressed by the rank r_i that a stimulus i has in a set of presentations relative to the lowest rank, 1, and the highest, N, of all stimuli. A category response C_i may thus be predicted from

$$C_i = (C_n - C_1) \left[(w) \, \frac{s_i - s_{min}}{s_{max} - s_{min}} + (1-w) \, \frac{r_i - 1}{N - 1} \right] + C_1. \qquad (27)$$

In this equation, w and $(1 - w)$ are relative weights reflecting the salience of the two tendencies of judgment compromise. Obviously, the model assumes that, if stimuli are spaced evenly on the subjective scale and if all are presented with the same frequency, the category response will be a linear function of subjective values. This assumption may not be tested directly, but some progress has been made in specifying the influence of stimulus skewing and range parameters on subjective values within stimulus comparison and combination tasks. Here, however, the additional question arises whether contextual influences precede the comparison operation or whether they alter the judgment only after the stimulus comparison has been accomplished. Experiments directed toward this question are reported in Birnbaum's chapter and are relative to his subtractive theory. Let k symbolize a specific context—for instance, a certain distribution of stimuli being either positively or negatively skewed. If f_2 is a judgment function reflecting a range-frequency compromise in accordance with Eq. 27, "difference" and "ratio" judgments may be reconstructed by the following model: $D_{ijk} = f_{2D_k} \{f_{2_k} (s_j) - f_{2_k} (s_i)\}$, $R_{ijk} = f_{2R_k} \{f_{2_k} (s_j) - f_{2_k} (s_i)\}$, where f_{2D_k} and f_{2R_k} are the overall judgment functions for "differences" and "ratios" respectively, while f_{2_k} is the judgment function for single stimuli. If there are two different contexts, one with positive and one with negative stimulus distribution, it is expected that the ordering for both contextual conditions differ with regard to both "difference" and "ratio" judgments. On the other hand, if the following model holds: $D_{ijk} = f_{2D_k} (s_j - s_i)$, $R_{ijk} = f_{2R_k} (s_j - s_i)$, the ordering of the "difference" and "ratio" judgments is independent of the stimulus distribution—that is, there is no contextual influence on the scale values prior to comparisons.

Empirical results suggest that the second of the models should be accepted because no drastic differences of rank order were obtained across both contextual conditions. Therefore, it can be concluded that, in comparison tasks, contextual effects obviously do not operate on single stimuli and that subjects compute "differences" and "ratios" between scale values that are independent of the distribution of stimuli with which they are presented. This result, however, was not substantiated when stimulus comparison was made *across* different modalities. In this case, the individual scale values are subject to a range-frequency compromise, that is, the stimuli of one modality are first evaluated within the stimulus sets of the involved modalities before their ranks are compared across modalities.

It is obvious that the recovery of subjective scale values needs to take contextual conditions into account. Moreover, the loci at which contextual effects intrude differ. Maybe what Luce and Galanter had deplored almost 20 years ago is still true—namely, that a "sophisticated theory of categorical judgment" is not available (Luce & Galanter, 1963, p. 268). However, what they had in mind was "a response theory which defines a scale of sensation that is invariant under the various experimental manipulations [p. 268]." This view implies that the inherent relativity of category ratings is an inconvenient source for disturbances of the *true* judgmental response. In recent research, however, it seems that a "relativistic turn" has taken place and that expansions of E_2 together with the growing knowledge of comparison and integration tasks may lead to empirical laws of categorical measurement of sensations. One must, however, be willing to look for situational components affecting the judgment task. Psychophysicists who assume constancy (primarily with regard to theories relative to E_1) will find constancy and will treat invariances as biases. Proponents of relativistic psychophysics, on the other hand, take invariance for granted and cannot help finding it every time. As Wittgenstein (1975) observed: "Tell me *how* you are searching, and I will tell you *what* you are searching for [p. 67]."

6.3. Social Psychophysics

A number of psychophysicists deny that social psychophysics is a part of psychophysics (e.g., Anderson, Chapter 5, this volume). Primarily, their claim is based on the elementary fact that there is no physical stimulus object in social attitude assessment and if psychophysics is defined as that discipline in which relations between physical and psychological intensities are sought, social attitude measurement falls outside the domain of psychophysics.

Apparently, this is a straightforward argument that must be accepted if the traditional definition of psychophysics is accepted. However, definitions—though they cannot be false—can be inappropriate. Restricting psychophysics to the study of psychophysical functions excludes major portions of the work that psychophysicists have been engaged in since Fechner. Moreover, the structure of psychophysical "paradigms"—taxonomized from a non-statement perspective—prohibits a strict division between sensory and social psychophysics. Both component disciplines rest on one identical structural core, and particular applications can be made by extending this common core. Thus, the basic structure of psychophysics is neutral with regard to how its primitives are interpreted. Indeed, for some expansions of the core H, particular sets of its predicates are interpreted as physical energy values of stimuli such that functional relationships between these and response variables may be studied. If an expanded theory of this sort additionally provides a rationale for deriving judgment functions, we have a psychophysical theory in the classic sense. For other expansions, however, the realm of intended applications is restricted to response variables only, and these responses may be responses to metric or nonmetric stimuli depending on the set of intended applications for which an expanded theory is designed. It should be evident, moreover, that this flexibility in choice of applications contributes to the "comprehensiveness" of the theory of sensation, the set-theoretical structure of which is outlined in this paper.

It follows that the term "psychophysics" may be defined in many ways, and any such definition must make reference to the level of theory to which it relates. Specifically, a definition of psychophysics has to be explicit about whether it refers to the abstract core, to some expansion, or to a specific strategy of application (cf. Marks, 1974, p. 4 for a similar notion). However, these relative definitions of psychophysics will not necessarily be disjunctive with regard to all areas of applications. One example for a definitional overlap is the *indirect* application of the family of power laws. Though the expanded core labelled E_1 and characterized by the set of power laws has been designed to apply to physical modalities, it lends itself for application to nonmetric stimuli as well.

Suppose that, using cross-modality matching experiments together with the convention of length veracity, the input functions f_{1i} and f_{1j} with regard to the modalities i and j have been established such that their respective exponents are known (cf. Eq. 20). If $\psi(a_i,b_i) \sim \psi(u_j,v_j)$, then $\psi(a_i,b_i) = (a_i/b_i)^{B_i} = (u_j/v_j)^{B_j}$. Let k be another continuum, and $\psi(x_k,y_k) \sim \psi(a_i,b_i) \sim \psi(u_j,v_j)$, then,

$$\psi(x_k,y_k) = (a_i/b_i)^{B_i} = (u_j/v_j)^{B_j}. \tag{28}$$

Equation 28 is true regardless of whether modality k is physically measurable or whether its elements can be placed only on a nominal scale. Therefore, the power law can be exploited to measure subjective values of nonmetric stimuli if the assumptions of E_1 are accepted. Moreover, ψ_k will be measured on a ratio scale because one of the psychophysical exponents, B_L, has been fixed. Also, Eq. 28 yields a consistency test for the scalability of ψ_k: Empirical exponent values in the indirect cross-modality matching task must approximate the ratio of exponents, B_j/B_i, found in direct cross-modality matching tasks. Assuming lognormal distribution of replicated responses, scale values ψ_a of k may be derived from $(a_i^{B_i} a_j^{B_j})^{1/2}$ if a_i and a_j are responses in modalities i and j respectively with regard to the stimulus a of the continuum k that is to be judged (cf. Cross, 1974; Stevens, 1966). Extensive use has been made of the indirect cross-modality matching paradigm, and examples are given in the chapters by Cross, Dawson, Lodge and Tursky, and Wegener in this volume.

It is well known that the alternative expanded core of psychophysics, E_2, which was—like E_1—originally designed for determining psychophysical relations, may be also applied to the measurement of nonmetric stimuli. Contrary to the indirect application of the power law, however, the application of E_2 to nonmetric stimulus variables calls for a revision of specific assumptions that characterize this expanded core. Let's briefly look into why this is so.

Recall condition X of Subsection 5.2. This condition expresses Fechner's *definition* (cf. Wendt, Chapter 12, this volume) of a psychological scale u that is obtained if just noticeable differences on the physical stimulus continuum are mapped into equal intervals on the subjective continuum u. Experimentally, this definition depends on the assumption that variability on the subjective continuum is constant. Only then can just noticeable differences of stimulus intensities be defined by specifying the relative frequency of discrimination between two stimuli. From these equally often noticed differences, Fechnerian scaling proceeds to construct u, in which equidiscriminable pairs of stimulus intensities mark off equal subjective intervals—which would be inadmissible if the variances of subjective magnitudes corresponding to a fixed stimulus intensity varied from occasion to occasion. Abandoning the assumption of constant subjective variability may, however, be advantageous if it is replaced by assumptions about the functional form of the distribution of subjective values. One such assumption was proposed by Thurstone (1927) yielding his *equation of comparative judgment*. Thurstone postulated that error variability of psychological magnitudes is due to distributions having a normal form. Therefore, distributions of subjective differences $u(a) - u(b)$ with regard to "comparable" stimuli a and b will be normal too, with mean $u(a) - u(b)$ and $\sigma^2(a, b) = \sigma^2(a) + \sigma^2(b) - 2\sigma(a)\sigma(b)r(a, b)$, if $r(a, b)$ is the correlation coefficient between the two normally distributed random variables a and b. Furthermore, the psychometric function expressing the probability density for a being judged larger than b is $p(a, b) =$

$\displaystyle\int_0^\infty$ N$\{u(a) - u(b), \sigma(a, b)\}$, where N$(\mu, \sigma)$ is the normal distribution with

mean μ and standard deviation σ. If $z(a, b)$ denotes the normal deviate corresponding to $p(a, b)$, that is, if N(μ, σ) is N$(0, 1)$, then

$$u(a) - u(b) = z(a,b)\sigma(a,b)$$
$$= z(a,b)\{\sigma(a)^2 + \sigma(b)^2 - 2\sigma(a)\sigma(b)r(a,b)\}^{1/2}.$$

For a matrix of pair-comparison judgments with regard to all pairs (a, b) ϵ A $\times$ A, a set of equations of the form just noted will result which unfortunately, is underdetermined because there are more unknown variances and correlation coefficients than equations. Several scaling models have been proposed that introduce additional assumptions in order to solve for the unknowns and to test the adequacy of these assumptions. For the present context, however, it is of importance that the family of Thurstonian models is neutral with regard to the stimuli to be measured. In contrast to a Fechnerian scale, which expresses subjective magnitudes in terms of just noticeable stimulus differences and thus in terms of *physical* units, Thurstonian scales are independent of any corresponding measurable quantities of stimuli. Therefore, Thurstonian models are particular applications of the discrimination paradigm for assessing attitudes—or any other distinguishable objects functioning as stimuli.

Summarizing from a structural point of view, applications of the set of theories and expanded theories of psychophysics to social phenomena are possible and as such they pose no qualitative new problems. Nevertheless, the foregoing discussion has left one problem unaccounted for: the problem of multiattributed stimuli. Social judgment situations are typically complex, and in most cases it will be inadequate to represent attitudinal stimuli on unidimensional psychological scales. Stevens (1975) optimistically claimed: "if we have some way of telling one stimulus from another . . . we can proceed to scale whatever common attribute of the stimuli the subjects are able to perceive as existing in amount or degree [p. 228].'' However, subjects have only a limited capacity to distinguish simultaneously different stimulus attributes that vary in degree or intensity, and their judgments on single dimensions are less accurate when presented with stimuli that vary on several dimensions (Miller, 1956). Therefore, Stevens' claim may not be valid for complex judgment situations in which subjects are unable to disentangle the various perceptive or evaluative dimensions. Nevertheless, a number of strategies have been developed to cope with problems of this nature. Two groups of strategies may be distinguished.

In one, the dimensions that are important to a subject are specified *by the experimenter,* and the stimuli are judged on these dimensions in turn in order to derive an integration model with regard to the overall judgment (one example is given by Sjöberg, Chapter 8, this volume). In addition, compound judgments may lead to integrative judgment models if stimuli can be presented in a factorial design, in which case functional measurement analyses may validate the model and response scales simultaneously. Ordinal requirements that must be satisfied by ideal data in order to be consistent with a specific integration model may be tested by conjoint-measurement analyses. In both cases, no stimulus metric is needed for evaluating the data. Furthermore, multiattributive integration theories introduce no new features that may not be reduced to the basic assumptions of the core or one of its expansions.

The other group of strategies for recovering multidimensional structures of judgments yields response scales on dimensions not prespecified by the experimenter. If subjects are able to establish a weak order of differences or dissimilarities between all pairs of a set of stimuli, a mathematical procedure has been proposed to represent the stimuli as points in a spatial configuration of minimal dimensionality such that there is a maximal agreement between the rank order of interpoint distances in the spatial configuration with the rank order of observed dissimilarities (Shepard, 1966). This configuration reflects the ''hidden structure'' in the data, and the dimensions of this configuration lend themselves to interpretations in terms of perceptual dimensions on which the projection values of the stimulus points form scale values for the different dimensions. This program of multidimensional scaling has been very successful in various areas of psychology and the social sciences. In this volume, it has been put to use to discover the structure of attitudinal and aesthetic judgments in the respective contributions by Feger (Chapter 9) and Eisler and Edberg (Chapter 10). Schneider (Chapter 13) makes use of the method to validate unidimensionality assumptions.

It should be understood that multidimensional scaling techniques—like the ordinal procedures of Coombs (1964)—assume that the data may be represented geometrically and that they seek the best fitting numerical solution for that representation regardless of whether or not the assumption is valid. Qualitative requirements that must be satisfied by the data in order to warrant their geometric representation have been studied by Beals, Krantz, and Tversky (1968) and Tversky and Krantz (1970). The proposed measurement structures are basically difference structures in conjunction with special conditions of additive conjoint structures, thus their structural properties may be reduced to those of the frame F of which they form specific expansions. If $\delta(a, a')$ denotes the dissimilarity or "difference" between a and a', and if a and a' have corresponding values $a_1, \ldots, a_m$ and $a'_1, \ldots, a'_m$ on m dimensions, the same being true for b and b', the basic representation takes the form:

$$\delta(a,a') \geq \delta(b,b') \quad iff \quad \sum_{i=1}^{m} \eta_i\{|\phi_i(a_i) - \phi_i(a'_i)|\} \geq \sum_{i=1}^{m} \eta_i\{|\phi(b_i) - \phi_i(b'_i)|\},$$

or

$$\delta(a,a') = F\left[\ \sum_{i=1}^{m} \eta_i\{|\phi_i(a_i) - \phi_i(a'_i)|\}\ \right],$$

where F is a strictly increasing function, ϕ_i are interval scales, and η_i are interval scales having identical units. A special case is the group of Minkowski r-metrics (or power metrics) defining a spatial configuration having additive segments, where

$$\delta(a,a') = F\left[\ \left(\ \sum_{i=1}^{m} |\phi_i(a_i) - \phi_i(a'_i)|^r\ \right)^{1/r}\ \right].$$

$r = 2$ corresponds to the familiar Euclidian metric. Other models with $r \geq 1$ have proved to be useful as well. The empirical verification of specific geometric properties poses several difficulties, however, which in part are due to the fact that the number of dimensions appropriate for a set of similarity data must be known in advance in order to test for the geometric properties.

7. CONCLUSION

With regard to the four "paradigms" of psychophysics introduced in Section 1, it has been demonstrated that despite their diversity, the paradigms may be subsumed under the framework of a common theory. This theory, however, is a very abstract calculus expressing, in effect, nothing more than the qualitative relations that must be satisfied if a scale of a certain type is to be constructed from ordinal data. In addition, the theory formulates a set of constraints for numerical representations. Together, the qualitative relations and the numerical constraints form a core for a theory of psychophysics, denoted $H = \langle F, C \rangle$, which for a set of intended applications I may yield the empirical theory $T = \langle H, I \rangle$. T is the theory basic to the four psychophysical paradigms. Due to the set-theoretical properties of T, the individual theories constituting the paradigms may be expressed as specific expansions of T. Two basic expansions are those in which psychophysical power relations or laws related to difference and discrimination scales are introduced. Relative to these expansions there are also particular strategies for applications that assume additional empirical laws and thereby form new expanded theories. All expanded theories may be reduced to the original theory T and its abstract core. Thus, the different paradigms converge to one comprehensive research program, the structural taxonomy of which has been outlined. Of special interest is that, within this taxonomy, social psychophysics may easily be located—depending on the intended applications to which a particular expanded theory of psychophysics is subjected. Therefore, the claim of "comprehensiveness" of psychophysics is justifiable. Whether or not, however, the empirical claims of the individual theories are justified and the extent to which the theories are able to contribute to an ultimate theory of sensation are problems that cannot be solved by structural analyses alone but must be attacked empirically.

ACKNOWLEDGMENTS

The editor thanks Bernhard Orth and Peter Schmidt for useful and critical comments on an early draft of this introduction.

REFERENCES

Anderson, N. H. *Introduction to cognitive algebra*. Preprint of Chap. 1 of Information integration theory: A case history in experimental science (Technical Report No. 85, La Jolla, 1979).

Aristoteles. *Metaphysik* (Vol. 1). H. Seidl (Ed.), Hamburg: Felix Meiner, 1978.

Attneave, F. Perception and related areas. In S. Koch (Ed.), *Psychology: A study of a science* (Vol. 4). New York: McGraw-Hill, 1962.

Beals, R., Krantz, D. H., & Tversky, A. Foundations of multidimensional scaling. *Psychological Review*, 1968, *75*, 127–142.

Beck, J., & Shaw, W. A. The scaling of pitch by the method of magnitude estimation. *American Journal of Psychology*, 1961, *74*, 242–251.

Birnbaum, M. H. Differences and ratios in psychological measurement. In N. J. Castellan, & F. Restle (Eds.), *Cognitive theory* (Vol. 3). Hillsdale, N. J.: Lawrence Erlbaum Associates, 1978.

Birnbaum, M. H., & Veit, C. T. Scale convergence as a criterion for rescaling: Information integration with differences, ratios, and averaging tasks. *Perception & Psychophysics*, 1974, *15*, 7–15.

Brentano, F. *Psychologie vom empirischen Standpunkt*. Leipzig: Duncker und Humblot, 1874.

Carnap, R. *Der logische Aufbau der Welt*. Hamburg: Felix Meiner, 1928 (3rd ed. 1966).

Carnap, R. *Testability and meaning*. New Haven, Conn.: Yale University Press, 1954.

Coombs, C. H. *A theory of data*. New York: Wiley, 1964.

Cross, D. V. Sequential dependencies and regression in psychophysical judgments. *Perception & Psychophysics*, 1973, *14*, 547–552.

Cross, D. V. Some technical notes on psychophysical scaling. In H. Moskowitz, B. Schaft, & J. C. Stevens (Eds.), *Sensation and measurement. Papers in honor of S. S. Stevens*. Dordrecht. The Netherlands: Reidel, 1974, 23–36.

Eisler, H. Magnitude scales, category scales, and Fechnerian integration. *Psychological Review,* 1963, *70,* 243-253.

Eisler, H. On psychophysics in general and the general psychophysical differential equation in particular. *Scandinavian Journal of Psychology,* 1965, *6,* 85-102.

Eisler, H., Holm, S., & Montgomery, H. The general psychophysical differential equation: A comparison of three specifications. *Journal of Mathematical Psychology,* 1979, *20,* 16-34.

Ekman, G. Is the power law a special case of Fechner's law? *Perception and Motor Skills,* 1964, *19,* 730.

Falmagne, J. C. The generalized Fechner problem and discrimination. *Journal of Mathematical Psychology,* 1971, *8,* 22-43.

Falmagne, J. C. Foundations of Fechnerian psychophysics. In D. H. Krantz, R. C. Atkinson, R. D. Luce, & P. Suppes, (Eds.), *Contemporary developments in mathematical psychology* (Vol. 2). San Francisco: Freeman, 1974, 127-159.

Fechner, G. T. *Elemente der Psychophysik* (2 Vols.). Leipzig: Breitkopf und Härtel, 1860.

Fechner, G. T. *In Sachen der Psychophysik.* Leipzig, 1877 (Photomechanical Reproduction, Amsterdam: E. J. Bonset, 1968).

Kant, I. *Kritik der reinen Vernunft.* R. Schmidt (Ed.). Hamburg: Felix Meiner, 1956.

Krantz, D. H. Integration of just noticeable differences. *Journal of Mathematical Psychology,* 1971, *8,* 591-599.

Krantz, D. H. Magnitude estimation and cross-modality matching. *Journal of Mathematical Psychology,* 1972, *9,* 168-199.

Krantz, D. H., & Tversky, A. Conjoint measurement analysis of composition rules in psychology. *Psychological Review,* 1971, *78,* 151-169.

Krantz, D. H., Luce, R. D., Suppes, P., & Tversky, A. *Foundations of measurement* (Vol. 1). New York: Academic Press, 1971.

Kuhn, T. *The structure of scientific revolutions* (2nd ed.). International Encyclopedia of Unified Science, II, 2, Chicago: University of Chicago Press, 1970.

Lakatós, I. Falsification and the methodology of research programmes. In I. Lakatós, & A. Musgrave (Eds.), *Criticism and the growth of knowledge.* Cambridge, U.K.: Cambridge University Press, 1970.

Luce, R. D. *Individual choice behavior. A theoretical analysis.* New York: Wiley, 1959. (a)

Luce, R. D. On the possible psychophysical law. *Psychological Review,* 1959, *66,* 81-95. (b)

Luce, R. D., & Edwards, W. The derivation of subjective scales from just noticeable differences. *Psychological Review,* 1958, *65,* 222-237.

Luce, R. D., & Galanter, E. Psychophysical scaling. In R. D. Luce, & E. Galanter, (Eds.), *Handbook of mathematical psychology* (Vol. 1). New York: Wiley, 1963, 245-307.

Luce, R. D., & Green, D. M. The response ratio hypothesis for magnitude estimation. *Journal of Mathematical Psychology,* 1974, *11,* 1-14.

Mach, E. *Analyse der Empfindungen.* Leipzig: Gustav Fischer, 1886.

Marks, L. E. *Sensory Processes. The new psychophysics.* New York: Academic Press, 1974.

Miller, G. A. The magical number seven, plus or minus two. *Psychological Review,* 1956, *63,* 81-97.

Parducci, A. Range-frequency compromise in judgement. *Psychological Monographs,* 1963, *77* (Whole No. 565).

Poulton, E. C. The new psychophysics: Six models for magnitude estimation. *Psychological Bulletin,* 1968, *69,* 1-19.

Putnam, H. What theories are not. In E. Nagel, P. Suppes, & A. Tarski, (Eds.), *Logic, methodology and philosophy of science.* Stanford, Calif.: Stanford University Press, 1962, 240-251.

Quine, W. V. O. Two dogmas of empiricism. In W. V. O. Quine, *From a logical point of view.* Cambridge, Mass.: Harvard University Press, 1953.

Quine, W. V. O. *Methods of logic.* New York: Holt, Rinehart and Winston, 1959.

Ramsey, F. P. Theories. In R. B. Braithwaite (Ed.), *The foundations of mathematics and other logical essays.* London: Routledge & Kegan Paul, 1965.

Savage, C. W. *The measurement of sensation*. Berkeley: University of California Press, 1970.

Shepard, R. Metric structures in ordinal data. *Journal of Mathematical Psychology*, 1966, *3*, 287–315.

Shepard, R. On the status of "direct" psychophysical measurement. In C. W. Savage, (Ed.), *Minnesota Studies in the Philosophy of Science* (Vol. 9). Minneapolis: University of Minnesota Press, 1978.

Sneed, J. D. *The logical structure of mathematical physics*. Dordrecht, The Netherlands: Reidel, 1971.

Stegmüller, W. *Probleme und Resultate der Wissenschaftstheorie und Analytischen Philosophie* (Vol. 2). Berlin: Springer, 1973.

Stevens, S. S. A metric for the social consensus. *Science*, 1966, *151*, 530–541.

Stevens, S. S. *Psychophysics. Introduction to its perceptual, neural, and social prospects*. New York: Wiley, 1975.

Teghtsoonian, R. Range effects in psychophysical scaling and a revision of Stevens' law. *American Journal of Psychology*, 1973, *86*, 3–27.

Teghtsoonian, R., & Teghtsoonian, M. Range and regression effects in magnitude scaling. *Perception & Psychophysics*, 1978, *24*, 305–314.

Thurstone, L. L. A law of comparative judgment. *Psychological Review*, 1927, *34*, 273–286.

Torgerson, W. S. Distances and ratios in psychological scaling. *Acta Psychologica*, 1961, *19*, 201–205.

Treisman, M. Laws of sensory magnitude. *Nature*, 1963, 198, 914–915.

Tversky, A., & Krantz, D. H. The dimensional representation and the metric structure of similarity data. *Journal of Mathematical Psychology*, 1970, *7*, 572–596.

Wagenaar, W. A. Stevens vs. Fechner: A plea for dismissal of the case. *Acta Psychologica*, 1975, *39*, 225–235.

Wegener, B. *Bewertung als Methodologie. Die epistemologischen Grundlagen der Angewandten Psychologie*. Frankfurt: Peter Lang, 1977.

Wever, E. G., & Zener, K. E. The method of absolute judgment in psychophysics. *Psychological Review*, 1928, *35*, 466–493.

Wittgenstein, L. *Philosophische Untersuchungen*. (German/English ed. by G. E. M. Anscombe, & R. Rhees). Oxford: Basil Blackwell, 1953.

Wittgenstein, L. *Philosophical remarks*. Oxford: Basil Blackwell, 1975.

APPROACHES TO SUBJECTIVE MAGNITUDE

1 Psychophysical Measurement: Procedures, Tasks, Scales

Lawrence E. Marks
John B. Pierce Foundation Laboratory
and
Yale University

1. INTRODUCTION

Having been asked to review psychophysical scaling procedures, I take the task quite literally, by which I mean to re-view certain basic topics, that is, to view them again—to take another look at them with the hope that examining them from a new perspective perhaps will give new insight into some of the complicated issues and perplexing problems that continue to beset psychophysics. Reviewing can mean taking a very fresh look; it can even mean reconsidering premises that previously may have seemed obvious. What I want to review are those methods that call upon people to make quantitative or quasi-quantitative judgments about their subjective states (about sensations, perception, attitudes, or whatever). By and large, these methods are magnitude estimation and magnitude production on the one hand, and various types of rating (numerical, adjectival, graphic) on the other.

The Enterprise of Scaling

The modern enterprise that Fechner may be said to have begun is the quantification of mental events. Interested as I always am in historical precedents, I pass along to you a passage in the *Republic* (IX, 587), where Plato (1961, p. 815) engages in a bit of psychological quantification. As Plato reports it, Socrates computes the relative happiness of king and tyrant, the result being that the king—the just king, that is—is said to be 729 times as happy as the tyrant (ratio of 3^6:1). Whether one wants to consider this as an antecedent or precursor to the method of ratio estimation is debatable, but surely it is an early attempt to quantify what we would call psychological values.

The use of mathematical symbolism to represent sensations or other internal, psychological events—the quantification of sensation that goes by the name psychophysical measurement—is really a most congenial part and parcel of the more general enterprise of science, much of which makes use of mathematics as a model, or, if you will, as a kind of metaphor. But it is interesting to note that the type of psychophysical measurement that forms much of the subject matter of this conference doubles or maybe even squares this metaphor; for when the subject matter of a science consists of "quantitative judgments" made by people, the metaphor is carried one step farther. When we study such judgments, we are examining people's metaphorical behavior, and when we quantify sensation by quantifying quantitative judgments, we are constructing metaphors for metaphors. It is good to keep in mind that many, maybe most, such quantitative judgments are metaphorical extensions through language or other symbolic systems, these systems being the media and sometimes the messages of many of our metaphors. In a sense, comparing the validity. reliability, or whatever other properties of different scaling methods is much like saying: "What are the good metaphors?"

If posing the question this way—in terms of "good metaphors"—makes one uneasy, perhaps this malaise will be relieved by considering that the criterion for "good" is, in some opinions anyway, largely pragmatic. Good metaphors are useful metaphors. Good psychophysical scales are useful psychophysical scales—scales that play a useful role in laws and theories of behavior. I do not think this is a very controversial point of view. It probably has the distinct advantage of being virtually tautological and, despite Plato or Keats, surely more defensible *for application to the realm of science* than other potential criteria for "good" such as simplicity or beauty. (Which is not to say that many a scientist's *Weltanschauung* does not rest on the latter criteria. See Marks, 1978c, especially chaps. 5 and 6.)

It's time to get into the real business. The remainder of this paper is divided into two major parts. In the first part, I give an overview of magnitude and rating procedures, pointing out in particular some of the problems and difficulties that befall their use and beset the interpretation of their results. In the last part of the paper, I present some new data in a context that, I hope, persuades you to re-view some of the old controversies.

2. PSYCHOPHYSICAL SCALING METHODS

Magnitude and Rating Procedures

Let me introduce here what is one of the main issues considered in this paper— the relationship between results obtained with magnitude procedures and with rating procedures. In certain respects, the methods of magnitude estimation and category rating do not appear so very different. They both ask subjects to try to assign numbers to psychological values. This makes it all the more puzzling why the two methods so often yield systematically different results—the well-known concave downward curve when ratings are plotted against the corresponding magnitude estimates. A few examples appear in Fig. 1.1.

What I would like to suggest is that, when these procedures do yield such a discrepancy, the discrepancy results from the two methods inducing the subjects to interpret the two tasks in (psychologically) different ways, with the consequence that the relative psychological values of the sensory/perceptual elements can differ. To those of us who have found the disagreement between rating scales and magnitude scales puzzling, one reason that we find it so is because we have made, implicitly at least, an assumption about converging operations—that in an ideal system the operations that define magnitude estimation and category rating will converge, nay should converge, on a single psychophysical function. Although sometimes they do—in some studies with continua like pitch, apparent position, length—more often they do not, especially with continua like loudness, brightness, weight, and size.

As an aside, let me mention that not everyone seems to find the relation a puzzle (Eisler, 1963, 1978). In fact, the experimental results that Eisler reported in 1963 are particularly instructive in this regard. He obtained magnitude estimates and category ratings of apparent length, which showed the systematic nonlinearity between them: The magnitude estimates were nearly proportional to physical length, whereas the category ratings were negatively accelerated functions of length. (As I just indicated, ratings and estimates of length are often collinear, as in the study by S. S. Stevens & Guirao, 1963, but not in this case.)

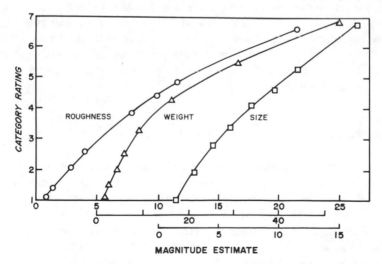

FIG. 1.1.   Category ratings (seven-point scale) of roughness of sandpapers, heaviness of weights, and size of circles, plotted against the corresponding magnitude estimates given to the identical stimuli. The same 12 subjects performed both tasks on all three continua. Data from Marks and Cain (1972).

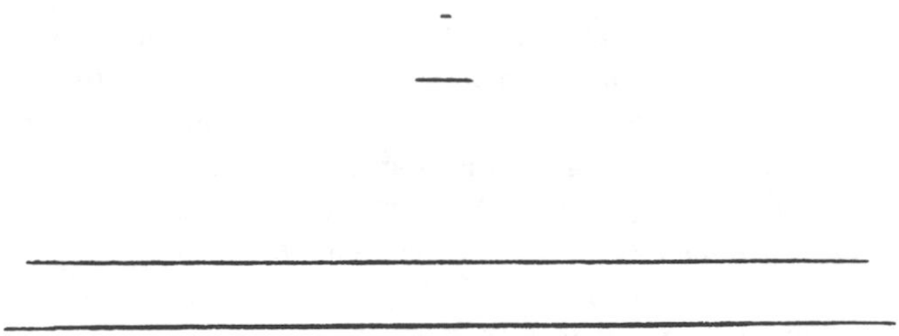

―

――

――――――――――――――――――――――――――――――

――――――――――――――――――――――――――――――――

FIG. 1.2.   Lines with relative physical lengths of 1, 6, 86, and 91 units.

Consider for a moment what subjects might be doing when they judge lengths of, say, 1, 6, 86, and 91 physical units (Fig. 1.2). When the method is magnitude estimation, the subjects give numbers approximately in the proportions of 1, 6, 86, and 91. But, when the method is rating on a 10-point scale on which 1 is defined by a 1-unit line and 10 by 91-unit line, a 6-unit line is often put in category 2, whereas an 86-unit line is often put in category 10. Thus, the magnitude estimates suggest that the differences between psychological values of 1 and 6 units and between 86 and 91 units are equal, whereas the ratings suggest they are not. My synthesis of this antinomy is as follows: I would suggest that, yes, the two psychological differences are unequal, as the ratings suggest, but also that the two differences between the pairs of psychological magnitudes are equal, as the magnitude estimates suggest.

Perhaps this statement itself is puzzling, so let me expand. Pairs of stimuli, such as lengths, can form a perceptual relationship that is readily identified as a psychological interval or difference. The pair 1–6 has a different value on this psychological scale than has the pair 86–91, and this difference expresses itself in the unequal spacing on the category scale. The perceptual relation on which the pairs differ is a psychological interval, but a psychological interval is not necessarily equal to a linear difference between psychological magnitudes. Some relevant data appear later.

Problems with the Methods of Psychophysics

Let me start off with a review of some of the features—both the good and the bad features—of magnitude and rating procedures. And if I seem to emphasize the latter at the expense of the former, it may be partly because, in actuality, the bad often seem to be intrinsically so much more appealing than the good (Satan after all is by far the most interesting character in Milton's *Paradise Lost*) and also because there are problems with all methods of psychophysics, and these problems must be taken seriously and dealt with at some point.

Every method has advantages and disadvantages of various sorts. With magnitude estimation and magnitude production, there is a basic uncertainty (variation) in the range of the responses, e.g., in the range of numbers assigned when the procedure is estimation, in the range of stimulus settings when the procedure is production. Such uncertainty generally cannot occur with rating procedures because the ranges of both stimuli and responses are set by the experimenter. But rating procedures have their own kind of uncertainty (variation), which manifests itself in the distribution of responses to stimuli within the (fixed) ranges.

Estimation Versus Production.   It is well-known that procedures of magnitude estimation and magnitude production tend to give results that differ systematically. S. S. Stevens and Greenbaum (1966) argued that subjects show a general tendency to contract the range of whatever variable they control. This compressing of range expresses itself, for example, in the exponent of power function relating numbers to stimuli. To give you some idea of the typical size of the difference between exponents obtained with estimation and production, I have culled out of the literature data from studies that scaled loudness by both magnitude-estimation and production procedures and that reported the results in terms of the exponent of a fitted power function. These values are listed in Table 1.1. On the average, the exponent of the loudness function is about 20–25% greater when magnitude production was used.

I suspect, though I do not know of relevant data, that similar differences will accrue to rating methods. One can turn category rating around into category production (e.g., S. S. Stevens, 1958; S. S. Stevens & Guirao, 1962, 1963) and ask subjects to produce the stimulus levels that typify each rating category. My suspicion is that, ceteris paribus, category production will tend to produce systematically different results from category estimation, in the same direction as the difference between results obtained with magnitude production and estimation.

TABLE 1.1
Exponents of Power Functions for Loudness
$$M = k\phi^\beta$$

Source	Magnitude Estimation		Magnitude Production	Ratio
Reynolds & Stevens, 1960	.56	(noise)	.67	1.21
	.50	(noise)	.63	1.26
S.S. Stevens & Guirao, 1962	.52	(noise)	.70	1.34
	.43	(tone)	.67	1.55
Hellman & Zwislocki, 1964	.53	(tone)	.57	1.08
Rowley & Studebaker, 1969	.48	(tone)	.56	1.17
Scharf & Fishken, 1970	.43	(tone)	.53	1.23
	.48	(tone)	.52	1.08
Hellman, 1976	.54	(tone)	.70	1.29
	.57	(tone)	.66	1.16

Effects of Stimulus Parameters—Range and Spacing.   Effects of stimulus range were noted very early in the psychophysical scaling game (e.g., S. S. Stevens, 1956), and these effects later received considerable discussion by Jones and Woskow (1962), Poulton (1968), and Teghtsoonian (1973). As stimulus range decreases, subjects fail to decrease the range of the numerical responses in appropriate proportion. In a log-log plot, the psychophysical (magnitude-estimation) functions are steeper when the range is smaller. In Teghtsoonian's study of loudness, as the stimulus range declined from 40 dB to 5 dB, the relative slope of the magnitude-estimation function increased by 50%, from .4 to .6.

Spacing within a range also exerts an effect, as J. C. Stevens (1958) demonstrated. Bunching stimuli causes a local steepening in a magnitude-estimation function.

Rating scales are also well known to bend with the stimulus. Parducci's extensive work (e.g., 1965) in particular has shown how variables like relative frequency of presentation influence ratings. On the basis of the relatively simple assumptions that the subject divides the psychological range into segments and tries to use the categories equally often, Parducci showed how one can account for many contextual effects on rating scales.

Effects of Standard and Modulus.   In the method of free magnitude estimation, the subject is told simply to match numbers to psychological magnitudes; no standard or modulus is used. Some experimenters prefer to give a standard stimulus, either one, twice, or ad lib., and sometimes to assign to the standard a numerical value. Systematic effects of standard and modulus were examined years ago. Typically, when the standard comes from near the bottom or top of the range, the magnitude-estimation function is less steep than it is when the standard comes from the middle of the range (Beck & Shaw, 1961, 1965; Hellman & Zwislocki, 1961; J. C. Stevens & Tulving, 1957; S. S. Stevens, 1956). Modulus also influences. Hellman and Zwislocki (1961) showed an interesting interaction between standard and modulus: Using an intense standard is like using a small modulus, and vice versa. The loudness scales came out much the same when a weak standard was used with a small modulus, a moderate standard with a moderate modulus, and an intense standard with a high modulus. This outcome suggests that there may be something like "natural" psychological scales. Recently, Zwislocki (1978) has presented evidence that subjects can do what he calls "absolute scaling," that subjects can match numbers to stimuli in a way that tends to be impervious to influences of variables like stimulus spacing and that is virtually constant from one group of subjects to another.

What about rating procedures? Probably the best analogy here is the effect of number of categories, which can exert some systematic effects on the form of the rating scale (Marks, 1968; S. S. Stevens & Galanter, 1957). Parducci discusses this topic in detail in Chapter 3 of this volume.

Individual Differences.   People differ. This could almost be a byword for a science of behavior (and probably is the most important facet of psychology to those who call themselves "humanistic"). Scales produced by magnitude estimation or by rating bear personal imprints, and these are often quite variable from individual to individual. To some extent, these differences may represent real sensory variations among people, but probably to a greater extent represent idiosyncratic "response biases," that is, differences in the ways that people go about making quantitative judgments—differences in their own number metaphors, if you will. To a first approximation, given a constant procedure, range, etc., individual subjects often produce data that have a common form, for instance, that are commensurate with a power function (Marks & Stevens, 1966; J. C. Stevens & Guirao, 1964). However, they do not always do so (Luce & Mo, 1965; Pradhan & Hoffman, 1963). Even when subjects do, for example, give data consistent with a power function, the spread of exponents is substantial, in a ratio from largest to smallest of two or even three to one.

Following Teghtsoonian (1973), one may reduce variation in exponent to variation in response range, that is, to the range from the smallest to the largest number assigned to a fixed pair of stimuli. Saying that subjects differ in exponent then becomes tantamount to saying that they differ in response range—the latter expression being in some ways preferable because it makes no a priori assumption about the appropriate form of the psychophysical function.

Rating scales have no directly comparable parameter because, as I have already said, the range is usually fixed by the experiment. However, one can look at, say, the relative curvature in the plot of ratings versus stimulus magnitude, that is, at the overall form the rating scale. Often, it is possible to fit power functions of the form $C = k\phi^c + c$ satisfactorily to rating-scale data (Marks, 1968). Curtis (1970) reported such fits to ratings of brightness, and his tabulation shows exponents for individual subjects that varied from near zero (essentially logarithmic functions) to values around one-third. A couple of years later, Marks and Cain (1972) reported data on individuals obtained by both magnitude estimation and category rating on three perceptual continua: roughness, weight, and area. These data also show large intersubject differences (see Table 1.2): The range of individual variation is much greater in the exponent of the power-function fit to the category scales than in the exponent of the function fit to the magnitude-estimation scales. It would be hard to argue that very much of the variation could have a sensory basis.

Variability as Noise.   Besides the forms of systematic variation, it is also the case—as anyone who has run scaling experiments surely can attest—that numerical judgments are just plain noisy. Even under tightly controlled conditions, a given stimulus does not elicit the same response from a subject as the stimulus is repeatedly presented over the course of a session; several investigators have

TABLE 1.2
Exponents of Power Functions Fitted to Magnitude Estimates $(M = k\phi^\beta)$
and Category Ratings $(C = k\phi^\alpha + c)$ Given by 12 Subjects on
Three Perceptual Continua.
From Marks and Cain (1972).[a]

	Heaviness		Roughness		Area	
Subject	Mag. Est.	Cat. Rat.	Mag. Est.	Cat. Rat.	Mag. Est.	Cat. Rat.
AA	1.32	.51	1.25	0.50	0.86	.14
JC	1.48	.11	0.93	0.84	0.83	.17
JE	0.82	−.31[a]	0.95	0.20	0.75	.17
HG	1.44	.51	0.75	1.15	0.60	.47
CL	0.82	.35	1.39	0.72	0.78	.26
KL	0.71	.37	1.11	1.11	0.64	.44
JL	0.93	.35	1.57	1.18	0.80	.91
LN	0.98	.86	1.65	1.04	0.75	.46
RP	1.20	.23	1.41	0.59	0.84	.44
AR	1.10	−.04[b]	1.13	0.56	0.58	.51
GS	1.33	.41	1.17	1.20	1.00	.94
RT	1.13	.50	1.04	0.27	0.58	.58

[a] Copyright (1972) by the American Psychological Association. Reprinted by permission.

[b] A negative exponent means that the best-fitting equation had the form $C = c\text{-}k\phi^{-\alpha}$, that is, the function relating ratings to stimulus magnitude has greater curvature than even a logarithmic function.

undertaken to assess this variability (e.g., Eisler, 1963; Green & Luce, 1974; Luce & Mo, 1965). In the experiment by Marks and Cain (1972), some of whose results were shown in Fig. 1.1., subjects gave magnitude estimates and category ratings of roughness, weight, and size. Actually, the same 12 subjects made eight judgments of each stimulus in each of the two tasks and for each of the three continua. This makes it possible to assess the variability around each data point by calculating the standard deviation of the eight judgments made by each subject to each stimulus. The averages of these individual measures of noise are plotted in Figs. 1.3 and 1.4 as a function of the mean judgments.

These graphs make several interesting points. First, they illustrate the well-known finding (see Eisler, 1963; Schneider & Lane, 1963; S. S. Stevens & Guirao, 1962) that variability in magnitude estimation tends to increase with size of the mean estimate (Fig. 1.3). Note, though, the difference between results for judgments of roughness and weight, which show relatively high noise, and judgments of size, which show relatively low noise.

Second, although the variability of category ratings is less nonuniform than the variability of magnitude estimates, it is still far from uniform (Fig. 1.4). The variability of the ratings also tends to increase with the mean rating, except for the dip at the highest levels. This dip at the top and the precipitous drop at the bottom are largely the result of end effects. But, I suspect that not all of the dip at

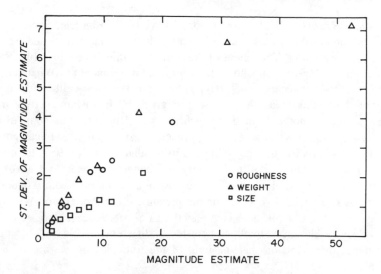

FIG. 1.3. Variability of magnitude estimates. Standard deviations were calculated separately for each subject, then normalized and averaged across subjects and plotted against the average estimates. The same 12 subjects judged stimuli on all three continua. Data from Marks and Cain (1972).

the high end is the result of end effect. As is seen later, some nonmonotonicity appears even when subjects are given "extra room" at the end of the scale. There is a final, interesting point: In rating, the difference in variability across continua virtually disappears.

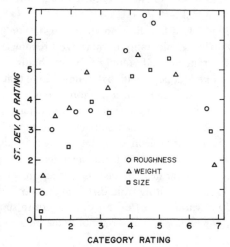

FIG. 1.4. Variability in category ratings. Standard deviations were calculated separately for each subject, then averaged across subjects and plotted against the average ratings. The same 12 subjects judged stimuli on all three continua. Data from Marks and Cain (1972).

Foxes and Hedgehogs. In this section, I have tried to indicate some of the uncertainties attached to scales obtained by procedures such as magnitude estimation and category rating. The extent of these uncertainties is considerable. Such uncertainty is troublesome and, to many scientists, it is anathema. What can we make of all this inconstancy? Clearly, people are not well-calibrated digital voltmeters. Does this mean that we should give up? In dismay, a few may consider turning to another branch of psychophysics. But given that some of us, at least, decide to stick with the scaling approach, it can be tempting to categorize each of us as either a fox or a hedgehog, to use Isaiah Berlin's (1953) terminology, either as one who basks in the glory of change and seeks out all of its pluralistic ramifications, or as one who inquires into the monistic unity underlying all of this superficial diversity. I do not presume that either approach is right or wrong—in both, what one does is to play the game of science and to search for the truth. Nevertheless, one may be interested in different aspects of the truth or operate under the suspicion that the bulk of the truth lies in one direction or another.

As you might guess, I work hard at being a hedgehog. The question I continually ask is: Where is the unity underlying the diversity of psychophysical scales? To try to reach an answer, let us first ask: What assumptions do we commonly make when we assume that there is unity? (Later, we see to what extent these may need be modified.) The assumptions are:

1. The underlying sensory or perceptual response, which as distinct from the overt response is inside the organism and never directly observed, is relatively uninfluenced by procedure. In its weakest form, we hope that all of the scaling procedures can at least operate indirectly as matching devices, preserving ordinality and equality. If two sounds are equally loud (determined by direct loudness matching), they should elicit, on the average, the same response in a rating or in an estimation task.

2. Individuals differ little in their sensory or perceptual responses, though they may differ considerably in their overt responses. Consider just one implication of a 2:1 range of individual exponents being largely sensory in origin. On a continuum like loudness, with a dynamic range that spans sound levels of 120 dB or a sound pressure range of a million to one, a person with an exponent at the bottom of the range, for example, .4, would have a ratio of greatest to smallest loudness of 250:1, whereas a subject at the top of the range, with an exponent of .8, would have a subjective loudness range, for the same stimuli, of 62,500:1.

3. A stronger assumption is that a single sensory or perceptual scale underlies all judgments, regardless of task or procedure. The idea is that differences in numerical scales resulting from different tasks or procedures (or from differences in procedural variables, or even from subject to subject) represent differences in judgment—in response bias—but not in the underlying psychological representation.

3. REPRESENTATION AND PROCESS:
PROCEDURE, TASK, SCALE

Rather than try to deal with research that has been carried out on a variety of continua, using a variety of procedures, on a variety of tasks, let me concentrate on a single continuum, namely loudness, where we can bring to a focus the concepts important to my argument. I choose loudness largely because: (1) so much of the scaling literature has used loudness as a medium—indeed, one might put the work of the 1930s by acoustical engineers as the modern beginning of the use of magnitude methods; (2) much of my own work over the last few years has been directed at auditory psychophysics.

I first draw what may seem a relatively simple picture of loudness, of a psychological scale for loudness, and of the role it plays in some models and theories of auditory intensity perception. I hope that this initial picture appeals to the hedgehogs among us. To be fair to the foxes, though, I follow the simple picture by showing how the scheme becomes more complicated.

The Sone Scale of Loudness

The original sone scale of the 1930s (S. S. Stevens, 1936) was based largely on loudness fractionations (mainly experiments where subjects set loudnesses in putative subjective ratios of 2:1). S. S. Stevens (1955) subsequently revised the sone scale to its present form, the revision based mainly on results of experiments using magnitude estimation and magnitude production. The present sone scale L is defined as $L = kP^{.6}$, where L is one sone when P, the sound pressure of a 1000-Hz tone, has a value of .002 N/m^2 (equivalent to 40 dB SPL). Although S. S. Stevens (1972) later suggested that the exponent might be a little higher than .6—specifically, about .67—the value of .6 represents a better average of results of magnitude estimation and production (Marks, 1974).

Is the sone scale a valid sensory scale? Recent work suggests that the transformation from sound pressure to loudness in sones does represent the result of sensory processing in the auditory system. This suggestion came about in the establishment of rules of loudness summation. In 1933, Fletcher and Munson proposed the possibility of generating a loudness scale by relying on an *assumption* about auditory processing. Fletcher and Munson (1933) assumed that the auditory system linearly adds the loudnesses of individual sound components in two paradigms: loudness summation by the two ears and loudness summation in multicomponent tones. Recent work suggests that their assumption about linearity was fundamentally correct.

Binaural Summation. With narrow-band signals (pure tones, narrow-band noises), binaural summation is in fact a linear process, as Fletcher and Munson conjectured. Levelt, Riemersma, and Bunt (1972) applied conjoint measurement theory to loudness matches and to paired comparisons of the loudness of 1000-Hz tones, which could be equal or unequal in intensity to the two ears; Levelt et al. concluded that the component loudnesses added linearly. Jankovic and Cross (1977) obtained magnitude estimates of the loudness of narrow-band noises (centered on 3150 Hz) and showed that the judgments were consistent with linear summation of values on (approximately) the sone scale. Some of my own data on pure tones (Marks, 1978a) appear in Fig. 1.5, which shows monaural and binaural loudness functions at three sound frequencies. At each frequency, the loudness of the binaural stimuli, as assessed by the method of magnitude estimation, equals the simple sum of the loudnesses of the monaural components, and the loudness scales approximate power functions of sound pressure, with exponent .6 at 1000 Hz and 400 Hz, .75 at 100 Hz. (The larger exponent at low frequencies is well-known—see Hellman & Zwislocki, 1968; S. S. Stevens, 1966.)

Actually, the data shown in Fig. 1.5 form a subset of results obtained in three experiments. In each experiment, nine levels of SPL delivered to the left ear were combined with the same nine levels delivered to the right ear, making 81 different stimuli in all. This factorial design, similar to that used by Jankovic and

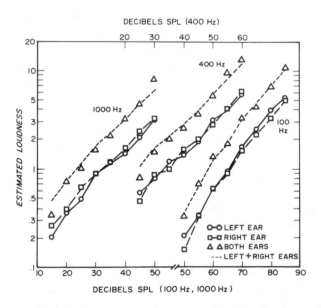

FIG. 1.5. Binaural summation of the loudness of pure tones. Plotted are magnitude estimates of 100-, 400-, and 1000-Hz tones presented binaurally and monaurally at various SPLs. The dashed lines give the sum of the judgments made to the monaural components and thus represent the prediction made by a model of linear loudness summation. Stimulus duration was 1 sec. Each data point gives the geometric average of two judgments made by each of 14 subjects. From Marks (1978a).

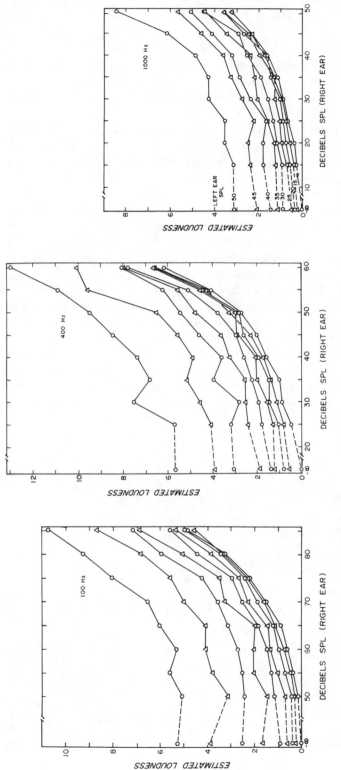

FIG. 1.6. Magnitude estimates of the loudness of pure tones of 100-, 400-, and 1000-Hz, plotted against the SPL delivered to the right ear. Each contour represents a constant SPL delivered to the left ear. The even spacing (parallelism) of the contours means that the estimates are consistent with a model of linear loudness summation. Stimulus duration was 1 sec. Each data point gives the geometric average of two judgments made by each of 14 subjects. From Marks (1978a).

Cross (1977), makes possible a rather strong test of a model of linear additivity (Anderson, 1970, 1974, and Chapter 5, this volume). The complete sets of data appear in Fig. 1.6, and they show the linear summation by means of the even spacing of the contours.

Subsequent experiments confirmed this finding: Narrow bands of noise, centered on 1000 Hz, show linear loudness summation in sones (Marks, 1980), as Jankovic and Cross (1977) showed for narrow bands of noise centered on 3150 Hz. (Interestingly, though, *wide*-band noise shows only partial summation [Marks, 1980].)

Let me mention one more experiment, which explored binaural summation of loudness of the same matrix of 1000-Hz stimuli used by Marks (1978a), but with a method of graphic rating rather than magnitude estimation (Marks, 1979a). Here, the subjects indicated the relative loudness of each sound by marking the appropriate position on a line segment with points near the ends defined by soft and loud anchor stimuli. The results appear in Fig. 1.7. Simple additivity is not clearly evident in the raw data because the graphic ratings are nonlinearly related to the magnitude estimates of Fig. 1.6. Binaural summation of pure-tone loudness is linear in sones, but the graphic ratings did not give the sone scale. Instead, the rating-scale data exhibit the typical concavity when plotted versus magnitude estimates, as shown in Fig. 1.8. Although the two sets of data are not collinear, they are consistent with the first assumption described earlier, that the two sets of judgments preserve equality and ordinality, and this in turn implies that the sone scale underlies binaural summation in the graphic ratings as well as in the

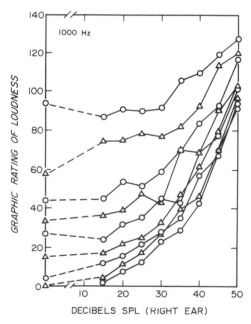

FIG. 1.7. Graphic ratings of the loudness of a 1000-Hz tone, plotted against the SPL delivered to the right ear. Each contour represents a constant SPL delivered to the left ear. The stimuli are identical to those of Fig. 1.6c. Each data point gives the arithmetic average of two judgments made by each of 15 subjects (from Marks, 1979a). Copyright (1979) by the American Psychological Association. Reprinted by permission.

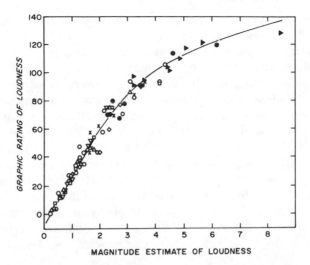

FIG. 1.8. The graphic ratings from Fig. 1.7, plotted against the corresponding magnitude estimates from Fig. 1.6c (from Marks, 1979a). Copyright (1979) by the American Psychological Association. Reprinted by permission.

FIG. 1.9. The graphic ratings of Fig. 1.7, rescaled to be collinear with the magnitude estimates of Fig. 1.6c. The rescaled graphic ratings show linear binaural summation (from Marks, 1979a). Copyright (1979) by the American Psychological Association. Reprinted by permission.

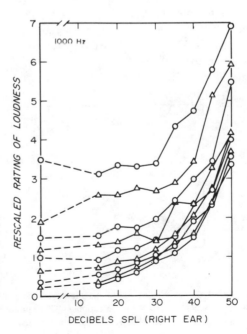

magnitude estimates. For if the ratings are rescaled by means of the curve drawn in Fig. 1.8, the rescaled ratings become additive (Fig. 1.9).

Let me interject a note about variability. In light of my previous remarks on variability in category ratings and magnitude estimates (vis-à-vis Figs. 1.3 and 1.4), it is instructive to look at the variability around these judgments of loudness. As Fig. 1.10 shows, the standard deviation of the magnitude estimates increases monotonically with the mean judgment. By contrast, the standard deviations of the graphic ratings are nonmonotonic, first increasing and then decreasing (Fig. 1.11). It is notable that the decrease at high levels takes place despite the fact that two precautions were taken to minimize end effects: (1) the anchor points of the rating scale were located 10 units from each end; (2) the subjects were told that they could extend the rating line as needed.

There is another curious feature: The variability in the ratings (Fig. 1.11) reaches its maximum right in the region where the rating scale begins to depart from proportionality to the magnitude-estimation scale (Fig. 1.8).

Summation Across Sound Frequency.   The sone scale also underlines loudness summation across frequency, given that the frequencies are relatively widely separated (separated by several critical bandwidths). Subjects gave magnitude estimates of each of 81 combinations of sound pressure of 300-Hz and 1000-Hz tones, presented binaurally (Marks, 1979b). The results, shown in the left-hand portion of Fig. 1.12, display nearly but not quite perfect addition on the response scale, the slight nonadditivity presumably related to the fact that the numerical responses in this case were not quite proportional to sones. To remove the nonadditivity, the averaged judgments were subjected to a mild positively accelerated transformation. I used the class of power transformations (with expo-

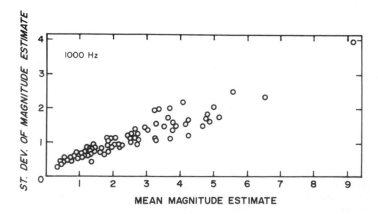

FIG. 1.10. Variability in the magnitude estimates of the loudness of a 1000-Hz tone, plotted against the mean estimates. The stimuli are those from the study of binaural summation (Fig. 1.6c). Data from Marks (1978a).

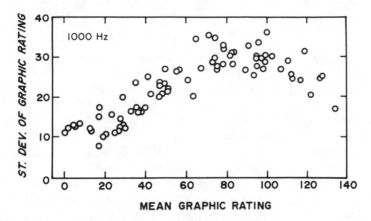

FIG. 1.11. Variability in the graphic ratings of the loudness of a 1000-Hz tone, plotted against the mean ratings. The stimuli are those from the study of binaural summation (Fig. 1.7). Data from Marks (1979a).

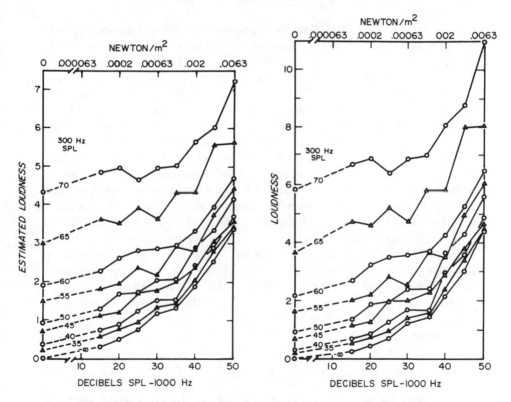

FIG. 1.12. *Left:* Summation of loudness of two-component tones. Magnitude estimates of the loudness of two-component sounds, plotted against the SPL of the 1000-Hz component. Each contour represents a constant level of the 300-Hz component. Stimulus duration was 1 sec. Each data point gives the geometric average of two judgments made by each of 20 subjects. *Right:* The same magnitude estimates raised to the 1.21 power. These rescaled estimates display parallelism, that is, linear loudness summation (from Marks, 1979b). Copyright (1979) by the American Psychological Association. Reprinted by permission.

nents greater than 1.0) and, by iteration, zeroed in on the transformation that eliminated the trend toward nonparallelism. This entailed raising the estimates to the 1.21 power; the transformed data, shown in the right-hand portion of Fig. 1.12, are again proportional to sones (exponent of .6 at 1000 Hz, .7 at 300 Hz). An analogous study of the summation of loudness of 2000-Hz and 5000-Hz tones gave much the same result (Marks, 1978b).

One can summarize the rule of summation on the sone scale, as applied to frequencies greater than 300–400 Hz, as follows: At all but very low sound levels, adding together two equally loud sounds augments the overall perceived magnitude to the same extent as increasing the sound pressure level of either sound alone by 10 dB. Adding two equally loud sounds is, given the rule of linear addition, a doubling of loudness. It follows, then, that the loudness of a given sound doubles with a 10-dB increase in its sound pressure. Therefore, loudness increases as the .6 power of sound pressure.

Processing Auditory Intensity. It is interesting to note that the identical rule of summation—summation of sones—governs additive processes of two rather different types, types that can be called synthetic and analytic. Binaural summation is synthetic: When sounds of the same spectral composition are delivered simultaneously to the two ears, the person hears a single sound whose loudness and lateral position depend on the absolute and relative levels, respectively, of the components. Perceptually, there is no direct access to the original components, only to the total sensory effect. Cross-frequency summation, by contrast, is analytic: When tones widely separated in frequency are delivered to the ears, the loudnesses, in sones, add, but access to the original components is not lost. Instead, the components may remain perceptually accessible, and it is often possible to judge the partial loudness of either component alone, as well as the loudness of the total. In fact, this analytic principle itself makes it possible to scale loudness by means of a simple intensity-matching procedure (Marks, 1978b)—by constructing a complex of two equally loud components, then matching to either component or to the total loudness—and the scale that results is commensurate with the sone scale. It seems difficult for me to conceive of the transformation from sound stimulus to sones, with the subsequent summation in the auditory system, as anything but a *psychoacoustic* process—by which I mean, a transformation instituted in the auditory system.

Sensory and Cognitive Summation

A noteworthy feature of the experiments that I just described is that, in all of them, the experimental task was one of judging loudness, of judging the subjective intensity of each of a set of single sounds. Even though each sound stimulus comprised two components, whose effects combined in a linear fashion to produce an overall loudness, there probably was no need for conscious integration of the sensory components, not even in the case of multicomponent tones, where the individual components perhaps could be parceled out perceptually. In fact, the instructions in all experiments were simply to judge loudness.

By contrast, it has been fashionable in recent years to study how people make relational (e.g., integrative) judgments of pairs of stimuli, as Anderson (Chapter 5) and Rule and Curtis (Chapter 3) describe in this volume. Let me put in my bit here. Analogous to the processes of sensory summation just described, one may ask about the processes of cognitive summation, where the task requires the subjects to integrate sensations consciously.

Taking the binaural-summation study with a 1000-Hz tone as a model, I duplicated (Marks, 1979a) the conditions in all respects save one; instead of presenting the left-ear and right-ear components simultaneously—so that the sensory effects combine synthetically to produce a single fused sound image—I separated them out in time so the subjects heard two sounds, separated from end of one to beginning of the other by 1 second. Rather than telling the subjects to judge loudness, I told them to judge total loudness. Figure 1.13 gives the results. Again, the magnitude estimates suggest linear summation of the psychological values, but the psychological values are not sones. Instead, the judgments of loudness follow roughly a .5, not a .6, power of sound pressure. Binaural and cognitive summation are compared critically in Fig. 1.14, which shows "monaural" and "binaural" functions obtained in the two paradigms. In both cases, the functions drawn through the data points represent perfectly linear

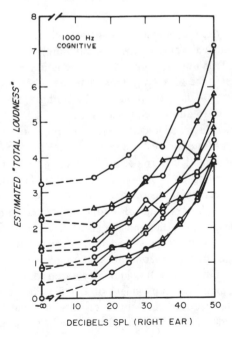

FIG. 1.13. Cognitive summation of loudness. Magnitude estimates of the "total loudness" of sequentially presented 1000-Hz tones, plotted against the SPL delivered to the right ear. Each contour represents a constant SPL delivered to the left ear. The successive stimuli lasted 1 sec. each, with a 1-sec. silent interval between them. Order of presentation to the left and right ears was counterbalanced. Each data point gives the geometric average of two judgments made by each of 15 subjects. From Marks (1979a). Copyright (1979) by the American Psychological Association, Reprinted by permission.

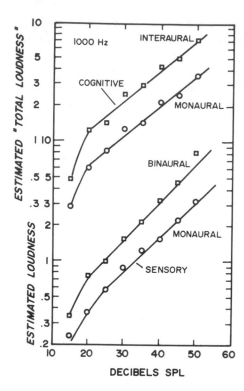

FIG. 1.14. Binaural and cognitive summation compared. Binaural gain (horizontal separation between monaural and binaural functions) equals 10 dB, whereas cognitive gain (corresponding horizontal separation) equals 12–13 dB. Data from Marks (1979a).

summation; the function drawn through each "monaural" function is half the psychological value of the corresponding "binaural" function. But the scales differ. True binaural summation—the gain produced by going from monaural to binaural in the sensory system—equalled about 10 dB. But cognitive (interaural) summation—the gain produced by going from "monaural" to "binaural" in conscious totalling—equalled about 12–13 dB. Some difference in process and/or scale must underlie the perception of loudness as magnitude and the relational (integrative) judgment of total loudness.

Subsequently, I repeated the cognitive-summation experiment with a graphic-rating procedure (Marks, 1979a). The ratings of "total loudness" displayed near parallelism, that is to say, linear additivity, this being in marked contrast with the ratings of loudness obtained in the binaural-summation experiment described earlier and shown in Fig. 1.7. (Whereas it is true that the ratings of "total loudness" revealed some ever so slight tendency for the functions to converge at the upper right, that trend was not statistically reliable—and to transform the data to full additivity required only a mild transformation, a power transformation with exponent of 1.095.) The scale underlying these ratings, as might be deduced, closely resembles the scale underlying the corresponding magnitude estimates of "total loudness"; the scales are the .43 and .49 powers, respectively, of sound pressure. The scales obtained from the two studies of "total loudness" do not differ reliably from one another, but both do differ reliably from the scale obtained from the study of binaural summation (Marks, 1979a). The amount of "summation," measured purely in units of physical intensity, is not the same in the two paradigms: Binaural summation (summation in the sensory system) averaged 10 dB, whereas cognitive summation (summation in an integrative judgment) averaged 13.5 dB.

Let me mention other work on integrative judgments of loudness. Dawson (1971) had subjects give magnitude estimates of total loudness of 1000-Hz tones presented in sequence, and his results suggest linear summation of psychological values that vary as the .52 power of sound pressure. Marks (1978b) reported magnitude estimates of the total loudness of sequentially presented pairs of tones—one at 2000 Hz, the other at 5000 Hz. These results also suggest linear summation, but with components that were the .44 power of sound pressure. Note, too, the study of Curtis and Mullin (1975) of judgments of *average* loudness of sequentially presented 1000-Hz tones. The scale underlying the magnitude estimates, after a transformation of the responses, is about the .4 power of sound pressure.

One possible conclusion is that, contrary to assumption 3, the scale of loudness, that is, the form of the internal psychological representation, is not independent of task. Instead, the representation may differ, depending on whether the task is one of judging loudness per se, or of judging some loudness relation. Instead of assuming that both judgments of magnitudes and judgments of relations between magnitudes rely on the same scale values, I would suggest considering some sort of hierarchical processing model (Marks, 1978b, 1979b), in which the representation depends on the task and hence on the stage in processing that the task taps.

Intervals and Magnitudes

This leads me to the last main topic, namely the psychological representations or scales for intervals and magnitudes. Having just said that judgments of an individual sound's loudness as a magnitude and judgments of at least one loudness relation, namely "total loudness," appear to rely on different underlying scales of "sensation," this provides a clue to what may be the basis for explaining the difference between category and magnitude scales discussed at the beginning of the paper. In a nutshell, I would conjecture that the procedures of category scaling (or more generally of rating, where two end points are specified in advance to the subject) usually induce the subject to deal not with sensations but with intervals, that is, not with magnitudes but rather with relationships. To the extent that the scales underlying interval and magnitude representations differ, and to the extent that the rating judgments provide an accurate measure of the representation of intervals, whereas the magnitude judgments provide an accurate measure of the representation of magnitudes, the rating judgments and magnitude judgments *should* differ. I present this as conjecture because the pertinent data are meager and somewhat circumstantial to say the least, but I think the evidence at hand is more congruent with this conjecture than with several other types of theory currently available.

Quite a few studies over the last number of years have attempted to determine the scale that underlies judgments of loudness intervals or loudness differences, and the results of these experiments generally agree very well in showing that such judgments cannot be based simply on linear differences in sones (Beck & Shaw, 1967; Birnbaum & Elmasian, 1977; Dawson, 1971; Parker & Schneider, 1974; Schneider, Parker, & Stein, 1974; Schneider, Parker, Valenti, Farrell, & Kanow, 1978). The upshot of all of these experiments, which have used methods of magnitude estimation, category rating, and paired comparisons in the study of loudness intervals, is that they point to an underlying representation for loudness that is much like Garner's lambda scale, where lambda can be defined by $\lambda = kP^{.26}$ That is to say, pairs of sound stimuli that are judged to have equal loudness intervals are separated by equal units on the lambda scale, not by equal units on the sone scale. The lambda scale, of course, was itself derived primarily from loudness equisections (Garner, 1954), which were assumed, in order to generate the scale, to give equal intervals of loudness.

It appears then that different sets of psychological values, different loudness scales, apply to loudness as a magnitude and to pairs of loudnesses that form the relation of loudness interval or loudness difference. The two scales seem to operate in different types of psychophysical task: the sone scale in the formation of loudness of an individual sound; the lambda scale in the way subjects evaluate certain relationships between sounds. If this is so, if both representations have a psychological reality in the way just stated, then it should be possible to exhibit the characteristics of both in a single experiment, from a single set of judgments. Simply stated, the experiment consists of asking subjects to make judgments (magnitude estimates) of loudness intervals of each of several pairs of sounds (this in order to display the psychological representation that underlies loudness intervals), but to allow the members of each pair to be presented either monaurally or binaurally (this in order to display binaural summation, and hence the psychological representation that underlies loudness magnitude).

The results of this experiment—actually, a mini-experiment (Marks, 1979b)—do in fact serve to demonstrate the simultaneous functioning of two perceptual scales for auditory intensity. First of all, the judgments of loudness intervals of pairs of 1000-Hz tones depended on differences defined on, approximately, the lambda scale (see Figs. 1.15 and 1.16). Thus, the lambda scale provides the psychological representation for the interval relationship between members of each pair of sounds. Second, the loudness of each individual sound depended on the total value in sones of the left-ear and right-ear components (Fig. 1.17). Thus, the sone scale provides the psychological representation for

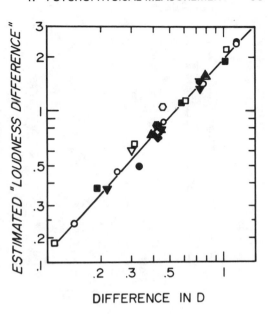

FIG. 1.15. Magnitude estimates of loudness intervals plotted against linear differences on the D scale, which approximates Garner's lambda scale. In each pair of stimuli, one or both could be either monaural (open symbols) or binaural (filled symbols). The successive stimuli lasted 1 sec. each, with a 1-sec. silent interval between them. Each data point gives the median of two judgments made by each of 14 subjects (from Marks, 1979b). Copyright (1979) by the American Psychological Association. Reprinted by permission.

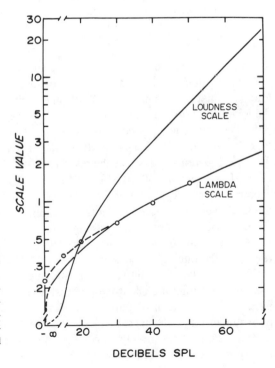

FIG. 1.16. Values on the D scale, plotted against SPL. The solid line gives values on the lambda scale. The loudness scale underlying binaural summation is plotted for comparison (from Marks, 1979b). Copyright (1979) by the American Psychological Association. Reprinted by permission.

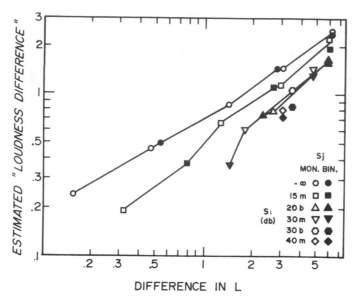

FIG. 1.17.   The magnitude estimates of loudness intervals from Fig. 1.15, plotted against linear differences in loudness. Whereas differences in loudness fail to predict the judgments (the data do not collapse onto a single function), they do predict binaural summation (for any given lower stimulus, monaural and binaural upper stimuli fall on a single function). From Marks (1979b). Copyright (1979) by the American Psychological Association. Reprinted by permission.

the magnitude of each sound. Let me give an example: The loudness interval of a monaural stimulus of 20 dB and a monaural stimulus of 50 dB equals the loudness interval of a monaural 20 dB and a binaural 40 dB. This is so because the lower stimulus marking each interval (20 dB monaural) is the same in the two pairs and thus equally loud, and the upper stimuli were selected to be equally loud (40 dB binaural equals 50 dB monaural, as summation in sones predicts). The two equations to describe the results are as follows: $L = L_1 + L_r = kP_1^{.6} + kP_r^{.6}$, P greater than 30 dB SPL, and $\Delta D = G(L_j) - G(L_i)$. The first equation accounts for the formation of the loudness as magnitude of each sound, whereas the second equation accounts for the perception of interval relationships between pairs of sounds. (Actually, the judgments were proportional to values of ΔD raised to the 1.07 power. That is, the response scale was slightly accelerated with regard to the intervals themselves.)

These results, like the results on judgments of total loudness, suggest the usefulness of thinking about the processing of auditory intensity information in terms of some sort of hierarchical model, with different perceptual representations underlying the psychological variables that operate at different stages in processing. This certainly makes a good deal of sense when one considers the purely sensory processes themselves. For instance, one of the earliest stages in processing sound intensity involves energy summation. When the frequency distribution of a sound falls wholly within limited range (within a critical bandwidth), loudness depends on total energy (Scharf, 1970; Zwicker, Flottorp, & Stevens, 1957). This in turn implies that one of the earliest stages of auditory processing operates on a representation that is fully proportional to sound energy. By way of contrast, binaural summation and summation across (widely separated) frequencies operate on sones, and thereby suggest that some subsequent transformation—that is, subsequent to the process of energy summation— operates to change the internal representation. It seems fairly natural to extend this scheme beyond the purely sensory realm to judgments of relations between sounds, where the results suggest yet another transformation.

Let me go back now to the question of why different scaling procedures often yield systematically different results and, in particular, to the difference between results that often obtain with magnitude estimation and rating. Quite simply, what I want to suggest is that the method of magnitude estimation (and the method of magnitude production) sets up for a subject the task of judging magnitudes, and much of the time the judgment scale that subjects produce comes pretty close to the mark, for example, comes close to producing the sone scale. This does not always occur, of course, as the review at the beginning of this paper should have made eminently clear. Still, the magnitude methods (estimation and production) aspire toward accurate representation of the underlying magnitude scale.

The second part of my suggestion is that rating methods set up for a subject the task of judging intervals, and much of the time the judgment scale that is produced also comes pretty close to the mark—close, for example, to producing the lambda scale. Again, this does not always happen, as the review earlier indicated. Any given rating scale, like any given magnitude-estimation scale, may exhibit slight or considerable response bias (as a recent study by Schneider et al., 1978, demonstrated). Nevertheless, it is interesting to note that when S. S. Stevens and Galanter (1957) sought to produce a "pure" category scale for loudness, that is, a scale as uncontaminated as possible by response biases, what they obtained is virtually identical to the lambda scale. If one plots the lambda scale against the sone scale, the result is a concave downward curve that can readily serve as a prototype for plots of ratings versus magnitude estimates.

4. SUMMARY

There are three main points to this paper, some of which have been made explicitly, others of which have been made only implicitly so far, but which can be made explicitly now:

1. Although there certainly are problems with the methods of psychophysics, this is not reason for despair. Despite systematic and unsystematic modes of variation, there is considerable order in scaling data. Moreover, there are under-

lying uniformities in the psychological representations, that is, in the scales underlying various tasks and procedures. It may even be that judiciously balanced experiments using magnitude and rating methods can produce the underlying scales directly.

2. I think it is time to give real consideration to the idea that the psychological representation—the scale, if you will—may in many circumstances depend on the task (see also Eisler, 1963). In particular, the scale underlying sensation as magnitude may not be the same as the scale underlying the psychological components of sensory or perceptual relationships. To the extent this is so, it obviously contradicts the assumption that a single scale underlies all tasks. Still, this assumption may hold on a more restricted level. For instance, I would expect the rule of addition of sones to describe binaural summation of the loudness of pure tones in virtually all tasks, using all procedures.

3. My third point is as follows: It is now time, in my opinion, to start looking at processing models or their equivalents. The new psychophysics of 1978 is not the new psychophysics of 1958. The prime issue is less scaling for scaling's sake and more the question of what are the functional roles of scales in sensory, perceptual, and other behavioral processes, so that the procedures and tasks of psychophysics become the tool of the student of sensory, perceptual, or social processes.

ACKNOWLEDGMENTS

Preparation of this paper was supported in part by grant BNS 76-09950 from the National Science Foundation.

REFERENCES

Anderson, N. H. Functional measurement and psychophysical judgment. *Psychological Review*, 1970, *77*, 153-170.

Anderson, N. H. Algebraic models in perception. In E. C. Carterette & M. P. Friedman (Eds.), *Psychophysical judgment and measurement. Handbook of perception* (Vol. 2). New York: Academic Press, 1974.

Beck, J., & Shaw, W. A. The scaling of pitch by the method of magnitude estimation. *American Journal of Psychology*, 1961, *74*, 242-251.

Beck, J., & Shaw, W. A. Magnitude of the standard, numerical value of the standard, and stimulus spacing in the estimation of loudness. *Perceptual and Motor Skills*, 1965, *21*, 151-156.

Beck, J., & Shaw, W. A. Ratio-estimations of loudness-intervals. *American Journal of Psychology*, 1967, *80*, 59-65.

Berlin, I. *The hedgehog and the fox*. New York: Simon & Schuster, 1953.

Birnbaum, M. H., & Elmasian, R. Loudness "ratios" and "differences" involve the same psychophysical operation. *Perception & Psychophysics*, 1977, *22*, 383-391.

Curtis, D. W. Magnitude estimations and category judgments of brightness and brightness intervals: A two-stage interpretation. *Journal of Experimental Psychology*, 1970, *83*, 201-208.

Curtis, D. W., & Mullin, L. C. Judgments of average magnitude: Analyses in terms of the functional measurement and two-stage models. *Perception & Psychophysics*, 1975, *18*, 299-308.

Dawson, W. E. Magnitude estimation of apparent sums and differences. *Perception & Psychophysics*, 1971, *9*, 368-374.

Eisler, H. Magnitude scales, category scales, and Fechnerian integration. *Psychological Review*, 1963, *70*, 243-253.

Eisler, H. On the ability to estimate differences: A note on Birnbaum's subtractive model. *Perception & Psychophysics*, 1978, *24*, 185-189.

Fletcher, H., & Munson, W. A. Loudness, its definition, measurement and calculation. *Journal of the Acoustical Society of America*, 1933, *5*, 82-108.

Garner, W. R. A technique and a scale for loudness measurement. *Journal of the Acoustical Society of America*, 1954, *26*, 73-88.

Green, D. M., & Luce, R. D. Variability of magnitude estimates: A timing theory analysis. *Perception & Psychophysics*, 1974, *15*, 291-300.

Hellman, R. P. Growth of loudness at 1000 and 3000 Hz. *Journal of the Acoustical Society of America*, 1976, *60*, 672-677.

Hellman, R. P., & Zwislocki, J. J. Some factors affecting the estimation of loudness. *Journal of the Acoustical Society of America*, 1961, *33*, 687-694.

Hellman, R. P., & Zwislocki, J. J. Loudness function of a 1000-cps tone in the presence of a masking noise. *Journal of the Acoustical Society of America*, 1964, *36*, 1618-1627.

Hellman, R. P., & Zwislocki, J. J. Loudness determination at low sound frequencies. *Journal of the Acoustical Society of America*, 1968, *43*, 60-64.

Jankovic, I. N., & Cross, D. V. *On the binaural additivity of loudness.* Paper presented at Eastern Psychological Association, Boston, Mass. April 1977.

Jones, F. N., & Woskow, M. H. On the relationship between estimates of loudness and pitch. *American Journal of Psychology*, 1962, *75*, 669-671.

Levelt, W. J. M., Riemersma, J. B., & Bunt, A. A. Binaural additivity of loudness. *British Journal of Mathematical and Statistical Psychology*, 1972, *25*, 51-68.

Luce, R. D., & Mo, S. S. Magnitude estimation of heaviness and loudness by individual subjects: A test of a probabilistic response theory. *British Journal of Psychology*, 1965, *18*, 159-174.

Marks, L. E. Stimulus-range, number of categories, and form of the category-scale. *American Journal of Psychology*, 1968, *81*, 467-479.

Marks, L. E. On scales of sensation: Prolegomena to any future psychophysics that will be able to come forth as science. *Perception & Psychophysics*, 1974, *16*, 358-376.

Marks, L. E. Binaural summation of the loudness of pure tones. *Journal of the Acoustical Society of America*, 1978, *64*, 107-113. (a)

Marks, L. E. PHONION: Translation and annotations concerning loudness scales and the processing of auditory intensity. In N. J. Castellan, Jr. & F. Restle (Eds.), *Cognitive theory* (Vol. 3). Hillsdale, N.J.: Lawrence Erlbaum Associates, 1978. (b)

Marks, L. E. *The unity of the senses: Interrelations among the modalities.* New York: Academic Press, 1978. (c)

Marks, L. E. Sensory and cognitive factors in judgments of loudness. *Journal of Experimental Psychology: Human Perception and Performance*, 1979, *5*, 426-443. (a)

Marks, L. E. A theory of loudness and loudness judgments. *Psychological Review*, 1979, *86*, 256-285. (b)

Marks, L. E. Binaural summation of loudness: Noise and two-tone complexes. *Perception & Psychophysics*, 1980, *27*, 489-498.

Marks, L. E., & Cain, W. S. Perception of intervals and magnitudes for three prothetic continua. *Journal of Experimental Psychology*, 1972, *94*, 6-17.

Marks, L. E., & Stevens, J. C. Individual brightness functions. *Perception & Psychophysics*, 1966, *1*, 17-24.

Parducci, A. Category judgment: A range-frequency model. *Psychological Review,* 1965, *72,* 407–418.

Parker, S., & Schneider, B. Non-metric scaling of loudness and pitch using similarity and difference estimates. *Perception & Psychophysics,* 1974, *15,* 238–242.

Plato. *The collected dialogues.* In E. Hamilton & H. Cairns (Eds.), New York: Pantheon, 1961.

Poulton, E. C. The new psychophysics: Six models for magnitude estimation. *Psychological Bulletin,* 1968, *69,* 1–19.

Pradhan, P. L., & Hoffman, P. J. Effect of spacing and range of stimuli on magnitude estimation. *Journal of Experimental Psychology,* 1963, *66,* 533–541.

Reynolds, G. S., & Stevens, S. S. Binaural summation of loudness. *Journal of the Acoustical Society of America,* 1960, *32,* 1337–1344.

Rowley, R. R., & Studebaker, G. A. Monaural loudness-intensity relationships for a 1000-Hz tone. *Journal of the Acoustical Society of America,* 1969, *45,* 1186–1192.

Scharf, B. Critical bands. In J. V. Tobias (Ed.), *Foundations of modern auditory theory* (Vol. 1). New York: Academic Press, 1970.

Scharf, B., & Fishken, D. Binaural summation of loudness: Reconsidered. *Journal of Experimental Psychology,* 1970, *86,* 374–379.

Schneider, B., & Lane, H. Ratio scales, category scales, and variability in the production of loudness and softness. *Journal of the Acoustical Society of America,* 1963, *35,* 1953–1961.

Schneider, B., Parker, S., & Stein, D. The measurement of loudness using direct comparisons of sensory intervals. *Journal of Mathematical Psychology,* 1974, *11,* 259–273.

Schneider, B., Parker, S., Valenti, M., Farrell, G., & Kanow, G. Response bias in category and magnitude estimation of difference and similarity for loudness and pitch. *Journal of Experimental Psychology: Human Perception and Performance,* 1978, *4,* 483–496.

Stevens, J. C. Stimulus spacing and the judgment of loudness. *Journal of Experimental Psychology,* 1958, *56,* 246–250.

Stevens, J. C., & Guirao, M. Individual loudness functions. *Journal of the Acoustical Society of America,* 1964, *36,* 2210–2213.

Stevens, J. C., & Tulving, E. Estimations of loudness by a group of untrained observers. *American Journal of Psychology,* 1957, *70,* 600–605.

Stevens, S. S. A scale for the measurement of a psychological magnitude: Loudness. *Psychological Review,* 1936, *43,* 405–416.

Stevens, S. S. The measurement of loudness. *Journal of the Acoustical Society of America,* 1955, *27,* 815–829.

Stevens, S. S. The direct estimation of sensory magnitudes—loudness. *American Journal of Psychology,* 1956, *69,* 1–25.

Stevens, S. S. Problems and methods of psychophysics. *Psychological Bulletin,* 1958, *55,* 177–196.

Stevens, S. S. Power-group transformations under glare, masking, and recruitment. *Journal of the Acoustical Society of America,* 1966, *39,* 725–735.

Stevens, S. S. Perceived level of noise by Mark VII and dB(E). *Journal of the Acoustical Society of America,* 1972, *51,* 575–601.

Stevens, S. S., & Galanter, E. Ratio scales and category scales for a dozen perceptual continua. *Journal of Experimental Psychology,* 1957, *54,* 377–411.

Stevens, S. S., & Greenbaum, H. B. Regression effect in psychophysical judgment. *Perception & Psychophysics,* 1966, *1,* 439–446.

Stevens, S. S., & Guirao, M. Loudness, reciprocality, and partition scales. *Journal of the Acoustical Society of America,* 1962, *34,* 1466–1471.

Stevens, S. S., & Guirao, M. Subjective scaling of length and area and the matching of length to loudness and brightness. *Journal of Experimental Psychology,* 1963, *66,* 177–186.

Teghtsoonian, R. Range effects in psychophysical scaling and a revision of Stevens' law. *American Journal of Psychology*, 1973, *86*, 3–27.

Zwicker, E., Flottorp, G., & Stevens, S. S. Critical band width in loudness summation. *Journal of the Acoustical Society of America*, 1957, *29*, 548–557.

Zwislocki, J. J. *Absolute scaling*. Paper presented to the Acoustical Society of America, Providence, R.I., May 1978.

2 On Judgments of Magnitude

David V. Cross
State University of New York at Stony Brook

S. S. Stevens discovered, in the summer of 1953, that if you ask individuals to give direct numerical estimates of the relative magnitudes of their sensory experiences, reliable empirical relationships obtain between their judgments and the physical magnitudes of the stimuli that produce them. As a sound or light varies in intensity, observers can easily describe the perceived changes in loudness or brightness (or in any other attribute they might discern) in numerical terms—just as they can use numbers to estimate the lengths of lines, the heaviness of lifted objects, or the duration of a timed event. Such judgments, of course, are fallible in that judgments of the same event repeated over time tend to be variable and they tend to be idiosyncratically influenced by contextual and procedural variables. Nevertheless, when averaged over trials or observers, numerical judgments of subjective magnitudes enter into highly reliable functional relationships with objective measures of stimulus magnitude and, although magnitude judgments are not actual *measurements* of sensations or perceptions, they can be relatively reliable *indicators* of how the experiences of these events are related conceptually for the individual experiencing them.

When magnitude estimation was first used to scale sensory magnitudes, it seemed natural to help the observer by specifying a standard stimulus to which there was made to correspond a designated modular response, but after a time it became clear that the practice of constraining the observer to use designated standards and moduli often produced spurious variance in experimental outcomes (Poulton, 1968). Observers frequently have difficulty accepting the experimenter's choice of modulus and standard, and their judgments tend to drift toward what is for them a more natural correspondence. The practice of designating these reference levels was eventually given up by most psychophysicists and current practice recommends imposing as few constraints as possible on the matching task, leaving the observer free to choose his own scale unit or modulus.

As a scaling procedure, the method of magnitude estimation has grown in popularity in recent years, particularly with social scientists in their quest for metric indicators of attitude and opinion (Hamblin, 1974). It has the considerable advantage of convenience compared to many other scaling procedures, especially in survey research where opinions on a variety of topics are sought and pair comparison methods would be impractical. However, Stevens (1975, pp. 286–287) points out that in reporting subjective magnitudes, people often use numbers in idiosyncratic ways, treating the number system as an array of discrete values rather than as a continuum and showing preferences for certain whole numbers like 1, 2, 5, 10, and some of their multiples while avoiding intermediate values. They might also have misconceptions about the number domain, believing, for example, that if they use numbers below five they risk running out of numbers if weaker stimuli are presented for judgment. Also, people are accustomed to using numbers in other kinds of judgments as in the expression os simple ordinal relations; if seven levels are discerned in the stimuli to be judged, a person might simply use the whole numbers 1 to 7, intending only to represent the order rather than the relative magnitudes of these stimuli. In addition, people have been trained through the widespread use of rating scales in social surveys and questionnaires to give numerical judgments in scales artificially constrained to a 5, 7, or 11 point range, hence ignoring ratios and the proportional relations actually perceived unless the top and bottom stimuli stand in the ratio 5, 7, or 11 to 1 by accident. In everyday speech, expressions like "on a scale of 10, I would give it a . . . " are commonplace. The tendency to use numbers in these idiosyncratic ways can intrude in numerical judgments of magnitude to distort the nature of the perceptual relationships that the judgments are intended to represent.

These problems can often be avoided or at least considerably reduced by introducing the procedure of magnitude estimation via a preliminary task in which the subject estimates the lengths of lines—not in conventional units of inches or centimeters, but in arbitrarily selected numbers whose magnitudes stand in the same ratio to one another as do the line lengths they represent (Stevens, 1966a). Generally, a line that is twice as long as another looks about twice as long unless it is differently oriented or embedded in a different context; lines similarly oriented and in identical contexts tend to be perceived veridically (Stevens & Guirao, 1963; Teghtsoonian, 1965). If the subject's number matches do not preserve these facts, then we are justified in regarding the judgments as biased—i.e., as deviating systematically from an accurate rendering of perceived relationships. Under certain conditions it might be reasonable to expect the same response bias to be operating when numbers are matched to other kinds of stimuli. A bias-free scale of subjective magnitudes can be constructed for these stimuli from transformed judgments using the inverse of the empirically determined function relating numbers to lines. Hence, preliminary practice at matching numbers to lines can serve the double purpose of clarifying for the subject that his judgments should preserve proportional relations as well as providing data enabling an objective assessment of response biases.

Magnitude scales can be constructed without direct recourse to numerical judgments. Experiments have shown that individuals can give reliable judgments of subjective magnitude—whether of a sensory, perceptual, or cognitive attribute—by squeezing a hand dynamometer (J. C. Stevens, Mack, & Stevens, 1960), or by varying the effort of a vocalization (Lane, Catania, & Stevens, 1961), or the amplitude of a vibration (Stevens, 1959), or the brightness of a light (J. C. Stevens & Marks, 1965), or loudness of a sound (Stevens, 1966b), or the extent of a temporal duration (Dawson & Mirando, 1975) or visual length (Stevens & Guirao, 1963), and so on, and that judgments given in these modes of expression are often even more reliable and less idiosyncratic than numerical judgments given under similar circumstances. In other words, if you present individuals with a sequence of stimuli that vary in magnitude along one perceptual or cognitive dimension and request that they "track" or respond to these changes by producing analogous changes in a different dimension, the task can usually be adeptly performed even when neither variable is given directly in numerical value. For example, a person can indicate his/her opinion of the desirability of various occupations by adjusting the intensity of a light, or the level of a noise burst, so that the levels of *brightness* and *loudness* produced are both proportional to the desirability of each occupation. If we know the exact functions relating these sensory attributes to their physical correlates, then measurements of the matching physical stimuli are sufficient to determine the relative magnitudes of the individual's perceptions. Unfortunately, although there is reason to believe that the sensory transformations in question are power functions, there is less certainty concerning the values of the exponents that govern the desired transformations. We cannot, for instance, simply adopt the value of ⅓ (which has been proposed as the characteristic exponent for both brightness and loudness) and calculate subjective magnitude as the cube root of the sound or light intensities produced because the production functions are generally not governed by the same exponents that determine the input sensory transformations; floor and ceiling effects (psychophysical regression) in the matching variables produce nonlinear biases in observed relationships that complicate the otherwise simple set of invariances characterizing sensory processes at the theoretical level. More will be said about this below. But just as response biases are detected in numerical judgments by having subjects first estimate line lengths, biases in loudness or brightness matching functions can be evaluated by having them first match these variables to numbers or lines. If doubling the number or the line length results in an increase, say, of nine decibels in the matching variable, whether it be sound or light intensity, then a similar increase of nine decibels when these stimuli are matched to two different occupations would imply that one occupation is twice as desirable as the other—assuming the response bias remains the same when occupations are substituted for lines or numbers as target stimuli.

A few years ago, as an undergraduate laboratory exercise, 37 Harvard students scaled the desirability of 16 occupations using only brightness and loudness as matching continua. As a prelude, they matched brightness to varying levels of loudness and they matched loudness to different brightness levels, thus gaining some practice using these modes of judgment as well as providing data calibrating each against the other (this is an alternative method for evaluating response biases in cross-modality matching functions when the corresponding input sensory transformations are presumed to be known). Two scales of occupational desirability were constructed, one based on the brightness and the other on the loudness matches, each slightly adjusted to compensate for the response biases determined in the calibration procedure. These scales are plotted in logarithmic coordinates, one against the other, in Fig. 2.1. The two subscales are clearly in very close agreement. The orthogonal projection of each point onto the unit slope regression line, and its representation in the spacing (in log scale) of the occupations listed on the right, corresponds to the geometric mean of the two scale values associated with that occupation. In linear scale, the occupation of physician is twice as desirable as that of high school teacher and over seven times more

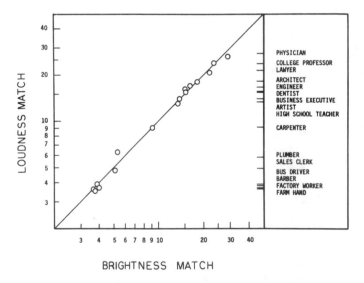

FIG. 2.1. Occupational desirability scale of 16 occupational titles derived from indirect cross-modality matches of loudness (y-axis) and brightness (x-axis). Judgments of both modalities are averaged by calculating the orthogonal projections of the points on the unit slope regression line and representing them in the spacing (in log scale) of the occupations listed on the right.

TABLE 2.1
Desirability or Prestige of Occupations

	Scale based on loudness & brightness matches	Scale based on loudness matches	Scale based on magnitude estimation	Treiman's Standard International Occupational Prestige Scale
Physician	28.1	28.3	28.0	78
College professor	24.2	25.3		78
Lawyer	21.7			71
Architect	18.5	18.3	19.4	72
Engineer	16.9	16.2	16.6	
Dentist	16.1			70
Business executive	15.8	18.7		67
Artist	14.3	12.0	16.3	57
High school teacher	13.8	22.0	16.9	64
Carpenter	9.4			37
Plumber	6.0			34
Sales clerk	5.1			34
Bus driver	4.0	5.0		32
Barber (hair dresser)	4.0	2.4	4.5	30
Farm hand	3.8	6.2	2.6	23
Factory worker	3.8	4.8	2.1	29

The scale values based on loudness and brightness matches were obtained from 37 students at Harvard University in 1971. The loudness matches were from 24 University of Notre Dame students as reported by Dawson & Brinker (1971). The magnitude estimations were made by 74 students at the University of Stockholm and reported by Künnapas and Wikström (1963). Treiman's Standard International Occupational Prestige Scale goes from 0 to 100 and is based on ratings of occupational prestige from 85 studies conducted since World War II in 60 countries. It covers 509 occupations.

desirable than factory worker. These numerical relations were derived not from numerical judgments but from sensory matches.

The numerical values for the occupations considered in this study are given in Table 2.1 along with the comparable results from three other studies. The scale values based on loudness matches were obtained from 24 male students at the University of Notre Dame (Dawson & Brinker, 1971). The magnitude estimations were made by 74 students at the University of Stockholm (Künnapas & Wikström, 1963), and Treiman's Standard International Occupational Prestige Scale is based primarily on rating scale data drawn from 85 studies conducted since World War II in 60 countries. It covers 509 occupations and scores their prestige from roughly 0 to 100 (Treiman, 1977). Although the magnitude scales were obtained from different populations (Harvard vs. Notre Dame and U.S.A. vs. Sweden) and at different times, there is remarkable agreement in some comparisons. For example, the occupation of physician is roughly 1.7 times more desirable than that of engineer for each of the magnitude scales. On the other hand, real differences emerge: whereas Harvard students regard teaching high school as less than half as desirable as college teaching, students at Notre Dame regard high school teaching as nearly $^4/_5$ as desirable as teaching in college. The important point to be made by the overall comparison of these scales is the consensual validity achieved; intercorrelations between scales range from .94 to .99 with an average r = .97.

How can individuals be expected to establish correspondences between magnitudes of such different qualities as, say, loudness on the one hand and prestige of occupation on the other? These are incommensurable magnitudes—one is the immediate sensory experience of a physical event, the other is an evaluation based on the individual's knowledge of the relative power, privilege, and prestige accorded to a member of a given occupation by society—and yet people have relatively little difficulty expressing one in terms of the other. What *is* comparable across different sorts of things is one's perception of *relative* magnitude. The size of an animal is not directly comparable to a measure of time, but the relation between a dog and a mouse with respect to their apparent size might be perceived to be of the same order of magnitude as that between a minute and a second in terms of experienced time. If so, the analogy "a dog is to a minute as a mouse is to a _____" would be completed by inserting the term "second" and if further asked to match time to an "elephant," the observer might respond with "hour." It is less likely that "hour," "minute," and "second" would be matched respectively to "deer," "pig," and "cat" even though the terms are similarly ordered and the proportions "hour:minute::minute:second" and "deer:pig::pig:cat" might be similarly endorsed, because the corresponding relative magnitudes are not perceived as equivalent; that is, the ratio of an hour to a minute seems larger than the ratio of a deer to a pig and the analogy "a deer is to an hour as a pig is to a minute" would be false. Hence, the analogies served by cross-modality matching functions tell us something about how the world is viewed by the observer and when a sound is matched to an occupation to indicate how desirable that occupation is, it is not because n units of loudness are equal to m units of social prestige but that if a given occupation is viewed as having x times more status than another, then a tone will be matched to it that is x times as loud as a tone matched to the other occupation.

The way people conceptualize magnitudes depends on the experiences they have had with numbers and numerical relations. Children learn when it is appropriate to use verbal phrases such as "twice as much" or "three times as long" when comparing quantities or lengths; the criteria for the correct use of such numerical judgments are explicit in the empirical operations that can be performed on physical objects and in the relations that hold among them. Typically, a child learns how to count, then it learns that "three times as long" means the long stick matches three of the short sticks laid end to end. It learns that ratios of numbers are equivalent to the ratios of lengths and that this property of proportionality can be extended to other kinds of magnitudes.

It is notable that the Greek word for magnitude (*megethos*) was used by Homer to mean *personal greatness* or *stature* (Bochner, 1966). The word was adopted by Eudoxus of Cnidus (c. 365 B.C.) and used for the first time in its mathematical sense in his theory of proportion (Mueller, 1974). To this day, these two meanings of personal greatness and mathematical magnitude are both contained in the French noun *grandeur* and in the German noun *grösse*. The Greeks never developed the concept of real numbers; their mathematics was based on the notion of magnitude. Lengths represented one kind of magnitude, areas were another kind, and volumes, weights, etc. were still other kinds of magnitudes. The Greeks could conceptualize the ratio M_1/M_2 for any two values of one kind of magnitude and the ratio N_1/N_2 for any two values of any other kind, and by a famous criterion credited to Eudoxus they could verify whether the proportion $M_1/M_2 = N_1/N_2$ does or does not hold for the four values given, thus generalizing the notion of magnitude as a relational property shared by diverse entities.

The Pythagoreans believed that the "worlds of beauty, of music, of architecture, and indeed of structure and symmetry of human thought, lie in the ordered relations of the numbers themselves" (Murphy, 1968, p. 12). They can be said to have been the first psychophysicists in that they were the first to discover a quantitative relationship between a subjective experience—that of musical harmony—and physical magnitudes associated with the stimulus. They discovered that when one string of a lyre is exactly twice as long as another, there is a pleasant blending or unity of tone and that other simple ratios such as 3 to 2 or 4 to 3 also produced sweet harmonious chords but discords were struck when the strings deviated slightly from these simple ratios.

Luce (1972) proposed that: "man—and any other organism—is, among other things, a measuring device, in function not unlike a spring balance or a voltmeter, which is capable of transforming many kinds of physical attributes into a common measure in the central nervous system [p. 96]." What is the character of this "common measure" that it will serve all subjective attributes? Luce and Green (1972) propose that subjective magnitudes of sensory experiences are represented in a common neural measure, namely, time between pulses. But this notion does not seem to serve the representation of other subjective magnitudes such as subjective utility, perceived seriousness of crimes, or desirability of occupations.

THE POWER LAW

Twenty-five years of research and literally hundreds of psychophysical studies involving an impressive number of psychological dimensions have provided a firm empirical basis for a weak form of Stevens' Law concerning cross-modality matching relations, namely, *proportional changes in a stimulus variable will be matched by proportional changes in a response variable*—an invariance that implies a power function relationship between the stimulus and response variables. This implies that equal ratios of physical magnitudes are subjectively equivalent. There is little dispute over the proposal that the power function is a statement of the simplest and most descriptive representation we can make of the cross-modality matches usually observed in scaling studies; a given stimulus ratio will produce a smaller, equal, or larger ratio of response magnitudes as the exponent of the power function describing the relationship takes on a value less than, equal to, or greater than unity. In general, power functions fit to group data from cross-modality matching experiments account for all but 1% or so of the total variance in average responding across levels of the independent variable. This law is so well established in psychophysics that exceptions to it in the form of statistically significant departures from the simple power function can alert attention to important second-order effects in the data such as a steepening of the curve near threshold.

It has been argued from evolutionary perspective that the power law has its basis in the emergence of a nervous system capable of stable homological representations of environmental events (Yilmaz, 1967). It has also been argued that the power law is the consequence of a simple perceptual constancy and the transitivity of the perceptual judgments that display this constancy (Shepard, 1978). In fact, both of these arguments parallel one given in biology to explain why the equation of allometry that describes the growth of a part of an organism in relation to the growth of the whole organism, or some other part of it, is a power function (Bertalanffy, 1968). Like the power law in psychophysics, the equation of allometry is a simplified approximation, but it applies to an astonishingly broad range of morphological, physiological, and biochemical phenomena. For instance, if growing animals of the same species are compared, basal metabolism increases generally as the ⅔-power of body weight. For many years, debate raged in biology over the precise value of this exponent. It is now recognized that the relationship is not invariable; the exponent can, and indeed does, vary as a function of the species in question, physiological conditions, and experimental factors. The exponents measured in psychophysical studies also vary significantly from person to person and from one experiment to another. Frequently, a different exponent describes the psychophysical relationship between say, A and B, depending on whether A is matched to B, or vice versa (Stevens & Greenbaum, 1966), or whether both A and B are each adjusted to match levels of a third variable and, hence, indirectly to match one another (Cross, 1974; Dawson & Brinker, 1971). Because the exponents relating psychophysical variables are not independent of the subject, and are not independent of nonsensory variations in experimental conditions, Luce (1972) argues that it is unlikely that an isomorphism will ever be found between the empirical invariances that remain and any formal measurement structure at all comparable to what exists for physical measures. Krantz's (1972) theory of magnitude estimation fails because the structure it provides is predicated on the invariance of relative magnitudes across subjects and conditions—an assumption that finds little support in empirical findings.

THE REGRESSION PROBLEM

Human judgments are notoriously unreliable in comparison to physical measurements. This is why grocers use a scale to weigh their packaged merchandise and carpenters use a measuring stick rather than trust their unaided judgment in determining the length of board needed to fit a given space. Judgments are variable because factors other than the stimulus to be judged contribute to the act of judgment. Let us assume the strong form of Stevens' Law: Subjective magnitude, ψ, grows as a power function of the objective magnitude of the stimulus, $\psi = S^\beta$, and the task of psychophysics is to determine the characteristic exponent for each stimulus continuum. Let us assume that numerical judgments directly match subjective magnitudes except for perturbations in the matching relation caused by unobserved random influences collectively represented by u. The causal relations I have just stipulated can be expressed diagrammatically as follows:

$$S \xrightarrow{\ \beta\ } \psi \longrightarrow N \longleftarrow u$$

The presentation of S leads to a perception of $\psi = S^\beta$, which, jointly with u, determines the judgment N. The effects of u are assumed to combine multiplicatively with ψ because, as in physical measurements of length, variability in N tends to increase with the magnitude of N, following a law of proportionate effect. Thus, the diagram represents the equation $N = \psi u$ or its equivalent, $N = S^\beta u$. With the additional assumption that the random variable u is lognormal with parameters $\mu = E(\ln u)$ and $\sigma^2 = \mathrm{Var}(\ln u)$, the model is completely specified. If ln u is independent of ln S, an unbiased estimate of the parameter β can be obtained by regressing ln N against ln S.

Most psychophysical studies employ a repeated measurement design in which different levels of S are presented in random order and subjects judge each presentation. The stimulus schedule is determined by such factors as the range and spacing of stimulus levels as well as the specific order in which they occur. In addition, judgments are often constrained by floor and ceiling effects because of arbitrary constraints imposed on the response range either by the observer or by the experimental procedure itself. These effects are obviously correlated with the stimulus. Such contextual and response bias factors are represented diagrammatically by the inclusion of another set of unobservable variables denoted by w

$$S \underset{w}{\overset{\beta}{\rightleftarrows}} \psi \longrightarrow N \longleftarrow u$$

The variables represented by w determine or influence both S and N and thus create a path of coordinated effects that parallels the direct path and which, because of the temporal priority of S, can be represented by the alternative diagram

The dashed arrow connecting S and N means that association is correlational rather than causal and the parameter ρ denotes the linear regression of ln N against ln S via this path. The equation modeled by this diagram is

$$N = \psi S^{\rho} u \text{ or, equivalently, } N = S^{\beta + \rho} u \qquad (2.1)$$

Linear regression of ln N against ln S estimates $\beta + \rho$ rather than β alone. The existence of floor and ceiling effects in judgment will result in a negative value for ρ and the empirical exponent will underestimate the true exponent as in the regression effect described by Stevens and Greenbaum (1966).

Let us now consider the magnitude-production procedure in which N is presented as the stimulus to be judged, and the observer adjusts S to match the subjective magnitude of N. The diagram for the causal relations involved in this situation parallels the prior case:

$$N \longrightarrow \psi \xrightarrow{\beta_*} S \longleftarrow v$$
$$\rho_*$$

A different set of random influences, v, is operating. The output exponent β_* relating S to ψ is assumed to be the inverse of the input exponent operating in the magnitude estimation experiment, hence $\beta_* = 1/\beta$. Again, ρ_* represents the correlation between N and S not accounted for by the direct causal relationship. The structural equation for this model is

$$S = N^{\beta_* + \rho_*} v \qquad (2.2)$$

If the regression effects ρ and ρ_* are zero, then magnitude estimation and production give the same exponent, β, otherwise they will be unequal (although it is possible, however unlikely, that ρ and ρ_* could be opposite in sign and with values that result in an equal but incorrect value for both exponents). If ρ and ρ_* are both negative and small relative to β and β_*, then the inequality

$$\beta + \rho < \beta < 1/(\beta_* + \rho_*)$$

should hold, which means the biased magnitude estimation exponent will be smaller than the biased magnitude production exponent but together they provide upper and lower bounds for the unbiased value. But even with the assumptions that the number exponent is unity, and $\beta_* = 1/\beta$, we have only two observational equations with three unknowns, so without further constraint there is no solution for β. Stevens (1971, 1975) suggested that a solution might be obtained by matching a third continuum to both number and the stimulus continuum whose exponent is to be determined, fitting the exponents for these two matching functions, and forming their ratio to obtain the unbiased exponent relating N and S. This makes the precarious assumption that the regression bias in the third continuum is the same in the two matching functions with no means of confirmation.

I previously believed (Cross, 1974) that a way out of this muddle is to match both N and S to any third variable, such as desirability of occupation, as in the following diagram:

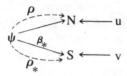

The indirect cross-modality matching relationship between N and S will have an exponent equal to $(\beta_* + \rho_*)/(1 + \rho)$. If magnitude estimation and production functions are also obtained, the three empirical exponents determine three equations involving the unknowns β, ρ and ρ_*. But in addition to the assumptions that have to be made to estimate the exponent of the indirect matching relation (because of error in both variables) this strategy depends on the regression biases remaining invariant in the two matching continua as the stimulus continuum is changed, an assumption I no longer feel comfortable about making.

MULTIVARIATE PSYCHOPHYSICAL SCALING

The use of two or more modes of judgment to scale the same stimulus domain offers several advantages over the traditional repeated measurement design using a single response measure. Although repeated measurements are intended to reduce measurement-error variance and provide more reliable estimates of "true scores," there are several sources of difficulty that make repeated measurements with the same response variable less useful. Successive measurements are frequently not independent—subjects recall their previous responses when they recognize a repeated stimulus, and they attempt to appear overly consistent. With multiple measures involving different operations, this difficulty is minimized. With single measures, subjects often become bored or lose motivation and become distracted as the task is carried out over a period of time. With multiple measures, interest may be sustained. Finally, greater construct validity can be achieved by basing a scale on multiple subscales that conform, in their interrelations, to expected functional form and that correlate highly with each other. The lawful relations shown to hold among the sensory variables used in social scaling reinforce the credibility of the scales of opinion that are derived from them.

The use of a multivariate procedure to scale another sensory continuum is illustrated in a study by Cross, Tursky and Lodge (1975). The study was undertaken in order to determine the exponent for electric shock because of some dispute in the literature over the question of whether apparent intensity of shock grows as the 3.5 power of electric current between the stimulating electrodes, as Stevens claimed, or as the 1.8 power, an exponent found by other investigators. Line length was used as a calibration continuum against which 30 observers matched force of handgrip, loudness of noise, and numerical judgments. The response mode called for was varied from one stimulus presentation to the next in a random manner. Power functions provided excellent fits to average judgment in each mode as a function of line length. The exponents of these functions were 1.46 for noise production, .83 for magnitude estimation, and .59 for force of handgrip. Only the number matching function showed a strong regression bias in yielding an exponent significantly smaller than its assumed value of unity. This is the only response mode in which the subject was apt to remember previous responses despite the intervention of other modes of responding in the stimulus sequence. Shock intensities were judged the same way, randomly alternating the mode of response called for. Scale values were constructed by taking the geometric mean of the three response measures after each was raised to a power equal to the reciprocal of the empirical exponent value obtained in the match to line length, i.e., $1/1.46 = .68$, $1/.59 = 1.70$, and $1/.83 = 1.20$. Hence, for the group data, the scaled subjective magnitude of a shock with intensity S_i is given by

$$\psi(S_i) = (P_i^{.68} F_i^{1.70} N_i^{1.20})^{1/3}$$

where P_i, F_i, and N_i denote the average noise level (in units of sound pressure), the average force of handgrip (in Newtons), and the average number matched to each shock intensity. These values plotted against shock intensity were well fit by a power function with an exponent of 2.26. Analysis of the matching functions relating noise, handgrip, and number separately to electric shock yielded exponent values which, when taken in ratio to the value 2.26, gives the numerical values 1.48 for noise (vs 1.46 when compared to line length), 0.62 for handgrip (vs .59), and .77 for magnitude estimation (vs .83)—an outcome that indicates the number continuum showed about the same amount of regression bias when matched to shock as when matched to lines; hence the calibration procedure appears to be vindicated in this application.

It would be very convenient if the exponents governing the relationship between a response variable and subjective magnitude could be determined without initial recourse to a calibration procedure in which the response is matched to a known continuum like line length in order to measure the amount of regression bias in the matching relation. When scaling nonmetric stimuli, we lack the opportunity to check the consistency of the regression effects between the calibration task and that of judging the nonmetric stimuli. I explored the possibility that perhaps in the pattern of interrelations among response measures in the multiple indicator approach, the values of the effective exponents might be identifiable. In a procedure involving k indicator variables, each is related to ψ by a power function

$$R_j = \psi^{\gamma_j} u_j \quad j = 1, \ldots, k \tag{2.3}$$

where the exponent $\gamma_j = \beta_j^{-1} + \rho_j$, and where β_j is the corresponding input exponent for modality j and ρ_j is the regression bias parameter which is presumed to vary with the conditions of judgment. The set of relations defined by equation (2.3) are linearized by logarithmic transformations of each variable. If we define

$$y_j = \log R_j \quad x^* = \log \psi \quad e_j = \log u_j$$

the structural equations corresponding to the psychophysical relations can be expressed in linear form

$$y_j = \gamma_j x^* + e_j \quad (j = 1, \ldots, k)$$

Here x^* and e_j are independent unobservables, but the moments of the observable variables, y_j, can be related to the structural parameters, γ_j, by $n(n+1)/2$ equations of the form

$$\text{Var}(y_j) = \sigma_j^2 = \gamma_j^2 \sigma_*^2 + \sigma_{e_j}^2 \quad \text{Cov}(y_i, y_j) = \sigma_{ij} = \gamma_i \gamma_j \sigma_*^2$$

assuming that $E(e_j) = 0$ and $\text{Cov}(e_i, e_j) = 0$ for all i, j (i $\neq$ j).

With only one response variable (k = 1), we have three unknowns γ_1, σ_*^2, and $\sigma_{e_1}^2$ and only one observable moment, σ_1^2, thus the structural parameters are not identifiable.

With two response variables (j = 1,2), the system produces three observable moments: σ_1^2, σ_2^2, and σ_{12}. But the three equations corresponding to these moments will not suffice to determine uniquely the five unknowns γ_1, γ_2, $\sigma_{e_1}^2$, $\sigma_{e_2}^2$, and σ_*.

With three response variables (j = 1,2,3) the picture changes. We have six equations involving the observable moments σ_1^2, σ_2^2, σ_3^2, σ_{12}, σ_{13}, and σ_{23} and seven unknowns γ_1, γ_2, γ_3, $\sigma_{e_1}^2$, $\sigma_{e_2}^2$, $\sigma_{e_3}^2$, and σ_*^2. Systems like this are sometimes normalized by setting $\sigma_* = 1$, leaving six unknowns with the following solutions fo the structural parameters:

$$\gamma_1 = (\sigma_{12}\sigma_{13}/\sigma_{23})^{\frac{1}{2}} \quad \gamma_2 = (\sigma_{12}\sigma_{23}/\sigma_{13})^{\frac{1}{2}} \quad \gamma_3 = (\sigma_{13}\sigma_{23}/\sigma_{12})^{\frac{1}{2}}$$

$$\sigma_{e_1}^2 = \sigma_1^2 - \sigma_{12}\sigma_{13}/\sigma_{23} \quad \sigma_{e_2}^2 = \sigma_2^2 - \sigma_{12}\sigma_{23}/\sigma_{13} \quad \sigma_{e_3}^2 = \sigma_3^2 - \sigma_{13}\sigma_{23}/\sigma_{12}$$

Unhappily, we are not free to set $\sigma_* = 1$. In strictly linear systems this has the effect of fixing a unit of measurement for the unobservable variable but in the present exercise the unit for ψ is fixed by setting $E(x^*) = 0$. Inasmuch as we can change the obtained values of σ_j^2 and σ_{ij} by choosing a different base for the logarithmic transformation used to linearize the psychophysical equations, the foregoing estimates of the structural parameters are not unique.

No matter how many indicator variables we add to the system, we will never be able to identify the output exponents γ_j uniquely. The best we can do is estimate the ratio of two exponents by

$$\gamma_i/\gamma_j = \sigma_{ih}/\sigma_{jh} \text{ for } i \neq j \neq h$$

By setting one exponent at an arbitrary value guided by other information we might have about the psychophysical relations involved, all of the others can be determined. This requires a minimum of three indicator variables.

With only two indicator variables, a reasonable estimate of γ_1/γ_2 can be obtained from the square root of the ratio of observable variances

$$\gamma_1/\gamma_2 \approx (\sigma_1^2/\sigma_2^2)^{\frac{1}{2}}$$

providing either the error variances are small relative to the observable variances ($\sigma_{e_1}^2 \ll \sigma_1^2$) or the error variances are related by $\sigma_{e_1}^2 = \lambda\sigma_{e_2}^2$ with $\lambda = (\gamma_1/\gamma_2)^2$.

ON THE SUBJECTIVE MAGNITUDE OF NUMBER

When numerical magnitudes are scaled by random production methods (Banks & Hill, 1974), by nonmetric scaling of ratings of the similarity of number pairs (Schneider, Parker, Ostrosky, Stein, & Kanow, 1974), by two-stage analyses of the input-output transformations required to linearize numerical judgments of differences of sums, or by analysis of the transformations of scale necessary to achieve additivity in a conjoint measurement design (Rule & Curtis, 1973), to cite only a few of the studies pertinent to the question, the results seem to indicate that subjective magnitude as defined in these various problems is not linearly represented by number.

From the perspective of a psychophysics based on cross-modality matching relationships, it makes little difference whether the exponent for number is taken as unity or some other value. As the exponents for other continua are defined relative to number as the reference continuum, to adopt a different value for the number exponent would merely involve multiplying all exponents by an appropriate conversion factor to re-establish their values. What is really at issue is the question of what we mean by subjective magnitude. It is easy to forget that numbers were invented by humans for purposes of reckoning and mensuration and that conventions such as the number 40 is 10 times as large as the number 4, that a length of 80 inches is 10 times as long as a length of 8 inches, that a box containing 10 objects has 10 times as many as a box contaiing only one, and so on, are true likewise simultaneously in both the objective and subjective sense. Of course, it could be argued that the numerical relation "ten times as great as" actually corresponds to a subjective numerical relation of only "4.8 times as great as." I prefer to assume that people perceive numerical magnitudes veridically. This does not entail that people necessarily use numbers to express their judgments in a veridical manner. Regression biases can be present in all judgments.

When an experimental finding indicates that we have not learned our school lessons very well—that the years spent memorizing the multiplication tables and learning how to work with units of measurement have not given us a firm concept of numerical relation—it might be appropriate to question the validity of the assumptions of the experimenter whose criteria for assessing subjective magnitudes lead to such violations of common sense.

REFERENCES

Banks, W. P., & Hill, D. K. The apparent magnitude of number scaled by random production. *Journal of Experimental Psychology*, 1974, *102*, 353–376 (monograph).

Bertalanffy, Ludwig von. *General system theory*. New York: Geoge Braziller, 1968.

Bochner, S. *The role of mathematics in the rise of science*. Princeton, New Jersey: Princeton University Press, 1966.

Cross, D. V. Some technical notes on psychophysical scaling. In H. Moskowitz, B. Scharf, & J. C. Stevens (Eds.), *Sensation and measurement: Papers in honor of S. S. Stevens*. Dordrecht, The Netherlands: Reidel, 1974.

Cross, D. V., Tursky, B., & Lodge, M. The role of regression and range effects in determination of the power function for electric shock. *Perception & Psychophysics*, 1975, *18*, 9–14.

Dawson, W. E. An assessment of ratio scales of opinion produced by sensory-modality matching. In H. R. Moskowitz et al. (Eds.), *Sensation and Measurement*. Dordrecht, The Netherlands: Reidel, 1974.

Dawson, W. E., & Brinker, R. P. Validation of ratio scales of opinion by multimodality matching. *Perception & Psychophysics*, 1971, *9*, 413–417.

Dawson, W. E., & Mirando, M. A. Sensory-modality opinion scales for individual subjects. *Perception & Psychophysics*, 1975, *17*, 596–600.

Hamblin, R. L. Social attitudes: Magnitude measurement and theory. In H. M. Blalock, Jr. (Ed.), *Measurement in the social sciences*, Chicago: Aldine, 1974.

Krantz, D. H. A theory of magnitude estimation and cross-modality matching. *Journal of Mathematical Psychology*, 1972, *9*, 168–199.

Kunnapas, T., & Wikstrom, I. Measurement of occupational preferences: A comparison of scaling methods. *Perceptual and Motor Skills*, 1963, *17*, 611–694.

Lane, H. L., Catania, A. C., & Stevens, S. S. Voice level: Autophonic scale, perceived loudness, and the effects of sidetone. *Journal of the Acoustical Society of America*, 1961, *33*, 160–167.

Luce, R. D. What sort of measurement is psychophysical measurement? *American Psychologist*, 1972, *27*, 96–106.

Luce, R. D., & Green, D. M. A neural timing theory for response times and the psychophysics of intensity. *Psychological Review*, 1972 *79*, 14–57.

Mueller, I. Greek mathematics and Greek logic. In J. Corcoran (Ed.), *Ancient logic and its modern interpretations*. Dordrecht, The Netherlands: Reidel, 1974.

Murphy, G. *Psychological thought from Pythagoras to Freud.* New York: Harcourt, Brace & World, 1968.

Poulton, E. C. The new psychophysics: Six models for magnitude estimation judgments. *Psychological Bulletin,* 1968, *69,* 1-19.

Rule, S. J., & Curtis, D. W. Conjoint scaling of subjective number and weight. *Journal of Experimental Psychology,* 1973, *97,* 305-309.

Schneider, B., Parker, S., Ostrosky, D., Stein, D., & Kanow, G. A scale for the psychological magnitude of number. *Perception & Psychophysics,* 1974, *16,* 43-46.

Shepard, R. N. On the status of "direct" psychophysical measurement. In C. W. Savage (Ed.), *Perceptions and cognition: Issues in the foundations of psychology,* (Vol. 9, Minnesota Studies in the Philosophy of Science). Minneapolis: University of Minnesota Press, 1978.

Stevens, J. C., Mack, J. D., & Stevens, S. S. Growth of sensation on seven continua as measured by force of handgrips. *Journal of Experimental Psychology,* 1960, *59,* 60-67.

Stevens, J. C., & Marks, L. E. Cross-modality matching of brightness and loudness. Proceedings *National Academy of Science,* 1965, *54,* 407-411.

Stevens, S. S. On the psychophysical law. *Psychological Review,* 1957, *64,* 153-181.

Stevens, S. S. Cross-modality validation of subjective scales for loudness, vibration, and electric shock. *Journal of Experimental Psychology,* 1959, *57,* 201-209.

Stevens, S. S. On the operation known as judgment. *American Scientist,* 1966a, *54,* 385-401.

Stevens, S. S. Matching functions between loudness and ten other continua. *Perception & Psychophysics,* 1966b, *1,* 5-8.

Stevens, S. S. Issues in psychological measurement. *Psychological Review,* 1971, *78,* 426-450.

Stevens, S. S. Psychophysics: *Introduction to its perceptual, neural, and social prospects.* New York: Wiley, 1975.

Stevens, S. S., & Greenbaum, H. B. Regression effect in psychophysical judgment. *Perception & Psychophysics,* 1966, *1,* 439-446.

Stevens, S. S., & Guirao, M. Subjective scaling of length and area and the matching of length to loudness and brightness. *Journal of Experimental Psychology,* 1963, *66,* 177-186.

Teghtsoonian, M. A. The judgment of size. *American Journal of Psychology,* 1965, *78,* 392-402.

Treiman, D. J. *Occupational prestige in comparative perspective.* New York: Academic Press, 1977.

Yilmaz, H. Perceptual invariance and the psychophysical law. *Perception and Psychophysics,* 1967, *2,* 533-538.

3 Category Ratings: Still More Contextual Effects!

Allen Parducci
University of California
Los Angeles

I am an unabashed advocate of category ratings as direct pipelines to the psyche. I realize that many experts on scaling believe that something must be done about the bad behavior of my clients. But these experts should be aware that rating scales have the support of a veritable mob—the thousands of psychologists and social scientists who use ratings to assess public opinion, consumer preferences, the psychological quality of life, and for a variety of other practical concerns. Rating scales are also widely employed for basic research on attitude change, perception, judgment, and other cognitive processes.

Why is my client so popular? I think the answer is obvious: *Category ratings are the way value judgments are expressed in everyday life.* We describe a book or movie as "extremely enjoyable" or perhaps as "not very good." Even the most devoted advocate of magnitude-estimation scales would hesitate to advise a friend, except perhaps in jest, that one movie is four times as enjoyable as another.

In choosing dependent variables for psychological research, consideration should be given to customary modes of response. Although it may be necessary to constrain the responses to simplify tabulation and interpretation, serious departures from everyday usage should be taken only with purposeful objective. Let us not lightly abandon the basic forms of expression for which millions of years of natural selection have adapted us.

This does not preclude improvement on everyday ways of expressing subjective experience. The late S. S. Stevens, for example, believed that sensation was measured better by magnitude estimation (e.g., Stevens, 1957). He questioned the validity of category scales, in part because of their notorious susceptibility to contextual effects (which I will be illustrating with some new data), but also because of their nonlinearity with magnitude scales. This, of course, begs the question. As Treisman (1964), Zinnes (1969), and so many others have pointed out, one could just as well question the validity of magnitude scales when they are nonlinear to category scales. I think that this whole problem has been enormously clarified by Norman Anderson's development of the functional approach to measurement (see Chapter 5, this volume). Anderson subsumes measurement to substantive theory, and he allows for rescaling the subject's responses to fit the theory. However, good fits to simple additive models are usually obtained without rescaling category ratings. Furthermore, Birnbaum and Veit (1974), using scale-free (ordinal) tests, demonstrated that "ratio" judgments were fitted best by a subtractive model without rescaling the ratings (see also Birnbaum, 1978, Chapter 17, this volume; Hagerty & Birnbaum, 1978; Veit, 1978).

This does not mean that the same stimulus must always evoke the same category rating. Good fits of substantive theory to empirical data can be obtained even when the experimental conditions are designed to *maximize* contextual effects. Thus, in my own research, a simple contextual model of judgment fits the data when the same stimulus evokes a much higher rating in one set of contextual stimuli than it does in another set (e.g., Parducci, 1974; Parducci & Perrett, 1971; see also Anderson, 1975; Birnbaum, 1974). I would have little interest in subjects' expressions of value experiences if these did not change with context. A particular income that might have seemed magnificent at an early stage in one's career would seem totally inadequate at a later stage. If a response scale did not reflect this change, it would miss the all important decline in experienced value.

There are, of course, problems of great substantive interest whose solutions can be obscured by contextual effects. In his extensive tests of algebraic models of information integration, Anderson has taken pains to restrict the nature of the response categories so that contextual effects are minimized. For example, in his studies of personality impression (e.g., Anderson, 1962), he presents as anchors or standards two extreme sets of adjectives that are either much less favorable or much more favorable to the personality being described than any of the regular sets; subjects are instructed to rate these standards "1" and "20," respectively; the result is that the regular sets are usually rated between 5 and 15. The purpose is to avoid ceilings or floors that might invalidate the ratings as tests of the integration model. I now believe that the use of a 20-category scale also reduces the disturbing contextual effects that would otherwise be produced by the particular frequency distribution of sets employed in the experimental design, e.g., contextual effects like those demonstrated by Birnbaum, Parducci, and Gifford (1971). What I am asserting is that the number of different categories prescribed by the instructions for judgment affects the form of the rating scale!

I did not always believe this. In fact, until very recently, I would have maintained vociferously that the form of the rating scale was independent of the number of different categories employed. My best evidence would have been the

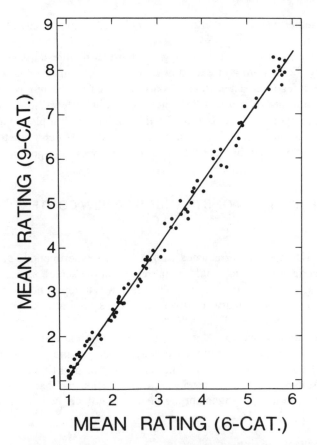

FIG. 3.1. Linearity of relationship between rating scales: Each point represents ratings on nine-category and six-category scales for a particular size presented in a particular set of contextual sizes. Adapted from Parducci & Perrett (1971), Copyright 1971 by the American Psychological Association. Reprinted by permission.

plot shown in Fig. 3.1 comparing nine-category with six-category scales for ratings of visual size. Although systematic manipulation of the sets of contextual sizes powerfully affected the ratings of any particular size of stimulus (i.e., some of the different points in Fig. 3.1 represent ratings of the same stimulus in different contexts), the effects were the same relative to the end points of the six- and nine-category scales. Figure 3.1 shows that the nine-category scale is a linear function of the six-category scale. It is as though we carry in our heads a little rubber ruler, which stretches or compresses anew for each particular context, measuring a value for each of its member stimuli. The overt rating is then simply a linear transformation of this "inner" value, a transformation applied to conform to the experimental instructions to use either six, nine, or any other number of categories.

The research I will now report suggests that this picture must be elaborated considerably. First, I am going to show that the scale *is* affected by the number of available categories. Then, that it is also affected by the number of stimuli! However, I must warn you that these new contextual effects do not undermine my faith in category ratings. Indeed, I will conclude with a plea that we try to capitalize on whatever we can learn about contextual effects, whether we are trying to assess public opinion or the value consequences of important decisions.

EMPIRICAL DEMONSTRATIONS OF NEW CONTEXTUAL EFFECTS

In this research, the undergraduates who served as experimental subjects were told that a series of squares would be projected on the screen several meters in front of them, one every five seconds. Their task was to report how small or large each size appeared in comparison with all the other sizes that would be presented. A short preview included all the sizes.

For the conditions we consider first, just five different sizes were projected: squares 1, 7, 13, 19, and 24 from a geometric series varying from 13 to 355 mm in width. The subjects never saw more than one size at a time, in each case a solid black square centered against a white, 750 × 1000-mm background (further details of the physical arrangement are given in Parducci & Perrett, 1971).

Number of Categories

The instructions restricted subjects to a particular set of categories: either two (Small and Large), three (Small, Average, and Large), four (Small, Slightly Smaller than Average, Slightly Larger than Average, and Large), five (Very Small, Small, Average, Large, and Very Large), nine (Very Very Small, Very Small, Small, Slightly Smaller than Average, Average, Slightly Larger than Average, Large, Very Large, and Very Very Large), 0–20 (with 0 for the smallest size and 20 for the largest), 0–100 (with 0 for the smallest and 100 for the largest), and Open (in which subjects were free to generate as few or many categories as seemed appropriate to them).

For each set of categories, the same five sizes were presented in a 50-trial, randomized sequence, with different frequencies to create either a negatively or positively skewed set. Figure 3.2 shows the resulting scales, each curve representing the mean transformed category ranks for approximately 20 subjects. Differences between the two curves in each panel thus represent the systematic effects of contextual skewing under restrictions to some particular number of

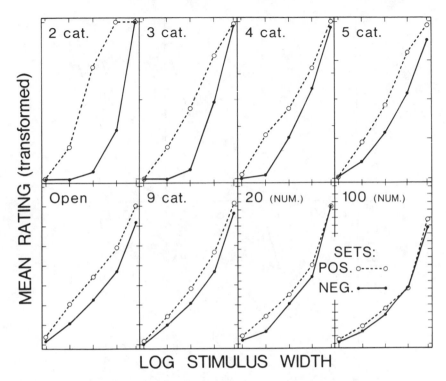

FIG. 3.2. Effects of skewing vary inversely with number of categories. Mean ratings of Squares 1, 7, 13, 19, and 24 (from geometric series 1–24) presented in one of two contextual sets: Positive with 10, 7, 4, 2, and 2 presentations per block of 25; Negative with 2, 2, 4, 7, and 10 per block. Categories ranked and linearly transformed to match end categories.

categories. Insofar as there are differences, the same stimulus receives a higher rating in the Positive Set, just what one would expect from previous research (cf. Parducci, 1974). However, what astonished me when I first made these plots was that the magnitude of this contextual effect varies inversely with the number of categories. The really big drops occur between two, three, and four categories, but the decline is systematic all the way out through the 0–20 and 0–100 scales. Figure 3.2 also shows a systematic drop in the use of the top categories as the number of permissible categories increases.

Range-Frequency Theory. This interaction between the skewing of the context and the number of available categories can be described in terms of my range-frequency theory of judgment. In the simplest interpretation of the theory (e.g., Parducci, 1974), the effects of contextual skewing reflect a tendency to assign the same number of stimulus presentations to each of the available categories. Insofar as subjects do equalize these frequencies, their rating scales

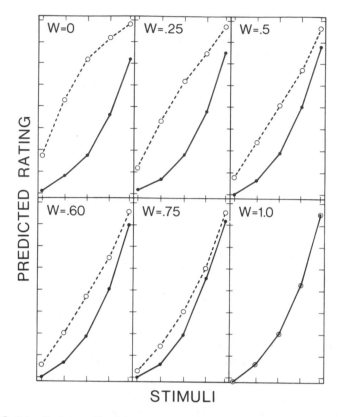

FIG. 3.3.   Ratings predicted from range-frequency model using different values
of *w*.

should be linear to the percentile ranks of the stimuli. These hypothetical equal-frequency scales are shown in the upper-left panel of Fig. 3.3.

According to range-frequency theory, the actual rating of any particular stimulus represents a compromise or weighted average between the frequency value and a hypothetical range value, the latter conceived as that proportion of the subjective range of contextual stimulus values falling below the stimulus being judged. The lower-right panel of Fig. 3.3 shows these hypothetical range values, estimated from the actual ratings. According to the theory, these range values are what the ratings would have been if subjects were not affected by the relative stimulus frequencies.

In algebraic form, these notions are expressed by the following equations:

$$Range\ Value:\ R_i = (S_i - S_{min})/(S_{max} - S_{min}), \tag{3.1}$$

where S_{min} and S_{max} represent the smallest and largest of the subjective values in the context of stimuli affecting the judgment of S_i, the subjective value of the ith stimulus in the contextual set. Since these subjective values are not known directly, range values must be estimated from empirical ratings.

Frequency Value: $F_i = (r_i - 1)/(N - 1)$,   (3.2)

where r_i is the rank of Stimulus i in the contextual set, and 1 and N are the ranks of the smallest and largest stimulus values. In the present case, r_i is obtained by arbitrarily assigning successive ranks to the different presentations of the ith stimulus and simply averaging these ranks. Thus, F_i approximates the conventional percentile rank, divided by 100.

Judgment: $J_i = wR_i + (1 - w)F_i$,   (3.3)

so that $(1 - w)$ is the relative weight or influence of the equal-frequency tendency, and J_i is the internal judgment on a scale from 0 to 1.

Category Rating: $C_i = bJ_i + a$,   (3.4)

where C_i is the rank of the overt category rating in the set of permissible verbal categories, b is the range of possible ranks (e.g., 4 for a five-category scale), and a is the rank assigned as the lowest rating (e.g., 1 on a scale from 1 to 5).

The reason the upper-left panel in Fig. 3.3 illustrates the frequency values is that these hypothetical ratings have been calculated assuming that $w = 0$; thus, each value is simply a linear transformation of the percentile rank of a stimulus in its respective set. The range values shown in the lower-right panel represent what the ratings would have been if subjects gave no weight to the contextual differences in skewing, i.e., $w = 1$. These range values were estimated using Eqs. 3.2, 3.3, and 3.4, and also the empirical ratings for all conditions (except the two-category ratings which were not used because of their extreme cutoffs). Separate estimates of w and then the range values were obtained for each pair of conditions, and these estimated range values were then averaged to obtain the range function plotted in the lower-right panel of Fig. 3.3.

This hypothetical range function is very close to one obtained previously for a six-category condition in which nine stimuli, 1–24, were presented in a rectangular set, i.e., with equal frequency and spacing of stimuli (Parducci & Perrett, 1971, Fig. 5D). The range function is intermediate in form between a purely logarithmic scale, which would plot here as a straight line, and a magnitude-estimation scale previously obtained using the same rectangular set (Parducci & Perrett, 1971, Fig. 2).

The other panels of Fig. 3.3 show hypothetical ratings for intermediate values of w. As w increases, the scales for the Positive and Negative Sets draw more closely together:

$$J_{i+} - J_{i-} = (1 - w)(F_{i+} - F_{i-}),$$ (3.5)

developing the positive acceleration of the pure range function. With two, three, and four categories, the empirical spread is too great near the middle of the scale for the degree of pinching at the ends, as though subjects wanted to extend the scale upward for the Positive Set and downward for the Negative Set but were cut off by the restriction to so few categories. The scales for five-category and Open conditions reflect a weighting of the common range values of about .70, with the nine-point, 0–20, and 0–100 scales having values for w of approximately .80, .85, and .95, respectively.

Adaptation-Level Theory.   An alternative measure of contextual effects is provided by the adaptation level (Helson, 1964). The adaptation level, defined as the stimulus judged "average" or at the center of the scale, was estimated by linear interpolation for each rating scale. As shown in Fig. 3.4, the differences in adaptation level are clearly greatest when subjects are restricted to just two categories, and they are almost nonexistent for either the 0–20 or 0–100 scales. Figure 3.4 also shows that the shifts in adaptation level are much greater for the Positive Set. In range-frequency terms, this reflects the positive acceleration of the range function, which is more similar to the frequency function for the Negative than for the Positive Set. Consequently, ratings of the Positive Set are much more sensitive to changes in w, the relative weighting of the range function.

The nonparallelism of the respective scales in Fig. 3.2 is inconsistent with

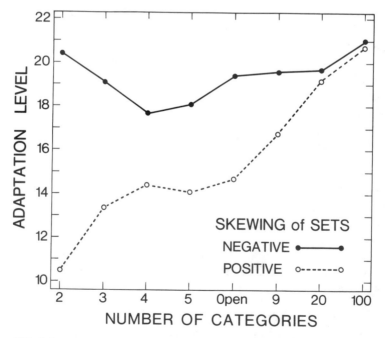

FIG. 3.4.   Differences in adaptation level also vary inversely with number of categories. Adaptation level determined by linear interpolation on scales plotted in Fig. 3.2.

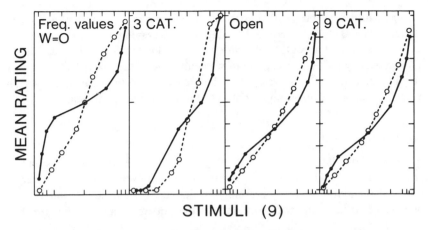

FIG. 3.5.   Effects of number of categories on intertwining of scales for sets varying in kurtosis: U-shaped set (solid points and lines) with log spacing of stimuli shown on lower abscissa and respective frequencies of 12, 10, 9, 7, 9, 10, and 12; Normal set (open spacing) with spacing shown on upper abscissa and frequencies of 6, 8, 9, 11, 13, 11, 9, 8, and 6.

adaptation-level theory (Helson, 1964), which postulates a subtractive model, with the subjective values of adaptation level (AL) and the stimulus being judged as component factors:

$$J_i = S_i - AL \tag{3.6}$$

This nonparallelism is illustrated most convincingly by Fig. 3.5, which shows the contextual effects for Normal and U-shaped sets of stimulus values. These two sets of contextual stimuli vary in their spacing of the sizes over the same 1–24 range and also in the proportions of presentations of each of the respective stimuli. The leftmost panel of Fig. 3.5 shows the ratings each set would have elicited if subjects simply put the same number of stimuli in each category (i.e., if $w = 0$). The other three panels show the empirical ratings obtained when subjects were instructed to develop either three-category, Open, or nine-category scales. Although each pair of empirical scales shows the expected intertwining, there is again a stronger equal-frequency effect (lower w) when subjects are restricted to just three categories and again a progressive dropping out of the top categories as the number increases. These crossovers provide powerful contradiction to the subtractive model of adaptation-level theory because no rescaling of the stimuli or responses could make them parallel (cf. Birnbaum, 1974).

The difference between the three-category and Open scales in Fig. 3.5 is of particular interest because, unlike any of the other conditions that have been described, they were obtained from the *same* subjects in the same experimental session. First, subjects rated a particular set using three categories; then they rated the same set under instructions to generate their own Open scales. These subjects could have continued to use the same three categories, viz., Small,

Average, and Large, but every subject added at least two categories, and all but two subjects added from three to 12 categories (averaging almost three times as many categories in the Open conditions). The fact that the decrease in the equal-frequency tendency (increase in w) is also found for Normal vs. U-shaped Sets, i.e., not just with skewed sets, adds generality to the conclusion that the number of categories is an important determinant of the rating scale.

Number of Stimuli

Figure 3.6 shows the joint effects of varying the number of categories and the number of stimuli. The upper half of Fig. 3.6 simply reproduces the scales for three of the conditions already presented in Fig. 3.2. The scales obtained for the lower half had the same two extreme stimuli, Squares 1 and 24; but for these

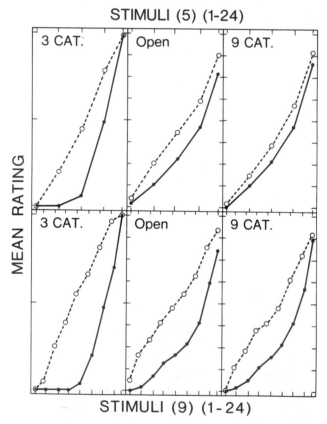

FIG. 3.6.   Effects of skewing vary directly with number of stimuli. For lower panels, nine stimuli in each of two sets: Positive with 5, 5, 6, 2, 2, 2, 1, 1, and 1, respectively, for each block of 25 presentations; Negative with frequencies 1, 1, 1, 2, 2, 2, 6, 5, 5. Upper panels are from Fig. 3.2.

conditions, there were always nine rather than just five stimulus values. In spite of the increased number of stimuli, the skewing of stimulus frequencies was designed to produce approximately the same pair of equal-frequency functions.

Figure 3.6 shows that although the effects of skewing again vary inversely with the number of categories (the separation between the two scales in each of the lower panels decreasing from three-category to Open to nine-category conditions), the magnitude of the skewing effect is in each case much greater when there are nine stimuli than when there are only five stimuli. It seems clear that the number of different stimulus values is another factor determining the form of the rating scale.

Stimulus Range

Figure 3.7 shows the effects of varying the stimulus range, again using Positive and Negative Sets with different numbers of categories. The lower panels of Fig.

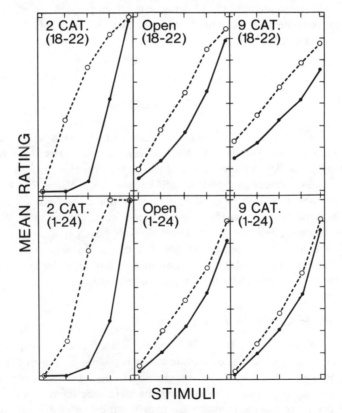

FIG. 3.7.   Small effects of stimulus range. Upper panels for narrow-range sets, Squares 18, 19, 20, 21, and 22, presented with same relative frequencies as five-stimulus, full-range sets. Lower panels are from Fig. 3.2.

3.7 reproduce three pairs of scales from Fig. 3.2; the top panels show the corresponding conditions modified to cover a much narrower range of stimuli. Although these 18–22 sets cover scarcely more than a sixth of the full log-range of sizes, this extreme reduction of range does not have very dramatic effects on the magnitude of the contextual effects. The biggest difference is with the nine-category scales for which the more extreme categories, especially Very Very Small and Very Very Large, are not used when the range of stimuli is so narrow.

The Open scales for Squares 18–22 (top-middle panel) also show marked avoidance of the extreme categories: No subject generated any category more extreme than Very Small or Very Large, and most subjects had Small and Large as their two most extreme categories. Thus, if the responses in the Open conditions had been plotted as though subjects had nine-category scales, the differences between the upper-middle and upper-right panels would have been greatly reduced. When the full 1–24 range of stimuli is presented, subjects in the Open conditions usually generate at least one category that is clearly more extreme than Very Small or Very Large. This difference between the 18–22 and 1–24 scales suggests that the stimulus range itself, or perhaps its relationship to the greatest possible range permitted by the background area, sets limits on what category labels can be appropriately matched to the end points of the stimulus range.

DISCUSSION

By this time, any reader devoted to the constancy of psychophysical scales must be thoroughly aghast. For the rating scale seems to be subject to a variety of contextual effects beyond the simple linear transformation that matches end categories to end stimuli, in itself a well-known range effect (cf. Volkmann, 1951). The nonlinear effects of skewing the stimulus context are also well-known, though perhaps a more bitter pill for those seeking constancy. What must be hardest to swallow is the notion that the psychophysical scale is so dramatically affected by the number of categories subjects are permitted to use, the number of stimuli presented for judgment, and perhaps also the appropriateness of the extreme category labels for the particular range of stimuli.

Inferred vs. Direct Scale Values

There may be some solice for such a reader in the relative constancy of the inferred range values. A single range function accounts for most of the data in Fig. 3.2, provided that the relative weighting of range and frequency values is permitted to vary. So, too, with the effects of increasing the number of stimuli: The shift from five to nine stimuli has virtually no effect on the inferred range function. Thus, this range function would seem to satisfy the requirement of constancy that some would impose on candidates for "the psychophysical law." Furthermore, in conformity with the prescriptions of functional measurement, this particular candidate comes out as a byproduct of the testing of range-frequency theory: The interest in the psychophysical relationship is subsidiary to the interest in the cognitive algebra implicitly performed by subjects asked to make category ratings.

I have no objection to calling the range function a "psychophysical law." However, I want to point out that the psychological states presumed to correspond to different range values may not be directly accessible to subjects making the judgments. It was only when subjects were instructed to rate the stimuli using 0 for the smallest and 100 for the largest that their ratings came at all close to the inferred range values. And yet subjects never voluntarily generate such scales. Indeed, even when told that the largest of just five squares was to be called "100," the average rating of this square was close to "75." When free to generate their own categories, as in the Open conditions, subjects are content with between five and seven categories. And the form of the scales relating these smaller sets of categories to the stimuli depend on the immediate stimulus context.

Even if one grants a psychological status to the inferred range values, treating them as something more than empirical constants estimated in the test of an algebraic model, they should not distract us from the overt ratings made by the subjects. It is these ratings that are the direct responses to our questions about the psychological values of the stimuli. These are what the subjects think best represent their subjective experiences.

The fact that subjective estimates vary so much with the instructions should not discourage us. As Marks points out in Chapter 1 of this volume, the psychological scale "may in many circumstances depend on the task." We have had to get used to the differences between category and magnitude-estimation scales. And I believe that we can get used to the idea that category scales depend on the number of categories and also the number of stimuli. If we can give up the Fechnerian assumption that one's subjective impression of magnitude is fixed for any particular physical stimulus, we can more readily accept what seems so apparent in the data I have been reporting: that the subjective impression, in the present case of size, depends on the relative position of the stimulus in a context of similar stimuli and also, in some poorly understood way, on the number of categories used to describe the stimuli and the number of different stimuli to be described.

Practical Consequences

My interest in psychophysics has, from the start, been motivated by a concern with everyday value judgments. Assessments of the pleasures and pains of life seem strikingly relativistic. Psychophysical research provides a special opportunity for exploring this relativism, using the power of experimental manipulation. The context of other psychophysical stimuli affecting the subject's judgment of any particular stimulus is largely under the control of the experimenter. Our present understanding of the effects of contextual manipulation is still in a primitive state—as demonstrated, perhaps, by my own surprise at the magnitude of the effects of number of categories and number of stimuli. But any advance on common sense in this area seems potentially useful.

Some people are disturbed by what they assume must be basic differences between the labile psychophysical scales and the sometimes more stable scales of multidimensional social judgment. Are these differences so basic? In the laboratory, as far as I can determine, such complex dimensions as the moral seriousness of crimes, the pleasantness of odors, or the satisfaction with different amounts of money, all seem to reflect the same kind of relativism (cf. Parducci, 1968). Of course, the context in which social judgments are made, even in the laboratory, may often include more from distant past experience with similar objects of judgment, and thus more stable standards, than is the case for simple psychophysical judgments. But this seems to be a problem of degree of experimental control rather than a basic difference.

More serious to me is the difficulty of dealing directly with the pragmatic aspects of value judgments, our attempts to influence each other's values by means of our own category ratings. Certainly, we sometimes dissemble in our self-reports, not just for the purpose of influencing others but also to shape our own experiences. Taken literally, our expressed judgments would often be deceptive. But even with these complications, the value judgments of everyday life reflect the contextual considerations that we find in our laboratory experiments. Consequently, an understanding of the nature of contextual effects can have practical consequences for how we conduct social research and even for how we make value decisions.

Consider, as an example, how in America we assess the public's opinion of our President. Before the recent Egyptian-Israeli negotiations at Camp David, President Carter had been receiving a high percentage of "poor" ratings in the national surveys. It would have been possible to ask the electorate to estimate the performance of Carter as a *ratio* of values, perhaps providing a predecessor (Nixon or Ford?) as a standard. It would even have been possible, though rather expensive, to elicit line productions (cf. Chapters 7 and 16, this volume) or dynanometer squeezes under instructions to express ratios of perceived quality. But such ratio estimations would be misleading. There is first the illusion that because we have a fundamental physical measure of length or handgrip, we therefore have a ratio measure of perceived quality of political performance. I agree with Marks (Chapter 1, this volume) that this is applying a metaphor on top of what is already a metaphor.

More crucial, from my standpoint, is the problem that our measurement procedure is likely to establish a context for judgment that is very different from the context in which political evaluations are ordinarily made. Consider again the assessment of Carter's performance as President. If we ask for magnitude estimations, the respondents to our survey must try to establish a ratio between Carter and some standard, such as the performance of an earlier President. But it seems quite unlikely that people ordinarily base their evaluations on such restricted comparisons. For example, ratio estimations of Carter relative to Nixon might remain fairly constant over a period in which category ratings of Carter's performance shift dramatically up and down. I would expect the ratio estimation to be much less affected by announcements of progress on plans for peace, by the emergence of other political personalities, or by changes in the economy. I see such factors as analogous in their effects to the contextual sets presented in our category-rating experiments. The assessment of a relatively unchanging performance by Carter can shift from "bad" to "good" if the context against which he is rated shifts sufficiently. But if the context really does change, we are obscuring the resulting change in evaluation when we design procedures that are less sensitive to context or that ask our survey respondents for a ratio judgment. A straight comparison between candidates is useful for predicting the outcome of an election. But if the President wants to know how satisfied the electorate is with his performance, he would be better served by category ratings for which the implied context is more likely to be whatever in fact influences people's everyday assessments.

There is no guarantee that a request for category ratings invokes the appropriate context. For example, in studies of the quality of life using category ratings of satisfaction with various aspects of work, health care, etc., our questions often seem to establish a philosophical context far different from the respondents' day-to-day experiences: People tell us that their jobs are great, and so they are if the context consists of poorer jobs or no job at all. I am particularly skeptical of the well-known positive "bias" coloring such reports. On the job, there may be very little of such philosophy, the important value judgments reflecting how some particular experience compares with a context of other experiences on the same job: "How I goofed on that one! I am too tired to go on without a coffee break." As in Anderson's personality-impression studies, we typically ask the respondent to integrate different experiences, in this case the memories of millions of separate experiences. But Anderson provides his subjects a context of similar sets that establish the standards for judgment. The respondent to quality-of-life surveys has to generate the context of other jobs or other lives himself. He is in the position of the subject on the first trial in the size-judging experiments in which I find that, if there is no preview, the very first rating is largely independent of the particular size presented first. And that may be why we find so little relationship between self-ratings of the quality of life and objective measures such as type of work (e.g., Schneider, 1975; *Social Indicators,* 1973).

The concern to evoke the appropriate context should also govern our use of category ratings when making decisions. When trying to envision the consequences of alternative choices, we should try to anticipate the different contexts in which the choices are likely to be experienced. A larger income is usually preferred to a smaller one in any particular context. However, if the larger income will be part of a life style in which associates are making still more, it is likely to be experienced as inadequate. Taking future contexts into account may induce us sometimes to choose the alternative that has less value when rated only in our present context. Students in America and Europe are desperate now to become doctors of medicine, attracted by the high projected incomes. But are these incomes experienced as high by doctors comparing themselves with other doctors and prosperous business associates?

Conclusion.   I take this structuring of the value problem as axiomatic: It is the relational character of events that determines their subjective values. Directing our research to category ratings, besides keeping us close to the way value judgments are ordinarily made, encourages us to think in terms of the contextual factors that become so obvious in this type of research.

REFERENCES

Anderson, N. H. Application of an additive model to impression formation. *Science*, 1962, *138*, 817-818.

Anderson, N. H. On the role of context effects in psychophysical judgment. *Psychological Review*, 1975, *82*, 462-482.

Birnbaum, M. H. Using contextual effects to derive psychophysical scales. *Perception & Psychophysics*, 1974, *15*, 89-96.

Birnbaum, M. H. Differences and ratios in psychological measurement. In N. J. Castellan & F. Restle (Eds.), *Cognitive theory* (Vol. 3). Hillsdale, N.J.: Lawrence Erlbaum Associates, 1978.

Birnbaum, M. H., Parducci, A., & Gifford, R. K. Contextual effects in information integration. *Journal of Experimental Psychology*, 1971, *88*, 158-170.

Birnbaum, M. H., & Veit, C. T. Scale convergence as a criterion for rescaling: Information integration with difference, ratio, and averaging tasks. *Perception & Psychophysics*, 1974, *15*, 7-15.

Hagerty, M., & Birnbaum, M. H. Nonmetric tests of ratio vs. subtractive theories of stimulus comparison. *Perception & Psychophysics*, 1978, *24*, 121-129.

Helson, H. *Adaptation-level theory: An experimental and systematic approach to behavior.* New York: Harper & Row, 1964.

Parducci, A. The relativism of absolute judgments. *Scientific American*, 1968, *219*, 84-90.

Parducci, A. Contextual effects: A range-frequency analysis. In E. C. Carterette & M. P. Friedman (Eds.), *Handbook of perception* (Vol. 2). New York: Academic Press, 1974.

Parducci, A., & Perrett, L. F. Category rating scales: Effects of relative spacing and frequency of stimulus values. *Journal of Experimental Psychology Monograph*, 1971, *89*, 427-452.

Schneider, M. The quality of life in large American cities: Objective and subjective social indicators. *Social Indicators Research*, 1975, *1*, 495-509.

Social Indicators. Washington: U.S. Department of Commerce, 1973.

Stevens, S. S. On the psychophysical law. *Psychological Review*, 1957, *64*, 153-181.

Treisman, M. Sensory scaling and the psychophysical law. *Quarterly Journal of Experimental Psychology*, 1964, *16*, 11-22.

Veit, C. T. Ratio and subtractive processes in psychophysical judgment. *Journal of Experimental Psychology: General*. 1978, *107*, 81–107.

Volkmann, J. Scales of judgment and their implications for social psychology. In J. H. Rohrer & M. Sherif (Eds.), *Social psychology at the crossroads*. New York: Harper, 1951.

Zinnes, J. L. Scaling. In P. H. Mussen & M. R. Rosenzweig (Eds.), *Annual review of psychology*. Palo Alto, Cal.: Annual Reviews, 1969.

4

Levels of Sensory and Judgmental Processing: Strategies for the Evaluation of a Model

Stanley J. Rule
Dwight W. Curtis
University of Alberta

A psychophysical judgment implicates both sensory and judgmental levels of processing. A framework and a methodology that have been helpful in attempts to explicate the sensory and judgmental aspects have been provided by the two-stage model of magnitude judgment. This paper summarizes some of the research strategies associated with this framework. The strategies to be presented relate to both experimental methodology and methods of data analysis. They are illustrated by some applications to issues in psychophysical judgment.

The two-stage model was initially conjectured by Attneave (1962) and was based on Stevens' (1959) model for cross-modality matching. The model partitions the psychophysical judgment into two stages: an input or sensory stage in which the subject evaluates the magnitude of the stimulus and an output or judgmental stage in which the evaluation is mapped onto a response. Each stage is assumed to be characterized by a power transformation such that the stimulus–response relation described by the empirical power function:

$$y = ax^n, \tag{4.1}$$

can be redefined as

$$y = ax^{km}. \tag{4.2}$$

In Eqs. 4.1 and 4.2, y denotes a magnitude judgment of a stimulus with physical measure x. The exponent k is an exponent of the input transformation between the physical stimulus and its central correlate, and the exponent m is a parameter of the output transformation between the central representation and the response. According to the model, the empirical exponent n is the product of input and output exponents, k and m.

Given that the model is correct, estimate of k and m provide very useful parameters for investigating sensory and judgmental phenomena. For example, one could determine whether an experimental factor had its influence on the sensory level or on the judgmental level by examining its effect on estimates of each parameter.

DIFFERENCE JUDGMENTS

The parameters k and m cannot be separately estimated by fitting Eq. 4.2 to magnitude judgments. However, Curtis, Attneave, and Harrington (1968) devised an expression for judgments of differences between stimulus magnitudes from which separate estimates can be obtained. The expression is:

$$y_{ij} = a(x_i{}^k - x_j{}^k)^m + b,\tag{4.3}$$

where y_{ij} denotes a judgment of the difference in magnitude of stimuli with physical measures x_i and x_j. The additive constant b in their expression was assumed to reflect a displacement of origin on the response scale. (See Rule & Curtis, 1973b and Rule, Laye, & Curtis, 1974, for evidence supporting inclusion of the constant.)

In fitting Eq. 4.3 to difference judgments, it was necessary to assume that the perception of a difference could be represented mathematically as the difference between two subjective impressions. Because this additional assumption was required, it was particularly important for Curtis et al. to relate their results back to the original judgment task. To do so, they also obtained magnitude estimates of the stimuli presented one at a time as a separate task. The following expression was fitted to the magnitude-estimation data

$$y = ax^n + b,\tag{4.4}$$

which also includes an additive constant.

This strategy permitted them to evaluate the two-stage model by comparing the estimate of n obtained by fitting Eq. 4.4 to magnitude estimates with its predicted value from the product of k and m obtained from fitting Eq. 4.3 to difference judgments. The procedure of obtaining estimates of k and m from judgments of paired stimuli and n from judgments of single stimuli has been employed since with a variety of stimulus continua, initially for purposes of evaluating the model and later in its application to sensory and judgmental issues. Table 4.1 presents a summary of results of these studies. In each case, the product of k and m closely approximates the exponent n obtained independently from magnitude estimation of single stimuli, a result consistent with the model. The prediction has been found to hold for data from individual subjects as well as data from groups.

TABLE 4.1
Estimates of Parameters from Magnitude and Difference Functions
for Several Continua

	$y_{ij} = a(x_i^k - x_j^k)^m + b$		$y = ax^n + b$	
Continuum	k	m	$k \times m$	n
Area[e]	.39	1.68	.66	.67
Brightness[a]	.16	1.34	.21	.26
Duration[d]	1.00	1.11	1.11	1.04
Lightness[c]				
High standard	.35	1.74	.51	.55
Low standard	.38	1.26	.47	.41
Lightness[f]	.29	2.06	.59	.57
Darkness[f]	.35	(−)1.83	(−).64	−.55
Roughness[e]	.71	1.76	1.24	1.26
Weight[b]	.64	1.14	.74	.75
Weight[e]	.73	1.43	1.04	1.09
Mean (absolute values)			.72	.72
q = 1/harmonic mean of m		.68		

[a] Curtis (1970).
[b] Curtis et al. (1968).
[c] Curtis & Rule (1972).
[d] Curtis & Rule (1977).
[e] Rule & Curtis (1973b).
[f] Rule et al. (1974).

It should be strongly emphasized that how well each expression fitted the data did not constitute the primary criterion for evaluating the model. Although a good fit is a necessary starting point, other expressions might fit as well. What was crucial was how well the parameters k and m predicted the exponent n from magnitude-estimation data. The point that goodness of fit is not considered the primary criterion in evaluating a mathematical model seems to be missed by some who would argue against fitting mathematical expressions to data. Note in this regard, how tidily the parameter estimates summarize the data and provide for the evaluation of the model.

SUBJECTIVE NUMBER

A similar strategy has been used to investigate the subjective number function. The subjective number function is an hypothesized relation between a subject's conception of number magnitudes and the numbers themselves. If magnitude estimation is treated as a special case of cross-modality matching in which subjective magnitudes of numbers are matched to subjective magnitudes of stimuli, the subjective number function is of considerable importance in interpreting the stimulus–response relation. According to the two-stage model, the number function is a power function with an exponent q equal to the reciprocal of m. That is,

$$q = 1/m. \tag{4.5}$$

A pooled estimate of the number exponent q is presented at the bottom of Table 4.1 as the mean reciprocal of m. It is .68. That the estimate is less then unity indicates that the number function is concave downward, and several studies of subjective number have provided results consistent with a negatively accelerated function (Banks & Hill, 1974; Birnbaum, 1974; Cinani, 1973; McKelvie & Shepley, 1977; Rule, 1969a, 1971, 1972; Rule & Curtis, 1973a; Schneider, Parker, Ostrosky, Stein, & Kanow, 1974).

In our attempt to scale subjective number (Rule & Curtis, 1973a), we employed a modification of the usual magnitude-estimation task. Instead of assigning numbers directly to stimuli, the subjects were presented with a number and a weight and were asked which had the greater magnitude. That is, the subject was presented with a weight and a number, say 5, and asked whether the heaviness of the weight was greater or less than the heaviness represented by the number 5. In the study, 36 subjects compared 15 weights with the integers 1 to 9. Each subject made 50 judgments for each number-weight pair.

The data of interest were the frequencies with which each number was judged greater than each weight. These frequencies were subjected to a nonmetric scaling analysis for a difference model. The program used was Roskam's (1977) UNICON, an algorithm for polynomial conjoint models. It was assumed in the analysis that the frequency with which a number was judged greater than a weight was monotone with the difference between subjective number and subjective heaviness. An expression for the relation fitted to the data is provided by

$$F_{ij} \overset{m}{\simeq} t_i - v_j, \tag{4.6}$$

where F_{ij} denotes the frequency with which the ith number was judged greater than the jth weight, and t_i and v_j represent scale values for subjective number and perceived heaviness. The symbol $\overset{m}{\simeq}$ denotes a weak monotone transformation fitted to a minimum-stress criterion.

Power functions, presented as Eqs. 4.7 and 4.8, were fitted to the relation between scale values for heaviness v and physical weight x and between scale values for number t and objective number N:

$$v = ax^k + b, \tag{4.7}$$

and

$$t = cN^q + d. \tag{4.8}$$

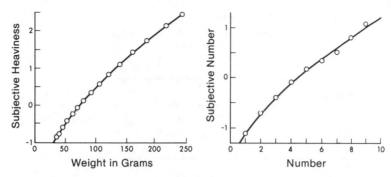

FIG. 4.1.   Scale values of subjective heaviness as a function of physical weight (left panel) and scale values of subjective number as a function of objective number (right panel).

The constants b and d were required in the expressions because the origins of the two scales are arbitrary. The constants required to recover the origins and the parameters of the power function can be estimated in a single analysis by fitting Eqs. 4.7 and 4.8 to the relation between scale values and stimulus measures. Figure 4.1 presents plots of these data. The curves through the points are based on the fits of Eqs. 4.7 and 4.8 to the data. Notwithstanding the earlier comments on goodness of fit, the plots are rather pretty.

Once again, however, it was particularly important to relate the results back to the original magnitude-estimation task. It seems obvious that any finding intended to have implications for a psychophysical judgment task must be shown to be consistent with data from that judgment procedure. Because the scales were derived from the data from a modification of the magnitude-estimation procedure, and because different psychophysical procedures can lead to different results, it was necessary to determine if these results are consistent with data from magnitude estimates of heaviness as a separate task.

The predicted exponent n from magnitude estimation is provided by the ratio

$$n = k/q. \tag{4.9}$$

Recall that q is the reciprocal of the output exponent m. The results are summarized in the first row of Table 4.2. The second row of the table presents results from a reanalysis of Cinani's (1973) data obtained in an experiment employing the same procedure but in which area rather than heaviness was compared with number. In both cases the predicted values are close to the magnitude-estimation exponent n.

Note as well, the close agreement between these estimates of q and the pooled estimate obtained from difference judgments shown in Table 4.1. This agreement in estimates of the number exponent provides converging results from different experimental operations, which also provides an important criterion in evaluating any model (Garner, Hake, & Eriksen, 1956).

TABLE 4.2
Estimates of Parameters from Magnitude Estimation
and Conjoint Scaling of Frequencies

	$v = ax^k + b$	$t = cN^q + d$	$y = ax^n + b$	
Continuum	k	q	k/q	n
Weight	.57	.63	.90	.90
Area[a]	.48	.75	.64	.68
mean		.69		

[a] Based on data from only three subjects.

Convergent results have also been found by other investigators of subjective number. In particular, Schneider et al. (1974) derived a scale of numbers from a nonmetric scaling analysis of judgments of the similarity of paired numbers. Their scale was found to be related to objective number by a power function with an exponent of .75. Another estimate in the same neighborhood was found by Banks and Hill (1974) from a task in which subjects were required to generate random number sequences. Their exponent is .67, which is very close to estimates in Tables 4.1 and 4.2.

The factors responsible for the curvature in the function are open to speculation. One possibility is that the curvature stems from subjects' experience with both the relative and additive properties of numbers used in measurement (Rule, 1972). If so, developmental changes in the number function might be expected. Perhaps for a child with only ordinal and cardinal concepts the number function is linear, and it becomes curved as relational concepts such as those of area and mechanical advantage are encountered. This line of thinking might lead one to suspect that experts in mathematics are afflicted with very bent subjective number functions. Whatever the antecedents may be, it should be kept in mind that the subjective number function differs from sensory functions in that its form is not constrained by operating characteristics of sensory transducers. Consequently, greater variability in number functions may be expected. They may even vary within an individual depending on how the numbers are used in a particular task.

INDIVIDUAL DIFFERENCES
IN POWER FUNCTIONS

Differences in subjective number functions may account for one source of the variability of individual exponents. That power functions for individual subjects vary between subjects has been noted (e.g., McGill, 1960), and several studies have yielded individual differences in exponents that are reliable within an experimental session (e.g., Rule, 1966) and perhaps over a longer period of time as well (see Engeland & Dawson, 1974, and Teghtsoonian & Teghtsoonian, 1971, for conflicting results). In addition, exponents have been found to be related between continua (Ekman, Hosman, Lindman, Ljungberg, & Åkesson, 1968; Jones & Marcus, 1961; Rule, 1966, 1968, 1969b), such that a subject with a high exponent for, say heaviness, also has a high exponent for perceived area. These results have been found to hold for other cross-modality matches as well as magnitude estimation (Duda, 1975; Rule & Markley, 1971). The findings from cross-modality matching have suggested that individual differences in exponents stem from idiosyncratic response factors rather than sensory differences.

The two-stage model has provided a useful framework for investigating these alternatives. If the individual differences stem from general differences in sensory processing of stimulus information, the input exponent k should be correlated across continua. Alternatively, if they are due to response factors, values of the output exponent m should be correlated, whereas values of k should not. These alternatives were investigated in an experiment in which subjects judged both differences in area and differences in numerousness (Rule & Curtis, 1977). The difference function given in Eq. 4.3 was fitted to each subject's data to provide estimates of k and m for each of the two tasks. The correlation coefficients for the relation between estimates of m obtained from the two tasks is .51, which is very close to correlations found for exponents obtained from magnitude estimation of single stimuli. The corresponding correlation coefficient for k is a near zero, .07. This low correlation for k would seem to discredit the possibility that individual differences between exponents from magnitude estimation reflect differences in perceived intensity that is general across continua. Instead, the differences in psychophysical functions stem from differences in judgmental processes involved in selecting a response.

From a strict interpretation of the two-stage model as initially formulated, the differences would be attributed to differences in subjective number functions. Although it seems likely that subjects may differ in this regard as we have noted, it seems equally likely that they differ with respect to other response factors as well. For example, Robinson (1976) has shown that numbers used as examples in instructions can affect the exponent. An interesting possibility is provided by Cross (1973), who has shown that sequential response dependency can affect estimates of parameters, which could account for some of the variability. It remains to be shown, however, whether the dependencies are associated with sensory or judgmental events in the stimulus–response sequence.

The framework and associated methodology developed within the context of the two-stage model have been applied to other sensory and judgmental problems as well. These have ranged from an investigation of the locus (sensory or judgmental) of the reciprocal relation between judgments of inverse attributes such as lightness and darkness (Curtis & Rule, 1978b; Rule, Laye, & Curtis, 1974), to an evaluation of the composition rules by which two monocular views combine to yield binocular brightness (Curtis & Rule, 1978a). Investigation of different problems has called for different analytic strategies as well as different experimental procedures.

ANALYTIC METHODS

Table 4.3 presents the symbolization of four strategies for data analysis that we have used within the framework of the two-stage model. Use of each procedure is illustrated on the right side of the table by showing the steps required to fit Eq. 4.3 to difference judgments. However, the methods have been useful for fitting other expressions as well. Analytic strategies for fitting expressions to data differ both with respect to the precision with which they estimate values of parameters and in the information that they provide regarding trends in the data. The first two procedures to be presented represent the extremes in the precision-information trade off. In the first, all parameters are directly estimated by fitting a specified equation to the data, whereas the second employs nonmetric scaling as an intermediate step. The third and fourth approaches are newer methods that share some of the properties of the first two procedures. When selecting an analytic strategy, the balance between information and precision required for the purposes of the experiment needs to be considered. However, often it is profitable to use two or more approaches to explore the data.

TABLE 4.3
Four Procedures for Estimating Parameters with
Applications to a Difference Equation

Analytic Sequence	Difference Equation
I. Metric parameter estimation	
$\quad y \simeq z = f(x;\theta)$	$\hat{y} = a(x_i^k - x_j^k)^m + b$
II. Nonmetric scaling analysis	
$\quad y \overset{m}{=} \hat{z} \simeq z = s(v)$	$z = v_i - v_j$
$\quad v \simeq \hat{v} = g(x;\theta_1)$	$\hat{v} = cx^k + d$
$\quad y \simeq h(z;\theta_2)$	$\hat{y} = az^m + b$
III. Metric scaling and parameter estimation	
$\quad y \simeq s(v;\theta_2)$	$\hat{y} = (v_i - v_j)^m + b$
$\quad v \simeq g(x;\theta_1)$	$\hat{v} = cx^k + d$
IV. Nonmetric parameter estimation	
$\quad y \overset{m}{=} \hat{z} \simeq z = f(x;\theta_1)$	$z = x_i^k - x_j^k$
$\quad y \simeq h(z;\theta_2)$	$\hat{y} = az^m + b$

Note: $\overset{m}{=}$ denotes a weak monotonic relation, $\simeq$ a (least squares) approximation, $\hat{z}$ fitted values, $\hat{v}$ and $\hat{y}$ predicted values.

Metric Parameter Estimation

Consider the first entry in Table 4.3. In this procedure, estimates of parameters θ of some specified function f are obtained such that values of the function denoted by z are approximately equal to the data y. The expression can also be fitted to some specified transformation of the responses, such as the logarithmic transformation that is often used for fitting a power function by linear methods. A number of numerical methods are available for solving nonlinear equations. We have found the Gauss-Newton method of solving nonlinear regression functions to a least-squares criterion (Hartley, 1961) particularly useful. It is a general method that can be used to solve a variety of expressions.

Directly fitting an expression to data has the advantage of yielding the most precise estimates of parameters in the sense that the standard errors of the parameters are smaller than for the other procedures. Consequently, it is the most useful approach when one wishes to predict the relation among parameters as in the case of the relation among estimates of k, m, and n, presented in Table 4.1.

Nonmetric Scaling

The second entry in Table 4.3 denotes an approach that involves, as an intermediate step, a nonmetric scaling procedure for estimating scale values associated with the stimulus set. Nonmetric scaling of the Kruskal (1964) variety is noted in which a set of scale values v and a set of fitted values $\hat{z}$ are obtained such that values of the scaling model z are a least-squares approximation to $\hat{z}$, which in turn are a weak monotonic transformation of the data y (notation due to Young, 1972). Parameters of specified functions may then be estimated from the outcome of the scaling analysis. A function can be fitted to the relation between scale values and physical measures, and an expression can also be fitted to the relation between the model's values z and the responses y. This latter relation defines the form of the monotonic transformation. Because only ordinal assumptions are required by the nonmetric analysis, the form of the monotonic transformation is not imposed by the analysis and may be recovered from the data.

The nonmetric strategy has the advantage of permitting evaluation of trends at each step in the analysis by allowing the examination of plots of scale values as a function of physical measures and of the judgments as a function of values predicted by the model. This approach was particularly useful in the early phases of evaluating the two-stage model because, according to the model, the relation between scale values and physical measures provides the form of the input transformation, and the relation between judgments and the scaling model's values gives the form of the output transformation. Consequently, this procedure allowed the separation of the two transformations to determine whether each was in fact characterized by a power function. Results of the Rule, Curtis, and

Markley (1970) study indicated that both transformations could be closely approximated by power functions, a finding that held for individual subject's data as well as group data.

The utility of the nonmetric analysis is not, of course, exclusive to tests of the two-stage model. It has an advantage in that it requires much weaker assumptions than the direct least-squares solution. No assumptions need be made concerning the form of the psychophysical function, and scales can be obtained when the form of the monotonic (output) transformation is unknown. A case in point is given by the experiment cited earlier (Rule & Curtis, 1973a) in which frequency data from paired comparisons were used to scale subjective weight and number simultaneously. Here the nonmetric solution required neither assumptions concerning the relations between the subjective and objective scales for number and weight nor assumptions concerning the form of the monotonic relation between frequency and subjective difference.

A disadvantage of an approach using nonmetric scaling as an intermediate step is that it yields the least precise estimates of parameters. Hence, it is more useful for examining trends in data than for evaluating relations among a model's parameters. In this regard, the estimate of the output exponent m from the two-stage model is particularly difficult with this approach because both variables in the expression are subject to error. An approach that remedies this problem is presented as the next procedure.

Metric Scaling and Parameter Estimation

The third approach is a particularly interesting procedure, one in which both scale values and some parameters are estimated in an initial step, and the remaining parameters can be estimated in a subsequent step from the relation between scale values and physical measures. This procedure yields more precise estimates of parameters than the nonmetric scaling approach, but it retains the advantage that visual inspection of the relation between scale values and physical measures is possible. The increased precision is at the expense of additional assumptions, however.

In applying this approach to solve the difference function presented as Eq. 4.3, scale values associated with the stimuli and parameters of the output transformation are estimated in the first step, which is followed in a second step by estimating parameters of the input transformation as in the nonmetric approach, presented earlier. The scaling solution is achieved by using dummy independent variables and solving a set of nonlinear equations by, say, the Gauss-Newton method. For a difference model, estimates of scale values are unique up to a linear transformation. Because the scale's origin is arbitrary, the lowest scale value v_0 can be conveniently set equal to zero. Consequently, for $t + 1$ stimuli, the equation to be solved is given by

$$y_{ij} = (v_1 x_1 + v_2 x_2 + \ldots + v_g x_g + \ldots + v_t x_t)^m + b, \qquad (4.10)$$

where x is a dummy independent variable with values

$$x_g = \begin{cases} 1 \text{ if } g = i \\ -1 \text{ if } g = j. \\ 0 \text{ otherwise} \end{cases}$$

(4.11)

Because the lowest scale value is set at zero, it can be excluded from the expression.

This method was initially devised to analyze judgments of differences in lightness of grays from a study by Curtis and Rule (1972) in which background reflectance was varied. The method provided a means by which contrast effects induced by the background could be evaluated by an examination of the relation between scale values and stimulus reflectance. The procedure was also used by Rule, Laye, and Curtis (1974) in an investigation of the reciprocal relation between judgments of lightness and darkness. The question was whether the reciprocal relation usually observed in this task stemmed from an inversion in perceptual processing or a judgmental effect due to subjects' reciprocal assignment of numbers. The data were found to be consistent with the latter interpretation.

In the two applications just described, the approach was applied to data from difference judgments, but it is possible to extend its application to other expressions as well. Assume, for example, that judgments of ratios of perceived magnitudes are obtained on a scale with interval scale properties. A scaling model for data of an experiment employing $t + 1$ stimuli is provided by

$$y_{ij} = \frac{v_i}{v_j} + b,$$

(4.12)

where the constant b is required because the origin of y is arbitrary. A solution for scale values can be obtained such that their estimates are unique up to multiplication by a positive constant. A solution to Eq. 4.12 using dummy independent variables is provided by solving the nonlinear equation

$$y_{ij} = v_1^{x_1} v_2^{x_2} \ldots v_g^{x_g} \ldots v_t^{x_t} + b,$$

(4.13)

where the values of x are given by

$$x_g = \begin{cases} 1 \text{ if } g = i \\ -1 \text{ if } g = j. \\ 0 \text{ otherwise} \end{cases}$$

(4.14)

Because the estimates of v are unique up to multiplication by a positive constant, the lowest scale value v_0 can be set equal to 1 and does not appear in the expression.

Each of these examples can be considered as an alternative to nonmetric scaling in which the form of the monotonic transformation is specified. It should be noted, however, that solutions for scale values and estimates of parameters are possible with this approach for some expressions for which nonmetric scaling would not be applicable.

Nonmetric Parameter Estimation

The fourth procedure to be considered also combines aspects of the nonmetric scaling approach and direct estimates of parameters. The basis of the approach is a method NOPE (Rule, 1979). NOPE is an acronym for NOnmetric Parameter Estimation. The NOPE method provides solutions to nonlinear equations from the ordering of data. It shares with nonmetric scaling analyses the advantage of requiring only ordinal properties of data. But, by estimating parameters directly from an ordering, it eliminates the scaling step and avoids the cumulation of error entailed in sequential analyses. Consequently, it yields more precise estimates. It has amazing flexibility and can be used to solve some expressions that would not be amenable to a nonmetric scaling analysis. However, the parameters of functions that can be estimated by this method are restricted to those which do not affect a monotonic transformation of the values of the function. Therefore, any parameter of the output transformation must be estimated in a second step. NOPE offers no advantage over nonmetric scaling analyses in this regard.

The essential aspect of the numerical method is that the monotonic regression feature of Kruskal's (1964) nonmetric scaling method is combined with the Gauss-Newton method of solving nonlinear regression functions. Monotonic regression and one step of the Gauss-Newton method are applied alternately until the iterative sequence converges. Convergence is often quite rapid. (See Carvellas & Schneider, 1971, for an application of monotonic regression in combination with a variation of the Gauss-Newton method to multidimentional scaling analysis.)

NOPE has been used to solve a variety of expressions, both from artificial data and from actual experimental results. Curtis and Mullin (1975) used the method in one of their analyses of judgments of average loudness. Its most fruitful application, however, has been a recent analysis of binocular brightness.

Binocular brightness. Any expression intended to describe binocular brightness must account for two trends in the data. One is Fechner's paradox, an effect observed when luminances at the two eyes differ greatly. Under these viewing conditions, perceived brightness falls between the brightnesses of each corresponding monocular viewing condition. This trend seems to suggest an inhibitory or averaging process. The other trend suggests partial brightness summation. When the stimulation of the two eyes is approximately equal, binocular brightness is greater than the brightness for either monocular view.

On the basis of trends that we (Curtis & Rule, 1978a) found in binocular brightness data in combination with certain mathematical constraints, a family of functions was derived to describe binocular brightness. An expression from this family that was fitted to the data by the NOPE method is given by

$$z_{ij} = (x_{Li}{}^{2k} + x_{Rj}{}^{2k} + 2\, x_{Li}{}^{k}\, x_{Rj}{}^{k}\, \cos \alpha)^{\frac{1}{2}}, \qquad (4.15)$$

where z_{ij} denotes binocular brightness, and x_{Li} and x_{Rj} denote luminances at the left and right eyes. Equation 4.15 has a geometric representation as the sum of two vectors with lengths $x_{Li}{}^{k}$ and $x_{Rj}{}^{k}$ and separated by an angle of α degrees. When α is between 90° and 120°, the model predicts both partial summation when the luminances are approximately equal and the interactions characterized by Fechner's paradox when they differ greatly. A similar expression had been employed earlier to describe the perceived intensity of odor combinations (Berglund, Berglund, & Lindvall, 1976).

Data for binocular brightness were obtained in three experiments. Magnitude estimation was used in two experiments, whereas category ratings were obtained in the third. Typically, magnitude-estimation and category-rating methods yield very different results. But, it has been an assumption within the framework of the two-stage model that differences found between the methods stem from judgmental factors, and that the perceptual relation does not depend on whether a subject rates sensory experience on a category scale or assigns to it a magnitude estimate. That is, the differences are assumed to be due to different output functions.

Because a NOPE analysis is not affected by monotonic output transformations, similar estimates of parameters were expected from the ratings and magnitude estimates. Similar estimates were found. A NOPE solution to Eq. 4.15 yielded estimates of k from the two sets of magnitude estimates of .12 and .14, as compared with .13 from category ratings. For α, the estimates are 112° and 114° from magnitude estimation and 112° from category rating. These results not only show the usefulness of a NOPE analysis, but they also demonstrate how results from different judgment tasks can converge once nonlinearities due to judgmental factors are removed from the data.

LEVELS OF SENSORY AND
JUDGMENTAL PROCESSING

Within the context of sensory and judgmental aspects of the psychophysical relation, there remain complex issues to be resolved, issues on which, at present, one can only speculate. A psychophysical judgment implicates many levels of processing during both the input and output stages. On the input side, sensory transducers transform impinging energy to a neural code that is forwarded to projection areas and elsewhere. Eventually, after a sequence of processing events, magnitude information is evaluated. The form of the neural code likely differs for different modalities, and there may even be coding and recoding at various levels before magnitude information is extracted. One clue to a representation for neural codes may be provided by findings that families of power functions for some modalities tend to converge toward a maximum level for the modality (Stevens, 1974). This suggests that intensity information may be coded relative to the maximum capacity for a sensory channel and, as such, has a simple mathematical representation as a proportion regardless of how the information is transmitted neurologically. Such a representation would provide a means by which magnitude information from different modalities could be interpreted by the central monitor, postulated by Teghtsoonian (1971), that serves as a common monitor for evaluating all subjective magnitudes.

The situation on the output side is at least as complex. Here are complicated processes by which the subject decides which response is appropriate to the perceived sensory relation. These are, we suspect, the processes that are the primary contributors to variability of responses both between and within subjects. They are also responsible for the different results that are obtained from different judgment tasks such as magnitude estimation and category methods.

Each of the many levels of processing in the stimulus–response sequence requires time to complete, thereby producing a persistence of sensory information throughout the sequence. Di Lollo (1977, 1980) has provided the interesting suggestion that those phenomena that have been attributed to a sensory memory store are actually due to processing time at various levels in the sensory system. This lingering of stimulus information during processing, together with the longer-term storage of stimulus–response relations in memory, provide opportunities for interactions with previous and subsequent stimulation both at the sensory level and at the judgmental level, producing effects due to adaptive state of receptors, time-order errors, contextual effects, sequential-response dependencies, and so on.

Within the sequence of processing events lies the subjective impression of stimulus magnitudes that has been the target of measurement for the psychophysicist. As more is learned about sensory and judgmental effects, the level of processing to which the measures refer is likely to become an important issue of debate. It is clearly of crucial importance, and can only be known by understanding sensory and judgmental levels of processing. Given the nature of the problem, it seems likely that understanding will initially be in the form of a mathematical description. The two-stage model and its associated methodology illustrate an initial attempt in this direction.

ACKNOWLEDGMENTS

This work was supported by Grants A0151 and A9582 from the Natural Sciences and Engineering Council, Canada.

REFERENCES

Attneave, F. Perception and related areas. In S. Koch (Ed.), *Psychology: A study of a science* (Vol. 4). New York: McGraw-Hill, 1962.

Banks, W. P., & Hill, D. K. The apparent magnitude of number scaled by random production. *Journal of Experimental Psychology,* 1974, *102,* 353-376.

Berglund, B., Berglund, U., & Lindvall, T. Psychological processing of odor mixtures. *Psychological Review,* 1976, *83,* 432-441.

Birnbaum, M. H. Using contextual effects to derive psychophysical scales. *Perception & Psychophysics,* 1974, *15,* 89-96.

Carvellas, T., & Schneider, B. Direct estimation of multidimensional tonal dissimilarity. *Journal of the Acoustical Society of America,* 1971, *51,* 1839-1848.

Cinani, J. M. *Scales of subjective number for individual subjects.* Unpublished master's thesis, University of Alberta, 1973.

Cross, D. V. Sequential dependencies and regression in psychophysical judgments. *Perception & Psychophysics,* 1973, *14,* 547-552.

Curtis, D. W. Magnitude estimations and category judgments of brightness and brightness intervals: A two-stage interpretation. *Journal of Experimental Psychology,* 1970, *83,* 201-208.

Curtis, D. W., Attneave, F., & Harrington, T. L. A test of a two-stage model of magnitude judgment. *Perception & Psychophysics,* 1968, *3,* 25-31.

Curtis, D. W., & Mullin, L. C. Judgments of average magnitude: Analyses in terms of the functional measurement and two-stage models. *Perception & Psychophysics,* 1975, *18,* 299-308.

Curtis, D. W., & Rule, S. J. Magnitude judgments of brightness and brightness difference as a function of background reflectance. *Journal of Experimental Psychology,* 1972, *95,* 215-222.

Curtis, D. W., & Rule, S. J. Judgment of duration relations: Simultaneous and sequential presentation. *Perception & Psychophysics,* 1977, *22,* 578-584.

Curtis, D. W., & Rule, S. J. Binocular processing of brightness information: A vector-sum model. *Journal of Experimental Psychology: Human Perception and Performance,* 1978, *4,* 132-143. (a)

Curtis, D. W., & Rule, S. J. Judgments of average lightness and darkness: A further consideration of inverse attributes. *Perception & Psychophysics,* 1978, *24,* 343-348. (b)

Di Lollo, V. Temporal characteristics of iconic memory. *Nature,* 1977, *267,* 241-243.

Di Lollo, V. Temporal integration in visual memory. *Journal of Experimental Psychology: General,* 1980, *109,* 75-97.

Duda, P. D. Tests of the psychological meaning of the power law. *Journal of Experimental Psychology: Human Perception and Performance,* 1975, *1,* 188-194.

Ekman, G., Hosman, B., Lindman, R., Ljungberg, L., & Åkesson, C. A. Interindividual differences in scaling performance. *Perceptual and Motor Skills,* 1968, *26,* 815-823.

Engeland, W., & Dawson, W. E. Individual differences in power functions for a 1-week intersession interval. *Perception & Psychophysics,* 1974, *15,* 349-352.

Garner, W. R., Hake, H. W., & Eriksen, C. W. Operationism and the concept of perception. *Psychological Review,* 1956, *63,* 149-159.

Hartley, H. O. The modified Gauss-Newton method for the fitting of non-linear regression functions by least squares. *Technometrics,* 1961, *3,* 269-280.

Jones, F. N., & Marcus, M. J. The subject effect in judgments of subjective magnitude. *Journal of Experimental Psychology,* 1961, *61,* 40-44.

Kruskal, J. B. Nonmetric multidimensional scaling: A numerical method. *Psychometrika,* 1964, *29,* 115-129.

McGill, W. The slope of the loudness function: A puzzle. In H. Gulliksen & S. Messick (Eds.), *Psychological scaling.* New York: Wiley, 1960.

McKelvie, S. J., & Shepley, K. Comparisons of intervals between subjective numbers, an extension. *Perceptual and Motor Skills,* 1977, *45,* 1157-1158.

Robinson, G. H. Biasing power law exponents by magnitude estimation instructions. *Perception & Psychophysics*, 1976, *19*, 80–84.

Roskam, E. E. A survey of the Michigan-Israel-Netherlands-Integrated series. In J. C. Lingoes (Ed.), *Geometric representations of relational data*, Ann Arbor, Mich.: Mathesis Press, 1977.

Rule, S. J. Subject differences in exponents of psychophysical power functions. *Perceptual and Motor Skills*, 1966, *23*, 1125–1126.

Rule, S. J. Subject differences in exponents for circle size and proportion. *Perceptual and Motor Skills*, 1968, *26*, 520.

Rule, S. J. Equal discriminability scale of number. *Journal of Experimental Psychology*, 1969, *79*, 35–38. (a)

Rule, S. J. Subject differences in exponents from circle size, numerousness, and line length. *Psychonomic Science*, 1969, *15*, 284–285. (b)

Rule, S. J. Discriminability scales of number for multiple and fractional estimates. *Acta Psychologica*, 1971, *35*, 328–333.

Rule, S. J. Comparisons of intervals between subjective numbers. *Perception & Psychophysics*, 1972, *11*, 97–98.

Rule, S. J. Solutions to some nonlinear equations from nonmetric data. *Psychometrika*, 1979, *44*, 143–155.

Rule, S. J., & Curtis, D. W. Conjoint scaling of subjective number and weight. *Journal of Experimental Psychology*, 1973, *97*, 305–309. (a)

Rule, S. J., & Curtis, D. W. Reevaluation of two models for judgments of perceptual intervals. *Perception & Psychophysics*, 1973, *14*, 433–436. (b)

Rule, S. J., & Curtis, D. W. Subject differences in input and output transformations from magnitude estimation of differences. *Acta Psychologica*, 1977, *41*, 61–65.

Rule, S. J., Curtis, D. W., & Markley, R. P. Input and output transformations from magnitude estimation. *Journal of Experimental Psychology*, 1970, *86*, 343–349.

Rule, S. J., Laye, R. C., & Curtis, D. W. Magnitude judgments and difference judgments of lightness and darkness: A two-stage analysis. *Journal of Experimental Psychology*, 1974, *103*, 1108–1114.

Rule, S. J., & Markley, R. P. Subject differences in cross-modality matching. *Perception & Psychophysics*, 1971, *9*, 115–117.

Schneider, B., Parker, S., Ostrosky, D., Stein, D., & Kanow, G. A scale for the psychological magnitude of number. *Perception & Psychophysics*, 1974, *16*, 43–46.

Stevens, J. C. Families of converging power functions in psychophysics. In H. R. Moskowitz, B. Scharf, & J. C. Stevens (Eds.), *Sensation and measurement: Papers in honor of S. S. Stevens*. Dordrecht, The Netherlands: Reidel, 1974.

Stevens, S. S. Cross-modality validation of subjective scales for loudness, vibration, and electric shock. *Journal of Experimental Psychology*, 1959, *57*, 201–209.

Teghtsoonian, M., & Teghtsoonian, R. How repeatable are Stevens' power law exponents for individual subjects? *Perception & Psychophysics*, 1971, *10*, 147–149.

Teghtsoonian, R. On the exponents in Stevens' law and the constant in Ekman's law. *Psychological Review*, 1971, *78*, 71–80.

Young, F. W. A model for polynomial conjoint analysis algorithms. In R. N. Shepard, A. K. Romney, & S. B. Nerlove (Eds.), *Multidimensional scaling: Theory and applications in the behavioral sciences* (Vol. 1). New York: Seminar Press, 1972.

5 Cognitive Algebra and Social Psychophysics

Norman H. Anderson
University of California, San Diego

The method of direct estimation for psychological measurement is simple and attractive. The subject is asked to assign numbers to represent psychological magnitude of loudness of a sound, for example, or likableness of a person, or subjective probability of some event. Subjects find this natural and easy to do. It seems to provide direct access to psychological sensation.

But the method of direct estimation has been severely criticized. The responses are really number-words; how can they be treated as true numbers? Many investigators have despaired of this question and have concluded that measurement theory must be built up using only ordinal, rank-order data.

Their reaction is understandable when it is realized that the two most popular methods of direct estimation do not yield equivalent results. As is well known, the common rating method gives generally different results than S. S. Stevens' method of magnitude estimation. Subjects find both methods natural and easy to use. That these two methods disagree raises serious doubts about both of them. If at least one is invalid, perhaps both are invalid.

Stevens, it is true, has argued vigorously that his method is the true method. However, his evidence has not generally been considered adequate. That does not mean his claim is incorrect, merely that he has failed to provide a convincing base of evidence.

1. FUNCTIONAL MEASUREMENT

A fundamentally new approach was provided by functional measurement theory (Anderson, 1962a, 1962b). Functional measurement is neutral in the controversy between ratings and magnitude estimation (Anderson, 1970, p. 166). It operates

123

at a deeper epistemological level. It provides a validational criterion against which ratings and magnitude estimation can be validated. It plays the role of a neutral judge.

1.1. Functional Measurement Diagram

The nature of functional measurement can be seen in Fig. 5.1. This diagram shows three successive stages between the physical stimuli S_i at left and the overt, observable response R at right.

The first stage transforms the physical stimuli S_i into psychological stimuli s_i. This is the province of the valuation function V. For simple sensory stimuli, V is the psychophysical law. However, the concept of valuation function also applies to verbal or symbolic stimuli that do not have any physical metric.

In the second stage, the several psychological stimuli are integrated to form an implicit or psychological response. This integration function I is also called the *psychological law* because it relates the psychological response to the psychological stimuli.

In the third and final stage, the psychological response r is transformed into the overt, observable response R. This is the province of the psychomotor law, M. When M is linear, then R is said to be a linear, or "equal interval" scale.

1.2. Psychological Law

The basic element in functional measurement is the psychological law or integration function. This is the foundation for measurement theory.

This approach is fundamentally different from that of Stevens. Stevens was

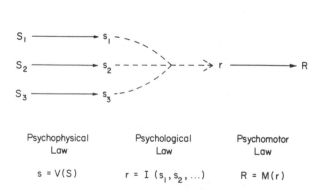

FIG. 5.1. Functional measurement diagram. Physical stimuli S impinge on the organism and are converted by the valuation operation or psychophysical law V into psychological stimuli s. The psychological stimuli are combined according to the integration function or psychological law I to yield an implicit response r. The implicit response is transformed into the overt observable response R according to the output function or psychomotor law M. From Anderson (1977).

concerned with the *psychophysical law*; functional measurement is primarily concerned with the *psychological law*. Functional measurement aims to derive the psychophysical law from the more basic psychological law.

A glance back at the functional measurement diagram shows that the three stages between physical stimulus and physical response present three distinct problems. Two of these are problems of measurement: measurement of the stimulus variables and measurement of the response. The other is a substantive problem of stimulus integration. The term "functional" reflects this foundation role of the integration function.

All three problems are to be solved simultaneously. That is, the two measurement problems are to be solved at the same time that the psychological law of stimulus integration is determined. That is quite simple in principle, and nature has fortunately made it work in practice. This is shown in the next two subsections.

1.3. Parallelism Theorem

The essential logic of functional measurement is well illustrated by the parallelism theorem. Suppose that two stimulus variables are hypothesized to add together to produce the observed response. To test this hypothesis, manipulate the two stimulus variables in a row × column matrix (factorial design). If the hypothesis is true, then the observed data will exhibit parallelism.

More specifically, let S_{Ri} and S_{Cj} denote the *physical values* of the stimulus variables in Row i and in Column j, respectively, of the factorial design. Let s_{Ri} and s_{Cj} denote the corresponding *psychological values,* and let r_{ij} denote the psychological response to the stimulus combination (S_{Ri}, S_{Cj}). Then the hypothesis may be stated:

$$r_{ij} = s_{Ri} + s_{Cj}. \tag{5.1}$$

This simple adding model is not directly testable because the response term and the stimulus terms are unobservables, inside the organism. To test this model, it must be related to something observable. That is done by the parallelism theorem.

Parallelism Theorem. If Eq. 5.1 is true, and if the observable response is a linear ("equal interval") scale, then:

1. *The factorial plot of the data will form a set of parallel curves.*
2. *The row (column) means of the factorial design will be estimates of the subjective values of the row (column) stimuli on validated linear ("equal interval") scales.*

The proof is simple, and can be obtained directly from Eq. 5.1, together with the assumption of response linearity. Response linearity means that the physical, observable response R_{ij} is a linear function of the psychological, unobservable response r_{ij}. As the proof has been given elsewhere, it is omitted here.

Note the power of this theorem. If the observed data exhibit parallelism, that supports the adding model. At the same time, it supports the other premise of the theorem, namely, the assumption of response linearity. For, if either assumption is incorrect, then parallelism will not in general obtain. Observed parallelism thus accomplishes three simultaneous goals:

1. It supports the adding model.
2. It supports the linearity of the response scale.
3. It provides linear scales of the stimulus variables.

Note that the test of parallelism is made directly in terms of the observed response. No stimulus values are needed for this test. Quite the opposite, the psychological values of the stimuli are derivative from the parallelism analysis.

1.4. Experimental Illustration

The parallelism theorem can be illustrated in the following experiment on grayness averaging. The subject is presented with two gray Munsell chips and asked to give a number that represents their average grayness. There are 25 pairs of chips, each ranging from black to white in a 5×5 factorial design. Because the subject is instructed to average, the data are expected to obey the adding model and so should exhibit parallelism—if the response scale is linear.

But this experiment used two response scales: the common rating scale and magnitude estimation. Both cannot give parallelism, of course, because they are nonlinearly related. Perhaps neither will give parallelism. However, both have equal opportunity: The parallelism theorem serves as an impartial judge between these two methods of direct estimation.

The results are shown in Fig. 5.2. The left panel shows the factorial plot of the rating data; these curves are approximately parallel. The right panel shows the factorial plot of the magnitude-estimation data; these curves are very nonparallel for the vertical spread changes by a factor of two to one from left to right. Judged by the criterion of the parallelism theorem, the rating method succeeds and magnitude estimation fails.

The main point of this experiment is to illustrate the functional measurement approach. This general method can be applied to many different problems. The essential feature is that measurement is grounded in the integration function or psychological law. This reflects a basic epistemological change from the philosophy that has been typical of work on magnitude estimation. Functional measurement provides a neutral, impartial judge between magnitude estimation and ratings.

This point deserves emphasis. Functional measurement does not conflict with

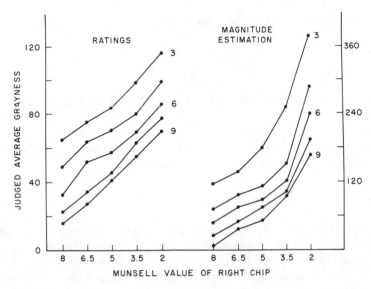

FIG. 5.2.   Test of grayness averaging. Subjects judged the average grayness of
two Munsell chips presented together. Value of the right-hand chip is shown on the
horizontal axis, with one curve for each value of the left-hand chip. Graphic rating
response in the left panel obeys the parallelism prediction of the integration model.
Magnitude estimations in the right panel disobey the parallelism theorem. This
nonparallelism reflects the nonlinear bias of this response procedure. Data from
Weiss (1972).

magnitude estimation because the two lie at different logical levels. Stevens has
been concerned with the *psychophysical law;* functional measurement is concerned with the *psychological law*.

However, I do not wish to argue about the relative merits of one or another
method of direct estimation. Instead, I wish to turn to the fundamental question.

1.5. Do Psychological Laws Have
Simple Algebraic Forms?

A large program of work over the last two decades has shown that many tasks do
obey simple algebraic models. This work originated in social judgment, but
applications have been made in many other areas including: psychophysics,
decision theory, learning and motivation, psycholinguistics, and developmental
psychology.

This outcome is not unexpected, of course, because many investigators have
hypothesized the operation of simple algebraic models. But without a capacity
for psychological measurement, progress on algebraic models has been halting
and limited. The functional measurement approach has provided an effective
solution to this problem.

But this approach only works if the algebraic models hold empirically. The true foundation of measurement lies in these substantive investigations. A few experimental applications are considered next.

2. COGNITIVE ALGEBRA: LINEAR MODELS

This section gives brief summaries of a few of the many investigations of stimulus integration with linear models. The main emphasis is on applications in social judgment as is appropriate to this symposium.

2.1. Person Perception

One of the first studies in the research program on information-integration theory is the study of person perception shown in Fig. 5.3 (Anderson, 1962a). Subjects received descriptions of nine different persons, each described by two personality traits. These descriptions formed the 3 × 3 design shown in the figure. Subjects rated likableness of each person on a 1–20 rating scale.

The important feature of Fig. 5.3 is the parallelism. Likableness of the person is a sum or average of the likableness values of the separate adjectives. This result has been confirmed many times since 1962.

Also notable in Fig. 5.3 is the difference between the two subjects in the relative location of the middle curve. For Subject FF, the middle curve is midway

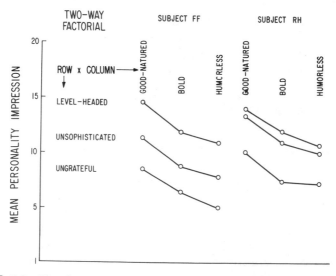

FIG. 5.3.   Test of averaging hypothesis in person perception. Data from Anderson (1962a).

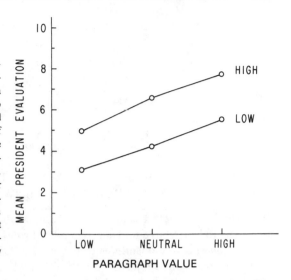

FIG. 5.4. Test of averaging hypothesis for attitudes toward U.S. Presidents. The six data points represent a 2 × 3 design according to which two informational paragraphs of graded value were presented about each of six Presidents. The two levels of the row factor were a low or high paragraph, as listed by the two curves. The three levels of the column factor were low, neutral, or high paragraphs, as listed on the horizontal axis (from Anderson, 1973.) Copyright (1973) by the American Psychological Association. Reprinted by permission.

between the other two. For FF, therefore, *unsophisticated* lies midway in value between *ungrateful* and *level-headed*. Subject RH has different values; for him, *unsophisticated* is nearly as desirable as *level-headed*. This last result illustrates how functional measurement can operate within the value system for each separate individual.

2.2. Attitudes Toward U.S. Presidents

This experiment tested the hypothesis that attitudes toward public and historical figures obey an averaging model. Subjects received paragraphs that described the lives and deeds of various Presidents of the United States. They rated each President on statesmanship. These results are in Fig. 5.4. The parallelism of the curves supports the hypothesis that the attitude is an average of the given information.

2.3. Subjective Probability

Many writers have speculated that human judgments of (subjective) probability might obey the algebraic rules prescribed by mathematical probability theory. Figure 5.5 shows a functional measurement test of one such algebraic model. The subject saw two urns, each with a specified proportion of red and white beads as listed in the figure. One urn was picked with specified probability, and one bead was drawn at random from that urn. The subject estimated the probability that the bead would be white.

Mathematical theory prescribes the model for *objective* probability:

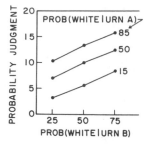

FIG. 5.5. Parallelism test of conditional probability model with allowance for subjective probabilities. Data from N. H. Anderson, unpublished experiment.

$$\text{Prob(White)} = \text{Prob(Urn A) Prob(White | Urn A)}$$
$$+ [1 - \text{Prob(Urn A)}] \text{Prob(White | Urn B)}.$$

The question is whether *subjective* probability obeys a similar model.

To test the subjective probability model, Prob(Urn A) was held constant, and the two conditional probabilities were varied in factorial design. If human judgment does obey this subjective probability model, then the data should exhibit parallelism. The results in Fig. 5.5 support this model.

2.4. Development of Cognitive Algebra

Where does cognitive algebra come from? Studies of children's judgments may shed some light on this question, and considerable work in this area has been

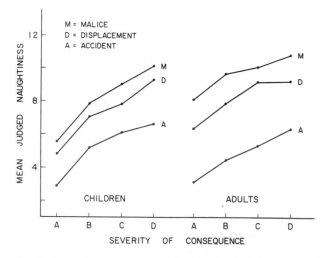

FIG. 5.6. Badness of act is the sum of the intention behind the act and the damage caused by the act. Subjects judge badness of story character who performed an act with one of three intentions: with purposive malice, by displaced aggression, or accidentally, as listed by the three curves. Amount of damage caused by the act is listed on the horizontal. Data from Leon (1980).

done in the last few years. The results show that children as young as 3 years and a few months possess a general-purpose adding rule, as well as the ability to use a graphic rating scale in a true linear manner.

Judged badness of an action depends on both the amount of harm or damage, and on the intention of the actor. The parallelism in Fig. 5.6 shows that both children and adults integrate these two pieces of information by an adding-type rule. The children place greater weight on the damage-consequence information, as shown by the slopes of the curves; they place less weight on the intent information, as shown by the vertical separation of the curves. Piagetian "centra-tion" was notable by its absence.

Other experiments have shown that children are quite good at intuitive calcu-lations. Indeed, children are showing much more cognitive ability than has been recognized in traditional child psychology (Anderson, 1980).

3. COGNITIVE ALGEBRA: MULTIPLYING MODELS

Many integration tasks obey multiplying models. Functional measurement pro-vides a simple analysis using the linear fan theorem.

3.1. Linear Fan Theorem

In terms of the notation used earlier, the multiplying model may be written:

$$r_{ij} = s_{Ri} s_{Cj}. \qquad (5.2)$$

Linear Fan Theorem.   If Eq. 5.2 is true, and if the observable response is a linear ("equal interval") scale, then:

1. *The appropriate factorial plot of the data will form a fan of straight lines.*
2. *The row (column) means of the factorial design will estimate the subjective values of the row (column) stimuli on linear scales.*

This theorem is very similar to the parallelism theorem. It provides a simple graphical analysis for multiplying rules of stimulus integration. Here are some empirical examples.

3.2. Subjective Probability and Utility

The classical problem in utility theory has been that of joint measurement of subjective probability and utility. Functional measurement provided the first general, practicable solution to this problem (Anderson & Shanteau, 1970). Subjects judged personal value of lottery tickets of the form: "*You have* _____

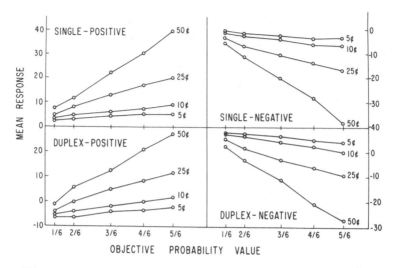

FIG. 5.7. Linear fan test of multiplying rule for subjective probability and utility (from Anderson & Shanteau, 1970.) Copyright (1970) by the American Psychological Association. Reprinted by permission.

chance to win _____.'' Chance to win was defined by the roll of a die; amount to be won was defined by coins.

The natural hypothesis is that these judgments obey the multiplying rule:

Personal Value = Subjective Probability × Utility.

If so, then the data will exhibit a linear fan pattern. The appearance of that pattern in Fig. 5.7 is evidence for the success of the multiplying model. This outcome has been confirmed in many experiments.

The spacing of the probability stimuli on the horizontal axis in Fig. 5.7 is in terms of their subjective value, as prescribed by the linear fan theorem. The unequal spacing means that subjective and objective probabilities are nonlinearly related. That is not surprising, but it emphasizes the necessity of a method that can allow for subjective values.

3.3. Fuzzy Logic

A central problem in semantic theory is to represent truth value as a continuous semantic variable. In traditional, two-valued propositional logic, class membership is all or none. In common thought, however, class membership is often a matter of degree. A sparrow and a penguin are both birds, but a sparrow seems to be a better or truer bird than a penguin. Information-integration theory provides a natural representation for degree of truth (Oden, 1977).

In one of Oden's studies, subjects responded to questions of the form: "How true is it that a sparrow is a bird, or a penguin is a bird?" The truth value of the

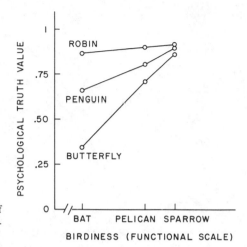

FIG. 5.8. Linear fan analysis of integration of fuzzy class membership. From Oden (1977).

first component is high; that of the second is medium to low. How are the truth values of these component statements integrated to determine the truth value of the compound statement?

One suggested integration rule has a multiplying form that can be stated thus: The falsity value of the compound equals the product of the falsity values of the components. The linear fan in Fig. 5.8 supports this multiplying rule. Other work by Oden has given further support to a cognitive algebra of fuzzy logic.

3.4. Other Applications

Numerous other applications of multiplying models have been made (see Anderson, 1974a, 1974b, 1974c, 1978, 1979, in press). There is little doubt but that the multiplying rule is a basic operation in cognitive algebra.

4. COGNITIVE ALGEBRA: OTHER MODELS

Other algebraic integration rules have also been studied. Subtracting rules for difference judgments are formally similar to adding rules and so may be tested using the parallelism theorem. Dividing rules for ratio judgments are formally similar to multiplying rules and so may be tested using the linear fan theorem. Two other models have also appeared quite often.

4.1. Averaging Model

The averaging model is ubiquitous in stimulus integration. In the experiment of Fig. 5.9, subjects rated preference value of meals. The left panel represents meals with a main course listed on the horizontal and a vegetable listed as curve

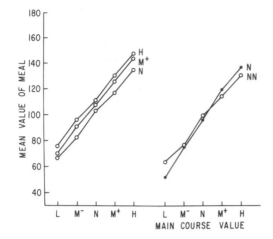

FIG. 5.9.   Critical test between adding and averaging hypotheses. From Oden and Anderson (1971).

parameter. The parallelism of these three curves supports an adding-type model. But, both adding and averaging models would account for this parallelism. How can they be distinguished?

A critical test between adding and averaging is shown in the right panel. The curve labelled N represents a main course with one neutral vegetable; the curve labelled NN represents the same meal but with an additional neutral vegetable.

The crossover of the N and NN curves eliminates the adding rule: If the added vegetable is positive (negative, or zero), then the adding rule requires that the NN curve lie above (below, or on) the N curve at every point.

The crossover is exactly as predicted by the averaging rule: Because the added vegetable is near neutral, it will average up the low main course and average down the high main course.

Numerous similar tests have been performed. Nearly all support the averaging model, an outcome that has far-reaching implications. Among other things, averaging represents a fundamental nonadditivity in cognitive processing.

4.2. Relative-Ratio Rule

What makes a fair division? This is an important social question. One view is that a person's *outcome O* should be proportional to his *input I*. If a fixed sum T is to be divided between two persons, A and B, then the fair outcome O_A for person A should obey the relative ratio rule $O_A = [I_A/(I_A + I_B)] T$.

When I_A and I_B are varied symmetrically from Low to High, then this model predicts a slanted barrel pattern of curves. This barrel pattern can be seen in Fig. 5.10. Thus, judgments of fairness and equity also appear to follow a cognitive algebra.

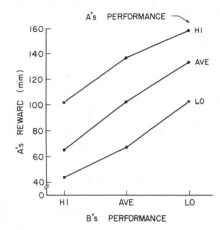

FIG. 5.10. Test of relative ratio rule for fair pay. From Anderson (1976a).

4.3. Cognitive Algebra

These experiments are only a small sample of the work that has been done. Not all tasks obey a simple cognitive algebra nor should they be expected to do so. There is no doubt, however, that much of human judgment does obey simple algebraic rules.

5.   MONOTONE ANALYSIS

Functional measurement would not be complete if it could not handle monotone ("ordinal") response measures. How to do this was indicated by Anderson (1962b): "The logic of the present scaling technique consists in using the postu-lated behavior laws to induce a scaling on the dependent (response) variable [p. 410]." This logic was in fact implicit in the foregoing experiments; the validity of the rating response was grounded on the algebraic models.

But not all response measures will be linear scales. Indeed, the rating response is linear only when certain precautions are used. This section illustrates how functional measurement provides a simple analysis of monotone response mea-sures.

5.1. Psychophysical Bisection

The century-old problem of psychophysical bisection seems simple—at first glance. To illustrate, suppose that the subject is presented with two stimulus chips, varied in reflectance or grayness, and chooses a response chip to lie halfway between in grayness. The great attraction of this bisection task is that no verbal response is required. It deals only with sense perceptions.

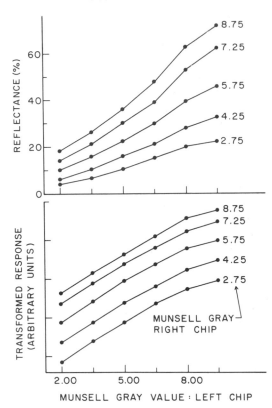

FIG. 5.11. Monotone analysis of bisection model for grayness. Subject selects response chip to lie halfway in grayness between two given stimulus chips. Munsell gray values of left and right stimulus chips are listed on horizontal axis, and as curve parameter, respectively. Upper panel plots reflectance value of bisector chip; lower panel plots monotone transformation of reflectance data. Parallelism supports bisection model. From Anderson (1976b).

The standard hypothesis is that the subject is equating two sense distances: $s_1 - r = r - s_2$, where s_1 and s_2 are the subjective values of the two stimulus chips, and r is the subjective value of the response. Solving for r yields a simple average: $r = \frac{1}{2}(s_1 + s_2)$.

Unfortunately, this simple model has long resisted analysis. The difficulty is that r, s_1, and s_2 are all unobservable subjective values. The investigator must make do with the physical reflectance measures.

The top panel of Fig. 5.11 plots the physical reflectance values from the factorial design used in this experiment. These data certainly do not obey the parallelism theorem.

But, if the bisection averaging model is correct, then some monotone transformation of physical reflectance will yield the psychological grayness value. This transformation can be determined, if it exists, for it is the one that will make the data parallel. Such a transformation was successfully obtained, as shown by the parallelism in the lower panel of Fig. 5.11. In this way, functional measurement was able to provide a general solution to the bisection problem.

5.2. The Psychophysical Law

By the parallelism theorem, the vertical elevations of the curves in the lower panel of Fig. 5.11 constitute a linear scale of subjective sensation of grayness. If a power function is fit to these data, it yields an exponent of approximately .2. That is quite different from the exponent of 1.2 that is obtained when magnitude estimation is used: One function is convex down, the other is convex up.

Stevens argues that magnitude estimation provides the true measure of sensation. But the exponent of .2 is based on the bisection model as a foundation. Thus it seems to have the better claim.

5.3. Cross-Task Validation

Further evidence on psychophysical scales can be obtained by asking whether the same scale is operative in different tasks. Figure 5.12 plots functional scales obtained from two other integration tasks, judging averages and differences, as a function of the bisection scale on the horizontal axis. The linearity of the relations show that all three tasks yield equivalent grayness scales. This *cross-task validation* lends further support to the bisection scale (Anderson, 1976b, 1977).

5.4. Methodology of Monotone Transformation

The idea of using monotone transformation is an old one, but only recently has it become practicable. Three main difficulties are involved.

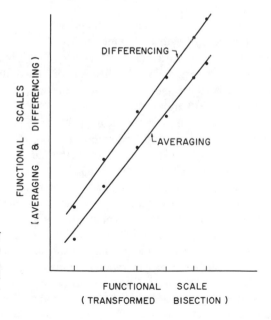

FIG. 5.12. Cross-task validation of psychophysical law. Linearity of the two curves implies that differencing, averaging, and bisection tasks all yield the same psychophysical function. From Anderson (1976).

First, there is the computational problem of obtaining the best possible monotone transformation. This seems to have reached a satisfactory solution with the development of Kruskal's (1965) MONANOVA, and the ADDALS program of de Leeuw, Young, and Takane (1976).

Second is the problem of testing goodness of fit. Krantz, Luce, Suppes, and Tversky (1971) comment on the "exceedingly perplexing problems raised by errors of measurement [p. xix]" in attempting to use conjoint measurement, but they do not provide a solution. Fortunately, recent developments in functional measurement have provided a solution to the problem of goodness of fit (Anderson, 1977, in press).

Third, and most basic, is the problem of algebraic models. Only if the algebraic models are empirically valid can they be used as the scaling frame for monotone transformation. The work on cognitive algebra previously cited points to the validity of this approach.

5.5. Monotone Indeterminacy

A number of writers have suggested that the question whether ratings or magnitude estimation provide a true linear scale is unanswerable. In practice it is often found that ratings are approximately a linear function of the logarithms of the magnitude estimations. It follows that an adding rule obtained with ratings will correspond to a multiplying rule obtained with magnitude estimations. The choice between these two alternative representations might seem to be a matter of arbitrary preference.

To help clarify this issue, consider an experiment in which subjects judge total apparent area of pairs of rectangles. An adding rule is naturally expected: Apparent area of the two rectangles taken together should equal the sum of the two separate apparent areas. The data support this adding rule—if the rating method is used. At the same time the apparent area of a single rectangle follows the natural multiplying rule, base × height.

But that means that the use of magnitude estimation would yield a product rule: Apparent area of the two rectangles taken together would equal the product of the two separate apparent areas. At the same time the area of a single rectangle would not be base × height but base^{height}.

Is the choice between these adding and multiplying rules arbitrary? Perhaps so on purely logical grounds. On any practical ground, however, there is sufficient reason to consider that apparent areas, like physical areas, add rather than multiply. Accordingly the rating method would be used.

Useful constraint on monotone transformation is available from two-operation models, in which two integration operations are involved. One operation may be used to define the monotone transformation while the other operation provides a basis for testing goodness of fit. Functional measurement can thus provide rigorous and powerful model tests with only rank order data. Further discussion of these matters is given elsewhere (Anderson, 1974a, pp. 227–233; 1977, pp. 210–213; in press).

6. COMMENTS ON MAGNITUDE ESTIMATION

The following observation (Anderson, 1975) is worth repeating: "Functional measurement is basically neutral in the controversy between ratings and magnitude estimation (Anderson, 1970b, p. 166) [p. 475]." It provides a validational base to assess any particular response method. The success of the rating method has been illustrated in Sections 3–5.

Stevens has repeatedly argued that magnitude estimation provides a true linear or even ratio scale. Equally often, he has been criticized for failing to provide a validational criterion. What evidence is available to support Stevens' claims?

6.1. Cognitive Algebra in Social Psychophysics

The results of Sections 3–5 demonstrate that the rating scale is a true linear scale. But, as Stevens has repeatedly emphasized, ratings and magnitude estimations are nonlinearly related on most stimulus dimensions. In Stevens' view, therefore, ratings and magnitude estimation cannot both be valid scales. But, if the foregoing evidence for ratings is accepted, then Stevens' position implies that magnitude estimation is biased and invalid. The program of research on information-integration theory thus presents a severe challenge to Stevens' position. He has never answered this challenge.

6.2. The Power Function

The fact that magnitude-estimation data usually fit a power function is sometimes taken as evidence for validity of magnitude-estimation data. But Marks (1968) has shown and Stevens has accepted the fact that category-rating data also fit power functions. Stevens' position is that not both power functions can be correct. So, fitting a power function tells us nothing.

6.3. Fluctuating Exponents

The first sign of bias in magnitude estimation was obtained by Stevens (1956) himself in his initial article on loudness where he advised: "Use various standards, for it is risky to decide the form of a magnitude function on the basis of data obtained with only one standard [p. 6]." But, Stevens' own data (e.g., 1956, Fig. 4) showed that different standards yielded markedly different exponents. Numerous later investigators have confirmed this inconsistency and have shown that many other biases will influence the exponent of a power function fit to the data. Stevens has never provided any criterion for deciding which exponent value might be unbiased.

6.4. Cognitive Algebra in Psychophysics

Algebraic models have been studied in numerous experiments using psychophysical stimuli. In general, magnitude estimation has failed in these experiments. Figure 5.2 provides one example. This class of experiments is reviewed by Marks (1974) who concludes: "The results of all these experiments agreed in their finding of nonlinear relations between estimates of intervals and the intervals predicted from estimates of magnitudes [p. 257]."

Stevens has attempted to account for this theoretical contradiction by assuming that the experimental tasks in question introduce a bias. This explanation is ad hoc. An alternative explanation is that the bias is in the magnitude-estimation method.

6.5. Cross-Modality Matching

At present, the main remaining support for magnitude estimation comes from studies of cross-modality matching. In addition to obtaining magnitude estimates for two sensory continua, one continuum may be judged directly in terms of the other. Three power functions are then available, and the ratio of two exponents should equal the third.

Unfortunately, as is well-known, this test is not conclusive. At best, it provides a result that is unique only up to a power transformation. This result fails to distinguish between ratings and magnitude estimation.

It has been suggested that this lack of uniqueness in cross-modality matching could be resolved by assuming that magnitude estimation produces a valid scale on some one dimension, such as length, time, or angle. This suggestion rests on a fallacy. Ratings and magnitude estimation do not always disagree. In fact, they give nearly equivalent results for angle, time, and perhaps even for length. These three dimensions are atypical, for they are nonenergetic or nonsensory. It could equally well be assumed that the rating method was valid for these dimensions. In that case, however, the argument for cross-modality matching would fail.

6.6. Multiple Scales?

Perhaps ratings and magnitude estimation are both valid, but measure different quantities. Stevens has explicitly rejected this possibility, but Eisler (1965) and Treisman (1964) have argued for two distinct scales: one of magnitude and one of discriminability. Marks (1974) adopted a similar position and suggested that magnitude estimation yields the magnitude scale whereas ratings yield discriminability scales. These two response measures would tap in at different stages in the processing claim between stimulus and response.

A more general stage view was suggested by Anderson (1975, p. 479; 1976b, p. 124) who noted that many successive stages lie between the physical stimulus and the observable response. This is consistent with the concept of valuation-integration operations in the functional measurement diagram. In principle, therefore, there might be many different scales, a position advocated by Marks (1978).

This hypothesis of multiple scales is certainly reasonable and deserves serious consideration. From the functional measurement view, it reduces to an essentially empirical question. However, what little evidence is available raises doubt about multiple scales for sensory dimensions such as loudness.

7.   RELATIONS TO OTHER WORK

This section presents brief discussions of some relations between integration theory and approaches that have been used by other workers.

7.1. S. S. Stevens

There is a fundamental difference between functional measurement and the approach used in the "new psychophysics" of S. S. Stevens. The two lie at different epistemological levels. Stevens' approach was centered on a search for the *psychophysical law;* functional measurement is centered on a search for the *psychological law*.

A sign of this epistemological difference appears in the experimental work. The typical experiment in the Stevens' tradition asks for judgments of single, one-dimensional stimuli. That is exactly in line with Stevens' emphasis on the *psychophysical law*, for the psychophysical law is a one-variable function. This one-variable representation reflects the phenomenological correspondence between physical dimensions and such sensory qualities as loudness or brightness.

The typical experiment with functional measurement asks for judgments of compound, multidimensional stimuli. That is exactly in line with the emphasis on the *psychological law*. The psychological law, or integration function, is in general a function of two or more variables. This many-variable representation is a natural consequence of the concern with stimulus integration.

This one-variable–several-variable distinction makes a decisive difference for measurement theory. A basic problem for any theory of measurement is to provide a basis for transforming an ordinal scale into an interval scale. A function of only one variable is inadequate because it provides no constraints on such monotone transformations. But with two variables in a factorial design, it is possible to allow for monotone transformation and still retain degrees of freedom for testing the psychological law [Anderson, 1975, p. 478].

The experimental base of traditional psychophysical scaling . . . is inherently too narrow to support a solution to its problems. Tasks based on psychophysical information integration provide a broader and potentially simpler approach to scaling. In this approach, the psychophysical law appears as a by-product of the substantive development [Anderson, 1970, p. 153].

Functional measurement provides a validational base for psychophysical scales. A great advantage of this approach is that it can be used for verbal or symbolic stimuli that do not have a physical metric—as in social psychophysics.

7.2. L. E. Marks

Marks (1974) has adopted a view that in some important ways is similar to integration theory and functional measurement. Thus, Marks' "psychosensory laws" appear to be the same as the psychological laws of functional measurement. He writes (1974): "In the present context it is worthwhile to mention Anderson's (1970) argument in favor of 'functional' measurement. Anderson regards psychophysical measurement and scaling to be coextensive with determination of behavioral—and, presumably, sensory—laws [p. 276]." And, "In a fundamental sense, Anderson's position is quite close to that taken in this book [p. 277]."

A practical sign of this similarity may be found in Marks' (1978) interesting paper on loudness summation. This experiment employs a factorial design to test an algebraic model of loudness summation. That is entirely in line with the functional measurement approach (Anderson, 1970, p. 168).

The magnitude-estimation response that Marks used in this experiment did not satisfy the parallelism theorem. However, Marks applied a monotone transformation as discussed in Section 5. That means, of course, that he treated the magnitude estimations as merely an ordinal scale.

This work by an investigator who was trained in the Stevens' school is an encouraging testimonial of the emergence of a common approach. This approach carries the problem of measurement to the deeper level of psychological law.

7.3. Conjoint Measurement

Conjoint measurement is so frequently confused with functional measurement that a few comments on similarities and differences may be advisable.

Similarities are obvious. Both are concerned with adding and multiplying models, both emphasize factorial design, and both allow for monotone analysis.

Because of these similarities, functional measurement is often confused with conjoint measurement.

Differences are of two kinds, the first being practical. Conjoint measurement has had near-zero experimental applications, whereas functional measurement has been applied in many empirical areas. Conjoint measurement has not solved the vital problem of goodness of fit for monotone analysis, whereas functional measurement has developed such a test. Further, conjoint measurement is inherently unable to handle certain nonlinear models such as the averaging model of Section 4.

Another important practical difference lies in the attitude toward direct numerical response methods. Numerical response methods are welcome in functional measurement but are disallowed in conjoint measurement. This includes monotone regression analysis such as Kruskal's (1965) MONANOVA and the ADDALS method of de Leeuw, Young, and Takane (1976). These and related methods are explicitly classed as numerical methods in writings on conjoint measurement, as opposed to true ordinal methods.

The difference of the second kind is epistemological. Functional measurement is an organic, working part of substantive theory. In contrast, conjoint measurement is founded on abstract axioms. But these abstract axioms are quite different in nature from ordinary scientific axioms. The axioms of thermodynamics, Euclid's axioms, or the axioms of probability theory have substantive referents. So do the axioms or assumptions of Thurstonian scaling, of von Neumann-Morgenstern utility theory, or of signal-detection theory. These are substantive premises from which substantive conclusions can be derived.

But the axioms of conjoint measurement are quite different. They refer merely to order relations among observable responses and have no referent to underlying psychological processes. Thus, the key axiom of double cancellation involves comparisons among responses on six different trials. These comparisons are made in the statistical analysis, not by the subject. The role of double cancellation in conjoint measurement is thus not really different from the role of analysis of variance in functional measurement. These are techniques of data analysis, not the foundations of measurement (Anderson, 1977, in press).

7.4. D. W. Curtis and S. J. Rule

An extensive series of experiments by Curtis, Rule, and their associates have employed a "two-stage model" in which stimulus input and response output are both assumed to be power functions. Much of the experimental work has studied judgments of sums or differences of two stimuli. The two-stage model can then be written: $R = c_1(S_1^k \pm S_2^k)^m + c_2$, where S_1 and S_2 are the physical values of the stimuli, c_1 and c_2 are constants, and the $\pm$ sign allows for sum or difference judgments. The constants k and m are exponents of power functions that are assumed to govern the input and output stages.

This two-stage approach has many similarities to functional measurement. Indeed, the two stages correspond to the V and M functions in the functional measurement diagram of Fig. 5.1. However, functional measurement is not restricted to power functions for input and output. Further, it also applies to verbal or symbolic stimuli that lack a physical metric and hence cannot obey a power law.

Finally, functional measurement places primary emphasis on a third stage, namely, the integration function I in Fig. 5.1. This integration function is the basic element; stimulus and response scaling rest on it. In this view, the essential feature of the two-stage model is not either of its two stages, but rather the third stage, namely, the $\pm$ algebraic integration operation.

8. LOOKING BACKWARD AND FORWARD

Looking back at the papers and discussion of this symposium, I am impressed especially by the happy outcome of increased harmony between the two schools of magnitude estimation and category rating. This outcome owes much to the statesmanlike presentation with which Larry Marks opened the symposium. Past interaction between the two schools has been rather polarized. Such polarizations tend to be self-perpetuating, and this one will no doubt remain with us for some time to come. As Marks points out, however, research emphasis has been shifting away from scaling per se to an increasing concern with various problems of process. In the course of this shift, the two schools appear less as antagonists and more as protagonists struggling with common problems.

8.1. Multiple Stimulus Tasks

The Zeitgeist can be seen at work in the wide concern with judgments based on multiple stimuli. Although the various participants have started from diverse origins, nearly every paper seemed to be converging on some problem involving response to a multiple stimulus field.

A simple and popular multiple stimulus task is that of judging the difference (or average) of two (or more) given stimuli. Such tasks can provide a theoretical basis for validated measurement. Pioneering work on this problem by Dawson and by Curtis and Rule is brought up to date by the Rule and Curtis paper. This work shows increasing sophistication and recognition of statistical problems, as can also be seen in the papers by Orth, Wegener, and especially Schneider. Also notable is the paper by Cross, which brings a new level of capability to the difficult problem of cross-modality matching.

However, the differencing and averaging tasks have mainly been of interest for the problem of scaling itself. Although they have been useful for that purpose, they have an element of artificiality in that the subject is instructed about the operation. Many advantages are available with tasks in which the integration is more natural. A good example is provided by Marks' work on loudness of multiple component tones, which involves a perceptual integration. These more natural integration tasks also offer the potential for scaling, but they go beyond mere scaling to questions of psychological process.

Social judgment characteristically requires response to a multiple stimulus field. In some cases, the stimulus attributes or dimensions can be experimentally controlled, as in the interesting studies of intuitive statistics by Wagenaar and in the utility judgments considered by Wendt. Such experimental control simplifies many problems of analysis. Indeed, the problem considered by Wendt—that of measuring subjective probability and utility—was solved almost 10 years ago (see Fig. 5.7).

Complex natural entities, in which the attributes or dimensions are not known or not under experimental control, present more difficult problems. The papers by Sjöberg and Feger both take up this fundamental problem of social judgment. As they emphasize, social attitudes have structure and content and cannot be understood with simple one-dimensional views. The careful paper by Eisler, although concerned with a more perceptual judgment, has a similar message. Measurement in the social realm and in most practical affairs must take account of multiple stimulus attributes.

8.2. "Social Psychophysics": A Contradiction in Terms?

The social realm involves problems for which the methods and concepts of past psychophysics appear to be both inadequate and misleading. Four aspects of this issue deserve notice.

First, there is no stimulus metric. Occupations and crimes, to name but two examples, are complex symbolic stimuli. Because they have no physical metric, the central concept of the form of the psychophysical law becomes vacuous.

Second, social stimuli often involve extreme individual differences. Marks has argued that individual differences are small for sensory stimuli, and the careful paper by Montgomery provides some support for this. As I noted in my talk, however, the social realm is quite different. Indeed, the scales for two individuals may even be disordinal, as in preferences for foods, automobiles, and for other persons. Here, as before, the concept of psychophysical law must give way to something more general, such as the valuation function of Fig. 5.1.

Third, the social stimulus field is typically complex. This important point has been stressed by Feger and by Sjöberg. Sjöberg's paper had special interest to me because of the interesting light that it shed on the valuation operation and on the constructivist concept of attitude (e.g., Anderson, 1974b, p. 89).

Fourth, social situations have a multiplicity of possible response dimensions. Person perception is a good example, for there are many different dimensions on which a person might be judged. The operative dimension in any situation depends on a variety of contextual factors, including the social setting and the momentary goals of the judge.

All these reasons indicate that the conceptual framework of traditional psychophysics is inadequate to meet the demands of the social realm. Even simple social tasks have an essential difference from traditional tasks of psychophysics. I think this point deserves reflection because of the very natural tendency to transfer old methods to new problems. That has its uses, but it can also be treacherous. At the risk of appearing ungracious, two otherwise valuable papers seem to me to show symptoms of such inappropriate transfer.

Parducci has long been concerned with the problem of contextual effects in social judgment, and his emphasis is in some respects similar to that of Sjöberg. However, Parducci's main weapon is the category-distribution effect, certainly interesting per se, but a relic from Helson's psychophysics that seems mainly irrelevant to most social judgment. Lodge and Tursky, similarly, seem to construe the scaling problem in outdated terms from Stevens' psychophysics as a confrontation between direct methods. Oddly enough, their preferred method, although somewhat complex, may not be essentially different from the graphic rating procedure used in integration theory. More effective analyses could be obtained with the parallelism theorem.

8.3. Future Work

An evolutionary trend in psychophysics, already discussed, is toward the study of multiple stimulus tasks. If this trend is extrapolated to the social realm, where does it lead? No general answer is attempted here, but two concrete suggestions may help illustrate some possibilities for future work in social judgment.

Are there any natural social judgments in which the stimulus field can be experimentally controlled? I believe that there are and that they deserve more consideration. One example concerns judgments of groups of people. Stereotypes about national, ethnic, or occupational groups are well-known examples of a common kind of social judgment. Judgments of groups provide an analog to the sum or average judgments of psychophysics. Thus, the badness of a group of criminal offenders, say, or the attractiveness of a work group might be expected to be a sum or average of the values of the individual group members. Such group judgments offer much greater flexibility than psychophysical sum and average judgments, in stimulus structure and in choice among many possible response dimensions. They are also fairly natural and, of course, they provide a method for social scaling.

A second example is provided by the concept of occupational prestige, which has been considered in a number of scaling studies. It is inadequate and, I believe, misleading to consider occupational prestige as a function of occupation alone. Not all university professors, to take a relevant example, have equal prestige. Rather, their prestige depends on a number of factors, including university affiliation and scholarly accomplishment, not to mention such less central factors as physical appearance. These judgments are naturally multidimensional and a one-dimensional approach will not get very far. Any actual social judgment involves the values placed on these various determinants and the rule by which they are integrated. Previous work on integration theory suggests that an averaging rule will hold (see Figs. 5.3, 5.4, and 5.9).

Both of these examples seem amenable to study with cognitive algebra. Each involves a natural integration of social values, and there is a reasonable expectation that the integration will follow a simple algebraic rule. In the functional measurement view, this integration rule is basic, and the social values may be obtained with its help.

REFERENCES

Anderson, N. H. Application of an additive model to impression formation. *Science,* 1962, *138,* 817–818. (a)

Anderson, N. H. On the quantification of Miller's conflict theory. *Psychological Review,* 1962, *69,* 400–414. (b)

Anderson, N. H. Functional measurement and psychophysical judgment. *Psychological Review,* 1970, *77,* 153–170.

Anderson, N. H. Information integration theory applied to attitudes about U.S. Presidents. *Journal of Educational Psychology,* 1973, *64,* 1–8.

Anderson, N. H. Algebraic models in perception. In E. C. Carterette & M. P. Friedman (Eds.), *Handbook of perception* (Vol. 2). New York: Academic Press, 1974. (a)

Anderson, N. H. Cognitive algebra. In L. Berkowitz (Ed.), *Advances in experimental social psychology* (Vol. 7). New York: Academic Press, 1974. (b)

Anderson, N. H. Information integration theory: A brief survey. In D. H. Krantz, R. C. Atkinson, R. D. Luce, & P. Suppes (Eds.), *Contemporary developments in mathematical psychology* (Vol. 2). San Francisco: Freeman, 1974. (c)

Anderson, N. H. On the role of context effects in psychophysical judgment. *Psychological Review,* 1975, *82,* 462–482.

Anderson, N. H. Equity judgments as information integration. *Journal of Personality and Social Psychology,* 1976, *33,* 291–299. (a)

Anderson, N. H. Integration theory, functional measurement, and the psychophysical law. In H.-G. Geissler & Y. M. Zabrodin (Eds.), *Advances in psychophysics.* Berlin: VEB Deutscher Verlag, 1976. (b)

Anderson, N. H. Note on functional measurement and data analysis. *Perception & Psychophysics,* 1977, *21,* 201–215.

Anderson, N. H. Progress in cognitive algebra. In L. Berkowitz (Ed.), *Cognitive theories in social psychology.* New York: Academic Press, 1978.

Anderson, N. H. Algebraic rules in psychological measurement. *American Scientist,* 1979, *67,* 555–563.

Anderson, N. H. Information integration theory in developmental psychology. In F. Wilkening, J.

Becker, & T. Trabasso (Eds.), *Information integration by children*. Hillsdale, N.J.: Lawrence Erlbaum Associates, 1980.

Anderson, N. H. *Foundations of information integration theory*. New York: Academic Press, in press.

Anderson, N. H., & Shanteau, J. C. Information integration in risky decision making. *Journal of Experimental Psychology*, 1970, *84*, 441-451.

Curtis, D. W., & Rule, S. J. Magnitude judgments of brightness and brightness difference as a function of background reflectance. *Journal of Experimental Psychology*, 1972, *95*, 215-222.

de Leeuw, J., Young, F. W., & Takane, Y. Additive structure in qualitative data: An alternating least squares method with optimal scaling features. *Psychometrika*, 1976, *41*, 471-503.

Eisler, H. The connection between magnitude and discrimination scales and direct and indirect scaling methods. *Psychometrika*, 1965, *30*, 271-289.

Krantz, D. H., Luce, R. D., Suppes, P., & Tversky, A. *Foundations of measurement* (Vol. 1). New York: Academic Press, 1971.

Kruskal, J. B. Analysis of factorial experiments by estimating monotone transformations of the data. *Journal of the Royal Statistical Society* (Series B), 1965, *27*, 251-263.

Leon, M. Integration of intent and consequence information in children's moral judgment. In F. Wilkening, J. Becker, & T. Trabasso (Eds.), *Information integration by children*. Hillsdale, N.J.: Lawrence Erlbaum Associates, 1980.

Marks, L. E. Stimulus-range, number of categories, and form of the category-scale. *American Journal of Psychology*, 1968, *81*, 467-479.

Marks, L. E. *Sensory processes*. New York: Academic Press, 1974.

Marks, L. E. Phonion: Loudness scales and the processing of auditory intensity. In N. J. Castellan & F. Restle (Eds.), *Cognitive theory* (Vol. 3). Hillsdale, N.J.: Lawrence Erlbaum Associates, 1978.

Oden, G. C. Integration of fuzzy logical information. *Journal of Experimental Psychology: Human Perception and Performance*, 1977, *3*, 565-575.

Oden, G. C., & Anderson, N. H. Differential weighting in integration theory. *Journal of Experimental Psychology*, 1971, *89*, 152-161.

Stevens, S. S. The direct estimation of sensory magnitudes-loudness. *American Journal of Psychology*, 1956, *69*, 1-25.

Treisman, M. Sensory scaling and the psychophysical law. *The Quarterly Journal of Experimental Psychology*, 1964, *16*, 11-22.

Weiss, D. J. Averaging: An empirical validity criterion for magnitude estimation. *Perception & Psychophysics*, 1972, *12*, 385-388.

PSYCHOPHYSICAL MEASUREMENT IN SOCIAL APPLICATION

6

On the Parallel Between Direct Ratio Scaling of Social Opinion and of Sensory Magnitude

William E. Dawson
University of Notre Dame

The early use of direct ratio scaling methods with social, and other nonsensory, variables mainly used number matching. That is, subjects were asked to give magnitude estimations, numbers in proportion to the intensity of their opinions about each of a set of items that were felt to vary along a single dimension. At the outset it should be noted that although many direct ratio methods ask subjects to make ratio judgments, they do not necessarily do so nor are scales that result from the data collected necessarily ratio-level scales. Further assessment of scale properties is needed to determine the level of scale achieved. The scales are called direct ratio scales in this paper because the scaling methods involved request subjects to respond directly in terms of subjective ratios of impressions. Through the work of several investigators, mainly Ekman and Künnapas (1960, 1963), it was learned that the magnitude-estimation and ratio-estimation scales obtained using number responses were related in an invariant manner to other types of scales for the same set of items from the social domain. For example, the category scale was related in a concave-downward fashion to the magnitude scale (Perloe, 1963; Stevens, 1966b). Also, the pair-comparison scale (Thurstone's Case 5) was approximately a logarithmic function of the magnitude scale based on ratio estimation (Ekman, 1962).

Because these relationships were the same interscale relationships observed with nonsocial, physical variables in studies in sensory psychophysics, their occurrence suggested that reliable and consistent opinion scales for social variables could be formed using direct ratio judgments. Some of the most basic parallels between social opinion scales and psychophysical sensory scales had been shown to exist. In 1966, Stevens reviewed and summarized some of this early work. It was a case of history repeated. Some fifty years earlier, L. L.

Thurstone (see Thurstone, 1959) had also bridged the gap between the sensory psychophysical domain and the measurement of attitudes in the social domain. Now, Ekman, Stevens, and others were doing the same with the new direct ratio methods. In a series of studies in our laboratory, starting in 1969, we looked for and found further parallels between opinion scaling and sensory scaling.

THE PARALLEL BETWEEN SENSORY-MODALITY MATCHING AND CROSS-MODALITY MATCHING

The first parallel sought and found had to do with cross-modality matching. Cross-modality matching had been introduced earlier into sensory psychophysics (see Stevens, 1961 for an early review of the method). This method, in which subjects match the sensory effects of one physical continuum against those of another, permitted scaling using other than number matching. It also allowed for a consistency check because any two magnitude-estimation scales implied that a

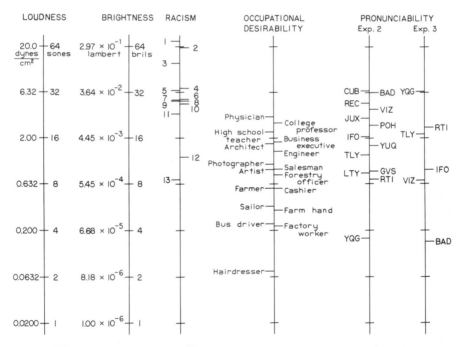

FIG. 6.1.   A comparison of ratio scales for two sensory continua and three attitudinal continua. The reference scale is the sone scale of loudness. The bril scale has been aligned with it such that one bril equals one sone. Scale position on the opinion scales was determined by the sound pressure matched to the stimulus as shown along the loudness scale. Numbers on the racism scale refer to the behaviors listed in Table 6.1. From Dawson and Brinker (1971).

power function with a specific exponent should be found in the cross-modality match involving the two sensory variables (Stevens, 1961). The predicted exponents were found to describe such matches.

The first question that we asked was, "Can subjects indicate the strength of their opinions by matching the sensory effects of a physical continuum in proportion to their opinion strength?" Magnitude estimation and ratio estimation, the main ratio methods used to scale opinions up to that time, both required the subject to indicate the strength of his or her opinion by producing numbers representative of this opinion. The task we employed is analogous to a cross-modality match but, because two sensory modalities are not involved, it seemed inappropriate to call this procedure cross-modality matching also. Therefore, this procedure was called *sensory-modality matching* (Dawson & Brinker, 1971) to reflect the fact that a sensory modality was being matched to opinion strength. It was found that people could match various sensory modalities to indicate their opinions on topics such as racism, occupational desirability, and trigram pronunciability. Figure 6.1 shows these scales along with two thoroughly studied psychophysical scales, the sone scale of loudness and the bril scale for brightness. Knowing the interscale relations here, one can move freely from one scale to the other, whether it is of the sensory or of the social variety.

Validation by Multimodality Matching

It appeared that people could perform the sensory-modality matching task to indicate their opinions, but was there any way to validate the scales so produced? Could a validation somewhat like the one used in cross-modality matching be found for the sensory-modality matching of opinions? Even though many social variables of interest possess no clear metric, scales of social opinion can be constructed and tested for consistency using two or more sensory-modality matches. When two or more such matches are made—a procedure called *multimodality matching* (Dawson & Brinker, 1971)—we have what is needed for an analogous type of test. When the same set of items is scaled using two (or more) sensory modalities, each pair of scales can be plotted, one as a function of the other. Because the *same* items are matched by both sensory modalities, the relationship between the two scales should be approximately the same as that holding for a direct cross-modality match between the two sensory continua. That is, if $R_1 = S_1^n$ and $R_2 = S_2^m$ describe two sensory-magnitude scales, and if $R_1 = R_2$, either because of a direct cross-modality match or because the two modalities have been matched against the same items, then $S_1^n = S_2^m$. In log-log form, this gives $\log S_1 = (^m/_n) S_2$ where S_1 is one physical continuum and S_2 is the other. Hence, the interscale relation is predicted to be a power function, linear in log-log axes, and having a predicted slope of $^m/_n$.

Figure 6.2 shows the results of multimodality matches for occupational desirability, racism, and pronunciability. In each case, subjective force of handgrip

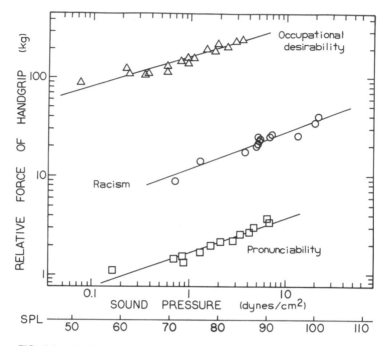

FIG. 6.2. Results of multimodality matches. The top curve has been shifted upward one long unit, and the bottom curve downward one log unit. From Dawson and Brinker (1971).

and the loudness of a 1000-Hz tone were matched by subjects to a series of items to indicate the intensity of their opinion. For occupational desirability, subjects judged each of the occupations that appear on Fig. 6.1. In the case of racism, they judged each of the behaviors listed in Table 6.1 as to the amount of racism it implied. For pronunciability, the trigrams listed under Exp. 2 on Fig. 6.1 were evaluated as to the ease with which they could be pronounced. Each datum point corresponds to the median of the sensory-modality matches produced.

The fact that the data for the three nonsensory continua are summarized well by a straight line on log-log axes serves as a validity check because it implies the predicted form for the interscale relation between the two sensory-modality matching scales, i.e., a power function. As a further test, the predicted value of the slopes should be $^{m}/_{n}$. Since the reported exponent for handgrip is in the neighborhood of 1.7 (Stevens & Mack, 1959) and that for loudness around .64 (Stevens, 1966a), the predicted slope for the lines in Fig. 6.2 is about $^{.64}/_{1.7}$ or .38. The best-fitting lines drawn through the datum points have slopes of .29 for occupations, .39 for racist behaviors, and .34 for trigrams. Although the slope for occupations is somewhat low, the other two are quite close to the predicted value. Clearly, the prediction of multimodality matching exponents is on a par with the prediction of cross-modality matching exponents.

TABLE 6.1
Behaviors Scaled for Racism

Code Designation	Behavior
1	A group of white men hanged and mutilated a Negro man who was observed talking to a young white girl on the street.
2	A white man joined several of his neighbors in setting fire to a home owned by a Negro family, the first such family to move into the man's neighborhood.
3	A white man joined the Ku Klux Klan.
4	The white owner of a small business company who had hired the man doing the best on a competitive examination for a job fired him when he saw that he was a Negro.
5	A white administrator of a southern university refused to admit Negro students.
6	The white owner of a motel refused to rent a room to a Negro family that was traveling.
7	A white guest at a small party loudly criticized the hostess for inviting a Negro couple and immediately left the party.
8	A white man gave a speech urging that segregation be enforced in order that neither of the two races would contaminate one another.
9	A white woman refused to send her son and daughter to a school when some Negro children were permitted to enroll.
10	A white judge upheld a state law that prevented a Negro man from marrying a white girl.
11	A white man said that he couldn't understand why Negroes complained—they had as much of an opportunity as anyone else to get ahead in life.
12	A white girl avoided social gatherings at which the majority present were Negroes.
13	A white student stated that he felt uneasy around black militants.

As a further check on the consistency of the sensory-modality matches made by the groups of subjects, rank-order correlations were obtained between median handgrip force and median sound pressure for each of the three sets of items scaled. If the subjects as a group were consistent in their evaluation of the items, then these correlations, which are an index of cross-modality reliability, should be large and positive. The correlations obtained were .94, .97, and .98 for occupations, racist behaviors, and trigrams, respectively. Groups of subjects obviously use different sensory modalities in a consistent manner to indicate the strength of opinion.

Comparison with a Cross-Modality Match

For a still more direct test of the parallel between sensory-modality matching and cross-modality matching, 24 subjects were asked to perform both a multimodality match to indicate trigram pronunciability and direct cross-modality matches of the sensory modalities used. To help assess the generality of our findings, some changes were made in the variables involved in these tasks. *Difficulty* of pronunciation, rather than *ease*, was to be indicated by the sensory-modality matches. Only the six trigrams listed under Exp. 3 on Fig. 6.1 were scaled.

Loudness was again taken as one of the sensory modalities, but apparent time duration replaced apparent force of handgrip. Subjects were asked to match time duration, as indicated by the amount of time they caused a small lamp to remain lighted, in proportion to their impression of how difficult it was to pronounce the presented trigram. For cross-modality matching, each person matched apparent time duration to apparent loudness and vice versa. In an effort to counterbalance for order, half of the subjects performed the sensory-modality matches first, whereas the other half did the cross-modality matches first.

Figure 6.3 gives the medians of the matches for the various tasks. The squares and the top line through them summarize the multimodality matches to difficulty of trigram pronunciation. Again, a power function describes the data. The predicted slope is given by the ratio of the exponents for loudness, .64, and time duration, 1.1. That is. $\cdot^{64}/_{1.1}$, or .58, is the predicted value; the best-fitting line through the squares has a slope of .60. Thus, the interscale relation predicted is very close to that obtained. The cross-modality reliability, as given by the rank-order correlation of the medians for the trigrams for the two matches, was again quite strong at a value of .94.

The median results for the cross-modality matches are given by the circles (time duration adjusted) and the triangles (sound pressure adjusted). The slopes of the best-fitting lines, as determined by a least squares criterion, are .44

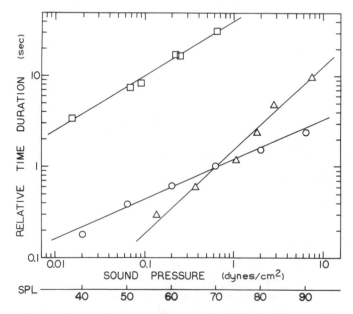

FIG. 6.3.   Results of the multimodality match (top curve) and the cross-modality matches (bottom curves). Circles indicate that Ss adjusted time duration; triangles indicate that sound pressure was adjusted. The top curve has been shifted both upward and to the left by one log unit. From Dawson and Brinker (1971).

and .91, respectively. As Stevens and Greenbaum (1966) have noted, it is the usual case to find two different such power functions in cross-modality matching, depending on which variable is the adjusted one. The latter, when plotted as the dependent variable along the ordinate, leads to the flatter slope. Stevens and Greenbaum suggest that the best power function relating the two dimensions is an average: the one that has as exponent the geometric mean of the exponents of the two lines. In the present case, the geometric mean of .44 and .91 is .63, a value quite close to the .60 produced by the same subjects in the multimodality matches described earlier.

A parallel between cross-modality and sensory-modality matches seems to have been established. People can match sensory intensity to represent opinion intensity just like they can match it to indicate some other sort of sensory intensity. Social and other nonsensory variables can be scaled using sensory matches just as they can be scaled using numbers. When two or more scales are constructed, their interscale relation or relations can be predicted as to form (a power function) and as to quantity (the exponent of the power function).

Figure 6.1 summarizes the opinion scales that have been discussed to this point. Each of the opinion scales has been drawn with reference to the loudness scale (the sone scale) given at the left. That is, each of the items scaled was matched by loudness. The leftmost scale lets us read the sound pressure so matched and also the corresponding number of sones. The latter gets us back to a number scale because the sone scale is basically in accord with magnitude estimation (Stevens, 1956). A second psychophysical scale, the bril scale of brightness, has been added for purposes of comparison and to show the potential for an endless catalog of psychophysical and social opinion scales. Knowing the interscale relations, which are obtainable from cross-modality and sensory-modality matching, one can move from one group-consensus scale to another at will. If the number scale is taken as the basic reference scale as Stevens (1975) suggests, then one can determine the supposed appropriate numerical scale values for any set of scaled items whether the actual scaling was conducted via number matching, as with magnitude estimation, or via sensory-modality matching.

Other notable methodological work involving sensory-modality matching has been conducted by Cross and his colleagues. In 1974, as part of a paper on psychophysical scaling, Cross further examined and made clear the mathematical underpinnings of the sensory-modality and multimodality matching procedures. In addition, Cross, Tursky, and Lodge (1975) have developed "a calibration procedure" for scaling that uses multimodality matches. They have used the method, which appears to compensate for regression effects (Stevens & Greenbaum, 1966), to scale the psychological effects of both physical (e.g., Cross et al., 1975) and social variables (e.g., Lodge, Cross, Tursky, & Tanenhaus, 1974). The method involves making three (or more) cross-modality matches to a physical calibration continuum and subsequently to the items to be scaled. Using the scales obtained in the calibration phase, they modify the scale values for the scaled items such that the regression effect (or centering tendency) is largely controlled for.

THE PARALLEL WITH INVERSE ATTRIBUTES

One procedure used early to assess the consistency of numerical and cross-modality ratio judgments, and the scales resulting from them, was the examination of the relation between the judgments of a primary attribute and those of its inverse attribute for the same set of scalable items. The idea was that if people can give consistent ratio estimates of attributes, then their judgments of an inverse attribute should be inversely related to those of the primary attribute. Many pairs of such attributes, starting with Torgerson's (1960) scaling of the lightness and darkness of Munsell grays, have been examined in this manner. Often, for magnitude estimation and cross-modality matches, the scales tend to be related by a power function having an exponent of negative one (Schneider & Lane, 1963; Stevens & Guirao, 1962; Stevens & Guirao, 1963; Stevens & Harris, 1962). In some of these cases, the relationship is only approximately reciprocal. For example, when Torgerson (1960) plotted scaled darkness as a function of scaled lightness on log-log axes, the relationship was approximately linear with a slope of minus one as predicted, but the "line" displayed a fair amount of concave-downward curvature. Dawson and Miller (1978) have summarized some of the reciprocality studies and, on the basis of additional experiments, have concluded that curvilinearity may be more common than heretofore indicated in the literature.

In the search for a parallel finding with the scaling of opinions, the question asked was, "Do inverse ratio scales of opinion show a similar relationship?" Dawson and Mirando (1976) used sensory-modality matching to scale primary and inverse attributes for two different sets of items. They asked subjects to indicate the ease and difficulty of trigram pronunciation by matching the apparent force of handgrip on a hand dynamometer; subjects indicated the desirability and undesirability of occupations by adjusting the amount of time that a small lamp remained lighted. For pronunciability, 24 subjects matched handgrip force to both ease and difficulty for each of 10 trigrams. A second set of 38 subjects evaluated each of 17 occupations for both their desirability and their undesirability. Different stimuli, different matching continua, and different subjects were used in the two tasks in order to establish some generality for the findings. To minimize order effects, counterbalancing was used with half of the subjects in a task starting with one attribute and the other half starting with the inverse attribute.

Geometric means of matched handgrip forces and of matched light durations were calculated for each of the items for both of the attributes judged. These

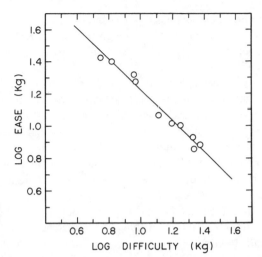

FIG. 6.4.   The relationship between sensory-modality scales for ease and difficulty of trigram pronunciation. From Dawson and Mirando (1976).

averages have been appropriately plotted in Figs. 6.4 and 6.5, which show the results of the sensory-modality matches for the inverse attributes. Perfect reciprocality here would be indicated by a best-fitting line having a slope of negative one. Best-fitting lines were determined again using the curve-fitting method described by Kenney (1939); it leads to a straight-line fit for data pairs for which both variables are subject to error. The line for the trigrams has a slope of $-.98$ whereas that for the occupations has a slope of -1.1. Neither of these values is significantly different from -1.0 statistically. For group data, it appears that judgments, and hence scales, are almost reciprocally related. This result, then, is similar to that found for the sensory scales of pairs of inverse attributes. In fact, Figs. 6.4 and 6.5 are much like sensory results in that Fig. 6.4 shows good

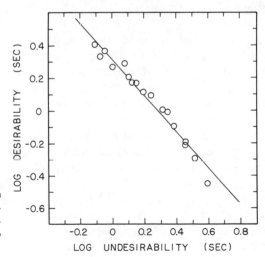

FIG. 6.5.   The relationship between sensory-modality scales for desirability and undesirability of occupations. From Dawson and Mirando (1976).

reciprocality whereas Fig. 6.5 shows some of the concave-downward curvilinearity alluded to earlier. Although ratio consistency might not be all that could be hoped for, the parallel between sensory scales and opinion scales is firmly established.

A further aspect of the data for the two reciprocality checks deserves some attention. Of interest are the standard deviations of the logarithms of the matching responses made for both of the pairs of inverse attributes in each of the two tasks. The variability of the responses for each of the scales' items is essentially constant in magnitude within each attribute, but the average standard deviation tends to be larger for one attribute than for its paired inverse (see Dawson & Mirando, 1976, for lists of these standard deviations). Stevens and Guirao (1963) found similar results for various sensory-magnitude scales.

The fact that for each of the four sensory-modality matches the standard deviations of the logarithms of the matches tend to be equal suggests that error tends to grow in proportion to the apparent magnitude of opinion. Similar results for psychophysical sensory-magnitude scales led to the conclusion that the correct error distribution for magnitude estimation and cross-modality matching is lognormal (Stevens, 1971; Stevens & Guirao, 1962). This distribution seems to be appropriate for sensory-modality matching as well. The proper measure of central tendency for the lognormal distribution is the geometric mean. It is the average used in several of our studies although the median, which is acceptable but less efficient, has also been used.

THE PARALLEL WITH INDIVIDUAL SUBJECTS

The Individual Subjects Problem

One of the most damaging criticisms directed toward so-called ratio scales of sensory magnitude has been the claim that the wide variation in the results obtained for individual subjects makes the scales' acceptability questionable. Whereas group data results show some stability from group to group, individual data display considerable variation from person to person. Actually, there are two questions here that can be, and have been, asked. First, could Stevens' power law be an artifact of averaging across individuals, none or few of whom produce the same form of mathematical function—i.e., a power function? Jones and Marcus (1961) asked this question fairly early in the history of the power law. Some investigators (Luce & Mo, 1965; Pradhan & Hoffman, 1963) on occasion have found individual functions not describable by power functions. Others (Marks & J. C. Stevens, 1966; Stevens & Guirao, 1964) have found that individual data are fitable by a power function. The second question, accepting the form as the same for both group and individuals, asks whether the exponents found in the two cases are the same. Further it is asked, if they are not the same, why do the exponents for individuals show such extreme variation? Often, exponents vary from the highest to the lowest by more than a two to one ratio. In addition, it is not uncommon to find, for a number of individuals, exponents that are less than one mingled with those that are greater than one. Our knowledge of other measures for sensory processes, e.g., absolute and differential thresholds, does not lead us to expect such large intersubject variation.

To determine whether individuals' exponents implicit in scales for social opinion showed a comparable high level of variation, Dawson and Mirando (1975) conducted multimodality matches of handgrip force and time duration to the pronunciability of trigrams. Two such sensory-modality matches are necessary because with items having no clear physical metric, one such match does not lead to an exponent. Several other questions were asked about individual subject performance on sensory-modality matching tasks as well. Are subjects reliable in their matches over repeated sessions? Are their matches to the same attribute of the items using two different matching modalities consistent? That is, are their cross-modality correlations high? And finally, is there a good level of agreement among the individuals regarding the pronunciability of the trigrams, or do individuals vary widely in this regard as well?

In the experiment, 16 male subjects judged 12 trigrams that varied in pronunciability: BAD, CUB, REC, VIZ, POH, YUQ, LTY, RTI, NDR, QZP, RZQ, and YQG. Each person took part in two sessions. In the first session, half of the subjects matched handgrip force first and then apparent duration second. The other half started with duration and ended with handgrip force. For the second session, further counterbalancing was used: Half of the subjects who had started with handgrip force again started with it whereas the other half started with duration. Similar counterbalancing was employed for subjects who had started with apparent duration in the first session. All subjects made three settings to each trigram for each type of match in both sessions.

For purposes of data analysis, medians were obtained for each subject's matches to each trigram for his first session, his second session, and the sessions combined. Before examining the data of individuals, the group data were examined for intersession reliability, cross-modality reliability, and the predictability of multimodality exponent of the sort discussed in the first part of this paper. Analyses of variance for both the handgrip force and duration data found no significant differences in judgments across the two sessions indicating intersession reliability, a result similar to that previously reported for cross-modality matching (Wanschura & Dawson, 1974). Cross-modality reliability, as indicated by product-moment correlations between median force and median duration for the 12 trigrams, was very high with values of .98, .99, and .99 for first session, second session, and combined sessions, respectively. Exponent prediction was fairly good also. The predicted slope is $^{1.1}/_{1.7}$, or .65; the empirical values using the Kenney procedure were .70, .73, and .71 for first, second, and combined sessions, respectively. In all three cases, the multimodality plots of handgrip force as a function of duration yielded power functions.

The multimodality plots for individual subjects varied in appearance from one subject to another. Figure 6.6 shows a random selection of plots for eight of the subjects. The datum points correspond to their median matches for both sessions combined. As can be seen from the example, these plots possess considerable variability, both as to slope and about the lines of best fit. However, they are describable by power functions and they tend to resemble the comparable psychophysical scales reported for individual judgments of loudness (Stevens & Guirao, 1964) and of brightness (Marks & Stevens, 1966). Thus, the *form* of the function appears to be the power function, but the intersubject variation in exponent is quite large, just as it is for the sensory scales of loudness and brightness. The results of the analyses for all of the individuals are given in Table 6.2. The variation in exponent for multimodality matches is greater for opinion magnitude than for sensory magnitude. For example, coefficients of variation reported for loudness by Stevens and Guirao (1964) were .29 and .22 for first and second sessions, respectively. The exponents in Table 6.2 have coefficients of .52 and .50 for first and second sessions. Many different variables might be responsible for the greater variability, but much of the additional variation may be due to the fact that exponents for the opinions here are based on two sensory-modality matches whereas the scales of sensory magnitude are usually based on one matching task.

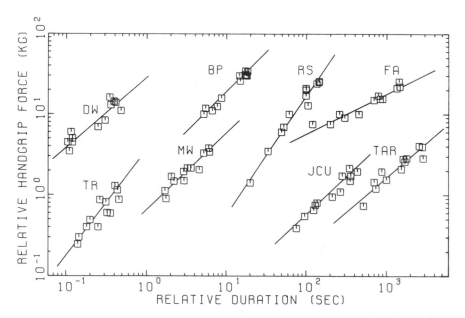

FIG. 6.6. Multimodality matches for eight individuals. Coordinates are correct for Subject D.W.; data for others in the top row are displaced successively one log unit to the right. Data in the bottom row are similar but were displaced downward a log unit also. From Dawson and Mirando (1976).

TABLE 6.2
Multimodality Exponents, Cross-Modality Correlations,
and Intersession Reliabilities for Individual Subjects

Subject	Multimodality Exponent			Cross-Modality Correlation			Intersession Reliability	
	Session 1	Session 2	Combined	Session 1	Session 2	Combined	Force Adjusted	Duration Adjusted
T.A.R.	.92	.57	.85	.93	.90	.94	.96	.92
P.S.	.33	.46	.36	.92	.90	.94	.90	.83
B.M.	.57	.81	.65	.94	.93	.99	.92	.95
D.W.	.90	.92	.87	.89	.87	.92	.81	.97
B.P.	1.06	1.04	.99	.84	.92	.98	.69	.86
J.G.	1.55	1.47	1.56	.86	.85	.90	.95	.99
T.R.	1.55	1.73	1.31	.77	.92	.89	.41	.95
P.M.	.48	.55	.54	.84	.95	.93	.83	.96
B.N.	.28	.35	.31	.87	.83	.83	.94	.85
J.C.U.	.58	1.26	.94	.89	.97	.97	.88	.89
M.W.	1.00	.65	.95	.86	.83	.94	.84	.80
G.S.	1.06	.55	.83	.96	.84	.96	.91	.93
R.S.	1.02	1.76	1.47	.95	.98	.98	.96	.93
J.C.L.	1.81	1.06	1.37	.92	.96	.98	.94	.95
F.A.	.44	.52	.50	.93	.90	.97	.90	.96
P.F.	.57	.70	.64	.96	.95	.99	.95	.96
Mean	.883	.900	.884	.896	.906	.944	.862	.919
SD	.459	.450	.385	.053	.050	.044	.140	.056

Intersession reliabilities for individuals, i.e., product-moment correlations for matches in the first vs. second session, are high showing that, although individuals differ with regard to exponent, they do respond in a stable, consistent manner. This sort of stability is also found with sensory-magnitude scales (Wanschura & Dawson, 1974). The cross-modality correlations for individuals, just as for the group data, show a high degree of consistency in subjects' matches across the two sensory-modality matches. Subjects, thus, were able to indicate, in effect, the same opinion irrespective of the sensory modality matched to the trigrams.

But, are subjects in agreement about the pronunciability of the set of trigrams? It is possible for the individuals to be consistent across both sessions and modalities and yet not be in agreement about the relative pronunciability of the various trigrams. For example, a subset of subjects could consistently have indicated that BAD is difficult to pronounce and YQG easy, whereas the rest of the subjects could have responded in the opposite, more usual manner. Neither the cross-modality correlation nor the intersession reliability would show this fact. Thus, a check on agreement among the subjects is necessary if one wishes to ensure that the averages of the group data can be used as scale values that are representative of the individuals making up the group. To check on agreement,

TABLE 6.3
Kendall's *W* for the Subjects by Trigrams Matrices

Adjusted Continuum	Session 1	Session 2	Combined
Force	.84	.86	.88
Time	.88	.88	.90

$p < .001$ for all entries.

the median matches for the 16 subjects were arranged in Subjects X Trigrams matrices, one for each combination of matching continuum and session, and Kendall's coefficient of concordance (*W*) was computed. As Table 6.3 shows, all *W*s were equal to or greater than .84 and significant at the .001 level. Individuals, in the present instance, are in excellent agreement regarding the relative pronunciability of the trigrams. Note that in the case of sensory-magnitude scales, an examination of the individuals' psychophysical plots tells us at once whether a group of individuals is in agreement as to relative sensory magnitudes. The datum points should be in the same monotonic order. Only for opinion scales, where the exponents are obtained somewhat indirectly via two sensory-modality matches, does one have to check in other ways for agreement.

In summary, individual opinion scales are very much like individual sensory scales. Both are consistent with Stevens' power law. Both are plagued by an unusually large, and yet unexplained, intersubject variation in actual or implicit exponent. For both, intrasubject variation is much less than intersubject variation.

TABLE 6.4
Slopes Relating Log Ease to Log Difficulty Obtained
from Individual Subjects

Subject	Slope	Subject	Slope
1	−.59	13	−1.17
2	−1.39	14	−.68
3	−1.19	15	−.85
4	−.78	16	−1.13
5	−.97	17	−1.42
6	−.78	18	−1.30
7	−2.90	19	−.68
8	−2.75	20	−.54
9	−1.10	21	−.50
10	−.93	22	−.67
11	−.98	23	−1.05
12	−1.06	24	−.84

Inverse Attributes

Additional examples of sizable variation in individual exponents show up in the previously described study of inverse opinion scales (Dawson & Mirando, 1976). Although group data suggest that scales for inverse attributes are nearly reciprocally related, this relationship for individuals making up the group is much more varied and departs widely from reciprocity. Tables 6.4 and 6.5 record the slopes for individuals of the best-fitting lines relating log ease to log difficulty and log desirability to log undesirability. As you may remember, trigrams were judged in one case and occupations in the other. Perfect reciprocality, which was approximated by the group data, would be indicated by a slope of minus one. Clearly, the subjects vary considerably as to the slope their data produces. Such radical departure from reciprocality throws doubt on the validity of any assumption suggesting that persons can judge perceptual ratios in a straightforward and consistent manner. Or else why would not all subjects approach more closely the group result of negative one? Nonetheless, we are still left with the intriguing question: "If individuals are poor with regard to reciprocality, why do the group results come out so good so often?" Perhaps there is some sort of constant bias we have yet to identify. In any case, the variation is great. The matching data for individuals, which result in the slopes in Tables 6.4 and 6.5, show the same large variation about the fitted lines as that found in Figure 6.6. (See Dawson & Mirando, 1976, for some plots of these data.) Again, the data for subjects support the power function, but the exponent (which should be negative one in the power function) varies widely from person to person.

How does the foregoing result compare with the result for individuals on sensory-magnitude scales? There have been few, if any, reciprocality studies that have examined reciprocality for individuals, and so it is difficult to say. One study that may be instructive, as it employed a related task, is that by Lilienthal

TABLE 6.5
Slopes Relating Log Desirability to Log Undesirability Obtained from
Individual Subjects

Subject	Slope	Subject	Slope	Subject	Slope	Subject	Slope
1	−1.48	11	−2.25	21	−.83	31	−.84
2	−1.12	12	−.49	22	−.51	32	−1.72
3	−1.53	13	−1.57	23	−1.03	33	−.52
4	−.97	14	−1.46	24	−1.22	34	−1.16
5	−1.15	15	−2.47	25	−1.44	35	−1.41
6	−.78	16	−2.27	26	−1.06	36	−.81
7	−.79	17	−1.97	27	−.64	37	−.79
8	−1.34	18	−1.34	28	−.89	38	−.77
9	−1.25	19	−1.44	29	−1.05		
10	−1.21	20	−1.83	30	−.54		

and Dawson (1976). They requested subjects to make cross-modality matches in both the usual, directly proportional manner and in an inversely proportional manner. Then they examined the relationship between the inverse cross-modality scales and the direct cross-modality scales that were produced. Group data showed nearly a reciprocal relationship, but individuals again varied widely with some persons displaying reciprocality and some departing substantially from it. These results for sensory scales seem to parallel the described findings for opinion scales.

To compare the individual variability of the reciprocality exponents for sensory and social scales, one can look at the coefficients of variation for each to see whether one type of scale involves more fluctuations than the other does. Values of $-.30$ and $-.24$ were obtained for sensory scales (Lilienthal & Dawson, 1976, Table 4) and $-.54$ and $-.41$ for the opinion scales reported in Tables 6.4 and 6.5, respectively. It appears that individuals may show even greater variation for opinion scales than they do for sensory scales. At this point, the cause of the individual differences in direct ratio scaling is not clear. For efforts to delineate the cause, one might look at some of the papers from our laboratory (Dawson & Waterman, 1976; Engeland & Dawson, 1974; Wanschura & Dawson, 1974). A particularly promising result is reported by Rule and Curtis (1977). This study, along with an earlier one by Rule and Markley (1971), suggests that the variation is due to idiosyncratic matching responses by subjects rather than to any major differences in sensory functioning.

APPLICATIONS

Usage of Ratio Scales of Opinion

Up to this point, emphasis has been placed on the methodological assessment of direct ratio methods, via an examination of the parallels between sensory magnitude and opinion scales, in an attempt to see what may be gained in using them to scale social and other nonsensory variables. In sensory psychophysics, these methods have been quite useful in the systematic study of suprathreshold sensory phenomena (e.g., Marks, 1974). For some time, these same methods have been employed in the study of nonsensory variables. As noted earlier, Stevens (1966b, 1972, 1975) provided occasional summaries of the research carried out along these lines. Hamblin (1971a, 1971b, 1974), among others, has made efforts to introduce the methods into sociology. Cross, Lodge, and Tursky (Cross et al., 1975; Lodge et al., 1974), as mentioned earlier, have made methodological improvements and have applied the methods in political science. Starting with Sellin and Wolfgang's (1964) study of delinquency, social science books that use the methods have begun to appear. Hamblin, Jacobsen, and Miller (1973) deal with social change; Coleman and Rainwater (1978) treat social status.

Some of the more recent studies employ sensory-modality matching in addition to, or in place of, the number matching characteristic of magnitude estimation (Dawson and Brinker, 1971; Galanter & Pliner, 1974; Latané & Harkins, 1976; Lodge et al., 1974; Lodge & Tursky, Chapter 7, this volume; Wegener, Chapter 16, this volume). Galanter and Pliner have examined the utility of money in a systematic set of experiments, some of which involved matching loudness to money gain and money loss. Latané and Harkins have showed that anticipated stage fright may be a multiplicative power function of two variables—audience size and audience status. They used loudness and brightness sensory-modality matches to scale fright. Latané (1976), on the basis of a number of social audience studies, has introduced a theory of social impact theorizing that audience effects, along with some other social phenomena, are power functions of group size. Such use of direct ratio scaling methods, of both the number and sensory matching variety, is likely to continue.

Two Sample Applications

Two studies from our laboratory (Brennan, Ryan, & Dawson, 1975; Dawson & Mirando, 1973) were conducted to ascertain whether scales obtained by sensory-modality matching can be used effectively in the study of substantive problems. Essentially, the answer comes down to the question: "Are the scales obtained relatable in meaningful ways to other stimulus and response variables of psychological interest?" For it is largely through an ability to interrelate with other variables and concepts in an effective manner that we can justify the scaling of any variable. It is the existence of such relationships, of either theoretical or practical interest, that serves to justify the construction of a scale. If the effectiveness of the parallel search to answer this question in the domain of sensory psychophysics is any indication, then we should expect that opinion scales will also enter into effective relationships. Indeed, some of the studies mentioned in the previous section of this paper show that this is actually the case.

In our first study, Dawson and Mirando (1973) examined whether a sensory-modality scale for trigram pronunciability was related to: (1) the free recall learning of the set of trigrams scaled; (2) a previously used nine-point rating scale for pronunciability (Underwood & Schulz, 1960). If the new scale could be useful, presumably the answer to both questions should be yes. In the experiment, 25 subjects first scaled difficulty of trigram pronunciability by matching force on a hand dynamometer to each of the 18 trigrams listed in Table 6.6. The table gives the median match for each of the trigrams along with its Underwood and Schulz rating-scale value. In their scale, a value of "one" stands for "easy to pronounce" and "nine" for "hard to pronounce." The sensory-modality and rating-scale values are closely related as a product-moment correlation of .96 (p < .001) between them indicates. The two methods appear to tap the same variable. A plot of the rating-scale values as a function of their sensory-

TABLE 6.6
Trigrams, Pronunciability Scales, and Proportion Recalled

Trigram	Underwood & Schulz Rating	Sensory Match (kg)	Proportion Recalled Trial 1	Proportion Recalled All	Trigram	Underwood & Schulz Rating	Sensory Match (kg)	Proportion Recalled Trial 1	Proportion Recalled All
BAD	1.50	7.0	.90	.96	LTY	7.03	22.0	.23	.73
CUB	1.80	9.0	.80	.87	RTI	7.43	22.0	.23	.67
REC	2.43	11.0	.50	.82	GVS	8.04	24.5	.20	.66
VIZ	3.03	14.0	.33	.68	NDR	8.14	24.0	.40	.78
POH	3.64	12.0	.37	.80	QZP	8.28	29.0	.00	.44
IFO	4.34	13.0	.37	.76	YLV	8.37	27.5	.03	.43
JUX	5.08	12.0	.23	.61	RZQ	8.59	26.0	.17	.46
TLY	5.75	21.0	.33	.73	VXK	8.64	30.0	.07	.54
YUQ	6.60	19.5	.13	.53	YQG	8.77	31.0	.10	.41

modality scale counterparts shows the typical concave-downward function usually reported for the category scale to ratio scale relationship (Stevens & Galanter, 1957).

In the second part of the study, 30 new subjects were given 12 trials to learn the 18 trigrams by the method of free recall. To see whether difficulty of pronunciation as scaled by sensory-modality matching was related to free recall, the trigrams were divided into three groups of six each: high, medium, and low pronunciability. The high group consisted of the six trigrams having the smallest medians of handgrip force, and the other two groups were composed accordingly of the trigrams having the middle and highest six medians of force. Mean proportion of correct recall on each of the 12 trials is listed in Table 6.6 and plotted in Fig. 6.7. Clearly, pronunciability as measured by sensory-modality matching is strongly related to the rate of learning. Further evidence of this relationship is indicated by highly significant product-moment correlations. Pronunciability (in kilograms) correlated $-.82$ with recall on Trial 1 and $-.81$ with recall over all trials. The comparable correlations with the nine-point rating scale were $-.84$ and $-.79$, respectively. Hence, the correlations involving sensory-modality pronunciability are significant and are of the same order of magnitude as those obtained for the rating scale. Clearly, the new scale is effectively related to performance in a verbal learning task. It appears to be just as useful as its rating scale counterpart—and we know more about its relationship to a large number of other scales (cf. Fig. 6.1).

The second study, concerned with the use of sensory-modality matching for a substantive problem, was one directed toward the perception of the accent in

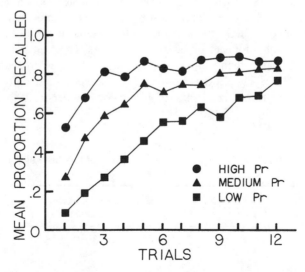

FIG. 6.7.   Mean proportion of trigrams recalled on each trial as a function of pronunciability (Pr). From Dawson and Mirando (1973).

speech. It is known that the manner in which persons speak a language influences the attitudes that others have toward them. Such language attitudes (see Shuy & Fasold, 1973) appear to depend in part on perceived accent. One problem in the study of the effect of accent on language attitudes has been to find a good measure of the amount of perceived accent for naive, nonlinguistically trained listeners (Ryan, 1973). If listeners' behavior reflects how they perceive others' speech, then a scale for accent would aid in the exploration of these effects. The study by Brennan, Ryan, and Dawson (1975) asked several questions. First, can a group of naive listeners evaluate the accent in a selection of speech samples in a consistent and concordant manner? Second, if judgments are obtained using magnitude estimation and sensory-modality matching, will the relation between the two scales be that predicted on the basis of the power function exponents obtained in earlier psychophysical research? Finally, are there any relationships between perceived accent and the incidence of accented pronunciations?

Three replications of the same experiment were carried out using two different experimenters. In each, 24 subjects listened to a taped speech sample from each of eight Spanish-English bilinguals. They matched both numbers (magnitude estimation) and force of handgrip (sensory-modality matching) to amount of perceived accent. For each replication, and for the combined 72 subjects, Kendall's coefficient of concordance (W) was computed on the appropriate subjects by speakers matrix. As Table 6.7 shows, all Ws were statistically significant indicating that there was consistent agreement among the listeners as to the relative amounts of accent in the samples. Table 6.7 also presents cross-modality reliabilities for the two types of matches. These correlations are all .95 or higher showing that listeners tended to be consistent across matching continua also. The last column in the table gives the fitted slopes for the multimodality plots of Fig. 6.8. The datum points in the figure represent the geometric means for the number and handgrip matches for each of the speech samples. The predicted exponent for the best-fitting lines, which were obtained using the Kenney procedure, is given by the ratio of the psychophysical exponents for handgrip force (between 1.6 and 2.0 according to Stevens & Mack, 1959) and for numbers (1.0 as assumed by

TABLE 6.7
Measures of Intersubject Agreement, Cross-Modality Reliability,
and Power Law Exponent

Experiment	Kendall's W		Cross-Modal Reliability	Estimate of Slope
	ME	SMM		
1	.77	.42	.955	1.95
2	.70	.67	.980	1.74
3	.69	.70	.995	2.00
Combined	.71	.56	.986	1.92

$p < 0.001$ for all entries.

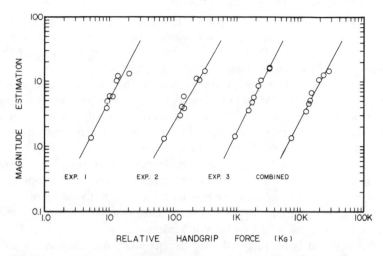

FIG. 6.8. Results of multimodality matches for the three experiments and for the data combined. The left curve has appropriate abscissa values; the other curves have been arbitrarily shifted 1, 2, and 3 log units to the right for ease of reading the display. From Brennan et al. (1975).

Stevens, 1975). Hence, the exponent predicted for the lines in Fig. 6.8 should lie between 1.6 and 2.0. The empirical values in Table 6.7 all fall in this range.

Further evidence of the usefulness of the direct ratio scales of accent was found when rank-order correlations between scale values and frequencies of mispronunciations were examined. Here, for speakers ranked for accent according to average magnitude estimates from all subjects combined, both the total frequencies of accented pronunciations and the relative frequencies of some types of accented pronunciations were significantly correlated (see Brennan et al., 1975 for details). The relative frequencies of the various types of mispronunciations tended to increase monotonically with increasing speaker accent. For example, stressed /a/, and final consonant clusters tended to be frequently mispronounced and the relative frequencies of each of these were significantly correlated with the average magnitude estimations of accent for the speakers. It appears that the newly developed accent scales might be helpful in the investigation both of the role of accent in the development of language attitudes and of the finer grain structure of perceived accent.

GENERAL ASSESSMENT

On the Parallel

To arrive at an overall assessment of the parallel between scales of opinion and sensory magnitude, attention now focuses on the question: How similar are so-called ratio scales of opinion to those for sensory intensity, and what does the similarity mean? As we have seen, parallel interscale relationships were reported to exist by the early investigators of ratio scales of opinion. Most of these studies used number matching methods. The research summarized in this paper shows that other parallels also hold. People are able to produce nonnumerical, sensory matches in a consistent manner reminiscent of performance on cross-modality matches. There is a similar ability to predict in advance one match from two previous matches. In another parallel, subjects' efforts to judge inverse attributes lead to the same quasi-inverse relationship between the scales for the two attributes as is found for pairs of sensory inverse attribute scales. The problem of individual differences in the power functions for sensory magnitudes is mirrored by a comparable one in the multimodality matches for intensity of opinion. In addition, both types of scales can be effectively applied to the study of substantive problems. In sum, many of the qualitative and quantitative features found for sensory scales also are found for opinion scales.

At this point, it is instructive to ask the question: Are there *any* clear-cut instances in which the properties of ratio opinion scales are different from those of ratio sensory scales? Although further parallels, assuredly, remain to be investigated, up to this time no big qualitative difference has emerged. Quantitatively, variability (or error) seems to be consistently larger with the opinion scales, but this does not constitute any sharp difference in the nature of the two types of scales. By and large, the parallel seems almost complete. The fact that some physical metric is often available with sensory scales—allowing us to look at a psychophysical relation—whereas there is often no clear physical metric with opinion scales, says nothing about any difference in the nature of the scales produced in the two cases.

On What It Means

Assuming a close parallel, what does it mean? One thing it does *not* mean is that either or both kinds of scales are, of necessity, adequate scales. The parallel can be complete, and the so-called ratio scales produced can turn out to be poor scales. However, it does suggest—if we are willing to make the tentative, parsimonious assumption that both kinds of scales have the same characteristics—that the broad, far-ranging use of direct ratio scales in sensory psychophysics may have an equally valuable counterpart role in the scaling of nonsensory variables. It means that we can study either class of scales and learn something about the other class. We can use psychophysical tasks with careful stimulus control to examine more closely the nature of the sensory scales knowing that, most likely, the nonsensory scales will behave similarly. Of course, we must always be on the lookout for instances where the social scales differ from the sensory scales. A few strong instances would destroy the parallel.

The parallel also suggests that the scales obtained reflect on the nature of human judgments in general, and not just on the nature of "sensory systems" as some of the early psychophysical articles seemed to imply (e.g., Stevens, 1961). It would urge caution in too readily creating *sensory mechanisms* to explain scaling results. After all, if analogous results hold for opinions, might not a sensory explanation be inappropriate? A possible example of inappropriate sensory mechanisms may be the use of the concepts of *effective threshold* and *physiological noise* to explain the low-intensity departures from simple power functions. Evidence seems to be accumulating that suggests the curvature is due to a response bias and not a sensory mechanism per se (Dawson & Miller, 1978). Similar low-end curvature has been found with some nonsensory functions (e.g., Stevens, 1975, p. 265), a fact that seems at odds with a sensory explanation. Many of the functions reported by Hamblin (1974) for social variables also have the low-end curvature.

Another thing that the parallel implies is that any problems with sensory scales are apt to be mirrored as problems with nonsensory scales. Stevens (1971, 1975) has discussed at length some of the problems and issues that arise in psychophysical scaling. Range effects, individual differences, sequential effects, and the why of virtual exponents are just some of the difficulties that have been encountered. Presumably, all such problems will show up in the social, and any other nonsensory, domain as well. In fact, a list of such problems provides a list of further potential parallels that remain to be investigated. Baird and Noma (1978) provide a recent, somewhat more impartial, list of the problems facing the direct ratio scaling enterprise.

Does the existence of such problems vitiate the scales or the data emerging from direct ratio judgments? In one sense, the answer is no; in another, it is yes. In terms of practical utility, the methods have been most helpful in providing us with valuable data that help us to understand psychological phenomena. A comparison of the first and second editions of Geldard's classic, *The Human Senses* (1953, 1972), shows what is meant. The second edition is replete with many valuable direct scaling results—results descriptive of suprathreshold phenomena. Such measures were sparse in the first edition, which relied more on sensitivity data—i.e., results expressed in terms of absolute and differential threshold measures. The progress has been healthy and noteworthy.

In terms of a more ultimate utility, however, the answer may well be yes. The weaknesses in the scales may result in their replacement when and if more acceptable, and less problem-laden, scales are developed. At this point in time, there remain so many problems with all of the various sorts of psychological scales that it seems imprudent to throw out any methods that have demonstrated practical utility. There is an interesting parallel here between the various scaling methods that we have and the various psychophysical methods that we use to measure absolute and difference thresholds. In both cases, different methods often lead to inconsistent, but practically useful, results. In both cases, there are those who say our intent is ill-conceived. The adequacy of the threshold concept has been questioned just as has the possibility of psychological measurement.

What is not in doubt is that progress has come from trying to measure sensitivity and suprathreshold impressions. Likely, similar progress will occur in the future for social and other nonsensory scaling.

REFERENCES

Baird, J. C., & Noma, E. *Fundamentals of scaling and psychophysics.* New York: Wiley, 1978.

Brennan, E. M., Ryan, E. B., & Dawson, W. E. Scaling of apparent accentedness by magnitude estimation and sensory modality matching. *Journal of Psycholinguistic Research,* 1975, *4,* 27-36.

Coleman, R. P., & Rainwater, L. *Social standing in America: A new dimension of class.* New York: Basic Books, 1978.

Cross, D. V. Some technical notes on psychophysical scaling. In H. Moskowitz, B. Scharf, & J. C. Stevens (Eds.), *Sensation and measurement.* Dordrecht, The Netherlands: Reidel, 1974.

Cross, D. V., Tursky, B., & Lodge, M. The role of regression and range effects in determination of the power function for electric shock. *Perception & Psychophysics,* 1975, *18,* 9-14.

Dawson, W. E. An assessment of ratio scales of opinion produced by sensory-modality matching. In H. Moskowitz, B. Scharf, & J. C. Stevens (Eds.), *Sensation and measurement.* Dordrecht, The Netherlands: Reidel, 1974.

Dawson, W. E., & Brinker, R. P. Validation of ratio scales of opinion by multimodality matching. *Perception & Psychophysics,* 1971, *9,* 413-417.

Dawson, W. E., & Miller, M. E. Inverse attribute functions and the proposed modifications of the hower law. *Perception & Psychophysics,* 1978, *24,* 457-465.

Dawson, W. E., & Mirando, M. A. Sensory-modality scale for pronounceability of trigrams and its relation to free-recall learning. *Perceptual and Motor Skills,* 1973, *36,* 1219-1224.

Dawson, W. E., & Mirando, M. A. Sensory-modality opinion scales for individual subjects. *Perception & Psychophysics,* 1975, *17,* 596-600.

Dawson, W. E., & Mirando, M. A. Inverse scales of opinion obtained by sensory-modality matching. *Perceptual and Motor Skills,* 1976, *42,* 415-425.

Dawson, W. E., & Waterman, S. P. Effects of session and intrasession repetition on individual power law exponents. *Bulletin of the Psychonomic Society,* 1976, *7,* 306-308.

Ekman, G. Measurement of moral judgment. *Perceptual and Motor Skills,* 1962, *15,* 3-9.

Ekman, G., & Künnapas, T. Note on direct and indirect scaling methods. *Psychological Reports,* 1960, *6,* 174.

Ekman, G., & Künnapas, T. A further study of direct and indirect scaling methods. *Scandinavian Journal of Psychology,* 1963, *4,* 77-80.

Engeland, W., & Dawson, W. E. Individual differences in power functions for a 1-week intersession interval. *Perception & Psychophysics,* 1974, *15,* 349-352.

Galanter, E., & Pliner, P. Cross-modality matching of money against other continua. In H. Moskowitz, B. Scharf, & J. C. Stevens (Eds.), *Sensation and measurement.* Dordrecht, The Netherlands: Reidel, 1974.

Geldard, F. A. *The human senses* (1st ed.). New York: Wiley, 1953.

Geldard, F. A. *The human senses* (2nd ed.). New York: Wiley, 1972.

Hamblin, R. L. Mathematical experimentation and sociological theory: A critical analysis. *Sociometry,* 1971, *34,* 423-452. (a)

Hamblin, R. L. Ratio measurement for the social sciences. *Social Forces,* 1971, *50,* 191-206. (b)

Hamblin, R. L. Social attitudes: Magnitude measurement and theory. In H. M. Blalock (Ed.), *Measurement in the social sciences.* Chicago: Aldine, 1974.

Hamblin, R. L., Jacobsen, R. B., & Miller, J. L. L. *A mathematical theory of social change.* New York: Wiley, 1973.

Jones, F. N., & Marcus, M. J. The subject effect in judgments of subjective magnitude. *Journal of Experimental Psychology*, 1961, *61*, 40–44.

Kenney, J. F. *Mathematics of statistics* (Part 1). New York: Van Nostrand, 1939.

Latané, B. *Theory of social impact*. Paper presented at Symposium on Social Influence at XXI International Congress of Psychology. Paris, Summer 1976.

Latané, B., & Harkins, S. Cross-modality matches suggest anticipated stage fright a multiplicative power function of audience size and status. *Perception & Psychophysics*, 1976, *20*, 482–488.

Lilienthal, M. G., & Dawson, W. E. Inverse cross-modality matching: A test of ratio judgment consistency for group and individual data. *Perception & Psychophysics*, 1976, *19*, 252–260.

Lodge, M., Cross, D., Tursky, B., & Tanenhaus, J. *The psychophysical scaling and validation of a political support scale*. Paper presented at 1974 Annual Meeting of American Political Science Associations, Chicago, Ill., Aug.-Sept., 1974.

Luce, R. D., & Mo, S. S. Magnitude estimation of heaviness and loudness by individual subjects: A test of a probabilistic response theory. *British Journal of Mathematical and Statistical Psychology*, 1965, *18*, 159–174.

Marks, L. E. *Sensory processes: The new psychophysics*. New York: Academic Press, 1974.

Marks, L. E., & Stevens, J. C. Individual brightness functions. *Perception & Psychophysics*, 1966, *1*, 17–24.

Perloe, S. I. The relation between category-rating and magnitude-estimation judgments of occupational prestige. *American Journal of Psychology*, 1963, *76*, 395–403.

Pradhan, P. L., & Hoffman, P. J. Effect of spacing and range of stimuli on magnitude estimation judgments. *Journal of Experimental Psychology*, 1963, *66*, 533–541.

Rule, S. J., & Curtis, D. W. Subject differences in input and output transformations from magnitude estimation of differences. *Acta Psychologica*, 1977, *41*, 61–65.

Rule, S., & Markley, R. P. Subject differences in cross-modality matching. *Perception & Psychophysics*, 1971, *9*, 115–117.

Ryan, E. B. Subjective reactions toward accented speech. In R. Shuy & R. Fasold (Eds.), *Language attitudes: Current trends and prospects*. Washington, D.C.: Georgetown University Press, 1973.

Schneider, B., & Lane, H. Ratio scales, category scales, and variability in the production of loudness and softness. *Journal of the Acoustical Society of America*, 1963, *35*, 1953–1961.

Sellin, J. T., & Wolfgang, M. E. *The measurement of delinquency*. New York: Wiley, 1964.

Shuy, R., & Fasold, R. (Eds.). *Language attitudes: Current trends and prospects*. Washington, D.C.: Georgetown University Press, 1973.

Stevens, J. C., & Guirao, M. Individual loudness functions. *Journal of the Acoustical Society of America*, 1964, *36*, 210–213.

Stevens, J. C., & Mack, J. D. Scales of apparent force. *Journal of Experimental Psychology*, 1959, *58*, 405–413.

Stevens, S. S. The direct estimation of sensory magnitudes–loudness. *American Journal of Psychology*, 1956, *69*, 1–25.

Stevens, S. S. The psychophysics of sensory function. In W. A. Rosenblith (Ed.), *Sensory communication*. New York: Wiley, 1961.

Stevens, S. S. Matching functions between loudness and ten other continua. *Perception & Psychophysics*, 1966, *1*, 5–8. (a)

Stevens, S. S. A metric for the social consensus. *Science*, 1966, *151*, 530–541. (b)

Stevens, S. S. Issues in psychophysical measurement. *Psychological Review*, 1971, *78*, 426–450.

Stevens, S. S. *Psychophysics and social scaling*. Morristown, N.J.: General Learning Press, 1972.

Stevens, S. S. *Psychophysics: Introduction to its perceptual, neural, and social prospects*. New York: Wiley, 1975.

Stevens, S. S., & Galanter, E. H. Ratio scales and category scales for a dozen perceptual continua. *Journal of Experimental Psychology*, 1957, *54*, 377–411.

Stevens, S. S., & Greenbaum, H. B. Regression effect in psychophysical judgments. *Perception & Psychophysics*, 1966, *1*, 439–446.

Stevens, S. S., & Guirao, M. Loudness, reciprocality, and partition scales. *Journal of the Acoustical Society of America*, 1962, *34*, 1466–1471.

Stevens, S. S., & Guirao, M. Subjective scaling of length and area and the matching of length to loudness and brightness. *Journal of Experimental Psychology*, 1963, *66*, 177–186.

Stevens, S. S., & Harris, J. R. The scaling of subjective roughness and smoothness. *Journal of Experimental Psychology*, 1962, *64*, 489–494.

Thurstone, L. L. *The measurement of values*. Chicago: University of Chicago Press, 1959.

Torgerson, W. S. Quantitative judgment scales. In H. Gulliksen & S. Messick, (Eds.), *Psychological scaling: Theory and applications*. New York: Wiley, 1960.

Underwood, B. J., & Schulz, R. W. *Meaningfulness and verbal learning*. New York: Lippincott, 1960.

Wanschura, R. G., & Dawson, W. E. Regression effect and individual power functions over sessions. *Journal of Experimental Psychology*, 1974, *102*, 806–812.

7 The Social-Psychophysical Scaling of Political Opinion

Milton Lodge
Bernard Tursky
State University of New York at
Stony Brook

Recent developments in the theory and practice of psychophysics now make it possible and feasible to build magnitude scales of political judgments and preferences. Paralleling explicitly the logic and procedures developed by psychophysicists for the scaling of sensory sensations (Cross, Tursky, & Lodge, 1975), our Laboratory for Behavioral Research has developed (Lodge, Cross, Tursky, & Tanenhaus, 1975), tested in the field (Lodge, Cross, Tursky, Tanenhaus, & Reeder, 1976), and adapted to survey settings a simple paper and pencil technique (Lodge, Cross, Tursky, Foley, & Foley, 1976) for the magnitude scaling and validation of strength of political opinion in survey instruments (Lodge & Tursky, 1979).

POLITICAL ATTITUDE MEASUREMENT

Most of what we as social scientists claim to know about opinions and attitudes is founded on the analysis of responses to semantic stimuli. From a reading of the literature, it is clear that much of the empirical research on social, psychological, and political behavior is based on the analysis of one type of behavioral response—some variant of verbal behavior—what people say or, more typically, what people check on a labelled category scale, to one type of stimulus, words, typically words and phrases embedded in questionnaires administered to survey respondents.

As social scientists interested in individual political behavior, we often need to determine what attributes people associate with political parties, incumbents and candidates, institutions, policies and issues, and also how intensely people feel about the attributes they perceive. How strongly do people identify with a political party? How much confidence do people have in the Supreme Court? How deeply do people oppose the use of busing to integrate the elementary schools in their area? How worried are people about an increase in taxes, an impending recession, a war? How committed are people to democratic processes? When dealing with queries like these, measurement of the strength of opinion response is a major concern. Whether we want only to typify or characterize the opinions that people express, or whether we want to go beyond this and use these expressions of opinion as data for constructing models of behavior, it is desirable to scale the relevant variables in as informative a way as possible.

Physical properties such as light, weight, temperature, and sound pressure, as well as their psychological attributes, brightness, heaviness, warmth, and loudness, are readily scalable. Social variables such as socio-economic status, stress, racism, and the seriousness of crimes can also be defined in terms of scalable attributes, despite their apparent lack of metric properties. The level of measurement attainable for these attributes depends on the isomorphism that can be established between the assumptions underlying each level of measurement and the reality of the perceptual or conceptual relations that obtain among instances of these attributes.

The technique most commonly used by political scientists for scaling strength of attitude is category scaling. A variety of standard two-, three-, four-, five-, and seven-point category formats is available. Often, we ask a respondent to select one of the category options associated with the garden variety of Likert scale. Or, we may ask respondents to position themselves on a seven- or nine-point bipolar adjectival scale of the kind associated with Osgood's semantic differential. Or, we may ask individuals to designate the strength of their feelings by selecting an appropriate position on a feeling thermometer:

$$
\begin{array}{rl}
\text{Warm} & 100° \underline{\hspace{2cm}} \\
& 85° \underline{\hspace{2cm}} \\
& 70° \underline{\hspace{2cm}} \\
& 60° \underline{\hspace{2cm}} \\
& 50° \underline{\hspace{2cm}} \\
& 40° \underline{\hspace{2cm}} \\
& 30° \underline{\hspace{2cm}} \\
& 15° \underline{\hspace{2cm}} \\
\text{Cold} & 0° \underline{\hspace{2cm}}
\end{array}
$$

If multiple observations are recorded, as is normal practice when using any of these category formats, a respondent's scale position is determined by averaging the responses.

Queries about the character of the intensity measures developed by such category-scaling procedures are hardly trivial because experience with decades of attitude research consistently reports that the degree of correspondence between measures of attitude and behavior is typically low to moderate (Deutscher, 1973). Although weak measurement is not the sole explanation for the disappointing degree of correspondence between attitude and behavior, what makes the measurement problem important is that, as a consequence of weak measurement, we cannot know whether our failure to find a closer correspondence between attitude and behavior results from weaknesses in our theoretical formulations or deficiencies in our measurements. There is a pressing need, it follows, to scale the intensity of verbal response in a manner commensurate with the metric implicit in the judgments respondents can and do make (Hamblin, 1974; Shinn, 1974).

The aim of this paper is to describe the adaptation of social-psychophysical scaling methods to survey settings and to review a number of applications to the magnitude scaling of political judgments and preferences.

THE MAGNITUDE SCALING OF POLITICAL OPINION

In our adaptation of the psychophysical methodology to the scaling of political judgments, we employ both forms of the cross-modality matching paradigm— *direct* cross-modality matching to confirm that subjects are using the response modalities to make proportional (and not merely ordinal) judgments and the *indirect* cross-modality paradigm for the magnitude scaling and verification of social judgments.[1] The collection of response data for the scaling and validating of judgments proceeds in two stages.

The first stage involves the calibration of response modalities. It is a straightforward sensory psychophysical scaling task—subjects match two response modalities to a metric, a calibrating continuum, e.g., force of handgrip and sound pressure matched to a randomly presented geometric sequence of line lengths. In addition to providing training and practice in the use of the response modalities in making magnitude judgments, this calibration task makes it possible to test subjects' ability to make proportional judgments and, if necessary, to correct for regression bias (Cross, 1974). When the matches are logged, averaged, and regressed directly against the logarithms of the metric stimuli, the empirically derived exponent should include the established exponent within its 95% confidence limits. This criterion test constitutes the calibration of response modalities.

The social scaling task, preceded by 5-6 minutes of instruction and practice in the use of the response modalities in making social-psychological judgments, is

---

[1] See Lodge & Tursky, Workshop on the magnitude scaling of political opinion in survey research. *American Journal of Political Science,* forthcoming May, 1981, for a full description of procedures.

directly analogous to the scaling of physical stimuli. The indirect cross-modality matching paradigm is simply two direct matching tasks combined: The same two response modalities matched to a metric in the calibration task are now used to estimate the perceived intensity of a social continuum. Because both modalities are matched to the same social stimuli, they are brought into a functional relationship on the principle of equivalence—objects equal to the same object are equal to each other.

The power of the indirect cross-modality matching paradigm, and what especially recommends it for social scaling, is that the empirical exponent derived from the two matches is primarily a function of the response modalities, *not* the stimuli. Thus, the criterion for psychophysically validating a scale is the same whether the matches are made to physical or social stimuli. Within the indirect cross-modality matching paradigm, a social scale is criterion-validated by predicting in advance the slope relating the two response modalities (Cross, 1974; Dawson & Brinker, 1971; Hamblin, 1974; Stevens, 1969, 1975). When the matches made to the scale items are logged, averaged, and regressed one against the other, the empirical exponent relating the two response modalities should be a good first-order approximation of the characteristic exponent. "A good first-order approximation" here means that the exponent characteristic of the relationship between modalities is included within the 95% confidence limits constructed around the empirically obtained exponent. When this criterion is met, the social scale derived from the cross-modality matches is judged psychophysically valid.

An Adjectival Scale for Measuring Political Support

In contrast to most social-psychophysical scaling studies that employ specific instances or attributes of a dimension as scale items (as, for example, specific dollar values of income, years of schooling, and occupational titles in Hamblin's [1974] study of social status, or verbal descriptions of specific criminal acts in Sellin & Wolfgang's [1964] seriousness of crime scale), we opted to construct a scale made up of adjectival modifiers implying degrees of approval–disapproval, which would be flexible and general enough to permit the measurement of support for different political institutions, leaders, and policies.

From a pool of 160 words and phrases used in everyday language and existing social-science scales, a set of 30 adjectives and adjectival phrases ranging from "absolutely perfect" to "disgusting" were selected as scale items. To determine whether or not these adjectival modifiers conveyed quantitative information, and if so their generalizability as expressions of support for different political objects, a series of magnitude-scaling experiments were carried out beginning with student subjects in the laboratory, then moving out to adult subjects in local field studies, and finally moving into a national survey.

Forty-eight student subjects participated in the first laboratory study using magnitude estimation (ME), force of handgrip (HG), and sound pressure (SP) as response modalities to estimate the amount of support conveyed by the 30 adjectival descriptors, among them "excellent," "very good," "good," "so-so," "bad," "very bad," "terrible." Each of the modifiers was embedded in a simple declarative statement describing political institutions, the U.S. Senate (e.g., The U.S. Senate is. . . .) and the local Suffolk County Police, a public policy, the Supreme Court's decision on abortion, and the performance of a political figure (then–President Nixon's handling of domestic affairs).

The scaling experiment proceeded in stages. First, to calibrate each response modality, all 48 subjects matched ME, HG, and SP to a geometric sequence of line lengths. Although each of the empirical estimates is somewhat regressive, the fit of the linear regression equation is good in each case, implying that these subjects were using the three response modalities to make proportional judgments and thereby enabling us to later correct for regression bias in the calculation of social scale values (Cross, 1974).

In the second stage of this scale-building study, three groups of 16 subjects each made ME, HG, and SP estimates of the amount of support expressed by different subsets of the adjectival descriptors when applied to the U.S. Senate, or

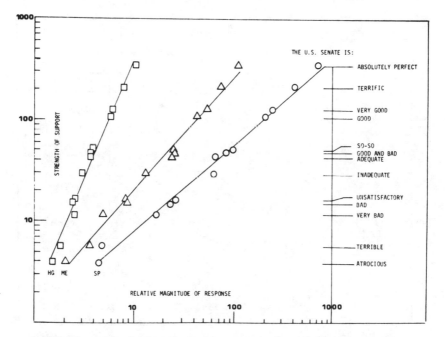

FIG. 7.1. Handgrip (HG), magnitude estimation (ME), and sound pressure (SP) responses (x-axis) as a function of the measure of strength of support for the U.S. Senate (y-axis) based on all three response measures, each corrected for regression. Each point is the geometric mean of 16 responses. (From Lodge, Cross, Tursky, & Tanenhaus, 1975.)

the police, or the Supreme Court's decision on abortion, and for all 48 subjects, Nixon's handling of domestic affairs. Thirteen adjectival descriptors made up each scale, and all judgments were made relative to the standard "so-so," which was assigned 50 units of support for ME and a "comfortable" squeeze and noise level for HG and SP.

Scale values for the adjectives describing the U.S. Senate are plotted against the ME, HG, and SP responses in Fig. 7.1. The correlation between the logs of the geometric means are high, implying a high degree of linear dependence between measures, and each of the empirical exponents approximates the expected within 95% confidence limits. The Senate scale—adjusted for regression bias—ranges from 343 for "absolutely perfect" to 3.8 for "atrocious," a magnitude range of 90:1.

Plots for the local police, Supreme Court's decision on abortion, and Nixon's handling of domestic affairs look and behave similarly and are presented here in Fig. 7.2, 7.3, and 7.4 for the reader's perusal.

The results across scales are summarized in Table 7.1. All 30 adjectival descriptors are listed in order of magnitude down the left side of the table. The

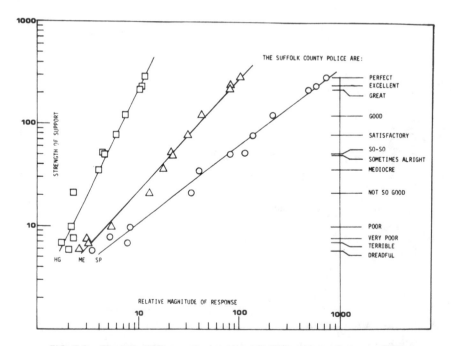

FIG. 7.2.   Handgrip (HG), magnitude estimation (ME), and sound pressure (SP) responses (x-axis) as a function of the measure of strength for the Suffolk County Police (x-axis) based on all three response measures, each corrected for regression. Each point is the geometric mean of 16 responses. (From Lodge, Cross, Tursky, & Tanenhaus, 1975.)

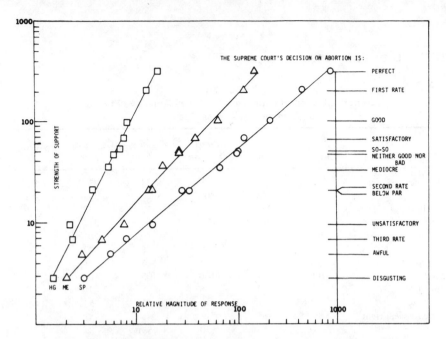

FIG. 7.3. Handgrip (HG), magnitude estimation (ME), and sound pressure (SP) responses (x-axis) as a function of the measure of strength of support for the Supreme Court's decision on abortion (y-axis) based on all three response measures, each corrected for regression. Each point is the geometric mean of 16 responses. (From Lodge, Cross, Tursky, & Tanenhaus, 1975.)

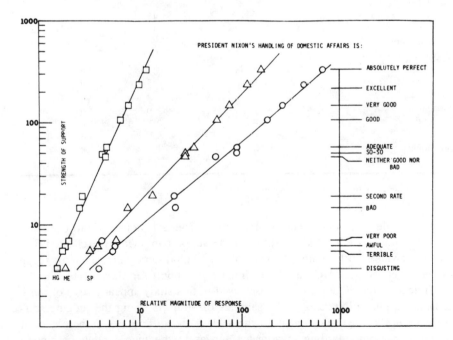

FIG. 7.4. Handgrip (HG), magnitude estimation (ME), and sound pressure (SP) responses (x-axis) as a function of the measure of strength of support for President Nixon's handling of domestic affairs (y-axis) based on all three response measures, each corrected for regression. Each point is the geometric mean of 48 responses. (From Lodge, Cross, Tursky, & Tanenhaus, 1975.)

TABLE 7.1
Strength of Support Expressed by Thirty Adjective Phrases:
Comparison Across Scales*

Adjective Phrase	Senate	Police	Court Decision	Nixon's Policy	Geometric Mean	C.V. (× 100)
absolutely perfect	343			328	332	2.2
perfect		286	307		296	3.5
excellent		237		232	233	1.1
great		217			217	
terrific	207				207	
first rate			200		200	
very good	126			146	141	7.3
good	106	121	100	105	107	7.3
satisfactory		77	66		71	7.7
adequate	42.6			57	53	14.5
sometimes all right		51			51	
so-so	(50)	(50)	(50)	(50)		
good and bad	47				47	
neither good nor bad			47	46	46	1.1
mediocre		35	34		34	1.4
inadequate	29				29	
not so good		21			21	
below par			20		20	
second rate			20	19	19	2.6
bad	16			15	15	3.2
unsatisfactory	15		9.3		12	23.5
very bad	11.5				11.5	
poor		9.8			9.8	
very poor		6.8		7	6.9	1.4
third rate			6.7		6.7	
terrible	5.6	7.7		6.5	5.9	16.2
dreadful		5.8			5.8	
awful			4.8	6.2	5.8	12.7
atrocious	3.8				3.8	
disgusting			2.8	3.7	3.4	13.8

*From Lodge, Cross, Tursky & Tanenhaus (1975).

first four column headings indicate the context (Senate, Police, Court decision, Nixon) within which subjects estimated the support implied by each modifier. The scale value (fifth column) for each of the 30 modifiers is the geometric mean pooled over the ME, HG, and SP estimates of support for all subjects.

Sixteen of the 30 adjectival phrases used in this study appear in two or more scales. Despite differences in the samples of subjects doing the judging, differences in the linguistic content of the scales, and differences in the object of description, some startling invariances appear in the metric relations among adjectives. The description "absolutely perfect," for example, is 6.9 times more favorable than "so-so" on the Senate scale and 6.6 times more favorable on the Nixon scale. On the Police scale "mediocre" expresses 70% of the support expressed by "so-so," and on the Court scale it is 68%. The description "good" appears on all four scales; its magnitude relative to "so-so" for each is 2.1, 2.4, 2.0, and 2.1. On average, "good" is 2.14 times more favorable than the standard with a coefficient of variation across scales of only 7.3%. Coefficients of variation for all 16 descriptors that appear on two or more scales are shown in the last column of Table 7.1. Half of these coefficients are 3.5% or less. The greatest disagreement arises in the reproducibility of the support expressed by "unsatisfactory." Values of 15 on the Senate scale and 9.3 on the Court scale represent a relative error of 23.5%.

An additional source of invariance can be found in the effect of the modifier "very" on a descriptor word. When modifying the words "good," "bad," or "poor," the magnitude of the increase or decrease in the word's scale value relative to "so-so" is approximately the same. On the Nixon scale, "very good" is 1.4 times more supportive than "good"; "very bad" on the Senate scale is 1.4 times worse than "bad"; "very poor" on the Police scale is 1.4 times worse than "poor"; and on the Senate scale "very good" is 1.2 times more supportive than "good." At this juncture, the reader may find it helpful to compare the scale values, relative to "so-so," for some of the more popular adjectives used to anchor category scales or designate the range and dimension of popular social science scales. Compare, for example, such pairs as: good vs. bad, very good vs. very bad, satisfactory vs. unsatisfactory, adequate vs. inadequate, excellent vs. terrible, and first rate vs. second rate. In no case are the polar adjectives equally distant from the standard "so-so." Note, too, that the most popular polar adjectives provide a narrow range.

A summary measure of the reliability of support values across scales is the .99 product-moment correlation for the 16 repeated words between each word's strength on one scale and its strength on another. In general, the pattern or invariances found here suggests that these scales are highly reliable and valid indicators of strength of support.

Testing the Support Scale in the Real World

These laboratory results indicate that some of the adjectival modifiers of support convey more precise information about the relative magnitude of opinion strength than heretofore expected. But, the possibility remains that these apparent invariances are peculiar to the linguistic behavior of college students in a laboratory setting. Before the scale items could be tested in a survey setting, two questions need be addressed: First, could "real-world" people make proportional judgments of the support implied by these words and phrases? And, equally important, would the metric relations between the adjectival modifiers of support found for students hold for adults outside the laboratory?

For this validation experiment—administered in the individual's home using portable equipment with the capability of delivering line length and word stimuli and eliciting ME, HG, and SP responses—111 of 123 local area adults completed the calibration and social scaling task. These subjects provide adequate distribution by sex, age, education, and income for a number of tests of the generalizability of the support scale. Each subject first made ME, HG, and SP estimates of a sequence of line lengths, then estimated the amount of support implied by 26 of the adjectival modifiers from the laboratory study. Once again the scale items were embedded in simple declarative sentences, here the Supreme Court's decision on abortion and either the Democratic or Republican Party.

TABLE 7.2
Strength of Support Expressed by Each Adjective in the Party Support
and Court Decision Scales as Determined by Magnitude Estimation (N),
Force of Handgrip (F), and Loudness (P) Matches with Correction for
Regression Biases*

	$N^{1.15}$	$F^{2.0}$	$P^{0.86}$	Ψ
Party Support				
Perfect	215	234	262	252
First Rate	142	154	154	160
Great	162	174	112	157
Good	96	77.4	115	101
Good & Bad	51	71.4	52.4	61
So-So	50	50.3	40.9	50
Below Par	20.5	19.9	22.2	22.2
Second Rate	20.5	11.6	17.4	17.1
Poor	14.5	10.7	8.4	11.7
Very Poor	8.3	13.1	8.9	10.6
Third Rate	10.6	6.5	11.9	10.0
Awful	6.1	9.2	7.5	8.0
Atrocious	3.1	3.6	4.2	3.8
Court Decision				
Absolutely Perfect	224	222	243	282
Excellent	192	203	240	258
Very Good	130	149	169	182
Good	91	66	103	105
Satisfactory	81	78	55.4	86
So-So	50	32.5	41.7	50
Neither Good Nor Bad	48.8	40.7	33.7	49.8
Mediocre	35.4	28	31.4	38.6
Unsatisfactory	15.4	13.7	16.1	18.4
Bad	10.6	12.9	20.2	17.2
Very Bad	6.5	8.8	4.7	7.9
Terrible	5.2	6.9	5.2	7.0
Disgusting	4.4	6.3	4.2	6.0

*From Lodge, Cross, Tursky, Tanenhaus & Reeder (1976).

The results of this study are reported in detail in Lodge, Cross, Tursky, Tanenhaus, & Reeder (1976). Synoptically, despite problems related to our use of a linear rather than sone potentiometer for loudness judgments, these adult subjects reveal an ability to make proportional judgments of the relative intensity of a metric continuum. The ME, HG, and SP matches to line length are well-described by power functions, which in each case approximate the expected relationship between modalities.

Scale values for the support items—adjusted for regression bias—are tallied in Table 7.2 for each of the three response modalities separately, with all scale units set relative to the modulus 50 used as the standard for "so-so" in magnitude estimation. The three subscales show remarkable agreement: The intercorrelations between modalities for the three Party Support scales are .98, .93, and .91, and for the Court scale, .98, .97, and .98. The high intercorrelations constitute high construct validity and strong evidence for an underlying psychological continuum corresponding to strength of support.

To test the generalizability of the Support scale, the scale values derived from the ME, HG, and SP matches of this local area adult sample were plotted against the scaled values obtained from the laboratory subjects for the 26 words common to both samples. The correlation between the scale values is .995, with a least squares error-in-both-variables estimate of the regression coefficient in log-log coordinates of .94. This is not statistically different from the expected unit exponent at the $p < .05$ level, indicating the linearity between scales. What is more, these results suggest a good deal of consensus among people as to the information conveyed by these adjectival modifiers of support.

Testing the Support Scale in a National Survey

Having shown that adult subjects can use established psychophysical response measures to make proportional estimates of the amount of support implied by some adjectival descriptors, a number of laboratory experiments were carried out to test various response modalities and interview formats for the magnitude scaling of political opinion in survey instruments (Lodge, Cross, Tursky, Foley, & Foley, 1976).

The obvious first choice for one response modality was magnitude estimation because it has a well-established, stable exponent within the 100:1 response range that we oftentimes uncover in the expression of social-psychological preferences. Of the psychophysical response measures that meet the requirements of survey research, line production (LP, drawing a line proportional to the perceived magnitude of a stimulus) was selected (Stevens & Guirao, 1963; Teghtsoonian & Teghtsoonian, 1965). As a paper-and-pencil measure, LP—like ME—is linear within the 100:1 range, portable, inexpensive to administer, record, and score, and relatively easy to incorporate into a more or less conventional survey instrument.

A number of laboratory and local field tests were conducted to test the characteristics of LP under survey conditions using different survey formats. Rather than review these tests and checks here, let it suffice to report the compromise—our survey protocols are printed on legal-sized paper (35.5 cm in length), which although obviously not ideal, provide sufficient length for respondents to make relatively expansive line-production estimates.

At this juncture, Murphy and Tanenhaus (1974) elected to employ the Support scale in a national survey carried out by the Survey Research Center of the University of Michigan on a national representative sample to measure support for the U.S. Supreme Court (see Lodge, Cross, Tursky, Foley, & Foley, 1976).

Employing ME and LP as response modalities in the indirect cross-modality matching paradigm, 375 of 404 respondents matched each modality to a common metric—LP matched to a sequence of number stimuli, and ME matched to an identical set of nine line lengths, which ranged from 3 to 300 mm in length—and then used both response modalities to estimate the amount of support implied by 13 adjectival modifiers, with the standard "so-so" assigned a 5 cm line for LP and 50 units of support for ME. Figure 7.5 displays the LP and ME estimates—pooled over 375 respondents and adjusted for regression bias—matched to the 13 Support scale items. The product-moment correlation between geometric means of the line and number estimates of support is .99, with a regression coefficient of 1.27 ± .08.

Following the calibration and social scaling tasks—whenever a judgment of support was called for—the respondent was presented with a card listing each of the adjectival scale items in alphabetical order and asked to select that word or

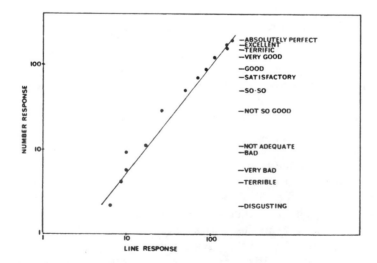

FIG. 7.5.   National Sample. Magnitude estimates (x-axis) of the 13 Support scale items plotted as a function of line production estimates (y-axis) in log-log coordinates. The solid line represents the empirical exponent (1.3).

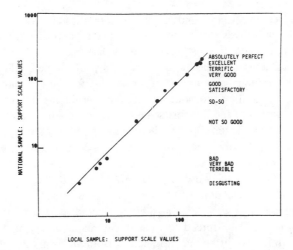

FIG. 7.6.   The Support scale items common to the national sample conducted by the Survey Research Center at the University of Michigan (y-axis) and a local sample selected from New York Suburban communities (x-axis) are plotted against each other in ratio-ruled coordinates. (From Lodge, Cross, Tursky, Foley, & Foley, 1976.)

phrase which best expressed his or her evaluation of political institutions, including the U.S. Supreme Court, its decisions, and performance. Given the strength of the magnitude scaling results summarized in Fig. 7.5, Murphy and Tanenhaus assigned magnitude weights to each adjectival modifier to test quantitative hypotheses of support.

To test the generalizability of the Support scale, we compared the scale values derived from the LP and ME estimates of this national sample to the scale values obtained from the ME, HG, and SP responses of our local area sample. This procedure provides a commanding ''back-translation'' criterion test of the generalizability of the adjectival descriptors of support. In Fig. 7.6, the 12 scale items common to our suburban New York study and the national survey are plotted in log-log coordinates. The relationship between magnitude scale values is linear and shows an extraordinary close match: a product-moment correlation of .999 with a regression coefficient of .98, which is not significantly different from the expected unit slope.

The Direct Magnitude Scaling of Political Judgments and Preferences

The results of the studies reviewed here demonstrate that the cross-modality matching paradigm is a powerful procedure for eliciting magnitude judgments from people under survey conditions. Further, the comparisons across diverse populations, research settings, and response modalities clearly indicate that the adjective modifiers convey metric information about support when used to judge different political institutions, policies, and leaders.

There are problems with the Support scale as well. Some could be corrected easily (e.g., the arbitrary assignment of a modulus for the standard), but others are endemic to the scaling procedure itself. Two problems in particular undermine the applicability of the Support scale in survey research. First, the adjectival modifiers are specific to support, whereas most political surveys are omnibus instruments that typically elicit responses to dozens of different social-psychological dimensions. A related problem is that once the items are scaled, respondents must choose the word or phrase that best approximates their strength of opinion about a political object. Assuming a geometric sequence of scale items could be developed and were to hold their magnitude weights for the sample, respondents would still be forced to treat the items as categorical options and thereby make similarity–difference judgments. Both problems stem from the fact that this scaling approach is *indirect*—respondents express their strength of opinion through the scale items rather than directly by using the response modalities.

The Direct Magnitude Scaling of Political Judgments

To address this problem, direct magnitude scaling procedures were tested extensively in the laboratory and in field studies. Rather than review this work here, let it suffice to highlight the results of a scale confrontation study pitting direct magnitude scaling against the standard category scales employed in American election research (Lodge & Tursky, 1979).

Comparing Magnitude to SRC-Type Category Scales. Prior to the 1976 Presidential election, 103 local area adults were interviewed in May, another 108 in October immediately before the election. The interview instruments were similar and proceeded in stages: First, the respondents matched lines and numbers to a common set of geometrically spaced physical stimuli—LP to numbers and ME to line lengths. Following this calibration task, the respondents used LP and ME to express their strength of political opinion on 28 standard questions used by the Center for Political Studies in the Survey Research Center's national election studies. And finally, each respondent responded categorically to the same 28 items presented word for word and option by option exactly as specified in the SRC/CPS code books, among them, such variables as party identification, candidate preference, political efficacy and trust, as well as items relating to such issues as unemployment, inflation, energy, abortion, and school busing.

The social-psychophysical scaling task proceeded in discrete steps for each survey question: (1) After reading the question, the respondents were presented with the polar options that define the dimension (e.g., the labels Democrat and Republican for the party identification item, or Agree and Disagree for the efficacy and citizen duty items, or the policy positions for each issue question) and asked to select the option that is closer to . . ., agrees with . . ., supports . . ., or best expresses one's opinion. In doing this, the respondent indicated the direction of response. Next, (2) the respondents drew a reference line (a standard) to represent a middle position in between the options, and, then, (3) relative to this reference line, drew another line (a response line) to express proportionately their strength of opinion. On a separate page, (4) each respondent assigned a number to represent a middle position between the options on the given dimension and then assigned a number relative to this standard to express his or her strength of opinion. Finally (5), if, as here, category scales are also used, the respondent checked the most appropriate categorical option.

The procedure for the party identification question illustrates the way in which questions were responded to psychophysically. Each of the respondents first checked the appropriate position on the standard format to indicate whether one was a Democrat, a Republican, or an Independent. Then, those respondents who indicated they were Republican or Democrat next checked whether they were "strong" or "not so strong" partisans; or, if an Independent, whether one felt closer to the Republican or Democratic party. Next, each respondent drew a reference line to represent a middle position between Democrat and Republican. Then, relative to this reference line, the respondent drew a response line to indicate his or her strength of partisanship. So, for those respondents who think of themselves as Independents, their response lines would be approximately the same length as their standard lines. The more partisan respondents felt themselves to be, the longer—relative to their own reference line—the response line would be.

Number responses were made on the following page of the interview schedule without referring back to the line-length responses. The same procedure was used. First, each respondent assigned a reference number to represent a middle position between the categorical options Democrat and Republican, and then a response number was made relative to the standard number to express strength of party identification. Similar procedures were used for all 28 variables: After indicating the direction of opinion by making a choice between the polar options provided by the SRC/CPS items, respondents expressed their strength of preference by means of line and number responses relative to a standard "middle position."

The construction of magnitude-scale values for the responses to each question is a simple procedure. Because two ratios are created for each question—one for the response line to the reference line and one for the response number to the reference number—the calculation of scale values involves averaging the two response ratios to produce a single magnitude measure of response and then

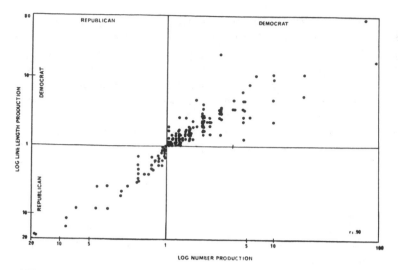

FIG. 7.7.   Scattergram of line Length Production (y-axis) with Magnitude Estimation (x-axis) for the October sample. The variable is the party identification question. (From Lodge & Tursky, 1979.)

examining the function relating the ratios to determine the degree to which the predicted unit is obtained.[2]

For illustrative purposes, let us examine the party identification question, as it is one of the most heavily researched independent variables in political science. First, an examination of the relationship between the two magnitude measures of partisanship in Fig. 7.7 reveals a product-moment correlation between LP and ME measures of .90. As is clear from visual inspection of this scatterplot, the two measures are linear in log-log coordinates, which indicates an underlying power function relationship. The (geometric) mean-to-mean magnitude range from Republican to Democrat is about 15:1.

Figure 7.8 plots the category against magnitude measures of party identification in semilog coordinates for both the May and October samples combined:

_____

[2]Of special note here is that within this direct cross-modality matching paradigm—unlike the scale-building studies reviewed earlier in which subjects judge a series of stimuli on a dimension, and each point on a plot represents the pooled estimates of all subjects to each stimulus—in this procedure subjects use two measures to express a single judgment on a dimension, and each point on a plot represents the combined LP and ME judgment of a single subject. Correlation and regression coefficients are then computed across subjects. That linear functions in log-log coordinates can be retrieved from these between-subject estimates attests to the underlying power of the power law.

An analogy from sensory psychophysics would be to present a single noise level to subjects seated varying distances from the noise source, asking each subject to estimate the loudness of the single noise. When the estimate of each subject is plotted against the db level of noise measured at each distance from the noise source, one would predict an exponent of two thirds for loudness from the estimates across subjects.

pooled ME and LP estimates on the ratio-ruled x-axis against the categorical position of all respondents who chose each of the categorical options on the linearly ruled y-axis. The point on each magnitude response is the geometric mean of all respondents who selected that option. The lines surrounding each point represent ± 1 standard deviation each side of the mean.

As is apparent from this display, there is a broad range of partisanship within each category level, with the greatest amount of variance occurring in the end-most categories, indicating that the most partisan respondents are the most constrained by the arbitrary constraints imposed by this standard category scale. Further, it is clear from Fig. 7.8 that "Leaning" and "Moderate" partisans are closer to one another than are "Moderate" and "Strong" partisans. In fact, it is impossible to distinguish those who chose either the "Leaning" or "Not so strong" labels. It is a consequence of the strength of partisanship evoked by the party identification question, which when arbitrarily constrained on the standard seven-point category scale, produces the loss of information and misclassification of respondents uncovered for this and each of the other 27 political variables compared in this study.

As these comparative data illustrate, weak measurement, the loss of information, and misclassification of respondents are direct consequences of the fixed

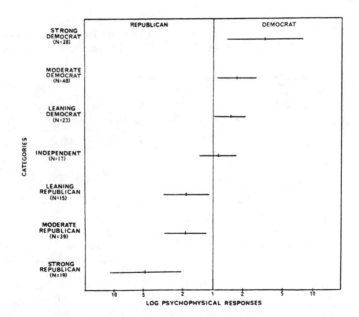

FIG. 7.8. Psychophysical responses (x-axis) for each of the Party Identification category values (y-axis) for the October sample. Psychophysical responses are shown as a mean plus/minus one standard deviation. The x-axis is ratio-ruled. (From Lodge & Tursky, 1979.)

range of standard SRC category scales. Essentially, category scaling distorts the expression of political opinion in systematic and predictable, but uncontrollable ways. When the range of social opinion is greater than the category scale can measure, as is typically the case, or when the range of opinion is less, there is a distortion of responses: The greater the discrepancy between true and constrained range, the greater the distortion of opinion intensity (Baird, Kreindler, & Jones, 1971; Marks, 1968; Stevens, 1975). Further, when the range of categories available to respondents for expressing their opinion is small relative to the strength of opinion held toward the item, most of the distortion appears to occur in the end categories. This is particularly serious because many theories of behavior posit a relationship between strength of opinion and the likelihood of a congruent behavior. That is, those expressing the strongest beliefs and preferences are most likely to behave in accordance with their opinion, whereas those who are less strongly engaged are less likely to act in behalf of their opinions. Because of the wide range of opinion that we observe in the endmost categories, a researcher cannot be confident that a respondent choosing a polar category is expressing an intense opinion. Attempts, therefore, to predict subsequent behavior as a function of categorical expressions of strength of opinion will, predictably, experience poor results solely as a result of the arbitrary constraints imposed by category scales.

Candidate Preference as a Function of Party Identification.   Another item that appeared in both surveys dealt with candidate preference—specifically

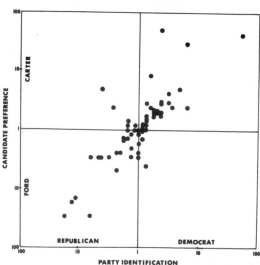

FIG. 7.9a. Candidate preference for Ford vs. Carter (y-axis) as a function of party identification (x-axis) for the May sample. Both variables are measured psychophysically and the relationship is plotted in logarithmic coordinates. The slope is 1.4 and the correlation is .83. (From Lodge & Tursky, 1979.)

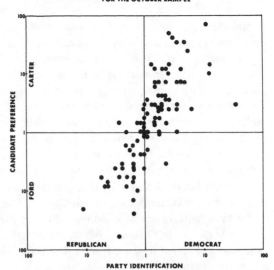

CANDIDATE PREFERENCE AS A FUNCTION OF PARTY IDENTIFICATION
FOR THE OCTOBER SAMPLE

FIG. 7.9b. Candidate preference for Ford vs. Carter (y-axis) as a function of party identification (x-axis) for the October sample. Both variables are measured psycho-physically and the relationship is plotted in logarithmic coordinates. The slope is 2.0 and the correlation is .81. (From Lodge & Tursky, 1979.)

whether the respondent favored Gerald Ford or Jimmy Carter for President. Figure 7.9a plots the relationship between candidate preference and party identification for the May, 1976 sample with each variable scaled by means of line and number matching. The correlation between variables is .83, but more importantly it is possible to examine the slope of the relationship. The best-fitting function relating candidate preference to party identification for the May sample is a power function with a slope of 1.4: A twofold increase in party identification produces a 2.8-fold increase in candidate support. For the October, 1976 sample (Fig. 7.9b) the correlation is again high, .81, virtually the same as for May, but with a significant steepening of the power function exponent to 2.0. Here, in the weeks immediately preceding the election, party identification produces a greater change in candidate support: A twofold increase in party identification produces a fourfold increase in preference for one's party's candidate.

This comparison of slopes between May and October for candidate preference as a function of partisanship points to what may be a major advantage of magnitude over rating scales in the development of social science theory and the testing of hypotheses. When an investigator is interested in the magnitude of change in a relationship between variables—how much an exponent increases or decreases as a function of some intervention (campaign effects implied here between May and October)—magnitude-scaling methods are superior, for the comparison of regression coefficients provides a quantitative measure of the strength of relationship. Because regression analysis is one of the most powerful tools available to the social sciences, further discussion of this point is in order.

DISCUSSION

A major consequence of weak measurement is weak theory. Given ordinal-level data, one is unable to test quantitative hypotheses rigorously: One can state only that an increase in X is likely to accompany an increase in Y. The magnitude of change in either variable, or in the relationship between variables, cannot be specified. As a consequence, a researcher is unable to measure precisely the impact of some intervening variable on an established relationship between variables. What is lost is a sensitive measure of the extent to which some experimental manipulation or environmental change alters a relationship. Although the data from our political survey are not ideal, the change in relationship between candidate preference and party identification illustrates the general argument. The relationship between variables changed between May (Fig. 7.9a) and October (Fig. 7.9b), presumably as a function of the Presidential campaign. The effect of the Presidential campaign did not influence the correlation between variables (.83 in May, .81 in October), but strengthened the preference for one's party's candidate (a change in slope from 1.4 to 2.0). The change in slope is primarily a function of an increase in the standard deviation of Candidate Preference from .688 to .838, whereas the standard deviation for Party Identification decreased slightly from .494 to .422.

Conventional category scaling could not provide this information. These empirical results indicate that category scaling does not produce regression coefficients that can be meaningfully interpreted as quantitative expressions of the relationship between variables. Regression coefficients are arbitrary when produced by variables measured categorically because of the arbitrariness of the categorical measure—first in the number of categories imposed by the format of the scale and second in the numbers assigned to the categories.[3]

The key problem with category scales is their inability to reflect changes in range. Because the range of response is fixed, category scales cannot adjust to changes in the true range of stimuli or track the magnitude of opinion strength. Because the range of social stimuli is not known beforehand, varies from question to question, and varies across individuals over time, category scaling denies effective access to quantitative measures of change in the relationship between variables. Regression coefficients computed from categorical judgments are

---

[3]The problem is of course that category scaling is oblivious to range. As a consequence, the number of categories imposed by the format of the category scale and the numbers assigned the categories arbitrarily fix the value of the regression coefficient. If one were to compute a regression coefficient for two variables, which were in perfect linear agreement across the full range of values, the obtained slope would be a function of the number of categories, not the true magnitude of relationship between variables. Under ideal conditions, two linearly related seven-point scales will produce a slope of about 1.0, whereas the same two variables, again in linear agreement, one measured on a 10-point scale, the other on a five-point scale, will yield a slope of about .5. Relatedly, the numbers assigned the categories will alter the slope.

indeterminate. Essentially, where the stimulus range is greater than the response range, the slope will be lower than it should be, and where the stimulus range is less than the response range, the slope will be steeper than it should be— solely as a result of the arbitrary constraints imposed by the format of the scale. Because all the SRC-type scales compared in our scale-confrontation study provide a far smaller range than the opinion ranges they purport to measure, and because magnitude measures track the stimulus range relatively well as a result of the lack of constraints on the respondent, one routinely finds that the regression coefficient for category scales numbered in the conventional fashion is lower than that obtained with magnitude measures (Curtis, 1970; Marks, 1974; Ward, 1972, 1973).

Given the power of regression analysis in social science research, Tufte (1969) and others (Heise, 1975; Namboodiri, Carter, & Blalock, 1975) suggest that investigators assign numbers to the categories that use their knowledge about the meaning of the response to reflect more accurately the true relationships between the responses. The first problem, of course, is the arbitrariness of the method, which depends on some consensus among researchers as to the meaning of responses and agreement on the numbers assigned to the categories. The second problem is that the movement toward seven-point category scales, with only the endpoints labelled, makes it difficult to do other than assume that the categories are equally spaced—an empirically untenable assumption.

On the basis of the comparisons between scale types presented here, we conclude that category and magnitude scales measure judgments differently. In measuring strength of political opinion—as with the perceived intensity of physical variables—category scales appear to measure the perceived similarity- dissimilarity of stimuli, whereas magnitude scales measure the relative intensity of stimuli. In practice, then, where a researcher requires simple difference judgments to test ordinal hypotheses, category scales suffice. Where, on the other hand, researchers propose to test quantitative hypotheses, magnitude scaling provides more sensitive, quantitatively interpretable information.

ACKNOWLEDGMENTS

Research funded by National Science Foundation Grant SOC 77-25539.

REFERENCES

Baird, J. C., Kreindler, M., & Jones, K. Generation of multiple ratio scales with a fixed stimulus attribute. *Perception & Psychophysics,* 1971, *9,* 399–403.

Cross, D. V. Some technical notes on psychophysical scaling. In H. Moskowitz, B. Scharf, & J. C. Stevens (Eds.), *Sensation and measurement: Papers in honor of S. S. Stevens.* Dordrecht, The Netherlands: Reidel, 1974.

Cross, D. V., Tursky, B., & Lodge, M. The role of regression and range effects in determination of the power function for electric shock. *Perception & Psychophysics,* 1975, *18,* 9–14.

Curtis, D. Magnitude estimations and category judgments of brightness and brightness levels: A two-state interpretation. *Journal of Experimental Psychology,* 1970, *83,* 201–208.

Dawson, W. E., & Brinker, R. P. Validation of ratio scales of opinion by multimodality matching. *Perception & Psychophysics,* 1971, *9,* 413–417.

Deutscher, I. *What we say/what we do: Sentiments and acts.* Glenview, Ill.: Scott, Foresman, 1971.

Hamblin, R. L. Social attitudes: Magnitude measurement and theory. In H. M. Blalock, Jr. (Ed.), *Measurement in the social sciences: Theories and strategies.* Chicago: Aldine, 1974.

Heise, D. *Causal Analysis.* New York: Wiley, 1975.

Lodge, M., Cross, D., Tursky, B., Foley, M. A., & Foley, H. The calibration and cross-modal validation of ratio scales of political opinion in survey research. *Social Science Research,* 1976, *5,* 325–347.

Lodge, M., Cross, D., Tursky, B., & Tanenhaus, J. The psychophysical scaling and validation of a political support scale. *American Journal of Political Science,* 1975, *19,* 611–649.

Lodge, M., Cross, D., Tursky, B., Tanenhaus, J., & Reeder, R. The psychophysical scaling of political support in the "real world." *Political Methodology,* 1976, *2,* 159–182.

Lodge, M., & Tursky, B. Comparisons between category and magnitude scaling of political opinion employing SRC/CPS items. *American Political Science Review,* 1979, *73,* 50–66.

Lodge, M., Tursky, B. Workshop on the magnitude scaling of political opinion in survey research. *American Journal of Political Science,* 1981, *25,* forthcoming.

Marks, L. E. Stimulus-range, number of categories, and the form of the category scale. *American Journal of Psychology,* 1968, *81,* 467–479.

Murphy, W., & Tanenhaus, J. Explaining diffuse support for the United States Supreme Court: An assessment of four models. *Notre Dame Lawyer,* 1974, *49,* 1037–1044.

Namboodiri, N., Krishnan, L., & Blalock, H. *Applied multivariate analysis and experimental designs.* New York: McGraw-Hill, 1975.

Pachella, R. G. The interpretation of reaction time in information-processing research. In B. Kantowitz (Ed.), *Human information processing: Tutorials in performance and cognition.* Hillsdale, N.J.: Lawrence Erlbaum Associates, 1974.

Sellin, J. T., & Wolfgang, M. E. *The measurement of delinquency.* New York: Wiley, 1964.

Shinn, A., Jr. Relations between scales. In H. M. Blalock, Jr. (Ed.), *Measurement in the social sciences: Theories and strategies.* Chicago: Aldine, 1974.

Stevens, S. S. On predicting exponents for cross-modality matches. *Perception & Psychophysics,* 1969, *6,* 252–256.

Stevens, S. S. *Psychophysics: Introduction to its perceptual, neural, and social prospects.* New York: Wiley, 1975.

Stevens, S. S., & Guirao, M. Subjective scaling of length and area and the matching of length to loudness and brightness. *Journal of Experimental Psychology,* 1963, *66,* 177–186.

Teghtsoonian, M., & Teghtsoonian, R. Seen and felt length. *Psychonomic Science,* 1965, *3,* 465–466.

Tufte, E. Improving data analysis in political science. *World Politics,* 1969, *21,* 641–654.

Tursky, B., Lodge, M., Foley, M. A., Reeder, R., & Foley, H. Evaluation of the cognitive component of political issues by use of classical conditioning. *Journal of Personality and Social Psychology,* 1976, *34,* 865–873.

Tursky, B., Lodge, M., & Reeder, R. Psychophysical and psychophysiological evaluation of the direction, intensity, and meaning of race-related stimuli. *Psychophysiology,* 1979, *16,* 452–462.

Ward, L. Category judgments of loudness in the absence of an experimenter-induced identification function: Sequential effects and power-function fit. *Journal of Experimental Psychology,* 1972, *94,* 179–184.

Ward, L. Repeated magnitude estimations with a variable standard: Sequential effects and other properties. *Perception and Psychophysics,* 1973, *13,* 193–200.

8

Beliefs and Values as Attitude Components

Lennart Sjöberg
University of Göteborg,
Sweden

People experience and express evaluations, likes and dislikes, for social objects and concepts. Such likes and dislikes are called attitudes, and they may be measured by means of a number of methods available for scaling subjective experience. In other chapters of the present volume, much attention is devoted to scaling problems, and here I simply assume that such scaling is possible. The quantitative details may give rise to problems such as those encountered in comparisons of magnitude and category scales, but the fact that the assumption of unidimensional preference continua usually is supported by data is quite robust (Sjöberg, 1968), although exceptions do exist (Tversky, 1969). In particular, in the empirical work reported here I have used category ratings. A monotonic transformation, approximately exponential, to a magnitude scale would probably not affect the gross trends in data that are at present the focus of interest. This is not to say, of course, that the scaling method is not of crucial importance in other applications.

The overall evaluation of a social object may be sufficient for many purposes, but often there is also a desire to investigate further what constitutes such evaluation. It is often natural to assume that evaluation is based on some basic value dimensions and that the global evaluation of an object is a function of its position on such underlying value dimensions. How should one go about finding which value dimensions are relevant in a certain case, what the loadings of particular attitude objects are, and how the different value dimensions are combined?

In a number of papers and in one extensive book (Fishbein & Ajzen, 1975), Fishbein and his coworkers have proposed and investigated a procedure for finding the value dimensions and a model for combining them. The ideas are quite straightforward. First, a list is made of the most salient dimensions aroused by consideration of a set of attitude objects. These salient dimensions are found by means of a semistructured interview method. Then, these value dimensions are scaled as to their overall evaluation (good or bad), and finally each attitude object is scaled according to which degree it is characterized by a certain value dimension. Evaluation scale values and degrees of beliefs concerning single attitude objects are then multiplied, and the sum of products is formed across all of the value dimensions for each attitude object. This sum of products is expected to reproduce the overall evaluation of the attitude object. The degree of fit of the model and the procedure for eliciting the value dimension is investigated by means of correlation statistics. The correlation between the sum of products and the global evaluation of objects is usually in the neighborhood of .7, which is then taken to imply that the model fits well to data. Concerning this procedure for model testing, it has been argued quite persuasively by Norman Anderson a number of times that a closer scrutiny of data is necessary and that correlations should not be used as a sole method for investigating the degree of fit of an attitude model (e.g., Anderson, 1977).

Beliefs and values may well constitute a basis for likes and dislikes, but this is not necessarily true for experienced or rated beliefs and values. The procedures of Fishbein presuppose that beliefs and values, as they occur in the rating procedure, are prior to evaluation and that the causal relation goes from beliefs and values to evaluations. Furthermore, beliefs and values should be independent. This condition has been checked by correlating beliefs and values across individuals and value dimensions simultaneously. The typical finding is a correlation around zero. However, if patterns are idiosyncratic and occur in different directions for different individuals, the pooled result may well be a zero correlation, which should then not be taken as an indication of independence of beliefs and values.

Fishbein's attitude model assumes that value and probability scales are measured on a ratio scale level. The predicted overall evaluation of an attitude object is not independent of scale origins in the case of a multiplicative model, such as the one proposed by Fishbein. Furthermore, nonlinear relations between values and probabilities are not expected in the model and cannot easily be accounted for by the way of thinking that Fishbein's model exemplifies. Deviations from the model may be due to faulty scaling procedures or to errors in more substantial psychological assumptions. The latter possibility is of major concern here.

This paper presents an alternative approach to the relationships between evaluation, beliefs, and values (cf. Sjöberg, 1976). Evaluations are no longer seen as a function of the rated beliefs and values. Rather, evaluations, beliefs, and values are all seen as indicators of the same underlying belief system that is striving for consistency in order to preserve self-esteem. According to this suggestion, people with low self-esteem should have a larger amount of overall consistency in their beliefs and values. Also, the reasoning that people use in order to justify their judgments should reveal some of the underlying tendencies toward consistency among beliefs and values. And finally, a closer scrutiny of individual data may suggest further properties of the belief system that may not be readily discovered if one only uses a straightforward quantitative model such as the Fishbein model where idiosyncratic and possibly nonlinear individual patterns are not readily discovered and attended to.

In the following, I report five studies that were performed in order to test these ideas. I conclude my presentation with some more general remarks concerning attitude models, attitude research, and decision making.

STUDY 1

The purpose of the first study was to test in a preliminary manner the approach just outlined. It was considered to be particularly important to devote attention to the study of interactions between beliefs and values at the individual level and to try to understand the dynamics of any such interactions.

Method

Pilot Studies.   The first problem was to choose a suitable area for investigation in the population of subjects who were to participate. For this reason, 137 subjects were recruited from boarding high schools (in Swedish "Folk-högskolor") in the neighborhood of Göteborg. The subjects were asked to rate their degree of interest in 23 specified problem areas. Alcohol was then selected as a suitable problem area because it was both high in overall rating and helped to define one major factor.

In a second pilot study, 41 students of psychology at the University of Göteborg participated as subjects. They were asked to perform the following tasks:

1. The subjects were asked to write down 15–25 words that they associated with the concept of alcohol consumption.

2. Forty possible effects of drinking a certain specified amount of alcohol were presented. The subjects were instructed to rate how likely the effects were. It was specified that the effects referred to drinking the stated amount of alcohol on one single occasion and that the subjects should not be concerned with long-term effects of alcohol consumption. The scale consisted of seven categories and used the figures 0 to 6, with 0 defined as "completely incredible" and 6 as "very credible." The amount of alcohol specified was "half a bottle of red wine (34 cls) or four bottles of medium strong beer or three bottles of strong beer or two drinks of aquavite." (These different definitions were all considered to denote the same amount of alcohol.)

3. The next task of the subjects concerned ratings of value. The same 40 possible effects of drinking alcohol as in the previous task were presented, and the instructions were in relevant aspects the same as in that task. The rating scale contained 13 categories and was presented as follows: 6 5 4 3 2 1 0 1 2 3 4 5 6. The first six categories were denotated as being negative, with 6 as the most negative and 1 the least negative. The six last categories were denotated as being positive, 6 the most positive and 1 the least positive value. The category 0 was to be used when an effect was considered as neutral from the standpoint of the value system of the subject.

4. Twenty-nine statements and questions concerning alcohol and its effects were then presented. The purpose of this section was to test suitable questions for measuring the knowledge of subjects concerning alcohol.

5. Half of the subjects had first rated probabilities of alcohol effects, and the other half had first rated values of alcohol effects. In the sixth section of the questionnaire, they were asked to estimate to what extent they felt that their ratings in the second task had been affected by their ratings in the first task. They were provided with a seven-category scale for this task, going from "to a very large extent" to "not at all."

Several analyses were performed on these data. Means and standard deviations of the probability and value ratings of the alcohol effects were obtained. Factor analyses of the probability and value ratings were performed. Twenty one of the 40 effects, presented in the following subsection, were selected for the main study on the following criteria:

1. High communality.
2. Small standard deviation.
3. All factors obtained should be represented.
4. The probability and value continua should be covered as well as possible.

Three of the questions concerning knowledge of alcohol and its effects were deleted because the answers given were difficult to score. The first section of the pilot questionnaire, requiring subjects to associate to the concepts of alcohol consumption, was used in constructing items for the measurement of logical deductions.

A preliminary analysis of the interaction between beliefs and values was considered to be of interest. For each individual, probability ratings were plotted against value ratings over the 40 suggested effects. Correlations significant at the .05 level were noted. Under the hypothesis of no interaction and for 41 subjects being independent of each other, we would expect two negative and two positive interactions to occur at the .05 level. The result was five negative and 18 positive correlations. It was thus tentatively concluded that many strong interactions could be expected and that they could be expected to occur both in the negative and the positive direction for about half of the sample of subjects.

Main Study: Procedure.   Ninety-two subjects participated in the main study. They were students of boarding high schools in the neighborhood of Göteborg. The main questionnaire contained the following tasks:

1. Ratings of the value of alcohol effects. The instructions were the same as in the pilot studies. Twenty-one effects were used, viz.: brain damage, positive social contacts, happiness, bad breath, sadness, disinhibition, clumsiness, calmness, vitamins, grumpiness, relaxation, curing colds, improved complexion, less skill as a car driver, destruction of social atmosphere in the home, increased self-confidence, loss of self-respect, escape from everyday life, illness, nervousness, decreased shyness.

2. Following the value ratings, subjects were asked to rate probabilities of the effects. The instructions were the same as in the pilot studies, and the effects were the same as in the value ratings just described.

3. Eleven syllogistic reasoning items were then presented. Each item contained two premises and four possible conclusions. The task of the subject was to indicate which of the conclusions was correct, given that the two premises were true. Only one conclusion could be selected for each item. (This part of the questionnaire was responded to by 75 subjects.)

4. Finally, the main questionnaire contained a number of statements and questions designed to measure knowledge of alcohol and its effects. In all, 34 statements and questions were presented. Fifty-seven subjects answered these questions. Syllogistic reasoning and knowledge of alcohol were scored in terms of the number of correct responses.

Finally, a few selected subjects were interviewed at a special occasion in order to find out more information about what thought processes had generated their ratings of probability and value.

Results

For all subjects, probability ratings were plotted against value ratings over all the 21 proposed alcohol effects. Probabilities and values were correlated for each subject. Scatter plots were obtained to study any nonlinearities. F and eta values were also computed to test deviations from linearity. Based on these plots and the computed correlations, the subjects were classified in four different groups. The first group, consisting of 45 subjects, had low correlations between probabilities and values and had no systematic trends in their plots. In a second group, consisting of seven subjects, there was a clear indication of positive intercorrelation be-

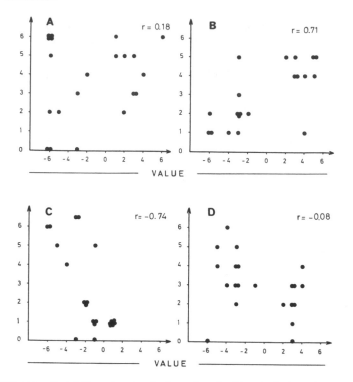

FIG. 8.1.   Probability-value plots for four selected subjects in Study 1. The plots exemplify an inconsistent relation (A), a positive relation (B), a negative relation (C), and a U-shaped relation (D).

tween probabilities and values, whereas a third group, consisting of 14 subjects, gave clear evidence of the opposite: a negative interrelationship between probabilities and values. Finally, a fourth group, consisting of 26 subjects, gave some indications of a nonlinear, U-shaped relationship when probabilities were plotted against values. The minimum probability value most often coincided approximately with a rating of 0 value on the bipolar rating scale of value. Typical examples from the four groups of subjects are given in Fig. 8.1.

The mean scores on the test of alcohol knowledge and the syllogistic-reasoning test are given in Tables 8.1 and 8.2 respectively. The tables also give standard deviations within the four groups. There is a weak trend indicating that the group with no clear relationship between probabilities and values had the largest amount of knowledge, but there is no evidence that this group also was superior in syllogistic reasoning. Furthermore, the differences in Tables 8.1 and 8.2 are not significant in the expected direction.

Finally, four selected subjects were interviewed and asked to explain in more detail certain of their ratings. The ratings were selected so as to cover the entire

TABLE 8.1
Knowledge of Alcohol Related Questions in Four Groups of Subjects

	Inconsistent	Positive Relation	Negative Relation	U-shape
Mean	15.36	15.23	14.67	14.46
Standard deviation	2.82	2.55	3.86	2.86

area of the scatter plot of probabilities against values of the 21 alcohol effects. The subjects were selected so as to represent each of the four groups of types of relationships.

The interviews suggested that the concept of alcohol gave rise to images that were either positive, negative, or both. A subject with a U-shaped relationship between probabilities and values had both positive and negative images of values and indicated some ambivalence about the concept of alcohol. The subject who had a very strong negative relationship between probabilities and values also had strong negative images referring back to childhood experiences. She had a morally condemning attitude toward alcohol and, although she accepted on the surface that alcohol might have some positive effects, she felt that these effects were not positive as long as they were due to alcohol. For example, she believed that relaxation was in itself positive but that this as an affect of alcohol, could lead to addiction.

Subjects tended to reason about probabilities in a value-free manner, but their reasoning concerning values often was contaminated by considerations of probability and by their unwillingness to rate value in the abstract. They seemed to refer their ratings to other goal states instead of the simple effect of alcohol that we had considered in constructing our questionnaire.

The interviews suggested to us that the images aroused by the concept of alcohol were the immediate basis of evaluation of the attitude object. Images were also directing the search for arguments, and they were more directive the stronger they were. The directive influence of the images influenced the value conceptions and put the values into a larger moral framework according to the original evaluation of the attitude object. In this way, consistency was achieved for subjects who had either a dominance of strong positive or strong negative

TABLE 8.2
Syllogistic Reasoning Scores in Four Groups of Subjects

	Inconsistent	Positive Relation	Negative Relation	U-shape
Mean	6.34	6.33	6.14	6.67
Standard deviation	2.48	3.84	2.17	2.73

images, and the ambiguous U-shaped pattern was obtained for the subject with both negative and positive images. The neutral subject gave no clear consistent relationship.

Discussion

The main investigation of Study 1 showed the same trend as the pilot study. A sizable portion of the subjects showed interaction between beliefs and values, and these interactions were different for different subjects. Pooling these data (a procedure commonly used by Fishbein) to compute a group intercorrelation would yield an overall correlation around 0, concealing the important and different consistent relationships found at the individual level.

The achievement and reasoning test did not indicate any clear differences in cognitive strategies and efficiency of the four groups of subjects when subjects were classified according to the type of relationship between probabilities and values. However, suggestive observations were obtained from interviews with four selected subjects. These interviews tended to support the idea that evaluations were not based on probabilities and values but were rather prior to them and were contained in images aroused by the attitude concept. These images tended to direct reasoning and in particular values seemed to be vulnerable to all sorts of redefinitions and twistings.

Fishbein's procedure calls for ratings of value in the abstract. Our results indicate that people may not wish to consider values in the abstract, i.e., without reference to a specific attitude object, unless utmost care is taken in defining the goal structure applied by the subjects. This point obviously calls for more empirical work.

STUDY 2[1]

The purpose of Study 2 was to follow up the findings of Study 1 in three respects. First, the finding of common and consistent patterns of interaction was to be generalized to a new type of content. Second, the suggestion that the sign of the interaction is dependent on whether the subject has a positive or negative attitude to the object was to be tested. Third, the suggestion that the interactions should be stronger when people are more involved in an object was also to be tested. The predictions were thus:

1. People with a positive attitude toward an object should have a positive interaction between beliefs and values concerning that object. The reverse should be true for people with a negative attitude to the object.

---

[1]This study was made possible through the courtesy of Dr. Martin Fishbein, who provided the data.

2. People with a high degree of stated interest or involvement in the area in question should show higher degrees of interaction than people with low degrees of interest.

Method

Subjects. The data analyzed here concerned political attitudes in Great Britain just before the parliamentary elections of the fall of 1974. Data were provided from a larger study. All of the subjects in the present analysis came from the same constituency. The constituency was a marginal one that switched during the election from Conservative to Labour. The total number of subjects analyzed and reported was 90.

Procedure. The subjects were interviewed about a number of background variables and their political attitudes. For the present purposes, two background questions are utilized: the party preference stated (Labour, Conservative, Liberal, or do not know) and the degree of interest in politics. The degree of interest in politics was stated in four categories (extremely interested, quite interested, slightly interested, and not interested at all). The present data analysis utilized two categories: extremely interested and not interested at all.

The subjects were then asked to rate 16 possible political actions on a value scale with seven categories going from extremely good to extremely bad. The political actions were:

1. Selling council houses to tenants.
2. Subsidies on essential foods.
3. Public ownership of building land.
4. Statutory wage control.
5. Curbing inflation with policies that increase unemployment.
6. The wealth tax.
7. Increased help for farmers.
8. Stricter immigration laws.
9. Government price control.
10. Nationalization of large companies.
11. Membership in the Common Market.
12. Private pay beds in National Health Service Hospitals.
13. Comprehensive schools.
14. Reducing mortgage rates.
15. Reducing the power of the Trade Unions.
16. Stronger measures to maintain law and order.

The subjects were then asked to rate the probability for each party, party leader, and local candidate of being in favor of each one of the 16 political actions. These ratings were made on a seven-category scale going from extremely likely to extremely unlikely.

Thus, value ratings in the abstract of the political actions were obtained and also nine sets of probability ratings, three sets for each party (the party itself, the party leader, and the local candidate). In the following analyses, the party, the party leader, and the local candidate have been pooled, thus generating 48 data points for each plot of probabilities versus values and three plots for each subject: one Conservative plot, one Liberal plot, and one Labour plot.

Results

As already mentioned, there were three plots of subjective probability versus values for each subject. All of the plots were analyzed according to the same

TABLE 8.3
Intercorrelations Between Beliefs and Values for Subjects
"Extremely Interested" in Politics[a]

| | Rated Party | | |
	Labor	Conservative	Liberal
Labor Subjects:			
1.	95	−70	13
2.	96	−72	21
3.	64	−66	−37
4.	30	−18	07
5.	71	−12	14
6.	83	−89	−81
7.	81	−19	—[b]
8.	60	−53	−14
9.	73	−20	37
10.	84	−57	−25
Conservative Subjects:			
1.	09	45	30
2.	−27	76	23
3.	−36	60	17
4.	−95	98	−76
5.	−56	86	−27
6.	−54	17	19
7.	−20	80	41
Liberal Subjects:			
1.	21	01	64
2.	−30	61	93
3.	49	−19	83
4.	−67	11	40
5.	40	14	92
6.	−38	48	79

[a]Zeroes and decimal points omitted.
[b]Ratings not available.

general strategy as in Study 1. Scatter plots were obtained and eta values and F ratios were computed to find any deviations from linearity. A few such deviations were found, but they showed no systematic tendencies in the present study and need not be dealt with further. The tendencies of the data were well-described by linear product-moment correlations.

The first prediction to be tested was the prediction that positive correlations will be obtained for positively evaluated objects and negative correlations for negatively evaluated objects. The signs and sizes of the correlations for the group of subjects stating that they were "extremely interested ' in politics can be found in Table 8.3.

A glance at Table 8.3 shows immediately that the prediction was confirmed. Subjects in favour of Labour had positive Labour correlations and negative correlations for the Conservative party. The reverse was true for those who were in favor of the Conservatives, and a similar trend may be detected for the Liberals. It may also be noted that the Liberal party apparently was considered as somewhere in between the Labour party and the Conservative party. Those who were in favor of the Labour party tended to have a negative correlation for their Liberal plots, but not as strongly negative correlations as they had for the Conservative party. A similar trend can be pointed out for the plots of Conservatives regarding the properties of the Liberal party.

The second prediction to be tested was that smaller correlations would be obtained in subjects who were not interested in politics. Those subjects who stated that they were not at all interested in politics may be found in Table 8.4. A glance at Table 8.4 is sufficient to prove the point. The correlations are generally

TABLE 8.4
Intercorrelations Between Beliefs and Values for Subjects
"Not Interested at All" in Politics[a]

	Rated Party		
	Labour	Conservative	Liberal
Labour Subjects			
1	36	−26	17
2	19	39	22
Conservative Subjects			
1	−01	20	31
2	08	62	22
3	10	68	00
Liberal Subjects			
1	−13	36	38
2	09	18	33
3	08	31	12
4	12	03	10

[a]Zeroes and decimal points are omitted.

quite low with few exceptions, and the contrast is striking when compared to Table 8.3.

Discussion

Results such as the ones reported in Study 2 may arise due to several different types of individual differences. People may differ as to values, probabilities, or both. It is very likely that some of the trends of Table 8.3 and Table 8.4 are due to differences in value. An interesting further step in the study of interactions between beliefs and values in the field of political attitudes would be to obtain enough information to make possible a separate study of effects where values do not differ among different groups of subjects. If interactions still exist in such a case, one may conclude more strongly that beliefs and values interact. Examples of such properties with possibly invariant value would be highly evaluated concepts such as honesty and realism.

STUDY 3

The purpose of Study 3 was to replicate and further generalize the findings of Study 1 and 2. In particular, it was considered to be of interest to investigate further the relationship between degree of involvement and size of interaction and between attitude and direction of interaction. Also, further interviews were to be performed with subjects selected to represent different types of relationships between probabilities and values.

Method

The 21 alcohol effects of Study 1 were investigated also in this study, and the ratings of the effects both as to value and probability were made in the same manner as in Study 1. However, the ratings were preceeded by two questions— one concerned with interest in alcohol questions to be rated on a scale from 0 to 6 and one concerned with the attitude toward alcohol to be rated on a bipolar scale from −3 to +3.

Sixty-five subjects participated in the study. They were students of a boarding high school in the neighborhood of Göteborg. Because several subjects either misunderstood the instructions or submitted incomplete ratings, only 51 could be used for data analysis. All of the following analyses are based on 51 subjects.

A few weeks after the main data collection, interviews were performed with eight subjects who represented different types of relationships.

Results

Plots of probabilities against values again produced four types of relationships: no consistent relationship (16 subjects); a consistent negative relationship (23 subjects); a consistent positive relationship (2 subjects); and a U-shaped relationship (10 subjects). No representative plots are given here because they are very much similar to the ones in Study 1. However, it is noteworthy that there were so few positive correlations in the present data.

The expected relationship between attitude and direction of relationship was present, although not strongly. When sign of intercorrelation between probabilities and values was cross-tabulated with attitude (combining neutral and positive ratings to one category), a χ^2 of 2.84 was found (.05 < p < .10). A regression analysis of size of correlation regardless of sign plotted against degree of interest in alcohol questions resulted in a correlation of .18 (.05 < p < .10). Thus, the prediction of a relationship between degree of consistency and degree of involvement was also supported by the present data.

As mentioned earlier, eight subjects were selected for further interviews and asked about their reasons for rating alcohol effects the way they had done. These interviews confirmed, in general, the findings of Study 1. The subjects who had exhibited either clear positive or negative relationships between probabilities and values were quite inclined to redefine the values of the effects according to considerations above and beyond the context of the questionnaire. A subject with a positive relationship would be inclined to accept in the abstract the positive value of, say, being happy or relaxed from drinking alcohol, but he or she would at the same time deny or belittle any long-term effect of negative events. The same kind of strategies but with opposite content were used by the subjects with negative linear relationships. Thus, accepting effects in the abstract and sticking to the defined concrete situation was done only when it fitted the general attitude of the subject. Otherwise, various supportive arguments were brought forward to strengthen or belittle the value in question according to the general trend of the ratings. Sometimes the probabilities themselves were also affected by the attitude, but this happened only rarely.

An amusing phenomenon was the double denial of one subject who was negative toward alcohol and claimed both that it would be very negative to be calm by drinking alcohol and also that it was quite improbable that such an effect would occur. (Such double denial should show up as bad fit in Fishbein's attitude model.) One interviewed subject had a U-shaped relationship. She was more inclined to stay with the definition of the effects in the questionnaire but also tended to bring in more long-term considerations of a negative nature. Finally, one subject had no consistent relationship. This subject tended to bring in factors in his value ratings that were quite unrelated to alcohol, saying that people differed, that the value depended on the context, time, situation, and so on.

Discussion

The findings of this study supported previous work reported in this paper. The fact that there were strikingly few positive correlations may be attributed to a widespread negative attitude toward alcohol in this sample. The extreme difficul-

ties subjects had to stick to the definition of alcohol effects given in the questionnaire and to differentiate values and probabilities further testified to the validity
of the suggestion that values and probabilities are caused by attitudes rather than
the other way around. This was particularly true for values as revealed in the
interviews performed with eight selected subjects.

STUDY 4

Consistency of belief systems may be related to self-esteem (Aronson, 1968;
Greenwald & Ronis, 1978; Sjöberg, 1976; Wicklund & Brehm, 1976). Beliefs
that are central to a person's self-esteem should be particularly vulnerable to all
sorts of cognitive distortions, both in acutely threatening situations and in neutral
situations due to the need to construct and persist in having relatively stable
cognitive systems. One implication from this theory has already been tested: the
relationship between degree of consistency and involvement. In the present
study, the purpose was to test the hypothesis of a relationship between degree of
consistency and self-esteem, the assumption being that people with low self-
esteem tend to have more vulnerable belief systems and hence tend to succumb
more easily to cognitive distortions leading to consistency. It was, therefore,
predicted that subjects low in self-esteem should have more consistency in their
belief value systems.

Method

Sixty subjects participated in this study. Of these, 36 were students of a boarding
high school in the neighborhood of Göteborg and 24 were students of psychology
at the University of Göteborg. One of the subjects showed a highly divergent
value of self-esteem and was discarded from the analysis.

The subjects were instructed to give ratings of alcohol effects including alcohol attitudes and degree of interest in the same manner as in Study 3. When
they had concluded their alcohol ratings, they were given a Swedish version of
the Tennessee Self-Concept Scale (Fitts, 1965; Löfvander & Ulveson, 1977).
This scale allows for a number of different scoring systems to be applied to the
self-concept as revealed by responses to the items. However, in this study, use
was only made of the simple score measuring the overall evaluation of the self.
This score has a satisfactory reliability in the Swedish version.

Results

Correlations between probabilities and values were computed for each subject,
and the self-concept score was plotted against these correlations. The plot
showed the expected inverted U-shape. Correlations between self-concept scores

and correlations between probabilities and values were computed separately for positive probability-value correlations and negative probability-value correlations. The first mentioned correlation was $-.39$ (p $<$ .05), and the latter correlation was .34 (p $<$ .05). The number of subjects who had positive probability-value correlations was 24 and the number of subjects with negative probability-value correlations was 35.

The relations between direction and intensity of attitude and degree of belief-value correlation were studied here as well as in Study 3. Sign of correlation was cross-tabulated with direction of attitude, pooling neutral and positive attitudes in one category. The resultant value of χ^2 with 1 df was 3.84 (p $<$ .05), according to the prediction. However, degree of interest did not correlate with belief-value correlation (r $=$ .08). There was a certain correlation between degree of interest and self-esteem (r $=$ .37) and, when self-esteem was partialled out, degree of interest again correlated with belief-value correlation (r $=$ .24; .05 $<$ p $<$ .10).

Discussion

The prediction of a straightforward relationship between self-evaluation and degree of consistency in the belief system under study was confirmed by the present data. The trends in the negative and positive parts of the plot seemed to be about equally strong.

Recently, Greenwald and Ronis (1978) pointed out that contemporary approaches to cognitive consistency tend to stress self-esteem motives rather than an abstract drive toward logical consistency, which seems to be more in line with the original proposal by Festinger (1957). The present data are in line with that suggestion.

STUDY 5

In several of the sets of data reported, there was an indication that some subjects had a U-shaped relationship between probabilities and values. Such a relationship may indicate ambivalence toward the attitude object because both very positive and very negative properties are rated as highly likely whereas more neutral properties are rated as unlikely. The purpose of Study 5 was to test this interpretation of the U-shaped relationship by means of investigating a group believed to have deeply ambivalent attitudes toward the attitude object of alcohol. We predicted a general trend of a U-shaped relationship for this group.

Method

Ten subjects were recruited from a clinic for severe abusers of alcohol. They responded to the questionnaire in the same manner as the subjects of Studies 3 and 4. Two of the alcoholics did not complete the questionnaire in such a way as to make it possible for us to use their data. Hence, the reported analyses utilized the data for eight subjects only.

Results

Individual data were plotted, and trends toward U-shaped relationships were clearly evident. In order to describe the results in a concise and quantitative manner, all of the ratings were pooled according to the sign of the value rating (value ratings of 0 were deleted from the analysis). Hence, all effects with a positive value rating were pooled in one plot, and all effects with a negative value rating were pooled in another plot of probabilities against values. Correlations between probabilities and values were computed in these two plots. It was found that for positive values the correlation was .55 (N = 47, p < .01). For negative values, however, the correlation was not significant (r = .05). Clearly, there was a difference between the correlations in the two plots. But, we had expected a clear negative correlation in the plot of negative values. This prediction was not confirmed.

A reason for the lack of a negative correlation can be found in a strong tendency toward bimodality in probabilities or very negative effects. In Fig. 8.2 there is a plot of the ratings of probability for both extremely positive and extremely negative effects. The plot of positive effects shows the expected distribution, which is in line with a positive intercorrelation between probabilities and values for that plot. However, for negative values there is a bimodal distribution. The subjects denied a large number of very negative effects, but they also confirmed a large number of negative effects. This oscillation between confirmation and denial is in line with the general concept of ambivalence toward the attitude object.

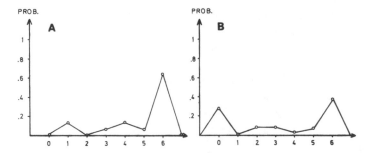

FIG. 8.2. Distributions of probability ratings for extremely positive (A) and extremely negative (B) ratings of value in Study 5.

Discussion

Although present data came from only eight subjects, the results were clear enough to warrant the conclusion that they supported the interpretation of a U-shaped relationship as an indication of ambivalence. It may be noted once more that this ambivalence would not have been discovered if data analysis had not been performed with individual subjects, making it possible to discover idiosyncratic trends and to introduce considerations beyond the simple linear model approach.

GENERAL DISCUSSION

The present results suggest that interactions between probabilities and values are strong and common. In the present section, I relate these findings to the reasoning of the introduction and to some general aspects on attitude and decision-making models.

People with a strong interaction appear to be both strongly concerned with the area in question and to have a pronounced viewpoint. Their belief systems appear to be "frozen": They do not easily or willingly differentiate probabilities and values. Their values are lacking in robustness, and they do not differentiate clearly between properties and effects in the abstract and properties and effects due to the attitude object. Such people appear to be, as it were, unidimensional in their way of functioning. Those who had no pronounced degrees of interaction, on the other hand, showed some subtlety in their value conceptions and did differentiate values and probabilities and also values and the attitude object. It would be of interest to study further whether people with low belief-value correlations can, or accept to, make ratings of value in the abstract.

It is interesting to speculate about whether the interactions we observed were the result of acute stress or due to more stable structures of a chronical nature. Possibly the latter is a more likely interpretation, although some subjects in the alcohol study and possibly some subjects in the political-attitude study may have been emotionally aroused. This means that we have studied mostly the products of belief distortion rather than the distortion itself. The point may be too subtle, however. In the process of constructing probabilities and values, those of our subjects who had a large degree of interaction also showed evidence of various distortion mechanisms. Saying something good about a bad object or something bad about a good object was simply something they wanted to avoid at the cost of some loss of intellectual honesty and distorted reasoning. Still, it would be of interest to investigate more directly if the degree of belief-value interaction increases as a function of emotional arousal and if such arousal is related to imagery. Shepard's studies of imagery point to the importance of images in mental functioning (Shepard, 1978) and provide an important example of the rising interest in imagery in studies of thinking.

Attitude objects may also be seen as choice objects. The consequences that various alternative choice objects lead to may be seen as their properties, and it is well-known that decision theory specifies which choice object to select given certain values of the outcomes and their subjective probabilities. Lack of rationality is often seen as lack of ability to combine values and subjective probabilities in a manner specified by some optimal decision rule. The present approach, however, suggests that the question of rationality goes much deeper (see Sjöberg, 1979).

Hence, various decision rules may differ rather little as compared to the distortions that may be brought about in generating probabilities and values themselves. What is really at stake may be mostly that individuals are not clear about their own needs and intentions and that they deceive themselves. In so doing, they construct a rigid and unidimensional view of the world with a lack of contact with reality. In such cases, what is called for is not decision analysis and application of an optimal decision rule. Rather, it is the clarification of the person's needs and true intentions. Toda (1981) has recently suggested that there are two modes of decision making that one may loosely describe as intuitive and analytical, corresponding to two mental systems of different phylogenetic origins and age. Now, decision making and consequent action may be primarily performed in the intuitive mode. Sometimes, however, there may be delay of action and analytical scrutiny according to the analytical mode. However, it may be far more common to find the analytical mode used for the justification of decisions already made and acts already carried out. In such cases, beliefs and values are humble servants under the rule of imagery, useful to justify decisions but never the cause of decisions. And their fragile ability as information processors shows up in "frozen" belief-value systems, reflected in belief-value intercorrelations of different types and sizes.

In the analyses performed on Studies 1–4, there have also been some indications of still other types of nonlinearities. These have, however, been rather rare and less clear than the U-shaped relationship. Obviously, it is hard to decide on just what relationship is revealed in plotting data like the present ones, particularly with rather few data points. Further studies with more dense sampling of properties and more data points would be of interest, as would attempts to relate properties of belief systems in different areas to each other. Would, for example, subjects with high consistency in one belief area also have high consistencies in other areas? Is ambivalence to be expected more generally or is it restricted to one belief area?

ACKNOWLEDGMENTS

This study was supported by a grant from the Swedish Council for Social Science Research. The author is indebted to Per Håkan Ekberg and Tommy Jonsson (Study 1) and

Lillemor Adrianson (Studies 2-5) for their help in planning and carrying out data collection and data analyses.

REFERENCES

Anderson, N. H. Note on functional measurement and data analysis. *Perception & Psychophysics,* 1977, *21,* 201-215.

Aronson, E. Dissonance theory: Progress and problems. In R. B. Abelson, E. Aronson, W. J. McGuire, T. M. Newcomb, M. J. Rosenberg, & P. H. Tannenbaum (Eds.), *Theories of cognitive consistency: A sourcebook.* Chicago: Rand McNally, 1968.

Festinger, L. A. *A theory of cognitive dissonance.* Stanford, Cal.: Stanford University Press, 1957.

Fishbein, M., & Ajzen, J. *Belief, attitude, intention and behavior: An introduction to theory and research.* Reading, Mass.: Addison-Wesley, 1975.

Fitts, W. *Tennessee Self Concept Scale. Manual.* Nashville, Tenn.: Counsellor Recordings & Tests, 1965.

Greenwald, A. G., & Ronis, D. L. Twenty years of cognitive dissonance: Case study of the evolution of a theory. *Psychological Review,* 1978, *85,* 53-57.

Löfvander, M.-B., & Ulveson, N. *Psykoterapi och självuppfattning.* Master's thesis, Department of Psychology, University of Stockholm, 1977.

Shepard, R. N. The mental image. *American Psychologist,* 1978, *33,* 125-137.

Sjöberg, L. The dimensionality paradox in comparative judgment: A resolution. *Scandinavian Journal of Psychology,* 1968, *9,* 97-108.

Sjöberg, L. Self esteem and information processing. *Göteborg Psychological Reports,* 1976, *6,* No. 14.

Sjöberg, L. Strength of belief and risk. *Policy Sciences,* 1979, *11,* 39-57.

Toda, M. What happens at the moment of decision? Meta decisions, emotions and volitions. In L. Sjöberg, T. Tyszka, & J. Wise (Eds.), *Decision processes.* Lund, Sweden: Doxa, 1981.

Tversky, A. Intransitivity of preferences. *Psychological Review,* 1969, *76,* 31-48.

Wicklund, R. A., & Brehm, J. W. *Perspectives on cognitive dissonance.* Hillsdale, N.J.: Lawrence Erlbaum Associates, 1976.

9 Multidimensional Scaling of Attitudes: Intra- and Interindividual Variations in Preferences and Cognitions

Hubert Feger
Universitat Hamburg, West Germany

1. SOME THEORETICAL BACKGROUND

This paper is mainly concerned with the analysis of attitude structure by models of nonmetric multidimensional scaling (MDS). We think that the analysis of attitude structure is fundamental for attitude research. We do not believe that every person has an attitude toward every object, as is suggested by the application of classical attitude measurement procedures to representative samples. On the contrary, we consider it necessary to prove that an individual holds an attitude toward one or more objects, called the attitude domain. Then it seems necessary to specify criteria that allow one to judge whether an attitude exists or not. In the literature, several characteristics of attitudes are mentioned, among them:

1. Attitudes are related to social objects—in contradistinction to personality traits, which are not oriented toward a specific external object.
2. Attitudes are relatively stable, usually more stable than motives and less stable than personality traits.
3. Attitudes are learned.
4. Attitudes generalize over different aspects of a social object or over different objects of the same domain.
5. Attitudes show structure, e.g. cognitive, evaluative, and intentional components.

Some of these characteristics are not well-suited to serve as criteria for testing whether an attitude exists. This seems to be the case for the time-related properties such as learning and stability. The most appropriate criterion seems to be that attitudes have structure. All procedures of direct attitude measurement can be understood as attempts to project structural assumptions into self-descriptive statements of persons whose attitudes are about to be measured. Partly in contrast with older techniques of attitude measurement the following study—as well as previous ones (Feger, 1974, 1975, 1976; Feger & Wieczorek, 1980)—is based on the following assumptions:

1. An attitude is a psychological organization of a single person, not a group. Therefore, the individual is the basis for beginning an analysis of attitudes. If one wants to study attitudes of a group, then one has to make explicit and to justify the steps and assumptions chosen in the process of aggregation.

2. Although one may plan to measure the attitude toward a single object or aspect of an object, we assume that the psychological organization extends over several objects in an attitude domain or over several aspects of an attitudinal object. This organization may be analyzed as a structure and as a process. Thus, in measuring cognitive, affective, or other orientations toward one attitudinal object, one is comparing this object with other objects. And this fact—that all measurement implies comparison—should be explicitly considered, e.g., by including several objects or aspects in the structural analyses.

3. An analytical (not necessarily an empirical) distinction can be drawn between a cognitive and an evaluative orientation toward attitude objects or aspects. Other distinctions are possible, of course, but in this study we concentrate on these two. We assume that in every attitude structure we can distinguish between relations that express the cognitive orientation and others that express evaluations. The relationship between cognitions and evaluations is one basic problem in attitude structure research, and this paper tries to clarify this problem.

4. If we gather data on several subjects or repeatedly on the same subject, there will be variability. We consider it reasonable to partition the information in the data into one part that is common to all subjects or constant over replications and into another part that varies. Because attitudes are mainly learned, and differences or changes in attitude are also assumed to be learned, we expect constancies and interindividual agreement in those parts of attitudinal organizations, where the learning history was the same for all subjects or the learning environment did not change during the time of observation.

2. MAIN EMPIRICAL QUESTIONS

The analysis of attitude structure, guided by the principle mentioned before, is done in four steps. In the first step, we investigate the reliability of the data. The basic observations in direct attitude measurement are verbal judgments. These judgments are related to states and processes which are observable only by the subject making the judgments. Because attitudes are supposed to have a certain temporal stability, we demand that the data generated by every single person show high reliability. In the second step, we ask whether there is structure in the data of every individual. Specifically, we investigate whether the cognitive and evaluative relations between political parties or institutions as reported by a person are representable by an MDS solution with low dimensionality. In the third step, we turn to the relations between repeated measurements on the same subject and try to describe constancies and changes in individual attitude structure by a model of MDS with intra- and interindividual differences. In the fourth step, the same model from the PINDIS approach of Lingoes and Borg (e.g., Borg, 1977) is applied to represent intra- and interindividual differences simultaneously.[1]

3. A LONGITUDINAL ANALYSIS OF ATTITUDE STRUCTURE

3.1. Data Collection[2]

Nine subjects participated voluntarily and without payment in this study. Three were majors in psychology, two others were also students. The remaining four subjects were of about the same age (21 to 33 years) but working in different fields. Four were female. There were 12 measurement trials, the first on June 2, 1976. The intervals between these measurement trials were approximately 3 weeks. The whole time covered was thus 36 weeks. A written instruction was given to each subject individually. It asked the subject to rate the closeness of several stimuli. We used 10 stimuli:

1. NPD: Nationalist party.
2. CSU: Bavarian Christian party.
3. CDU: Conservative party.
4. FDP: Liberals.
5. SPD: Social Democrats.
6. DKP: Communists.
7. Gewerkschaften: trade unions.
8. Kirche: the church.
9. Arbeitgeberverband: employers union.
10. ich selbst: I myself (Explained as the own position of the subject giving the ratings.)

---

[1]To avoid misunderstandings, we are not interested in causal analysis of attitude change and therefore not in the effects of repeated measurement.

[2]Data were collected by Ms. H. Hocke and Ms. D. Immig, whom we want to thank very much for their patient and skillful work.

All 45 pairs of these 10 stimuli were formed, and each subject was asked individually to give a rating on a scale ranging from 1 = außerordentlich nahe (extremely close) to 21 = außerordentlich fern (extremely far). On every measurement trial this was done three times, giving 135 ratings per trial, and 12 × 135 = 1620 over all 12 trials per subject. The position of a stimulus in a pair and the sequence position of a pair were randomized for every subject. The pairs of stimuli were presented in a booklet, one pair on each page. Subjects were to work at their own pace giving judgments for every pair in succession without turning back to responses already made.

In the postexperimental interviews, the subjects described the task as boring and tiring. It demanded a lot of concentration. Also, some subjects felt stimulated to think about relations that they previously had not thought about. Some subjects reported changes of the judgmental criteria during and between the trials. Preference judgments, i.e., those including the stimulus "I myself," were reported to be easiest. Some subjects remarked that a choice of some different stimuli would have changed their ratings considerably.

3.2. Reliability Analysis

As is well-known, results of studies on single subjects and of studies with repeated measurement are very vulnerable, if the data are not reliable. As some of our analyses are on repeated measurements of a single person, the question of reliability is a very important one. We choose to study the reliability by means of analysis of variance, as described in Winer (1971, pp. 283-296). With nine subjects and 12 replications, there are 108 analyses of the design reported in Table 9.1, with three measurements per replication and 45 pairs of stimuli to be judged by the subject on every trial, three times per replication, leading to 135 ratings per replication. The results of these analyses are given in Table 9.2. In this table, the unbiased estimates of r_k, the reliability of the mean of the k = 3

TABLE 9.1
Design for Reliability Analysis[a]

Pair of Stimuli	Measurement		
	First	Second	Third
1. (A,B)			
2. (A,C)			
45. (I,J)			

[a] In each of the 3 × 45 = 135 cells there is one rating given by the same subjects. As there are nine subjects and 12 replications, there are 108 analyses of this type, the results of which are reported in Table 9.2.

TABLE 9.2
Results of Reliability Analyses[a]

	Subject								
Replication	1	2	3	4	5	6	7	8	9
1	.95	.94	.92	.94	.97	.99	.93	.99	.97
2	.96	.96	.96	.97	.98	.99	.97	.99	.97
3	.97	.97	.98	.99	.98	.99	.97	.99	.97
4	.96	.94	.98	.99	.95	.99	.99	.99	.98
5	.97	.95	.95	.99	.97	.99	.95	1.00	.98
6	.96	.98	.94	.99	.99	.99	.98	1.00	.99
7	.99	.99	.99	.99	.98	.99	.96	.99	1.00
8	.99	.99	.98	.97	.99	.99	.98	1.00	.99
9	.99	.99	.97	.99	.96	.99	.99	.99	1.00
10	.99	1.00	.90	.99	.96	.99	.98	1.00	1.00
11	.98	.99	.99	.97	.99	1.00	.98	1.00	.99
12	.99	.99	.92	.97	.99	.99	.99	.99	.99
x	.98	.97	.96	.98	.98	.99	.97	.99	.99
s	.01	.02	.03	.02	.01	.00	.02	.00	.00

[a] This table reports the values of the unbiased estimation of r_k according to Winer, 1971, pp. 283–296.

ratings per pair, is reported because we intend to base the later analyses on these means. The reliability, i.e., the reproducibility over the three measurements within one replication, is very high—almost perfect—for all subjects. The nine subjects were apparently able to give stable judgments of the "closeness" of two stimuli, especially as far as the relative rank of the closeness of pairs of stimuli is concerned.

These positive results depend, of course, on the validity of the assumptions of the analysis of variance approach for our data. The error of measurement should be uncorrelated with the true score, which could be tested, e.g., using procedures of path analysis. The pairs of stimuli and the three measurements in a replication should be considered a random sample, which might be reasonable for the measurements. The pairs could be considered as a fixed factor, which would increase the values of the reliability coefficients (see Cronbach, Gleser, Nanda, & Rajaratnam, 1972).

An alternative to our method of reliability analysis could have been to apply MDS to every measurement first and then analyze the internal consistency of the scaled values. One reason not to go this way was—as could be expected—the lower reliability of a single measurement, r_1 in Winer's notation. Not that these coefficients were generally much lower than the r_k values, but they showed more variability and would have led to some MDS analyses of unreliable data. Another reason was that some of the MDS solutions, based on one rating per pair only, showed very high stress values (> .15 with 10 points and two dimensions), and we did not want to base further analyses on these solutions. As the rank order of the ratings is the information we intend to use, one could have calculated the average τ or Spearman's ρ (among others) between the three measurements of each replication. With our data, this leads to very similar results. The purist might then demand picking the median rank for further analyses. But then, we think, we would throw away too much information.

We thus feel justified to conclude that the reproducibility over the three measurements in the same situation—at the same hour, so to speak—is given.

3.3. Individual Representation for One Replication

Following our theoretical considerations, we next have to check whether there exists an attitude structure for every one of the nine subjects and at each of the 12 replications. It is not possible, of course, to check exhaustively whether any structure exists. So one has to make a choice among possible and plausible structural representations and to justify this choice by showing that the assumptions of the chosen representation model have interesting psychological interpretations. We have chosen the geometric model underlying MDS for the following reasons:

1. Similarity or closeness and preference are binary relations, and MDS models allow to represent binary relations, the intensity of which are represented by the length of distances between points.

2. The representation of attitude objects by points implies, in this case, that every object is most similar to itself (and that the ideal is preferred most). In contrast with some representations in quantitative sociometry (e.g. Feger, 1977), this seems plausible in analyzing attitude structure.

3. The model assumes symmetric distances between the points. This seems reasonable with the objects chosen in our investigation because none of the objects seem to be more prominent or more suited as a reference point when comparing two objects—conditions which according to Tversky (1977) might lead to asymmetric proximity relations.

4. The MDS model allows for variation in higher dimensional spaces. As previous work in this area has shown, the perception of political institutions or parties varies along more than one dimension, the "left-right" attribute is present almost always, and quite often one finds a dimension "moderate-extreme." Preference is thought of as being unidimensional by definition, but preference could be imbedded in a multidimensional structure.

5. A MDS representation implies transitivity and the triangular inequality for the distances. There is no general psychological theory under which conditions a metric representation of subjective judgments should be possible, but we think

that two conditions would help to elicit judgments suitable for a metric representation:

a. The objects to be judged should be well-known to the subject, and the relation to be judged should be in existence before the experiment begins—in contrast to requiring elaboration during the experiment.

b. The objects should be clearly distinguishable among each other. Therefore, we selected objects from the full range of political institutions.

We did $9 \times 12 = 108$ analyses of the mean ratings for every S on every replication with the program SSA-I (Lingoes, 1973) with one, two, and three dimensions. The coefficient of alienation for the unidimensional solution was too high in absolute terms ($> .15$), generally, and there were some degenerate solutions. Two dimensions seem to be sufficient. The average coefficient of alienation $= .056$, $s = .035$. The maximum stress observed was $.122$. There were no remarkable differences over replications, but over subjects with maximum average $= .097$ and minimum average $= .007$. As $.056$ is "good" according to Kruskal (1964) in absolute terms and acceptable relative to a null hypothesis of randomness (Wagenaar & Padmos, 1971, report $s = .15$ for 10 points), we decided that a MDS representation in two dimensions is possible for all 108 cases and continued the analysis with these two-dimensional SSA solutions.

3.4. Intraindividual Longitudinal Analysis of Attitude Structure

We now turn to the question of how the structure of attitudes toward the political institutions changes over 36 weeks. Inasmuch as this may be different for different subjects, we want to analyze each subject separately first and generalize later. To represent the intertrial variations as well as the intraindividual constancies we chose the PINDIS program, which contains several models. We were interested in three of these models to describe the data:

1. One that finds the centroid configuration that best represents the spaces of all intraindividual replications by using only admissible transformations. Transformations are admissible if they add no new information to that contained in the single configuration; admissible are rotation, translation, and central stretching or shrinking).
2. One model that allows additionally for different dimension weights per replication.
3. One model that uses the admissible transformation and vector weight from an origin to be chosen by the researcher or to be determined by the program to obtain the best fit.

The vector weights stretch or shrink the distances from the origin to every object point differently, and the weights may differ from one replication to the next. We chose stimulus 10 ("I myself") as the origin for the vectors, thus allowing intraindividual variability in preference to the social objects from trial to trial.

The results, reported in Table 9.3, come to us as a surprise because we expected less stability. The table gives fit coefficients R^2, which describe the degree of configurational similarity. The first column describes the fit of the model Z, X; this is the model that relates the single configuration X to the centroid space Z by admissible transformations only. As can be seen from Table 9.3, this model fits the data very well. This means that for most subjects the similarity of the political institutions as well as their own preference for these attitude objects did not change noticeably during the 36 weeks of observation, during which there was an intensive campaign for the election of the federal government.

Because the level of fit is already very high with the Z, X model, there could not be a large increase of fit for the models with more parameters. The models ZW, X—with dimensional weights W—gives a decrease of fit of only 1.6%. For subjects 3, 5, and 7 we have some increase of fit when comparing the Z, X model with the model VZ, X with vector weights. This increase is produced by $12 \times 9 = 108$ vector weights per person, and it is questionable whether such a large number of parameters is worth the small percentage (4.8% on the average) better fit. The data seem well-represented by a model that basically assumes no change in the perceived and evaluated configuration of the objects over the time of observation.

TABLE 9.3
Fit (R^2) for Nine PINDIS-Solutions Over 12
Intraindividual Replications Each

Subject	Z, X	ZW, X	VZ, X
1	.953	.956	.976
2	.926	.945	.968
3	.846	.898	.970
4	.931	.946	.949
5	.895	.899	.962
6	.978	.981	.995
7	.863	.879	.941
8	.946	.970	.984
9	.943	.948	.970
mean	.920	.936	.968
variance	.002	.001	.000

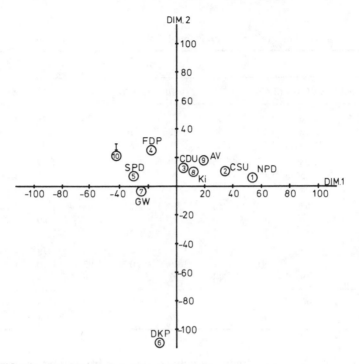

FIG. 9.1.   Centroid configuration of subject 3.

Applying these models to represent intraindividual change of attitude structure has some implications to which we turn now. Change is not represented by a trend model or by a stage model. These models seemed inappropriate for attitudes already well-established. The models chosen conceive—in this context—of structure as the potential of change. The psychological meaning of the centroid or joint space in these applications is—as we interpret it—basically a description of change potential. To illustrate this interpretation, we select subject 3 as an example, for whom we might be most willing to accept the vector model, and thus some intertrial variability in the configuration. Figure 9.1 shows the centroid configuration of this subject; Table 9.4 reports the vector weights of VZ, X for subject 3.

The vector weights are coefficients with which the distances between the origin in stimulus 10 and the points representing the other stimuli are to be multiplied to get the best fit between the centroid space and an individual space. They thus indicate a change in preference to the respective object relative to the preference as depicted in the joint configuration of Fig. 9.1. The larger the value, the less preferred is this object relative to the centroid space. So, as in trial 8 the distance to NPD and FDP are almost one half, this indicates a much larger change in attitude toward NPD because the distance to FDP is relatively small in

TABLE 9.4
Vector Weights for Intraindividual PINDIS Solution of Subject 3

	Stimulus								
Replications	(1)NPD	(2)CSU	(3)CDU	(4)FDP	(5)SPD	(6)DKP	(7)GW	(8)KI	(9)AV
1	1.70	1.26	1.33	1.42	.88	.76	1.19	1.40	1.19
2	1.22	1.26	1.30	1.50	1.10	.71	1.37	1.26	1.39
3	1.18	1.27	1.24	.98	1.33	.78	1.57	.97	1.31
4	1.08	1.12	1.16	1.68	1.14	.93	1.72	1.10	1.07
5	1.13	1.06	.97	1.20	.63	.81	1.22	1.06	1.10
6	1.09	.94	1.16	.74	2.12	.91	2.34	1.03	1.10
7	.67	.59	.55	.38	1.21	.92	1.48	.54	.62
8	.56	.61	.66	.51	1.14	.93	1.49	.79	.56
9	.60	.53	.53	.40	1.26	−.96	1.23	.45	.57
10	1.13	1.19	.98	1.15	2.17	.79	.79	1.03	.17
11	.97	.91	1.01	1.46	1.07	1.02	1.10	1.04	.82
12	.19	.24	.18	.03	−.13	1.16	.14	.23	.21
mean	.96	.92	.92	.95	1.16	.73	1.30	.91	.84
variance	.16	.12	.13	.29	.37	.30	.28	.12	.17

the centroid configuration compared with the distance from stimulus 10 to NPD. The negative weights indicate a change of the direction of the vector by 180°; this feature of the program should have been depressed in this application. We did not report the vector cosine values, which indicate how much the vector direction in the joint and in the single space agree, because there was very high agreement except for replication 12; the results of this replication could therefore be the starting point for new analyses with different models.

In Table 9.4, we see some change in preference for subject 3, especially a pronounced turn to more conservative political institutions on the seventh replication, which remains so for the eighth and ninth trials as well. This is in agreement with our assumption that changes usually do not occur for only one stimulus or few unrelated stimuli but for similar stimuli at the same time. This would correspond to a homogeneous stretching or shrinking of various coherent parts of the space over trials. We hope to further analyze this in a future study. One could calculate the variance of the vector weights as a measure of stability of the preference for a political institution. But then one should realize that the fitting procedure of PINDIS affects more variability for vector weights of stimuli close to the origin. Change measures on absolute distances are to be preferred.

Up to this point, we have discussed only changes in preferences. But the vector weights do not only change preferences relative to the joint configuration. They also simultaneously change the distances between stimuli other than the one in the origin. The dissimilarity between stimuli A and B, S_{AB}, is a function of the preference (to be precise: the disliking) for A, P_A, and of P_B, and of α, the angle between the preference vectors (see Fig. 9.2).

The exact function is taken from trigonometry: $S_{AB}^2 = P_A^2 + P_B^2 - 2P_A P_B \cos \alpha$, with two interesting special cases. If $\alpha = 0°$, we have $S_{AB} = P_A - P_B$. This is the unidimensional case with both stimuli on the same side of the ideal point. If $\alpha = 180°$, then $S_{AB} = P_A + P_B$. In this case the ideal point is between two stimuli on one dimension. Inasmuch as α is fixed, it is always possible to predict the third element if two of S_{AB}, P_A, and P_B are given. Thus, in our interpretation of the MDS model with vector weight, also called the perspective model, the relationship between similarity and preference is exactly specified. Similarity depends on the preferences and on α, which is a structural parameter independent of the preferences. If α gets larger, then the increase in similarity between two objects gets larger, if there is a homogeneous increase in the dislike for these two objects. It is assumed to be constant over replication for a pair of stimuli. The very good fit of the MDS models means that, indeed, over all replications for every individual there is a structural constancy as expressed in fixed alphas for all 36 pairs of social objects. What is stable in the structure even for subject 3, where we might have to resort to the perspective model, is the position of a stimulus in a certain segment of the space. Another possible way to imagine the variability that the model describes is to conceive of a star of vectors originating in the ideal point. The direction of these vectors is fixed. On the vectors, the points representing the stimuli move toward and away from the origin, thus at the same time representing changes in preference and strictly related changes in similarity. The strong implications of the model could also be

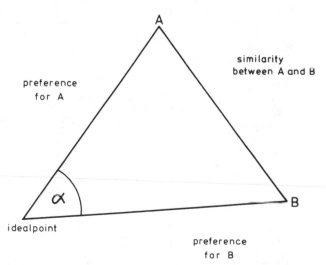

FIG. 9.2. Relationship between similarity and preferences in model VZ, X with stimulus 10 interpreted as ideal point.

formulated as follows: P_A is predictable from P_B and S_{AB}, but also from P_C and S_{AC}, etc. It does not matter which stimulus I chose. If I know the preference for this stimulus and the similarity to another stimulus, I can predict the preference for that stimulus.

Interpreting these MDS models with allowances for individual differences as models of change seems justified for well-established attitudes in a situation where the subject gets influencing messages of all kinds. The attitude system reacts to these messages flexibly, contracting or yielding and lashing back again. We assume that the degree of covariation between the preferences for two parties over time is positively correlated with their average similarity (in the centroid configuration). The MDS model, of course, does not describe all change that is possible in the system. The procedure of aggregating used by first calculating the means of three ratings within a measurement trial and then determining the SSA solution on which then the PINDIS application is based, can not detect changes of the overall mean. In such a change, a person would like or dislike all stimuli more than before, in proportion to his previous feelings. We used only the rank-order information. A common loss of prestige for all parties, as assumed to have happened recently, could therefore not be registered with this approach.

For subjects with a lower fit of the Z, X model, a large set of change-related questions open up, now analyzable with reliable data on a high scale level. For

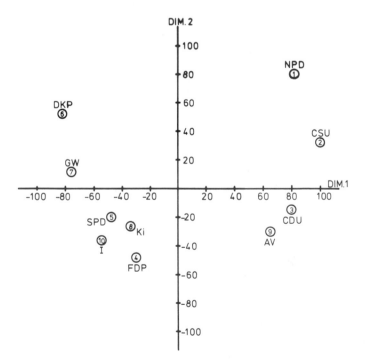

FIG. 9.3.   Centroid configuration of subject 1.

example, how is the preference for A in t = 1 related to P_A in t = 2? How is it related to P_B in t = 1 or t = 2? How is S_{AB} in t_1 related to P_A and P_B in t_2? Is the perceived closeness at a later time more determined by earlier preferences, or is preference change caused by previous change in perception? But, this question is answered by the model: Changes in similarity and in preferences are strictly simultaneous.

There are, as was to be expected, interindividual differences in attitude structure. To give some impression of the kind of differences, Figs. 9.3 and 9.4 give the joint configuration for subjects 1 and 2. For subject 2 the structure could probably be well-approximated by a simplex. Church, NPD, and DKP form a cluster despised equally, maybe experienced as ideological agencies. For all pairs of stimuli it holds that increasing the difference in preference means decreasing their similarity. This is in contrast to subject 3 where relatively large variations among the preferences and similarity between all pairs would not change those relations very much, in which the communist party is one member of the pair. The DKP is very dissimilar to all other stimuli, and the preference for this party strongly covaries with the similarity of this party to all other stimuli simultaneously. Whereas for subject 3 the second dimension was necessary mainly to describe the position of the DKP, the structure for subject 1 approximates a circumplex, leaving a large empty space between NPD and DKP for a party like the National-Socialists.

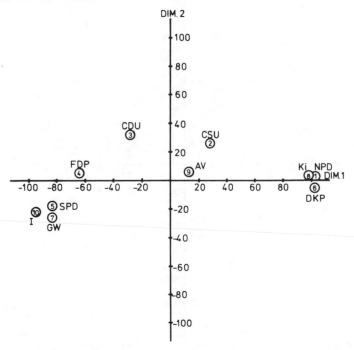

FIG. 9.4.   Centroid configuration of subject 2.

3.5. Simultaneous Representation of Inter- and Intraindividual Differences

The question now arises whether it is possible to represent the different subjects and their intraindividual variation by one model with a common configuration for all systematic variation in the data. What would be gained is obvious: If the perspective model fits, the constant alphas describe a structure common to all inter- and intraindividual replications despite large differences in preferences and similarities. Figures 9.1, 9.3, 9.4, and the other results of the intraindividual PINDIS solutions suggest that we might need just the vector model to represent all 108 SSA solutions. We tested Z, X, ZW, X, and VZ, X with the origin in stimulus 10 for all 108 SSA solutions simultaneously.

We found R^2 for Z, X = .787, for ZW, X = .829, and for VZ, X = .913. Although there is only a 4% increase in fit from the first to the dimension weight model, the increase to the vector model is 13%. We pay for this increase with 972 more parameters, and it is hard to say whether this price is too high. We suspect that the Z, X model would not fit as well if we had not such a small and homogeneous group of subjects, but a representative sample with a larger variability of the position of the ideal point.

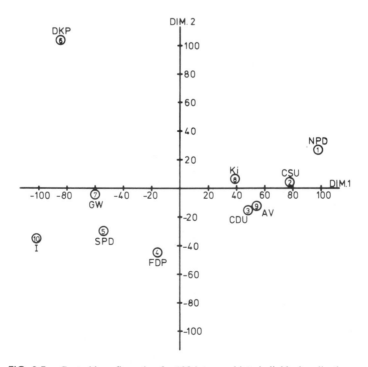

FIG. 9.5.   Centroid configuration for 108 inter- and intraindividual replications.

Figure 9.5 shows the centroid configuration of all intra- and interindividual replications. As in previous research, we find the simplex configuration from NPD over CSU, CDU, FDP, SPD to DKP, perhaps including the trade unions between SPD and DKP. The communist party is experienced as an outsider. The average preference is highest for the social democrats, lowest for NPD and DKP. The data reduction is considerable: from 14,580 ratings, to 4860 means, to 2160 SSA coordinates, and finally to 20 coordinates of the joint solution plus 972 vector weights.

The model suggests statements like: The preference of subject 3 for CDU is stronger than the preference of subject 7 for FDP. Thus, interindividual comparability is assumed, a problem usually not treated explicitly in attitude measurement. But, because we took only rank-order information about distances from every subject, assumptions must have been made to create the comparability. One relevant assumption was made when in applying the PINDIS algorithm we stretched or shrinked every SSA solution so that the overall scale factor was the same for every SSA solution. The overall scale factor is the square root of the sum of squares of the coordinate values of all stimuli (Borg, 1977, p. 610). Thus, the average intensity of the nine preferences and 36 similarities of one solution taken simultaneously is the same for every solution. (This does not mean that the average preference strength or the mean similarity taken separately are the same for every replication.) So, if distance $\overline{AB}$ in one solution is larger than $\overline{CD}$ in another solution, it is in both solutions relative to, or normed by, the same overall scale factor. Whether this procedure is psychologically meaningful for our data cannot be decided by clear-cut criteria. We think that by selecting stimuli that cover the whole range and almost exhaust the whole range, all subjects are led to make their judgments relative to this context. But, it would perhaps be a good idea to do sensitivity analyses with different normative assumptions.

4. DISCUSSION

We chose to gather both kinds of data—preferences and similarities—simultaneously and with the same observational method. We also chose to analyze them simultaneously—one analytical procedure handled all data together. There are, of course, alternatives to both decisions. We prefer to use one observational method only because this avoids confounding of possible differences between preferences and similarities by differences between judgmental processes created by two different data-gathering methods.

We do not intend here to compare the perspective model empirically with other models that relate preferences for and similarities between stimuli. But, we would like to make a few theoretical comments on just two basic models: Tucker's (1960) vector model and Coombs' (1964) unfolding theory with its multidimensional generalizations. Internal analyses, described by Carroll (1972) as:

". . . based entirely on the preference data for a set of individuals without reference to an outside or a priori set of stimulus dimensions [p. 114]," are not interesting in this context because they do not use similarity judgments in addition to preference judgments, and this rules out the detection of discrepancies between the configuration of stimuli in cognitive spaces and the configuration of stimuli in preference spaces.

Both Tucker's and Coombs' models assume a stimulus configuration that is identical for all replications. This is in contrast with the tradition in attitude research, which has found various interdependencies between cognitions and preferences, e.g., for attitudes toward political parties (Sjöberg & Capozza, 1975). In both models, individual differences are allowed to exist in preferences: Tucker's model accounts for them by varying the direction of the vectors, and Coombs' model by representing each individual by his or her own ideal point. The cosine theorem mentioned earlier is, of course, valid in both models. But, in the unfolding model there are different angles for the same pair of stimuli viewed from different ideal points, thus the α-values are not fixed. The vector model, as is well-known, can be seen as a special case of the unfolding model. To quote Carroll (1972):

> One can see this by conceptually moving the ideal point for an individual farther and farther out along a fixed line from the origin, while holding the stimuli constant. As one does this the rank order of distances from the ideal will approach (and will asymptotically be identical to) that of *projections* of stimuli onto a vector whose direction is the same as that of the line along which the ideal point is moved [p. 118].

The further out the ideal point is moved, the more α approaches zero, and in the limit we have the special case that for every subject considered separately in the vector model the equation holds: $S_{AB} = |P_A - P_B|$. Psychologically, this means that for a single subject only those differences between the stimuli that exist along the vector representing this subject are taken into account. In this sense, we have in this vector model an identity of the similarity dimension and the preference dimension for every subject, although different dimensions are provided for different subjects.

Thus, the perspective model is similar to external analyses in that it explicitly accounts for similarity as well as for preference data. It differs from the unfolding model in that it allows individual variation in the cognitive spaces and at the same time identifies a common segmental structure of the cognitive space. And it differs from the vector model in that it does not equate for every subject preference–differences with similarity–differences. It seems desirable to elaborate these differing theoretical implications of the models further and to base comparative model tests on them, not just on goodness-of-fit measures.

REFERENCES

Borg, I. Geometric representation of individual differences. In J. C. Lingoes (Ed.), *Geometric representations of relational data*. Ann Arbor, Mich.: Matheses Press, 1977.

Carroll, J. D. Individual differences and multidimensional scaling. In R. N. Shepard, A. K. Romney, & S. B. Nerlove (Eds.), *Multidimensional scaling* (Vol. 1). New York: Seminar Press, 1972.

Coombs, C. H. *A theory of data*. New York: Wiley, 1964.

Cronbach, L. J., Gleser, G. C., Nanda, H., & Rajaratnum, N. *The dependability of behavioral measurements: Theory of generalizability for scores and profiles*. New York: Wiley, 1972.

Feger, H. Die Erfassung individueller Einstellungsstrukturen. *Zeitschrift für Sozialpsychologie*, 1974, *5*, 242–254.

Feger, H. Längsschnittliche Erfassung intraindividueller Unterschiede bei Einstellungsstrukturen. In U. Lehr & F. Weinert (Hrsg.), *Entwicklung und Persönlichkeit*. Stuttgart: Kohlhammer, 1975.

Feger, H. *Einstellungsanalyse am Einzelfall*. Vortrag anläßlich des 12. Seminars des Institutes für die Pädagogik der Naturwissenschaften, Universität Kiel, 1976.

Feger, H. Quantitative sociometry: Problems, methods, and first results. In H. J. Hummell & R. Ziegler (Eds.), *Anwendung mathematischer Verfahren zur Analyse sozialer Netzwerke*. Duisburg: Sozialwissenschaftliche Kooperative, 1977.

Feger, H., & Wieczorek, T. Multidimensionale Skalierung in der Einstellungsmessung. In F. Petermann (Hrsg.), Einstellungsmessung-Einstellungsforschung. Göttingen: Hogrefe, 1980.

Kruskal, J. B. Multidimensional scaling by optimizing goodness of fit to a nonmetric hypothesis. *Psychometrika*, 1964, *29*, 1–27.

Lingoes, J. C. *The Guttman-Lingoes nonmetric program series*. Ann Arbor, Mich.: Matheses Press, 1973.

Sjöberg, L., & Capozza, D. Preference and cognitive structure of Italian political parties. *Giornale Italiano di Psicologia*, 1975, *2*, 391–402.

Tucker, L. R. Intra-individual and inter-individual multidimensionality. In H. Gulliksen & S. Messick (Eds.), *Psychological scaling: Theory and applications*. New York: Wiley, 1960.

Tversky, A. Features of similarity. *Psychological Review, 977, 84*, 327–352.

Wagenaar, W. A., & Padmos, P. Quantitative interpretation of stress in Kruskal's multidimensional scaling technique. *British Journal of Mathematical and Statistical Psychology*, 1971, *24*, 101–110.

Winer, B. J. *Statistical principles in experimental design* (2nd Ed.). New York: McGraw-Hill, 1971.

10 The Visual Perception of Texture: A Psychological Investigation of an Architectural Problem

Hannes Eisler
University of Stockholm

Gösta Edberg
*Royal Institute of
Technology,
Stockholm*

Whereas in the good old days building materials were few and "natural," like stone and wood, architects are now able to choose from a plethora of substances, both natural and artificial. Very often it is economic rather than esthetic considerations that dictate their choice. This development seemed to require a systematization of the available materials, not so much from a technical as from an experiential (psychological) point of view—what one might call the visual perception of texture.[1] Our interest in the study of textures also derives from the work of Gibson (1950, 1966). These considerations led Dr. Gösta Edberg to initiate the investigation that I am about to report. For a complete, detailed report (in Swedish) see Edberg, 1968, 1971, 1976, 1977.

SKETCH OF THE PROBLEM

The ultimate aim of the investigation was to construct a chart with standardized scales of textures, and for this the following problems had to be solved:

1. Which attributes does an observer of a texture spontaneously pay attention to?

---

[1]We use the term "texture" to denote both the surface structure of a material ("out there," "physically") and the perceived "visual texture" in the sense of Gibson (1950).

2. Can these attributes be related in a simple way to physically measurable properties (or relations between them) of surface structures? (Note the distinction between [subjective] attributes and [physical] properties.)
3. Can real textures be replaced by stylized textures suitable for a chart of relevant attributes?
4. How much do the attributes—relative to each other—contribute to the total impression of a surface texture?

EMPIRICAL APPROACH

Method

Subjects

In all experiments, the subjects were students of architecture. In order to have subjects who are fairly naive regarding systematic experience of textures, mostly students in their first two years at the Royal Institute of Technology, Stockholm, were chosen. In general, moreover, each subject participated in only one experiment.

Stimulus Material

1. Real Surfaces.   From a collection of 100 samples, three judges chose 50 "slabs" as being fairly representative of common surface qualities of building materials. Strongly colored items were avoided. The slabs were approximately of A4-format (297 mm × 210 mm) and varied in thickness. Seventeen of these 50 slabs were used in the Main Experiment 1 and are shown in Fig. 10.4.

2. Dot Patterns.   These were used as the stylized textures mentioned earlier (point 3 in the section "Sketch of the Problem"). Twenty-four two-dimensional dot patterns with four different diameters of the black dots and six center distances were used. Table 10.1 gives a description.

Experimental Setup

In most experiments, a carrousel formed as a regular hexagonal prism with a vertical axis was used. The sides were located 125 cm above the floor, in front of the seated observer's eyes. Each side was provided with two windows into which the slabs or dot patterns could be inserted. The carrousel was covered with gray cardboard, and the same cardboard covered the inside of each window, being visible when no stimulus was inserted. The distance between the subject's eyes and the windows was 125 cm, so that minor details of the slabs could be discerned, but not the texture of the cardboard. The experimenter and five subjects were seated facing the sides of the carrousel. While the subjects wrote down

TABLE 10.1
Measures of the 24 Dot Patterns as Shown on the
Small Screen and in the Carrousel

Dot Pattern Number	Total Number of Dots	Dot Diameter $\emptyset$ mm	Center Distance cd mm
1	1 656	0.89	6.3
2	1 656	1.50	6.3
3	1 656	2.34	6.3
4	1 656	3.70	6.3
5	690	1.35	9.6
6	690	2.30	9.6
7	690	3.60	9.6
8	690	5.70	9.6
9	221	2.40	17.0
10	221	4.00	17.0
11	221	6.30	17.0
12	221	10.00	17.0
13	63	4.50	31.8
14	63	7.50	31.8
15	63	11.80	31.8
16	63	18.70	31.8
17	27	7.30	52.0
18	27	12.30	52.0
19	27	19.30	52.0
20	27	30.60	52.0
21	12	11.00	78.0
22	12	18.50	78.0
23	12	29.00	78.0
24	12	46.00	78.0

their judgments, the experimenter changed the stimuli. Then, the carrousel was rotated $\frac{1}{6}$ revolution, and the procedure was repeated. Thus, each group of five subjects saw the stimuli in the same order. Each presentation took 10–20 seconds, depending on whether one or two stimuli were changed, which gave the subjects enough time to make their judgments without being stressed.

Though the same room was not used for all experiments, the conditions were practically uniform. The rooms had white walls, the illumination was artificial, of about 250–300 lux emanating from above, causing some shadow formation on the slabs, and was strong enough for detailed viewing of the slabs without causing glare.

When the dot patterns were shown alone, they were projected on two screens, either two small ones near the subjects or a small and a larger one, the latter farther away. Measurement of the illuminance on the screens showed satisfactory homogeneity within dots and between dots both of the same and of different patterns. The visual angle was always about 13° × 8°, the same as for the carrousel windows. In these experiments, three subjects participated in each session.

The subjects were asked to write down their judgments on prepared forms. Other experimental arrangements are described in connection with the particular experiment.

Pilot Studies

These studies were designed to indicate how textures can be handled by subjects in psychophysical experiments.

Pilot Study 1. Estimation of Texture-strength and Pleasantness in Real Textures

Thirty-two subjects carried out texture-strength estimations and 31 subjects pleasantness estimations. Most subjects participated in both tasks. The 50 slabs were presented to them in the carrousel (using only one window on each side), and the task was to estimate the experienced "strength" of the texture presented. No interpretation or definition of the attribute "texture-strength" was given. The method was magnitude estimation without standard, and it was exemplified by having the subjects judge straight lines of varying lengths on a blackboard. In the same way, pleasantness estimations were collected. Each slab was judged eight times (four times for texture-strength, four times for pleasantness). The whole experiment took about 1 hour for each subject and variable.

The individual means were correlated with the grand mean for both texture-strength and pleasantness estimations. Figure 10.1 shows the distribution of these correlations. For texture strength, with the exception of five subjects whose correlations lie below .5, the homogeneity in the judgments is high. This implies that texture strength is a rather robust attribute that can be judged consistently. The outcome is less favorable for pleasantness, showing lower correlations on the average and relatively more low correlations. Six subjects correlated low (< .4) throughout (see Fig. 10.1). Among the remaining 25 subjects, compara-

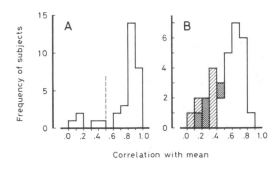

FIG. 10.1. Histograms for the correlations between individual means and the grand mean for texture strength (A) and pleasantness (B) estimations (32 and 31 subjects, respectively). The five subjects to the left of the dashed line in A were excluded in subsequent data treatment. In B, the hatched areas indicate the six excluded subjects; the filled areas show the subjects belonging to the deviant but coherent group of four subjects.

tively high intercorrelations were found for 21, as well as for the remaining four. A factor analysis in which these 25 subjects were treated as variables supported the grouping.

For subsequent data treatment, the deviant subjects were excluded, and only the data of the remaining 27 (texture-strength) and 25 (pleasantness) subjects were used.

A plot of pleasantness vs. texture strength indicates that high pleasantness appears only with medium texture strength; the reverse is not true, because a number of slabs with medium texture strength are low in pleasantness.

Pilot Study 2. Estimation of Texture-Strength and Pleasantness in Dot Patterns

The experiments described in Pilot Study 1 were repeated with the 24 dot patterns, projected either on the small or the large screen, as stimuli. Each dot pattern was presented four times on each screen. The experiment took about 1 hour. Fifty-seven subjects estimated texture strength and 58 pleasantness; of these, 27 had not participated in Pilot Study 1. The subjects who carried out all four tasks (texture strength and pleasantness judgments of both slabs and dot patterns) were partitioned into four groups with different orders between the tasks.

There was practically no difference between judgments from the small and the large screen, as was shown by separately correlating for each of the four groups the group means obtained for each screen over the 24 dot patterns. The correlations lay between .87 and .99.

A scrutiny of the correlation pattern for both texture strength and pleasantness suggested a partitioning of the subjects into several groups (three for texture strength and four for pleasantness). A factor analysis supported the grouping. This outcome indicates that the concept of texture strength for dot patterns is ambiguous and interpreted differently by different subjects. Therefore, the suitability of these dot patterns as substitutes for real surface textures seems questionable. The result for pleasantness underlines this conclusion.

General Plan

From the outcome of the pilot studies it was concluded that the subjects were capable of carrying out psychophysical tasks with the stimulus material at hand, at least with the real surfaces. Therefore we decided to proceed by investigating the real surfaces and the dot patterns both separately and together, using the method of similarity estimation with subsequent multidimensional analyses of the data (Main Experiments 1–3). Depending on the results, these experiments were to be followed by validation studies and control experiments. To answer point 2 of the section ''Sketch of the Problem'' a number of measurements of physical properties of the real surfaces were carried out.

REAL SURFACES

Main Experiment 1. Similarity Estimation of Slabs

The method of unspecified similarity estimation with subsequent multidimensional analyses was adopted in an attempt to solve problems 1 and 4 (see "Sketch of the Problem") in an unprejudiced way. If the subject's task is specified in too much detail, there is a risk that the results will reflect the experimenter's conceptions rather than the subjects' experiences.

Stimuli, Subjects, Procedure

To keep the experiment manageable, 17 of the 50 slabs were chosen as stimuli. This was the smallest number that seemed to represent the different types among the 50 used in the pilot study. These slabs can be seen in Fig. 10.4. All 136 different pairs were presented in the carrousel to 20 subjects, of whom five repeated the experiment to obtain a measure of reliability. Each pair was shown twice, with right–left position changed so that every subject made 272 estimates. The experiment took 2 hours, including a rest of half an hour. The similarity between each pair was to be indicated on a 0–10 scale, where 0 stood for "no similarity at all" and 10 for "identity." For subsequent data treatment, the estimates were divided by 10 so that similarity varies between zero and unity. Table 10.2 gives the means of the similarity estimates.

Reliability and Homogeneity

Reliability.   The correlations between the first and second session for the five subjects who repeated the experiment amounted to .84, .81, .83, .69, and .67. These values can be considered acceptable.

Homogeneity.   The correlations between the individual means and the grand mean for the 20 subjects varied between .47 and .67. Factor analysis with the subjects as variables indicated no decomposition into groups. The homogeneity can be considered fair, taking into account the unstructuredness of the task.

Data Treatment: General Remarks

Two models (e.g., Ekman & Sjöberg, 1965) were tried out for the multidimensional analyses. The *content model* works with scalar products and uses component analysis to determine the dimensions. If the vector lengths are equal, similarity estimates are regarded as scalar products and component analyzed untransformed. The *distance model* is well-known, and algorithms for both nonmetric and metric scaling are available.

TABLE 10.2
Means (Divided by 10) of the Similarity Estimates of the 17 Slabs

Slab Number	2	3	4	5	6	7	8	9	10	11	12	13	14	15	16	17
1	.6381	.3017	.2665	.5975	.1467	.0525	.1117	.5037	.0538	.1912	.8307	.5212	.7337	.4400	.2700	.5167
2		.3825	.4312	.7280	.3030	.1542	.3325	.8122	.1682	.3055	.6325	.3765	.1980	.6766	.3000	.5812
3			.1385	.2725	.4027	.3940	.2862	.3065	.2120	.2850	.3745	.3247	.3062	.2825	.2512	.3125
4				.3500	.1567	.1137	.3040	.3540	.1702	.2257	.2465	.1530	.3562	.3600	.2977	.2112
5					.3392	.2290	.1827	.6212	.1155	.2925	.6212	.3825	.6350	.5972	.3375	.6575
6						.6912	.2850	.2937	.2770	.3380	.2305	.1890	.2825	.3852	.3667	.3117
7							.4360	.1942	.3327	.3345	.1130	.1680	.1270	.2147	.2662	.1615
8								.2940	.5182	.4862	.1252	.1525	.2425	.2787	.4575	.1850
9									.3575	.3700	.5887	.3225	.8450	.6410	.3812	.4437
10										.6237	.1172	.1092	.2077	.3750	.5287	.0950
11											.2900	.1600	.4387	.5687	.8350	.1675
12												.5462	.7172	.5587	.2879	.5300
13													.2955	.2140	.1325	.4437
14														.8231	.5412	.5012
15															.7450	.3587
16																.1552

Component Analysis

Four factors were extracted and varimax-rotated. Dimensionality was judged from an analysis of eigen values, communalities, and proportion of explained variance. To achieve comparability with the outcomes of the multidimensional scalings according to the distance model, the stress was computed and found to be 15%. This is quite high, even when one considers that component analysis is based on a highly restrictive model that is not only metric but also assumes ratio-scaled factor loadings. Somewhat surprisingly, the factor loadings showed rather high intercorrelations: 1-2 −.32, 1-3 .15, 1-4 −.57, 2-3 −.57, 2-4 −.10, 3-4 −.40. The four factors were difficult to interpret; Factor 1 somewhat resembled texture strength. In view of the comparatively high stress, the high intercorrelations between the dimensions, and the interpretational difficulties, the content model was discarded for the problem at hand.

This outcome does not necessarily mean that the content model cannot be applied. As shown by Eisler and Roskam (1977a, 1977b), the similarity estimates can be considered scalar products only for equal vector lengths. For unequal vector lengths, other tasks are required (multidimensional ratio estimation and commonality ratio estimation) to obtain vector lengths and cosines for the angle between pairs of vectors, from which the scalar products can be computed. Sjöberg (1975) shows distributions of similarity estimations that are reversed J-shaped (many estimates of low and few of high similarity) for data with equal vector lengths and roughly symmetric for one set of data with unequal vector lengths. The distribution for the present data set is shown in Fig. 10.2. Though it is not symmetric, it is not J-shaped either and indicates probably varying vector lengths.

Nonmetric Multidimensional Scaling

The analyses were carried out with the similarity estimates as input, using TORSCA (Young & Torgerson, 1967). Both the city-block and Euclidean metric were tried, yielding stress values of 10% and 7%, respectively, for the three extracted dimensions. In spite of the somewhat higher stress, the city-block metric was

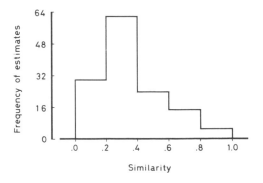

FIG. 10.2. Histogram of the 136 similarities for the 17 slabs, cf. Table 10.2.

TABLE 10.3
The Coordinates of the 17 Slabs for the Three Dimensions Obtained by
Nonmetric City-block Analysis

Slab Number	Dimension 1	Dimension 2	Dimension 3
1	0.983	.062	.126
2	0.410	.145	−.082
3	−0.089	−.641	.309
4	0.111	.592	−.629
5	0.421	−.082	−.125
6	−0.534	−.526	−.029
7	−1.024	−.549	−.036
8	−0.823	.085	−.388
9	0.163	.108	.041
10	−1.188	.351	.108
11	−0.564	.337	.276
12	0.689	.009	.254
13	0.831	−.657	.031
14	0.405	.242	.170
15	0.052	.327	.112
16	−0.403	.522	.156
17	0.557	−.325	−.295

accepted because it fixes the positions of the axes. (The correlations between the coordinates of the city-block and the Euclidean model amounted to .99, .98, and −.98 for the three dimensions, implying a practically identical configuration.) Pairwise correlations between the dimensions were negligible. The three dimensions obtained from the city-block analysis are given in Table 10.3. A preliminary interpretation of the dimensions was as follows:

Dimension 1. Texture-strength.
Dimension 2. Regularity of forms (details).
Dimension 3. Hard–soft, cold–warm, grainy–fibrous.

Metric Multidimensional Scaling

The mean similarity estimates s were transformed into distances d according to (a) $d = K - s$ and (b) $d = -\log s$. Roskam's (1972) algorithm MRSCAL (we had only the algorithm with Euclidean metric at our disposal) was used, yielding stress values of 7% for both transformations with four dimensions extracted. The pairwise intercorrelations between dimensions were all 0; correlations between coordinates for each dimension between the two transformations were .99, .97, .93, and −.88, indicating practically the same configuration. The interpretation of the first three dimensions was the same as for the nonmetric analysis; the fourth did not yield to our attempts at interpretation.

Validation Studies

Pilot Study 1: Naming of Attributes

For each of the three dimensions from the city-block analysis, the three slabs with the highest and the three with the lowest coordinates were displayed on a table. Eighty subjects were asked to write down the attribute or attributes in which the two sets of three slabs differed most.

The most frequent attributes for the first dimension described the evenness of the surfaces, like rough, coarse, and dented—as opposed to smooth, fine, or even. Also, dark–light was a common attribute. As is seen later, the attribute of unevenness, even if given different names, seems to be identical with texture-strength.

The second dimension concerns the regularity of the texture of the surfaces, with regular–irregular as the most frequent attribute. But, also, the attributes cold–warm and hard–soft were not uncommon.

The attributes of the third dimension did not receive names as unambiguous as the first two. Hard–soft was the most frequent, followed by heavy–light and cold–warm. Perhaps more interesting attributes, though less common, were solid–porous and stony–wooden.

Pilot Study 2: Confirmation of Attributes

The following 14 slabs were shown, one at a time, in a "frame" on a table: 1, 3, 4, 6, 8, 10, 11, 12, 13, 15, 17, 31, 35, 39. The 19 subjects were given forms that listed 26 attributes. For each slab, they had to mark using +, −, or 0, whether the slab presented had the attribute, had the opposite attribute, or whether the attribute was irrelevant, respectively. The 26 attributes were derived from theoretical considerations, from attributes commonly used among architects to describe textures, from the preliminary interpretations of the dimensions obtained by multidimensional scaling, and from the results of Pilot Study 1. They are given in Table 10.4.

For each attribute and slab, the judgments were summed algebraically with "+" as +1, "−" as −1, and "0" as 0, and the mean of the absolute values of these 14 sums was computed. The larger this mean, the more unambiguous and applicable the attribute. The result of Pilot Study 2, together with other considerations, made us retain 15 of the 26 attributes, in addition to texture strength and pleasantness. They are indicated in Table 10.4.

Main Validation Experiment
Relation Between Dimensions and Attributes

The 15 selected attributes were divided into three groups of five, and to each such group 24 or 25 subjects were assigned. The subjects estimated all 50 slabs on five attributes each, with separate sessions for each attribute. Both the experimental procedure and the data treatment were the same as in the texture-

TABLE 10.4
The 26 Judged Attributes

1. Heavy[a]	14. Glossy[a]
2. Fibrous[a]	15. Inorganic
3. Outdoor material	16. Natural
4. Coarse[a]	17. Shadow-forming
5. Porous	18. Deep[a]
6. High density of texture elements[a]	19. Regular[a]
7. Even	20. Light (opposite: dark)[a]
8. Colored	21. Malleable
9. Angular	22. Hard[a]
10. Large texture elements[a]	23. Warm[a]
11. Clear	24. Clearly composed of units[a]
12. Constructional material	25. Alive[a]
13. Rough[a]	26. Directed[a]

[a] Denotes attributes that were retained for the main validation study.

strength and pleasantness ratings. Homogeneity of estimates, evaluated from the individual correlations with the mean values, was quite good (though a few deviant subjects' data were removed) except for density. This attribute was obviously interpreted differently by different subjects, who seemed to split up into four groups.

As a preliminary, mechanical attempt at interpreting the three dimensions obtained from the city-block analysis, stepwise multiple regression of each dimension on the 15 attributes (plus texture strength and pleasantness) was carried out. Coarseness explained 90% of the variance of Dimension 1 (texture strength 87%), directedness explained 59% of Dimension 2 (a value that increased to 89% when depth was added), and fibrousness explained 85% of the variance of Dimension 3. Further gains from adding more attributes amounted to only a small percentage of the explained variance in all three dimensions.

Physical Measurements of the Properties of the Textures

This part of the investigation was carried out in an attempt to solve Problem 2 (see "Sketch of the Problem"). Let me say at the outset that it was very time-consuming and not too rewarding. The following four properties of texture elements of the 50 slabs were measured: (1) depth; (2) density; (3) area; (4) fibrousness (by two methods).

Method

1. Depth. Of the 50 slabs, 22 were so even that there was no variation in depth. The remaining 28 slabs were viewed under magnification, and a profile curve of a randomly selected section was drawn. On this curve, 50 points were selected at random, and their distance from a baseline measured. As the measure of depth, the standard deviation of the 50 points was chosen.

2. Density.   All slabs were photographed, and the enlarged prints were divided into 35 squares, of which 1–5 were selected at random for measurement of the texture elements. The remaining part of the photograph was covered with opaque cardboard. The same procedure was used for the measurement of the remaining properties.

The number of texture elements in each square was counted and divided by the area. As the measure of density, the mean value of this ratio was chosen.

3. Area.   The area of all texture elements within a square was measured by means of a planimeter or, for small elements, by means of mm-graph paper. As the measure of area, the mean over all elements measured was chosen.

4. Fibrousness.   The fibrousness of a texture element was defined in two ways:

(a) $F_1 = \dfrac{\text{perimeter of element}}{\text{perimeter of circle of equal area}} = \dfrac{\text{perimeter of element}}{2\sqrt{\pi \cdot \text{area of element}}}$.

For this definition, fibrousness for a circular element is unity and increases with increasing elongation of the element. The perimeter of an element was measured with a "map meter" for large elements and with mm-graph paper for smaller elements. The area was measured as just described. As before, the mean of F_1 over all elements measured was computed.

(b) $F_2 = \dfrac{\text{length of element}}{\text{width of element}}$, where "length" is the longest straight distance between two points on the periphery of the element, and "width" is the width of the smallest rectangle circumscribing the element with its long side parallel to the line measuring the length of the element.

Results

Reliability.   All properties (except depth) were measured for four of the slabs by two assistants independently. All correlations between the two sets of measures exceeded .99.

Relation Between Estimated Attributes and Measured Properties.   A stepwise multiple regression of the measured properties (some transformed to achieve linearity) on the estimated attributes did not result in much of interest. The most important measured variable seemed to be depth, which explained more than 80% of the variance of the estimated attributes depth, coarseness, and roughness.

DOT PATTERNS

Main Experiment 2. Similarity Estimation of Dot Patterns

The series of experiments with the slabs was repeated with the 24 dot patterns. Though the subjective experience of dot patterns is psychologically interesting, not much of value was obtained for the problem at hand. Therefore, only a brief account is given.

Twenty subjects carried out similarity estimation of all 300 pairs of the dot patterns (identical ones included). Each pair was estimated twice. The experiment consisted of two sessions of 1 hour each for every subject. The analyses were, as before, component analysis (six factors were extracted, stress = 6.8%), and nonmetric and metric multidimensional scaling, with four extracted dimensions (TORSCA: stress for city-block metric = 6.7%, for Euclidian metric = 4.2%; MRSCAL: stress for linear transformation 5.4%, for logarithmic transformation 6.7%). Preliminary interpretation of the dimensions resulted mostly in other attributes than those employed for the slabs, perhaps with the exception of texture-strength.

Pilot Study 1 (cf. section "Validation Studies") for validation did not give any clear-cut results. Rather independently of the presented dimension, the most common attributes were size and density. Twenty-two attributes were used for Pilot Study 2, and 10 of these were retained for the main validation study. However, no multiple regressions were carried out.

REAL SURFACES AND DOT PATTERNS TOGETHER

Main Experiment 3. Similarity Estimation of Slabs and Dot Patterns Mixed

In order to keep the experiment manageable, the number of stimuli was reduced to 15 slabs and 15 dot patterns. From the 17 slabs used in Main Experiment 1, numbers 2 and 14 were removed; from the 24 dot patterns used in Main Experiment 2, nine (2, 5, 6, 7, 8, 10, 14, 18, 22) were removed. The attributes characterizing these stimuli were considered to be covered by those retained. To check that the reduction of the stimulus sets did not change the experienced dimensions, two control experiments were carried out, viz. similarity estimation of the 15 slabs and the 15 dot patterns separately. These two control experiments can also be regarded as stability studies.

Similarity Estimation of Mixed Stimuli

The similarity of the 435 pairs formed from the 30 stimuli was estimated twice by 25 subjects, of whom five repeated the task. The time required for the experiment was 4 hours for each subject, divided into five sessions. Again, similarity was estimated on a 0 to 10 scale.

Reliability and Homogeneity

Reliability. The correlations between the first and the second experiment for the five subjects who carried out the experiment twice were .96, .85, .90, .82, and .58, yielding an average of .82. Thus, the reliability was good.

Homogeneity. The correlation between single subjects and the mean varied between .63 and .93, a satisfactory outcome.

Multidimensional Analyses

Component analysis divided the factors into slab- and dot-pattern factors. Of the five extracted factors, the first two had high loadings ($>$ .5) only for the dot patterns (with the exception of the perforated asbestos-cement board with regular round holes, slab no. 3, which resembles a dot pattern), and the last three only for the slabs. The *TORSCA analysis* (city-block), likewise with five dimensions extracted (stress 8.1%), did not give a similar partitioning. However, the first dimension there distinguished between slabs and dot patterns in such a way that the slabs obtained positive coordinates and the dot patterns negative coordinates (again with the exception of slab no. 3).

Control Experiments

Fifteen subjects made similarity estimations of the 15 slabs, and another 15 subjects of the 15 dot patterns. The data showed acceptable homogeneity (the correlations of single subjects with the mean varied between .62 and .92 for the slabs, and between .79 and .95 for the dot patterns). Both component analysis and city-block analysis (TORSCA) were carried out with both data sets.

There are three sets of similarities for the same 15 slabs: from the Main Experiment 1, where the stimuli consisted of 17 slabs; from the Main Experiment 3, where the stimuli were slabs and dot patterns mixed; and from the first control experiment with 15 slabs alone. Furthermore, there are two multidimensional analyses carried out for all three data sets, viz. component analysis and nonmetric multidimensional scaling according to the city-block metric. The same holds for the dot patterns.

Validation is carried out by correlating the coordinates for each dimension over the 15 stimuli. Inasmuch as the dimensions need not correspond to each other by numbers, the pair of dimensions yielding the highest correlation are given. It is worth noting that the similarity values (means) were linearly related between the mixed and control experiments.

Slabs

Table 10.5 shows the correlations between the factors obtained by component analysis in the control experiment and in Main Experiments 3 and 1. (Only the highest values in any row and column are given.) One sees that "Slab Factors" 3 to 5 from Main Experiment 3 are recovered as Factors 1 to 3 from the control experiment. Likewise, when three factors are extracted from the data of Main Experiment 1, they agree very well with the first three of the control experiment. Extraction of four factors in Main Experiment 1 does not yield such a clear-cut picture. It seems more probable that data allow an extraction of only three factors than that one factor disappeared when slabs no. 2 and 14 were removed.

The city-block analysis, likewise given in Table 10.5, shows an unclear relation between Main Experiment 3 and the control experiment, but the agreement between Main Experiment 1 and the control experiment with three dimensions is very good.

Dot Patterns

Corresponding correlations between factor loadings obtained by component analysis are given in Table 10.6. The agreement between the control experiment and Main Experiment 3 is fair.

It is noteworthy that the correlations for Factors 3-5 of Main Experiment 3 are high despite their low loadings. This outcome can be interpreted to mean that the same dimensions are experienced for both slabs and dot patterns but that the intensity for dot patterns is weak compared to slabs.

The agreement between the control experiment and Main Experiment 2 is surprisingly good. The "loss" of Factor 4 of Main Experiment 2 is probably due to the considerably reduced number of stimuli.

The outcome for the city-block treatment is not good when the control experiment is compared with Main Experiment 3. It is more than acceptable for the comparison between the control experiment and Main Experiment 2, though the reality of the fourth dimension may be doubted.

Conclusion

Two conclusions can be drawn from the results:

TABLE 10.5
Highest Correlations Between Dimensions Obtained From the Control Experiment and From Main Experiments 3 and 1 Over 15 Slabs

Component Analysis

Control Exp.	Main Exp. 3					Main Exp. 1 (4 dimensions)				Main Exp. 1 (3 dimensions)		
	1	2	3	4	5	1	2	3	4	1	2	3
1	-.27					.61						
2			.93				.90			.98		
3				.93	.94			.84	.96		.94	.96
4		-.74					-.51					

City-block Analysis

Control Exp.	Main Exp. 3					Main Exp. 1		
	1	2	3	4	5	1	2	3
1	-.64					.98		
2		-.90	.66				-.93	
3				.57	.14			.88

TABLE 10.6
Highest Correlations Between Dimensions Obtained From the Control Experiment and From Main Experiments 3 and 2 Over 15 Dot Patterns

Component Analysis

Control Exp.	Main Exp. 3					Main Exp. 2					
	1	2	3	4	5	1	2	3	4	5	6
1	-.84					.89					
2		-.92									
3			-.73	.93				.88	.81		
4				-.70					.57		
5					.77					.75	
6	.60										.98 .54

City-block Analysis

Control Exp.	Main Exp. 3					Main Exp. 2			
	1	2	3	4	5	1	2	3	4
1	.89	-.88	.66	.71	-.76	.96	-.88	-.85	-.44
2			.50		-.37			.31	

1. Dot patterns are not suitable as substitutes for real textures because the dimensions for the former are either different or weaker in intensity.
2. The methods employed (experiments and data analysis together) show more than satisfactory stability.

INTERPRETATIONS

The subjective interpretations were made by placing the stimuli (slabs and/or dot patterns) in the rank order given by the dimension to be interpreted, while attempting to make the distances between the stimuli proportional to the coordinate differences. The members of the research group tried to specify and name the variables indicated by the arrangement, first individually and then together. About 50 "interpretation meetings" were held.

Here we deal only with the dimensions obtained from the (nonmetric) city-block analyses. As mentioned earlier, the results of the component analyses were often difficult to interpret, besides showing other drawbacks; the Euclidean spaces agreed well with the city-block structures but still would have caused some worry regarding the most suitable rotation.

1. Main Experiment 1: Slabs

Dimension 1

The range of the coordinates was -1.19 through $+.98$. Slabs with high positive coordinates were even, with small texture elements, unclear, weak; high negative coordinates indicated depth, roughness, large texture elements, clearness, coarseness (see Table 10.7). Dimension 1 could clearly be interpreted as texture strength. The correlation between Dimension 1 and texture strength as estimated amounted to $-.93$ ("cross-validation": $-.92$ with Dimension 1 of the control experiment).

Denotations.   Texture strength, pregnancy.

Description.   Unclear, even, shallow, elements small; vs. clear, coarse, deep, elements large.

Dimension 2

The range was smaller than for Dimension 1, viz. $-.66$ through $+.59$. Slabs with high positive coordinates could be described as soft, amorphous, crude, with irregular surface, dull, without form, not orderly, unpatterned. Those with high negative coordinates could be described as structured, orderly, endowed with form, glossy, hard, machined, with regular surface, checkered, patterned, directed (see Table 10.8).

TABLE 10.7
The 17 Slabs Ranked According to
City-block Dimension 1 With Corresponding
Coordinates

Rank Number	Slab Number	Coordinate
1	1	+0.983
2	13	0.831
3	12	0.689
4	17	0.557
5	5	0.421
6	2	0.410
7	14	0.405
8	9	0.163
9	4	0.111
10	15	0.052
11	3	−0.089
12	16	−0.403
13	6	−0.534
14	11	−0.564
15	8	−0.823
16	7	−1.024
17	10	−1.188

TABLE 10.8
The 17 Slabs Ranked According to
City-block Dimension 2 With Corresponding
Coordinates

Rank Number	Slab Number	Coordinate
1	4	.59
2	16	.52
3	10	.35
4	11	.34
5	15	.33
6	14	.24
7	2	.15
8	9	.11
9	8	.09
10	1	.06
11	12	.01
12	5	−.08
13	17	−.33
14	6	−.53
15	7	−.55
16	3	−.64
17	13	−.66

Dimension 2 correlated $-.77$ with the attribute directed ("cross-validation": .77 with Dimension 2 of the control experiment), .60 with regular, .66 with glossy, .46 with live, and .45 with warm. It seems clear that Dimension 2 has irregular and regular patterns at the endpoints, whereas slabs with diffuse or unclear patterns ("no pattern") lie near the origin. The attributes "alive" and "warm" are probably secondary; they seem to require a pattern, and a pattern that is not too orderly.

Denotation.   Texture pattern, texture order, order of elements.

Description.   Irregular, undirected vs. regular, directed.

Dimension 3

The range is still smaller, $-.63$ through $+.31$. No obvious interpretations could be made that seemed to hold for all slabs (see Table 10.9). Correlations with estimated attributes were: fibrousness $-.92$ ("cross-validation": $-.75$ with Dimension 3 of the control experiment), warmth $-.80$. We settled for:

Denotation.   Appearance of elements.

Description.   Granular, grainy vs. streaked, fibrous.

TABLE 10.9
The 17 Slabs Ranked According to
City-block Dimension 3 With Corresponding
Coordinates

Rank Number	Slab Number	Coordinate
1	3	.309
2	11	.276
3	12	.254
4	14	.170
5	16	.156
6	1	.126
7	15	.112
8	10	.108
9	9	.041
10	13	.031
11	6	−.029
12	7	−.036
13	2	−.082
14	5	−.125
15	17	−.295
16	8	−.388
17	4	−.629

2. Main Experiment 2: Dot Patterns

The dimensions of the dot patterns obtained were throughout much more difficult to interpret than the dimensions of the slabs. Also, it was almost impossible to disregard the clear physical properties, size of dots, and distance between centres or relations between them. Though the results obtained may be of interest with reference to visual perception in general, their contribution to the problem at hand is small, as mentioned before. Dot patterns cannot be used as a satisfactory substitute for real textures. Therefore, we do not give a precise account of what we found.

3. Main Experiment 3: Slabs and Dot Patterns Mixed

Dimension 1

Dimension 1 divides the stimuli into slabs (positive coordinates) and dot patterns (negative coordinates). Exceptions are slab no. 3, perforated grey asbestos-cement board, and dot pattern no. 1, the densest one with the finest spots. Both lie closest to the origin. Within each group, the order seems to indicate clearness or "readability."

Dimension 2

For the slabs, Dimension 2 seems to agree with texture strength; for the dot patterns it agrees with texture strength for one of the groups of subjects. The range for this dimension is much shorter for the dot patterns ($-$ 6.6 through $+$ 3.1) than for the slabs ($-$ 10.2 through $+$ 12.2).

Dimension 3

Dimension 3 seems to indicate orderliness or regularity, if one assumes that contrast caused by shadows or colors "displaces" slabs toward the positive (orderly) direction. It is noteworthy that Dimension 3 is monotonic with the center distances of the dot patterns.

Dimension 4

Dimension 4 resembles Dimension 3 from Main Experiment 1 (fibrousness: granular, grainy vs. streaked, fibrous). However, the slabs are to be found at the extremes of the scale and the dot patterns around the origin.

Summary

By and large, dimension 1-3 from Main Experiment 1 are recovered—at least qualitatively—as dimensions 2-4 from Main Experiment 3. Dimension 1 of Main Experiment 3 distinguishes between the two types of stimuli, slabs and dot patterns.

OVERALL RESULTS

Referring to the section "Sketch of the Problem," we can summarize our findings as follows:

1. There seem to be three primary visual attributes of textures an observer pays attention to: (a) texture strength (intensity of the experience of texture); (b) pattern of texture, orderliness (regularity) among the texture elements; (c) form of the individual texture elements (grainy–fibrous).

2. It proved very difficult to find physical properties and relations between these properties that can be used as predictors for subjective attributes. Our only real success was the relation between texture-strength and the standard deviation of measured depth of the surface.

3. Dot patterns proved unsuitable as standard textures to substitute for real textures, probably because they lack important attributes such as depth, irregularity, and fibrousness.

4. The relative importance of the three attributes can be assessed by their relative range of variation (extension of the dimensions).

The main goal—construction of a texture chart—was achieved. Figure 10.3 shows scales of the three attributes with the 17 texture samples in place. Figure 10.4 demonstrates how each texture sample is specified in three attributes, together with the relative importance of the attributes.

Final Remark

The results obtained indicate a rather satisfactory stability. The same attributes have been obtained in different experiments and contexts. It has also been shown that the attributes corresponding to the dimensions function in isolation and thus are not artifacts of the data treatments. However, the problem of generalizability of the results remains. Although we did try to work with typical samples of textures, the size of the sample was rather limited. And this holds still more for our subjects—students of architecture are not even a typical sample of people confronted with buildings endowed with surfaces.

ACKNOWLEDGMENTS

This work was supported by the Swedish Council for Building Research and the Swedish Council for Research in the Humanities and Social Sciences. It was carried out by the authors in collaboration with M. Ericson, O. Pernholm, P. Sporrong, and A. Toomingas.

BUILDING MATERIALS ("SLABS"). THE FIRST TEXTURE DIMENSION TEXTURE STRENGTH. TEXTURE PREGNANCY.

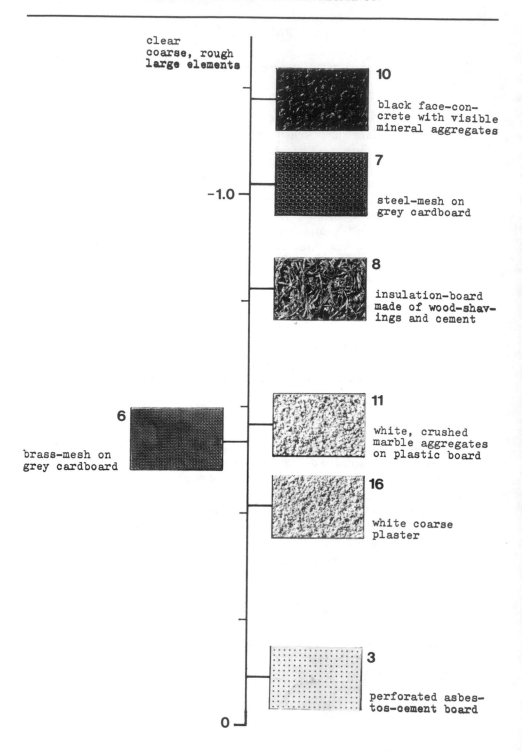

clear
coarse, rough
large elements

10 black face-con-
crete with visible
mineral aggregates

7 steel-mesh on
grey cardboard

-1.0

8 insulation-board
made of wood-shav-
ings and cement

6 brass-mesh on
grey cardboard

11 white, crushed
marble aggregates
on plastic board

16 white coarse
plaster

3 perforated asbes-
tos-cement board

0

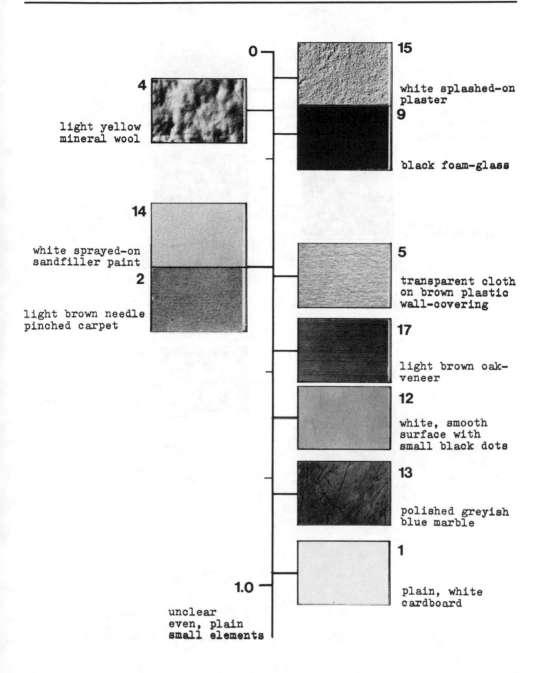

FIG. 10.3. Scales of the three visual attributes of surface textures, with the 17 slabs in place (see p. 257 and Tables 10.7–10.9). (From Edberg, 1977.)

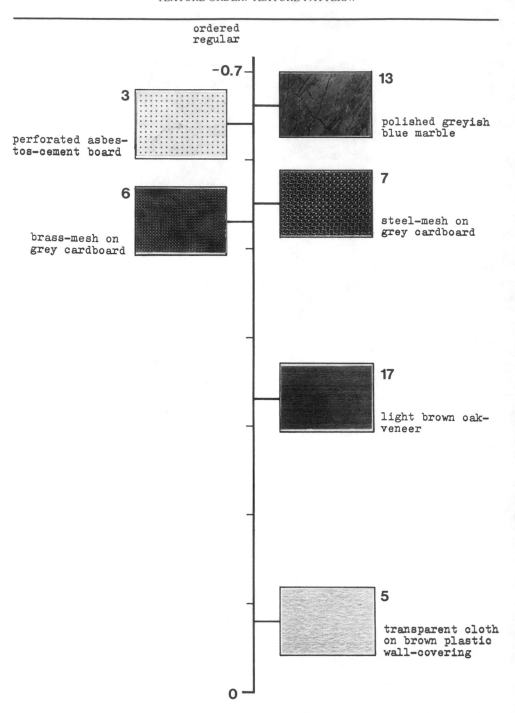

ordered
regular

−0.7

3
perforated asbes-
tos-cement board

13
polished greyish
blue marble

6
brass-mesh on
grey cardboard

7
steel-mesh on
grey cardboard

17
light brown oak-
veneer

5
transparent cloth
on brown plastic
wall-covering

0

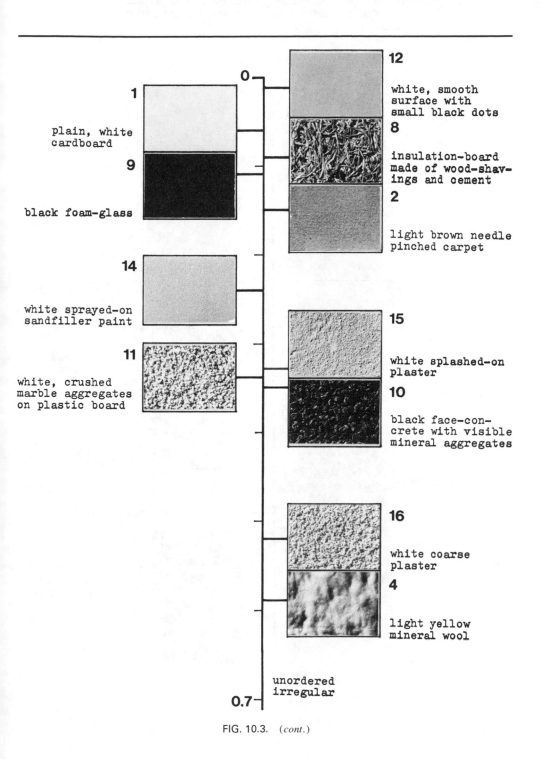

1 plain, white cardboard

9 black foam-glass

14 white sprayed-on sandfiller paint

11 white, crushed marble aggregates on plastic board

0

12 white, smooth surface with small black dots

8 insulation-board made of wood-shavings and cement

2 light brown needle pinched carpet

15 white splashed-on plaster

10 black face-concrete with visible mineral aggregates

16 white coarse plaster

4 light yellow mineral wool

0.7 unordered irregular

FIG. 10.3. (*cont.*)

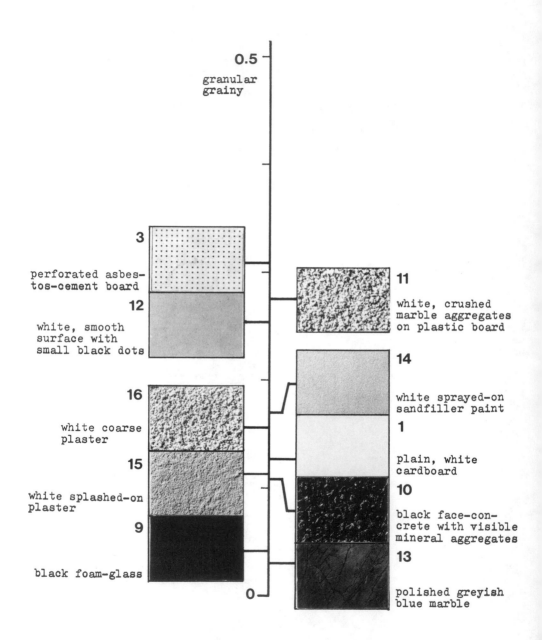

0.5

granular
grainy

3

perforated asbes-
tos-cement board

11

white, crushed
marble aggregates
on plastic board

12

white, smooth
surface with
small black dots

14

white sprayed-on
sandfiller paint

16

white coarse
plaster

1

plain, white
cardboard

15

white splashed-on
plaster

10

black face-con-
crete with visible
mineral aggregates

9

black foam-glass

13

polished greyish
blue marble

0

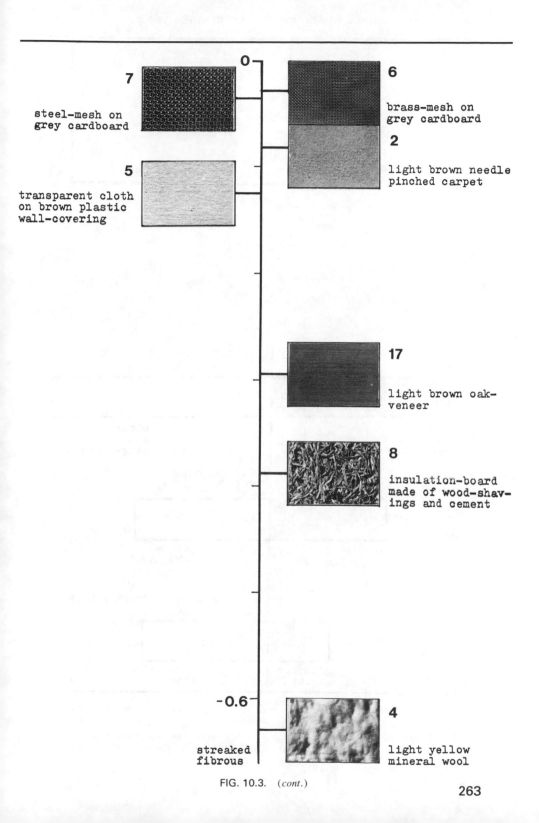

7
steel-mesh on
grey cardboard

6
brass-mesh on
grey cardboard

5
transparent cloth
on brown plastic
wall-covering

2
light brown needle
pinched carpet

17
light brown oak-
veneer

8
insulation-board
made of wood-shav-
ings and cement

4
light yellow
mineral wool

streaked
fibrous

0

-0.6

FIG. 10.3.   (*cont.*)

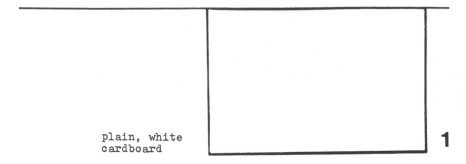

plain, white
cardboard

1

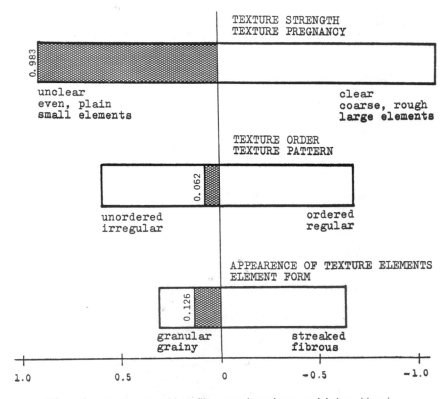

TEXTURE STRENGTH
TEXTURE PREGNANCY

0.983

unclear   clear
even, plain   coarse, rough
small elements   large elements

TEXTURE ORDER
TEXTURE PATTERN

0.062

unordered   ordered
irregular   regular

APPEARANCE OF TEXTURE ELEMENTS
ELEMENT FORM

0.126

granular   streaked
grainy   fibrous

1.0   0.5   0   -0.5   -1.0

FIG. 10.4. The 17 slabs, with profile curve when relevant, and their positions in the three visual-attribute scales of texture (see p. 257). (From Edberg, 1977.)

light brown needle
pinched carpet

2

Profile of surface.   Scale: magnified 5:1
Exemplifies amplitude or depth.

TEXTURE STRENGTH
TEXTURE PREGNANCY

0.410

unclear   clear
even, plain   coarse, rough
small elements   **large elements**

TEXTURE ORDER
TEXTURE PATTERN

0.145

unordered   ordered
irregular   regular

APPEARENCE OF TEXTURE ELEMENTS
ELEMENT FORM

-0.082

granular   streaked
grainy   fibrous

1.0   0.5   0   -0.5   -1.0

FIG. 10.4.   *(cont.)*

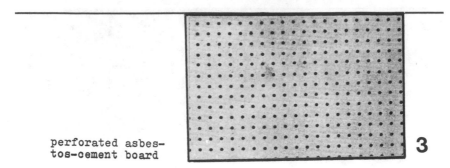

perforated asbes-
tos-cement board

3

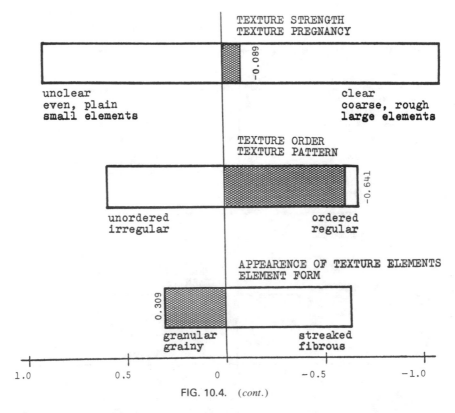

TEXTURE STRENGTH
TEXTURE PREGNANCY

-0.089

unclear
even, plain
small elements

clear
coarse, rough
large elements

TEXTURE ORDER
TEXTURE PATTERN

-0.641

unordered
irregular

ordered
regular

APPEARENCE OF TEXTURE ELEMENTS
ELEMENT FORM

0.309

granular
grainy

streaked
fibrous

1.0   0.5   0   -0.5   -1.0

FIG. 10.4.   (*cont.*)

light yellow
mineral wool

4

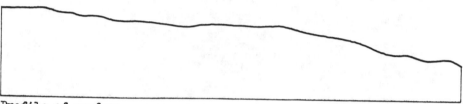

Profile of surface.   Scale: magnified 5:1
Exemplifies amplitude or depth.

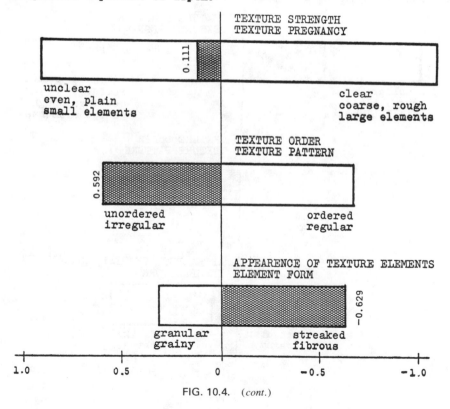

TEXTURE STRENGTH
TEXTURE PREGNANCY

0.111

unclear   clear
even, plain   coarse, rough
small elements   large elements

TEXTURE ORDER
TEXTURE PATTERN

0.592

unordered   ordered
irregular   regular

APPEARENCE OF TEXTURE ELEMENTS
ELEMENT FORM

-0.629

granular   streaked
grainy   fibrous

1.0   0.5   0   -0.5   -1.0

FIG. 10.4.   *(cont.)*

267

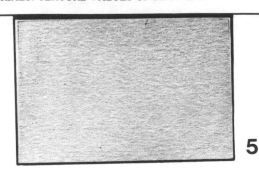

transparent cloth
on brown plastic
wall-covering

5

Profile of surface. Scale: magnified 5:1
Exemplifies amplitude or depth.

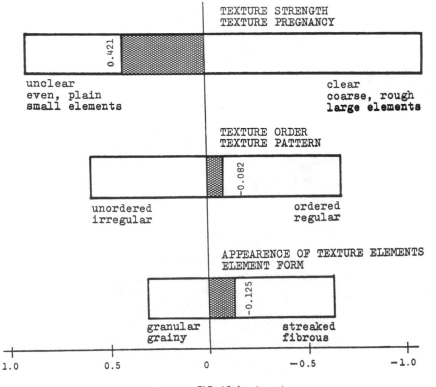

TEXTURE STRENGTH
TEXTURE PREGNANCY

0.421

unclear
even, plain
small elements

clear
coarse, rough
large elements

TEXTURE ORDER
TEXTURE PATTERN

-0.082

unordered
irregular

ordered
regular

APPEARENCE OF TEXTURE ELEMENTS
ELEMENT FORM

-0.125

granular
grainy

streaked
fibrous

1.0   0.5   0   —0.5   —1.0

FIG. 10.4. (cont.)

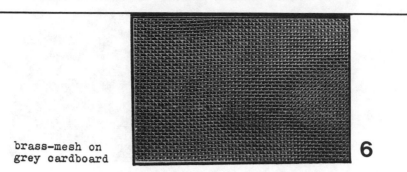

brass-mesh on
grey cardboard

6

Profile of surface.   Scale: magnified 5:1
Exemplifies amplitude or depth.

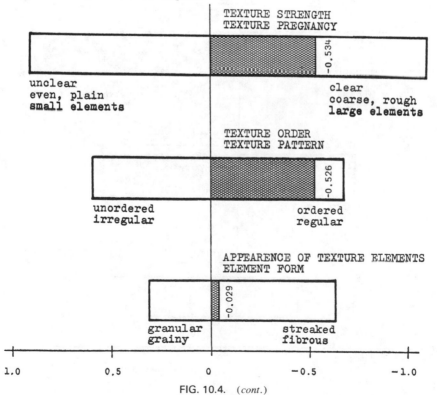

TEXTURE STRENGTH
TEXTURE PREGNANCY

−0.534

unclear
even, plain
small elements

clear
coarse, rough
large elements

TEXTURE ORDER
TEXTURE PATTERN

−0.526

unordered
irregular

ordered
regular

APPEARENCE OF TEXTURE ELEMENTS
ELEMENT FORM

−0.029

granular
grainy

streaked
fibrous

| 1.0 | 0.5 | 0 | −0.5 | −1.0 |

FIG. 10.4.   (*cont.*)

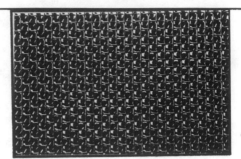

steel—mesh on
grey cardboard

7

Profile of surface.   Scale: magnified 5:1
Exemplifies amplitude or depth.

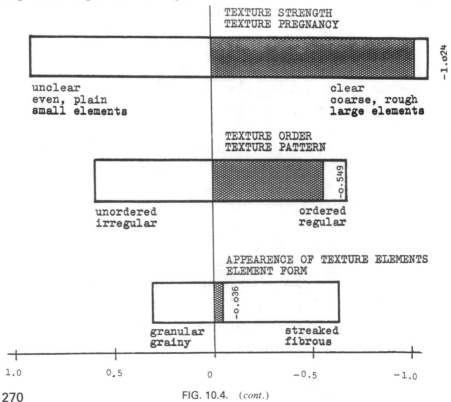

TEXTURE STRENGTH
TEXTURE PREGNANCY

−1.o24

unclear   clear
even, plain   coarse, rough
small elements   **large elements**

TEXTURE ORDER
TEXTURE PATTERN

−0.549

unordered   ordered
irregular   **regular**

APPEARENCE OF TEXTURE ELEMENTS
ELEMENT FORM

−0.o36

granular   streaked
grainy   **fibrous**

| 1.0 | 0.5 | 0 | −0.5 | −1.0 |

FIG. 10.4.   (*cont.*)

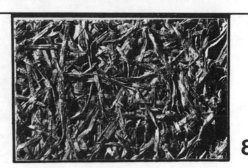

insulation-board
made of wood-shav-
ings and cement

8

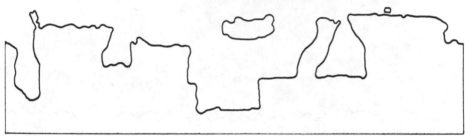

Profile of surface.   Scale: magnified 5:1
Exemplifies amplitude or depth.

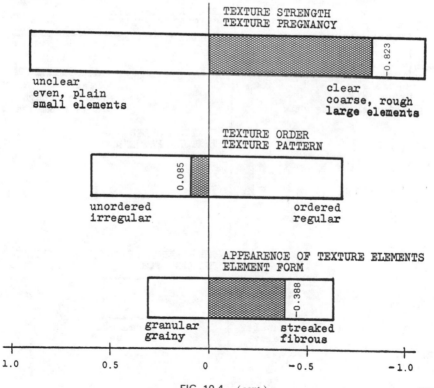

TEXTURE STRENGTH
TEXTURE PREGNANCY

−0.823

unclear   clear
even, plain   coarse, rough
small elements   large elements

TEXTURE ORDER
TEXTURE PATTERN

0.085

unordered   ordered
irregular   regular

APPEARENCE OF TEXTURE ELEMENTS
ELEMENT FORM

−0.388

granular   streaked
grainy   fibrous

1.0   0.5   0   −0.5   −1.0

FIG. 10.4. (cont.)

black foam-glass

9

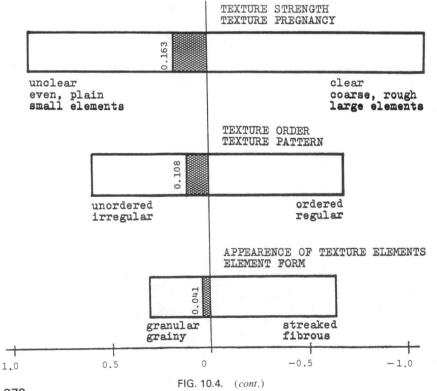

Profile of surface.   Scale: magnified 5:1
Exemplifies amplitude or depth.

TEXTURE STRENGTH
TEXTURE PREGNANCY

0.163

unclear   clear
even, plain   coarse, rough
small elements   large elements

TEXTURE ORDER
TEXTURE PATTERN

0.108

unordered   ordered
irregular   regular

APPEARENCE OF TEXTURE ELEMENTS
ELEMENT FORM

0.041

granular   streaked
grainy   fibrous

1.0   0.5   0   −0.5   −1.0

FIG. 10.4.   (cont.)

black face-con-
crete with visible
mineral aggregates

10

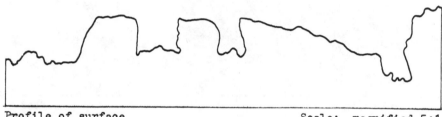

Profile of surface.   Scale: magnified 5:1
Exemplifies amplitude or depth.

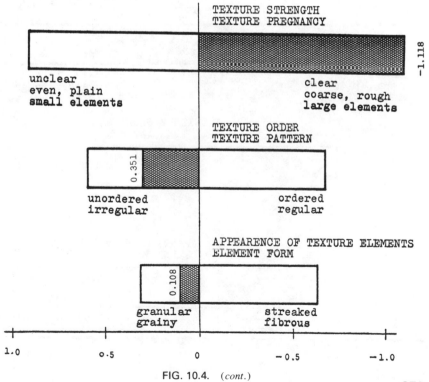

TEXTURE STRENGTH
TEXTURE PREGNANCY

-1.118

unclear   clear
even, plain   coarse, rough
small elements   large elements

TEXTURE ORDER
TEXTURE PATTERN

0.351

unordered   ordered
irregular   regular

APPEARENCE OF TEXTURE ELEMENTS
ELEMENT FORM

0.108

granular   streaked
grainy   fibrous

1.0   o.5   0   - 0.5   - 1.0

FIG. 10.4.   *(cont.)*

white, crushed
marble aggregates
on plastic board

11

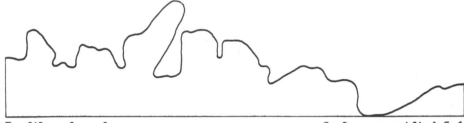

Profile of surface.   Scale: magnified 5:1
Exemplifies amplitude or depth.

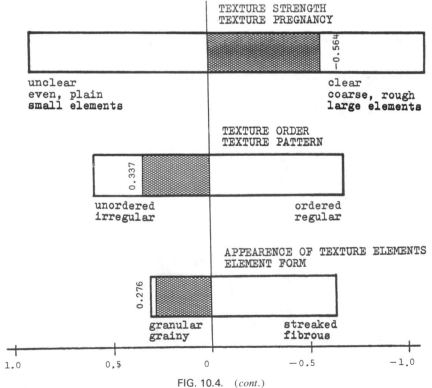

TEXTURE STRENGTH
TEXTURE PREGNANCY

−0.564

unclear   clear
even, plain   coarse, rough
small elements   **large elements**

TEXTURE ORDER
TEXTURE PATTERN

0.337

unordered   ordered
irregular   regular

APPEARENCE OF TEXTURE ELEMENTS
ELEMENT FORM

0.276

granular   streaked
grainy   fibrous

| 1.0 | 0.5 | 0 | −0.5 | −1.0 |

FIG. 10.4. (cont.)

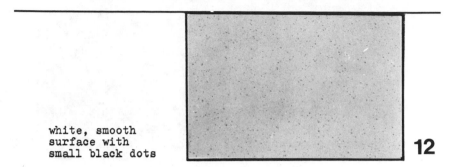

white, smooth
surface with
small black dots

12

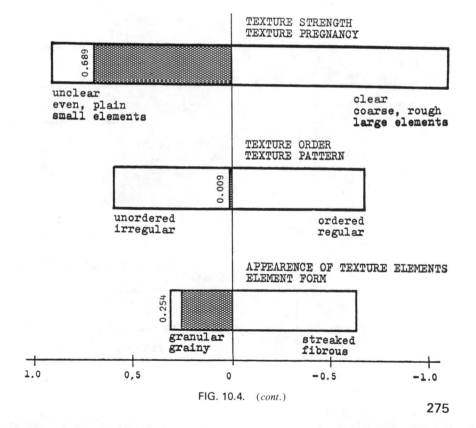

TEXTURE STRENGTH
TEXTURE PREGNANCY

0.689

unclear
even, plain
small elements

clear
coarse, rough
large elements

TEXTURE ORDER
TEXTURE PATTERN

0.009

unordered
irregular

ordered
regular

APPEARENCE OF TEXTURE ELEMENTS
ELEMENT FORM

0.254

granular
grainy

streaked
fibrous

1.0   0,5   0   -0.5   -1.0

FIG. 10.4. *(cont.)*

polished greyish
blue marble

13

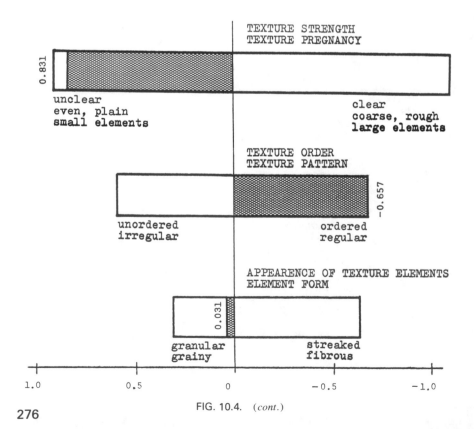

TEXTURE STRENGTH
TEXTURE PREGNANCY

0.831

unclear
even, plain
small elements

clear
coarse, rough
large elements

TEXTURE ORDER
TEXTURE PATTERN

−0.657

unordered
irregular

ordered
regular

APPEARENCE OF TEXTURE ELEMENTS
ELEMENT FORM

0.031

granular
grainy

streaked
fibrous

| 1.0 | 0.5 | 0 | − 0.5 | − 1.0 |

FIG. 10.4. (*cont.*)

white sprayed-on
sandfiller paint

14

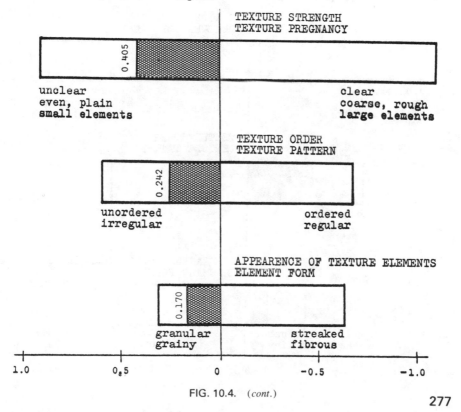

Profile of surface.
Exemplifies amplitude or depth.

Scale: magnified 5:1

TEXTURE STRENGTH
TEXTURE PREGNANCY

0.405

unclear
even, plain
small elements

clear
coarse, rough
large elements

TEXTURE ORDER
TEXTURE PATTERN

0.242

unordered
irregular

ordered
regular

APPEARENCE OF TEXTURE ELEMENTS
ELEMENT FORM

0.170

granular
grainy

streaked
fibrous

1.0   0.5   0   -0.5   -1.0

FIG. 10.4.   (cont.)

277

white splashed-on
plaster

15

Profile of surface.   Scale: magnified 5:1
Exemplifies amplitude or depth.

TEXTURE STRENGTH
TEXTURE PREGNANCY

0.052

unclear
even, plain
small elements

clear
coarse, rough
large elements

TEXTURE ORDER
TEXTURE PATTERN

0,327

unordered
irregular

ordered
regular

APPEARENCE OF TEXTURE ELEMENTS
ELEMENT FORM

0,112

granular
grainy

streaked
fibrous

| 1.0 | 0.5 | 0 | —0.5 | —1.0 |

FIG. 10.4.   *(cont.)*

white coarse
plaster

16

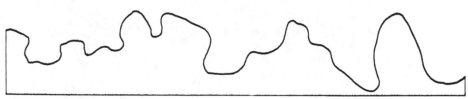

Profile of surface.   Scale: magnified 5:1
Exemplifies amplitude or depth.

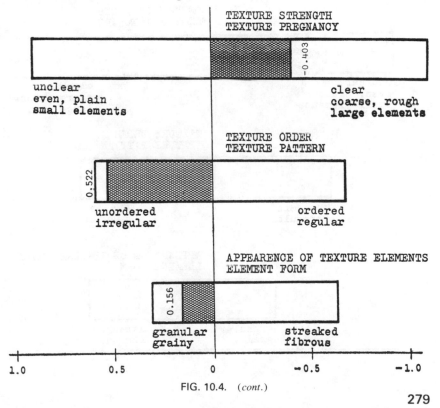

TEXTURE STRENGTH
TEXTURE PREGNANCY

-0.403

unclear
even, plain
small elements

clear
coarse, rough
large elements

TEXTURE ORDER
TEXTURE PATTERN

0.522

unordered
irregular

ordered
regular

APPEARENCE OF TEXTURE ELEMENTS
ELEMENT FORM

0.156

granular
grainy

streaked
fibrous

1.0   0.5   0   -0.5   -1.0

FIG. 10.4.   (*cont.*)

light brown oak-
veneer

17

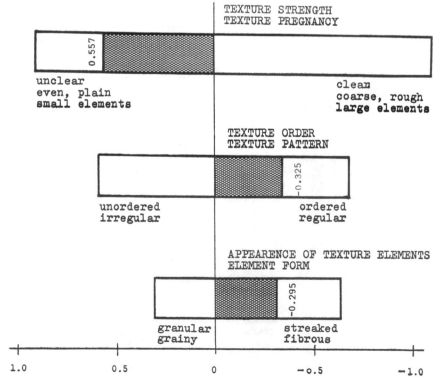

TEXTURE STRENGTH
TEXTURE PREGNANCY

0.557

unclear
even, plain
small elements

clean
coarse, rough
large elements

TEXTURE ORDER
TEXTURE PATTERN

-0.325

unordered
irregular

ordered
regular

APPEARENCE OF TEXTURE ELEMENTS
ELEMENT FORM

-0.295

granular
grainy

streaked
fibrous

| 1.0 | 0.5 | 0 | -0.5 | -1.0 |

REFERENCES

Edberg, G. *Systematisering av texturer. Texturers egenskaper* (Statens råd för byggnadsforskning's Reports No. Bb 345:1, Bb 345:2, Bb 345:3-4). Stockholm, Sweden: Royal Institute of Technology, 1968, 1971, 1976.

Edberg, G. *Systematisering av texturer. Texturers egenskaper* (Report No. R90:1977). Stockholm, Sweden: Statens råd för byggnadsforskning, 1977.

Eisler, H., & Roskam, E. E. Multidimensional similarity: An experimental and theoretical comparison of vector, distance, and set theoretical models. 1. Models and internal consistency of data. *Acta Psychologica,* 1977, *41,* 1-46. (a)

Eisler, H., & Roskam, E. E. Multidimensional similarity: An experimental and theoretical comparison of vector, distance, and set theoretical models. 2. Multidimensional analyses: The subjective space. *Acta Psychologica,* 1977, *41,* 335-363. (b)

Ekman, G., & Sjöberg, L. Scaling. *Annual Review of Psychology,* 1965, *16,* 451-474.

Gibson, J. J. *The perception of the visual world.* Boston, Mass.: Houghton Mifflin, 1950.

Gibson, J. J. *The senses considered as perceptual systems.* Boston, Mass.: Houghton Mifflin, 1966.

Roskam, E. E. Multidimensional scaling by metric transformation of data. *Nederlands Tijdschrift voor de Psychologie,* 1972, *27,* 486-508.

Sjöberg, L. Models of similarity and intensity. *Psychological Bulletin,* 1975, *82,* 191-206.

Young, F. W., & Torgerson, W. S. TORSCA: A Fortran-4 program for Shepard-Kruskal multidimensional scaling analysis. *Behavioral Science,* 1967, *12,* 498.

11 Misperception of Exponential Growth and the Psychological Magnitude of Numbers

Willem A. Wagenaar
Institute for Perception TNO
Soesterberg, The Netherlands

In this paper, I first sketch how people tend to underestimate exponential growth. Next, I discuss what has been said about the psychological magnitude of numbers, the number scale being just another continuum susceptible to psychophysical transformation. Finally, I attempt to link the two phenomena, explaining the first by the second.

1. MISPERCEPTION OF EXPONENTIAL GROWTH

1.1. Introduction

Many worldwide problems of today are related to growth. Economic growth and population growth induce shortages of energy, raw materials and food, and an increase in cost of living and pollution. These processes show a marked exponential character that is going faster and faster. Any attempt to control these processes will depend on the cooperation of individual citizens. These citizens should appreciate how fast the growth will be before they can reasonably weigh the growth problem against a number of alternative issues, such as religion or personal comfort. In the past 5 years, I have conducted a number of experiments on perception of exponential growth by human subjects. The growth processes were presented directly by means of graphs or tables, and subjects were asked to predict future events on the basis of prior history. Here is a simple example.

Pollution in the upper air space was measured in 5 consecutive years. Expressed as a 'pollution index' the outcomes were: 3, 7, 20, 55, 148. Subjects were asked: If nothing will stop this growth process, what do you expect the index to be after another 5 years? The estimates of 30 subjects are presented in Table 11.1 (Wagenaar & Sagaria, 1975). You should notice that 20 out of 30 subjects estimate below 2500, which is only 10% of the best normative prediction. If you present the best extrapolation and ask in which year it will be reached, 20 out of 30 subjects do not expect that event within the next 10 years. Half of the subjects expect the event a long time after the year 2000!

The growth series presented in the example is described by:

$$y = e^x \tag{11.1}$$

where y = pollution index and x = number of years. Complication of this function may lead to three different sets of stimuli.

Absolute size of the pollution index is varied by

$$y = a\, e^x, (a = 1, 2, 4, \dots 128) \tag{11.2}$$

The growth tendency is varied by using

$$y = e^{bx}, (b = 1.0, 1.1, 1.2, \dots 1.7) \tag{11.3}$$

The initial level is varied by using

$$y = e^x + c, (c = 0, 100, 200, \dots 700) \tag{11.4}$$

This illustration examplifies the condition $a = 1$, $b = 1.0$, $c = 0$. Results of two groups of subjects are discussed here. These two groups were assigned to the following tasks:

Group 1. Estimate how large the index will be after 5 more years.
Group 2. Estimate how large the index will be next year, the following year, etc., up to 5 years (stepwise extrapolation).

The results led us to propose a mathematical model for misperception of exponential growth, which is presented first because it may serve as a framework for the discussion of the results.

TABLE 11.1
Subjective Extrapolations: Air-Pollution Example
(a = 1, b = 1.0, c = 0)

Extrapolation	Number of Subjects	Cumulative Percentage
250–500	11	37
501–1000	5	53
1001–2500	4	67
2501–10.000	5	83
10.001–25.000	2	90
>25.000	3	100

1.2. The Mathematical Model and Some Data Supporting It

The model assumes that underestimation results from misperception of the growth rate b. The subjects can compensate for this misperception through adjustment of the absolute magnitude of their responses.

For the a-series, the predictions in group 1 would be described by:

$$\hat{y} = a\ e^5 \cdot (\alpha e^{\beta})^5 \tag{11.5}$$

or

$$Ln\ \hat{y} = Ln\ a + 5\ Ln\ \alpha + 5(1 + \beta) \tag{11.6}$$

which means that plots of Ln $\hat{y}$ versus Ln a would yield linear functions with unit slope.

For the b-series, the predictions in group 1 would be described by:

$$\hat{y} = e^{5b} \cdot (\alpha\ e^{\beta b})^5 \tag{11.7}$$

or

$$Ln\ \hat{y} = 5\ Ln\ \alpha + 5\ b(1 + \beta) \tag{11.8}$$

which means that plots of Ln $\hat{y}$ vs. b would yield linear functions with a slope $5(1 + \beta)$ and intercept 5 Ln α.

In Fig. 11.1, plots of Ln $\hat{y}$ vs. Ln a are presented for the 25%, 50%, and 75% points of the distributions of responses. The plots indeed have unit slopes, as shown by the dotted lines, which were obtained by substituting in Eq. 11.6 the values of α and β as determined in Fig. 11.2.

Figure 11.2 presents plots of Ln $\hat{y}$ vs. b. The linear components account for 96%, 82%, and 69% of the variance (first to third quartile). The differences between subjects are caused by the values of α (intercept differences) whereas β (slope) is approximately .20 for all subjects.

Results of the c-series and of group 2 can be briefly summarized. In group 1, the c-series elicited strong effects of underestimation; this is illustrated in Fig. 11.3 by the dramatic drop of $\hat{y}$ when c goes from zero to 100. The results of group 2 (step-by-step extrapolation) were very similar to the results of group 1. Additionally, they reveal, as prescribed by the model, that underestimation is already present in the first value predicted and that it remains the same for all following steps (Fig. 11.4). The conclusions of these experiments are:

1. Underestimation of exponential growth presented through tabulated data is caused by the fact that people take into account only 20% of the exponent, which means applying too small a multiplier the correct number of times.
2. Individual differences are caused by different adjustments of the absolute magnitude of the responses (a kind of willingness to produce large numbers).

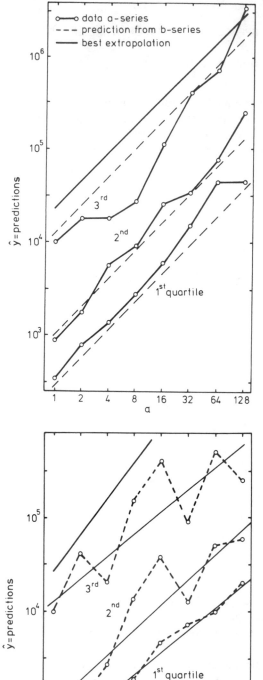

FIG. 11.1. A plot of predictions of group 1 (on a logarithmic scale) vs. a, the absolute size of the input series (also on a logarithmic scale). Dotted lines have unit slopes; intercepts are based on estimates of α and β derived from Fig. 11.2.

FIG. 11.2. A plot of predictions of group 1 (on a logarithmic scale) vs. b.

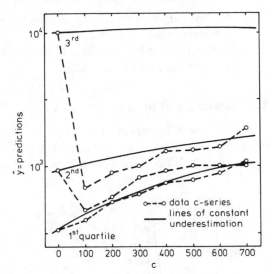

FIG. 11.3. A plot of predictions of group 1 (on a logarithmic scale) vs. c. The drawn lines represent the response level to be expected when addition of c does not change underestimation.

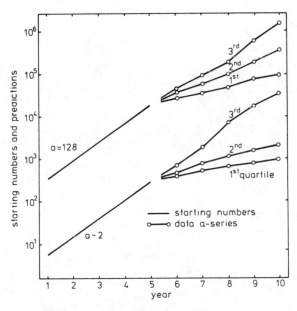

FIG. 11.4. A plot of predictions of group 2 (on a logarithmic scale) as a function of x (years).

3. The absolute magnitude of the stimulus numbers has no effect on the underestimation.
4. Underestimation is more liable to occur when the growth is superimposed on a constant, nonzero, level.

1.3. Extension of the Experiments

It was attempted to improve perception of growth by substituting graphs for tables, keeping in mind that "a picture is worth a thousand words." The graphs represented the b-series described earlier and were manufactured with three

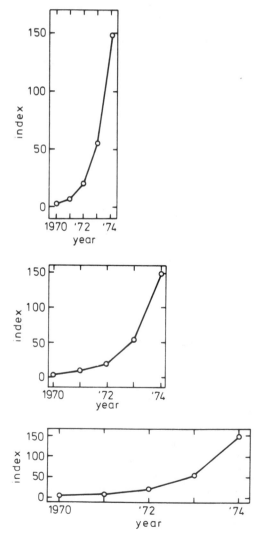

FIG. 11.5. Examples of graphical representations of $y = e^x$.

length-to-width ratios (Fig. 11.5), each presented to a different group. Estimates of α and β can again be obtained from plots of Ln $\hat{y}$ vs. b. The results, presented in Fig. 11.6, show that the plots are linear as well as that individual differences were again due to α and not to β. The values of β, which were virtually similar in the three groups, ranged from $-.07$ to $.28$, with a median value of .04.

The graph experiment was also conducted with very sophisticated subjects. One group consisted of college students who first received a 1 hour lecture on exponential growth and the tendency to underestimate. Another group consisted of members of the Conservation Committee of the Senate and House of Representatives of the State of Pennsylvania, U.S.A. The results of both groups indicate that sophistication affects α (the willingness to use high numbers) but not β (the sensitivity to growth). We conclude from the graph experiments:

1. Underestimation of growth is not reduced when data are presented graphically. Rather it is increased.
2. Sensitivity to growth is not related to the length-to-width ratio of the graphs.

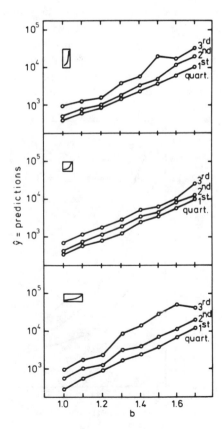

FIG. 11.6. Plots of predictions in the graph experiment (on a logarithmic scale).

3. Sensitivity to growth is fairly constant across subjects, irrespective of their level of sophistication.

In another series of experiments (Wagenaar & Timmers, 1979), growth was presented on a scope display by small duckweeds growing in a pond. At a certain point the display was halted, and the subject had to indicate how long it would take to get the pond completely covered with duckweeds. In this manner, growth was presented by numerousness instead of by numbers. Also, a time factor was involved because the results of the growth process were shown as they developed in time. Some results of this experiment are shown in Fig. 11.7.

A remarkable result was obtained when the number of duckweeds was updated a limited number of times (3, 5, or 7). It appeared that underestimation tended to be less when the rate of updating became smaller (Fig. 11.8). This effect is not incongruent with our daily experience: Persons continuously involved in a process often fail to notice gradual changes that are easily discerned by people who have been away for some time. From the duckweed experiments, we conclude:

1. Underestimation is absent when the growth is almost linear (b = .1), but values of β drop considerably when b increases.
2. It helps when a larger portion of the process is shown (presentation is stopped at t = 33, 50 or 67% of the time needed to get the pond covered), but this advantage tends to disappear when b increases.
3. Underestimation may be less when a process is updated less frequently.

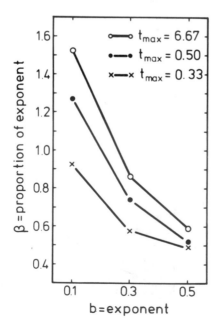

FIG. 11.7. β-scores in the pond-and-duckweed experiment; t_{max} is the proportion of time needed to get the pond filled that was shown to the subjects.

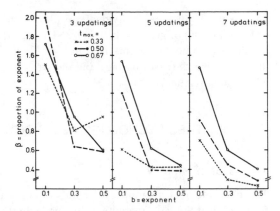

FIG. 11.8. β-scores in the pond-and-duckweed experiment with limited updating rates.

The effect of updating frequency was also studied in number series (Wagenaar & Timmers, 1978). The results were nicely replicated. The three series—3, 20, 148; 3, 7, 20, 55, 148; 3, 5, 10, 20, 39, 76, 148—were perceived to grow slower in that order.

A full release from underestimation can be obtained when growth functions with a negative exponent are presented. Such "decline" functions are obtained

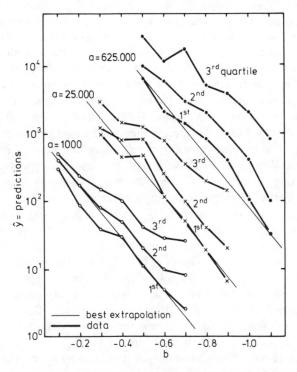

FIG. 11.9.   A plot of predictions (on a logarithmic scale) in the decline functions experiment. (From Timmers & Wagenaar, 1977).

when square miles per individual are plotted instead of individuals per square mile, or amount of gasoline bought by $10 instead of the price per gallon. Results of such experiments are presented in Fig. 11.9. Values of β are close to 1.0 for the best subjects (first quartile), but the worst subjects (third quartile) still have β's of approximately .20.

2. THE PSYCHOLOGICAL MAGNITUDE OF NUMBERS

2.1. A Brief History

The psychological magnitude of numbers is a much discussed topic within the framework of Stevens' magnitude-scaling techniques. Garner, Hake, and Eriksen (1956) were probably the first to doubt that subjects use the number scale in the way prescribed by simple arithmetic rules. Attneave (1962) elaborated on this idea, suggesting that a *phenotypical* exponent provided by magnitude scaling is the product of a *genotypical* exponent (the "real" one) and the exponent of the subjective number scale. In his view, the psychophysical function that relates subjective number to objective number is a power function with an exponent of about .4. Some intuitive appreciation of the phenomenon can be obtained from Attneave's example (1962): "Suppose we agree that *one* is a very small number and that a *million* is a very large number. Now give me a good example of a medium-size number [p. 626]." You may feel comfortable with the mean response of Attneave's subjects: 186, 575. This number would lie halfway between one and a million after a power transformation with an exponent of .41.

A more extensive discussion of the role of subjective number in psychophysical scaling is presented by Wagenaar (1975). Here we concentrate on some experiments designed to assess the exponent of the psychophysical function of subjective number. In some of the experiments, numbers were not used as stimuli but as the dependent variable. Thus far, however, it was always assumed that the function relating subjective number to numerical response is just the inverse of the function that relates numerical stimuli to subjective number.

According to the two-stage model of magnitude judgment as formulated by Attneave, phenotypical exponents consist of two factors: the genotypical exponent and the exponent of subjective number. By adroit experimentation, it is possible to estimate the contributions of both factors. One possibility is to obtain magnitude judgments for stimuli and for *differences* between stimuli. Exponents for subjective number, estimated on the basis of such data, reached values of .88 (Curtis, Attneave, & Harrington, 1968), .6 to .9 (Rule, Curtis, & Markley, 1970), and .75 (Curtis, 1970). Curtis and Fox (1969) found a value of .7 in an experiment employing magnitude judgments of sums.

A more direct approach to the scaling of subjective numbers is to use numbers as stimuli in scaling experiments. An obvious obstacle is that subjects might use previously learned arithmetic rules (such as taking absolute differences for similarity ratings). In two successive publications on this matter, Rule (1969, 1971) reported concave functions with exponents in the range .4–.5. Schneider, Parker, Ostrosky, Stein, and Kanow (1974) observed exponents in the range .7–.8. Rule and Curtis (1973) report an exponent of .63 in a nonmetric conjoint measurement of subjective number and weight. Finally, Rule (1972), using triadic comparisons, found that subjective number is a negatively accelerated function of objective number. Taken together, the experimental evidence reveals that subjective number is a power function of objective number with an exponent below 1.0, probably even below .6.

2.2. New Experimental Evidence

The exponential growth experiments cited earlier provided as a byproduct some additional data on the psychological magnitude of numbers. The reasoning is as follows. In the first experiment discussed, exponential series had the general form presented by Eq. 11.2: $y = a\,e^x$, $a = 1, 2, 4, \ldots 128$. With sufficient spacing of the values of a, extrapolation will monotonically increase with a. When two values of a are close to each other the resulting series might become quite similar. In that case, it is possible that a subject produces the smaller response for the series with the larger numbers. Now the occurrence of these inversions in the rank ordering of responses to two stimulus series are taken as an index for the similarity between the series. These similarities are then scaled by a Thurstone case-V technique (Torgerson, 1958), which yields measurement of subjective magnitude on an interval scale (Suppes & Zinnes, 1963).

The absolute magnitude of the stimulus series is expressed by a, as division by a will render all stimulus series equal. Any variable c.a, in which c is a constant, would represent magnitude as well. Hence a represents magnitude on a ratio scale. In order to prove meaningfulness of the scale it is necessary to show how the obtained relation between absolute and subjective number depends on the admissible scale transformations. A power law would describe the relation thus:

$$S = a\,I^b + c \tag{11.9}$$

where S = subjective number, I = absolute number, and a, b, and c are constants. Application of the admissible transformations (linear transformation on S, similarity transformation on I) results in:

$$pS + q = a(rI)^b + c \tag{11.10}$$

(p, q, and r are constants). Equation 11.10 can be rewritten as:

$$S = \frac{ar^b}{P} \cdot I^b + \frac{c-q}{P} \tag{11.11}$$

In this expression $\frac{ar^b}{P}$ and $\frac{c-q}{P}$ are constants. Thus, the admissible transformations only affect some constants in the power law, not the structure or the value of the exponent.

The raw results entering the proposed analysis consist of the number of times the *smaller* extrapolation was produced with a starting series with *larger* numbers. For each pair of the eight conditions (a = 1, 2, 4, ... 128) this inversion of the rank ordering could occur for maximally 30 subjects. The complete matrix of inversions is presented in Table 11.2.

The scale values obtained for a = 1, 2, 4, ... 128 are presented in Fig. 11.10. A Mosteller test for goodness of fit (Mosteller, 1951) yielded $\chi^2 = 17.43$, df = 21, p > .70.

Fitting an exponential curve through these data relies heavily on the estimation of the additive constant c. The extreme estimates of c are between 0 and −3.09. The resulting values of the Stevens exponent b are between .48 and .14. The linear component in the plot of log (scale value +3.09) vs. log a accounts for 99.4% of the variance.

The exponent for subjective number thus obtained is quite a bit below the values reported by Curtis, Rule, and their associates, and its minimum is even below Attneave's estimate. Possibly, we are dealing with a range effect. Curtis, Rule, and associates worked with numbers in the range from 1 to 100, or two log units. As argued by Teghtsoonian (1971), estimates of exponents based on different ranges could be linked by the simple formula:

$$\text{exponent} \times \log \text{stimulus range} = \text{constant} \tag{11.12}$$

Now it could be argued that the a-series growth functions confront the subject with a range of about six log units if the numerical responses are included. With this range, the exponent is expected to be one third of the exponents usually reported. Hence, a value of about .20 would not be extremely low.

TABLE 11.2
Inversions in the Rank Orderings of Extrapolations

a	1	2	4	8	16	32	64
2	6						
4	5	7					
8	3	4	6				
16	2	2	5	8			
32	0	1	3	6	6		
64	0	0	1	2	2	3	
128	0	1	1	2	3	3	6

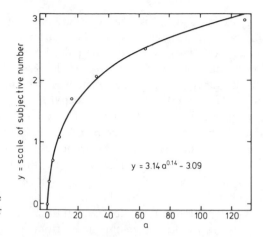

FIG. 11.10.   Subjective vs. absolute number (open circles) and the power function best fitting the data.

$$y = 3.14\,a^{0.14} - 3.09$$

2.3. Subjective Number and Utility Functions

In the previous subsection, we saw that the objective number scale behaves like a physical continuum that has a subjective counterpart, a subjective number. A two-stage model of magnitude scaling was discussed in which two types of transformations are postulated. Type 1 is the sought psychophysical transformation from intensity to sensation; then sensation is matched with subjective number, whereafter the type 2 transformation occurs: from subjective number to numerical response. The exponent for subjective number cannot be measured by simple magnitude scaling because it is assumed that in that case the two transformations become reciprocal, one neutralizing the other. The exponent for subjective number is to be measured by isolating one of the two transformations. In this subsection, I present a much discussed case in which, in my opinion, we are dealing with a type 1 transformation, from numerical stimulus to subjective number, "tapped halfway" before the type 2 transformation was applied.

The issue deals with the so-called "utility of money." The following example may serve as an illustration: You are invited to play in a lottery with a 10% probability of winning. Alternatively, you may choose to receive 10% of the

TABLE 11.3
Lotteries, Illustrating the Utility of Money

Win	with Probability	or Receive Immediately
$ .10	.1	$ .01
$ 10	.1	$ 1
$ 1000	.1	$ 100
$ 100,000	.1	$ 10,000
$ 10,000,000	.1	$ 1,000,000

prize without playing. As the expected values of the lotteries equal 10% of the prize, any rational person should be indifferent with respect to playing or not playing. As it appears, subjects are indeed indifferent or prefer to play when the prize is small, but with high prizes subjects would rather take 10% than bother with the lottery. This phenomenon was explained by the introduction of the "utility" concept: Utility is the subjective value attached to a commodity, and it can be measured on an interval scale (Neumann & Morgenstern, 1944). Utility of money is the subjective counterpart of amount of money, and in this respect it bears a close conceptual resemblance to subjective number. The utility curve for money is a psychophysical relation, plotting the subjective value of money against its monetary value. Various techniques have been designed to measure this curve, and all were based on the idea that a subject should not be asked to apply a type 2 transformation on utilities. One can say that utility functions represent two type 1 transformations: from number to subjective number and from value to utility. The exponent of a utility function is the product of the exponents of these two transformations. Hence, the genotypical exponent for utility is to be obtained by division. This will result in a value unequal to 1.0 only if the exponents of utility functions are outside the range of exponents for subjective number.

The most classic studies on utility functions are by Mosteller and Nogee (1951), Davidson, Suppes, and Siegel (1957), and Tversky (1967a, 1967b), three of which are reprinted in a paperback volume edited by Edwards and Tversky (1967). A qualitative description of the general form of the utility curve was given by Friedman and Savage (1948), and the most prominent feature of this curve is its concave character. Inasmuch as utility is supposed to be measured on an interval scale and monetary value on a ratio scale, concavity is a meaningful property. Also, as shown before, values of the Stevens exponent extracted from the data are constant under admissible transformations. Concavity was reported by Mosteller and Nogee (11 out of 15 subjects) and Davidson et al. (12 out of 15 subjects). Values of the Stevens exponents extracted from averages across subjects are .78 and .90. Tversky observed almost linear utility functions (exponent = 1.0). These estimates, divided by the exponent of number (.4 to .6) all yield genotypical Stevens exponents for utility above 1.0. The general form described by Friedman and Savage seems to be determined by subjective usage of numbers, rather than by utility.

The next example, which is known as the St. Petersburg paradox (Bernoulli, 1738), comes a little closer to the exponential growth situation: You are invited to bet on the outcome of flipping a coin. If heads turns up first you win two roubles; if not, you neither win nor lose anything. As long as heads keeps turning up your gains will be doubled, but at the first appearance of tails the game is over. What price are you willing to pay as a fee to enter the game? Most subjects do not pay more than a maximum of 10 roubles. Yet the expected value of the gains is:

$$2 \times \tfrac{1}{2} + 4 \times \tfrac{1}{4} + 8 \times \tfrac{1}{8} \dots = 1 + 1 + 1 \dots = \infty \qquad (11.13)$$

Hence, one should be willing to pay any fee. The traditional explanation of the nonnormative behavior is that the utility curve for money is concave: The higher terms of the expected value approach to zero, which makes the expected value go to a finite value. This explanation assumes that the psychophysical transformation of the money-number dimension is not in the same way applied on the series of declining probabilities. In fact, if money is transformed by raising it to the power .8 (estimate based on the data provided in this subsection) whereas probabilities are raised to the power .4, terms of the expected value would be squared instead of reduced.

On the basis of our exponential growth studies, we can offer a slightly different solution to the St. Petersburg paradox. We assume that subjects do not compute 10 or 20 terms of which the expected value is composed. Rather, they consider a few initial values like 2, 4, 8 and ½, ¼, ⅛, which are extrapolated subjectively. We know already that extrapolations of increasing series tend to be low, whereas the decline of the second series may be perceived correctly. Thus, the terms of the expected value would go to zero quite soon. The difference with the classical account is that computation is replaced by intuitive extrapolation. The underestimation of growth comes in lieu of the concave utility function, but this distinction may boil down to a matter of words, as it is not impossible that underestimation of growth is also a product of the psychophysical transformation of the number scale. This is the topic of the next section.

3. A PSYCHOPHYSICAL EXPLANATION OF GROWTH MISPERCEPTION

3.1. General Outline

A subject presented with the exponential series 1, 10, 100, 1000, . . . would correctly continue with 10,000, 100,000, etc. The continuation would be independent of psychophysical transformations, strategies, or problem-solving processes. The task is executed according to the norms because the mathematical rule is obvious and overlearned. Problems arise only when the time series is relatively unfamiliar, such as in the example 3, 7, 20, 55, 148, . . . ($y = e^x$). In order to extrapolate, we have to go through two stages at least: discovery of the rule and application of the rule. As demonstrated in section 1 of this paper, subjects usually discover the fact that time series are exponential, and they apply the exponential rule consistently. They only judge the growth rate to be smaller than its actual value (e in the example), and this underestimation is thought to occur in the first stage. An account of this effect could be given by postulating that subjects do not *compute* the growth rate by taking the ratio of two successive numbers, but rather that they *estimate* growth rate by looking at the type 1 transformation of the input series. The exponent q of this psychophysical transformation would be present in the ratio of successive transformed numbers:

$$\frac{e^{n_q}}{e^{(n-1)q}} = e^q \tag{11.14}$$

The objective ratios ranged from 2.7 to 5.0 in our experiments; the power transforms will range considerably less, provided that $1 > q > 0$. In the case q = .4, the power transforms lie between 1.5 and 2.0; in the case q = .2, the extremes are 1.2 and 1.4. The subjective correlates of growth rate are thus within a very narrow range. How are these transformed into numerical values, to be used in stage 2? Normally, the type 2 transformation results in a wide range of numbers, anchored by a modulus ("give the number 10 to this standard stimulus"). Because, in our case, the resulting number must be on an absolute scale, the subject cannot give a value relative to a modulus. Comparison to another dimension such as line length (cf. Krantz, 1972) will neither increase the range nor provide a modulus. I propose that subjects translate the subjective correlates of ratios into proportions: A ratio of 1.5 then means that extrapolation is performed by increasing previous numbers by 50%. Mapping estimated growth onto the proportion scale is a partitioning activity, which according to Stevens is executed without a power transformation, provided that the numerical proportion scale is metathetic (Stevens, 1975, Ch. 5). Formally, one can only determine whether a scale is prothetic or metathetic by looking at the way a dimension behaves in category scaling. Intuitively, however, proportions are more like pitch than like loudness: .75 is not only more than .25, it is also qualitatively different, and time error will not easily diffuse .75 into .25, notwithstanding what has been said by Rule (1969). Thus, accepting the proportion scale as metathetic, we can picture the translation of estimated growth rate into a number without a type 2 transformation. A schematic representation of the proposed theory looks like this:

input numbers	type 1 transf.	subj. numbers	relation judgment	estimated growth	linear transf.	proportion

The underestimation β of the exponent, which was found to be around .2, would according to this view be identical with q, the Stevens exponent for number. The value .2 coincides with our estimate of this exponent, which was obtained in the context of a growth experiment.

The previous reasoning does not add so much to what has been said about underestimation: It only links the phenomenon with the more basic processes of psychophysical transformations. It still needs further explanation why the underestimation is less when the growth is described by fewer data points, and why the effect may even be absent when the growth is presented as a decline. Specifically, we should explain why the psychophysical transformation of the starting numbers is different in these two instances.

3.2. Specific Explanations

Why is it that people underestimate the increase of the series 3, 7, 20, 55, 148, and correctly perceive the decline of 22,026, 8103, 2981, 1097, 403? If it is to be attributed to different psychophysical transformations, why would they differ? I can tentatively indicate four lines of explanation.

Magnitude. The growth and decline functions differ with respect to magnitude of the numbers. It is not impossible that the Stevens exponent for number is not constant along the number scale, but in that case one would rather imagine that the exponent decreases with increasing magnitude. There is no experimental evidence to this effect, but then, of course, many experiments used only numbers below 100, or even below 10. The exponential growth experiments, however, did not reveal better performance with larger numbers, and finally the difference between growth and decline extrapolations seems to be present even in the following example, where magnitude differences have been removed: 55, 148, 403, 1097—how many steps to 22,000? 1097, 403, 148, 55—how many steps to 3?

Order. In the growth series, all numbers except the first are preceded by smaller numbers, whereas in the decline series the reverse is true. Two different effects of order could be expected. One is nicely illustrated by Cross (1973): Magnitude estimations tend to be larger when a stimulus is preceded by a larger one, and smaller when a stimulus is preceded by a smaller one. This is interpreted as a strategy effect: The previous numerical response serves as an anchor from which insufficient adjustment is made (cf. Tversky & Kahneman, 1974). An opposite effect is predicted by adaptation-level theory (Helson, 1964): A high preceding stimulus raises the adaptation level, which in turn lowers the subjective impression of the stimulus presented. Stevens (1975, p. 278) argues that Cross' (1973) results are in conflict with adaptation-level theory, but this may not be the case. If in magnitude-scaling fluctuations of the adaptation level are thought to affect the type 1 transformation whereas anchoring is thought to influence the type 2 transformation, both effects could occur simultaneously. The stronger one wins and shows up in the results. According to this view, we might expect contrast effects of preceding numbers in the judgment of exponential growth because we are dealing only with the type 1 transformation. Why then should these contrast effects be larger in case of decline functions? One possibly is that the magnitude of contrast is determined by *differences* between successive numbers and not by *ratios*.

Contrast effects could nicely account for the fact that growth is more accurately perceived when fewer data points are presented. A comparison of the series 3, 20, 148; 3, 7, 20, 55, 158; and 3, 5, 10, 20, 39, 76, 148 shows that steps between numbers are increased when the number of data points is reduced, and contrast likewise.

Boundedness.   When subjects start to read the growth series, they can attach scale values to the successive numbers with no risk of striking against the upper limit of the scale; when reading the decline series, however, they may have reserved a scale value for the number zero, the lower limit of the numerical response. In other words, the scale for increasing series is unbounded whereas the scale for decreasing series is bounded. This boundary dictates how the other scale values are used; subjects cannot respond to relative magnitudes by placing them in their appropriate place on a ratio scale. Instead, they must spread the range of stimuli over the limited set of scale values. This is in fact a partitioning operation, and again we can say that it involves no power transformation, provided that the number scale is metathetic. Accepting this, it is to be expected that the exponent for subjective number is equal to 1.0 for exponential decline series.

Inverse Attributes.   This final explanation is offered as an aside, because it presumes that the continuum scaled by the observer is not number, but growth as presented by numbers. In that case, two inverse attributes are judged: growth and decline. The exponents for these two need not be equal.

I would like to conclude by reiterating that an important societal phenomenon—the continuous intuitive underestimation of growth—is caused by simple psychophysical transformations applied on the number and numerousness dimensions. Developments that are perfectly in line with what we already know will often come as a complete surprise, and we will not be prepared for them unless we recognize this problem and act accordingly.

REFERENCES

Attneave, F. Perception and related areas. In S. Koch (Ed.), *Psychology: A study of a science* (Vol. 4). New York: McGraw-Hill, 1962.

Bernoulli, D. Specimen theoriae novae de mensura sortis. *Commentarii academiae scientiarum imperiales petropolitanae*, 1738, *5*, 175–192. (English translation in G. A. Miller [Ed.], *Mathematics and psychology*. New York: Wiley, 1964.)

Cross, D. V. Sequential dependencies and regression in psychophysical studies. *Perception & Psychophysics*, 1973, *14*, 547–552.

Curtis, D. W. Magnitude estimations and category judgments of brightness and brightness intervals: A two stage interpretation. *Journal of Experimental Psychology*, 1970, *83*, 201–208.

Curtis, D. W., Attneave, F., & Harrington, T. L. A test of a two-stage model of magnitude judgment. *Perception & Psychophysics*, 1968, *3*, 25–31.

Curtis, D. W., & Fox, B. E. Direct quantitative judgments of sums and a two-stage model for psychophysical judgments. *Perception & Psychophysics*, 1969, *5*, 89-93.

Davidson, P., Suppes, P., & Siegel, S. *Decision making: An experimental approach.* Stanford, Cal.: Stanford University Press, 1957.

Edwards, W., & Tversky, A. (Eds.). *Decision making.* Harmondsworth: Penguin, 1967.

Friedman, M., & Savage, L. J. The utility analysis of choices involving risk. *Journal of Political Economy*, 1948, *56*, 279-304.

Garner, W. R., Hake, H. W., & Eriksen, C. W. Operationism and the concept of perception. *Psychological Review*, 1956, *63*, 149-159.

Helson, H. *Adaptation level theory.* New York: Harper & Row, 1964.

Krantz, D. H. A theory of magnitude estimation and cross-modality matching. *Journal of Mathematical Psychology*, 1972, *9*, 168-199.

Mosteller, F., & Nogee, P. An experimental measurement of utility. *Journal of Political Economy*, 1951, *59*, 371-404.

Neumann, J., & Morgenstern, O. *Theory of games and economic behavior.* Princeton, N.J.: Princeton University Press, 1944.

Rule, S. J. Equal discriminability scale of number. *Journal of Experimental Psychology*, 1969, *79*, 35-38.

Rule, S. J. Discriminability scales of number for multiple and fractional estimates. *Acta Psychologica*, 1971, *35*, 328-333.

Rule, S. J. Comparison of intervals between subjective numbers. *Perception & Psychophysics*, 1972, *11*, 97-98.

Rule, S. J., Curtis, D. W., & Markley, R. P. Input and output transformations from magnitude estimations. *Journal of Experimental Psychology*, 1970, *86*, 343-349.

Rule, S. J., & Curtis, D. W. Conjoint scaling of subjective number and weight. *Journal of Experimental Psychology*, 1973, *97*, 305-309.

Schneider, B., Parker, S., Ostrosky, D., Stein, D., & Kanow, G. A scale for the psychological magnitude of number. *Perception & Psychophysics*, 1974, *16*, 43-46.

Stevens, S. S. *Psychophysics.* New York: Wiley, 1975.

Suppes, P., & Zinnes, J. L. Basic measurement theory. In R. D. Luce, R. R. Bush, & E. Galanter (Eds.), *Handbook of mathematical psychology* (Vol. 1). New York. Wiley, 1963.

Teghtsoonian, R. On the exponents in Stevens' law and the constant in Ekman's law. *Psychological Review*, 1971, *78*, 71-80.

Timmers, H., & Wagenaar, W. A. Inverse statistics and the misperception of exponential growth. *Perception & Psychophysics*, 1977, *21*, 558-562.

Torgerson, W. *Theory and methods of scaling.* New York: Wiley, 1958.

Tversky, A. Additivity, utility, and subjective probability. *Journal of Mathematical Psychology*, 1967, *4*, 175-201. (a)

Tversky, A. Utility theory and additivity analysis of risky choices. *Journal of Experimental Psychology*, 1967, *75*, 27-36. (b)

Tversky, A., & Kahneman, D. Judgment under uncertainty: Heuristics and biases. *Science*, 1974, *185*, 1124-1131.

Wagenaar, W. A. Stevens vs. Fechner: A plea for dismissal of the case. *Acta Psychologica*, 1975, *39*, 225-235.

Wagenaar, W. A., & Sagaria, S. Misperception of exponential growth. *Perception & Psychophysics*, 1975, *18*, 422-426.

Wagenaar, W. A., & Timmers, H. Extrapolation of exponential time series is not enhanced by having more data points. *Perception & Psychophysics*, 1978, *24*, 182-184.

Wagenaar, W. A., & Timmers, H. The pond-and-duckweed problem; Three experiments on the misperception of exponential growth. *Acta Psychologica*, 1979, *43*, 239-251.

12

On S. S. Stevens' Psychophysics and the Measurement of Subjective Probability and Utility

Dirk Wendt

Christian-Albrechts-Universität, Kiel, West-Germany

In this paper it is shown that Stevens' and Fechner's approaches to psychophysics are not necessarily contradictory, and that both can be and have been successfully applied to the measurement of subjective probability and utility. Moreover, a more axiomatic approach is advocated.

1. HISTORY

Going back far enough into history, we find that (except for early astronomers constructing scales for the magnitude or brightness of stars) psychophysics started with an assessment-of-utility problem. Way back in 1728, Gabriel Cramer proposed a square-root function, i.e. a power function for the assessment of the utility of money: $U = k \, D^{.5}$, where U indicates utility, D monetary value, and k a scaling constant. Ten years later, in 1738, Daniel Bernoulli found another function that he considered more appropriate, namely a logarithmic function: $U = k \log D$, which constitutes, in principle, Fechner's psychophysical law. S. S. Stevens (1975) considered Bernoulli's statement a serious mistake that threw psychophysics back, or at least halted it for about 200 years (p. 19).

Weber's law, Fechner's law (which was based on it), and the more general Fullerton and Cattell principle (1892) that equally often noticed differences are (subjectively) equal unless always or never noticed, led to Thurstone's law of comparative judgment (1927). The law of comparative judgment enabled psychophysicists to measure commodities or variables where no physical measures exist, using the same principles as applicable to physically measurable stimuli. Stevens (1975) however, considered the Fullerton/Cattell principle "a false but appealing notion [p. 232]." He apparently did not recognize that this "false but appealing notion" constituted—at least in part—the basis for his own work.

Moreover, Stevens seems not to have seen that the Fullerton/Cattell principle was meant (or at least interpreted and used) as a *definition* of subjective distances, not as an observational *statement* about them. As a definition the Fullerton/Cattell principle cannot be "false" but only more or less appropriate.

S. S. Stevens never made use of the idea of measuring variables or commodities by means of the uncertainties involved in judgments of intensities. (He termed measures based on uncertainties "poikilitic measures,"[1] e.g., in Stevens 1975, p. 231.) Instead, in his review of L. L. Thurstone's book *The measurement of values* (1959), he added a "Case VI" to Thurstone's famous five cases of the law of comparative judgment. Stevens called this additional case "the equal-ratios assumption." It assumes that "equal units of dispersion represent not equal distances but equal ratios along the subjective continuum (Stevens 1959b, p. 389; Stevens 1975, p. 232)."

Stevens himself, instead of using dispersions or variability, used "direct scaling methods": (1) magnitude measures, i.e., direct assessment of numbers to stimuli, events, or their respective sensations; (2) cross-modality-matching, i.e., the assessment of the stimulus intensity on one physical continuum to that of another; (3) fractionating methods where the subject's task is to divide the (subjective) distance between two given stimuli proportionally to some given numbers—mostly to a fifty-fifty ratio (midpoint scaling). These scaling procedures yield numbers to represent the measured variable directly whereas so-called classical methods like pair comparisons are based on Thurstone's law and yield numbers only through special algorithms involving theoretical assumptions about distributions of sensory magnitudes.

Stevens' psychophysical methods have also been applied to variables and commodities where no physical stimulus continua are available. This is also true of the methods of determining difference limens, which where used to establish Fechner's psychophysics, e.g., in Thurstone's pair comparison (Thurstone, 1927). In a series of studies, G. Ekman demonstrated that Stevens' psychophysical methods could be applied to nonphysical stimulus variables. These studies have been reviewed by Ekman and Sjöberg (1965). In a sense, therefore, Ekman did for Stevens' approach what Thurstone did for Fechner's. Both applied methods of sensory psychophysics to nonphysical variables.

The accumulating results of studies in both the sensory and attitudinal realm in which Stevensian scaling methods were used led Stevens to formulate his famous power law $U = kD^\nu$. This law is a generalization of Cramer's function and Stevens proposed it as an alternative to Fechner's law. Being confronted with

---

[1]From $\pi o \iota \kappa \iota \lambda \lambda \omega$ = to model artificially (Editor's addition).

two competing psychophysical laws, it was hoped that comparisons of subjective scales that were constructed by different scaling methods—i.e., by rating procedures, magnitude estimation, paired comparisons, successive intervals—would yield a decision with respect to which of the two laws was empirically more appropriate. Such studies are reported in Cliff (1973), but they do not lead to any conclusive generalization. Results of scale comparison studies are also reported by Marks, by Schneider, by Orth, and by Wegener in this volume.

2. RELATIONS BETWEEN STEVENSIAN AND FECHNERIAN PSYCHOPHYSICS

In the following paragraphs I discuss two points of criticism on Stevens' psychophysics and its application:

> (1) Stevens, in all his lifelong engagement against Fechnerian/Thurstonian psychophysics, apparently never saw that he himself was applying Fechner's law in his own power law. He did so even *twice:* he applied Fechner's law to the stimulus scale *and* to the response scale.
> (2) Stevens never took up the ideas of axiomatic measurement theory, although he himself (1951) introduced the four famous levels of scale quality: nominal, ordinal, interval, and ratio.

But let us first go into a little more detail in Stevens' psychophysics: In order to obtain the typical psychophysical function, we plot stimulus intensity on the abscissae, and sensation on the ordinate. If we use a (Fechnerian) jnd scale for sensation, and a logarithmic scale for stimulus intensity, the result is a linear function *if Fechner's law holds*. If, however, we use logarithmic scales on both axes, i.e., a logarithmic stimulus intensity scale on the abscissae, and a logarithmic response scale (of number responses for magnitude estimation, or of physical intensity for cross-modality matching) on the ordinate, then a linear function results *if Stevens' power law holds*.

This means that with Fechner's law, linearity is established if we "logarithmize" the stimulus scale and have the sensation scale in jnd units. With Stevens' law, a linear relationship results if we plot *sensations* on both scales, i.e., if we "logarithmize" both scales according to Fechner's law. In this case, the response scale is actually considered as the representation of another stimulus scale. Consequently, in magnitude estimation experiments the numerical judgments are equivalent to "just one form of cross-modality matching" (Cliff 1973, p. 493) where we assume that Fechner's law holds for the internal representation of numerals.

What results as the power exponent in Stevens' law from this procedure is nothing but the ratio of the proportionality factors of the Fechnerian (i.e., logarithmic) transformations of both stimulus continua (one of which serves as response continuum).

I demonstrate this a little more formally. For any two "prothetic" modalities X and Y with X and Y as vectors of physical intensities on the respective continua, and R(X) and R(Y) as the arrays of the respective subjective intensities or "sensations," Stevens' power law pretends: Intensities X_i and Y_i "match", i.e. are perceived equally strong or $R(X_i) = R(Y_i)$, if and only if $X = Y^p$. Note that this relation is completely symetric, i.e. we could just as well write: $Y = X^q$ with $q = \frac{1}{p}$.

It is obvious that $X = Y^p \Leftrightarrow \log X = p \log Y \Leftrightarrow R(X) = R(Y)$. This indicates that the perception, or subjective representation of X and Y are represented by the respective logarithms of their physical intensities, i.e., it is assumed $R(X) = \log X$, $R(Y) = p \log Y$. This is nothing but Fechner's law applied to *both* modalities, and the scale factor between them is Stevens' power exponent p. Thus, Stevens found nothing different from, nor better than Fechner's law. Actually, his power law supports Fechner's law twice.

All this is not new. Auerbach (1971), Cliff (1973), Krantz (1972), Teghtsoonian (1971), and probably others mentioned that Weber's law can be reformulated as: equal stimulus ratios are equally discriminable. Cliff (1973) has written: "Since equal stimulus ratios form equal subjective ratios, equidiscriminable stimuli form equal subjective ratios [p. 494]." Ekman (1964) considered the power law as a special case of Fechner's law. His argumentation is similar to the one given here.

3. NUMBERS AS A PSYCHOPHYSICAL STIMULUS CONTINUUM

Guilford (1954) mentioned the idea of a non-linear relation between the arithmetic and the psychological number continuum already in his "Psychometric methods", and so do Garner (1954), Garner, Hake and Erikson (1956), Goude (1962), Attneave (1962), and Cliff (1973). Cross, Wagenaar, and Rule and Curtis in this volume deal with the problem of the subjective representation of the number continuum, and they cite some further references on this topic.

In a sense, numbers are abstract concepts representing numerousness i.e., the size of sets. Psychophysical laws holding for the perception of sets of elements should hold as well for the internal representation of their respective sizes, i.e. numerousness. Therefore, comparisons of different subjective scales should parallel psychophysical regularities. Studies comparing category and ratio scaling often yield that the category scale is a logarithmic function of the ratio scale. This has been shown by Eisler (1962a, 1962b; see also Montgomery, this volume). More examples of such studies are quoted in Ekman and Sjöberg (1965, p. 464). An interval scale constructed by means of pair comparisons under the assumption of Thurstone's Case V, too, is usually a logarithmic function of a ratio scale obtained by the complete method of ratio estimation (Stevens, 1975, pp. 231 ff). This evidence supports the conjecture that the relationships between internal representations are logarithmic in nature. However, Ekman and Sjöberg (1965), in their review article, conclude that: "Fechner's logarithmic law was replaced by the power law [p. 467]," pointing at the large amount of experimental work accomplished in the 1950s by Stevens and his coworkers. They also think that the power law is "established beyond any reasonable doubt, possibly more firmly than anything else in psychology [p. 467]." I have no doubts about the power law—it just does not differ from Fechner's law applied to both stimulus continua, as shown earlier.

Stevens' own main point seems not to have been the rejection of Fechner's law either. His main point against the Fechnerian/Thurstonian tradition was his objection to accept variability as a basis for a metric, a point most clearly made in Stevens (1959a), and in his review (1959b) of Thurstone's book *The measurement of values* (1959). Furthermore, contrary to Fechner and Thurstone, Stevens' interest seems to have been comparison of physical continua, and the number continuum used in magnitude estimation (ME) is just one. Thus, the application of Fechner's law to magnitude estimation reads: jnd $= a \log (\text{ME}) + b$. A similar argument is found in Ekman (1964): $R(\text{numbers } X) = a + b \log X$; $R(\text{stimulus } Y) = c + d \log Y$. If the number X_i is chosen such that for the subject $R(X_i) = R(Y_i)$, then: $a + b \log X = c + d \log Y$, and thus $\log X = (c-a)/b + d/b \log Y$, which leads to the power function $X = g Y^h$ with $g =$ antilog $[(c-a)/b)]$ and $h \doteq d/b$.

However, although all this may look acceptable on theoretical grounds, it is hard to imagine what "sensation" corresponds to in the ("physical") magnitude of numbers.

4.   APPLICATION TO DECISION MAKING: UTILITY AND SUBJECTIVE PROBABILITY

4.1. Direct Scaling

In decision analysis and multiattribute utility assessment the objective is quite similar to that of psychophysicists: Decision analysts consider objects specified by a multitude of physical variables (including their probability of occurrence). They call these variables attributes, or aspects, and they measure, and/or compose their respective subjectively perceived intensities under the special aspect of preference. In terms of psychophysics, utility is a sensation of physical attributes or variables of options, perceived with respect to preference. In principle, these evaluations of options are ultimately due to their physical attributes, i.e. physical stimuli.

Here we return to Cramer and Bernoulli. The measurement of utility and assessment of value and probability is essentially psychophysics, although many decision analysts may not be aware of this fact. So, let us consider some standard procedures of uni-dimensional or multiattribute utility and subjective probability assessment under a psychophysical point of view.

Of course, decision analysts have used direct estimates, i.e. magnitude estimation, as did Stevens. (If you don't know how to scale an attribute, why not ask your subject to do it?) Some authors did so with direct reference to Stevens (Galanter 1962). A typical result of this procedure with probability assessment was an overestimation of small probabilities and an underestimation of large ones. Approximately, this result fits Fechner's law. Stevens' law, however, is also supported with an exponent less than 1, if we only consider "objective" probabilities P below .5. For probabilities above .5 we have to consider (1-P) rather than P to fit a power function.

Unfortunately, those early data from probability estimates are not sufficient to prove either a logarithmic or a power relation between "true" probabilities and numbers assessed to them. Therefore, any psychophysical interpretation remains rather hypothetical. The term "early data," by the way, does not mean that this phenomenon of overestimating low probabilities is nowadays not found any more. It is still being observed under the label of "overconfidence" (Slovic, Fischhoff, & Lichtenstein, 1977).

4.2. Training Assessors to Estimate Subjective Probabilities

Today, decision analysts use more sophisticated techniques to elicit probability estimates, namely the so-called scoring rules. With this technique a subject—the probability assessor—is reinforced by means of a function which insures that the expected payoff is larger the closer an estimate approaches the "true" probability (usually measured as relative frequency). Actually, a scoring rule is not really a scaling technique but rather a reinforcement schedule, an incentive to be as correct as possible. Utilized as the core of a training procedure, scoring rules cause any "natural" psychophysical relation between "true" probability and its estimate ("magnitude measurement") to disappear—probably the same way experienced postal employees get more and more skilled to assess the correct weight to letters. As far as I can see, similar training and feedback procedures (trying to teach subjects what numbers to assess to stimuli) have never been applied in classical or Stevensian psychophysics. However, reflections on the possible results can be found in the literature. Cliff (1973) has suspected that the exponent in Stevens' power law "merely reflects how to use the number scale [p. 492]." This view is particularly supported by the finding by Beck and Shaw (1967) that magnitude estimates of differences between stimuli were exponentially related to the numbers of jnds separating them.

Teghtsoonian (1965) found that subjects are able to use two different psychophysical functions, depending on instruction, either a subjective scale or a scale veridically corresponding to the physical scale. That is, subjects are able to choose a strategy by which to arrive at their judgments. They are flexible in their use of numbers and not rigidly tied to some innate function.

In general then, one has to consider the fact that internal connections between stimuli and responses, albeit physical or verbal (or numeral), are based on associations within our nervous system, and these connections are learned. It would be worthwhile to find out how the intuitive or unlearned connections between physical stimulus intensities and responses look—but probably we will never find out. Subjects do not enter our laboratories like naive *tabulae rasae*, they all have experienced and learned "appropriate" connections elsewhere. Thus, we do not know if there exists something like an innate function relating stimulus intensities to responses, and if it exists, we cannot elicit it unspoiled by prior learning. In contrast to psychophysical research, decision analysts when measuring subjective probabilities are interested in veridical judgments to base their composition rules on. They see no harm in teaching subjects to elicit veridical probability judgments, and therefore they do not encounter the epistemological problem of finding the intuitive stimulus-response connections.

However, reinforcing subjects (or professional probability assessors) is just a means of teaching them the appropriate use of numerals. There is no theory of measurement or axiomatic behind it. Therefore the metric qualities of resulting probability scales are unknown—even if the scales are veridical. In this respect, an approach recently taken by Ksiensik (1978) to elicit winning probabilities in horse races is much more sophisticated because it is directly designed to test certain measurement axioms in a probability assessment task. She asked bettors at the race track to rank order winning probabilities and (mostly disjunctive) combinations thereof. Bettors were asked, for instance, whether or not they considered the probability of the event that one of the most favored two horses won larger than the probability that any other horse came in first. This procedure enabled Ksiensik to gain ordered metric information from such pairwise comparisons and to test basic axioms of a probability measurement structure.

4.3. Techniques to Assess Utilities

In the measurement of utility the perspective of an axiomatic foundation of scaling is more firmly established. Of course, decision analysts do use direct estimates as well—which could, again, be considered as a Stevensian magnitude-measurement scaling procedure—but there also exist scaling procedures based on axioms like those originally proposed by von Neumann and Morgenstern (1947).

What is typically done in these procedures is this: Given a set of options or alternatives, subjects are asked first to rank order these alternatives according to their preference, or at least to select the best and the worst of the options. Next, they are instructed to assess the utility of any other alternative by finding the indifference point. At this point the subjects are indifferent between obtaining the respective alternative for sure, and a lottery in which they might either get the best alternative with probability P or the worst one with probability (1-P). This is done with all alternatives in turn, attributewise if the alternatives are characterized by more than one aspect, and likewise with weight factors for these aspects or attributes. In the spirit of S. S. Stevens, we could call this procedure an elaborated fractionation method. It corresponds roughly to Comrey's method of constant sum (see, Torgerson 1958) where the subject is required to divide a given number of points between the objects such that the ratios between these numbers correspond to the subjective "ratios" between the objects. The difference between Stevens' and Comrey's procedures is that in Stevens' fractionation scaling, subjects are asked to find a *stimulus* that is located between the two anchors such that a given proportion of the distances is reflected, whereas here the task is to find the *proportion* of the distances that corresponds to a given stimulus with regard to the two anchors. Formally, both methods should also be equivalent to bisection or midpoint scaling as a special case of this procedure, with $P = .5$. Thus, any axiomatic applicable to bisection or midpoint scaling (like those by Pfanzagl 1962, Kristof 1968) should be applicable to this kind of utility assessment as well. However, in spite of this formal equivalence, experimental findings have shown that these two procedures result in different scales (Stevens & Galanter, 1957).

4.4. Independence of Subjective Probability and Utility

Normative decision theory assumes, at least in most cases, that the decision maker maximizes expected utility. This assumption requires simultaneous but independent measurement of utility and subjective probability. Independence of subjective probability and utility posed a major problem until the invention of conjoint measurement by Luce and Tukey (1964). Tversky (1967) successfully applied conjoint measurement to the simultaneous scaling of subjective probability and utility. This approach was rather satisfactory from an axiomatic point of view, but, of course, completely unstevensian. Anderson and Shanteau (1970) measured subjective probability and utility by means of Anderson's (1962a, 1962b, 1970, and this volume) functional measurement model and tested basic consequences of the respective models.

4.5. Stevensian Methods in the Assessment of Utility

There are a few studies where Stevensian methods have been explicitly used for the measurement of utility and subjective probability. For example Galanter (1962) asked his subjects about how much money would make them twice as happy as a certain given amount. This method worked and resulted in a power function between value and perceived utility. However, reverse methods (asking subjects how large a loss would make them twice as unhappy as a specified loss, and asking them how much money would make them half as happy as a given amount) led to inconsistent results. Eliciting the amount of money that would make subjects "twice as happy" resulted in a power function with an exponent of .43 (which is close to Cramer's .5). In another experiment, Galanter (1974) had subjects increase the loudness of a 400-Hz tone such that it matched given monetary increments. It resulted in a power exponent of .45.

Sjöberg, in a series of studies (1968), had subjects rate the favorableness of gambles and, thus implicitly, he assessed subjective probabilities and utility of money. The ratings were obtained from the subjects by having them mark a cross on a bar—a kind of direct scaling technique. However, Sjöberg tested a consequence of the decision making model without measuring probability and utility explicitly, so we cannot infer anything about the measurement of these scales from this experiment.

The fact that we find only so few references using Stevensian techniques in the assessment of subjective probability and utility does not necessarily mean that these techniques are not applicable for these purposes. Possibly it may be due only to the fact that decision analysts do not look into psychophysics. We could easily imagine how to use techniques like those presented by Dawson, Lodge and Tursky, and Wegener in this volume for the measurement of utility as well.

5. ADVANTAGES OF AN AXIOMATIC APPROACH

Although many scaling procedures both based on classical and on Stevens' psychophysics, have been proven useful for the measurement of utility and subjective probability, rather little has been done to test the assumptions underlying these procedures. The advantages of a more formal, axiomatic approach to measurement lie in a clear distinction between assumptions (the axioms)—in most cases a set of almost self-evident statements—and their consequences which lead to scales. Cliff (1973) categorized psychologists concerned with scaling into two categories: (1) the *axiomatizers* "who are concerned with the construction of exquisite mathematical structures," and (2) the *representationalists* "who are concerned with methods for wringing a numerical result from given data sets [p. 497]." If we accept this distinction between *axiomatizers* and *representationalists,* we would have to categorize S. S. Stevens with the latter. Therefore we need approaches towards axiomatization of Stevensian scaling techniques, like, e.g., Krantz (1972) who presented a formalization and theory of magnitude estimation and cross-modality matching that could give an axiomatic foundation to these methods (see also Orth's chapter and the Introduction to this volume).

Stevens was not very much concerned about axiomatic approaches to measurement, although he (1951) gave one of the most frequently quoted definitions of measurement: the "assignment of numerals to objects according to rules [p. 1]." To accept this definition, however, we should require that the "rules" governing the assessment of numbers to events must include something like a representation and uniqueness theorem derived from a set of axioms that are at least partly testable. However, Stevens never took up the idea of axiomatic measurement theory. Even in his last book on *Psychophysics* (1975), he nowhere quotes the paper by Suppes and Zinnes (1963) which is considered rather fundamental for a foundation of axiomatic measurement theory. On the other hand, Stevens had the principle of "invariance under admissible transformations" (which is essentially the statement of a uniqueness theorem) already formulated in 1939, and he presented it to the International Congress for the Unity of Science in 1941.

Obviously, *representationalists,* including Stevens, are not aware of the advantages of an axiomatic approach in terms of philosophy-of-science considerations. Perceiving nature, observables and relations between these, is never a nontheoretical endeavour.[2] We do not passively "see," but actively "look for" reality. We select what we want to see and what we wish to neglect, and by doing so, we are guided by implicit assumptions or hypotheses about real events.[3] These assumptions and hypotheses may well turn out to be wrong or improper but they are there to begin with. Any improvement of our knowledge presupposes that we make our prior assumptions on which observations are based explicit, clearly separating them from new findings. Actually, this is exactly what is proposed by the axiomatic approach. It enables us to make our assumptions, hypotheses, and background theories specific, call them axioms, and test these against the empirical reality. Some approaches to the measurement of subjective probability and utility make use of this scientific maxim, as we have seen, and they manage to keep assumptions and findings apart. Definitely, Stevens' approach is not free from assumptions either, but it is hard to see in his results what has been assumed and what has been found.

---

[2] All observations are "theory-laden" (Hanson, 1969, p. 84) or "theory-impregnated" (Popper, 1973, p. 71) (Editor's addition).

[3] "In science it is *observation* rather than perception which plays the decisive part. But observation is a process in which we play an intensely *active* part. An observation is a perception, but one which is planned and prepared. We do not 'have' an observation (as we may 'have' a sense experience) but we 'make' an observation.... An observation is always preceded by a particular interest, a question, or a problem—in short, by something theoretical. After all, we can put every question in the form of a hypothesis or conjecture to which we add: 'Is this so? Yes or no?' Thus we can assert that every observation is preceded by a problem, a hypothesis (or whatever we may call it); at any rate by something that interests us, by something theoretical or speculative. This is why observations are always selective, and why they presuppose something like a principle of selection." (Popper, 1973, pp. 341 f) (Editor's addition).

REFERENCES

Anderson, N. H. Application of an additive model to impression formation. *Science*, 1962, *138*, 817–818. (a)

Anderson, N. H. On the quantification of Miller's conflict theory. *Psychological Review*, 1962, *69*, 400–414. (b)

Anderson, N. H. Functional measurement and psychophysical judgment. *Psychological Review*, 1970, *77*, 153–170.

Anderson, N. H., Krantz, D. H., & Tversky, A. An exchange on functional and conjoint measurement. *Psychological Review*, 1971, *78*, 457–458.

Anderson, N. H., & Shanteau, J. Information integration in risky decision making. *Journal of Experimental Psychology*, 1970, *84*, 441–451.

Attneave, F. Perception and related areas. In S. Koch (Ed.), *Psychology: A study of a science*. Vol. 4, New York: McGraw-Hill, 1962.

Auerbach, C. Interdependence of Stevens' exponents and discriminability measures. *Psychological Review*, 1971, *78*, 556.

Beck, J., & Shaw, W. A. Ratio-estimation of loudness intervals. *American Journal of Psychology*, 1967, *80*, 59–65.

Cliff, N. Scaling. *Annual Review of Psychology*, 1973, *24*, 473–506.

Eisler, H. Empirical test of a model relating magnitude and category scales. *Scandinavian Journal of Psychology*, 1962, *3*, 88–96. (a)

Eisler, H. On the problem of category scales in psychophysics. *Scandinavian Journal of Psychology*, 1962, *3*, 81–87. (b)

Ekman, G. Is the power law a special case of Fechner's law? *Perceptual and Motor Skills*, 1964, *19*, 730.

Ekman, G., & Sjöberg, L. Scaling. *Annual Review of Psychology*, 1965, *16*, 451–474.

Fullerton, G. S., & Cattell, J. Mck. *On the perception of small differences*. Philadelphia: Publications of the University of Pennsylvania, Philosophy Series, No. 2, 1892.

Galanter, E. The direct measurement of utility and subjective probability. *American Journal of Psychology*, 1962, *75*, 208–220.

Galanter, E. Psychological decision mechanisms and perception. In E. C. Carterette & M. P. Friedman (Eds.), *Handbook of perception* Vol. 2. New York: Academic Press, 1974.

Garner, W. R. A technique and a scale for loudness measurement. *Journal of the Acoustic Society of America*, 1954, *26*, 73–78.

Garner, W. R., Hake, H. W., & Erikson, C. W. Operationism and the concept of perception. *Psychological Review*, 1956, *63*, 149–159.

Goude, G. *On Fundamental Measurement in Psychology*. Stockholm: Almquist & Wiksel, 1962.

Guilford, J. P. *Psychometric Methods*, (2nd ed.). New York: McGraw-Hill, 1954.

Hanson, N. R. Logical positivism and the interpretation of scientific theories. In P. Achenstein & S. F. Barker (Eds.), *The legacy of logical positivism*. Baltimore: Hopkins Press, 1969.

Krantz, D. H. A theory of magnitude estimation and crossmodality matching. *Journal of Mathematical Psychology*, 1972, *9*, 168–199.

Krantz, D. H., & Tversky, A. Conjoint measurement analysis of composition rules in psychology. *Psychological Review*, 1971, *78*, 151–169.

Kristof, W. Structural properties and measurement theory of certain sets admitting a concatenation operation. *British Journal of Mathematical and Statistical Psychology*, 1968, *21*, 201–229.

Ksiensik, M. I. Anwendungen der Meβstruktur von Krantz et al. zur Messung subjektiver Wahrscheinlichkeiten. *Bericht aus dem SFB 24, Universität Mannheim*, 1978.

Luce, R. D., & Tukey, J. W. Simultaneous conjoint measurement: A new type of fundamental measurement. *Journal of Mathematical Psychology*, 1964, *1*, 1–27.

Pfanzagl, J. *Die axiomatischen Grundlagen einer allgemeinen Theorie des Messens.* Psysica-Verlag, Würzburg, 1962.

Popper, K. R. *Objective knowledge. An evolutionary approach.* Oxford: Clarendon Press, 1973.

Sjöberg, L. Studies of the rated favorableness of offers to gamble. *Scandinavian Journal of Psychology,* 1968, *9,* 257-273.

Slovic, C. P., Fischhoff, B., & Lichtenstein, S. Behavioral decision theory. *Annual Review of Psychology,* 1977, *28,* 1-39.

Stevens, S. S. *Handbook of experimental psychology.* New York: Wiley, 1951.

Stevens, S. S. Measurement, psychophysics, and utility. In C. W. Churchman & P. Ratoosh, (Eds.), *Measurement: Definitions and theories.* New York: Wiley, 1959. (a)

Stevens, S. S. Review: L. L. Thurstone's *The measurement of values. Contemporary Psychology,* 1959, *4,* 388-389. (b)

Stevens, S. S. *Psychophysics and social scaling.* Morristown. General Learning Press, 1972.

Stevens, S. S. *Psychophysics: Introduction to its perceptual, neural, and social prospects.* New York: Wiley, 1975.

Stevens, S. S., & Galanter, E. H. Ratio scales and category scales for a dozen perceptual continua. *Journal of Experimental Psychology,* 1957, *54,* 377-411.

Suppes, P., & Zinnes, J. L. Basic Measurement Theory. In R. D. Luce, R. R. Bush, & E. Galanter (Eds.), *Handbook of Mathematical Psychology,* Vol. 1, New York: Wiley, 1963.

Teghtsoonian, M. The judgment of size. *American Journal of Psychology,* 1965, *78,* 392-402.

Teghtsoonian, R. On the exponents in Stevens' law and the constant in Ekman's law. *Psychological Review,* 1971, *78,* 71-80.

Thurstone, L. L. A law of comparative judgment. *Psychological Review,* 1927, *34,* 273-286.

Thurstone, L. L. *The measurement of values.* Chicago: University of Chicago Press, 1959.

Torgerson, W. S. *Theory and methods of scaling.* New York: Wiley, 1958.

Tversky, A. Additivity, utility, and subjective probability. *Journal of Mathematical Psychology,* 1967, *4,* 175-201.

von Neumann, J. v., & Morgenstern, O. *Theory of games and economic behavior,* (2nd ed.). Princeton, N. J.: Princeton University Press, 1947.

DIFFERENCES AND RATIOS IN SENSORY AND SOCIAL PSYCHOPHYSICS

13

The Nonmetric Analysis of Difference Judgments in Social Psychophysics: Scale Validity and Dimensionality

Bruce Schneider
Erindale College
University of Toronto, Canada

In the scaling of sensory or social events using direct judgments of single stimuli, subjects usually are instructed to assign numbers or categories to reflect the magnitude of some attribute of the stimulus. For instance, in magnitude estimation of loudness, pure tones are presented one at a time, and subjects are requested to assign numbers to the tones such that the numbers are proportional to the loudnesses of the tones. These instructions assume that subjects can base their judgments on loudness alone—ignoring any variations that may occur in the pitch of the tones. To focus attention on the attribute of loudness, the experimenter usually holds the frequency of the tone constant while varying only the intensity. Because pitch variations with intensity are relatively small compared to the loudness variations, it is reasonable to assume that the subjects' judgments reflect only loudness variations in the tones. Hence, with respect to loudness, the question of the dimensionality of the judgment is seldom if ever raised.[1]

However, in the social domain, the issue of the dimensionality of the judgment becomes more critical. For instance, suppose one is requested to judge the desirability or prestige of various occupations (Dawson & Brinker, 1971; Kunnapas & Wikstrom, 1963). Occupations vary along several dimensions, e.g., amount of remuneration, blue collar versus white collar, service oriented versus production oriented, etc. Each of these factors might be expected to influence the desirability or prestige of an occupation. Inasmuch as it is very difficult, if not impossible, to find a set of occupations that differ along only one of the dimen-

---

[1]It is interesting to note that the unidimensionality of loudness ratio judgments has been questioned. Richards (1974) has claimed that judgments of loudness ratios require a two-dimensional representation (however, see Schneider, Parker, Farrell, & Kanow, 1976, for a reply).

sions that might influence desirability, it seems plausible that the desirability or prestige of various occupations may *not* be a unidimensional experience. This means that the assumption of unidimensionality, which is implicit in magnitude- or category-estimation techniques, may not be warranted in this case. Hence, in order to speak of a scale of social prestige, it appears that one must first justify that social prestige is indeed a unidimensional attribute of a set of occupations and that subjects can assign numbers to a set of occupations such that variations in numerical assignments reflect only variations with respect to occupational prestige and not simultaneously reflect variations with respect to any of the other dimensions along which the stimuli might vary. A similar caution would hold for the scaling of other social events. Because direct judgments of single stimuli cannot be used to establish the dimensionality of an attribute, we must turn to scaling techniques that require the subject to judge a relation on two or more stimuli.[2]

Judgments of relations among two or more stimuli generally fall into two classes—those that deal with additive operations (conjoint measurement, Luce & Tukey, 1964; functional measurement, Anderson, 1977) and those that deal with difference operations (Fagot, 1959; Krantz, Luce, Suppes, & Tversky, 1971). My work has been primarily concerned with the establishment of valid sensory scales based on difference judgments, and I would like to review the evidence showing that measurement based on psychological differences can establish the unidimensionality of an attribute such as loudness and validate the numerical assignments intended to measure it. The measurement-theoretical framework I am using is borrowed from measurement theorists such as Suppes and Zinnes (1963) and Krantz et al. (1971), and the scaling techniques are derived from the work of Shepard (1966) and others in the area of nonmetric multidimensional scaling. Finally, after showing how difference judgments can be used to construct valid unidimensional scales of loudness, I would like to report some preliminary results of the application of these techniques to the measurement of occupational prestige.

DIFFERENCE STRUCTURES

Unidimensionality

One way of testing the unidimensionality of a psychological attribute is in terms of difference judgments. If a sensory dimension such as loudness is unidimensional, then we can specify the experience of loudness difference by two numbers,

---

[2]An approach such as this is advocated by Norman Anderson in his chapter on cognitive algebras in this volume.

$$D(i, j) = L_i - L_j \qquad\qquad (13.1)$$

where $D(i, j)$ is the experienced loudness difference, and L_i, L_j are the loudnesses of the tones i and j. Furthermore, if loudness is unidimensional, we should be able to represent the loudnesses of tones as points on a line segment where the *distance* between points represents the experience of loudness difference. Therefore, loudness difference judgments should behave like distances along a line segment. Measurement theorists concerned with difference structures have spotlighted three properties of differences along a line segment that are critical for unidimensionality in the sense that they are testable.[3] The first of these properties of distances is transitivity. Consider points on a line segment and distances, $d(x, y)$ between these points. For points a, b, c, e, x, and y on such a line segment, if $d(a, b) \geq d(c, e)$ and $d(c, e) \geq d(x, y)$, then it must follow that $d(a, b) \geq d(x, y)$. This property of distances between points on a line segment can be easily translated into relationships among loudness difference judgments. When an observer experiences two tones in sequence, they appear to differ in loudness. It seems reasonable, therefore, to interpret this experience as equivalent to distance along a line segment where the coordinate values of the points represent the loudness values of the tones. If this interpretation is valid, however, these loudness difference judgments must satisfy the property of transitivity, i.e.,

$$D(r, s) \geq D(t, u) \text{ and } D(t, u) \geq D(x, y) \text{ implies } D(r, s) \geq D(x, y) \quad (13.2)$$

where $\geq$ stands for a judgment of the first pair having the same or greater loudness difference than the second pair.

In addition to the property of transitivity, there are two other properties of distances along a line segment worthy of mention in the sense that they are testable in the psychological realm. The first is that for any three points a, b, and c, which increase in magnitude in that order, $d(a, c) \geq d(a, b)$ and $d(b, c)$. In terms of loudness difference, consider a comparison between a 50–75 dB interval and either a 50–60 dB interval or a 60–75 dB interval. If the tones vary along a single psychological dimension, and if the loudnesses are monotonic with intensity, then the 50–75 dB interval will have a greater loudness difference than either of the two other intervals. This is almost certainly true of loudness dif-

---

[3]In addition to testable axioms such as the ones specified here, different measurement systems have a number of technical axioms as well (see Krantz et al., 1971, for example). It is doubtful that events in the social realm satisfy some or all of these axioms. For example, in the theory of positive differences, there are existence axioms whose purpose is to establish the continuity of the property being measured. Inasmuch as a social attribute such as occupational prestige is not continuous (the number of occupations is clearly finite), these axioms are violated. However, in practical terms, if difference judgments satisfy the testable properties previously specified, they can be interpreted as distances along a line segment, and scale values can be assigned that are *approximately* unique up to addition and multiplication by a constant. But, if these testable axioms are violated, such an interpretation is ruled out.

ference judgments (Schneider, Parker, & Stein, 1974). Hence, we would expect that loudness difference judgments satisfy the following property:

$$L(c) \geq L(b) \geq L(a) \text{ implies } D(a, c) \geq D(a, b), D(b, c). \qquad (13.3)$$

The last property of distances between points along a straight-line segment that we may consider is the so-called monotonicity condition. For points on a line segment such that $c \geq b \geq a$ and $z \geq y \geq x$, $d(a, b) \geq d(x, y)$ and $d(b, c) \geq d(y, z)$ imply that $d(a, c) \geq d(x, z)$. This condition is illustrated in Fig. 13.1, and is fairly obvious geometrically.

However, it is not so obvious that its interpretation in the psychological domain will hold. For in the psychological domain it requires that for $L(c) \geq L(b) \geq L(a)$ and $L(z) \geq L(y) \geq L(x)$:

$$D(a, b) \geq D(x, y) \text{ and } D(b, c) \geq D(y, z) \text{ then } D(a, c) \geq D(x, z). \quad (13.4)$$

In an experiment by Schneider et al. (1974) properties 13.2 and 13.4 were tested. In this experiment, subjects were required on each trial to directly compare two pairs of tones and indicate which pair of tones had the greater loudness difference. Ten 1200 Hz tones differing only in intensity were employed. Subjects made binary comparisons among the 45 tone pairs that were formed from the set of 10 tones. Hence, in each trial the subjects were required to judge whether the tones in pair A or pair B were more widely separated in loudness. These data then can be used to check whether Eqs. 13.2 and 13.4 are satisfied For example, Schneider et al. (1974) found only five instances where comparisons of loudness intervals were inconsistent with eq. 13.2. Inasmuch as only five violations of transitivity occurred, they concluded that transitivity (Eq. 13.2) essentially was satisfied.

In a similar fashion, property 13.4 was tested and found to hold for loudness difference judgments. Schneider (1977) also has shown that the same results hold for individual subjects.

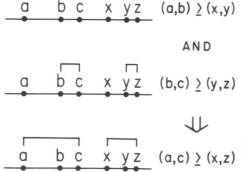

FIG. 13.1. Illustration of the monotonicity axiom for a line segment.

Hence, it can be argued that for all practical purposes, a set of events whose differences have been compared can be adequately represented as points on a line segment if difference judgments satisfy conditions 13.2–13.4. In this way the unidimensionality of the sensory attribute can be established, and it can be shown that measurement is possible on an interval scale.[4] Note that conditions 13.2–13.4 refer to judgments that can be interpreted as differences between points on a line segment. It should be noted at this point that other kinds of psychological judgments exist. For example, in functional measurement two events are also presented, but the observer is requested to respond to the joint effect (average) of the two events. Naturally, the joint effect is interpreted as additive. In order for this additive interpretation to be valid, the psychological judgments must also satisfy certain conditions that are, of course, appropriate for an additive structure (see Anderson, this volume). Hence, we are dealing in this paper with only one kind of judgment (namely, a difference judgment) and the conditions it must satisfy in order to justify a unidimensional interpretation.

The Determination of Scale Values for a Unidimensional Attribute

Let us suppose that we have reason to believe that we are dealing with a unidimensional attribute. Naturally, we actually want to locate the events on a line segment. For once we do that we can determine the coordinate values of the points and use them as our measure of the psychological magnitude of the event. Because the coordinate values of points on a line segment are unique up to addition and multiplication by a constant, we will have constructed an interval scale of the attribute in question.

The nonmetric techniques developed by Roger Shepard (1966) can be used to generate scale values for the stimuli whose differences have been estimated or compared. Generating scale values from difference judgments has a distinct advantage over many other numerical assignment techniques in that only the ordinal properties of the distance judgments are used. Hence, one need not make the much stronger metric assumptions that are characteristic of magnitude estimation.

In magnitude estimation, subjects are asked to assign numbers to stimuli such that the ratio of any two numbers reflects the ratio of the corresponding psychological magnitudes. Stevens (1962) has shown that for a number of sensory continua, the numerical assignments obtained in this fashion are a power function of stimulus intensity, that is $N = kI^n$, where N represents the observer's numerical judgments, I denotes the physical value of the stimulus, n is the exponent of the power function, and k is a constant of proportionality. This

---

[4]Again, for this statement to be strictly true, all axioms, including the technical ones, must be satisfied.

robust relationship between numerical judgments and physical intensity has led a number of investigators to believe, at least implicity, that this technique succeeds in the measurement of sensation. However, there are difficulties with this interpretation of the numerical judgments. First, it assumes that numerical judgments are directly proportional to sensation (S), that is,

$$N = kS. \tag{13.5}$$

A number of investigators (Anderson, 1974; Attneave, 1962; Curtis, Attneave, & Harrington, 1968; Curtis & Rule, 1972; Rule, Curtis, & Markley, 1970; Rule, Laye, & Curtis, 1974; Schneider, Parker, Valenti, Farrell, & Kanow, 1978; Weiss, 1972, 1975) have argued that magnitude estimates of sensory events or sensory differences are biased, that is, Eq. 13.5 is not true. In that case, it is quite difficult to argue that one has succeeded in measuring sensation. Another problem for social psychophysists using this technique is that there is no independent physical scale of the event being judged. Hence, it is impossible to appeal to the existence of a robust relationship between judgments and physical scale.[5] In the case of social events, to accept the results of magnitude estimation alone as measurement on a ratio scale is equivalent to assuming the validity of Eq. 13.5 without any empirical justification. This can be quite dangerous especially when one is dealing with social events whose unidimensionality has not been proven.

Hence, it is quite difficult to argue successfully that interval or ratio scale measurement has been achieved when judgments of single stimuli are involved. In fact, most measurement structures require that stimuli be compared either implicitly or explicity. This holds true even for magnitude estimation. Krantz (1972) has considered in detail the kinds of interpretations (theories) that have been used to account for the data collected via direct estimation procedures (primarily magnitude-estimation and cross-modality matching) and comes to the conclusion that in these tasks: "the fundamental object judged by an observer is not a single stimulus, but a pair of stimuli [p. 172]." What this means is that in a magnitude-estimation task, the subject is not judging the magnitude of a stimulus but rather the relation of one stimulus to another, in particular, the "sensation ratio." If, indeed, subjects judge or report relations even when asked to judge single magnitudes, experiments in which pairs of stimuli are explicitly presented

---

[5]This lack of a physical metric in the measurement process in the social realm has led to the development of a technique called sensory-modality matching (Dawson, this volume) in which two or more sensory attributes (e.g., loudness and brightness) are matched to the same social attribute (e.g., occupational prestige). The fact that one sensory-modality match (e.g., brightness-prestige) can be predicted from the other (e.g., loudness-prestige) using the results from a cross-modality matching of the two sensory continua (loudness vs. brightness) leads one to place more faith in the scales constructed using these techniques (Dawson, this volume; Lodge, this volume). However, as Cross (this volume) has pointed out, these scales can be shown to be unique only up to a power transformation—that is, they constitute measurement on a log-interval scale. It is yet to be shown that they result in measurement on a ratio scale.

to the observer (and therefore known to the experimenter) should be employed for the construction of sensory scales.

Hence, it seems reasonable to use judgments of pairs of stimuli for construction of sensory scales. In this way, the sensory values of the stimuli can be determined at the same time that the axioms required for unidimensionality are being tested.

Analysis of Difference Judgments

In the analysis of difference judgments we are able to use a much weaker nonmetric assumption. Suppose we have a set of points on a line segment whose coordinate values (x_i) are known. For n such points there are $n(n - 1)/2$ distinct interpoint distances. These interpoint distances can be ranked from largest to smallest. Shepard (1966) has shown that the rank order of these distances is sufficient to determine a set of projection values P_i on a second line segment such that $P_i = ax_i + b$. That is to say, provided that the number of points is sufficiently large ($n \geq 10$), the rank order of interpoint distances can be used to determine projection values along a line segment that are, for all practical purposes, unique up to addition and multiplication by a constant. Figure 13.2 illustrates this principle.

The reason why we need only the ordinal properties of the distances is not always intuitively obvious to those who are first introduced to this fact. Figure 13.3 illustrates why ordinal properties of distances are sufficient for interval scale

The rank order of the distances between points, X_i, on a line segment is sufficient to determine a set of projection values, P_i, on another line segment such that:

$$P_i = aX_i + b$$

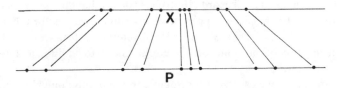

FIG. 13.2. Illustration of basic principle involved in nonmetric scaling of unidiminsional stimuli.

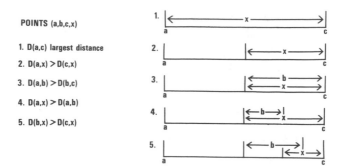

FIG. 13.3. An example of the kind of constraints imposed on the location of points along a line by the rank order of their interpoint distances.

measurement with a unidimensional attribute. Suppose we start off with four points (a, b, c, x) and suppose we know that the distance between a and c, d(a, c), is the largest interpoint distance. We can arbitrarily locate a and c any place along the line segment. We then know that all the other points (namely, b and x) must lie between a and c; otherwise d(a, c) could not be the largest distance. Suppose we also know that d(a, x) > d(c, x). If this is true, then x must be located somewhere in the right-hand half of the line segment between a and c. Suppose also that d(a, b) > d(b, c). By the same logic b must be located in the right half of the same segment. Note, however, that we do not know whether b is to the left or right of x. If we also determine that d(a, x) > d(a, b), we know that x must be to the right of b. Finally, suppose that d(b, x) > d(c, x). This can only be true if the location of x is restricted to the rightmost quarter of the line segment. For suppose we tried to put x anywhere else. Then, d(b, x) > d(c, x) would mean that b would have to be located in the left-hand half of the line segment, something that is forbidden by d(a, b) > d(b, c).

The inequalities just mentioned are sufficient to restrict the location of x to ¼ of the line segment. Suppose we had more points and more inequalities. Then, of course, the portion of the line segment over which x could range (its neighborhood) would be decreased. In general, as the number of inequalities increases, the neighborhood over which x can range becomes progressively smaller. It follows that with a sufficiently large number of inequalities the location of x would be restricted, for all practical purposes, to a single point on the line segment between a and c. Shepard (1966) has shown that this point is effectively reached for $n \geq 10$. Because the choice of coordinate values for points a and c was arbitrary, it follows that the rank order of interpoint distances is sufficient to recover the location of the points on a line segment up to addition and multiplication by a constant.

To illustrate how we can use this principle in the psychological realm, we can consider an experiment on estimation of loudness differences. Parker and Schneider (1974) had subjects give magnitude estimates of loudness differences for tonal pairs. The 10 tones used to construct the 45 pairs used in that experiment were identical in frequency and ranged in intensity from 50 to 104 dB. These magnitude estimates of loudness difference were regarded as analogous to estimates of distance along a line segment. Hence, the rank order of these loudness difference judgments was used to determine projections along a line segment for the 10 tones. These projection values then represent an interval scale of loudness if:

$$D(x_i, x_j) = m[L(x_i) - L(x_j)] \qquad (13.6)$$

where m is strictly monotone function.

Note that Eq. 13.6 requires much less of the subject's judgments than Eq. 13.5. Equation 13.5 (M.E. Assumption) requires that the subject's judgments be strictly proportional to sensation. Equation 13.6, on the other hand, simply requires that the subject's numerical judgments be monotonic with loudness difference, i.e., that whenever $|L(x_i) - L(x_j)|$ is greater than $|L(x_k) - L(x_m)|$, $D(x_i, x_j)$ will be greater than $D(x_k, x_m)$. The extent to which one places faith in the validity of a psychological scale depends on the extent to which the assumptions are met. Clearly, it is much more likely that numerical judgments be monotonic with some psychological property than that they be directly proportional to it. Consequently, whenever there is some possibility that numerical judgments might be biased, it is much safer to use a nonmetric scaling technique with its weaker assumptions.[6]

We have seen, therefore, that there are two steps in the construction of a valid scale of a psychological attribute using difference judgments. First, it is necessary to show that the difference judgments behave as distances along a line segment. One way to do this is to show that they satisfy conditions 13.2–13.4. If a set of judgments fails to satisfy these conditions, we are not justified in con-

---

[6]Under some circumstances even the relatively weak assumption specified by Eq. 13.6 is not necessary. Consider the Schneider et al. (1974) study mentioned earlier. In this study, subjects were required to compare pairs of tones directly and indicate which pair of tones had the greater loudness difference. This, of course, required only a binary decision on the part of the subject, i.e., either the tones in pair A or pair B were judged to be more widely separated in loudness. These binary comparisons were used to generate a rank order of loudness differences. The rank order was in turn used to generate scale values for the loudnesses of the tones. Note that this analysis assumed only that a subject can accurately report which of two tone pairs had the greater loudness difference. The nonmetric analysis of these data agreed quite closely with that of Parker and Schneider (1974). Hence, even the relatively weak assumption of Eq. 13.6 is unnecessary if one undertakes the direct comparison of psychological intervals. The drawback of this approach is the massive amount of data involved. For example, with 10 tones there are 45 tone pairs. If a scaling technique such as magnitude estimation is used to rank order these tone pairs, the experiment is of a manageable size. However, for the same number of stimuli, we have 45 pairs and $45 \times 44/2 = 990$ comparison pairs. A fairly long period of time is required to collect this amount of data from a single subject. Hence, although the comparison of psychological intervals is preferred, it is not always as practical as the direct numerical estimation of the magnitude of the individual psychological intervals.

structing a unidimensional scale based on these difference judgments. However, if these conditions or their equivalents are satisfied, then we can proceed to the second step, which is to construct a psychological scale using a nonmetric scaling technique.

We next turn to the question of what sort of judgments can be best interpreted as distances along a line segment.

Difference Judgments, Similarity Judgments, and Ratio Judgments

Earlier we mentioned that almost all measurement theories in psychology require either explicitly or implicitly that the subject compare stimuli. Typically, there are three kinds of psychological judgments that involve comparisons: judgments of psychological differences, judgments of psychological ratios, and judgments of psychological similarity. I have argued earlier that judgments of psychological intervals or differences can be regarded as distances along a line segment if we are dealing with a unidimensional structure. Psychological similarity, in most cases, turns out to be the monotonic inverse of distance (Parker & Schneider, 1974). Inasmuch as the nonmetric techniques are not bothered by monotonic response biases, this inverse relation between similarity and difference means that with respect to scale construction, it is irrelevant whether one uses category or magnitude techniques or one judges loudness differences or similarities. For example, Schneider et al. (1978) derived interval scales of loudness from category and magnitude estimates of loudness differences and loudness similarities using the nonmetric techniques previously described. The scale values derived from the nonmetric analyses of each of these four experiments (category estimation of loudness difference, magnitude estimation of loudness difference, category estimation of loudness similarity, and magnitude estimation of loudness similarity) are plotted as a function of decibels of sound pressure in Fig. 13.4. Note that all four loudness scales are equivalent. Hence, the nonmetric techniques offer the additional advantage that it does not matter whether one uses magnitude or category estimation or whether one judges similarity or difference. As long as biases are monotonic and similarity is the monotonic inverse of difference, the same underlying scale will be recovered.

This still, however, leaves us with the question of how we are to interpret judgments of psychological ratios. Again, the answer is as intervals along a line segment. Suppose we have a set of points along a line segment and we determine the ratios of the coordinate values of every pair of points, i.e., we determine (x_i/x_j) for pairs of points x_i, x_j. If we now take the logarithm of these ratios, $\log(x_i/x_j) = \log(x_i) - \log(x_j)$. That is, the logarithm of a ratio is the same as a difference in logarithms and is an interval on a line segment. Consequently, if we are dealing with a unidimensional psychological attribute, ratio judgments of pairs should satisfy Eqs. 13.2–13.4.

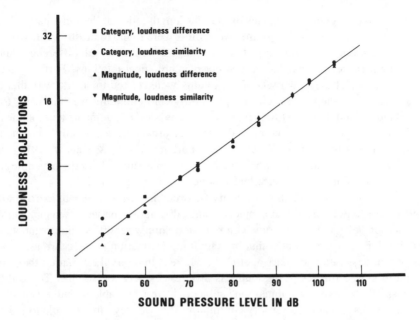

FIG. 13.4. Adjusted loudness projections obtained from the nonmetric analyses of category and magnitude judgments of loudness differences and similarities as a function of dB (SPL). Notice that the ordinate is spaced logarithmically. A straight line in these coordinates indicates that loudness is a power function of sound pressure. (From Schneider et al., 1978, by permission of the American Psychological Association.)

If both interval judgments and ratio judgments can be interpreted as intervals along a line segment, how, then, are we to distinguish between them? Suppose that a subject is capable of judging the psychological ratios as well as the psychological intervals of pairs of stimuli. Let us hypothesize that we have two pairs of stimuli, (A, B), whose psychological values are (1, 3) and (5, 8) respectively. If a subject is asked to estimate the psychological difference between two stimuli, and if the judgments satisfy Eq. 13.6, then the subject should say that pair B (8 − 5 = 3) has a greater psychological difference than pair A (3 − 1 = 2). If, on the other hand, the subject was asked to judge psychological ratios, he or she would respond that pair A (3/1) had a greater ratio than pair B (8/5).

In general, then, the rank order of ratio judgments for pairs of stimuli should be different from the rank order of difference judgments if the subject is judging the stimuli with respect to a single psychological scale and if the subject is capable of making both difference and ratio judgments. An example of a case where the two kinds of judgments satisfy these criteria is for judgments of perceived line-length differences and perceived line ratios. Parker, Schneider, and Kanow (1975) had one group of subjects magnitude estimate the perceived line-length difference for each of 36 pairs of line lengths. A second group of subjects gave magnitude estimates of the line-length ratios of the same pairs. The rank orders of the judgments for the two groups were found to be different, which is what we would expect if subjects could judge both line-length differences and line-length ratios as separate and distinct psychological relations. Furthermore, the rank order of these two sets of judgments were related in such a way that it was possible to show that the same psychological continuum was the basis for both kinds of judgments. However, when loudness ratio judgments and loudness difference judgments were compared, the rank orders are essentially equivalent (Birnbaum & Elmasian, 1977; Schneider, Parker, Farrell, & Kanow, 1976). If the rank orders are identical, what, then, are we to assume about the psychological basis of loudness difference and loudness ratio judgments?

A possible reason for this similarity in order has been given by Torgerson (1961). He hypothesized that subjects cannot distinguish between sensory ratios and sensory differences for some continua and simply report but one perceptual relationship. Torgerson noted that in magnitude estimation subjects are asked to judge loudness ratios for pairs of stimuli, whereas in interval estimation they are asked to give estimates of the loudness differences between stimuli. To do this successfully, Torgerson pointed out, subjects have to be able to judge two distinct relationships along a sensory continuum; that is, they must be able to judge the loudness difference between two sounds as well as the loudness ratio of one sound to another. Torgerson's conjecture was that they could not do both. He argued that there was only one perceptual relationship defined on a pair of stimuli from an intensive continuum.

The implication of Torgerson's hypothesis for a nonmetric analysis of difference and ratio judgments is clear. If subjects cannot distinguish between psychological differences and psychological ratios, then the rank order of a set of difference judgments should be essentially the same as the rank order of ratio judgments. Furthermore, if the rank orders are the same, the projection values must be the same.[7] Schneider et al. (1976) had subjects give magnitude estimates of loudness differences and loudness ratios. The rank orders of the two sets of judgments were essentially the same. Hence, it appeared that these subjects did not distinguish between loudness differences and loudness ratios—when presented with a pair of tones, subjects apparently experienced but one perceptual relationship. The effect of different instructions, then, was simply to change in a

---

[7]If subjects can judge both differences and ratios along a psychological continuum, then the rank orders of these judgments will be different. Consequently, the representations obtained in the two cases will be different. Krantz et al. (1971) have shown that if ratios and differences are both defined then the relationship that holds between the two sets of projection values will be $\log(P_d - b) = aP_r + c$, where P_d and P_r are the projection values obtained from the difference and ratio judgments respectively and a, b, and c are constants. Of course, if Torgerson's hypothesis is correct, the two sets of values should be identical up to addition and multiplication by a constant ($P_d = k'P_r + k$). Hence, the two alternatives have clearly defined predictions.

monotonic fashion the reporting strategy employed by the subject but not the nature of the perceptual relationship reported.

In a way, it is a disappointment that judgments of loudness ratios are not distinct from judgments of loudness differences.[8] For if they were, then as Krantz et al. (1971) noted, it would be possible to construct a ratio scale of loudness from a nonmetric analysis of ratio judgments and difference judgments. Furthermore, if direct comparisons of sensory intervals and sensory ratios both satisfied Eqs. 13.2-13.4, then the ratio scale so constructed would be well-founded in a measurement-theoretical sense. However, it is still possible that when we move to the social realm, subjects might be capable of judging both ratios and differences of some social event. In that case, it would be possible to construct a ratio scale of that social attribute from a nonmetric analysis of ratio and difference judgment—something that has not yet been done for some sensory continua such as loudness.

APPLICATION TO THE SOCIAL REALM

As the purpose of this conference is the application of psychophysical methodology to the social realm, I would like to give an example of how difference judgments might be used to establish a scale of a social attribute and determine at the same time whether the attribute is, in fact, one dimensional. The attribute I would like to consider is the prestige of occupations. This attribute has been scaled previously by Kunnapas and Wikstrom (1963) using magnitude estimation and by Dawson and Brinker (1971) using a loudness-matching technique. Using these techniques, they were able to assign numbers to represent the psychological prestige of the various occupations. Stevens (1972) has argued that because the subjects made magnitude estimations, the scale values are such that ratios have meaning. This is equivalent to assuming the validity of Eq. 13.5. However, also implicit in this technique is the assumption that the prestige of an occupation can be represented one dimensionally.

Hence, it seemed reasonable to test these assumptions using a nonmetric technique. In the experiments reported later, 11 occupations (see Table 13.1) were used to construct 55 occupation pairs. These occupations are a subset of those used by Kunnapas and Wikstrom (1963) and Dawson and Brinker (1971). In experiment 1, subjects were asked to magnitude estimate the difference in

---

[8]It is always possible that better trained or better instructed subjects might be able to distinguish between the two kinds of relationships. Because group data were used in the studies just reported, it is also possible that individual subjects might be capable of distinguishing between the two. What is discouraging is that using relatively standard instructions for groups of subjects resulted in ordinal rankings, which were essentially identical. However, Schneider (1980), in a more extensive analysis of these data found one subject who was actually judging loudness ratios.

TABLE 13.1
Prestige Values from Nonmetric Analyses

Occupation	Experiment 1 (Difference Est.)	Experiment 2 (Ratio Est.)	Experiment 3 (Difference Est.)
Physician	5.50	5.50	5.50
Engineer	5.03	4.89	4.95
Architect	4.73	4.58	4.64
Business executive	4.35	4.41	4.31
High school teacher	3.21	3.23	3.15
Forestry officer	2.85	2.77	2.80
Photographer	2.55	2.44	2.41
Farmer	1.76	1.73	1.70
Hair dresser	1.07	1.05	1.14
Bus driver	0.99	0.98	1.05
Cashier	0.71	0.88	0.79

prestige for each pair of occupations. In experiment 2, they were asked to estimate the ratio of the prestige of the first occupation in a pair to the second occupation in the pair. The instructions for these two experiments were presented to them on a sheet of paper (see Appendix for instructions) followed by the pairs of occupations in a random order. Each of 100 subjects rated all 55 pairs once for each experiment. The order of the occupations in a pair was also randomized. Subjects were university students at Erindale College of the University of Toronto. A different set of subjects were employed for experiments 1 and 2.

If occupational prestige is a unidimensional experience, then the judgments of differences in prestige can be considered as distances along a line segment. And if these judgments of occupational prestige difference are at least monotonic with prestige difference, then nonmetric techniques can be employed to obtain scale values of occupational prestige. In experiment 1, each subject's judgments were ordinally ranked. That is, for subject 1 the pair of occupations receiving the highest difference estimate was assigned the number 55, the pair receiving the next highest was assigned the number 54, and so on. The average ranking for each occupation pair was then determined across subjects, and these average ranks served as input to a nonmetric scaling program (Carvellas & Schneider, 1972). This program produces numerical assignments (projection values, Ps, along a line segment) for each of the 11 occupations such that the differences in numerical assignments between all pairs of occupations best predict the ranks of the 55 pairs of prestige differences used as input for the program. Furthermore, these projection values are unique up to addition and multiplication by a constant, that is, these values constitute interval scale measurement.

Goodness of fit was evaluated by computing stress (Kruskal, 1964). Stress measures the discordance between the predicted distances, ds, and a set of

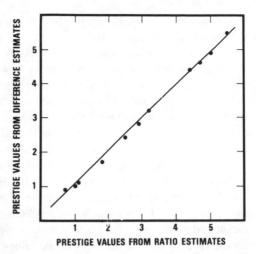

FIG. 13.5. Prestige values obtained from a nonmetric analysis of difference judgments plotted against prestige values obtained from a nonmetric analysis of ratio judgments.

distances, d̂s, that are (a) monotonically related to the rank order of the difference judgments and (b) as much like the ds as they can be within the restrictions imposed by (a). Stress is given by $[\Sigma(d - \hat{d})^2/d^2]^{\frac{1}{2}}$, often expressed as a percentage. Notice that perfect ordinal agreement produces $d = \hat{d}$, and in this case, stress = 0.

Stress in this experiment was 7.88%, which indicates only a fair amount of agreement between the ds and d̂s. The scale values obtained for the prestige of the various occupations are listed in column 1 of Table 13.1.

A similar procedure was followed for the analysis of the ratio judgments. Stress, in this instance was 7.12%—about the same as for the difference judgments.[9] Furthermore, the scale values of the various occupations are nearly identical (see Table 13.1, column 2) to those obtained from the difference judgments. Recall that this is what we would expect if subjects did not distinguish between ratios and differences as Torgerson (1961) argued. Figure 13.5 plots the projections obtained from the analysis of the difference judgments against those obtained from an analysis of the ratio judgments. The two sets of projections are

---

[9] Young (1970) has used the index of metric determinancy to evaluate stress in a scaling experiment. M is the squared Pearson correlation coefficient between the true distances (whose rank ordering serves as the input to the algorithm) and the ds produced by the algorithm. Hence, M varies between 0 and 1, and M = 1 means that the true distances have been perfectly recovered. In no empirical investigations using these techniques are the true distances known, but Young provides a nomogram for estimating M from the number of points, number of dimensions, and stress—all of which are available. The result is that, in nonmetric analyses, if M is sufficiently high (above .98, say) the point coordinates produced by the algorithm are properly regarded as an interval scale representation of the original points. In the present experiments, stress values of about 6-7% yield an estimate of M = .96. Hence, the degree of metric recovery is not as good as we might like if the underlying representation is unidimensional.

linearly related (r = .999). Hence, Torgerson's hypothesis seems to be confirmed for judgments of social prestige.

In both of these experiments stress values for a unidimensional scaling were quite high. This could be due to two reasons—an excessively large amount of variability within and/or across subjects or the fact that occupation prestige is not a unidimensional structure. To check to see whether the high stress was simply a function of variability, another 100 subjects were run in the prestige-difference condition. The results of this replication of the difference condition are shown in column 3 of Table 13.1. Stress was somewhat lower (6.21%), but the projection values were about the same as in the previous experiment (correlation between projection values from experiments 1 and 3 is .998). The fact that experiment 3 produced the same results suggests that the high stress values are not due to random error. For if the high stress values were due to random error, we might have expected more divergent sets of projection values from the two experiments (experiments 1 and 3). If the high stress values are not due to excessive variability, then they must indicate that the judgments deviated in a systematic way from what we would predict on the basis of a unidimensional model. To check this possibility, two-dimensional Euclidian solutions were obtained for each of the experiments. If there are systematic deviations of judgments from a unidimensional model, then the two-dimensional solutions for all three experiments should have not only lower stress but the same two-dimensional configuration. But, if the deviations were random in nature, they should show up in different places in the rank order of judgments in the three experiments and lead to different two-dimensional representations.

Figure 13.6 shows the two-dimensional solutions for the three experiments. Note that the two-dimensional solutions are nearly identical in all three cases. Stress was 3.62, 3.57, and 3.45% for experiments 1, 2, and 3.

Note that the deviations from unidimensionality are not extreme. The dotted line in Fig. 13.6 represents a possible rotation of the axes in this two-dimensional representation. (In a Euclidian space, the location of points is unique only up to rotation, translation, and expansion.) If we were to plot the projection values of each of the points onto this new dimension, the projection values would be roughly the same as those we obtained from the unidimensional solution. Clearly, then, these data deviate systematically but only slightly from unidimensionality.

It is interesting to note that the rank order of the occupations obtained in the unidimensional solution in this study does not agree with that of Dawson and Brinker (1971) or Kunnapas and Wikstrom (1963). The ranks of their occupations are listed in Table 13.2. The major differences are that the profession of high school teacher has slipped a notch or two from its position in both the Dawson and Brinker and Kunnapas and Wikstrom studies whereas that of engineer has climbed to second place in the present study. It is possible that these differences represent differences in the subject populations or changes in occupa-

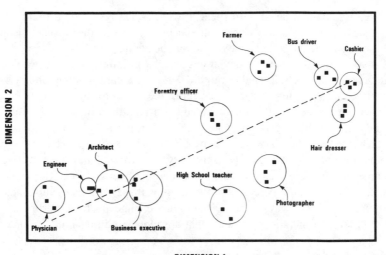

FIG. 13.6.   Two-dimensional representations of occupational prestige for experiments 1, 2, and 3. The dotted line represents a possible rotation of the coordinates
in this two-dimensional representation.

TABLE 13.2
Rank Order of Prestige of Occupations

Occupation	Dawson & Brinker	Kunnapas & Wikstrom
Physician	1	1
College professor	2	
High school teacher	3	3
Business executive	4	
Architect	5	2
Engineer	6	4
Photographer	7	5
Salesman	8	8
Artist	9	6
Forestry officer	10	7
Farmer	11.5	9
Manufacturer		10
Painter		11
Cashier	11.5	14
Sailor	13	12
Farmhand	14	16
Bus driver	15	
Bus conductor		15
Factory worker	16	17
Hair dresser	17	13

tional prestige over time. In retrospect, it would have been interesting to obtain magnitude-estimation data of occupational prestige from the same subjects we tested in experiments 1–3. However, it was not done.

It is also possible that the deviations from a unidimensional representation found here might be eliminated or minimized if more careful attention is given to the instruction set (greater care in defining the meaning of prestige) or other variables in the experiment. More detailed specification of the stimuli could have reduced some of the uncertainty and variability in the judgments. Also, a more homogeneous population would be desirable. The subjects were psychology students at Erindale College of the University of Toronto. They are a diverse mix of people from different ethnic and socioeconomic backgrounds. Consequently, the ways in which they perceive the prestige of these various occupations may differ. Hence, it is always possible that some change in the experiment might lead to difference or ratio judgments that are more unidimensional in nature.

CONCLUDING REMARKS

Social psychophysics is at a disadvantage in at least three ways when compared to sensory psychophysics. First, social data are considered to be inherently more variable than sensory data. Second, there is greater difficulty in determining the dimensionality of a social attribute than a sensory attribute. And third, social scales usually lack clearly defined physical counterparts so that the problem of determining their validity is more complicated.

With respect to the first point, it is clear that, at least within a well-defined population, the underlying interval scale representation responsible for judgments of differences and ratios of prestige can be determined with a fair degree of reliability. All that is needed is a sufficient number of subjects.

Second, the issue of dimensionality can be tackled if we use judgments of differences and/or ratios of pairs of stimuli. We have seen that occupational prestige, although roughly unidimensional, does show systematic deviations from unidimensionality. It is possible that increased precision in the instruction set or some other experimental variable might lead to judgments that are more unidimensional in nature. However, the close approximation to unidimensionality shown here might be good enough for many practical applications.

Finally, once one is convinced that a particular social dimension is unidimensional, it is possible to test the unidimensionality of the attribute more rigorously within the framework of the theory of positive difference structures. All that is needed is the collection of an enormous amount of data within the paired comparisons of differences framework. Even if occupational prestige is ultimately found not to be unidimensional, it is quite possible that other social scales will indeed turn out to be unidimensional. If this is the case, it should be possible to construct unidimensional scales of social attributes that are well-founded in the measurement-theoretical sense.

In conclusion, then, I think the use of difference judgments might be particularly suited for the construction of social scales. They require only the ordered properties of subjects' judgments, they can be used to determine the dimensionality of the attribute in question, and it is possible to show, provided that the testable axioms of a positive difference structure are satisfied, that they approximate measurement on an interval scale.

ACKNOWLEDGMENT

The research reported here was supported in part by a grant from the Natural Sciences and Engineering Research Council of Canada. I would like to thank Dr. Patricia Pliner for her comments on a preliminary draft of this manuscript.

REFERENCES

Anderson, N. H. Cross-task validations of functional measurement using judgments of total magnitude. *Journal of Experimental Psychology,* 1974, *102,* 226–233.

Anderson, N. H. Note on functional measurement and data analysis. *Perception & Psychophysics,* 1977, *21,* 201–205.

Attneave, F. Perception and related areas. In S. Koch (Ed.), *Psychology: A study of a science* (Vol. 4). New York: McGraw-Hill, 1962.

Birnbaum, M. H., & Elmasian, R. Loudness "ratios" and "differences" involve the same psychophysical operation. *Perception & Psychophysics,* 1977, *22,* 383–391.

Carvellas, T., & Schneider, B. Direct estimation of multidimensional tonal dissimilarity. *Journal of the Acoustical Society of America,* 1972, *51,* 1839–1848.

Curtis, D. W., Attneave, F., & Harrington, T. L. A test of a two-stage model of magnitude judgment. *Perception & Psychophysics,* 1968, *3,* 25–31.

Curtis, D. W., & Rule, S. J. Magnitude judgments of brightness difference as a function of background reflectance. *Journal of Experimental Psychology,* 1972, *95,* 215–222.

Dawson, W. E., & Brinker, R. P. Validation of ratio scales of opinion by multimodality matching. *Perception & Psychophysics,* 1971, *9,* 413–417.

Fagot, R. F. A model of ordered metric scaling by comparison of intervals. *Psychometrika,* 1959, *24,* 157–168.

Krantz, D. H. A theory of magnitude estimation and cross-modality matching. *Journal of Mathematical Psychology,* 1972, *9,* 168–199.

Krantz, D. H., Luce, R. D., Suppes, P., & Tversky, A. *Foundations of measurement.* (Vol. 1), *Additive and polynomial representations.* New York: Academic Press, 1971.

Kruskal, J. B. Multidimensional scaling by optimizing goodness of fit to a nonmetric hypothesis. *Psychometrika,* 1964, *29,* 1–27.

Kunnapas, T., & Wikstrom, I. *Measurement of occupation preferences: A comparison of scaling methods.* Reports from the Psychological Laboratory, No. 156, University of Stockholm (Sweden), 1963.

Luce, R. D., & Tukey, J. W. Simultaneous conjoint measurement: A new type of fundamental measurement. *Journal of Mathematical Psychology,* 1964, *1,* 1–27.

Parker, S., & Schneider, B. Nonmetric scaling of loudness and pitch using similarity and difference estimates. *Perception & Psychophysics,* 1974, *15,* 238–242.

Parker, S., Schneider, B., & Kanow, G. Ratio scale measurement of the perceived lengths of lines. *Journal of Experimental Psychology: Human Perception and Performance,* 1975, *104,* 195–204.

Richards, A. M. Nonmetric scaling of loudness. I. 1000 Hz tones. *Journal of the Acoustical Society of America*, 1974, *56*, 582–588.

Rule, S. J., Curtis, D. W., & Markley, R. P. Input and output transformations from magnitude estimation. *Journal of Experimental Psychology*, 1970, *86*, 343–349.

Rule, S. J., Laye, R. C., & Curtis, D. W. Magnitude judgments and difference judgments of lightness and darkness: A two-stage analysis. *Journal of Experimental Psychology*, 1974, *103*, 1108–1114.

Schneider, B. *Individual loudness functions determined from direct comparisons of sensory intervals*. Paper presented at the Mathematical Psychology Meetings, Los Angeles, August 1977.

Schneider, B. A technique for the nonmetric analysis of paired comparisons of psychological intervals. *Psychometrika*, 1980, *45*, 357–372.

Schneider, B., Parker, S., Farrell, G., & Kanow, G. The perceptual basis of loudness ratio judgments. *Perception & Psychophysics*, 1976, *19*, 309–320.

Schneider, B., Parker, S., & Stein, D. The measurement of loudness using direct comparisons of sensory intervals. *Journal of Mathematical Psychology*, 1974, *11*, 259–273.

Schneider, B., Parker, S., Valenti, M., Farrell, G., & Kanow, G. Response bias in category and magnitude estimation of difference and similarity for loudness and pitch. *Journal of Experimental Psychology: Human Perception and Performance*, 1978, *4*, 483–496.

Shepard, R. N. Metric structures in ordinal data. *Journal of Mathematical Psychology*, 1966, *3*, 287–315.

Stevens, S. S. The surprising simplicity of sensory metrics. *American Psychologist*, 1962, *17*, 29–39.

Stevens, S. S. *Psychophysics and social scaling*. Morristown, N.J.: General Learning Press, 1972.

Suppes, P., & Zinnes, J. L. Basic measurement theory. In R. D. Luce, R. R. Bush, & E. Galanter (Eds.), *Handbook of mathematical psychology*. New York: Wiley, 1963.

Torgerson, W. S. Distances and ratios in psychophysical scaling. *Acta Psychologica*, 1961, *19*, 201–205.

Weiss, D. J. Averaging: An empirical validity criterion for magnitude estimation. *Perception & Psychophysics*, 1972, *12*, 385–388.

Weiss, D. J. Quantifying private events: A functional measurement analysis of equisection. *Perception & Psychophysics*, 1975, *4*, 351–357.

Young, F. W. Nonmetric multidimensional scaling: Recovery of metric information. *Psychometrika*, 1970, *35*, 455–473.

APPENDIX

Difference Instructions

This is an experiment on how you rate the prestige of various occupations. The sheet which you have been given contains pairs of occupations. What we would like you to do is to indicate how much the two occupations in a pair differ in prestige. To do this use the difference in prestige between a retail clerk and a fireman as a reference difference. Consider the difference in prestige between these two occupations to be 40. For any other pairs of occupations, if the occupations in that pair seem to you to be twice as different in prestige as those in the reference or standard pair, assign the number 80 to that pair. If in some pairs, the occupations seem to differ only half as much as in the standard pair, assign the number 20. If they seem 4 times as different, assign the number 160. If the pair is 1/10 as different, assign the number 4 and so on. You may use any positive number—integer, fraction, or decimal. You may not use negative numbers or zeros. Are there any questions?

Ratio Instructions

This is an experiment on how you rate the prestige of various occupations. The sheet which you have been given contains pairs of occupations. We would like you to judge the prestige ratio of the first occupation to that of the second. For example, if the first occupation in a pair seems twice as prestigious as the second, assign the number 2 to that pair. If, on the other hand, in some other pairs, the first occupation seems to be ¼ as prestigious as the second, assign the number ¼ or .25. If the first occupation of a pair seems 5 times as prestigious, assign the number 5, if 1/10 as prestigious, assign the number 1/10 or 0.1, and so on. You may use any positive number—integer, or decimal. You may not use negative numbers or zero. Are there any questions?

Subjects were discarded and replaced if: (1) they failed to complete the questionnaire; (2) they used the same number for each item; (3) they used negative numbers or zero. In experiment 1, 33 questionnaires had to be replicated for these reasons; 30 were replicated in experiment 2, and 44 in experiment 3.

14

Intra- and Interindividual Variations in the Form of Psychophysical Scales

Henry Montgomery
University of Göteborg, Sweden

A continuing problem in modern psychophysics is the variations in psychophysical scales that occur across different judgmental tasks and/or different subjects. That is, when the *same* subjects participate in *different* judgmental tasks, the form of the resulting scale may change. For example, scales based on subjective ratios (e.g., magnitude scales) do not agree with those based on subjective differences (e.g., category scales). Moreover, the form of a psychophysical scale may also change considerably across *different* subjects who participate in the *same* judgmental tasks. For example, the exponents of power functions relating magnitude scales of loudness for individual subjects to physical stimulus values may change from .05 to .35 (McGill, 1960).

The purpose of this paper is to present a common framework for the study of intra- and interindividual variations in psychophysical scales. This framework is based on the General Psychophysical Differential Equation (the GPDE), which originally was developed for describing *intra*individual variations in psychophysical scales. The GPDE states that the following relation holds between two subjective variables x and y, say a magnitude and a category scale, with the subjective Weber functions $W_1(x)$ and $W_2(y)$ (usually defined as intraindividual SDs as a function of the central tendencies):

$$\frac{dy}{dx} = \frac{W_2(y)}{W_1(x)} \tag{14.1}$$

It can be seen from Eq. 14.1 that one subjective variable, say *y*, can be predicted from the other provided that both Weber functions are known. The transformation y = f(x) is obtained by integrating Eq. 14.1.

$$\int_{y_0}^{y} \frac{dy}{W_2 (y)} = \int_{x_0}^{x} \frac{dx}{W_1 (x)} \qquad (14.1a)$$

(The limits x and y correspond to the same stimulus; subscript 0, to the lowest one.)

The GPDE has been shown to yield a close fit to empirical data on *intra*individual relations, such as the relation between ratio and similarity estimates (Eisler, 1963b), between category and magnitude scales (Eisler, 1962, 1963a, 1963b, 1963c; Eisler & Montgomery, 1974; Montgomery & Eisler, 1974), and between magnitude scales of softness and loudness of white noise (Eisler, 1962). In this paper, I propose that the GPDE also holds for *inter*individual variations in psychophysical scales. That is, it is proposed that x and y in Eq. 14.1 may denote scales for two single individuals who have judged the same set of stimuli implying that one subject's psychophysical scale can be predicted from another subject's psychophysical scale when both Weber functions are known.

Before discussing the GPDE in general and the extension of the GPDE to interindividual relations in particular, the validity of the GPDE is examined across intra- and interindividual relations in psychophysical scales. The test of the GPDE was conducted on individual data from a series of magnitude-estimation and category-rating experiments (Eisler & Montgomery, 1974). In all experiments, subjects judged the loudness of white noise.

METHOD

Twelve persons served as subjects in the experiments. All subjects participated in a magnitude-estimation task and a category-rating task. In both tasks, the subjects were presented with 10 different noise intensities ranging from 40 dB to 110 dB (re 20 microbar/m²). Each stimulus was presented 50 times in each task. In the magnitude-estimation task, a standard stimulus of medium intensity was presented to the subject and called 10 (the standard). The subject was asked to estimate a series of noise intensities so that the ratio between his (her) own estimate and 10 reflected the ratio between the sensations of the stimulus presented and the standard.

In the category-rating task, the weakest and strongest intensities were presented and were labelled 1 and 7, respectively, (or 1 and 15, see later). The subjects were instructed to assign to each stimulus noise an integer between 1 and 7 (or 1 and 15) so that subjective sensation intervals between successive numbers were equal. The standards were presented only once, at the beginning of the experiments.

The subjects were randomly assigned in groups of four to three different experiments, in the following denoted as experiments ERA, ED1, and ED2. In experiment ERA, the stimuli were spaced so that subjects' response ambiguity was approximately equal for all stimuli (Attneave, 1959). In experiments ED1 and ED2, stimuli were spaced so that successive stimuli were approximately equally discriminable (Garner, 1952). The standards in the category-rating task were called 1 and 7 in experiments ERA and ED1 and 1 and 15 in experiment ED2. For more details concerning the experimental procedure, the reader is referred to Eisler and Montgomery (1974).

RESULTS

Figures 14.1 and 14.2 present individual Weber functions, i.e., SDs as a function of scale values (arithmetic means) in the magnitude-estimation and category-rating experiments, respectively. The Weber functions of the magnitude scale exhibit various forms, such as an approximately linear function (subjects MW and BJ), a more or less parabolic function (subjects EE and TJ), and an almost constant function (subjects KJ and DM). The Weber functions of the seven-point category scale (experiments ERA and ED1) usually are approximately constant with some exceptions for one or both extreme points. The Weber functions of the

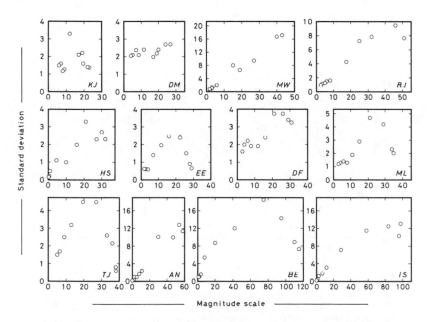

FIG. 14.1. SDs as a functions of magnitude scales of loudness for individual subjects. First row: experiment ERA. Second row: experiment ED1. Third row: experiment ED2.

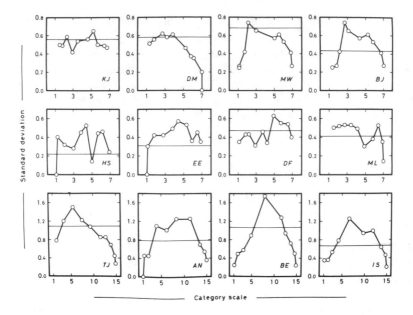

FIG. 14.2. SDs as a function of category scales of loudness for individual subjects. First row: experiment ERA. Second row: experiment ED1. Third row: experiment ED2.

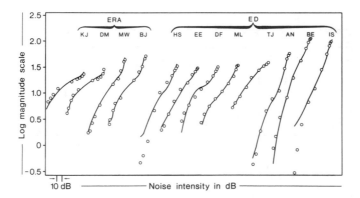

FIG. 14.3. Log magnitude scales of loudness for individual subjects as a function of noise intensity. The curves constitute predictions by the GPDE based on magnitude-estimation data from other subjects. The predicted magnitude scales were selected randomly from each set of three and seven predicted magnitude scales, that were obtained for each subject in experiment ERA and experiments ED1 and ED2, respectively.

15-point category scale (experiment ED2), on the other hand, decrease from the middle of the stimulus range toward both ends.

Figure 14.3 shows log-log plots of magnitude scales as a function of stimulus values. The slope of these scales varies considerably across different subjects. For many subjects, the scale values deviate systematically from a power function, particularly in experiment ERA in which all scales exhibit a sigmoid form. Moreover, in both experiments, single scales deviate in idiosyncratic ways from a power function. The category scales (see Fig. 14.4) exhibit varying forms across different experiments. The variability across subjects, however, is comparatively small within a particular experiment for the seven-point category scales (experiments ERA and ED1) and somewhat greater for the 15-point category scales (experiment ED2).

The GPDE was tested by numerical integration because explicit expressions could not be found for all the Weber functions. For all possible pairs of individuals i and j in each experiment, the following two integrals (both derived from Eq. 14.1) were calculated by the trapezoid method for each stimulus:

$$I_1 = \int \frac{\sigma\psi_j(\psi_j)}{\sigma\psi_i(\psi_i)} \, d\psi_i \text{ and } I_2 = \int \frac{\sigma\psi K_j(K_j)}{\sigma\psi_i \, (\psi_i)} \, d\psi_i, \qquad (14.2)$$

where σ denotes the SD, ψ magnitude scale, and K category scale values. I_2 was also calculated for magnitude and category scales for the same individuals.

To predict the seven-point category scale, the following integral was also calculated for each individual i:

$$I_3 = \int \frac{d\psi_i}{\sigma\psi_i(\psi_i)} \, . \qquad (14.3)$$

In I_3, the category scale is regarded as a Fechner integral of the magnitude scale. That is, in this integral the Weber function is assumed to be constant

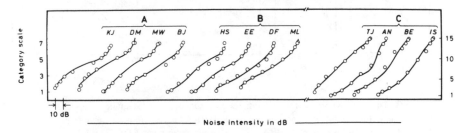

FIG. 14.4. Category scales of loudness for individual subjects as a function of noise intensity. The curves constitute predictions by the GPDE based on magnitude-estimation data from the same subjects.

implying that the category scale may be regarded as a discrimination scale (Eisler & Montgomery, 1974). The deviations from constancy in the empirical Weber functions for the seven-point category scale were assumed to be due to response bias (cf. Eisler & Montgomery, 1974).

For each of the three integrals I_1 I_2, and I_3, the method of least squares was used for fitting the straight lines:

$$y = \alpha I + \beta, \tag{14.4}$$

where y denotes the empirically obtained scale values to be predicted by I_1, I_2, and I_3, respectively. If the GPDE as given in Eq. 14.1 is correct, the slope α should equal unity in I_2 and the "constant" Weber function for the category scale in I_3. Thus, the agreement between empirical and predicted values of α reflects the extent to which the *absolute* sizes of the two sets of SDs are comparable in terms of the GPDE.

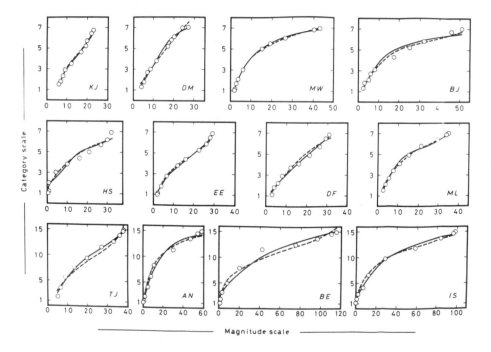

FIG. 14.5.   Category scales of loudness as a function of magnitude scales of loudness for individual subjects. Both scales were obtained from the same subjects. First row: experiment ERA. Second row: experiment ED1. Third row: experiment ED2. The curves constitute predictions of the category scales based on magnitude-estimation data from the same subject. (Solid curve: GPDE in general. Dashed curve: Fechnerian integration.)

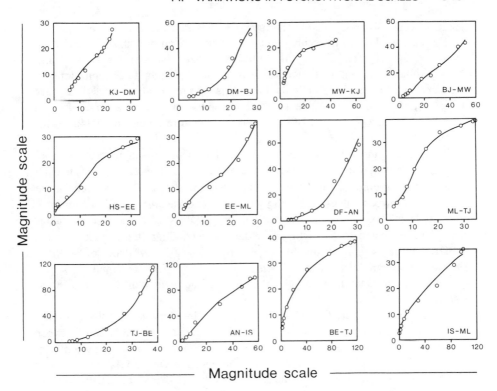

FIG. 14.6.   Interindividual relations between magnitude scales of loudness. First row: experiment ERA. Second row: experiment ED1. Third row: experiment ED2. The curves constitute predictions of the abscissa scale based on data from the subject corresponding to the ordinata scale. The predicted magnitude scales were obtained from each set of three and seven predicted magnitude scales, that were obtained for each subject in experiment ERA and experiments ED1 and ED2, respectively.

The goodness of fit of the scale values predicted by Eq. 14.4 was evaluated by computing the stress, defined as:

$$\sqrt{\frac{\Sigma(y'-y)^2}{\Sigma y^2}}, \tag{14.5}$$

where y' denotes predicted scale values and y denotes the values obtained empirically. It can be seen that the stress is independent of the absolute size of the y' and y values and, hence, permits comparisons between different subjects and experiments.

Figures 14.5 and 14.6 show empirical and predicted scales (Eq. 14.4) for all intraindividual relations studied and for a sample of the interindividual relations. It can be seen that the fit of the empirical to the predicted scales is good in the great majority of cases (see also the stress values in Table 14.1). Note that the GPDE can predict such peculiar relations between empirical scales as those exhibited by subjects EE and ML (intraindividual relations) and KJ-DM and ML-TJ (interindividual relations). Table 14.1 shows that the fit is approximately the same for intra- and interindividual relations with respect to predicted category scales (cf. S_2 and S_2^* in Table 14.1). The median of the stress value for the predicted category scales is .0400 for intraindividual relations and .0440 for interindividual relations.

To evaluate the stress values for the GPDE with respect to the predicted magnitude scales, a straight line was fitted by the method of least squares to each possible pair of empirical magnitude scales, and the stress was computed for the deviations between values predicted by this line and the corresponding empirical magnitude scale values. To the extent that the GPDE is valid, these stress values should be expected to be higher than the corresponding stress values for the GPDE. Figure 14.7 shows that this expectation is largely fulfilled. For 54 of the 68 pairs of magnitude scales, the stress for the line fitted to empirical scales exceeds the corresponding stress for the GPDE. The median of the former stress values is .1002. For the latter ones it is .0545.

As indicated earlier, the GPDE implies that the slope α (Eq. 14.4) should equal unity. The means of α for (a) the 12 intraindividual relations between category and magnitude scales, (b) the 68 interindividual relations between category and magnitude scales, and (c) the 68 interindividual relations between magnitude scales were .92, .92, and .97, respectively. (No strict statistical test of

TABLE 14.1

Medians of Stress Values (Eq. 14.5) for Predicted Magnitude Scales (S_1) and Predicted Category Scales (S_2) Across Different Subjects, and Slopes (Eq. 14.4) and Stress Values (S_2^*) for Predicted Category Scales Within Same Subjects

Experiment	S_1	S_2	Slope	S_2^*
ERA (KJ)	.0414	.0357	1.07	.0248
ERA (DM)	.0498	.0384	1.22	.0572
ERA (MW)	.0930	.0554	1.14	.0134
ERA (BJ)	.0544	.0574	0.76	.0462
ED1 (HS)	.0956	.0484	0.57	.0741
ED1 (EE)	.0386	.0440	0.69	.0120
ED1 (DF)	.0510	.0491	1.06	.0559
ED1 (ML)	.0437	.0331	0.92	.0280
ED2 (TJ)	.0213	.0439	1.10	.0337
ED2 (AN)	.1096	.0353	0.80	.0554
ED2 (BE)	.0414	.0637	1.05	.0704
ED2 (IS)	.0673	.0297	0.83	.0338

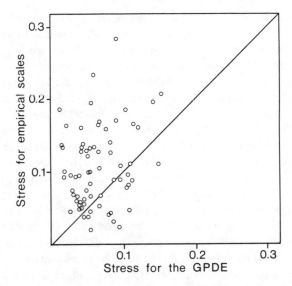

FIG. 14.7. Stress (Eq. 14.5) for deviations of empirical magnitude scale values from a straight line fitted by the method of least squares to each possible pair of magnitude scales for individual subjects in experiments ERA and ED, respectively, as a function of stress for predictions by the GPDE of magnitude scales for the corresponding pair of subjects.

whether α deviated from unity was carried out due to possible dependencies among the α-values.) The SDs of α for the three types of relations listed above were .203, .274, and .328, respectively. To evaluate whether these SDs reflected systematic differences among individual α-values the standard error of α was estimated for individual α-values (see Draper & Smith, 1966, p. 19). Ninety per cent of these estimates were at least five times lower than the corresponding empirical SDs and none was less than three times lower. It seems safe to conclude that there were systematic differences among individual α-values and, hence, that the *absolute* sizes of SDs from different scales for single individuals may not be strictly comparable in terms of the GPDE.

DISCUSSION

The present data show that the GPDE not only yields a close fit to empirical data from the same subject but also that it allows good prediction across different subjects. That is to say, a subjective scale for one subject can be predicted either from a different scale for the same subject or from the same or a different scale for a different subject provided that the Weber functions of both scales are known. To interpret these results I now discuss some implications of the GPDE.

First, the GPDE implies that the Weber functions of two scales are identical if, and only if, the scales themselves can be made identical by fitting one free parameter, i.e., the integration constant in Eq. 14.1a (or two free parameters if the absolute sizes of the Weber functions are disregarded, see Eq. 14.4). Hence, if the GPDE is used for transforming two scales (x_1 and x_2) to two other scales (y_1 and y_2 both with the same Weber functions), then these two scale transformations should result in the same scale. That is, to the extent that the GPDE is valid across scales from different experimental conditions and/or different individuals, it should be possible to use the GPDE for transforming all these scales to the same scale provided that a particular Weber function is specified for the latter scale. If such a scale has some psychological counterpart in a particular individual and if the GPDE holds for the relationships between this scale and other scales from the same individual or from other individuals, then it follows that the GPDE also holds for the relationships between these other scales. Thus, the GPDE is compatible with the assumption that all variations in psychophysical scales for a given set of stimuli are due to different transformations of an underlying subjective variable whose scale values and Weber function remain unchanged across different judgmental tasks or subjects for a given set of stimuli. It might be conjectured, for example, that subjects' *sensations* of a given set of stimuli as well as the Weber function of these sensations do not change across different judgmental tasks or subjects, whereas the overt response may change.

The idea that the overt responses made by subjects in a scaling experiment can be seen as a transformation of an underlying subjective variable has been put forth by researchers using the so-called functional measurement paradigm (Anderson, 1970; Birnbaum, 1978; Veit, 1978). These authors maintain that sensations are independent of the judgmental task (nothing is assumed with respect to interindividual variations in the sensations) and that discrepancies between the overt responses across different tasks are due to different transformations of the underlying sensations. To take a specific example, judgments of differences in a category-rating task are assumed to be linearly related to sensations whereas ratio judgments in a magnitude-estimation task are assumed to be an expotential function of sensation differences. Hence, according to these authors, a scale based on difference judgments (such as the category scale) is more appropriate than a scale based on ratio judgments. Experimental support for this proposition has been presented by Birnbaum (1978) and Veit (1978). (See, however, Eisler [1978] for a critical discussion of these experimental results.)

As indicated earlier, the present results are in line with the assumption that sensations do not change across different judgmental tasks (or across different subjects). However, the fact that the GPDE yields a close fit to empirical data does not in itself imply anything about which type of scale primarily reflects subjects' sensations.

On the other hand, the large interindividual variations in the form of the magnitude scale cannot be reconciled with the assumption that the magnitude scale is close to a sensation scale that is invariant across different subjects. In contrast, the category scale varied little across individuals within a particular experiment. Hence, it cannot be excluded that the category scale is close to a subject-invariant sensation scale. (Notice that the extension of the GPDE to interindividual relations implies that the category scale *should* be invariant across different subjects, if its Weber function is assumed to be a constant for all subjects, see Eq. 14.4).

Another implication is that if the GPDE is specified such that the scale values are medians and the Weber functions percentile distances (cf. Eisler, Holm, & Montgomery, 1979), then the discriminability among different stimuli should be invariant or practically invariant across scales that could be related by the GPDE. That is, the extent to which the response distributions for different stimuli overlap should be the same or practically the same regardless of the type of response scale used by subjects. Consider as an example two variables x and y with medians x_1 and y_1 for stimulus ϕ_1. If x_1, in addition, corresponds to, say, the tenth percentile of the distribution of x responses for stimulus ϕ_2, then the median y_1 is also the tenth percentile of the y distribution for stimulus ϕ_2 (Eisler, Holm, & Montgomery, 1979).

The present data indicate that the *absolute* level of the Weber functions and, hence, also of subjects' ability to discriminate between different stimuli varies considerably across scales from different subjects as well as across different scales from the same subject. However, if the absolute levels of the Weber functions are corrected (see Eq. 14.4) then the GPDE holds well for both inter- and intraindividual relations. Hence, the present data may imply that the *relative* discriminability among different stimuli, that is, a discriminability measure unique on the ratio scale level, is invariant across different subjects as well as across different types of response scales. In this connection, a scale with a constant Weber function is of particular interest because such a scale may be regarded as a discriminability scale. That is, a constant Weber function implies that equal probabilities of confusing two stimuli correspond to equal subjective distances provided that certain other assumptions of the scaling model are valid (cf. Torgerson, 1958, Ch. 10). In the present study as well as in other tests of the GPDE (Eisler, 1962, 1963a, 1963c; Montgomery & Eisler, 1974), it has been shown that if the (unbiased) Weber function of the category scale is assumed to be constant then the GPDE allows good prediction of this scale. For this reason, the category scale may be regarded as a discriminability scale. Moreover, the present data seem to imply that the category scale is a subject-invariant discriminability scale, at least approximately.

In summary, it has been found that the GPDE holds not only for intraindividual relations but also across different subjects. These results are compatible with the assumption that the sensations of a given set of stimuli are invariant both across different response scales and across different subjects. Moreover, the present data indicate that the relative discriminability among different stimuli is approximately invariant across different scale types and/or subjects. Finally, it seems that the category scale has two advantages over the magnitude scale. These are: (1) it varies less across different subjects and, hence, is more likely to be close to a subject-invariant sensation scale; (2) it has a clear-cut interpretation, that is, it may be regarded as a discriminability scale.

REFERENCES

Attneave, F. *Applications of information theory to psychology*. New York: Holt, 1959.

Anderson, N. H. Functional measurement and psychophysical judgment. *Psychological Review,* 1970, *77,* 153–170.

Birnbaum, M. H. Differences and ratios in psychological measurement. In F. Restle & N. J. Castellan, Jr. (Eds.), *Cognitive theory* (Vol 3). Hillsdale, N.J.: Lawrence Erlbaum Associates, 1978.

Draper, N. R., & Smith, H. *Applied regression analysis*. New York: Wiley, 1966.

Eisler, H. Empirical test of a model relating magnitude and category scales. *Scandinavian Journal of Psychology,* 1962, *3,* 88–96.

Eisler, H. How prothetic is the continuum of smell? *Scandinavian Journal of Psychology,* 1963, *4,* 29–32. (a)

Eisler, H. A general differential equation in psychophysics: Derivation and empirical test. *Scandinavian Journal of Psychology,* 1963, *4,* 265–272. (b)

Eisler, H. Magnitude scales, category scales and Fechnerian integration. *Psychological Review,* 1963, *70,* 243–253. (c)

Eisler, H. On the ability to estimate differences. A note on Birnbaum's subtractive model. *Perception & Psychophysics,* 1978, *24,* 185–189.

Eisler, H., Holm, S., & Montgomery, H. The general psychophysical differential equation: A comparison of three specifications. *Journal of Mathematical Psychology,* 1979, *20,* 16–34.

Eisler, H., & Montgomery, H. On theoretical and realizable ideal conditions in psychophysics: Magnitude and category scales and their relation. *Perception & Psychophysics,* 1974, *16,* 157–168.

Garner, W. R. An equal discriminability scale for loudness judgments. *Journal of Experimental Psychology,* 1952, *43,* 232–238.

McGill, W. The slope of the loudness function: A puzzle. In H. Gulliksen & S. Messick (Eds.), *Psychological scaling: Theory and applications*. New York: Wiley, 1960.

Montgomery, H., & Eisler, H. Is an equal interval scale an equal discriminability scale? *Perception & Psychophysics,* 1974, *15,* 441–448.

Torgerson, W. S. *Theory and methods of scaling*. New York: Wiley, 1958.

Veit, C. T. Ratio and subtractive processes in psychophysical judgment. *Journal of Experimental Psychology: General,* 1978, *107,* 81–107.

15

A Theoretical and Empirical Study of Scale Properties of Magnitude-Estimation and Category-Rating Scales

Bernhard Orth
Christian-Albrechts-Universität, Kiel, West Germany

1. INTRODUCTION

Since the invention of magnitude estimation, it has commonly been assumed that the scales obtained by this method are ratio scales, i.e., unique up to similarity transformations. It has been argued further that this assertion holds because magnitude estimates are based on ratio judgments.

Similarly, category ratings are most often supposed to yield scales that are unique up to positive linear transformations, i.e., interval scales. This assumption is commonly justified by noting that category ratings are based on judgments of differences or intervals.

From measurement theory, however, it is known that matters are not that simple. To get an interval scale from difference judgments, certain qualitative laws must be shown to be empirically satisfied. So, if we merely assume that category ratings are based on subjective differences, it is by no means guaranteed that these judgments yield an interval scale—no matter how reliable they are. It has also been shown that ratio judgments—taken by themselves—lead at best to what has been called a logarithmic interval scale, a scale that is unique up to power transformations. But again, the assumption that magnitude estimates are mediated by judgments of ratios turns out to be insufficient for the existence of a log-interval scale. (Necessary and/or sufficient conditions for obtaining the desired scale type from either difference or ratio judgments are given, e.g., in Krantz, Luce, Suppes, & Tversky, 1971; Orth, 1974; Pfanzagl, 1968). Nevertheless, ratio scales may be obtained by means of ratio judgments, but this can only be accomplished either by supplementary use of difference judgments (Krantz et al., 1971) or by cross-modality matching (Krantz, 1972b).

Even upon the assumption that magnitude estimates are based on ratio judgments, it is thus not possible to determine the scale type of a magnitude-estimation scale. Necessary conditions cannot be tested simply because the available data are magnitude estimates and not ratio judgments. Magnitude estimates themselves are just numbers and thus give us no information at all concerning their uniqueness, i.e., scale type. An analogous argument applies, of course, to the uniqueness of category-rating scales.

On the other hand, knowing the level of a scale is important on several grounds. The decision of whether or not a numerical statement is meaningful depends critically on the scale type of the measurements involved (Suppes & Zinnes, 1963). The scale type is also necessary to determine the appropriateness of statistical methods in data analysis (Stevens, 1946, 1951, 1959). In addition, quantitative models as well as quantitative laws require at least interval scale measurement of the variables involved and hence knowledge about their uniqueness.

In this paper we examine the problem of how to determine the uniqueness of scales constructed either by magnitude estimation or by category rating. As just demonstrated, there is no direct way to determine the type of those scales. What is required, then, is a model involving empirically testable assumptions that are mathematically sufficient to establish the desired uniqueness result. The next three sections are devoted to the development of such models. We begin with a model designed for the application of category ratings (Section 2); we next give a model with respect to magnitude estimation (Section 3); and in Section 4, we discuss a possible combination of both models yielding ratio scale measurement. All models are based on a measurement-free approach.

These theoretical considerations are followed by empirical applications of the proposed models. Section 5 describes an experiment on line length, which provides empirical tests of the models under study. Relevant results of group data as well as of individual subject data are presented. In Section 6, we present empirical results (in relation to the model of Section 4) concerning both the relationship between category-rating and magnitude-estimation scales and that between difference and ratio judgments. Some concluding remarks are given in the final section.

2. A CATEGORY-RATING MODEL

A mathematical proof of what is called a uniqueness theorem specifies the set of admissible transformations of a scale, and these transformations define the scale type. For instance, if the only admissible transformations turn out to be positive linear transformations, the type of the scale under consideration is an interval scale.

Transformations of a scale are called admissible if they preserve the representation, i.e., those properties of the attribute to be measured that are represented by properties of the scale numbers. For an empirical ordering of subjective differences, for example, the most natural representation is to state that this rank order is preserved by the ordering of numerical differences between corresponding scale values. Specifying the set of admissible transformations thus requires the representation to be known. Whether or not a certain representation holds, however, has to be shown mathematically by proving a representation theorem stating that under explicit conditions a scale possessing the desired representational properties does exist. Therefore, without a representation theorem, there can be no uniqueness theorem.

To understand the uniqueness problem of category-rating scales more fully, it is useful to consider a typical measurement theoretical task (e.g., Suppes & Zinnes, 1963). Given an empirical relational system (i.e., a set of stimuli together with at least one relation that formally characterizes some judgmental task), one has to find conditions that are necessary and/or sufficient for proving the desired representation and uniqueness theorem. A relational system together with a set of conditions imposed, a representation, and uniqueness theorem is called a measurement structure.

From a formal point of view, the conditions given by a measurement structure are to be regarded as axioms, whereas from an empirical viewpoint, they are to be considered as empirical hypotheses and, if satisfied, as (qualitative) empirical laws (Krantz, 1972a).

With category ratings, however, the problem of how to establish the desired uniqueness theorem differs in important ways from the typical approach just outlined. Take a set, say, A of stimuli to be rated and a real-valued function, say, CR on A denoting the (numerical) category ratings; the relational system will then be written $\langle A, CR \rangle$. However, there is no way to impose empirically testable constraints on the function CR. We are unable to determine whether or not the numbers given by the subjects represent anything of interest of the attribute to be measured. Without axioms, no representation can be shown to hold, and thus no result on uniqueness can be obtained.

In some sense, what is lacking is information—information about what is represented by category ratings. From this point of view, there is a need for more information and hence for more data, that is, for data other than category ratings. This amounts to saying that we have to look for an enrichment of the relational system $\langle A, CR \rangle$.

As previously mentioned, category ratings are commonly assumed to be based on difference judgments. Therefore, it seems most natural to enrich the relational system $\langle A, CR \rangle$ by a binary relation $\succsim_D$ on $A \times A$ (the Cartesian product of the set A) to be interpreted as an ordering of subjective differences. That is, we propose to use—supplementary to category ratings—difference judgments of the same stimuli as an independent source of data to get the information required. As discussed later, this approach provides sufficient information to establish both a reasonable representation and the desired (interval scale) uniqueness result for category-rating scales.

The model proposed may be outlined as follows: Given are both category ratings and difference judgments on the same set of stimuli. Suppose first that the ordering of subjective differences is well-behaved in the sense that it satisfies certain empirical laws (soon to be stated), which insure the existence of an interval scale for the difference judgments, and suppose secondly that this rank order of subjective differences coincides with the rank order of numerical differences between the corresponding category ratings. It is then easily shown that the category-rating scale under consideration is an interval scale, i.e., unique up to positive linear transformations. Thus, the basic idea of the present approach is that category ratings coincide with difference judgments.

A formal statement of the model can be presented in terms of a definition of a "category-rating structure." (As usual, we use "iff" as an abbreviation for "if and only if." Furthermore, we denote subjective differences, i.e., elements in $A \times A$, by ab, cd, etc. where a, b, c, d are elements in A; we have to distinguish between ab and ba. The relation $\sim_D$ can be defined in terms of $\gtrsim_D$ and denotes indifference. Similarly, $>_D$ is defined as usual and denotes strict dominance.)

Definition 1.   Let A be a nonempty set, CR be a real-valued function on A, and $\gtrsim_D$ be a binary relation on $A \times A$. The relational structure $\langle A, CR, \gtrsim_D \rangle$ is called a *category-rating structure* iff, for all a, b, c, d in A, the following two conditions hold:

1. $\langle A \times A, \gtrsim_D \rangle$ is an algebraic difference structure.
2. Compatibility between $\gtrsim_D$ and CR holds, i.e., ab $\gtrsim_D$ cd iff
   $CR(a) - CR(b) \geq CR(c) - CR(d)$.

Theorem 1.   Suppose that $\langle A, CR, \gtrsim_D \rangle$ is a category-rating structure. Then the function CR is unique up to positive linear transformations, i.e., CR is an interval scale.

For an explicit statement of an algebraic-difference structure, see Krantz et al. (1971, p. 151); it involves the testable axioms of weak ordering (i.e., transitivity and connectedness), sign reversal, weak monotonicity, and two nontestable conditions (solvability an an Archimedean axiom). Those axioms that are tested in the present study are stated in Section 5. The proof of Theorem 1 is a direct consequence of the representation and uniqueness theorem of an algebraic-difference structure and hence can be omitted here. The cornerstone of the present model is the compatibility condition relating the ordering $\gtrsim_D$ with the function CR. It asserts that subjective differences yield the same rank order as differences between corresponding category ratings.

A consequence of the category-rating model is its prediction of a linear function between the category-rating scale and the scale that can be constructed from the difference judgments (if these satisfy the axioms of an algebraic-difference structure). Let this scale be denoted by D. So, if the category-rating structure holds, it follows that there are real constants a and b, with a > 0, such that

$$CR = aD + b. \tag{15.1}$$

Note, however, that the converse is not true. If one finds a linear relation between the scales CR and D, it does not follow that either scale is an interval scale.

Although the category-rating model is primarily concerned with scale properties, it is based on psychologically plausible assumptions and hence might serve as a starting point for developing a more elaborated theory of category judgments. An analogous comment applies to the magnitude-estimation model to be given next.

3. A MAGNITUDE-ESTIMATION MODEL

A magnitude-estimation scale is often called a "ratio scale." Here, the term "ratio scale" refers to any scale that is obtained by instructing subjects to judge stimuli according to (subjective) ratios. This terminology, introduced by Stevens (1957), has given rise to some confusion because it is quite different from the technical meaning of the term "ratio scale," also introduced by Stevens himself some years earlier (Stevens, 1946, 1951). According to this meaning, a ratio scale is defined as a scale whose only admissible transformations are similarity transformations (i.e., multiplication by a positive constant). (Throughout this paper, the term "ratio scale" is used in this latter sense.) It is not at all clear, however, whether a magnitude-estimation scale is a ratio scale (i.e., unique up to similarity transformations). As Krantz et al. (1971) put it: "Stevens has not provided any argument showing that the procedure of magnitude estimation can be axiomatized so as to result in a ratio-scale representation; he has neither described the empirical relational structure, the numerical relational structure, nor the axioms which permit the construction of a homomorphism [p. 11]" (i.e., a scale).

This situation closely resembles the situation with category ratings. Though an empirical relational system can easily be set up—i.e., ⟨A, ME⟩ where A is a stimulus set, and ME is a function from A into the positive reals denoting numerical magnitude estimates—there is no way to impose empirically testable restrictions on the function ME. Accordingly, neither a representation theorem nor any uniqueness result can be established. There is a need for information from supplementary data sources and hence for enriching the relational system ⟨A, ME⟩ in order to obtain an appropriate uniqueness result for the magnitude-estimation scale.

The most natural candidate for an enrichment of $\langle A, ME \rangle$ seems to be a quarternary relation $\gtrsim_R$ on A (i.e., a binary relation on A $\times$ A) denoting an order relation of subjective ratios (corresponding to some "ratio" instruction). We thus suggest the use of ratio judgments on the same stimulus set in addition to magnitude estimates. Not surprisingly, then, the proposed magnitude-estimation model closely parallels the category-rating model. Assuming explicitly that magnitude estimates are mediated by judgments of ratios, the model provides conditions that assure the magnitude-estimation scale to be a log-interval scale.

To give an account of the model, suppose that both magnitude estimates and ratio judgments on the same set of stimuli have been obtained. Now, it is postulated first that the ordering of subjective ratios satisfies specific empirical laws that are required for the construction of a log-interval scale from these data, and second that this ordering agrees with the rank order of numerical ratios of corresponding magnitude estimates. These hypotheses, then, imply that the magnitude-estimation scale under consideration is unique up to power transformations and thus a log-interval scale. The essential assumption of this model is that magnitude estimates coincide with ratio judgments in regard of their respective orderings. It should be noted that the present approach is in close agreement with relation theory, as developed by Krantz (1972b).

Inasmuch as numerical ratios and differences share the same qualitative properties, the magnitude-estimation model becomes formally almost equivalent to the category-rating model if we replace the function CR by ME and the relation $\gtrsim_D$ by $\gtrsim_R$. The model is given in Definition 2. Here, we denote subjective ratios (elements in A $\times$ A) by ab, cd, etc. (with stimuli a, b, c, d in A). Again, we must distinguish between ab and ba etc.; the meaning of $\sim_R$ and $>_R$ should be obvious.

Definition 2. Suppose A is a nonempty set, ME a positive-valued real function on A, and $\gtrsim_R$ a binary relation on A $\times$ A. The triple $\langle A, ME, \gtrsim_R \rangle$ is a *magnitude-estimation structure* iff, for all a, b, c, d in A, the following two axioms are satisfied:

1. $\langle A \times A, \gtrsim_R \rangle$ is an algebraic difference structure.
2. Compatibility between $\gtrsim_R$ and ME holds, i.e., ab $\gtrsim_R$ cd iff ME(a)/ME(b) $\geq$ ME(c)/ME(d).

Theorem 2. If the relational system $\langle A, ME, \gtrsim_R \rangle$ is a magnitude-estimation structure, then the function ME is unique up to power transformations, i.e., ME is a log-interval scale.

As is well-known, an algebraic-difference structure is applied with regard to ratios or differences as representation (Krantz et al., 1971). Accordingly, the magnitude-estimation model is based on the same measurement structure as the category-rating model. The proof of the desired uniqueness result (Theorem 2) is entirely straightforward, too, and can be omitted.

Again, an implication of the model should be mentioned. Let R denote the scale that can be constructed from the ratio judgments whenever they are fairly well-behaved in the sense of satisfying Condition 1 of Definition 2. The magnitude-estimation model then predicts a power function between R and the magnitude-estimation scale, i.e., there exist positive constants a and b such that

$$ME = a\ R^b.\tag{15.2}$$

It should be noted that the magnitude-estimation model permits an empirical comparison with the category-rating model even on an individual data level. Moreover, a use of both models in conjunction might prove useful for thoroughly studying the interrelations between category-rating and magnitude-estimation scales and/or between difference and ratio judgments.

4. A COMBINED MODEL

Under what circumstances does the method of magnitude estimation yield a scale unique up to similarity transformation, i.e., a ratio scale?

One answer proposed by Krantz (1972b) involves cross-modality matching. Krantz developed conditions that insure the existence of a meaningful representation and of a uniqueness theorem involving as many scales as modalities. These scales are unique up to power transformations with the same exponent. If one exponent is fixed, the scales of the other continua are ratio scales.

Here, however, another approach is adopted. It is based on results obtained by Krantz et al. (1971) and makes use of difference judgments rather than cross-modality matchings. It can be shown that the magnitude-estimation model yields a ratio scale if it is properly linked together with the category-rating model. The result of this joining may be labeled a combined model.

The assumptions of the combined model may be summarized as follows: Suppose first that both the magnitude-estimation model and the category rating model hold, assume further that the ordering of subjective ratios does not agree with the ordering of subjective differences, and suppose finally that these two orderings are interlocked specifically. It is shown, then, that both the magnitude-estimation and the category-rating scale can be transformed in such a way that they yield a common ratio scale. A precise statement of the combined model is given in terms of the following definition.

Definition 3.   Let A, ME, CR, $\gtrsim_R$, and $\gtrsim_D$ be as in Definitions 1 and 2. The relational system $\langle A, ME, CR, \gtrsim_R, \gtrsim_D \rangle$ is called a *combined magnitude-estimation and category-rating structure* iff, for all a, b, c, d, e, f in A, the following four conditions hold:

1. $\langle A, ME, \gtrsim_R \rangle$ is a magnitude-estimation structure (Definition 2).
2. $\langle A, CR, \gtrsim_D \rangle$ is a category-rating structure (Definition 1).
3. The relations $\gtrsim_R$ and $\gtrsim_D$ are distinct.
4. The interlocking condition holds, i.e.,
   a. $ab \gtrsim_R aa$ iff $ab \gtrsim_D aa$;
   b. If $ad \sim_R be \sim_R cf$, then $ab \gtrsim_D bc$ iff $de \gtrsim_D ef$.

Theorem 3.   Let $\langle A, ME, CR, \gtrsim_R, \gtrsim_D \rangle$ be a combined magnitude-estimation and category-rating structure. Then there are real constants a, b, and c (with a, b > 0) such that

$$C = CR + c = a\ ME^b, \qquad\qquad (15.3)$$

where C is a (common) ratio scale.

The proof of Theorem 3 is a direct consequence of results obtained by Krantz et al. (1971, p. 154). It is interesting to note that exactly this relationship between category scales and magnitude-estimation scales has been suggested by Marks (1968). The interlocking condition, due to Krantz et al. (1971), states how difference and ratio judgments must be interrelated in order to yield a common scale. It should be noted, however, that this axiom is not easily testable because of the indifferences involved, which are either empirically unreliable or difficult to obtain.

The requirement that $\gtrsim_R$ and $\gtrsim_D$ do not coincide (Condition 3) is perhaps the most interesting assumption from an empirical viewpoint. Here, we are concerned with a problem that was posed for the first time by Torgerson (1960, 1961). Do subjects judge differences and do they judge ratios if they are told to do so? Or, do they give identical judgments regardless of instructions? What is it they judge then? Do they judge differences only? Do they judge ratios only? Or, do they judge according to some combination of both? Torgerson holds the view that both "difference" and "ratio" instructions lead to the same empirical ordering, and he reported some data in favor of this assertion. Further empirical evidence in support of Torgerson's hypothesis has been provided, e.g., by Birnbaum and coworkers (see Birnbaum, 1978).

To account for these findings, we provide an alternative to Theorem 3 (and Definition 3) by assuming explicitly that the empirical orderings $\gtrsim_R$ and $\gtrsim_D$ coincide. We then arrive at the following result (cf. Krantz et al., 1971).

Theorem 4.   Let A, ME, CR, $\gtrsim_R$, and $\gtrsim_D$ as in Definition 3. Suppose that the following hold:

1. $\langle A, ME, \gtrsim_R \rangle$ is a magnitude-estimation structure.
2. $\langle A, CR, \gtrsim_D \rangle$ is a category-rating structure.
3. The relations $\gtrsim_R$ and $\gtrsim_D$ are not distinct.

Then there are real constants a and b, with b > 0, such that

$$CR = a + b \log ME. \tag{15.4}$$

So, contrary to Theorem 3, there does not exist a common scale. Assuming $\gtrsim_R$ and $\gtrsim_D$ to be equal leads to the conclusion that CR and ME are two different scales that are logarithmically related. However, there is also empirical evidence against this consequence. Quite often the category scale cannot properly be described as a logarithmic function of the magnitude-estimation scale; its curvature is too flat (e.g., Stevens & Galanter, 1957).

We are now faced with a somewhat puzzling situation. If the conclusions of both Theorem 3 and Theorem 4 are empirically not valid (according to Torgerson's and Stevens' viewpoints, respectively), we cannot retain both the category-rating model and the magnitude-estimation model. That is, we must assume either that category ratings are not based on difference judgments or that magnitude estimates are not based on ratio judgments (in the sense of Definitions 1 and 2, respectively). Conversely, if both models can be shown to hold, then Theorem 3 and Theorem 4 cannot both be satisfied.

5. EMPIRICAL TESTS OF THE CATEGORY-RATING AND THE MAGNITUDE-ESTIMATION MODEL

In this section, an experiment on line length judgment is reported, which has been designed for testing the models discussed previously. Experimental results of both the category-rating model and the magnitude-estimation model are given in the present section; empirical findings with respect to the combined model are deferred to the next section.

Method

Subjects. Sixty-four first- and second-year undergraduates of the University of Kiel served as subjects in the experiment. They were naive with respect to the judgmental tasks and the purpose of the experiment.

Stimuli. Ten lines were used as stimuli, varying in length from 1.0 to 23.5 cm. The stimuli were chosen in such a way that neither their differences nor their ratios produced ties and such that the rank correlation between (physical) differences and ratios was fairly low (Kendall's τ was .55). Depending on the task, either one or two lines were printed horizontally on a single sheet of paper (size 30×21 cm).

Procedure.   The following six tasks were administered to each subject: (a) category rating on a numerical seven-point rating scale; (b) category rating on a 100-point rating scale; (c) magnitude estimation (no standard and no modulus); (d) difference judgments of all different pairs of stimuli on a 20-point rating scale; (e) ratio judgments of the same 45 stimulus pairs on a 20-point rating scale; (f) similarity judgments of all stimulus pairs on a 20-point rating scale. No use of the similarity judgment is made in this study, though. Different sheets of paper were used for different tasks. Within each task, stimuli or stimulus pairs were presented in a random order, which was different for all subjects.

All subjects had to perform each of the tasks, a, b, and c three times and each of the tasks d, e, and f once (the latter tasks were preceded by five warming-up trials). The order of tasks was counterbalanced and partially permuted according to the scheme aabbdaccfbce. All permutations of a, b, c and—at the same time—of d, e, f were used, making up six different orders that were given to 10 or 11 subjects each. No effects of task order, however, were notable.

Subjects received a booklet containing stimuli and stimulus pairs for all tasks, special instructions for every task, and—at the beginning—a general instruction that included the shortest and the longest line to familiarize subjects with the range of stimuli used in the experiment. The number of 240 judgments required was to be made in one session, lasting about 70 minutes. Subjects were free to pause.

Results

According to Sections 2 and 3, applications of the category-rating and the magnitude-estimation model amount to testing whether the orderings of subjective differences and ratios satisfy the empirical laws of an algebraic-difference structure (Condition 1 of Definitions 1 and 2) and whether the corresponding compatibility conditions hold (Condition 2 of Definitions 1 and 2).

Test of algebraic-difference structures of both models are discussed first. In the present study, transitivity is satisfied vacuously because the use of rating scales for obtaining difference and ratio judgments insures the transitivity of $\gtrsim_D$ and $\gtrsim_R$. Similarly, connectedness holds because all different pairs of stimuli have been used. The sign-reversal axiom cannot be rejected by the present experiment because stimulus pairs were not presented twice. With line-length judgments, however, this condition may safely be assumed to hold.

We are thus left with weak monotonicity, the most crucial condition of an algebraic-difference structure. It is the weakest axiom known for obtaining the desired results. With respect to empirical applications, however, it may be advisable to test some stronger necessary condition to account at least partially for an indirect test of solvability (cf. Adams, Fagot, & Robinson, 1970). We therefore employed empirical tests of the so-called quadrupel condition rather than weak monotonicity. It is not difficult to show that the quadrupel condition implies weak monotonicity, but not vice versa (Block & Marschak, 1960; Luce & Suppes, 1965). With regard to the category-rating model, this new empirical hypothesis reads as follows:

Quadrupel condition:
If ab $\gtrsim_D$ cd, then ac $\gtrsim_D$ bd (15.5)

(With respect to the magnitude-estimation model, simply replace $\gtrsim_D$ by $\gtrsim_R$.)

Although, in the present context, the quadrupel condition provides a sufficiently strong test of an algebraic-difference structure, still another necessary condition has been tested. It is a comparatively weak axiom, which is necessary for the category-rating scale (as well as for the magnitude-estimation scale) to be merely an ordinal scale, in the context of the present models. This condition can be referred to as independence because of its close relationship to a similar condition in conjoint measurement, and it may be stated as follows.

Independence:
  (i) If ac $\gtrsim_D$ bc, then ad $\gtrsim_D$ bd;
  (ii) If ac $\gtrsim_D$ ad, then bc $\gtrsim_D$ bd. (15.6)

(For a statement of independence within the framework of the magnitude-estimation model, simply replace $\gtrsim_D$ by $\gtrsim_R$.) Independence is most easily explained in terms of a matrix of subjective differences (or ratios). It asserts that the rank order of cell entries of any column agrees with that of every other column (i) and, similarly, that the ordering of values within any row coincides with that of every other row (ii). Testing independence, therefore, permits an estimate of a base line for number of empirical violations for a comparison with those of the crucial quadrupel condition. Independence should be especially suitable for this purpose because it can hardly be questioned that category ratings as well as magnitude estimates yield at least ordinal scales.

Computer programs[1] for testing the quadrupel condition and independence were applied to individual and pooled data (difference and ratio judgments). It should be noted that subjects were forced to produce ties because 45 different stimulus pairs were to be judged on a 20-point rating scale. To account for these ties induced by instruction, we replaced $\gtrsim_D$ by $>_D$ (and $\gtrsim_R$ by $>_R$) in the antecedents of both independence and the quadrupel condition, that is, we tested slightly weaker versions of both conditions. The results are summarized in Table 15.1.

For the averaged group data of both difference and ratio judgments, there is not a single failure of independence (out of 8100 possible tests), and there are only 1.27% violations of the quadrupel condition (32 violations each out of 2518 and 2520 possible tests for difference and ratio judgments, respectively). (A possible test refers to a case where the antecedent of a condition holds, i.e., where a prediction is made; a violation indicates an instance of a possible test where the prediction [conclusion] fails.)

TABLE 15.1
Violations of Independence and of the Quadrupel Condition of the
Category-Rating and Magnitude-Estimation Models for Group and
Individual Data

	Category-Rating Model		Magnitude-Estimation Model	
	Difference Judgments		Ratio Judgments	
	Quadrupel Condition	Independence	Quadrupel Condition	Independence
Group data (N = 64)	1.27 %	0.00 %	1.27 %	0.00 %
Individual subject data				
median	2.71 %	2.30 %	3.31 %	3.63 %
mean	3.44 %	2.95 %	4.13 %	4.12 %
SD	2.41 %	2.46 %	3.18 %	3.46 %

With respect to individual subject data, both independence and the quadrupel condition are very well-satisfied for both models. According to Table 15.1, the averaged percentages of violations are low for both conditions and both models. Note that the quadrupel condition and independence are about equally well-satisfied, indicating that the observed violations might be considered as random errors (if we accept the ordinal scale hypothesis for category ratings and magnitude estimates). Moreover, the percentages of violations of both conditions are highly correlated ($r = .89$ and $.91$ for difference and ratio judgments, respectively).

How many subjects have violated either model? Unfortunately, there is as yet no fully developed error theory available according to which a particular axiom has to be rejected. Therefore, some more or less arbitrary criterion must be used. We decided to choose 10% violations of the quadrupel condition as a cutoff point, a value that corresponds roughly to a stress value of 20%, which is considered as yielding a poor fit (Kruskal, 1964). According to this criterion, the category-rating model should be rejected for only two out of 64 subjects and the magnitude-estimation model for only three out of 64 subjects (where one of these subjects satisfies neither model).

We may thus conclude that difference as well as ratio judgments satisfy an algebraic-difference structure on both the individual and the group-data level. Hence, scales can be constructed for both kinds of judgments most easily by means of nonmetric multidimensional scaling procedure. The goodness-of-fit values may be used as an additional empirical evaluation of algebraic-difference structures because a unidimensional MDS solution provides a direct test of the representation.

Roskam's MINISSA (see, e.g., Lingoes, 1973) was applied to individual and group data of both difference and ratio judgments. The obtained stress values for unidimensional solutions are summarized in Table 15.2 and indicate results that are very similar to those reported in Table 15.1. Again, the group data satisfy both models almost perfectly, and the individual subject data (which are not very reliable, of course) of both difference and ratio judgments yield a good fit, as well. In general, stress values turned out to be about twice as large as the percentages of violations of the quadrupel condition. It should be noted that the highest stress values (about 20%) were obtained from the difference and/or ratio data of those subjects who have been said to violate the category-rating and/or magnitude-estimation model, respectively, according to the previously discussed criterion based on failures of the quadrupel condition. Hence, the MINISSA results are in good agreement with those of the axiomatic analysis; they confirm our conclusion that Condition 1 of both models holds for an overwhelming majority of subjects.

We now turn to tests of the compatibility conditions of the category-rating and the magnitude-estimation model. Compatibility asserts that two different empirical orderings of subjective differences (or ratios) should coincide, that is, that the rank correlation between both orderings should be very high. Both category ratings and magnitude estimates were averaged for each subject, and Kendall's tau coefficients (corrected for ties) between difference judgments and differences of category ratings as well as between ratio judgments and ratios of magnitude estimates were calculated for the group data and for individual subject data. The category-rating model is tested for the seven-point rating scale and for the 100-point rating scale. The main results are given in Table 15.3.

The tau coefficients of Table 15.3 are fairly high for both models, for both types of category ratings, and for both group data and individual data. We may

TABLE 15.2
Stress Values (obtained by MINISSA) of Unidimensional Solutions for
Difference and Ratio Judgments from Group Data and from
Individual Data

	Category-Rating Model	*Magnitude-Estimation Model*
	Difference Judgments	*Ratio Judgments*
Group data		
(N = 64)	< 1.00 %	< 1.00 %
Individual subject data		
Median	5.62 %	7.70 %
mean	6.29 %	7.89 %
SD	4.26 %	5.67 %

TABLE 15.3
Results of Testing the Compatibility Conditions of the Category-Rating Model
(for two rating scales) and the Magnitude-Estimation Model[a]

	Category-Rating Model		Magnitude-Estimation Model
	Seven-Point Scale	100-Point Scale	
Group data (N = 64)	.91	.84	.90
Individual subject data			
median	.75	.76	.82
mean	.75	.75	.79
SD	.10	.12	.13

[a] Values are Kendall's τ coefficients, given for pooled and individual data.

thus conclude that compatibility is satisfied for all three models (for convenience, we refer to the two versions of the category-rating model as two models). As with respect to the quadrupel condition, we may ask how many subjects violate compatibility for either model. Again, we have to find some criterion. If we allow for up to about 20% of the minimum number of possible pairwise reversals, we get a tau coefficient of .60 as a cutoff point. This value is just within the confidence interval of .85 (p = .01), which can be regarded as a value high enough for accepting compatibility. To account for the different numbers of ties in both types of category ratings and in magnitude estimates, a tau coefficient of .55, which is uncorrected for ties (and corresponds to a corrected value of .60), was used as the final criterion. There were only three, four, and four subjects out of 64, respectively, who failed to satisfy the category-rating models for the seven-point and 100-point scales and the magnitude-estimation model with respect to compatibility. Together with those subjects who have been said to violate the quadrupel condition, there are in total four, six, and six subjects out of 64 violating those three models, respectively; and there are only two subjects who satisfy neither model. Thus, each model is satisfied by more than 90% of the subjects.

It should be noted, however, that compatibility seems to be less well-satisfied than the quadrupel condition. The tau coefficients in Table 15.3 are not large enough to exclude the possibility that there are slight but systematic violations of compatibility. Indeed, there is some evidence for the existence of systematic violations. This can be seen from Fig. 15.1 where category ratings are plotted against scale values from difference judgments, obtained by MINISSA, and magnitude estimates are plotted against MINISSA scale values from ratio judgments.

Figure 15.1 thus provides a test of predictions of the models stated as Eqs. 15.1 and 15.2 in Sections 2 and 3, respectively. The problem that the scale values from ratio judgments are based on a difference representation rather than a ratio representation has been bypassed by taking logarithms of magnitude estimates; then, the predicted relationship becomes a linear one in semilog coordinates rather than in log-log coordinates (according to Eq. 15.2). Hence, all functions plotted in Fig. 15.1 should be linear. Although goodness of fit is quite high, all plots show some slight but systematic curvature. The magnitude-estimation function is curved downwards, whereas the function of the 100-point category ratings is positively accelerated. Even the function of the seven-point scale can be fitted slightly better by some positively accelerated function. We consider these deviations to be substantial. Further evidence in favor of this assumption is given later.

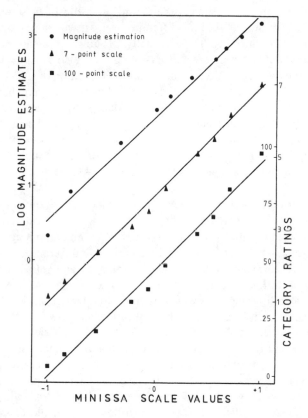

FIG. 15.1. Category ratings (from two different rating scales) as a function of scale values from difference judgments (obtained by MINISSA) and logarithms of magnitude estimates as a function of MINISSA scales values from ratio judgments. Each data point is based on 192 observations from 64 subjects. Straight lines are best-fitting functions as predicted by the category-rating and the magnitude-estimation models (Eqs. 15.1 and 15.2, respectively).

In the remainder of this section, we provide an explanation for the deviations from predictions of the models as well as for some systematic violations of the compatibility condition. These systematic errors are due to individual differences with respect to difference and ratio judgments. That is, they heavily depend on whether or not subjects do indeed judge differences and ratios when they are instructed to do so.

We first examine individual differences with respect to compatibility. Individual differences become readily apparent when we raise the criterion for accepting compatibility to $\tau \geq .75$, which corresponds roughly to the mean tau values. With three models, there are eight possible groups of subjects: subjects satisfying all three models, two models, one model only, or no model at all, yielding one, three, three, and one group of subjects, respectively. What is interesting is that almost all subjects belong to only four of these eight groups; there are only six subjects (in four different groups) who satisfy one category-rating model but not the other. Thus, virtually all subjects who are said to satisfy (violate) compatibility for either category-rating scale also satisfy (violate) compatibility for the other scale. According to this classification of subjects, there are 20 subjects satisfying all three models, 11 subjects satisfying both category models but not the magnitude-estimation model, 19 subjects satisfying the magnitude-estimation model but neither category-rating model, and eight subjects satisfying neither model at all. For convenience, we classify these latter eight subjects in one group together with the remaining six subjects mentioned before. We then end up with a classification of all 64 subjects into four different groups.

We consider now another classification of subjects based on a comparison of difference and ratio judgments with physical differences and ratios between stimuli. In order to examine whether or not difference and ratio judgments indeed rely on differences and ratios, respectively, subjective difference and ratio orderings were rank correlated with physical differences and ratios for individual subject data. With line length judgments, the rank correlations between subjective and physical differences (as well as ratios) should approach 1, whereas those between subjective differences and physical ratios and between subjective ratios and physical differences should be about .55 (the tau coefficient between physical differences and ratios). Again, large individual differences are found. If we say, for example, that subjects yielding $\tau \geq .80$ between subjective and physical differences and/or ratios (this value is close to the corresponding mean tau coefficients) presumably judge according to differences and/or ratios when they are required to do so, then we obtain the following fourfold classification of subjects. There are 17 subjects performing well with both difference and ratio judgments, 13 subjects performing well with difference judgments only, 24 subjects performing well with ratio judgments only, and 10 subjects performing well with neither difference nor ratio judgments.

An important result is that both classifications essentially coincide. This is easily seen from Table 15.4, which gives the number of subjects classified into the four groups of each classification. This table shows that almost all subjects who satisfy all three models perform well with both difference and ratio judgments, that all subjects satisfying the category-rating models perform well with difference judgments only, that all subjects satisfying the magnitude estimation model perform well with ratio judgments only, and that most subjects satisfying neither model (or just one category-rating model) perform well with neither difference nor ratio judgments. For convenience, we denote these four groups of subjects as the DR-group, D-group, R-group, and NN-group ("neither/nor"), respectively. (Because of the high agreement between both classifications, it is immaterial which classification these groups rely on.)

It is now logical to hypothesize that violations of compatibility as well as deviations from predictions of the models are due to individual differences in the performance of difference and ratio judgments. We thus expect the different groups of subjects to yield systematic differences in satisfying the compatibility conditions. Table 15.5 shows that this prediction holds very nicely. Compatibility of both category-rating models is satisfied very well by the DR-group and D-group subjects and holds only poorly for the R-group and NN-group subjects,

TABLE 15.4
Two Classifications of Subjects, Showing Their High Agreement
(Values Are Numbers of Subjects)[a]

		Classification According to Difference and Ratio Judgments				
		DIFF + RATIO +	DIFF + RATIO −	DIFF − RATIO +	DIFF − RATIO −	Σ
Classification According to Compatibility	CR + ME +	16	1	3	—	20
	CR + ME −	—	11	—	—	11
	CR − ME +	—	—	19	—	19
	CR − ME −	1	1	2	10	14
	Σ	17	13	24	10	64

[a] Row classification is according to goodness of satisfying compatibility of either model (at criterion $\tau \geq .75$); column classification is according to performance with difference and ratio judgments as determined by rank correlations between subjective and physical differences as well as ratios (at criterion $\tau \geq .80$). CR, ME, DIFF, and RATIO denote category-rating and magnitude-estimation model and difference and ratio judgments, respectively; + and − denote "above" and "below" corresponding criterion, respectively.

TABLE 15.5
Results of Testing the Compatibility Conditions of Both Models[a]

	Category-Rating Model		Magnitude-Estimation Model
	Seven-Point Scale	100-Point Scale	
DR-Group (N = 20)	.95	.96	.95
D-Group (N = 11)	.91	.93	.65
R-Group (N = 19)	.75	.66	.96
NN-Group (N = 14)	.85	.76	.83

[a] Values are Kendall's τ coefficients, given for pooled data and for different subgroups of subjects (for this classification, see text).

TABLE 15.6
Goodness-of-Fit Values (r^2) to Functions Predicted by the Category-Rating and the Magnitude-Estimation Models (Eqs. 15.1 and 15.2, respectively)

	Category-Rating Model		Magnitude-Estimation Model
	Seven-Point Scale	100-Point Scale	
DR-Group[a] (N = 20)	.993	.995	.994
D-Group (N = 11)	.992	.995	.902
R-Group (N = 19)	.944	.913	.997
NN-Group (N = 14)	.990	.970	.973

[a] Values are given for four different subgroups of subjects (for this classification, see text).

whereas compatibility of the magnitude-estimation model holds very well for the DR-group and R-group subjects and only poorly for the other groups. It has been mentioned previously that compatibility does not hold very well for the group data from all subjects and that there might be systematic violations. The results of Table 15.5 confirm this conjecture. At the same time, they clearly indicate that violations of compatibility are due to those subjects who perform comparatively bad with difference and/or ratio judgments.

A similar prediction can be made with respect to the deviations from the predicted linear functions shown in Fig. 15.1. For the four groups of subjects, the values of r^2 for the goodness of fit to a linear function are given in Table 15.6. This prediction holds very well, too. The results are in perfect agreement with those of Table 15.5 and thus provide further evidence for the assumption that there are small but substantial deviations from the predictions of both models. In Table 15.6, these deviations can be explained by individual differences in difference and ratio judgments. It can thus be argued that possible failures of the models are primarily to be attributed to difference and ratio judgments rather than to category ratings and magnitude estimates.

6.   AN EMPIRICAL TEST OF THE COMBINED MODEL

It has been shown that the magnitude-estimation model as well as both versions of the category-rating model are empirically satisfied for almost all subjects— except for some small but systematic violations of compatibility, probably due to confusion between difference and ratio judgments by some subjects. Hence, it may safely be assumed that Conditions 1 and 2 of the combined model (Definition 3 in Section 4) are empirically valid.

The next assumption of this model (Condition 3) asserts that the rank orders of subjective differences and ratios are distinct. (Note that the opposite assumption is a hypothesis of Theorem 4, which gives an alternative to the combined model.) In order to test both assumptions, tau coefficients between subjective difference and ratio orderings were calculated for both individual and group data. Again, because individual differences were to be expected, rank correlations were also calculated for those different groups of subjects mentioned in the preceding section. The results are summarized in Table 15.7. For the individual subject data, the tau coefficients are faily low. (Note that, for reasons already mentioned, the minimum tau to be expected is about .55.)

TABLE 15.7
Rank Correlations (Kendall's τ) Between Orderings of Subjective Differences and Ratios for Pooled Data and Individual Data from Different Subgroups of Subjects (see Section 5) and from the Total Group of Subjects (Last Column)

	DR-Group (N = 20)	D-Group (N = 11)	R-Group (N = 19)	NN-Group (N = 14)	All Subjects (N = 64)
Pooled Data	.67	.90	.94	.92	.87
Individual Subject Data					
median	.64	.72	.83	.71	.73
mean	.66	.78	.82	.71	.74
SD	.08	.12	.06	.07	.10

There are only nine subjects out of 64 yielding $\tau > .85$, only four subjects with $\tau > .90$, and no subjects with $\tau > .95$, whereas seven subjects yield $\tau \leq .60$ and 16 subjects $\tau \leq .65$. In view of the results of the preceding section, it is not surprising that the four groups of subjects yield different results. The low values of the DR-group subjects are to be expected because these subjects discriminate very well between subjective differences and ratios. Most subjects of other groups, however, discriminate rather poorly and thus yield higher values. The rank correlations of the pooled data are considerably higher than those of the individual data; this holds for all groups, except for the DR-group.

Another way of studying the relationship between difference and ratio judgments is provided by determining the function between respective scale values obtained by MINISSA. Inasmuch as both orderings satisfy the conditions of an

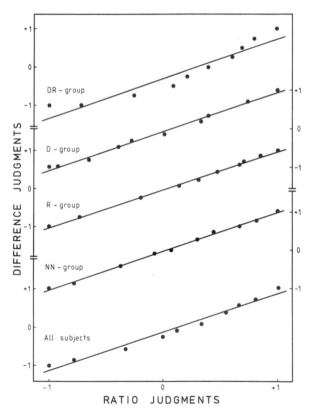

FIG. 15.2.   Relationship between scale values from difference and ratio judgments (obtained by MINISSA) for four different subgroups and the total group of subjects. (For classification of subjects, see Section 5.) Straight lines are predicted if orderings of subjective differences and ratios coincide (cf. Eq. 15.7 and following text).

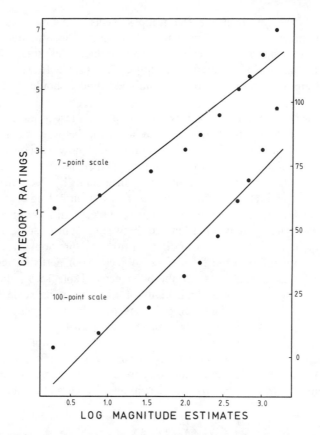

FIG. 15.3.   Category ratings (from two rating scales) as a function of logarithms of magnitude estimates. Each data point is based on 192 observations from 64 subjects. Straight lines are asserted by the conclusion of Theorem 4 (Eq. 15.4), an alternative to the combined model.

algebraic-difference structure, an agreement of difference and ratio orderings implies a logarithmic function between scale values:

$$D = a + b \log R, \tag{15.7}$$

where D and R denote the scale values obtained from difference and ratio judgments, respectively, and a and b are constants (b > 0) (cf. Krantz et al., 1971, p. 152). Again, it has to be taken into account that the MINISSA scale values from ratio judgments are based on a difference representation, too. Therefore, a linear function rather than a logarithmic one between obtained scale values is predicted if both orderings coincide. Figure 15.2 shows the results of testing this prediction for the pooled data from different groups of subjects. Although the fit is fairly good for the group data from all subjects ($r^2 = .982$), there are substantive deviations from a linear relationship. It is readily seen that these deviations are mainly due to the data from the DR-group subjects, showing some positively accelerated function. Hence, it seems to be justified to reject the hypothesis that the orderings of subjective differences and ratios coincide, especially if the fairly low rank correlations for the individual subject data (Table 15.7) are taken into account. Thereby, Condition 3 of the combined model should be assumed to hold.

Very clear results are obtained if we turn to a direct test of the conclusion of Theorem 4, which asserts a logarithmic relationship between category ratings and magnitude estimates (Eq. 15.4). Figure 15.3 shows unequivocally that Theorem 4, as an alternative to the combined model, must be ruled out. This result corresponds very well to the low rank correlations between differences of category ratings and ratios of magnitude estimates given in Table 15.8 for individual and pooled data from different groups of subjects. In addition, Table 15.8 shows that there are virtually no differences between groups of subjects, contrary to the results of Table 15.7. This finding confirms our previous hypothesis that failures of compatibility result from some subject's poor performance with differences and/or ratio judgments. On the other hand, Table 15.8 indicates some systematic differences between both kinds of category-rating scales: The rank correlations with respect to the seven-point scale are always larger than those for the 100-point scale. We return to this matter momentarily.

As already mentioned, the final assumption of the combined model—the interlocking condition—is somewhat difficult to test because of the indifferences involved. Therefore, the conclusion of Theorem 3 of the combined model must be tested directly. Moreover, this approach allows for a direct comparison of the

TABLE 15.8
Rank Correlations (Kendall's τ) between Differences of Category Ratings
and Ratios of Magnitude Estimates

		DR-Group (N = 20)	D-Group (N = 11)	R-Group (N = 19)	NN-Group (N = 14)	All Subjects (N = 64)
Seven-Point Scale	Pooled Data	.64	.64	.70	.73	.69
	Individual Subject Data					
	median	.67	.67	.66	.70	.67
	mean	.67	.66	.67	.68	.67
	SD	.09	.08	.10	.07	.08
100-Point Scale	Pooled Data	.60	.60	.61	.62	.62
	Individual Subject Data					
	median	.62	.64	.63	.63	.62
	mean	.61	.61	.61	.61	.61
	SD	.06	.06	.08	.06	.07

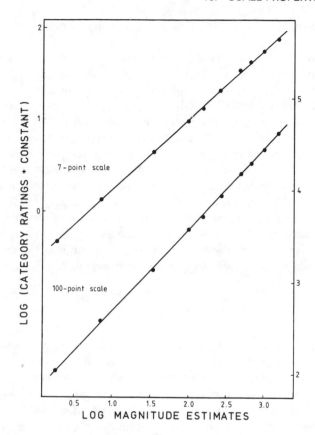

FIG. 15.4. Logarithms of sum of category ratings plus a constant (from two rating scales) as a function of logarithms of magnitude estimates. Each data point is based on 192 observations from 64 subjects. Straight lines confirm to the combined model (Theorem 3, Eq. 15.3).

empirical validity of Theorems 3 and 4. As a consequence of the combined model, Theorem 3 states that there is a generalized power function between category ratings and magnitude estimates (Eq. 15.3). Figure 15.4 shows how well this prediction holds. For both category-rating scales the fit is almost perfect ($r^2 = .9997$ and $r^2 = .9999$ for the seven-point and the 100-point scale, respectively).

In addition, a generalized power function can be fitted well to individual data from all subjects. Thus, the combined model is shown to be empirically valid. It should be emphasized that the relationship between category ratings and magnitude estimates has not been determined solely by curve fitting. Rather, this relationship is a consequence of a model that is based on simple and psychologically plausible assumptions and thereby provides a theoretical explanation for the obtained generalized power function between category-rating and magnitude-estimation scales.

One final remark should be made. According to the combined model, there exists a common ratio scale. This holds with respect to both category-rating scales. However, these scales are apparently not linearly related. Although the fit to a linear function between both category-rating scales is quite high (r^2 = .9966), there is a systematic curvature in the data plot. Furthermore, the exponents of the generalized power function between category ratings and magnitude estimates are different; they are .77 for the seven-point scale and .89 for the 100-point scale. It should be noted that this result is in agreement with those systematic differences between both rating scales that were shown in Table 15.8. As there are two different (i.e., nonlinearly related) category-rating scales, two different ratio scales can be constructed. These scales can be shown to be related by a power function (r^2 = .9994) with an exponent of .86. This somewhat disturbing result raises the problem of how to decide which scale, if any, would be the "true" scale. The present study gives no answer to that question.

7. DISCUSSION

Both difference and ratio judgments on line length have been shown to satisfy the conditions of an algebraic-difference structure very well. This has been demonstrated directly by empirical tests of the quadrupel condition and indirectly by applications of a nonmetric multidimensional scaling procedure. These results have been obtained for group data as well as for individual subject data. Hence, perceived line length is a unidimensional continuum that can be measured by means of difference judgments on the level of an interval scale and by means of ratio judgments on the log-interval scale level. Similar measurement-theoretical analyses (as well as applications of multidimensional scaling) have been successfully performed by Schneider, Parker, and Stein (1974) and Schneider (1977) for difference judgments of loudness. With respect to line length, a similar study yielding comparable results is reported by Wegener (1977). In this study sound production was employed as an additional response modality for ratio and difference judgments, but no use of multidimensional scaling was made. The present results also support those of Parker, Schneider, and Kanow (1975) who analyzed difference and ratio judgments of line length but did so by multidimensional scaling only. An axiomatic analysis, however, avoids problems inherent in multidimensional scaling, such as the problem with local minima. It is argued, therefore, that a joint approach would be most advantageous.

The cornerstone of the models developed in this paper, however, is so-called compatibility conditions linking together difference judgments and category ratings as well as ratio judgments and magnitude estimates. These conditions have been empirically tested, too, and shown to hold fairly well. According to our models, which are based on ideas borrowed from relation theory (Krantz, 1972b), both types of category-rating scales used in the experiment lead to interval scale measurement, and magnitude estimation yields a log-interval scale of perceived line length. Moreover, our data have been shown to support the combined model given in Section 4, leading to a common ratio scale. Consequently, the relationship between category ratings and magnitude estimates could be fitted very well by a generalized power function. This finding is in agreement with results obtained by others, e.g., by Marks (1968), Curtis (1970), Marks and Cain (1972), and Wegener (this volume). Within the framework of the present paper, however, we cannot determine whether a valid scale is obtained either by magnitude estimation only (e.g., Stevens, 1971, 1974, 1975), by category rating only (e.g., Anderson, 1972, 1974a, 1974b, this volume), or by both methods (e.g., Marks, 1974a). The latter point of view seems to be confirmed by our results. On the other hand, we obtained a nonlinear relationship between the seven-point and the 100-point category rating scale, a result not enhancing the validity of category ratings. Closely related findings have been reported, e.g., by Marks (1968) and Parducci (this volume).

Although the models presented in this paper have been confirmed, some small but substantive violations have been observed. It has been argued that these violations as well as deviations of predictions of the models result from some subject's poor performance in discrimination between judgments of differences and ratios. For most individual subject data as well as for the pooled data, however, the orderings of subjective differences and ratios are different. Hence, Torgerson's (1960, 1961) conjecture that subjects produce the same orderings if required to judge differences and ratios must be rejected. For judgments of line length, the same result has been obtained by Parker et al. (1975). On the other hand, Torgerson's hypothesis has been supported for several other continua, e.g., for loudness by Schneider, Parker, Farrell, and Kanow (1976) and Birnbaum and Elmasian (1977), for heaviness by Birnbaum and Veit (1974), for numerals by Rose and Birnbaum (1975), and for occupational prestige by Schneider (this volume). For further results in favor of Torgerson's assumption, see, e.g., Birnbaum (1978), Birnbaum and Mellers (1978), Hagerty and Birnbaum (1978), Veit (1978), and Birnbaum (this volume). It should be noted that these results are based on group data only, and that the present study reveals that the rank correlations between difference and ratio judgments are considerably higher for pooled data than for individual data (Table 15.7). Although this data-pooling effect is not strong enough to explain those divergent results, it is argued that individual differences should be considered more seriously. At any rate, further studies are needed in order to resolve the somewhat puzzling situation that perceived line length seems to be the only continuum on which subjects are able to discriminate between difference and ratio judgments.

REFERENCES

Adams, E. W., Fagot, R. F., & Robinson, R. E. On the empirical status of axioms in theories of fundamental measurement. *Journal of Mathematical Psychology,* 1970, *7,* 379-409.

Anderson, N. H. Cross-task validation of functional measurement. *Perception & Psychophysics,* 1972, *12,* 389-395.

Anderson, N. H. Algebraic models in perception. In E. C. Carterette & M. P. Friedman (Eds.), *Handbook of perception* (Vol. 2). New York: Academic Press, 1974. (a)

Anderson, N. H. Cross-task validation of functional measurement using judgments of total magnitude. *Journal of Experimental Psychology,* 1974, *102,* 226-233. (b)

Birnbaum, M. H. Differences and ratios in psychological measurement. In N. J. Castellan, Jr. & F. Restle (Eds.), *Cognitive theory* (Vol. 3). Hillsdale, N.J.: Lawrence Erlbaum Associates, 1978.

Birnbaum, M. H., & Elmasian, R. Loudness "ratios" and "differences" involve the same psychophysical operation. *Perception & Psychophysics,* 1977, *22,* 383-391.

Birnbaum, M. H., & Mellers, B. A. Measurement and the mental map. *Perception & Psychophysics,* 1978, *23,* 403-408.

Birnbaum, M. H., & Veit, C. T. Scale convergence as a criterion for rescaling: Information integration with difference, ratio, and averaging tasks. *Perception & Psychophysics,* 1974, *15,* 7-15.

Block, H. D., & Marschak, J. Random orderings and stochastic theories of responses. In I. Olkin, S. G. Ghurye, W. Hoeffding, W. G. Madow, & H. B. Mann (Eds.), *Contributions to probability and statistics.* Stanford, Cal.: Stanford University Press, 1960.

Curtis, D. W. Magnitude estimations and category judgments of brightness and brightness intervals: A two-stage interpretation. *Journal of Experimental Psychology,* 1970, *83,* 201-208.

Hagerty, M., & Birnbaum, M. H. Nonmetric tests of ratio vs. subtractive theories of stimulus comparison. *Perception & Psychophysics,* 1978, *24,* 121-129.

Krantz, D. H. Measurement structures and psychological laws. *Science,* 1972, *175,* 1427-1435. (a)

Krantz, D. H. A theory of magnitude estimation and cross-modality matching. *Journal of Mathematical Psychology,* 1972, *9,* 168-199. (b)

Krantz, D. H., Luce, R. D., Suppes, P., & Tversky, A. *Foundations of measurement* (Vol. 1). New York: Academic Press, 1971.

Kruskal, J. B. Multidimensional scaling by optimizing goodness of fit to a nonmetric hypothesis. *Psychometrika,* 1964, *29,* 1-27.

Lingoes, J. C. *The Guttman-Lingoes nonmetric program series.* Ann Arbor, Mich.: Mathesis Press, 1973.

Luce, R. D., & Suppes, P. Preference, utility, and subjective probability. In R. D. Luce, R. R. Bush, & E. Galanter (Eds.), *Handbook of mathematical psychology* (Vol. 3). New York: Wiley, 1965.

Marks, L. E. Stimulus range, number of categories, and form of the category scale. *American Journal of Psychology,* 1968, *81,* 467-479.

Marks, L. E. On scales of sensation: Prolegomena to any future psychophysics that will be able to come forth as science. *Perception & Psychophysics,* 1974, *16,* 358-376. (a)

Marks, L. E. *Sensory processes: The new psychophysics.* New York: Academic Press, 1974. (b)

Marks, L. E., & Cain, W. S. Perception of intervals and magnitudes for three prothetic continua. *Journal of Experimental Psychology,* 1972, *94,* 6-17.

Orth, B. *Einführung in die Theorie des Messens.* Stuttgart: Kohlhammer, 1974.

Parker, S., Schneider, B., & Kanow, G. Ratio scale measurement of the perceived lengths of lines. *Journal of Experimental Psychology: Human Perception and Performance,* 1975, *104,* 195-204.

Pfanzagl, J. *Theory of measurement.* New York: Wiley, 1968.

Rose, B. J., & Birnbaum, M. H. Judgments of differences and ratios of numerals. *Perception & Psychophysics,* 1975, *18,* 194-200.

Schneider, B. *Individual loudness functions determined from direct comparisons of sensory intervals*. Paper presented at the 10th Mathematical Psychology Meeting, Los Angeles, August 1977.

Schneider, B., Parker, S., Farrell, G., & Kanow, G. The perceptual basis of loudness ratio judgments. *Perception & Psychophysics*, 1976, *19*, 309-320.

Schneider, B., Parker, S., & Stein, D. The measurement of loudness using direct comparisons of sensory intervals. *Journal of Mathematical Psychology*, 1974, *11*, 259-273.

Stevens, S. S. On the theory of scales of measurement. *Science*, 1946, *103*, 677-680.

Stevens, S. S. Mathematics, measurement, and psychophysics. In S. S. Stevens (Ed.), *Handbook of experimental psychology*. New York: Wiley, 1951.

Stevens, S. S. On the psychophysical law. *Psychological Review*, 1957, *64*, 153-181.

Stevens, S. S. Measurement, psychophysics, and utility. In C. W. Churchman & P. Ratoosh (Eds.), *Measurement: Definitions and theories*. New York: Wiley, 1959.

Stevens, S. S. Issues in psychophysical measurement. *Psychological Review*, 1971, *78*, 426-450.

Stevens, S. S. Perceptual magnitude and its measurement. In E. C. Carterette & M. P. Friedman (Eds.), *Handbook of perception* (Vol. 2). New York: Academic Press, 1974.

Stevens, S. S. *Psychophysics*. New York: Wiley, 1975.

Stevens, S. S., & Galanter, E. H. Ratio scales and category scales for a dozen perceptual continua. *Journal of Experimental Psychology*, 1957, *54*, 377-411.

Suppes, P., & Zinnes, J. L. Basic measurement theory. In R. D. Luce, R. R. Bush, & E. Galanter (Eds.), *Handbook of mathematical psychology* (Vol. 1). New York: Wiley, 1963.

Torgerson, W. S. Quantitative judgment scales. In H. Gulliksen & S. Messick (Eds.), *Psychological scaling: Theory and applications*. New York: Wiley, 1960.

Torgerson, W. S. Distances and ratios in psychophysical scaling. *Acta Psychologica*, 1961, *19*, 201-205.

Veit, C. T. Ratio and subtractive processes in psychophysical judgment. *Journal of Experimental Psychology: General*, 1978, *107*, 81-107.

Wegener, B. Das Exponentenproblem bei der psychophysischen Skalierung "sozialer" Variablen. ZUMA-Arbeitsbericht, May 1977.

16

Fitting Category to Magnitude Scales for a Dozen Survey-assessed Attitudes

Bernd Wegener
Zentrum für Umfragen,
Methoden und Analysen (ZUMA)
Mannheim, West Germany

1. COMMENSURABILITY

Category scaling within the social sciences is ubiquitous. Dawes' (1972, p. 96) evaluation of 1 year's volumes of a well-known psychological journal states that 60% of the published empirical studies rely in one way or another on category measurement of dependent variables. In survey research, this percentage is by far exceeded. Attitude measurement within surveys virtually *is* measurement by some "agree-strongly/don't-agree-at-all" variety. At the same time, the detrimental properties of category scales are well-known (Luce & Galanter, 1963). The form of the category scale is determined by a multitude of contextual influences, but despite impressive recent progress in the study of contextual dependencies of category ratings (see Parducci, this volume), a comprehensive theory of relative categorical judgment has not been put forth to date. Instead, it seems, social researchers are still inclined to maintain the old categorical habit because of its striking simplicity of application in every imaginable field of research. By now, however, a serious alternative to the category paradigm is available that satisfies criteria of easy applicability and is also able to cope with a number of problems the category scale has posed for so long a time. As has been demonstrated repeatedly, the multimodal magnitude technique may effectively be transferred from the psychological laboratory (see both Dawson and Schneider, this volume) to the real-world setting of opinion surveys (Coleman & Rainwater, 1979; Lodge, Cross, Tursky, & Tanenhaus, 1975; Lodge, Cross, Tursky, Tanenhaus, & Reeder, 1976; Lodge, Tanenhaus, Cross, Tursky, Foley & Foley, 1976; Saris, Bruinsma, Schoots, & Vermeulen, 1977). However, only few nonexperimental field studies applying *multimodal* scaling have been carried out so far (Beck, Brater, & Wegener, 1979a, 1979b; Murphy & Tanenhaus, 1974).

Why is it that researchers of the social science disciplines are still hesitant to make use of the "new" method? It cannot be lack of insight into the methodological gains one will encounter, for there have been a number of attempts to formulate these advantages even for the methodological layperson (Hamblin, 1971, 1974; Lodge et al., 1975; Lodge, Cross, Tursky, Tanenhaus, & Reeder, 1976; Lodge, Tanenhaus, Cross, Tursky, Foley, & Foley, 1976; Shinn, 1969; Wegener, 1979). Neither is it plausible to assume that the mass of sociological practitioners has deliberately taken sides in the vigorous debate among psychophysicists about "differences" versus "ratios," giving a vote for the Helsonians every time they put a category scale to use. Rather, it seems that the reluctance to accept magnitude scaling is caused not by properties of the procedure as such but by the lack of comparability of results the new method may yield with those obtained by conventional methods.

The aim of this paper is to attack incommensurability of the two scaling methods by specifying the functional relation between both. Can an appropriate interrelationship be determined that is general enough to account for different sets of category-magnitude pairs of attitude scales? The attitude scales studied—a round dozen—are culled from several large-scale surveys involving almost 2500 respondents. The attitudinal objects and the populations of the interviews are sufficiently different in order to generalize findings of the category-magnitude interrelationship and to study the influences various contextual constraints exercise on this relationship.

In the following section, two proposals for a *scale convergence model,* with their implicit assumptions and consistency requirements are discussed. Next, a *mathematical procedure* for estimating the interscale relationships is introduced. In Section 4, the results of a nationwide study of *occupational prestige* are reported, and Section 5 is concerned with the effects that *judgmental ranges* of both scale types have on the individual form of the interscale relationships.

2. TWO MODELS

Within sensory psychophysics, a number of suggestions have been made as to how category and magnitude scales relate. For metathetic continua this relationship is usually reported as being a linear one (Stevens & Galanter, 1957); as a matter of fact, these continua are defined as a distinct class because this is so. Prothetic continua, on the other hand, evidence nonlinear relations between categorical and magnitude scales, giving rise to abundant speculations about the precise form of the relationship. A considerable number of researchers proposed that it might best be captured by a logarithmic function (Baird, 1970; Galanter, 1962; Helm, Messick, & Tucker, 1961; Torgerson, 1961). Others have pointed out that this is only true in exceptional cases because curvature of the interscale function is more often found to be rather flat (Marks, 1964; Stevens & Galanter, 1957) and might best be expressed as a power function in which the magnitudes are raised to a power less than unity. Both convictions are brought to the level of testable proposals within two models that introduce additional fitting parameters and stand out because they involve deductions from assumptions. One is the additive power model first suggested by Marks (1968) and supplied with additional data by Curtis (1970) and Marks and Cain (1972); the other may be termed quasi-logarithmic and was explored by Eisler in several instances (1962a, 1962b). Both models have also been formulated with respect to the relationship between category scales and physical intensity (Marks, 1968; Schneider & Lane, 1963).

The two models may be written as:

$$CJ_i + \kappa = a\ ME_i^{\alpha} \tag{16.1}$$

$$CJ_i = a' \log (ME_i + \kappa') + b \tag{16.2}$$

where CJ_i and ME_i are the components of the respective vectors of the category and magnitude responses to the ith stimulus, the other parameters being constants. Both models make use of the idea of scale transformations, although the logic applied differs in both cases.

The Additive-Power Model.   In the additive-power model (16.1), it is assumed that the category scale is an interval scale, whereas the magnitude scale is assumed to be a logarithmic interval scale. Inasmuch as the first is unique up to a positive linear transformation and the second up to $g_i = a_i J_i^{\alpha}$, Eq. 16.1 results if convergence of both scales is sought without violating the respective requirements of uniqueness. It is on these premises that the question is posed whether values for the parameters κ, a, and α may be specified such as to satisfy the model. Specifically, if A is a set of stimuli, Eq. 16.1 assumes that a scale ϕ on A exists that will yield a difference representation for CJ and a ratio representation for ME with regard to A if two different orderings $\gtrsim_D$ and $\gtrsim_R$ on A × A are available. Krantz (1972) and Krantz, Luce, Suppes, and Tversky (1971, pp. 152ff.) give the axioms for an algebraic-difference structure along these lines (see also Orth, this volume), proving, moreover, that any representation with the properties of ϕ will be a ratio scale. Consequently, if the numerical relation of Eq. 16.1 can be established with some degree of approximation for concrete instances, this will increase the confidence with which ϕ is labelled a scale of sensation (Krantz, 1972, p. 197). It should be kept in mind, however, which assumptions have been used to "buy" our results and which assumptions could be wrong in spite of the good numerical fit.

With regard to successfully accomplished fittings, it should be noted that Eq. 16.1, if multiplied by some constant, is unaffected with respect to the characteristic parameter α. This is a very useful property because the input of the magnitude vectors will often be available in a form already made subject to a similarity transformation in order to be able to compare magnitude scales of different subjects. As there is some evidence (Marks 1968, and this volume) that the size of the exponent α varies systematically with contextual conditions in both scales, its constancy with regard to scale transformations is of special value.

Another closely related property of the additive-power model is that its form corresponds to the way regression biases affect the magnitude scales. As Cross (1974, and this volume) has proposed, the unbiased magnitude scale is a power function of the biased one. If there is an independent and valid estimation of the magnitude regression bias, the structure of the model with the unbiased ME-scales inserted will remain unchanged, and fitting parameters will differ in value.

Supposing, finally, that there is more than one magnitude production modality (magnitude estimation and line production, say), Eq. 16.1 will yield two consistency tests for the estimated parameters. If M_1 and M_2 are vectors of magnitude values of identical stimuli i produced with two different response modalities two equations may result: $CJ_i + \kappa_1 = a_1 M_{1i}^\alpha$ and $CJ_i + \kappa_2 = a_2 M_{2i}^\beta$. Inasmuch as $a_1 M_{1i}^\alpha - \kappa_1 = a_2 M_{2i} - \kappa_2$, we may formulate the indirect cross-modality relation in terms of the estimated parameters of the additive-power model,

$$M_{1i} = \left(\frac{a_2}{a_1} M_{2i}^\beta + \frac{\kappa_1 - \kappa_2}{a_1} \right)^{1/\alpha}. \tag{16.3}$$

The additive-power model is valid only if this relationship is linear with the estimated parameters inserted. It should approximate the indirect cross-modality matching relation if the expression $(\kappa_1 - \kappa_2)/a_1$ comes close to being zero.

Moreover, an intramodal relationship can also be specified and tested,

$$a\, M_{2i}^\gamma = \left(\frac{a_2}{a_1} M_{2i} + \frac{\kappa_1 - \kappa_2}{a_1} \right)^{1/\alpha}; \tag{16.4}$$

γ is the empirically obtained indirect cross-modality exponent of the magnitude measurements.

Eisler's Quasi-Logarithmic Model.   Eisler's *quasi-logarithmic model* (16.2) is grounded in the poikilitic tradition basing the rationale for scale transformation on variation and Weber functions. In Eisler's view, the method of Fechnerian integration is not restricted to physical scales from which another, subjective scale may be constructed, but rather allows that the starting point might just as well be another subjective scale and its obtained Weber function. The integral of the general psychophysical differential equation, $dME/dCJ = \sigma_{ME}/\sigma_{CJ}$, yields the values of the new scale. For the special case of a *constant* Weber function of a resulting scale, which was derived from a magnitude scale with *linear* Weber functions, a close fit was found between category scales and the constructed values (Eisler, 1962a, 1962b, 1965; Eisler & Montgomery, 1974). Thus, it was not only concluded that the relation between category and magnitude scales could be expressed by Eq. 16.2 (employing the linear generalization of Weber's law), but also that the category scales under study were discrimination scales implying that equal probabilities of confusing two stimuli were indicative of equal subjective distances.

It is obvious that the method of Fechnerian integration can only be applied if empirical Weber functions are available and, of course, if one is willing to generalize the concept of Weber functions to subjective continua. Usually intraindividual SD's are taken as measures from which Weber functions are obtained, and this necessitates replications that are unfeasible in surveys. When applying Eq. 16.2, therefore, we make use of untestable assumptions. On the aggregated level of analysis, however, the Weber functions of both scales are readily given if one is willing to accept *inter*individual variation as a measure of uncertainty (see Montgomery, this volume). A successful fitting of both aggregated scales should be accompanied by a constant Weber function for the category and a linear one for the magnitude scale. Additionally, it should be noted that the value of the estimated κ' (Eq. 16.2) should equal the value of the ME-intercept of the linear generalization of Weber's law. No additional consistency tests, however, are available, and for individual interscale relations the quasi-logarithmic model gives—in the present context—no criteria for adequacy at all.

3. A PROCEDURE FOR ESTIMATING THE PARAMETERS IN MASS DATA

The estimation of parameters for the additive-power model involves the computations of logarithms that linearize the equation, the determination of value κ, and the regression of log $(CJ_i + \kappa)$ on log ME_i in order to find a and α. A high correlation is supposed to be indicative of approximate linearity. Because of the striking structural equivalence between the linearization of model 16.1 and model 16.2, the latter may be solved by a formally identical procedure, exchanging ME_i with CJ_i and entering the latter as exp (CJ_i).

As can be seen from the literature, the estimation of κ (κ' respectively) is usually accomplished by trial-and-error procedures (i.e., Marks, 1968; Marks & Cain, 1972; Parker, Schneider, & Kanow, 1975; Petrusic & Jamieson, 1979; Schneider, Parker, Ostrosky, Stein, & Kanow, 1974): A rather large value for κ (κ') is entered into Eq. 16.1 (Eq. 16.2) and the correlation coefficient between log $(CJ_i + \kappa)$ and log ME_i for model 16.1 and between log $(ME_i + \kappa')$ and $(CJ_i$

— b) for model 16.2 are computed. Gradually smaller values of κ and κ' are successively chosen, and that value for which the size of the correlation is largest is taken as a valid estimate. It is obvious that this is a suboptimal procedure because:

1. There is considerable danger of landing on a local maximum. This danger can even be magnified when generally available computer programs are employed—for example STEPIT (Chandler, 1969)—because any indicated maximum of $|r|$ will be a local maximum inasmuch as ranges for involved parameters are subject to a priori restrictions without the user being able to specify variation outside the considered boundaries.

2. The ad hoc techniques are totally unfeasible when the number of subjects or pairs of scales becomes large, as will usually be the case with survey research. It is therefore mandatory that an algorithm for a systematic estimation be designed and inserted into a computer program in which the decision process is executed under constraints supplied by the user in the form of parameters for that program.

Inasmuch as the optimal value for κ (in model 16.1, say) cannot be represented in a closed form, its value must be computed iteratively. This poses the problem of specifying the range within which the search for the optimizing κ should be carried out. The lower boundary B_ℓ of such a range is readily given by $(CJ_i + \kappa)$ > 0 for all values of CJ, because Eq. 16.1 can only be treated as a linear equation if logarithms of $(CJ_i + \kappa)$ are feasible, restricting the range for κ from the negative of the smallest CJ_i to ∞. A related argument is of course valid with regard to model 16.2 and κ'. The construction of the upper bound B_u is by far more sophisticated and is outlined just briefly and informally (see Wegener & Kirschner, 1981, for details).

It can be shown that the variation with respect to κ of the correlation coefficient $r(\kappa)$ between $\log (CJ_i + \kappa)$ and $\log ME_i$ about the value of the correlation coefficient between CJ_i and $\log ME_i$ can be bounded from above by a function $B(\kappa)$ *monotonically decreasing* to zero for all sufficiently large values of κ. This monotonicity property of $B(\kappa)$ implies that beyond the smallest κ with $B(\kappa) \leq \epsilon$, $\epsilon = 10^{-6}$, for example, there can be no substantial increase of $|r(\kappa)|$, and hence this value of κ is a proper choice for B_u. The value of the error term ϵ may be specified by convenience.

For mass data an OSIRIS-compatible computer program—ZUMAPSYCH2 (cf. ZUMAPACK-Manual, 1979)—has been designed, which as a first step, determines B_u. Then, by a powerful and well-known algorithm (Fletcher-Powell), a maximum of $|r(\kappa)|$ with optimizing argument κ is computed within the constructed range. Furthermore, the subsequent values of the other parameters of the models and goodness-of-fit indexes are computed.

4. A NATION-WIDE STUDY OF OCCUPATIONAL PRESTIGE

Twelve pairs of scales are being explored in this study. For purposes of demonstration, the analysis of only one of these—the comparative measurement of subjective prestige of occupations—is reported in detail, whereas the remaining 11 pairs of scales serve as background for generalizations, and it suffices to summarize results.

Procedure

A 60-minute cross-section survey interview dealing primarily with topics on politics and election behavior included a segment in which respondents were asked to give their opinion about the prestige of 16 occupations. The 16 occupational titles serving as stimuli were preselected from previous studies on social structure in Germany (Mayer, 1979; Wegener, 1979), such that a more or less even distribution along the range of prestige values could be expected. Respondents had to scale the occupations twice: first with a multimodal magnitude technique—line production (LP) and numerical magnitude estimation (ME)—and second, in a later part of the interview, on a nine-point category scale labelled at its end points ("very low prestige" and "very high prestige"). Two thousand and twelve interviews were conducted, and the sample was representative for the West German population (including West Berlin) of 16 years and older.

Since this was the first time that magnitude scaling was incoporated in a typical survey interview, special care was taken with regard to the training of the interviewers, all of whom were affiliated with a commercial survey institute. Three different levels of training were realized: written, verbal, and no training. Interviewers who had received written or verbal training were selected for participation in the study by means of their performance in a written test in which they had to apply the magnitude technique to a number of diverse scaling tasks. These test booklets were analyzed before fieldwork began, and 327 interviewers were selected from a field of about 400 on the basis of the goodness of intermodality correlations and indirect cross-modality exponents in the test results.

Interviewers were asked to instruct the respondents about the magnitude scaling in their own words. There was, however, a standard formulation of the instruction printed into the questionnaire, which they could turn to if needed. Respondents were briefly trained with the help of circles of different sizes, and they were asked to assign lines and numbers to these to estimate the sizes of the circles relative to each other. No standard was provided. A second exercise involved six offenses, the severity of which was to be scaled using lines and ME.

Only after these tasks were completed did the interview proceed to the scaling of the 16 occupations.

Respondents were handed booklets that displayed the stimuli and in which they could draw the lines and write the magnitude estimates. The physical format of these booklets was based on previous tests (Wegener, 1978, 1979) that indicated that a paper size of about 30 cm (11.8 in.) in width was appropriate. Several paper widths had been tried out and were evaluated with regard to cross-modality matching exponents and intermodality correlations. It should be noted that respondents were not restricted by the size of paper when drawing their lines, for they were to continue lines below one that reached the edge of the available paper if they wished to do so. No auxiliary devices were tolerated. On the average, the magnitude task (LP and ME, including exercises) took about 6 minutes.

The resulting data set consists of 1796 cases for which two complete scales—a magnitude scale computed as the geometric mean of the LP with the ME and a category scale—are available. About 9% of the subjects refused or were unable to perform the magnitude tasks; this amounts to 6% more missing data than in the conventional category tasks of prestige scaling.

Inasmuch as several demographic characteristics of respondents as well as those of interviewers were available in this study, it is possible to distinguish some of the characteristics of those respondents who refused to work with the method or were unable to apply it and, correspondingly, to isolate relevant attributes of the interviewers executing the questionnaire. Variables explaining the greatest proportion of variance are age and sex of subjects: Older respondents refuse more often than younger ones, and women more often than men (however, both of these groups are significantly better in doing the job once they accept the tasks). It is also interesting to note that the different training levels enjoyed by the interviewers were of no significant importance for the number of refusals an interviewer encountered, indicating that training of interviewers can be kept at a minimum.

Scale Construction

The first column of Table 16.1 contains mean relative scale values for the *magnitude scale of prestige* computed from the geometric means of both modalities for each subject (see Lodge & Tursky, this volume). Individual absolute scale values have been transformed by multiplication with a constant such that the occupation with the lowest rank to all (female manual worker) has a common relative scale value of 10. Four digit numbers behind the names of the occupations are International Standard Classification of Occupation indexes used for constructing comparative prestige scales. A recent example is the Treiman Scale (1977), which is shown in the third column of Table 16.1.

TABLE 16.1
Mean Magnitude and Category Scale Values for Estimated Prestige of
16 Occupations (N = 1796) and International Treiman Scores

	Magnitude Scores	Category Scores	Treiman
Manual worker (female) (0990)[a]	10.00	3.18	32
Construction worker (0950)	15.63	3.82	31
Mason (0951)	17.14	4.22	34
Mail carrier (0370)	17.83	4.20	30
Electrician (0855)	18.68	4.78	44
Machinist (0841)	20.62	4.55	42
Taxi driver (0985)	22.66	4.58	31
Garage mechanic (0843)	24.13	4.96	44
Office clerk (female) (0393)	24.16	4.92	44
Policeman (0582)	24.41	5.06	40
Clerical worker (0390)	29.36	5.34	38
Professional nurse (0071)	29.73	5.55	54
Primary teacher (female) (0133)	32.96	5.94	57
Civil engineer (0022)	35.56	6.23	70
High school teacher (0132)	42.48	6.76	60
Physician (0061)	64.30	8.03	78

[a] In parentheses, numbers of International Standard Classification of Occupations.

The indirect cross-modality analysis of the aggregated values yields a cross-modality correlation of .994 and an indirect cross-modality matching exponent of 1.154. This includes all subjects regardless of whether indirect cross-modality matching relations on the individual level are significant or not. Actually, the data for about 7% of the subjects result in cross-modality exponents differing significantly from the expected 1.0 (p = .999); the mean individual exponent value is 1.167 with a SD of .475. The mean inter-modality correlation of logarithmic modality values is .810 (SD = .173). Finally, the mean range of magnitude scales is 7.78:1, exhibiting individual variation from a scale of no distribution at all (1:1) to 250:1 and more.

Scale values for the *categorical judgments* are used as provided by the respondent in the interview, and arithmetic means for the occupations are used to compute aggregated scales. Table 16.1 displays the mean categories for the 16 occupations. No criterion for goodness of the scale or goodness of the individual values is available. Compared with the vast ranges of the magnitude scale, the category scale is compact. For all respondents it exhibits a mean difference from maximum to minimum category value of 5.49 (8.0, of course, being the largest difference possible with a nine-point scale).

Inasmuch as the indirect cross-modality paradigm (outlined by Dawson and by Cross, this volume) supplies a criterion for the goodness of individual magnitude scales, it is interesting to note which respondents produced "good" scales, which did not, and whether attributes of respective interviewers had any part in this (Wegener, 1980). Table 16.2 gives a summary of results of a first order multiple regression analysis with the significance of matching exponents as the dependent variable. Because a dichotomous variable is being predicted, it is not surprising that betas are relatively low. In the present context, however, the rank order of effects is of primary interest. It can be seen that the attributes of the interviewer—experience as an interviewer, level of education, age, sex, etc.— are of greater importance for good scaling results than the characteristics of the respondents. The sex of the respondents is, however, influential. Interestingly enough, women do better than men whereas male interviewers are more successful in stimulating respondents to do a good job than their female colleagues (some interaction between the sexes is, in fact, noticeable). It is obvious from these results that the goodness of attitude scaling is not only a matter of an appropriate scaling model, but is also considerably influenced by contextual effects of the complex nature exhibited.

Fitting the Models

Indifference functions between magnitude and category scales were established using both models. Fittings for the individual pairs of scales and for aggregated scales may be sought, and it is also possible to confront categorical values with both magnitude modalities separately. Table 16.3 summarizes results for both models.

As can be seen, the fit for the power model is always better than that for the logarithmic model. On the individual level, the mean values exclude cases that yield a correlation lower or equal to .5, or for which a monotonic function $r(\kappa)$

TABLE 16.2
Summary of Effects of Respondent's and Interviewer's Characteristics on
Goodness of Indirect Cross-Modality Matching

Rank	Beta	Variable[a]
1	.19089	Number of interviews carried out by interviewer within last year
2	.10131	Level of education of interviewer
3	.08550	Sex of respondent (male 1, female 2)
4	−.08186	Sex of interviewer (male 1, female 2)
5	.07917	Years/months interviewer has worked as interviewer
6	−.06514	Number of interviews carried out by interviewer in present study
7	−.05556	Age of interviewer
8	−.04841	Income of respondent
9	−.04716	Age of respondent
10	.04445	Prestige of interviewer's previous or concurrent occupation

[a] Dependent variable: Exponent is not significant = 1, is significant = 0.

TABLE 16.3
Goodness of Fit of Interscale Relationship with Additive-Power
and Logarithmic Models

	Power				Logarithm		
	R_κ	R_{INF}	α	%-NOFIT	R_κ	R_{INF}	%-NOFIT
MA	.9904	.9840	.550	0.0[a]	.9842	.9673	0.0[a]
ME	.9899	.9834	.517	0.0[a]	.9677	.9587	0.0[a]
LP	.9876	.9808	.585	0.0[a]	.9460	.9243	0.0[a]
MA	.8735	.7762	.590	10.5	.8680	.8453	26.9
SD	.1203	.2540	.734	—	.2232	.3810	—
ME	.8674	.7713	.557	10.5	.8453	.8445	26.9
SD	.1260	.2603	.658	—	.2539	.4021	—
LP	.8290	.7138	.612	12.4	.7751	.7608	34.6
SD	.1344	.2635	.773	—	.2457	.4067	—

[a]$N = 1796$.

Note: Upper part of table gives results for fitting aggregated, lower half gives mean values for fitting individual scales of prestige. R_κ: maximal correlation between transformed scales; R_{INF}: convergence value for κ approaching infinity. Values are calculated for magnitude estimation (ME), line production (LP), and the combined magnitude scale (MA), separately.

was detected. The percentage of both is given in the columns "%-NOFIT." For the logarithmic model, the percentage of failures when fitting the two scales was more than twice as high as that for the power model.

It is interesting to note that a considerable number of those cases for which the magnitude scales could not be fitted to the category scales also exhibit significant cross-modality matching exponents: Whereas only about 3% of the fitted cases had significant exponents in the indirect cross-modality tasks, there are more than 30% of significant exponents for those not having a fit between magnitude and category scales.

From a pragmatic point of view, it may be concluded that the additive-power model obviously provides the more adequate formulation for the relationship between both kinds of scales. There is, moreover, additional evidence that speaks against the logarithmic model. Looking at Figure 16.1, it is immediately apparent that the Weber function of the mean magnitude scale may in fact be viewed as linear, but the Weber function of the category scale is by no means constant. So at least for the case of aggregated data, we know that the quasi-logarithmic model of Eq. 16.2 is inadequate because its assumptions are not met empirically. This, of course, is only true insofar as one is willing to accept interindividual variation as indicative for uncertainty. On the individual level, no such inference is possible with the present data.

With regard to the additive-power model, on the other hand, internal consistency tests are available, as outlined in Eqs. 16.3 and 16.4. Plotting numbers

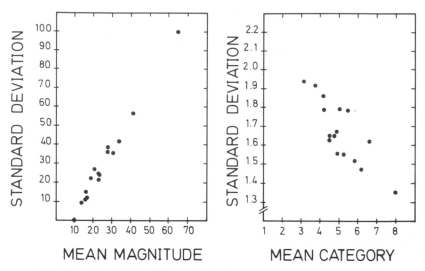

FIG. 16.1.   Interindividual Weber function for mean magnitude scale of 16 occupations (left panel) and for mean category scale (right panel).

against line length, which are transformed in accordance with the right side of Eq. 16.3, results in a correlation between these two variables of—on the aggregated level—.989 and .851 as the mean individual correlation. The slope of the line is .9995 (individual mean: .986) indicating a perfect agreement. Solving Eq. 16.4 for ME and LP respectively gives a very similar result. In addition, it is not surprising to find that the quotient of exponents, empirically found for Eq. 16.1 with regard to the two modalities, tends to equal the cross-modality matching exponents. This is true for about 75% of those cases for which model 16.1 is solvable if one provides for a range $.5 \leqq \beta/\alpha \leqq 1.5$ in correspondence with a mean matching exponent value of 1.0. Put differently: In all those cases in which the differences between the two estimated values for κ_1 and κ_2 are very small, the quotient β/α is approximately equal to the cross-modality matching exponent. In all other cases, we may take $(\kappa_1 - \kappa_2)/a_1$ as a correction term quantifying the amount of distortion when the indirect cross-modality relation is expressed by magnitude scales that were fitted to their categorical counterparts.

Even though there is an impressive numerical fit as well as consistency with regard to model 16.1, its application is contingent on premises not testable with the present data. Nevertheless, the model does serve the purpose of determining the relationship between both kinds of scales. To the social science practitioner who is applying one or both methods, it is also important to be able to isolate specific attributes of the mapping relation, that is, to distinguish individual differences. Obviously, there is variation, exponents differ, and quality of fit does, too. If commensurability is to be satisfied exhaustively, causal factors to which these differences can be attributed should be studied. With this goal in mind, additional data sets, employing different category scales, different attitudes, and different respondents were analyzed.

5.   RANGE EFFECTS

Data Sets 2-12

The 11 additional pairs of scales are drawn from five different surveys in which identical scaling procedures in comparison to the occupational prestige study were used. In every instance, magnitude estimation, line production, and category scaling were called for. The number of categories available in the latter task, however, differed and extended from four to 11 categories.

One interview was on consumer behavior. In particular, the opinion of respondents about the *utility* of certain attributes they might be willing to accept when buying a new car was scaled. Twelve items describing aesthetic and safety conditions, technical quality, comfort, etc. were included and had been selected from previous studies. ME, LP, and a five-point labelled category scale were employed. In a replication, the identical items were used, but the category scale had 11 points. Respondents in both surveys constituted representative samples with regard to several social attributes.

In the third study, apprentices were interviewed on topics concerning occupational choice. One of the attitude scales dealt with the *prestige of 13 apprentice occupations,* that is, with occupations being very similar in social esteem. Within the same interview an *occupational choice* scale was incorporated. Respondents were asked to express the extent to which they agreed with six statements relating to their own occupational choice, (e.g., "I was lucky, I got just the job I wanted." or, "It doesn't matter how one decides because all jobs at my level are more or less equivalent."). Again, numbers and lines had to be given, and the category responses were on a nine-point bipolar scale for prestige, and on a four-point labelled scale for the statements on occupational choice.

The fourth survey also dealt with occupational-choice matters, but it utilized a different population. This survey also included political-opinion scales. The one reported here was a scale of *party preference* with regard to seven German political parties. An 11-point bipolar response scale as usually employed for party preference indicators was given for the category task and magnitude scaling was again done with numbers and line production.

The final survey asked for the evaluation of attributes with respect to political parties and respondents' self-concept. Nine so-called *ideological labels* ("left," "conservative," "radical," etc.) were judged as to the extent to which they were an adequate description of the parties and to the extent respondents themselves identified with them. Eleven-point bipolar rating scales were used throughout, besides ME and LP. The interviews were carried out with students of different scientific disciplines and care was taken that their political affiliations were heterogeneous.

In all five interviews, the possibility of estimating the individual regression tendency of the subjects (Stevens & Greenbaum, 1966) was provided. In some of the studies, the two response modalities were matched against each other (Cross, 1974; Dawson & Brinker, 1971). In others, a third modality—visual area of circles—was introduced as a criterion against which numbers and lines had to be adjusted. Because the size of computed biases was usually not very decisive for scales construction, the following analysis does not take the corrected scale values into account. This keeps the results of the 11 scales comparable with the representative study in which no calibration procedure was included. It should also be noted that the rationale for eliminating bias given by Cross (1974; also Cross, this volume) rests on the untestable assumption that the extent of regression bias for a person is identical for the physical and nonmetric judgment. The congeneric test model (Jöreskog, 1974; Saris, Neijens, & Doorn, 1979) would be a better alternative for determining true scores, but no computation of these is possible with only two indicators of one construct because of identification problems.

Results

The results of magnitude-scale construction for all 11 attitude scales are summarized in Table 16.4 by displaying the indirect cross-modality exponents and intermodality correlations for the gross population. In Table 16.5, individual means of indexes of fitting category and magnitude scales for all 12 scales with the additive-power model are shown. The mean correlation of optimally fitted scales is .871.

Of special interest is the exponent α. As can be seen, the values for the exponents vary, having a mean value of about .5. To this extent, the results obtained coincide with those reported for physical stimuli (Marks, 1968; Marks & Cain, 1972; Stevens, 1975). Can the variation be attributed to any characteristics of the scales? Marks (1968, 1974) states that size of exponent is an index of stimulus range and the number of categories available. As both variables increase, the exponent also increases. Looking at Table 16.5, however, the picture seems to be more complex. Obviously, there is evidence that the size of exponent becomes larger as the number of categories increases. The range of magnitude judgments, however, seems to produce smaller exponents if it is growing.

It can be shown that Eq. 16.1 is, with regard to the exponent α, contingent on

TABLE 16.4
Indirect Cross-Modality Matching Exponent and Correlation Between
ME and LP for 11 Attitudes

Scale	β	R_{ICMM}	N	Items
1. Utility I	0.975	.9713	29	12
2. Utility II	1.027	.9827	30	12
3. Prestige II	1.000	.9760	122	13
4. Choice	1.003	.9762	120	6
5. Party preference	1.054	.9753	25	7
6. CDU[a]	1.068	.9954	17	9
7. FDP	1.056	.9954	17	9
8. SPD	0.967	.9913	17	9
9. CSU	1.010	.9838	17	9
10. DKP	.0859	.9967	17	9
11. Self	1.083	.9768	17	9

[a] Scales 6 through 11 are scales of "ideological labels" with regard to five political parties and the respondent's self-concept.

the variances of both variables involved, then as the variance of the category scale increases, the curvature of the power function will become more pronounced and the exponent will increase. If, however, the variance of the magnitude scale becomes greater, the exponent will become smaller, flattening the curvature of the function. Because variance is bounded by an expression in which

TABLE 16.5
Goodness of Fit for the Additive-Power Model for All 12 Attitude Scales[a]

Scale (MA)	R_κ	R_{INF}	α	% NOFIT	No. Cat.	R	D
1. Utility I	.8803	.8760	.445	3.4	5	43.4	3.9
2. Utility II	.8975	.8602	.898	6.7	11	22.3	8.0
3. Prestige II	.9052	.8534	.825	11.8	9	8.6	6.1
4. Choice	.9453	.8897	.379	21.6	4	8.5	2.8
5. Party	.9352	.9047	.435	16.0	11	25.5	6.3
6. CDU	.8481	.6963	.160	5.9	11	69.1	6.4
7. FDP	.8017	.6633	.274	23.5	11	24.7	5.0
8. SPD	.7337	.6462	.765	11.8	11	17.1	5.2
9. CSU	.8851	.8312	.525	5.9	11	62.9	6.9
10. DKP	.8228	.7086	.360	11.8	11	46.8	7.1
11. Self	.9207	.8975	.331	11.8	11	67.3	6.9
12. Prestige I	.8735	.7762	.773	10.5	9	7.8	5.5

[a] Values represent the mean of individual results. Last two columns contain the mean range of magnitude scale (R) and the mean range of category scale (D).

the difference of the minimal and maximal values ($x_{\{1\}}$ and $x_{\{n\}}$) is involved, namely:

$$\frac{(x_{\{n\}} - x_{\{1\}})^2}{2} \leqslant \sum_{1}^{n} (x_i - \bar{x})^2 \leqslant \left(1 - \frac{1}{n} \right) (n - 1) (x_{\{n\}} - x_{\{1\}})^2,$$

(16.5)

one can accept the ranges of both variables as being indicative for variation of variation. As the range of values—defined as the difference between the largest and the smallest value—is proportional to the upper bound of the variance in Eq. 16.5, it should be feasible to formulate a relationship between size of exponent α and range as an approximation of the variance dependency of the additive-power model for all individual subjects, for which a high degree of fit was established.

This will result in a model, extending Eq. 16.1, in which the fitting parameter α is expressed as a function of the two ranges of the involved scales: Let logR be indicative for the range of the magnitude scale where R is computed as the ratio of the extreme values, and let D be the range of the category scale, computed as the difference of the maximal and minimal response values. The model should read:

$$CJ_i + \kappa = a \ ME_i^{(w_1 D - w_2 \log R + C)}$$

(16.6)

with w_1 and w_2 as unstandardized regression coefficients and C a constant.

A linear regression analysis of individual data excluding all subjects having a correlation of fit below .99 (leaving 289 subjects from all 12 scales) results in a linear equation of the form $\alpha = 0.284D - 1.762\log R + 0.512$. This structural equation has a .83 multiple correlation between independent and dependent variables explaining about 70% of the variance. Standard error for the regression coefficient of the D-variable is .013 and .007 for the regression coefficient of the logR-variable. These values are highly satisfactory and model 16.1 may be specified approximately as

$$CJ_i + \kappa = a \ ME_i^{\frac{1}{2} + (0.3D - 1.8_{\log R})}$$

(16.7)

It should be noted that $\frac{1}{2}$ is the value for the exponent usually reported within sensory contexts. Equation 16.7 is able to explain deviations from this value by means of range parameters of both scales.

6. DISCUSSION

From the data presented, it can be concluded that the relationship between category and magnitude scales of opinion is of the additive-power form. The large number of pairs of scales, the heterogeneity of their topics, variation in number of categories and attitudinal ranges, modes of data collection, and, finally, the representativity of samples give some credibility to this conclusion. It should also be noted that a mathematically precise procedure was employed for estimating individual interscale functions.

The results agree with findings in the realm of sensory psychophysics (Curtis, 1970; Marks, 1968, 1974; Marks & Cain, 1972; Orth, this volume). The logarithmic interscale relationship (Eisler, 1962a, 1962b) was rejected because, on the average, it did not fit the data as well as the additive-power model. It should be noted, however, that as the value of the exponent α approaches zero, the category scale becomes more nearly a logarithmic function of magnitudes. In fact, for large magnitude-response ranges the exponent does become rather small, especially if the number of categories of the category scale is small.

It should be pointed out that, in spite of the impressive fit of the two types of scales in accordance with the additive-power model and in spite of the internal consistency of the additive-power model, nothing can be concluded about the *general* nature of the interscale relationship from these findings. We are dealing with nothing beyond empirical generalizations. As Birnbaum (this volume) points out, the interscale relation may not be a power function at all. Contextual effects other than judgmental range may infringe on the form of both types of scales in such a way that it is no longer possible to relate both by means of a power function. However, within survey settings and when scaling nonphysical stimuli, skewed spacing of stimuli, for instance, may not be controlled for. Having chosen the stimuli in the prestige of occupation studies to be "evenly spaced," sociological generalizations and information from other studies have been taken into account, but the series of occupational names might not be equally distributed for an individual subject.

In this chapter, the question was raised whether or not category and magnitude scales of nonmetric stimuli can be compared. The answer is yes, but the results show that there is not just one (and certainly not one unique) comparison or translation function. It seems, rather, that the form of such a function is determined by response parameters that are peculiar to the way in which the individual makes use of both scale types. Figure 16.2 presents values of magnitude range as functions of exponent values for the 10 category ranges of our studies (the largest number of categories being 11). As can be seen, a magnitude response range of 20:1, say, may result in an exponent value of about .25 when compared with a category range of seven (most likely an eight-point scale); a category difference of nine (10-point scale) will produce an α of about .85. Knowing only the magnitude range for an individual, the approximate curvature of the translation function may be inferred for any specific category scale if it is assumed that the expected category range is the number of categories minus one. Standard instructions for category scaling do, in fact, insist that subjects place the largest and smallest stimuli in the two extreme categories respectively.

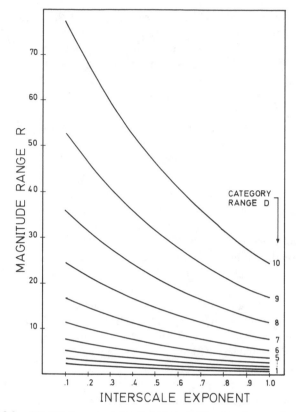

FIG. 16.2. Magnitude range as function of exponent values in accordance with Eq. 16.7 for category ranges of 1 to 10.

In applying rating scales, the social scientist is free to decide how many categories to use. As there is no criterion for the appropriate number of categories for a given scaling task, the choice is arbitrary. The present study, however, might provide a guideline. Obviously, it would be convenient to have a linear interscale relationship between magnitude and category scales in order to circumvent the problem of commensurability. Linearity may in fact be "produced." Prior to carrying out a survey, for instance, one would have to determine the expected magnitude range for a specific list of stimuli (by applying magnitude-scaling techniques to a representative pretest sample). From Eq. 16.7 the appropriate number of categories $(D + 1)$ may be calculated by inserting $\alpha = 1.0$. The determination of the proper number of categories should be made in relation to groups of respondents if drastic differences of ranges due to group characteristics are expected. As a consequence, it might turn out that different rating scales with different numbers of categories should be used within one and the same study. On the average, these category scales would be linearly related to each other and to a magnitude scale of the same set of stimuli.

ACKNOWLEDGMENTS

I wish to acknowledge the helpful comments by Willem E. Saris on an earlier version of this chapter.

REFERENCES

Baird, J. C. A cognitive theory of psychophysics. II. Fechner's law and Stevens' law. *Scandinavian Journal of Psychology*, 1970, *11*, 89–102.

Beck, U., Brater, M., & Wegener, B. *Berufswahl und Berufszuweisung. Zur sozialen Verwandtschaft von Ausbildungsberufen*. Frankfurt: Campus 1979. (a)

Beck, U., Brater, M., & Wegener, B. Soziale Grenzen beruflicher Flexibilität. *Mitteilungen des Instituts für Arbeitsmarkt- und Berufsforschung*, 1979, *4*, 584–593. (b)

Chandler, J. P. STEPIT—Finds local minima of a smooth function of several parameters. *Behavioral Science*, 1969, *14*, 81–82.

Coleman, R. P., & Rainwater, L. *Social standing in America: New dimensions of class*. London: Routledge & Kegan Paul, 1979.

Cross, D. V. Some technical notes on psychophysical scaling. In H. Moskowitz, B. Scharf, & J. C. Stevens (Eds.), *Sensation and measurement: Papers in honor of S. S. Stevens*. Dordrecht, Holland: Reidel Publishing Company, 1974.

Curtis, D. W. Magnitude estimations and category judgments of brightness and brightness intervals: A two-stage interpretation. *Journal of Experimental Psychology*, 1970, *83*, 201–208.

Dawes, R. M. *Fundamentals of attitude measurement*. New York: Wiley, 1972.

Dawson, W. E., & Brinker, R. P. Validation of ratio scales of opinion by multimodality matching. *Perception & Psychophysics*, 1971, *9*, 413–417.

Eisler, H. Empirical test of a model relating magnitude and category scales. *Scandinavian Journal of Psychology*, 1962, *3*, 88–96. (a)

Eisler, H. On the problems of category scales in psychophysics. *Scandinavian Journal of Psychology*, 1962, *3*, 81–87. (b)

Eisler, H. Magnitude scales, category scales, and Fechnerian integration. *Psychological Review*, 1963, *70*, 243–253.

Eisler, H. The connection between magnitude and discrimination scales and direct and indirect scaling methods. *Psychometrika*, 1965, *30*, 271–289.

Eisler, H., & Montgomery, H. On the theoretical and realizable conditions in psychophysics: Magnitude and category scales and their relation. *Perception & Psychophysics*, 1974, *16*, 157–168.

Galanter, E. H. Contemporary psychophysics. In E. H. Galanter, *New directions in psychology*. New York: Holt, 1962.

Hamblin, R. L. Ratio measurement for the social sciences. *Social Forces*, 1971, *50*, 191–206.

Hamblin, R. L. Social attitudes: Magnitude measurement and theory. In H. M. Blalock, (Ed.), *Measurement in the social sciences: Theories and strategies*. Chicago: Aldine, 1974.

Helm, C. E., Messick, S., & Tucker, L. R. Psychological models for relating discrimination and magnitude estimation scales. *Psychological Review*, 1961, *9*, 167–177.

Jöreskog, K. G. Analyzing psychological data by structural analysis of covariance matrices. In D. H. Krantz, R. D. Luce, R. C. Atkinson, & P. Suppes, (Eds.), *Contemporary developments in mathematical psychology* (Vol. 2), San Francisco: Freeman, 1974.

Krantz, D. H. Magnitude estimation and cross-modality matching. *Journal of Mathematical Psychology*, 1972, *9*, 168-199.

Krantz, D. H., Luce, R. D., Suppes, P., & Tversky, A. *Foundations of measurement* (Vol. 1). New York: Academic Press, 1971.

Lodge, M., Cross, D. V., Tursky, B., & Tanenhaus, J. The psychophysical scaling and validation of a political support scale. *American Journal of Political Science*, 1975, *19*, 611-649.

Lodge, M., Cross, D. V., Tursky, B., Tanenhaus, J., & Reeder, R. The psychophysical scaling of political support in the "real world." *Political Methodology*, 1976, *2*, 159-182.

Lodge, M., Tanenhaus, J., Cross, D. V., Tursky, B., Foley, M., & Foley, H. The calibration and cross-modal validation of ratio scales of political opinion in survey research. *Social Science Research*, 1976, *5*, 325-347.

Luce, R. D., & Galanter, E. Psychophysical scaling. In R. D. Luce & E. Galanter (Eds.), *Handbook of mathematical psychology* (Vol. 1). New York: Wiley, 1963.

Marks, L. E. On scales of sensation: Prolegomena to any future psychophysics that will be able to come forth as a science. *Perception & Psychophysics*, 1964, *16*, 358-376.

Marks, L. E. Stimulus-range, number of categories, and form of the category scale. *American Journal of Psychology*, 1968, *81*, 467-479.

Marks, L. E. *Sensory processes: The new psychophysics*. New York: Academic Press, 1974.

Marks, L. E., & Cain, W. S. Perception of intervals and magnitudes for three prothetic continua. *Journal of Experimental Psychology*, 1972, *94*, 6-17.

Mayer, K. U. Berufliche Tätigkeit, berufliche Stellung und beruflicher Status. In F. U. Pappi (Ed.), *Sozialstrukturanalysen mit Umfragedaten*. Königstein/Ts.: Athenäum, 1979.

Murphy, W. F., & Tanenhaus, J. Explaining diffuse support for the United States Supreme Court: An assessment of four models. *Notre Dame Lawyer*, 1974, *49*, 1037-1044.

Parker, S., Schneider, B., & Kanow, G. Ratio scale measurement of the perceived length of lines. *Human Perception and Performance*, 1975, *104*, 195-204.

Petrusic, W. M., & Jamieson, D. G. Resolution time and the coding of arithmetic relations on supraliminally different visual extents. *Journal of Mathematical Psychology*, 1979, *19*, 89-107.

Saris, W. E., Bruinsma, C., Schoots, W., & Vermeulen, C. The use of magnitude estimation in large scale survey research. *Mens en Maatschappij*, 1977, *52*, 369-395.

Saris, W. E., Neijens, P., & van Doorn, L. *Scaling social science variables by multimodality matching*. Unpublished Research Report, Vrije Universiteit Amsterdam, 1979.

Schneider, B., & Lane, H. Ratio scales, category scales, and variability in the production of loudness and softness. *Journal of the Acoustical Society of America*, 1963, *35*, 1953-1961.

Schneider, B., Parker, S., Ostrosky, D., Stein, D., & Kanow, G. A scale for the psychological magnitude of number. *Perception & Psychophysics*, 1974, *16*, 43-46.

Shinn, A. An application of psychophysical scaling techniques to the measurement of national power. *Journal of Politics*, 1969, *31*, 932-951.

Stevens, S. S. *Psychophysics: Introduction to its perceptual, neural, and social prospects*. New York: Wiley, 1975.

Stevens, S. S., & Galanter, E. H. Ratio scales and category scales for a dozen perceptual continua. *Journal of Experimental Psychology*, 1957, *54*, 377-411.

Stevens, S. S., & Greenbaum, H. Regression effects in psychophysical judgment. *Perception & Psychophysics*, 1966, *4*, 439-446.

Torgerson, W. S. Distances and ratios in psychological scaling. *Acta Psychologica*, 1961, *19*, 201-205.

Treiman, D. J. *Occupational prestige in comparative perspective*. New York: Academic Press, 1977.

Wegener, B. Das Exponentenproblem bei der psychophysischen Skalierung "sozialer" Variablen, *ZUMA-Arbeitsbericht*, Mannheim, 1977.

Wegener, B. Einstellungsmessung in Umfragen: Kategorische vs. Magnitudeskalen. *Zumanachrichten*, 1978, *3*, 3-27.

Wegener, B. Magnitude-Messung beruflicher Einstellungen. In U. Beck, M. Brater, & B. Wegener, *Berufswahl und Berufszuweisung. Zur sozialen Verwandtschaft von Ausbildungsberufen.* Frankfurt: Campus, 1979.

Wegener, B. Magnitude-Messungen in Umfragen: Kontexteffekte und Methode. *Zumanachrichten,* 1980, *6,* 4-40.

Wegener, B., & Kirschner, H. P. A note on estimating interscale relations in "direct" psychophysical scaling. *British Journal of Mathematical and Statistical Psychology,* 1981 (in press).

ZUMAPACK-Manual. Zentrum für Umfragen, Methoden und Analysen e.V. (ZUMA), Mannheim, 1979.

17 Controversies in Psychological Measurement

Michael H. Birnbaum
University of Illinois
Urbana –Champaign

Psychological measurement is the oldest area of scientific research in psychology and probably the area with the most sophisticated controversies. The chapters in this volume reflect a good deal of disagreement on the fundamental question: How should we measure subjective values? This chapter reviews some of these controversies and presents new points of view on some old, but unsettled, problems.

1. There are two popular methods for obtaining "direct measures" of psychological value—the methods of category rating and magnitude estimation. If category ratings and magnitude estimations are linearly related to subjective value, they should be linearly related to each other. Instead, magnitude estimations are often a positively accelerated function of category ratings. This apparent contradiction has long troubled psychologists, and several theories have been proposed to explain the discrepancy. Section A notes that the relationship between ratings and magnitude estimations varies because both depend on stimulus spacing and the range of responses implied in the instructions. Therefore, theories that assume an invariant relationship between the results of the two procedures face grave difficulties.

2. Because the instructions for magnitude estimation (M) seem to focus on "ratios" whereas the instructions for ratings (C) seem to focus on "intervals," it seems reasonable to speculate that the relationship between C and M could be better understood in terms of the comparison processes of the judge. Section B reviews experiments designed to test the hypothesis that judges use the same comparison operation despite instructions to judge "differences" or "ratios." (In this chapter, quotation marks are used to denote the instructions given to the subject or the

responses obtained with such instructions. It is possible to empirically test the hypothesis that "ratio" judgments, for example, fit a ratio model, so it is important to maintain the distinction between the task given the subject and the model used to represent the data.)

3. Many experiments, reviewed in Section B, are consistent with the hypothesis that subjects use the same comparison process to judge both "differences" and "ratios." If subjects use only one operation, is there any way to decide empirically how to represent that operation? Section C discusses more general theories of stimulus comparison that make predictions for tasks in which judges are asked to compare two stimulus relations, for example, to judge the "ratio of two differences" or the "difference between two ratios." In this wider realm, it is possible to test among theories that would otherwise be impossible to discriminate. Evidence from three studies suggests that the "basic" operation for comparing two stimuli is subtraction.

4. Contextual effects in scaling are discussed in Sections A, D, and E. In Section A, contextual effects due to stimulus spacing in category ratings and magnitude estimations are shown to be comparable in form for the two procedures. However, Section D shows that in stimulus-comparison experiments, it may be possible to derive scales that are largely independent of stimulus distribution. In certain situations it is possible to localize the effects of stimulus distribution in the final stage of processing (i.e., in the response function). Section D also presents evidence that in cross-modality comparisons a stimulus is compared in relation to other stimuli within its own modality, and contextually determined values within modality are compared between modalities. Hence, scale values derived from cross-modality comparison depend on the stimulus contexts.

5. Section E discusses philosophical implications of contextual effects for methodology. Some have argued that there is a "right" way to do psychophysical experiments and have advocated experimental designs that would preclude evaluation of the theories upon which the methodology is based. An alternative point of view is presented in which contextual effects are regarded as basic to studies of scaling, and they are therefore accepted and even welcomed.

6. Section F takes up controversies in measurement and model testing. The parallelism test of functional measurement is shown incapable of simultaneously establishing the validity of the response scale and model. Two areas of research, impression formation and the size-weight illusion, are reviewed to challenge previous conclusions of functional measurement and to show how methodological loopholes in simplistic application led to inappropriate conclusions. Improved techniques for model testing are discussed.

7. Section G evaluates related theories of psychophysics that attempt to encompass a wide array of data. It is shown that theories requiring different scales of sensation for different tasks are not yet needed by the data and simpler theories that assume a single scale of sensation remain consistent with a variety of data.

A. JUDGMENT FUNCTIONS IN SINGLE STIMULUS EXPERIMENTS

The overt response, be it a category judgment, magnitude estimation, linemark, physical estimate, cross-modality match, or physical adjustment, depends on the context: the stimulus range, spacing, frequency of presentation, etc. These effects cannot be "avoided" and should not be ignored either at the practical or theoretical level. One way to represent contextual effects is to express the overt response as a function of the subjective value of a stimulus, where the function is permitted to depend on the contextual features of the experiment.

Category Ratings vs. Magnitude Estimations

Let C_{ik} and M_{ik} be the category judgment and magnitude estimate of stimulus Φ_i in context k, having subjective value s_i. One can then express the judgments as follows:

$$C_{ik} = J_{C_k}(s_i); \tag{A.1}$$

$$M_{ik} = J_{M_k}(s_i); \tag{A.2}$$

where J_{C_k} and J_{M_k} are the strictly monotonic judgment functions for context k. Equations A.1 and A.2 make clear the distinction between subjective value, s, and the overt response. If the modulus in magnitude estimation or the number of categories in category rating were changed, the overt judgments would change, but one would not want to conclude that the sensations changed. The subscripts (k) for context include any change in procedure for responding that is likely to influence the judgment (or output) function. It seems reasonable to suppose that the functions J_{C_k} and J_{M_k} lawfully depend upon such contextual features as the number of categories, stimulus spacing, modulus, etc.

The relationship between category ratings and magnitude estimates in contexts k and n can be expressed as follows:

$$M_{ik} = J_{M_k}[J_{C_n}^{-1}(C_{in})] \tag{A.3}$$

where $J_{M_k}(J_{C_n}^{-1})$ represents the relationship between ratings and magnitude estimates of the same stimuli.

At one time it was thought that one could operationally define judgments as in Eqs. A.1 and A.2 to be "direct" measures of sensation, a definition that corresponds to assuming J_M and/or J_C are linear. However, category ratings and magnitude estimations are typically nonlinearly related (Stevens & Galanter,

1957). Therefore, if s is the same in both equations, then J_C and J_M cannot both be linear. Typically, $\mathbf{M}$ is positively accelerated relative to $\mathbf{C}$. Torgerson (1960) noted that log $\mathbf{M}$ is often linearly related to $\mathbf{C}$. Eisler (1962) found that $\log(\mathbf{M} + b)$ may be more nearly linear to $\mathbf{C}$. Marks (1974, 1979), Orth (this volume), Wegener (this volume), and others have represented this relationship with linear functions of power functions, $\mathbf{C} = a\mathbf{M}^b + d$, where a, b, and d are arbitrary constants.

Although $\mathbf{M}$ is typically a positively accelerated function of $\mathbf{C}$, the relationship between $\mathbf{M}$ and $\mathbf{C}$ changes as a function of contextual details of the experiments, as is illustrated in the next section.

Contextual Effects in "Direct" Scaling

The following experiment illustrates typical findings. Groups of subjects were instructed to judge the darkness of the dot patterns in either half of Fig. 17.1 using either category rating or magnitude estimation. There were eight different groups of subjects. Four groups made category ratings and four groups made magnitude estimations. Within either response procedure, two groups of subjects received stimuli spaced according to a positively skewed stimulus distribution (relative to logΦ), as shown in the left side of Fig. 17.1, and two different groups of subjects received stimuli spaced according to a negatively skewed distribution, as on the right of Fig. 17.1. Note that both distributions have six values in common. Patterns labeled 9, 11, 6, 10, 1, and 7 have 12, 18, 27, 40, 60, and 90 dots, respectively, in both contexts. If there were no effects of the other stimuli presented for judgment, then these common stimuli should receive the same judgments in both contexts.

Category Ratings.   For the category-rating experiments, two groups used a five-point scale in which 1 = *lightest* pattern and 5 = *darkest* pattern. The other two groups were given a 1–100 scale with the end points anchored to the end stimuli in the same way.

Results for the category-rating tasks are shown in Fig. 17.2. The upper panel shows the results for the 1–100 scale, and the lower panel shows the results for the 1–5 scale. The two curves within each panel show that mean ratings can be either positively accelerated or negatively accelerated relative to logΦ, depending on the spacing of the stimuli chosen for judgment. The general shape of the trends is consistent with Parducci's range-frequency theory. Parducci (this volume) has shown that the magnitude of the contextual effect due to stimulus distribution decreases with increasing number of response categories and increases as a function of the number of stimulus levels. The present data, obtained with 11 stimulus values, show that the contextual effect for the 100-point rating scale remains quite large.

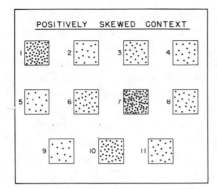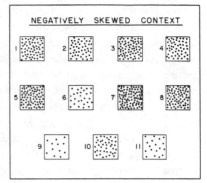

FIG. 17.1.   Two stimulus distributions (contexts). Subjects judged darkness of each dot pattern. Different groups of subjects received different stimulus distributions. Note that patterns numbered 9, 11, 6, 10, 1, and 7 are identical in both contexts; these stimuli have 12, 18, 27, 40, 60, and 90 dots, respectively. From Birnbaum and Mellers (1980a).

FIG. 17.2.   Contextual effects in category ratings. Mean ratings are plotted against stimulus values, spaced on abscissa in log scale. Dashed curves show ratings when stimuli are spaced according to the positively skewed stimulus distribution in Fig. 17.1; solid curves are for the negatively skewed distribution. Upper panel shows results for 1–100 rating scale, lower panel for 1–5 rating scale. Brackets show plus and minus one standard error. Trends are in direction predicted from Parducci's range-frequency theory. From Birnbaum and Mellers (1980a).

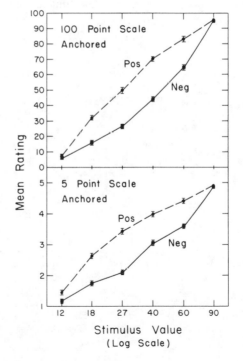

Magnitude Estimations. For the magnitude-estimation experiments, all subjects were told to call the lightest pattern "100" and to assign numbers to each stimulus so that the ratios of the numbers would match the "ratios of the subjective darkness of the sensations." Both groups were encouraged to use whatever numbers they wished, but different examples were given in the instructions to help explain the task. In one case, the examples went as high as "300" (if the pattern seems *three times as dark* as the lightest pattern, say 300). In the other case, the examples went as high as "900" (if the pattern seems *nine times as dark*). Note that this change in the magnitude-estimation instructions is subtle; according to early theories of magnitude estimation, this aspect of the instructions should theoretically have no effect. Instead, Fig. 17.3 shows that it has a great effect.

The magnitude estimations of the common stimuli are shown in Fig. 17.3, with a separate curve for each condition. If the stimulus values chosen had no effect on magnitude estimations, and if the examples used in the instructions had no effect, then all four curves should coincide. Instead, the difference between the open and solid points shows that when the examples range as high as "900," the subjects use numbers that average much higher than when the largest example is only "300." Inasmuch as the exponent obtained in a magnitude-estimation experiment depends largely on the (log) response range, it appears that the exponents obtained in magnitude-estimation studies may relate more closely to the experimenter's range of examples than to the subjects' range of sensations. Robinson (1976) and Poulton (1979) reached similar conclusions.

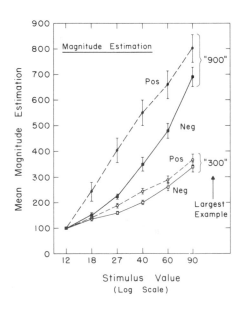

FIG. 17.3. Contextual effects in magnitude estimation. Mean magnitude estimations are plotted against stimulus values as in Fig. 17.2. The 12-dot stimulus was the standard and was assigned the value "100." Dashed lines show results when stimuli were spaced in a positively skewed distribution; solid lines are for negatively skewed conditions. Upper two curves show results when instructions included an example response as high as "900"; lower two curves show results when largest example was "300." Brackets show plus and minus one standard error. If there are no contextual effects in magnitude estimation, the curves should all coincide. From Birnbaum and Mellers (1980a).

Furthermore, Fig. 17.3 shows that magnitude estimations depend on the stimulus spacing. Magnitude estimations appear to show similar contextual effects to those for category ratings. Parducci (1963) found similar results.

Quite clearly, because the relationships between M and Φ and between C and Φ can have so many different forms, the relationship between M and C should not be theorized to be an invariant functional form.

Contextual effects due to stimulus distribution cannot be adequately approximated by power functions. By increasing the stimulus density in the center of the array or at the ends, the functions can be changed in their cubic components (sigmoidal trends). Therefore, the relationship between category ratings and magnitude estimations cannot be adequately represented by power functions, even allowing different exponents for different contexts. Because the relationship between stimulus and response can attain so many different functional forms, Nihm (1976) has suggested (satirically) that the power function be replaced by the polynomial, which given enough parameters can describe any finite set of data.

Reactions to Contextual Effects

Some investigators, having realized the existence of contextual effects, have reacted by adopting extreme positions. Some of these are discussed by Poulton (1968, 1979). One reaction is that contextual effects are undesirable and should be "avoided," averaged away, or ignored. In order to "avoid" contextual effects, it has been argued that everyone should use the same stimulus distribution, response examples, and so on. Then these different functions (as in Fig. 17.3) would not trouble us. But then, how do we decide which context (stimulus distribution, response procedure, etc.) is the "right" one? Will we not be accused of choosing the context to produce the desired effect?

The second reaction, which is also unfortunate, is that if the functional relationship between stimulus and response can be manipulated, then one cannot assume any metric properties in the response. It could be thought that because the response with one procedure (rating) is nonlinearly related to the response with another (estimation), one cannot assume any more than that the response is an unknown and perhaps unpredictable monotone function of subjective value. It is argued in sections D and E that this reaction is too pessimistic and ignores the lawfulness of the effects in Figs. 17.2 and 17.3. Instead, it can be argued that any complete theory of psychophysics must give an account of the response procedure and contextual effects in order to explain the lawful numerical changes that result as a function of these variables.

The effects of stimulus range, stimulus spacing, and frequency are best understood for category ratings and are well-described by Parducci's range-frequency theory (Parducci, 1963, 1965, 1974, this volume; Parducci & Perrett, 1971).

Indeed, the lawfulness of the stimulus-spacing effect can be used to define a psychophysical scale (Birnbaum, 1974c).

Range-Frequency Theory

A general form of Parducci's range-frequency theory can be written as follows:

$$\mathbf{C}_{ik} = a_k \left[\frac{s_i}{s_m - s_o} \right] + b_k G_k(s_i) + c_k \tag{A.3}$$

where $\mathbf{C}_{ik}$ is the category rating of stimulus i in context k; s_i is the subjective value of the stimulus; s_m and s_o are the subjective values of the maximum and minimum stimuli in context k; and $G_k(s_i)$ is the (cumulative) proportion of subjective values less than s_i in context k. The linear constants, a_k, b_k, and c_k reflect the weight of the range and frequency principles and may depend on the number of stimulus levels and the number of categories (Parducci, this volume).

Birnbaum (1974c) noted that when the stimulus and response ranges are held constant, and the stimuli are presented simultaneously, ratings can be well-approximated by the model:

$$\mathbf{C}_{ik} = as_i + bF_k(\Phi_i) + c \tag{A.4}$$

where $F_k(\Phi_i)$ is the cumulative proportion of stimuli less than Φ_i in context k; and a, b, and c are constants. It follows that

$$as_i + c = \mathbf{C}_{ik} - bF_k(\Phi_i) \tag{A.5}$$

Thus, because F_k is known, range-frequency theory provides a basis for estimating scale values. Instead of "avoiding" contextual effects by holding the stimulus distribution fixed to some arbitrary value, Birnbaum (1974c) argued that the systematic manipulation of the context allows one to test theories, such as range-frequency theory, and simultaneously estimate context-free scale values. This issue is taken up in greater detail in Section E.

B.   "RATIOS" AND "DIFFERENCES"

Torgerson (1961) postulated that the contradiction between magnitude estimations and category ratings might be explained by the premise that judges perceive only a single relation between a pair of stimuli, irrespective of instructions to judge "differences" or "ratios." This conjecture, which could not be tested in the early research, has received new support from recent studies that have independently manipulated stimulus levels (for reviews, see Birnbaum, 1978, 1979, 1980a). The following empirical findings have emerged from this research:

1. With certain experimental methods, magnitude estimations of "ratios" closely fit the ratio model. The raw data, when plotted against the estimated scale value of the comparison stimulus with a separate curve for each standard, show the appropriate pattern of bilinearity predicted by the ratio model.
2. Category ratings of "differences" fit the subtractive model, showing approximate parallelism, when the data are plotted in the same way.
3. Scale values derived from the fit of the ratio model applied to "ratios" are very close to an exponential function of scale value derived from the fit of the subtractive model applied to "difference" judgments.
4. Judgments of "ratios" and "differences" are monotonically related. These empirical findings are consistent with the hypothesis that the same operation and scale values underlie both procedures.

Theories of Ratios and Differences

Two-Operation Theory.   According to this theory, subjects perform both tasks using two operations on the same scale values. "Ratio" judgments are given by the equation:

$$\mathbf{R}_{ij} = J_{\mathbf{R}}[s_j/s_i] \qquad (\text{B}.1)$$

where $\mathbf{R}_{ij}$ is the "ratio" judgment of stimulus j relative to i, and $J_{\mathbf{R}}$ is the monotonic judgment function. "Difference" judgments are given by the equation:

$$\mathbf{D}_{ij} = J_{\mathbf{D}}[s_j - s_i] \qquad (\text{B}.2)$$

where $\mathbf{D}_{ij}$ is the "difference" response, and $J_{\mathbf{D}}$ is the judgment function for "differences."

This theory implies that $\mathbf{R}_{ij}$ and $\mathbf{D}_{ij}$ should *not* be monotonically related, in general, but instead that the rank orders of these matrices should be different but appropriately interrelated (Krantz, Luce, Suppes, & Tversky, 1971). For example, as a constant difference is moved up the scale (e.g., $2 - 1 = 3 - 2 = 4 - 3 = 5 - 4$, etc.), the corresponding ratios approach 1 ($\frac{2}{1} > \frac{3}{2} > \frac{4}{3} > \frac{5}{4}$, etc.). As a constant ratio is moved up the scale (e.g., $\frac{2}{1} = \frac{4}{2}$), absolute differences increase ($2 - 1 < 4 - 2$).

The left side of Fig. 17.4 plots actual ratios against actual differences for a 7 × 7, A by B, factorial design, using successive integers from 1 to 7 as levels of A and B. The ordinate plots A/B, the abscissa plots A − B, and separate curves connect points with the same value of B (curve parameters). The highest curve (solid points) plots A/1 vs. A-1. The curve with the lowest slope (solid diamonds) plots A/7 vs. A-7. Note that the relationship between actual ratios and differences cannot be expressed by any function of a single variable because for

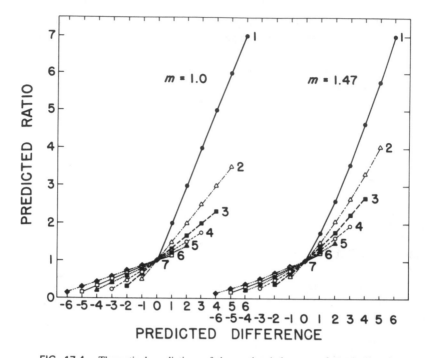

FIG. 17.4.   Theoretical predictions of theory that judgments of "ratios" and "differences" are governed by ratio and difference operations. Left: A/B plotted against A–B with a separate symbol (and separate curve) for each value of B. Predictions for 7 × 7 design using successive integers from 1 to 7 for A and B. Right: $(A/B)^{1.47}$ plotted against $2.17(A-B)$ in the same fashion, except the seven values of A and B were evenly spaced between 1 and 3.76 (i.e., 1 to $7^{.68}$). From Birnbaum (1980a).

any given difference there does not exist one unique ratio, but many, and for any ratio there exist many differences.

The judgment functions, J_R and J_D, serve to monotonically stretch the ordinate and abscissa of Fig. 17.4, but it should be clear that as long as A and B have been independently manipulated over a sufficient range, the ordinal pattern of ratios vs. differences of Fig. 17.4 should remain.

The right side of Fig. 17.4 shows the expected relationship between ratios and differences if the subjective stimulus range is only $7^{.68}$, or 3.76, and if the J_R function is a power function with an exponent of 1.47. The abscissa shows differences (times 2.17), and the ordinate shows ratios raised to the 1.47 power. Thus, the ordinate shows $(A/B)^{1.47}$, plotted against $2.17 (A - B)$ on the abscissa, using seven levels of A and B spaced evenly between 1.0 and 3.76.

This smaller stimulus range was chosen so that the largest "ratio" (7) would be consistent with typical results from "ratio" experiments, given the average output exponent (1.47) reported by Rule and Curtis (this volume). Thus, if magnitude estimations of "ratios" are a power function of subjective ratios with an exponent in the range of values reported by Rule and Curtis, "ratios" and "differences" should be quite distinct and have different rank orders as shown on the right of Fig. 17.4.

One-Operation Theory. If subjects use only one operation for both tasks, and if that operation can be represented by subtraction, then the data can be represented by the following:

$$\mathbf{R}_{ij} = J_{\mathbf{R}}[s_j - s_i] \tag{B.3}$$

$$\mathbf{D}_{ij} = J_{\mathbf{D}}[s_j - s_i] \tag{B.4}$$

where $J_{\mathbf{R}}$ represents the strictly monotonic judgment function for magnitude estimations of "ratios" and $J_{\mathbf{D}}$ represents the strictly monotonic judgment function for ratings of "differences." It follows that $s_j - s_i = J_{\mathbf{D}}^{-1}[\mathbf{D}_{ij}]$. Therefore, $\mathbf{R}_{ij} = J_{\mathbf{R}}[J_{\mathbf{D}}^{-1}(\mathbf{D}_{ij})]$. Because $J_{\mathbf{R}}J_{\mathbf{D}}^{-1}$ is monotonic, one-operation theory implies that "ratios" are monotonically related to "differences."

With the experimental procedures used in the research reviewed by Birnbaum (1980a), it has been found that the $J_{\mathbf{R}}$ function for magnitude estimation can be well-approximated by an exponential function, and $J_{\mathbf{D}}$ for ratings can be approximated by a linear function. In this case, the model can be written:

$$\mathbf{R}_{ij} = a_{\mathbf{R}}\exp[c_{\mathbf{R}}(s_j - s_i)] + b_{\mathbf{R}}, \tag{B.5}$$

$$\mathbf{D}_{ij} = a_{\mathbf{D}}(s_j - s_i) + b_{\mathbf{D}}, \tag{B.6}$$

where $a_{\mathbf{R}}$, $a_{\mathbf{D}}$, $b_{\mathbf{R}}$, $b_{\mathbf{D}}$, and $c_{\mathbf{R}}$ are constants. The comparison operation is subtraction in both cases. It follows that $\mathbf{R}_{ij}$ should be exponentially related $\mathbf{D}_{ij}$.

A Brief Review of Research on "Ratios" and "Differences"

Nine experiments that obtained "ratio" and "difference" judgments are summarized in Fig. 17.5. "Ratios" are plotted on the ordinate against "differences" on the abscissa, with separate symbols for each divisor, as in Fig. 17.4. Instead of resembling the predictions in Fig. 17.4 of the two-operation theory, the data appear more closely to fall on a single monotone function in each case. "Ratios" are roughly an exponential function of "differences," as shown by the resemblance of the data to the exponential curves, which have been fit through just two points (0, 1) and the highest point for each set of data.

Figure 17.5 shows that for experiments with heaviness (Birnbaum & Veit, 1974a), pitch of pure tones (Elmasian & Birnbaum, 1979), darkness of dot patterns (Birnbaum, 1978), darkness of grays (Veit, 1978), loudness of 1000 Hz tones (Birnbaum & Elmasian, 1977), likeableness of adjectives (Hagerty & Birnbaum, 1978), and easterliness or westerliness of U.S. cities (Birnbaum &

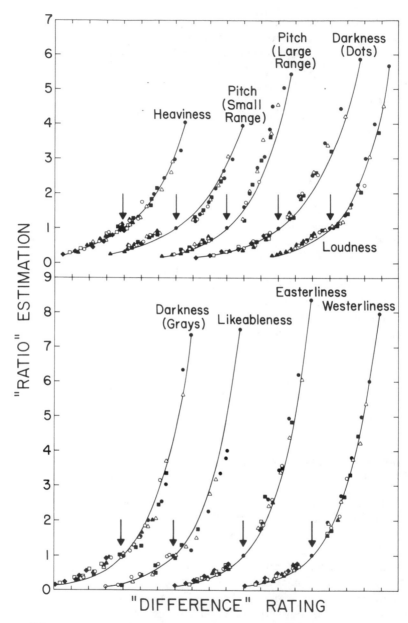

FIG. 17.5. Judgments of "ratios" and "differences," plotted as in Fig. 17.4, for nine experiments. Magnitude estimations of "ratios" are nearly a monotonic function of ratings (or estimations) of "differences," unlike the predictions of Fig. 17.4, but consistent with the theory that the same operation underlies both tasks. Exponential functions have been drawn through the point corresponding to a difference of "zero" and a ratio of "one" (arrows) and the highest point for each experiment. From Birnbaum (1980a).

Mellers, 1978), it appears that "ratios" and "differences" are monotonically related. Similar conclusions were reached by Rose and Birnbaum (1975) for numerical comparisons. Although Parker, Schneider, and Kanow (1975) concluded that judges use two operations for length, Schneider, Parker, Kanow, and Farrell (1976) reached the conclusion that "ratios" of loudness are governed by subtraction. Schneider (this volume) summarizes additional research consistent with the hypothesis that the same comparison process is used for judgments of "ratios" and "differences."

In summary, for a number of social and psychophysical continua, judgments of "ratios" and "differences" can be represented by the same comparison operation. If it is assumed that this operation is subtraction, the J_R function (for magnitude estimations of "ratios") can be approximated by the exponential, and the J_D function (for ratings of "differences") is approximately linear.

However, the subtractive representation,

$$\mathbf{R}_{ij} = a_R \exp(s_j - s_i) \tag{B.7}$$

$$\mathbf{D}_{ij} = a_D(s_j - s_i) \tag{B.8}$$

can be replaced by an equivalent ratio representation as follows:

$$\mathbf{R}_{ij} = a_R(s_j^*/s_i^*) \tag{B.9}$$

$$\mathbf{D}_{ij} = a_D \ln(s_j^*/s_i^*) \tag{B.10}$$

where $s^* = \exp(s)$. In other words, judgments of "ratios" and "differences" are consistent with the proposition that the *same* operation underlies both tasks, but they do not permit specification of what that operation might be.

Is it meaningful to ask whether judges are "really" comparing two stimuli by computing a difference or a ratio? The next section discusses a theoretical and methodological framework in which this question can be answered.

C. RESOLUTION OF THE RATIO-DIFFERENCE CONTROVERSY

The finding that judgments of "ratios" and "differences" are monotonically related is consistent with Torgerson's (1961) hypothesis that judges compare two stimuli by the same operation for both tasks. Torgerson (1961) concluded that if only one operation were used, it would not be possible to *discover* whether the operation is a difference or ratio. Whichever representation was chosen would be a "decision, not a discovery."

However, Birnbaum (1978) and Veit (1978) have shown that with a wider array of data involving both stimulus comparisons (A vs. B) and also comparisons of stimulus relations (AB vs. CD), it becomes possible to discriminate among different theories. Consider the stimuli shown in Fig. 17.6. The observer can be asked to judge the "ratio" (**R**) of A to B or the "difference" (**D**) between A

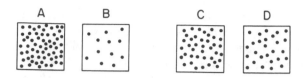

FIG. 17.6.   Stimulus array for one trial of a four-stimulus task. From Birnbaum (1980d).

and B, as before. It is also possible to ask the observer to judge the "ratio of the difference" between A and B relative to the difference between C and D, for example. Four of these four-stimulus tasks have been investigated: "ratios of ratios" [$RR = (A/B)/(C/D)$], "ratios of differences" [$RD = (A - B)/(C - D)$], "differences of ratios" [$A/B - C/D$], and "differences of differences" [$(A - B) - (C - D)$].

These four-stimulus polynomials can be diagnosed by ordinal and metric analyses (Birnbaum, 1978). Furthermore, by comparing the scale values for the same stimuli across the tasks, the information gained from such an experiment is increased. Veit (1978) employed a "ratio of differences" task in addition to the "ratio" and "difference" tasks for judgments of the darkness of papers of varied reflectance. Hagerty and Birnbaum (1978) used six tasks (**R, D, RR, RD, DR, DD**). (These experiments have been reviewed by Birnbaum, 1978). The next sections illustrate the major findings using data from a new experiment that employed stimuli as in Fig. 17.6, and which replicated the findings of Veit (1978) and those of Hagerty and Birnbaum (1978). The following conclusions have been drawn from this research:

1. Judgments of "ratios of ratios," "differences of ratios," or "differences of differences," can all be represented by the difference of differences model, using the same scale values for the stimuli for all three tasks.
2. However, judgments of "ratios of differences" can be represented by a ratio of differences model.
3. The scale derived from the ratio of differences model is consistent with the scale derived from the subtractive model applied to "difference" and "ratio" judgments.
4. The scale values derived from the fit of the difference of differences model applied to "ratios of ratios," "differences of ratios," and "differences of differences" agree with the scale derived from the ratio of differences model applied to "ratios of differences."
5. The judgment functions for magnitude estimations of "ratios" and "ratios of ratios" can be well-approximated by exponential functions, whereas the other judgment functions are approximately linear.
6. Therefore, the data are consistent with the hypothesis that the basic operation for comparing two stimuli in these continua is subtraction.

Theories of Stimulus Comparison

Figure 17.7 gives an outline for discussing theories of stimulus comparison and combination. In the outline, the physical and subjective values of the stimuli are denoted Φ and s, where $s = H(\Phi)$ is the psychophysical function; the subjective value of a comparison between two stimuli (or the combination of two stimuli) is denoted $\Psi_{ij} = C(s_i, s_j)$, where C represents the comparison (or combination) process. Two comparisons (or combinations) are compared (or combined) by the function $\delta = G(\Psi_{ij}, \Psi_{kl})$; the overt response, $\mathbf{R}$, is assumed to be a monotonic function of Ψ in the two-stimulus case and of δ in the four-stimulus case. For comparison with Table 17.1 and Fig. 17.7, let $s_j = A$, $s_i = B$, $s_l = C$, and $s_k = D$.

Table 17.1 shows five theories of stimulus comparison considered by Birnbaum (1978, 1979). It is useful to consider first the predictions of the theory that judges obey the instructions and use a single scale of subjective value. This theory is labelled Model = Task in Table 17.1.

Figure 17.8 shows calculated ratios and differences for a 7 × 7, A by B, factorial design, using integers from 1 to 7 as in the left of Fig. 17.4. In Fig. 17.8, A/B is plotted on the left as a function of A with a separate curve for each

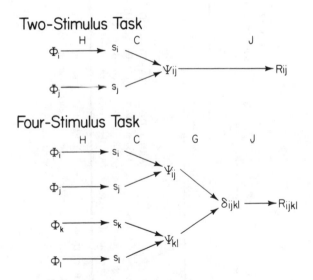

FIG. 17.7. Outline of stimulus comparison and combination for two- and four-stimulus tasks. In the outline, physical values, Φ, are mapped into subjective values, s, by the psychophysical function, H; subjective values are compared (or combined) by the function, $\Psi_{ij} = C(s_i, s_j)$. Two comparisons (or combinations) are compared (or combined) by the function, $\delta = G(\Psi_{ij}, \Psi_{kl})$. The overt response, $\mathbf{R}$ is assumed to be a monotonic function of the subjective impression, where J represents the judgment function. From Birnbaum (1979).

TABLE 17.1
Theories Discussed by Birnbaum (1978)[a]

	Theory				
Task	Model = Task	Subtractive	Ratio	Indeterminacy	Two-Worlds
"Ratios"	A/B	A−B	A/B	A−B	a/b
"Differences"	A−B	A−B	A/B	A−B	A−B
"Ratios of Ratios"	(A/B)/(C/D)	(A−B)−(C−D)	(A/B)/(C/D)	(A−B)−(C−D)	(a/b)/(c/d)
"Differences of Ratios"	(A/B)−(C/D)	(A−B)−(C−D)	(A/B)−(C/D)	(A−B)−(C−D)	(a/b)−(c/d)
"Ratios of Differences"	(A−B)/(C−D)	(A−B)/(C−D)	(A/B)/(C/D)	(A−B)−(C−D)	(A−B)/(C−D)
"Differences of Differences"	(A−B)−(C−D)	(A−B)−(C−D)	(A/B)/(C/D)	(A−B)−(C−D)	(A−B)−(C−D)

[a] A, B, C, D refer to s_j, s_j, s_i, s_k, s_l in Fig. 17.7, respectively. Each entry represents the model for each task predicted by each theory. Judgment functions are omitted for simplicity. For the two-worlds theory, $a = \exp(A)$, $b = \exp(B)$, etc.

416

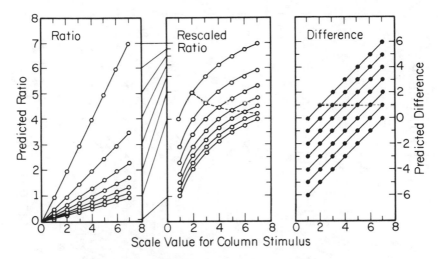

FIG. 17.8. Predicted ratios (A/B) and differences (A–B) for 7-by-7 design using successive integers from 1 to 7 for values of A and B. This figure replots the data of Fig. 17.4 to show bilinearity and parallelism predictions of ratio and subtractive models, respectively. Center panel shows that when ratios are rescaled to parallelism (by the log transformation), the curves would *not* coincide with differences. From Birnbaum (1978).

level of B. On the right of Fig. 17.8, A − B is plotted against A with a separate curve for each level of B. The curves are linearly related to A in each case. They form a bilinear divergent fan for A/B, and the curves are parallel for A − B. The center panel of Fig. 17.8 shows that when ratios are transformed by the log function, log(A/B) = logA − logB, the transformed ratios are parallel, but they are not linearly related to A. Figure 17.8 shows again that A/B and A − B are not monotonically related.

Figures 17.9 and 17.10 show predictions of the theory that Model = Task for the four-stimulus tasks (**RR, RD, DD**, and **DR**). To compute predictions, the 7 × 7 design (using successive integers from 1 to 7) was factorially combined with a 2 × 2, C by D design, in which the levels of C were five and seven and the levels of D were one and four. The design is thus a 7 by 7 by 2 by 2, A by B by C by D factorial. Therefore, C/D is always greater than 1, and C − D is always greater than 0.

Figure 17.9 shows that the **RR** and **DR** models [(A/B)/(C/D) and A/B − C/D] imply a bilinear interaction between A and B. The **DD** and **RD** models [(A − B) − (C − D) and (A − B)/(C − D)] imply no interaction (parallelism) between A and B. Figure 17.10 shows the form of the A by C by D interactions for the four tasks. Other aspects of these models are discussed by Birnbaum (1978).

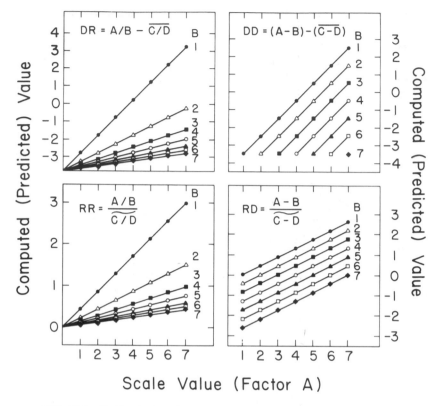

FIG. 17.9.   Predicted values for A-by-B cell means, averaged over levels of C and D, for the theory that the model is the same as the task. Note that curves are parallel for ratios of differences (**RD**) and differences of differences (**DD**), and that they show bilinear divergence for ratios of ratios (**RR**) and differences of ratios (**DR**). Note also that curves are all linearly related to scale values of A. From Birnbaum (1980d).

Comparing the Theories

As Birnbaum (1978) and Veit (1978) noted, the four-stimulus polynomials can be distinguished on the basis of ordinal tests analogous to those described by Krantz and Tversky (1971). By adding the extra leverage of the scale convergence criterion, the number of distinct outcomes (and therefore the total constraint of the experiment) is greatly increased.

In addition to the theory that Model = Task, there are four simple theories to consider. The subtractive theory assumes that simple "ratios" and "differences" are computed by subtraction. Once a subjective interval has been computed, however, the subject can compare this interval by either a ratio or difference operation. The ratio theory (comparably) assumes that ratios underlie

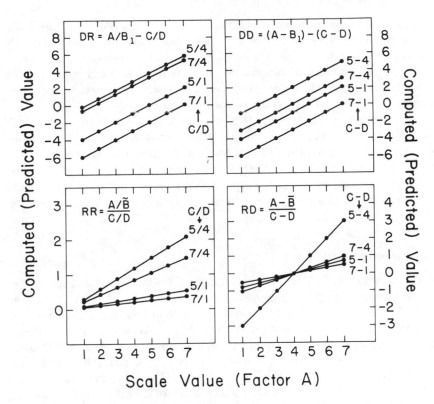

FIG. 17.10.   Predicted values for A by C by D, with B fixed to level 1 (for upper panels) and averaged over levels of B (for lower panels) based on the theory that model = task. Note that curves are linearly related to scale values of A in all panels. Note also that A is additive (parallel) with C/D and C–D for **DR** and **DD** models, respectively, and shows a bilinear interaction with C/D and C–D for **RR** and **RD** models, respectively. From Birnbaum (1980d).

the comparison of two stimuli and that judges can compare two ratios by either a ratio or by a difference. The indeterminacy theory assumes that only one operation is possible for comparison of two stimuli or two comparisons. If the data are consistent with this theory, they would not offer any basis for preferring a ratio or subtractive representation. The two-worlds theory assumes that there are two scales and two sets of corresponding operations. The two-worlds outcome could occur if observers in the four-stimulus tasks used arithmetic on their (implicit) judgments of **R** and **D**.

Except for Model = Task, all four theories predict that the **R**, **D**, **RR**, and **DD** data should be rescalable to a difference, or difference of differences, model using the same scale values for A. The theories differ in that the subtractive and two-worlds theories predict that "ratios of differences" should fit the ratio of differences model.

Veit (1978) found that "ratios of differences" of darkness of gray chips could indeed be fit to a ratio of differences model, but could *not* be monotonically rescaled to fit a difference of differences model, as they showed the appropriate violations of joint independence that refute the **DD** or **RR** models but which are characteristic of the **RD** model. Thus, her results were consistent with the subtractive theory but did not test the two-worlds theory.

The ratio theory and two-worlds theory predict that "differences of ratios" should fit the difference of ratios model. Hagerty and Birnbaum (1978) studied all six tasks for the likeableness of adjectives and found no evidence for ratio theory or two-worlds theory. With the assistance of Steven E. Stegner and Bernadette Setiadi, the author has replicated the major findings of Hagerty and Birnbaum (1978) in a new experiment using psychophysical stimuli as in Fig. 17.6.

Experimental Test

In this experiment, 227 undergraduates judged "ratios" and "differences" of the darkness of dot patterns presented in the format of Fig. 17.6 (except without C and D). The number of dots varied from 8 to 90 in seven equal log steps as in the experiment described by Birnbaum (1978, Fig. 4), which used a different stimulus presentation format. After performing both the simple **R** and **D** tasks, each subject served in one of the four-stimulus tasks: **RR**, **RD**, **DR**, or **DD** (there were 41 to 55 different subjects in each condition). The design for these tasks was a $7 \times 7 \times 2 \times 2$, $A \times B \times C \times D$, in which levels of C were levels five (40 dots) and seven (90 dots) and for D they were one (8 dots) and four (27 dots).

Experimental Results

Figures 17.11, 17.12, and 17.13 show the results for the six tasks, plotted for comparability with Figs. 17.8, 17.9, and 17.10. However, note that data for "ratios," and "ratios of ratios" are plotted against the antilog$_2$ of the estimated scale value, *unlike* Figs. 17.8 through 17.10.

The data were fit to the theories in Table 17.1, with the result that the subtractive theory gave the best overall fit. The predicted curves in Figs. 17.11, 17.12, and 17.13 are based on the following model (subtractive theory of Table 17.1 with *J* specified):

$$\hat{R}_{ij} = a_{\mathbf{R}} \exp(\Psi_{ij}) + b_{\mathbf{R}} \tag{C.1}$$

$$\hat{D}_{ij} = a_{\mathbf{D}}(\Psi_{ij}) + b_{\mathbf{D}} \tag{C.2}$$

$$\hat{RR}_{ijkl} = a_{\mathbf{RR}} \exp(\Psi_{ij} - \Psi_{kl}) + b_{\mathbf{RR}} \tag{C.3}$$

$$\hat{RD}_{ijkl} = a_{\mathbf{RD}}(\Psi_{ij}/\Psi_{kl}) + b_{\mathbf{RD}} \tag{C.4}$$

$$\hat{D}R_{ijkl} = a_{DR} (\Psi_{ij} - \Psi_{kl}) + b_{DR} \tag{C.5}$$

$$\hat{D}D_{ijkl} = a_{DD} (\Psi_{ij} - \Psi_{kl}) + b_{DD} \tag{C.6}$$

$$\Psi_{ij} = s_{A_j} - s_{B_i} \text{ and } \Psi_{kl} = s_{C_k} - s_{D_l} \tag{C.7}$$

Note that the unit of the Ψ values is determined by Eq. C.1. The same unit was assumed for Eq. C.3, as it was expected that judges would be consistent with their previous "ratio" judgments.

For each task, a proportion of variance unaccounted for was defined as follows:

$$P_T = \frac{\Sigma(X_T - \hat{X}_T)^2}{\Sigma(X_T - \bar{X}_T)^2} \tag{C.8}$$

where P_T is the proportion unexplained, X_T is the cell mean judgment, $\hat{X}_T$ the prediction (from Eqs. C.1 through C.7), and $\bar{X}_T$ the mean judgment for task **T** (over all cells). The summation is over all cells in the design for Task **T**. For the "ratio" and "ratio of ratios" tasks, X_T is the log cell mean response, $\hat{X}_T$ is the log of the predicted response, and $\bar{X}$ is the mean log response.

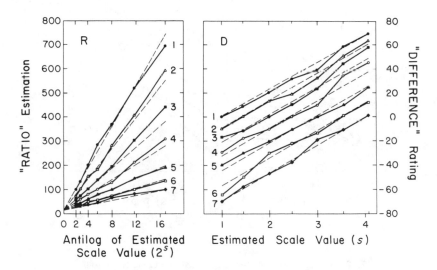

FIG. 17.11. Judgments of "ratios" and "differences" of darkness of dots. Dashed lines are based on the subtractive theory, fit to data of all six tasks simultaneously. Note that "ratios" are plotted against 2^s rather than s, whereas "differences" are plotted against s. Therefore, these data are *not* like predictions of Fig. 17.8, but instead are consistent with subtractive theory (dashed lines). From Birnbaum (1980d).

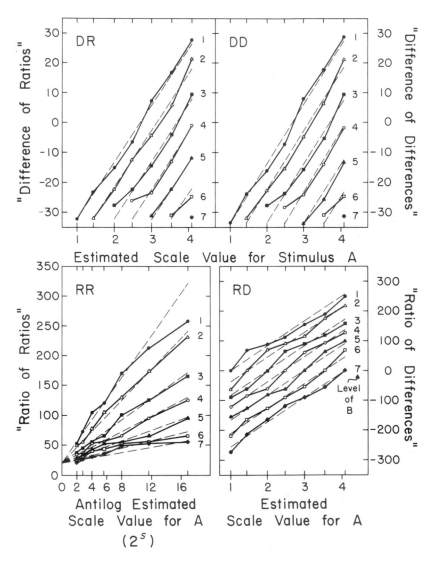

FIG. 17.12. Obtained A-by-B effects, averaged over C and D, for four-stimulus tasks, plotted for comparison with Fig. 17.9. Dashed lines are predictions of subtractive theory, simultaneously fit to all six tasks. Note that abscissa for **RR** task is 2^s rather than s. From Birnbaum (1980d).

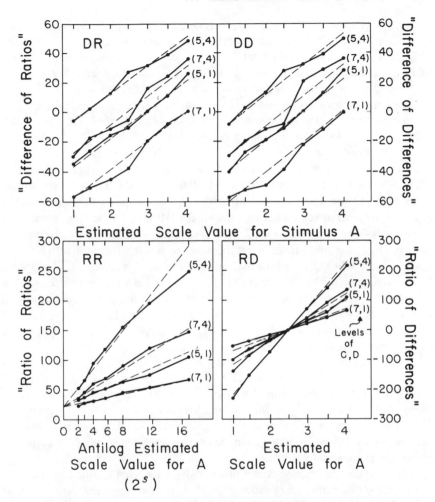

FIG. 17.13. Obtained A-by-C-by-D effects for four-stimulus tasks, plotted for comparison with Fig. 17.10. For **DR** and **DD** tasks, data are for first level of B only. For **RR** and **RD** tasks, data are averaged over levels of B. Dashed lines are predictions of subtractive theory, constrained to fit all six sets of data simultaneously. Abscissa for **RR** task is 2^s. From Birnbaum (1980d).

An overall index, L, was defined as follows:

$$L = \sum_{T=1}^{6} P_{\mathrm{T}},$$

where L is an index of badness of fit that is the sum over all six data arrays. The **R** and **D** arrays are each 7×7, symmetric A by B factorials; the **RR**, **RD**, **DR** and

DD arrays are each $7 \times 7 \times 2 \times 2$, A by B by C by D factorials. Therefore, there are 882 cells to be fit. In addition to the 12 linear constants in Eqs. C.1 through C.7, there were six scale values for A and B to estimate (the scale values for s_{A_1} and s_{D_1} are fixed to 1.0) and three scale values to estimate for C and D. Therefore, there are 21 parameters to be estimated from 882 data cells.

The same scale values are assumed for A (and B) throughout all six tasks. The estimated values for the seven levels of A (and B) are 1.00, 1.45, 2.00, 2.47, 3.00, 3.54, and 4.08. The estimated values for C are 3.83 and 4.90, and for D they are 1.0 and 2.58.

The values of P_T for the six tasks for the subtractive theory were .012, .014, .027, .026, .023, and .042 for the **D**, **R**, **DD**, **DR**, **RD**, and **RR** tasks, respectively. Attempts to fit the other theories in Table 17.1 led to poorer overall fits. For example, the sum of squared deviations for the **DR** task for the ratio theory and two-worlds theory was more than 2.7 times as great as for the subtractive theory, with the fit of the other tasks about the same or worse. The subtractive theory gives a reasonable account of the data in Figs. 17.11, 17.12, and 17.13 as shown by the similarity of the solid curves (data) and dashed lines (predictions). The largest deviations, for the **RR** task, may be due in part to the unnecessarily strict restriction that the unit of the exponential in Eqs. C.1 and C.3 were the same. A better fit was obtained by the following: $a_{RR}\exp[c_{RR}(\Psi_{ij} - \Psi_{kl})] + b_{RR}$, where c_{RR} is less than 1.0.

The subtractive theory assumes that "ratios of differences" can be represented by a ratio of differences model even though "ratios" and "ratio of ratios" are represented by subtraction (Birnbaum, 1978; Hagerty & Birnbaum, 1978; Veit, 1978). Consistent with this assumption, and with the corresponding assumptions concerning J in Eqs. C.1 through C.6, the **RD** data are nearly linearly related to scale values estimated from the other tasks, whereas the **R** and **RR** data are nearly exponentially related.

The other theories make distinct predictions that are not fulfilled by the data. For example, the ratio theory predicts that "differences between ratios" would fit a difference of ratios model. The data in Figs. 17.12 and 17.13 show that the **DD** and **DR** data are nearly identical and do not resemble the predictions of the difference of ratios model (Figs. 17.9 and 17.10).

The indeterminacy theory predicts that the **RD** data could be represented by subtraction. Instead, Figs. 17.12 and 17.13 show the appropriate pattern of parallelism for the A by B interaction and a cross-over interaction for the A by (C − D) interaction. Eisler's (1978) transformation theories (which are discussed in more detail in Section G) predict that **DD** and **DR** should be different and that **DD** should resemble the **RD** data, fitting a ratio of differences model.

In sum, the data of six tasks appear consistent with the pattern predicted by the subtractive theory. This result agrees with the conclusions of Birnbaum (1978, 1979), Veit (1978), and Hagerty and Birnbaum (1978). The results are consistent with the proposition that two stimuli are compared by subtraction whether the instructions are to report a "ratio" or a "difference." To argue that "ratio" judgments are represented by the ratio model appears to require a complex sequence of arguments (Birnbaum, 1978, 1979).

More Evidence

Rose and Birnbaum (1975) asked judges to divide a line segment to represent either the "ratio" or "difference" of two numbers. The pattern of responses was largely independent of the task. If it was assumed that the responses were represented by a ratio rule:

$$\Psi_{ij} = \frac{s_i}{s_i + s_j} \tag{C.9}$$

then the scale values, s, were found to be a positively accelerated function of numerical value. On the other hand, if the subtractive model was assumed, the scale values were found to be a negatively accelerated function of physical number. The scale values for number estimated from the subtractive model were approximately a linear function of scale values estimated from range-frequency theory (Birnbaum, 1974c) and scale values estimated by other procedures (Rule & Curtis, 1973).

Elmasian and Birnbaum (1979) found that the subtractive theory applied to judgments of "ratios" and "differences" of pitch led to scale values that were compatible with the musical scale, whereas the ratio theory led to scale values that were nonlinearly related to the musical scale of pitch.

Birnbaum and Mellers (1978) asked judges to estimate "ratios" and "differences" of easterliness and westerliness of U.S. cities. The task is a particular "inverse" judgment for which the *inverse* appears an unattractive theoretical interpretation. They used a factorial design that permits segregation of scale values from the response function for "inverse" judgments. As shown in Fig. 17.5, "ratios" were nearly exponentially related to "differences" for both easterliness and westerliness, consistent with the hypothesis that only one operation is involved for both tasks. The data can be well-described by the model:

$$\mathbf{DE}_{ij} = s_j - s_i \tag{C.10}$$

$$\mathbf{DW}_{ij} = s_i - s_j \tag{C.11}$$

$$\mathbf{RE}_{ij} = \exp[a(s_j - s_i)] \tag{C.12}$$

$$\mathbf{RW}_{ij} = \exp[a(s_i - s_j)] \tag{C.13}$$

where $\mathbf{DE}_{ij}$ and $\mathbf{DW}_{ij}$ are the predicted ratings of "differences" in easterliness and westerliness, and $\mathbf{RE}_{ij}$ and $\mathbf{RW}_{ij}$ are the predicted magnitude estimations of "ratios" of easterliness and westerliness, respectively. This theory requires only one cognitive map and one comparison operation (subtraction). Note also that the distinction between easterliness and westerliness is merely one of direction. Because $\exp(s_i - s_j) = 1/\exp(s_j - s_i)$, it follows that magnitude estimations of "ratios" of easterliness and westerliness are reciprocally related.

Figure 17.14 shows a summary of "mental maps" (scale values) derived from the data of Birnbaum and Mellers (1978). The figure shows that mental maps based on the ratio model depend on direction of judgment and are nonlinearly distorted relative to the actual map. The subtractive model (Eqs. C.10 through C.13) is preferred because it produces a single map for all four tasks that is independent of direction and resembles the actual map closely.

In summary, the ratio theory does not give an adequate account of the four-stimulus results, it leads to an unattractive psychophysical function for number, it contradicts the musical scale of pitch, and it yields mental maps that depend on

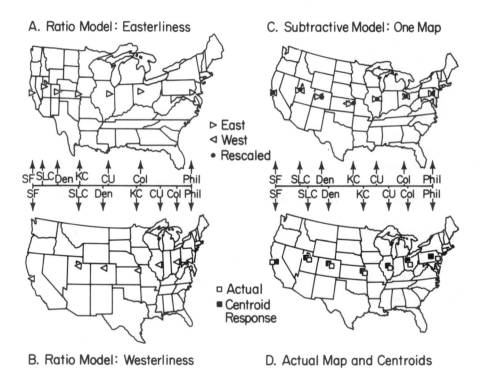

A. Ratio Model: Easterliness

C. Subtractive Model: One Map

▷ East
◁ West
• Rescaled

▫ Actual
▪ Centroid
Response

B. Ratio Model: Westerliness

D. Actual Map and Centroids

FIG. 17.14. Mental maps of the U.S. derived from ratio model applied to "ratios" of easterliness (Panel A) and "ratios" of westerliness (Panel B). The subtractive model can represent all four sets of data (including "differences") by means of a single map (Panel C). Actual map of U.S. is shown in Panel D. Subtractive theory is preferred over ratio theory because it uses a single map that resembles the actual map, whereas ratio theory requires different maps for different directions that are reciprocally related to each other and nonlinearly related to the actual map. From Birnbaum and Mellers (1978).

the direction of judgment and are nonlinearly related to the actual map. The subtractive theory gives a far simpler summary of these data.

D. CONTEXTUAL EFFECTS IN COMPARISON AND COMBINATION

There are several possible loci for contextual effects in stimulus comparison and combination (Birnbaum, Parducci, & Gifford, 1971) that can be discussed in terms of Fig. 17.7. Contextual effects could operate on the scale values prior to comparison or combination (i.e., on the function H in Fig. 17.7). They could operate *within* the set of stimuli presented for judgment (i.e., on C in Fig. 17.7). Contextual effects could operate on the *between-set* distribution of Ψ or δ in Fig. 17.7 (on the J function). Birnbaum and Mellers (1980b) and Mellers and Birnbaum (1980a, 1980b) have investigated possible loci of contextual effects and reached the following tentative conclusions:

1. When stimuli of the same modality are compared, the distribution of stimulus levels seems to have minimal effects on the scale values.
2. When stimuli from different modalities are compared or combined, the distribution of stimulus levels has large effects on the scale values in the general directions predicted by range-frequency theory.
3. When the context between sets was manipulated in a social judgment task, results were similar to those of Birnbaum et al. (1971, Exp. 5): The contextual effects could be attributed to changes in the judgment function (J).

Context Effects in Within-Mode Comparison

As shown in Fig. 17.3, the judged "ratio" of darkness of stimulus No. 7 (Fig. 17.1, 90 dots) relative to that of stimulus No. 9 (12 dots) can receive a mean judgment anywhere from 3.4, if the largest example is "3", to 8.0 if the largest example is "9". Although this effect was attributed to the judgment function, which describes the relationship between subjective comparisons and overt "ratio" responses, experiments in which the stimuli are varied in one factor (as in Fig. 17.3) do not permit unambiguous identification of the loci of contextual effects.

Given only the results of Fig. 17.3, it is possible that contextual effects operate on the scale values (on H) instead of the judgment function (J). When asked to judge the "difference" or "ratio" of two stimuli, as in Fig. 17.1, will the observer first *judge* each stimulus (with contextual effects) and then *compare* two implicit judgments? Or will contextual effects occur only after stimulus comparison?

These two ideas can be formalized as follows: Let $\mathbf{D}_{ijk}$ and $\mathbf{R}_{ijk}$ be the judged "difference" and "ratio" between stimuli j and i in context k. Suppose J represents the contextual effect (range-frequency). Model 1 states:

$$\mathbf{D}_{ijk} = J_{\mathbf{D}_k} [J_k(s_j) - J_k(s_i)] \tag{D.1}$$

$$\mathbf{R}_{ijk} = J_{\mathbf{R}_k} [J_k(s_j) - J_k(s_i)] \tag{D.2}$$

where $J_{\mathbf{D}_k}$ and $J_{\mathbf{R}_k}$ are the judgment functions (presumably based on the distribution of subjective differences), and J_k is the judgment function for the single stimuli (presumably based on the distribution of s).

Note that if this model holds, then the rank order of "difference" judgments obtained for the positively skewed context (stimuli on the left of Fig. 17.1) would be quite different from the rank order of "differences" for the negative context (on the right). In other words, the estimated scale values $[J_k(s_j)]$ would depend on the stimulus distribution.

Model 2 is a special case of Model 1 that assumes that the scale values are independent of context and that context influences only the transformation from subjective differences to overt judgments. This model can be written:

$$\mathbf{D}_{ijk} = J_{\mathbf{D}_k} [s_j - s_i] \tag{D.3}$$

$$\mathbf{R}_{ijk} = J_{\mathbf{R}_k} [s_j - s_i] \tag{D.4}$$

According to this model, the rank order of "difference" and "ratio" judgments should be independent of stimulus spacing because the scale values are independent of context.

To test these theories, Mellers and Birnbaum (1980b) asked four groups (about 20 undergraduates per group) to judge either "differences" or "ratios" of the darkness of dots spaced in either a positively or negatively skewed context (as in Fig. 17.1). Nested within each 11×11 design was a 6×6 design of stimuli common to both distributions.

Figure 17.15 shows mean "ratios" plotted against mean "differences" with a separate point for each divisor/subtrahend, plotted as in Fig. 17.4 and Fig. 17.5. Data are shown for the 6×6 common design, with the results for the positively skewed condition on the left and the results for the negatively skewed condition on the right. Note that the data appear reasonably consistent with the premise that one operation underlies both tasks, i.e., that "ratios" are approximately a monotonic function of "differences."

Accordingly, the two data sets for each context were fit to the subtractive model:

$$\hat{D}_{ijk} = a_{D_k} [s_{jk} - s_{ik}] + b_{D_k} \tag{D.5}$$

$$\hat{R}_{ijk} = a_{R_k} \exp[s_{jk} - s_{ik}] + b_{R_k} \tag{D.6}$$

where the k subscript on the scale values indicates that different scale values are permitted for each context (though the same scale values and comparison process is assumed for both "ratio" and "difference" tasks). The proportions of variance unaccounted for were computed as in Eq. C.8, and the sum of these proportions was minimized. Parameter estimates were derived from the entire 11 × 11 design in each case. Similar results were obtained when only the 6 × 6 common stimuli were used to fit the model. For the common design, the overall indexes (as in Eq. C.8) were .011 and .014 for positively and negatively skewed conditions, respectively, indicating that the model deviations constitute about half of 1% of the variance for each of the four matrices.

Figure 17.16 shows estimated scale values from two sets of both 11 × 11 matrices. The solid points fall nearly on the identity line, indicating minimal contextual effects. The broken line shows the predicted relationship based on the single judgments for the 100-point scale (Fig. 17.2). The scale values shown in

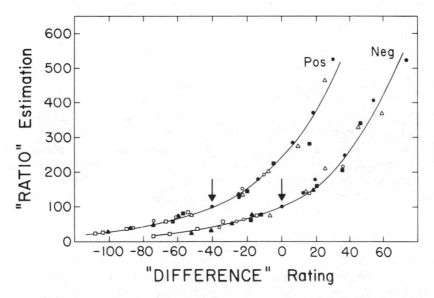

FIG. 17.15. Estimations of "ratios" plotted against estimations of "differences," as in Fig. 17.5. Data on the left are for the positively skewed context (see Fig. 17.1). Positively skewed context data are shifted 40 units to the left relative to the abscissa labels. Curves are best-fit solutions to a special case of the one-operation theory. From Mellers and Birnbaum (1980b).

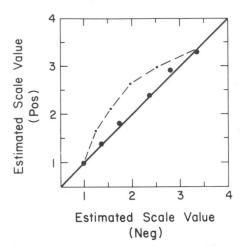

FIG. 17.16. Scale values derived from subtractive theory (applied to both tasks) are largely independent of context. Large solid points show estimated scale values for positively skewed context plotted against estimated scale values for negatively skewed context. Broken curve shows relationship predicted from the 100-point ratings in Fig. 17.2. From Mellers and Birnbaum (1980b).

Fig. 17.16 do not differ as much as would be expected from Model 1, assuming the expected range-frequency compromise. Instead, it appears that one can give a good approximation to the data by the simpler theory (Eqs. D.3 and D.4) that scale values for the subtractive model (applied to both "differences" and "ratios") are independent of stimulus spacing.

Figure 17.2 shows that for the positively skewed condition the difference in judgment between stimulus 90 and 40 is *less than* the difference in judgment between 27 and 12, whereas for the negatively skewed distribution the order of these differences in judgment is reversed. However, when judging "differences" (or "ratios"), the judged "difference" (and "ratio") between 90 and 40 *exceeds* the "difference" (and "ratio") between 27 and 12 for all four comparisons of means for the negative skew and three of four for the positive skew.

Thus, these data do not provide evidence that contextual effects operate on *s* in within-mode stimulus comparisons. Instead, it appears that the rank order of "ratios" and "differences" can be reproduced by assuming that judges compute differences between scale values that are independent of the stimulus spacing.

Cross-Modality Combination and Comparison

Aside from the psychophysics laboratory, cross-modality questions such as "Who was the greater, Babe Ruth or Roman Gabriel?," "Does the punishment fit the crime?," "Is this salary fair for this job?" are often asked. It seems likely that responses to such questions would not depend solely on absolute values but would depend on the joint distribution of the two modalities.

Krantz (1972) discussed mapping and relation theories of cross-modality "matching." According to the mapping view, sensations in different modalities are somehow mapped into a common scale of magnitudes that can be compared.

According to the relation view of Shepard (1978) and Krantz (1972), relation-ships (e.g., ratios) between pairs of stimuli can be compared. In other words, it is possible to compare the ratio of two heavinesses to the ratio of two loudnesses. By analogy with physical measurement (in which lengths cannot be compared with masses, but ratios of lengths can be compared with ratios of masses), the relation theory seems sensible.

Another view can be called psychological relativity theory (Birnbaum & Mellers, 1980b). In this theory, each stimulus is compared to its distribution, and the relative positions of the two stimuli in the two modalities are compared. Thus, a loudness will be "matched" to a brightness when the two stimuli hold the same position in the distributions of their respective modalities.

To study possible dependence of the scale values on the stimulus distribution, Birnbaum and Mellers (1980b) investigated two tasks: cross-modality "dif-ference" judgments and "total" intensity judgments. "Total" intensity judg-ments have been studied by Feldman and Baird (1971) and Anderson (1974a).

A typical stimulus presentation is shown in Fig. 17.17. The "difference" task was to compare the size of the circle to the darkness of the dot pattern and judge which is greater and by how much. The "total" task was to combine the size of the circle and the darkness of the dot pattern. On some trials, only one stimulus (dot pattern or circle) was presented. On these occasions, the unpresented stimulus value was assumed to be zero.

The experimental design paired each of six circles, varying from 8 to 25 mm in diameter factorially with six common dot patterns geometrically spaced from 12 to 90 dots. In two conditions, the positively and negatively skewed distri-butions (of Fig. 17.1) were factorially combined with the six circles. In two other conditions, more extreme patterns of 10 and 135 dots were added for the medium range; or patterns of 6 and 180 dots were added for the wide range.

The models were as follows:

$$\mathbf{D}_{ijk} = a_{\mathbf{D}_k} (c_j - d_{ik}) \tag{D.7}$$

$$\mathbf{T}_{ijk} = a_{\mathbf{T}_k} (c_j + d_{ik}) + b_{\mathbf{T}_k} \tag{D.8}$$

where $\mathbf{D}_{ijk}$ and $\mathbf{T}_{ijk}$ are the judgments of "difference" and "total intensity" of circle j and dot pattern i in context k, c_j and d_{ik} are the scale values of the circles and the dot patterns, respectively, and $a_{\mathbf{D}_k}$, $a_{\mathbf{T}_k}$, and $b_{\mathbf{T}_k}$ are linear constants for each context.

FIG. 17.17. Example stimulus array for one trial of cross-modality comparison. From Birnbaum and Mellers (1980b).

In the subtractive model, when the response is "no difference" it is assumed that $c_j = d_{ik}$, i.e., a cross-modality "match." In the additive model, the additive constant, b_T, is determined by the constraint that when a stimulus is not presented its value is zero. Therefore, $T_{i0k} + T_{0jk} - T_{ijk} = b_T$, where T_{i0k} and T_{0jk} are judgments of the ith dot pattern alone and jth circle alone in context k.

Scale values for the dot patterns were estimated separately for "totals" and "differences" for each context. Inasmuch as the distribution of circles was the same for all conditions, circle scale values were assumed to be the same for all conditions. Because the scale values for the circles are assumed to be the same across conditions, once the unit of the circle scale values is fixed, the estimated scale values for dot patterns in the different contexts are uniquely determined for the "total" task. Similarly, once the unit and additive constant for the scale values of circles is fixed, the scale values of the dot patterns for the "difference" task are uniquely determined by the data.

Estimated scale values are shown in Fig. 17.18 as a function of log Φ with separate curves for each context. Note that for both "differences" and "totals," the slopes are greater for the narrow-range conditions (positive and negative skew) than for the medium- or wide-range conditions. The wide-range condition was the lowest in slope. Note also that the scale value of a medium-level dot pattern (e.g., 27 or 40) receives a greater scale value in the positively skewed context than it does in the negatively skewed context. These contextual effects, which are in the general direction of the usual contextual effects in ratings, cannot be attributed to the J functions between Ψ and response, for different circles are judged to "match" the same dot patterns in different contexts.

In previous tests of cross-modality "matching," experiments have controlled the stimulus distributions to be comparable in the magnitude estimation and cross-modality "matching" experiments. It seems likely that if the stimulus and response ranges were systematically manipulated, then the conclusions of cross-modality matching experiments would be altered. Let ΔR be the log response range and ΔS be the log stimulus range, then the power-function exponent in a magnitude-estimation experiment will be $b = \Delta R / \Delta S$. If ΔR is a constant (Teghtsoonian, 1971), then exponents for two modalities will be $b_1 = \Delta R / \Delta S_1$ and $b_2 = \Delta R / \Delta S_2$. Thus, the predicted cross-modality exponent is $b_1/b_2 = (\Delta R / \Delta S_1)/(\Delta R / \Delta S_2) = \Delta S_2 / \Delta S_1$. In other words, one should be able to predict cross-modality exponents either from the stimulus ranges or from the magnitude-estimation exponents.

To unconfound these different interpretations, cross-modality "matching" experiments should systematically manipulate the stimulus and response ranges. For force of handgrip, the response range is not under the experimenter's control but rather under the subject's control. A better procedure would be to use a dimension such as loudness for the response and to vary the range and taper of the control knob. It seems likely that the cross-modality "matching" function will depend heavily on the range and distribution of responses under the subject's control. As

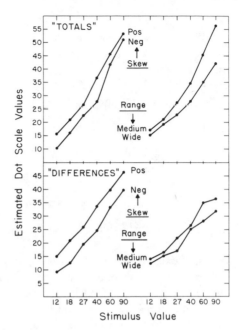

FIG. 17.18. Estimated scale values for dot patterns from studies of cross-modality comparison and combination. If there were no contextual effects, curves should all coincide. Differences in height and slope of curves are generally in the direction predicted by range-frequency theory. From Birnbaum and Mellers (1980b).

another example, the response could be lifted weight. The experimenter could present a number of bottles with the judge's task being to select the bottle whose heaviness "matches" the stimulus. The distribution of weights is clearly under the experimenter's control.

In summary, experiments show that in cross-modality comparison or combination, the range and spacing of the stimuli affect the scale values. It is as if stimuli must be judged within the context of other stimuli in the same modality before they can be compared across modalities. This result is compatible with a relativity theory of cross-modality "matching" rather than the mapping or relation views.

Contextual Effects in Social Information Integration

Mellers and Birnbaum (1980a) applied the approach of Birnbaum et al. (1971, Experiment 5) to a social judgment task in which judges evaluated the performance of students on the basis of their scores on two exams.

The joint distribution of exam scores for the positively skewed context is shown in Fig. 17.19. Each symbol represents the exam scores of one or more hypothetical students. The solid squares show the common stimuli that were presented in both contexts. The common stimuli consist of the union of 4 by 7 and 7 by 4, first exam by second exam, factorial designs. Each open circle represents a contextual trial; each open triangle represents three such trials. Thus,

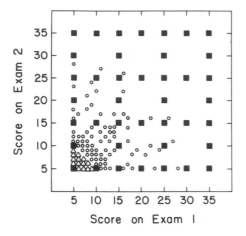

FIG. 17.19. Joint distribution of exam scores for experiment on contextual effects in social-information integration. Figure shows distribution for positively skewed condition. Each open circle or solid square represents the performance of one hypothetical student. Each triangle represents three students with the same scores. Solid squares were the same for both contexts. Contextual trials for negatively skewed distribution were the mirror image of those in this figure, reflected about the axis, exam 1 + exam 2 = 40. From Mellers and Birnbaum (1980a).

the total of both exam scores ranges from 10 (i.e., 5 + 5) to 70 (i.e., 35 + 35). The distribution of total score and the marginal distributions of each exam score are positively skewed. The open triangles show that 42 students (of the total of 160) had scored scores between 10 and 15 for the positively skewed distribution. There were none in this open interval for the negatively skewed context, which had a mirror-image distribution, reflected about the axis, exam 1 + exam 2 = 40.

Assuming the scores are combined by an additive (or parallel-averaging) model, the general model of context can be written:

$$\mathbf{G}_{ijk} = J_k^*[J_k(s_i) + J_k(s_j)] \tag{D.9}$$

where $\mathbf{G}_{ijk}$ is the evaluation of the student with scores i and j in context k, J_k^* is the judgment function (presumably based on the distribution of Ψ_{ij}), and J_k represents the contextual effect on the scale values. In general, if J_k is nonlinear, then the rank orders for different contexts will be different.

A variation of the model that assumes parameter invariance but does not assume additivity can be written

$$\mathbf{G}_{ijk} = J_k^*[\Psi_{ij}] \tag{D.10}$$

where Ψ_{ij} is the integrated impression, which may or may not be additive. This model implies that the rank order of the data should be independent of context.

There were four groups. Half of the judges received either the positively or negatively skewed distributions. Half of each of these groups were given histograms depicting the marginal distributions of exam 1 and exam 2 to use while making their judgments. It was thought that presentation of these histograms might enhance any tendency to evaluate performance first and then combine, as in Eq. D.9. There were about 25 subjects in each of the four groups.

The mean judgments are plotted in Fig. 17.20 as a function of the score on exam 1 with a separate curve for each level of exam 2. Parallelism would be consistent with an additive (or parallel-averaging) model. Instead of being parallel, however, the curves for the positively skewed context show systematic convergence to the right (the vertical separations between the curves decrease as the score on exam 1 increases). The curves for the negatively skewed context show the opposite: divergence to the right. Thus, the apparent interaction between the exam scores depends on the stimulus distribution. This result is consistent with the results of Birnbaum et al. (1971), who used psychophysical stimuli.

The interaction can be represented in this case by assuming that only the J^* function (rather than the scale values or combination process) depends on the stimulus distribution, as in Eq. D.10. Note that the rank orders of the data points are essentially the same in all four panels. The rank orders would be systematically different in the different panels had the subjects made separate (context-dependent) judgments of each exam score and averaged their separate judgments.

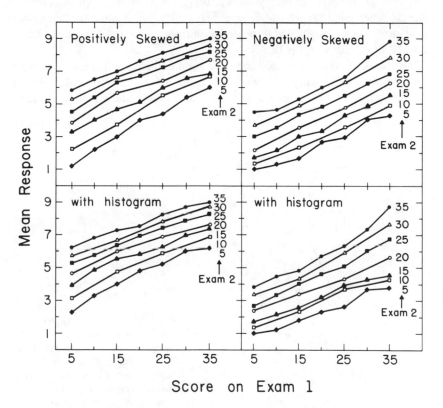

FIG. 17.20.   Mean evaluations of the performance of students, as a function of score on exam 1, with a separate curve for each level of score on exam 2. Note that curves converge for positively skewed distribution (left panels), and they diverge for the negatively skewed distribution (right panels). From Mellers and Birnbaum (1980a).

(To check this, another group of subjects was asked to judge performance based on exam 1 only. Indeed, when these judgments were substituted into Eq. D.9, the rank order of predictions differed for different contexts.)

The data of Fig. 17.20 were rescaled to parallelism, and scale values estimated from the additive model applied separately to the four conditions were found to be nearly identical across conditions. These estimates were averaged and used to compute $s_i + s_j$. The mean responses are plotted in Fig. 17.21 as a function of $s_i + s_j$, with a separate curve for each context. (The data were averaged over the histogram vs. no histogram manipulation, which showed minimal effects in Fig. 17.20.) The mean judgments have been linearly calibrated to the same zero to one scale in Fig. 17.21. The solid curves show the cumulative density functions for the two contexts, based on the density of the sum of the exam scores (see Fig. 17.19).

According to range-frequency theory, if $\Psi_{ij} = s_i + s_j$, then the obtained values for each condition should be an average of the solid curve for that context (frequency) and a straight line through the end points (range). The dashed lines show the predictions of this theory.

The dashed curves give a good approximation to the data. It is also possible to use range-frequency theory to solve for the values of Ψ_{ij} in order to determine if the assumption that $\Psi_{ij} = s_i + s_j$ is reasonable. The model was fit as follows:

$$\mathbf{G}_{ijk} = aF_k(\mathbf{G}_{ijk}) + \Psi_{ij} + c \qquad (D.11)$$

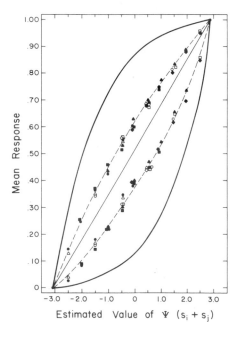

FIG. 17.21. Mean judgments of student performance from Fig. 17.20 (recalibrated to a 0–1 scale) as a function of estimated value of Ψ, with separate dashed curves for each contextual distribution. Solid curves are cumulative density functions for the two contexts, dashed curves are predictions of range-frequency theory. Symbols are consistent with Fig. 17.20. From Mellers and Birnbaum (1980a).

where G_{ijk} is the rating of a student with test score levels i and j in context k, F_k is the cumulative proportion of students receiving lower judgments (curves in Fig. 17.21), Ψ_{ij} are estimated parameters, and a and c are fitted constants. The model was fit by means of multiple regression using dummy variables. The estimated values of Ψ_{ij} were very nearly parallel (with a very small divergence). This analysis gave only a slightly better fit than the special case that assumed $\Psi_{ij} = s_i + s_j$. The additive model therefore appears to provide a satisfactory approximation.

In summary, Figs. 17.20 and 17.21 show that the data are consistent with the hypothesis that manipulation of the distribution of totals (as in Fig. 17.19) can manipulate the judgment function, according to the principles of range-frequency theory, applied to the distribution of totals. No evidence was found to require the interpretation that the scale values for the test scores depended on the marginal distributions. Indeed, had the scale values changed according to range-frequency theory, the rank order of the points in Fig. 17.20 would have changed.

These results show the potential importance of contextual effects in studies of information integration in which the parallelism test is of interest for evaluating theories. In this case, it should be clear that the change from convergence to divergence was brought about by the change in stimulus distribution and can be explained in terms of a range-frequency analysis of the judgment function. This experiment shows that it should often be possible to select stimuli to produce parallelism, even though the model is not additive. The implications of this finding for functional measurement are further discussed in Section F.

Contextual Effects in Similarity Judgments

Tversky (1977) argued that distance theories of "similarity" judgments cannot account for violations of the three basic axioms of a distance function, δ:

Minimality: $\delta(x,y) \geq \delta(x,x) = 0$
Symmetry: $\delta(x,y) = \delta(y,x)$
Triangle inequality: $\delta(x,y) + \delta(y,z) \geq \delta(x,z)$

Tversky notes that judgments of the form, "North Korea is like Red China" often violate symmetry because "Red China is like North Korea" is less preferred. He has also questioned the other axioms. Tversky's (1977) theory, which extends developments of Restle (1959), is that judgments of "x is like y" depend on the common psychological features of x and y, the features that x possesses that are absent from y, and those features belonging to y but not x. In Tversky's theory, measures of these sets are permitted to depend on the context, but no theory is advanced to describe the effects of context.

Krumhansl (1978) argued that the distance concept can be saved by introducing a particular theory of contextual effects in "similarity" judgments. Her theory assumes that "similarity" judgments depend on both distance in a context-free multidimensional space (that satisfies the axioms) and also on local stimulus densities in the regions of the points.

There are many possible loci for contextual effects in the distance model. Investigating them empirically would require a large experimental effort. Figure 17.19 can be relabelled to facilitate discussion of possible loci of contextual effects. Suppose the abscissa represents (psychological) dimension I, and the ordinate represents (psychological) dimension II. There are then three likely loci for contextual effects: (1) projections of points on the dimensions (scale values); (2) distance calculations (Ψ_{ij}); (3) the judgment function relating overt judgments of similarity to subjective distances.

Suppose, for example, the judge's task was to rate the "similarity" between pairs of squares that vary in size and reflectance. There are three kinds of distributions to consider: (1) the marginal distribution of square sizes and the marginal distribution of square darknesses; (2) the joint distribution of sizes and darknesses; (3) the distribution of distances (which depends on the pairs presented for similarity judgment).

Manipulation of the marginal distributions in such a task seems analogous to the cross-modality experiments of Mellers and Birnbaum (1980a). It seems likely that manipulation of the range and spacing of the levels will affect the scale values (projections on the axes). It also seems likely that the difference in size coordinates between two given squares will vary with the total range of squares and the number of squares intermediate in size. Variation in stimulus spacing would presumably produce nonlinear changes in the projections (of the stimuli on the axes) in the usual multidimensional scaling solution.

Variation in the joint distribution would be expected to affect distance judgments so as to increase the judged dissimilarity between two points that have a large number of points "between" them in space. Krumhansl's (1978) model attempts to deal only with this aspect of contextual effects. However, her model does not reduce to range-frequency theory in one dimension, because it deals only with the densities in the regions of the points rather than in the space between them. It may be preferable to define the density term as a weighted integral of the stimulus density within an ellipsoid (based on the two points x and y as foci) where the weights are a function of the distance from x. It seems likely that the judged distance between two points will be greater when the stimulus density in this region "between" points is greater. This version would reduce to range-frequency theory in one dimension with suitable ellipse and weighting function.

E. SYSTEXTUAL DESIGN

There is a fundamental difference between physics and psychophysics that has long troubled psychologists (Baird & Noma, 1978; Luce, 1972). In classical physics, the measuring devices do not "remember" their previous measurements. Measurements of length or mass, for example, do not depend on the other lengths or masses previously measured. However, human judges give different responses to the same stimulus depending on the other stimuli forming the context for judgment, as illustrated in Sections A and D. Obviously, numerical judgments of subjective values cannot be regarded as analogous to the readings of voltmeters or thermometers. Figures 17.2 and 17.3, for example, show that category ratings and magnitude estimations of single stimuli depend on the stimulus spacing and response range. Figure 17.18 shows that scale values derived from cross-modality comparisons and "total" intensity judgments depend on the stimulus distribution. Figure 17.20 shows that the test of parallelism depends on the distribution of combinations.

Because the results of psychological experiments depend on the distribution of treatments to which the subject is exposed, psychologists have become concerned with the implications for generalization. At least four distinct methodological positions have emerged: standardized design, representative design, between-subjects design, and systextual design. In standardized design, the context is fixed to some conventional value. In representative design, the aim is to survey the environment and use the context to which generalization is desired. Between-subjects designs hope to "avoid" the context by allowing each subject to choose his or her own context. Systextual design systematically manipulates context.

Standardized Design

In standardized design, procedures for the conduct of research are agreed upon. If scientists all agree to do the same experiment, they should all obtain the same results. This position assumes that certain variables can cause a nuisance when left uncontrolled by different experimenters. In physics, for example, a calorie has been defined as the amount of heat required to raise one gram of water one degree Celsius at 4°C. Because the heat required to raise water temperature by a given amount depends on the temperature, it is necessary to qualify the temperature, that is, to agree to standardize our measurements. Much can be said in favor of the reasonableness of this approach. If psychology can develop consistent laws that hold in some restricted domain (no matter how restricted), we will have the beginnings of a science.

One unfortunate offshoot of the approach of standardization has been what can be called a *standardization of circularity* (perhaps analogous to the use of persuasive definition in philosophy). The circular standardization argues that the "right" way to do research is by the method that yields results compatible with a pet theory and therefore anyone who deviates from the approved method cannot be taken seriously. For example, it is possible to adjust the spacing of the stimuli so that the data for a magnitude-estimation study actually approximate a power function of physical value. It is also possible to select the stimulus spacing to produce deviations from a power function (as in Fig. 17.3). Because the power function was once thought to be the "right" function, any procedure that maximized the fit of it was deemed a "good" procedure. As Poulton (1979) has remarked, finding a stimulus spacing that produces a fit to the power function does not provide support for the power function; it merely demonstrates that the researcher has knowledge (at some level, perhaps implicit) of the stimulus spacing effect. Surprisingly, Poulton (1979) advocates geometric spacing as the "right" procedure, though he offers no theoretical justification. Stevens, Anderson, and others have given (conflicting) pronouncements concerning proper procedures for psychophysical studies, and their suggestions have unfortunately become orthodoxy to many persons.

Perhaps a time may come for psychologists to agree to adopt a set of standardized procedures. However, such agreement should not (and hopefully will not) occur until the scientific questions under investigation have been settled. Until that time, there is a danger that a theory will be accepted prematurely and will bring with it a set of orthodox, "right" procedures that will prevent its modification or falsification.

Criteria for Evaluating Methods

A set of criteria for evaluating psychophysical methods would seem useful. The following criteria, which have been implicitly suggested, do *not* seem appropriate ones:

1. Proper methods are those that yield results consistent with the power law. (Problem: The power law may not be appropriate.)
2. Proper methods are those that yield data that are parallel (fit the additive model). (Problem: The model predicting parallelism may not be valid.)
3. Proper methods are those that avoid the possibility of testing invariance properties of the scales. (Problem: By avoiding the possibility of testing the invariance properties, one does not establish invariance, one merely avoids the issue.)

The following considerations seem more useful for evaluating psychophysical methods and theories.

1. A psychophysical scale consists of a set of scale values used to reproduce the rank order of empirical data in terms of a theory.
2. The value of the scale is enhanced if it can be shown that the scale values cannot be arbitrarily transformed (beyond the uniqueness of the model) and still reproduce the rank order of the data. In other words, the more the scale is constrained by the data the better. (One can consider the scale values to be parameters estimated from data.)
3. A psychophysical scale should not only operate in a single situation, but it should show generality across situations (scale convergence). Thus, a theory involving one set of scale values and a pair of theories for two

empirical situations is preferred to one using two different scales and two different theories.

Methods that allow one to assess the scales in terms of these three considerations should be preferred over methods that do not permit these tests.

Consider Poulton's (1979) suggestion to use equal geometric spacing of the stimuli in magnitude-estimation experiments. How can one decide if this suggestion is reasonable? How do we know we are obtaining the "true" result? The experimental design *precludes* the possibility of establishing contextual invariance or demonstrating that the "true" result has been obtained.

Between-Subjects Design

Poulton (1979) has listed many of the factors that influence the outcome of direct scaling studies (as in Figs. 17.2 and 17.3) and has argued that contextual effects (which he regards as "biases") can and should be "avoided." Poulton (1973) suggested that such effects can be "avoided" by using a special type of standardized design in which the observer is presented with only one level of the treatment. A standardized design in which each subject receives only one treatment combination is called a between-subjects design.

The idea behind between-subjects designs (and certain other suggestions by Poulton for experimental procedure) is that there is an ideal laboratory condition that can and should be achieved in psychology. In physics, for example, Galileo's law of falling bodies would not be verified in the atmosphere. Galileo's critics noted that when two objects are dropped, the coin strikes the earth before the feather. In Galileo's time, nature still abhorred the vacuum, so it was not possible to conduct the experiment under reduced atmospheric conditions. But today, many museums demonstrate a low pressure tube in which coin and feather do fall together. Being confident in Galileo's premise, we now feel that the vacuum is the "right" context for conducting the study.

Poulton's (1973, 1979) suggestions to "avoid" contextual effects seem based on the proposition that they are analogous to friction in the physics lab. For example, in response to the stimulus spacing effects and effects of examples in the instructions (as in Fig. 17.3), Poulton (1979) recommends presenting the subject with only one stimulus and giving the subject no examples. Unfortunately, we cannot achieve a psychological vacuum in our judges' minds by presenting them with only one stimulus. Just because we have not presented other stimuli for judgment does not mean that our subjects, who are usually adults, have never before experienced a stimulus. There are two kinds of contexts: the context the subject brings to the laboratory and the context provided in the laboratory. Subjects' judgments depend on both. Therefore, when a subject is given a single stimulus to judge, the subject brings extralaboratory contexts to the task. It is even possible that when a different stimulus is presented to each subject that the context will be confounded with the stimulus.

Confounding of Contexts in Between-Subjects Designs

It may be that many of the counterintuitive findings so well-liked in social psychology are merely results of the *confounding of contexts* that can occur in between-subjects designs. To explain this point, consider an experiment by Jones and Aronson (1973) on the judged fault of rape victims. Which victim is most at fault for her own rape: the housewife, virgin, or divorcée? Jones and Aronson (1973) presented each subject with *only one* case history and found that the divorcée was rated *least* at fault and the virgin and married woman were *more* at fault (see Fig. 17.22). They interpreted this result in terms of a "just world" hypothesis. In a "just world," you get what you deserve. What you deserve (presumably) depends on *who you are* and *what you do*. If the victim did not deserve to be raped because of *who she was* (e.g., respectable, married), she must have *done something* to deserve it, and therefore, according to this theory, the more respectable victim should be rated *more* at fault.

It is difficult, but possible, to replicate the Jones and Aronson (1973) experiment using a between-subject design. In 1973 at Kansas State University, the effect was observed in a between-subject design only if the fault of the defendant was not rated, but the effect was reversed if both victim and defendant were rated (see Fig. 17.23). At the University of Illinois, at a time when a local rapist was causing great concern on campus, in a between-subjects design it was found that 10.5%, 10.4%, and 4.7% of 76, 67, and 85 subjects thought the virgin, housewife, and divorcée, respectively, were at fault exceeding 15 (on a 1–20 scale) for their own rape.

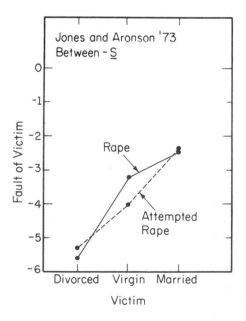

FIG. 17.22. Judged fault of rape victim as a function of victim's respectability in a between-subject design (Jones and Aronson, 1973). One group of subjects rated the fault of the divorced victim to be less than the average rating of fault given by another group of subjects who rated only the raped virgin. From Birnbaum (1980c).

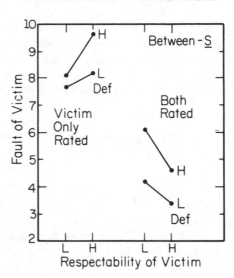

FIG. 17.23. Mean judgments of fault of victim as a function of victim's respectability, with a separate curve for each level of defendant's respectability. Each point is based on the mean judgment of a different group of judges who received only one type of case history. Data on left are for judges who rated only the victim. Data on the right are for judges who rated the fault of both victim and defendant. From Birnbaum (1980c).

However, in a within-subject design (Birnbaum, 1980c), it has been found that the judged fault of a victim *decreases* with increasing victim respectability. Judged fault of the victim is also greater when the defendant is higher in respectability and is lower for more severe crimes. These results are shown in Fig. 17.24, which plots judged fault as a function of the respectability of the victim, with a separate curve for each level of respectability of the defendant. It there-

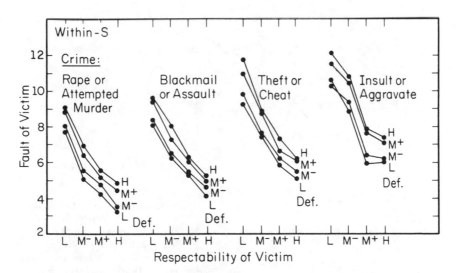

FIG. 17.24. Mean judgments of fault of victim as a function of victim's respectability in within-subject design, with a separate curve for each level of respectability of the defendant and a separate set of curves for each level of crime. From Birnbaum (1980c).

fore appears that the conclusion of Jones and Aronson (1973) can be reversed by changing from a between-subject to a within-subject design.

One can understand the finding that results change for between- vs. within-subject designs in this case by realizing that *in the between-subjects design, the stimulus and the context are completely confounded.* It is like the old stand-up joke:

Person 1. "How's your wife?"
Person 2. "Compared to what?"

Similarly, in a between-subjects experiment, the judge may ask him or herself, "How much at fault is this (former) virgin for her own rape? Compared to what? Compared to *other virgins,* perhaps."

Figure 17.25 shows a range-frequency analysis, assuming that virgins on the average are perceived to be more "innocent" than divorcées. In this analysis, a *raped virgin* is *more* innocent than a *raped divorcée* (see arrows on abscissa). But, she will be rated *less* innocent (more at fault) because *relative to the distribution of virgins,* a raped virgin is less innocent than a divorcée is *relative to the distribution of divorcées.* The curves show the predictions of range-frequency theory applied to the (presumed) distributions for this social judgment task. This interpretation explains how within- and between-subjects designs can give different results.

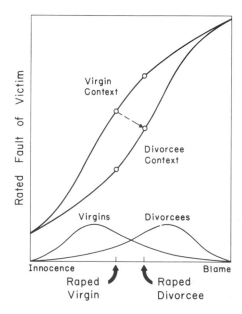

FIG. 17.25. A range-frequency analysis of social judgment in between-subject designs. Stimulus value and context are confounded in a between-subject design. In this case, the raped virgin is psychologically *less* at fault than a divorcée, but rated *more* at fault in a between-subjects design. Distributions show assumed contexts for different groups; curves are based on range-frequency theory. From Birnbaum (1980c).

It is not unusual in a between-subject design for the smaller stimulus to be judged greater. For example, in Figs. 17.2 and 17.3, the 27 dot pattern (in the positive context) is judged darker than is the 40 dot pattern (in the negative context). However, *within* each context (i.e., within subjects), the 40 dot stimulus is always judged darker. Therefore, comparing judgments of stimuli between groups of subjects who experience different contexts can be misleading.

Representative Design

Brunswik (1956) contended that the effects of psychological variables could depend on the experimental design—that is, on the range, spacing, and intercorrelations of the independent variables. Brunswik was concerned because in the natural environment, variables are correlated; whereas, in systematic research, variables are made independent in order to test theories of causation. He argued that if the correlation between variables is crucial to the subjects' performance and if the correlation is altered in the lab, then the results of systematic experiments would not generalize beyond the lab.

As an alternative to systematic design, Brunswik (1956) suggested representative design (see also Petrinovich, 1979, for a recent review). In representative design, the experimenter surveys the ecology (the subject's environment) and attempts to sample from it representatively. Brunswik also introduced the idea of *hybrid* design, discussing an example in which a factorial design of facial features (with schematic faces) was altered to produce a more representative correlation between two facial features.

Representative design is based on two ideas. First, it is based on the theory that the results of psychological investigations depend on the experimental design. This contention is reasonable in light of experimental evidence, including that presented in Section D. Second, it is based on the assumption that the foundation of generalization is representative sampling. In order to generalize from a political survey to an election, for example, pollsters attempt to obtain a representative sample. Statistical theory gives a rational basis for making inferences about population parameters on the basis of statistics computed from random samples. Problems of attempting to generalize from biased samples are well-known. Representative design emphasizes that treatments and situations should be sampled as well as subjects.

From these two ideas, Brunswik (1956) argued that psychologists should be willing to sacrifice experimental control for the sake of representativeness. He contended that systematic experiments are necessarily nonrepresentative because they are designed to unconfound variables that are actually confounded in nature.

There are two major problems with representative design. First, without experimental control, inferences of causation are unsound and dangerous. Second, the key element for generalization is not representative sampling but theory.

Let us consider, for example, a possible representative design for the study of health as a function of medical care. In each 6 month interval, the number of visits to a doctor and the state of the patient's health are recorded. In a representative design, people who see doctors more often have poorer health. This apparent harmful effect would persist even if the patient's diagnosis was partialed out; for example, among cancer patients, those seeing the doctor more often are in worse health. Only in a *very peculiar and nonrepresentative sample,* in which patients are randomly assigned to treatment vs. placebo conditions, is it possible to detect a beneficial effect of modern medicine. This example shows that correlations in representative samples can show relationships *opposite* of the direction of causation as inferred from systematic experimental research.

Reviewing the history of science, one finds many good examples of research that could not have succeeded with representative design. For example, the development of penicillin, television, the electric generator, Mendel's laws of genetics, and atomic and subatomic theory could not have occurred in representative research. These successes occurred because scientists were able to control simple situations in their laboratories and create new situations that do not occur in nature. It is difficult to find good counterexamples, where representative observation led to important results. The contributions of Jenner and Semmelweiss may fall in this category, but even their discoveries, which at first were based on observation of correlations, were doubted until verified by systematic research.

Two Notions of Generalization: Sampling vs. Theory

Let us consider two notions of generalization for an example experiment. An experimenter has tested a new drug using five fixed levels of concentration: .01, .02, .04, .08, and .16 moles/liter. Of the rats who have ingested lg per kg body weight of this mixture, the percentage who die within 1 hour is 2.5%, 16%, 50%, 84%, and 97.5% for the five levels of increasing dosage. According to the logic behind representative design, there is no basis for generalizing to levels intermediate in value or beyond the levels tested. There is also no basis for generalization from rats to humans. However, few people would be willing to ingest lg per kg body weight of a .32M concentration of this drug. The reason for this reluctance is that one generalizes to levels not tested from a *theory,* such as the following:

$$\text{Proportion killed} = F \text{ (dosage)} \tag{E.1}$$

where F is a monotonic function. We also theorize that if the drug kills rats, it would likely kill humans even though the drug has never been tested on humans before. This prediction is based on the very primitive theory that what kills one mammal is likely to kill another, a theory supported by considerable evidence. Furthermore, we might be willing to fit F to a particular function (cumulative normal log dose) and predict that if a concentration of .0566 moles/liter were used, about 69% of the rats would die. Such prediction and extrapolation is based on *theory*, not representative sampling.

Let us return to the problem of psychophysical judgment and examine the consequences of different design strategies. Suppose we were interested in obtaining judgments of the heaviness of lifted weights. A standardized design would use a given stimulus range with a given stimulus spacing (a large range with geometric spacing has been advocated). A between-subjects design would present each subject with only one weight to lift. A representative design would survey the objects lifted in everyday life. This could be done by following people around and asking them to judge the heaviness of every object they happened to lift. The experimenter would then record the weights and other characteristics of the objects. By means of multiple regression, one would establish the effect of weight, size, etc. on heaviness judgments.

What can be made of the equation that predicts heaviness as a function of weight and other characteristics of the objects? Providing it is based on sufficient data, the function for weight obtained from this study can be used to give a reasonable statistical estimate of heaviness judgments as a function of weight in the population of objects from which the experiment can be considered a random sample. One *cannot* generalize beyond this population to other populations. Thus, representative design holds the context fixed to the context to which generalization is desired, and it provides no basis for generalization beyond the context studied. In order to generalize to all contexts, systematic manipulation of the contexts and development of contextual theory are required.

Systextual Design

Systextual design refers to systematic manipulation of the context (Birnbaum, 1975). The logic of systextual design is based on two premises: (1) it is necessary to manipulate the context in order to learn its effect; (2) one needs to develop a theory of context in order to generalize across contexts.

In the physics example, the approach of systextual design would be to develop a theory of the friction and thereby to predict observed departures from simple physical laws. By means of the theory, one could extrapolate to the frictionless situation or predict the results in a friction-filled one.

In the case of psychophysics, Parducci's research can be seen as an example of systematic manipulation of the range, stimulus spacing, frequency, response procedure, and so on. Parducci's range-frequency theory provides the possibility of predicting the judgment of a stimulus in any context—not just the standard context, or a subject's personal context, or the ecological context—but in principle it allows prediction to results across different contexts. Birnbaum (1974c) has shown how one can use range-frequency theory to derive a psychophysical scale from contextual effects in a fashion that demonstrates the invariance of the derived scale as a byproduct of fitting the theory.

In Birnbaum's (1974c) experiment, subjects judged the magnitude of numbers presented in one of nine stimulus spacings. Because the stimulus end points are fixed and because the psychophysical function was assumed to be strictly monotonic and error free, Birnbaum's (1974c) development of range-frequency theory yields:

$$\mathbf{C}_{ik} = aF_k(\Phi_i) + s_i \tag{E.2}$$

where $\mathbf{C}_{ik}$ is the rating of stimulus i in context k, $F_k(\Phi_i)$ is the cumulative proportion of stimuli less than Φ_i in context k, a is the weight of the frequency principle, and s_i is the scale value of stimulus i (calibrated on a linear scale). Once a has been estimated (which can be done using multiple linear regression with dummy variables for s), the equation can be written:

$$s_i = \mathbf{C}_{ik} - aF_k(\Phi_i) \tag{E.3}$$

Thus, by subtracting $aF_k(\Phi_i)$ from each category rating, it should be possible to derive a scale of psychological value that is the same for all contexts. Plotting $\mathbf{C}_{ik} - aF_k(\Phi_i)$ versus Φ_i should produce a set of curves for different contexts that all coincide, as in Birnbaum (1974c, Fig. 5).

Another example of systextual design is given in Birnbaum (1975). Judges were asked to press down on one end of a lever, lifting a weight at some distance from the fulcrum, and judge the force required to do so. The judge who understands the physics of the lever should expect the force required (to lift a weight) to vary directly with the distance of the weight from the fulcrum. However, in the systextual design, different weights were used to produce different correlations between force and position for different groups. A factorial design of force and position was embedded in an overall positive, negative, or zero correlation. In accord with Birnbaum and Veit (1973) and Birnbaum, Kobernick, and Veit (1974), it was theorized that judgments reflect a contrast between required force and expected force and that expected force depends on both the position and the subjective correlation between force and position. The model can be written

$$\mathbf{E}_{ijk} = Q_i - P_j R_k \tag{E.4}$$

where $\mathbf{E}_{ijk}$ is the judgment of the effort required, P_j is the position (distance from the fulcrum), R_k is the subjective correlation in context k, and Q_i is the effect due to actual force required. The results were consistent with the model and showed that the effect of position can indeed be reversed by reversing the correlation between force and position.

This experiment together with those of Birnbaum and Veit (1973) and Birnbaum et al. (1974) show that Brunswik was justified in his concern that the correlations among variables can affect the results of psychological experiments. Indeed, the effect of position can be reversed by changing its correlation with the variable to be judged. However, contrary to Brunswik's contention, it is possible to nest a systematic factorial design inside an overall correlation between variables and to systematically manipulate the overall correlation. Furthermore, by means of such systextual design, it is possible to demonstrate the effect of the correlation and to develop a theory that permits generalization across correlations.

In summary, systematic design and representative design both hold the context fixed, and between-subject design confounds the context and the stimulus. Therefore, these designs do not permit tests of the empirical propositions upon which they are based. Systextual design calls for systematic manipulation of context and development of theory for generalization across contexts.

F. METHODOLOGY: ON MODEL TESTING AND MEASUREMENT

Conclusions regarding psychophysical processes are no better than the experimental, theoretical, and methodological foundations upon which they are based. In the study of psychophysical theories, it is useful to examine the logic of model testing and measurement carefully.

Anderson's functional measurement approach has had great impact on recent developments in psychophysical theory. The approach has many strong points in comparison with certain other approaches that have been well-expounded elsewhere (Anderson, 1970, 1977, 1979; Birnbaum, 1973, 1974b) and need not be repeated here. Instead, this section takes a critical look at the logic of functional measurement, from the skeptic's point of view. It is hoped that progress can be made by working to detect and strengthen weaknesses.

The following subsections review two substantive issues, impression formation and the size-weight illusion, to illustrate how weaknesses in the application of functional measurement led to the erroneous conclusion that these two processes could be represented by a parallel-averaging model. These two issues have been cited by Anderson (1979) to illustrate advantages of functional measurement, but they also serve well to illustrate limitations of the approach. Papers that have proposed methods to remedy defects in functional measurement are reviewed to show that previous conclusions regarding impression formation and the size-weight illusion do not stand up under improved experimental and analytical methods.

Six problems with simplistic applications of functional measurement are discussed. Several of these issues have been acknowledged by Anderson, but they have not been given sufficient attention. The following conclusions are discussed:

1. The fit of a model does not simultaneously validate the model, stimulus scale, and response scale.
2. Functional measurement is not a "neutral judge" between category rating and magnitude estimation.

3. Agreement of estimated scale values across tasks does not validate functional measurement.
4. Marginal means may not be linearly related to scale values even if the additive model fits the data (when the experiment lacks constraint).
5. The logic of two-stage integration analysis is inconsistent.
6. Methods involving the use of scale convergence and scale-free tests yield results that contradict previous conclusions from scale dependent research regarding the size-weight illusion and impression formation.

Parallelism Test

In functional measurement, a key method of analysis is the use of factorial design and analysis of variance. For example, the subject could be asked to judge the "average" sensation produced by two stimuli, A_i and B_j, where A_i and B_j have been factorially combined. The responses are plotted as a function of A_j with a separate curve for each level of B_i. Parallelism of the curves is equivalent to zero interaction between A and B.

In terms of the outline in Fig. 17.7, a set of premises that lead to parallelism can be listed as follows:

1. stimulus independence (e.g., s_{A_i} is independent of j)

2. $\Psi_{ij} = \dfrac{w_0 s_0 + w_A s_{A_i} + w_B s_{B_j}}{w_0 + w_A + w_B}$

3. $\mathbf{R}_{ij} = a\,\Psi_{ij} + b$

where s_{A_i} and s_{B_j} are scale values for the rows and columns, respectively, s_0 is the scale value of the initial impression and w_0 is its weight, w_A and w_B are the weights of the row and column factors, respectively, Ψ_{ij} is the subjective impression, $\mathbf{R}_{ij}$ is the overt response, and a and b are constants. Premise 2 is called the parallel-averaging model.

This model predicts that when $\mathbf{R}_{ij}$ is plotted against the column marginal mean ($\bar{\mathbf{R}}_{.j}$) with a separate curve for each row, the curves should be linear and parallel. Thus, if the curves are *not* parallel, one should question the premises. If the curves *are* parallel, the premises can be retained.

However, parallelism does not validate the model, stimulus scale, and response scale all at once. True conclusions can be deduced from false premises. There are many sets of premises from which parallelism could be deduced. Some of these alternatives are shown in Table 17.2.

For example, the model could be multiplicative, and the judgment function could be logarithmic. It follows that $\mathbf{R}_{ij} = a\log \Psi_{ij} + b = a\log(s_{A_i} s_{B_j}) + b = a\log s_{A_i} + a\log s_{B_j} + b = s^*_{A_i} + s^*_{B_j} + b$ where $s^*_{A_i} = a\log s_{A_i}$. Therefore, a multi-

TABLE 17.2
A Few Ways to Explain Parallelism

Theory[a]	Psychophysical Function H	Combination Function C	Judgment Function J
1	(independence)	$\Psi_{ij} = s_{A_i} + s_{B_j}$	$\mathbf{R}_{ij} = a\Psi_{ij} + b$
2	(independence)	$\Psi_{ij} = s_{A_i} s_{B_j}$	$\mathbf{R}_{ij} = a\log\Psi_{ij} + b$
3	(independence)	$\Psi_{ij} = \sqrt{s_{A_i}^2 + s_{B_j}^2}$	$\mathbf{R}_{ij} = a\Psi_{ij}^2 + b$
4	$s'_{A_{i(j)}} = s_{A_i} + ks_{B_j}$		
	$s'_{B_{j(i)}} = s_{B_j} + ks_{A_i}$	$\Psi_{ij} = s'_{A_{i(j)}} + s'_{B_{j(i)}}$	$\mathbf{R}_{ij} = a\Psi_{ij} + b$

[a]Theory 1, 2, 3, and 4 can be titled the additive model, multiplicative model, Pythagorean model, and change of value model, respectively. These are some of the many alternative representations of parallelism.

plicative model could produce parallel data if the *J* function is logarithmic. Therefore, parallelism does not establish the validity of the response scale unless the additive (or parallel-averaging) model is assumed. Parallelism does not test the validity of the additive model unless the linear *J* function is assumed. Some additional constraint is needed (beyond arbitrary stipulation) to specify the functions of functional measurement.

Suppose the curves are nonparallel. How can nonparallelism be interpreted? There are two cases. In the first case, it may be possible to reject the additive or parallel-averaging model on the basis of the ordinal information in the data, when the data systematically violate independence or double cancellation (Krantz & Tversky, 1971). In the second case, the numerical data are not parallel, but they can be rescaled to parallelism by means of a monotonic transformation. In this case, it is not possible without additional constraint to specify whether the nonparallelism is due to a nonadditive integration function or to a nonlinear *J* function. This point is expanded upon in the discussion of impression formation and the size-weight illusion.

A debate between proponents of conjoint measurement (Krantz et al., 1971) and Anderson occurred over the propriety of rescaling data from Sidowski and Anderson (1967) who found an interaction between cities and occupations for judgments of job desirability. Krantz et al. (1971) rescaled the mean judgments to parallelism and argued that the interaction analyzed by Sidowski and Anderson could be without psychological significance.

Thus, if the data are parallel, many combinations of $J[C(s_i, s_j)]$ are possible. If the data are not parallel, but can be rescaled to parallelism, many combinations of $J[C(s_i, s_j)]$ are still possible. Some have concluded that the parallelism test is therefore nondiagnostic. However, it does have value because the realm of possibilities for *J* and *C* in the parallel and nonparallel cases are different.

Is Functional Measurement a Neutral Judge?

Anderson (1972, and this volume) argued that functional measurement serves as a "neutral judge" between magnitude estimation and category rating. This contention was illustrated with reference to an experiment by Weiss (1972), who obtained magnitude estimations and graphic ratings of the "average" darkness of two gray chips. Anderson argued that because subjects were instructed to "average," one should postulate a parallel-averaging model. The rating data were approximately parallel whereas the magnitude-estimation data showed bilinear divergence. Anderson concluded that ratings are "valid," but magnitude estimations are "biased and invalid."

At least three other studies have directly compared magnitude estimation with rating methods in situations employing factorial designs and the same task. Sarris and Heineken (1976) used these two procedures for the judgment of heaviness of size-weight blocks. Curtis and Rule (1978) extended the study of Weiss (1972) to include "average" lightness and darkness using the two-response procedures. Veit (1978) obtained ratings and magnitude estimations of "differences." Marks (1979) had subjects rate the "overall loudness" of a multicomponent tone using magnitude estimation and a graphic rating procedure. In each case, the effect of the response procedure was represented by changes in the J function. In each case, magnitude estimations were positively accelerated relative to ratings. In three of the studies, the *assumption* of an additive (or subtractive) model would lead to the conclusion that the J function for ratings is nearly linear, and the J function for magnitude estimation is positively accelerated. Marks (this volume) found that to *assume* the additive model for loudness summation required negatively accelerated J functions for both response procedures.

The size-weight experiment of Sarris and Heineken (1976) obtained results similar to those of Weiss (1972). Using magnitude estimations, the data were nearly consistent with a geometric averaging model (multiplicative). If one *assumes* that grayness "averaging" and the size-weight illusion can be represented by the parallel-averaging model (as did Anderson, 1972), one would conclude that the J function for magnitude estimation is nonlinear. If one were to *assume* that grayness "averaging" and the size-weight illusion should be represented by a geometric averaging model, however, one would conclude that magnitude estimations are "valid" and that ratings are "biased." Thus, the situation is circular. In order to decide on the "valid" scale, one must *assume* the model. To choose the appropriate model, one must *assume* the "valid" scale. Birnbaum and Veit (1974b) termed this problem "scale-dependence," in which the conclusions regarding the model depend on the arbitrary decision to place faith in the particular dependent variable and the particular context that led to either parallelism or bilinearity.

To argue that Weiss (1972) has shown magnitude estimation to be biased requires the assumption either that ratings are valid (making the argument completely circular) or that the appropriate model is additive (which is semicircular). Were one to assume that the model is multiplicative (as in a geometric averaging model), it would be concluded that magnitude estimation is "valid" and category rating is "biased and invalid." Unless the model is assumed, the conclusion is scale dependent (Birnbaum & Veit, 1974b); unless the scale is assumed, the conclusion is model dependent.

Therefore, if functional measurement was truly neutral (i.e., did not prejudge the validity of the response scale or model), then the experiments cited by Anderson would be inconclusive on the question of the "validity" of ratings and magnitude estimations in experiments like that of Weiss (1972) and Sarris and Heineken (1976).

Anderson (1977) argued that the circularity of his conclusion regarding magnitude estimation can be ameliorated by considering the success of the parallelism test using category ratings in impression-formation research. However, it is shown next that the early work in impression formation was inadequate and reached erroneous conclusions.

Impression Formation

Perhaps no paper has been as often cited to illustrate Anderson's approach as his first article on impression formation (Anderson, 1962). Anderson (1962) had 12 subjects judge the likeableness of hypothetical persons described by sets of adjectives, using a 20-point rating scale. Anderson's theory of these data can be written as follows:

$$\Psi = \sum_{i=0}^{k} w_i s_i \bigg/ \sum_{i=0}^{k} w_i, \tag{F.1}$$

where Ψ is the integrated impression, w_i and s_i are weight and scale value of adjective i, and w_0 and s_0 are the weight and scale value of a postulated initial impression.

The adjective combinations were generated from a factorial design. Anderson noted that: (1) if the weights are independent of scale value; (2) if the scale value of each adjective is independent of the other adjectives with which it is paired; (3) if the response scale is "valid" (i.e., J is linear); and (4) if impressions are governed by Eq. F.1, then the data would show parallelism, and there would be nonsignificant interactions among the adjective factors in analysis of variance. Anderson (1962) found that the majority of his 12 subjects had nonsignificant interactions.

What can be concluded from the experiment? It has been contended that the fit of the model simultaneously "validates" the stimulus scale, response scale, and model all at once. However, as just noted, this view is oversimplified, for the conclusion in principle is scale dependent. Furthermore, it can also be shown that the basic finding does not replicate.

A Divergent Finding.   Anderson's (1962) conclusions regarding impression formation were challenged by Birnbaum (1974a, Exp. 1), who obtained a large divergent interaction for ratings of likeableness. The left of Fig. 17.26 shows mean judgments of likeableness as a function of one adjective with a separate curve for each level of the other. The means in Fig. 17.26 are averaged over six different sets of adjectives. Each off-diagonal point is the average of 600 judgments by 300 subjects. Results for individual adjectives are given in Birnbaum (1974a, Fig. 2). Although there are other aspects of individual adjective and subject data that are of interest (see Birnbaum, 1974a), the divergence shown in Fig. 17.26 was characteristic of individual data.

The interaction obtained by Birnbaum (1974a, Exp. 1) reopens all of the issues of impression formation. Nonparallelism indicates that impression formation may violate the parallel-averaging model, that J could be nonlinear, that the scale values of the adjectives could change as a function of the adjectives with which they are paired, or any of a number of other possibilities.

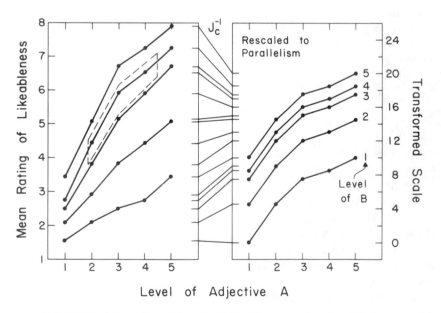

FIG. 17.26.   Mean ratings of (combined) likeableness as a function of the level of likeableness of adjective A, with a separate curve for each level of adjective B. Mean ratings (left panel) are not parallel, but they can be monotonically rescaled to parallelism, as shown in panel on the right. Dashed box shows that domain of Lampel and Anderson (1968) was small in comparison with that of Birnbaum (1974a). From Birnbaum (1980b).

A more prosaic possibility is that the difference in results between Anderson (1962) and Birnbaum's Experiment 1 (1974a) is due to differences in experimental procedure. It was once argued that the parallel-averaging model held, but only under very special experimental conditions. Birnbaum (1974a) systematically varied the experimental procedures to see if any of the following manipulations would remove the interaction experimentally: The category scale labels were reversed, a 20-point anchored scale was used, a line mark response scale was used, a matching procedure (analogous to method of adjustment) was used to eliminate numerical response, and "equal accuracy and importance" instructions were tried. No evidence was found that the interaction could be removed by these variations in the experimental procedure. The divergent interaction appeared with all of these procedures.

Rescaling to Parallelism.   In order to rescue the parallelism-predicting averaging model (Eq. F.1), it is possible to rescale the data in the left of Fig. 17.26 to parallelism, as shown on the right of Fig. 17.26. The scale values 0, 4.5, 7.5, 8.5, and 10 for the five levels can be added or averaged to produce the parallel curves on the right of Fig. 17.26. The rank order of the means can be perfectly reproduced by the parallel-averaging (or additive) model. Therefore, the divergence in the left of Fig. 17.26 could be explained either by the assumption that C (the model representing impression formation) contains an interaction, or that J (the judgment function) is nonlinear and C is a parallel-averaging (or additive) model.

The Rescaling Debate

It is instructive to discuss a possible debate between a mentalist measurer and a behaviorist model tester concerning the data in Fig. 17.26. The behaviorist declared that the data on the left of Fig. 17.26 allow one to refute Anderson's (1962) additive (or parallel-averaging) model of impression formation. The mentalist declared the data ordinally consistent with the parallelism model and used the model to measure scale values for the adjectives, as on the right of Fig. 17.26.

"But you're *assuming* the model I just disproved!" the model tester exclaimed.

The mentalist replied, "The data can be rescaled to additivity, so I see no problem."

"But the violation of parallelism in the raw data is inconsistent with the additive model," the behaviorist noted.

"Only if you assume that J is linear," the measurement mentalist said, becoming edgy. "It is simpler and more reasonable to assume that the parallel-averaging model described the combination process. After all, subjects can't be trusted to do any more than rank order their impressions."

The behaviorist grew confident, "I see no reason to postulate a J function at all. I have operationally defined likeableness in terms of my rating procedure. As a behaviorist, I want a model that describes the raw data I obtained. The raw data do not fit the additive model. As a model tester, I therefore reject the additive model in favor of a model with an interaction. You are fudging the data with your transformation. You are rescaling the data to fit the model and then trying to tell me that the model fits!"

The mentalist grew irritated and looked away as he said, "I find no reason to reject the model if the data satisfy the ordinal (rank order) requirements. The data are perfectly additive, in the ordinal sense that $R_{ij} > R_{kl}$ whenever $s_i + s_j > s_k + s_l$. You assume that J is linear and are trying to reject the model for no valid reason. Category ratings are nonlinearly related to magnitude estimations. How can we be convinced that the ratings shouldn't be monotonically transformed?"

"Anderson validated ratings by showing that impression-formation data are parallel," the behaviorist replied weakly.

The mentalist looked him in the eye and snapped, "Now you've contradicted yourself! You are *assuming* the model in order to *validate* the response scale you must assume for your test, and then you reject the model you assumed in the first place! Parducci has shown repeatedly that category ratings in two situations can be nonlinearly related if the stimulus distribution is changed. The change in stimulus distribution doen't change the rank order of the points, but it *does* change the apparent parallelism. Look at Fig. 17.20 in this chapter! You can't be sure that ratings are linearly related to subjective value because ratings in one context are nonlinearly related to ratings in another context, as in Fig. 17.21. Therefore, we must allow for nonlinear transformation of the data."

Just then, an aged philosopher stepped up with a look of condescension and said: "You two are arguing over a meaningless distinction. What difference does it make whether the interaction comes from C or J? You'll never be able to settle your dispute on empirical grounds, because the two theories are equivalent."

The next subsections show that, contrary to the philosopher, it is possible to design new experiments that can test between the two theories, if one is willing to accept the principle of scale convergence and the logic behind the scale-free test.

Scale-Convergence Criteria

To decide whether the interaction shown in Fig. 17.26 was "real" (i.e., due to C in Fig. 17.7) or reflecting only response "bias," (i.e., due to J) Birnbaum (1974a) advanced the criteria of stimulus and response scale convergence. The stimulus scale convergence criterion assumes that the likeableness scale values of adjectives should be independent of the task, which in this case was to judge "differences" in likeableness or "combinations" (integrated impressions). The response scale convergence criterion states that consistent principles determine the J function. It was postulated that if the same subjects used the same response procedure to judge the same stimuli on the same dimension presented in the same distribution, the J functions should be the same for both tasks (see Birnbaum, 1974a).

The stimulus scale convergence theory can be written as follows:

$$\mathbf{D}_{ij} = J_{\mathbf{D}}[s_j^* - s_i^*] \tag{F.2}$$

$$\mathbf{C}_{ij} = J_{\mathbf{C}}[\Psi_{ij}] \tag{F.3}$$

$$\Psi_{ij} = \frac{w_0 s_0 + w_A s_i + w_B s_j}{w_0 + w_A + w_B} \tag{F.4}$$

$$s_i^* = s_i \text{ (scale convergence)} \tag{F.5}$$

where $\mathbf{D}_{ij}$ and $\mathbf{C}_{ij}$ are the ratings of "differences" in likeableness between two different people, each described by an adjective, and overall (combined) likeableness of a person described by both adjectives. Equation F.5 explicitly assumes that $s^* = s$, i.e., that the scale value for the likeableness of an adjective is the same for both "combination" and "difference" tasks. The response scale convergence theory would allow s^*_i and s_i to be different, but would assume that $J_{\mathbf{C}}$ and $J_{\mathbf{D}}$ have the same functional form, within a linear transformation.

The data of Birnbaum (1974a, Exp. 3) required rejection of both scale convergence criteria if the parallel-averaging model was assumed. However, both criteria could be retained if the parallel-averaging model was rejected. Figure 17.27 shows the results for the "differences" experiment (Birnbaum, 1974a, Exp. 3). Note that the data for "combinations" show a divergent interaction (left of Fig. 17.26) whereas the data for "differences" are nearly parallel. To retain the premise that $J_{\mathbf{D}}$ and $J_{\mathbf{C}}$ are both linear would require the rejection of the parallel-averaging model. To retain the subtractive model of "differences"

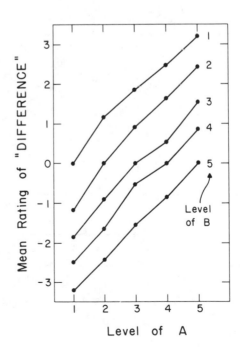

FIG. 17.27. Mean rating of "difference" in likeableness between two persons, each described by one adjective. From Birnbaum (1980b).

and the parallel-averaging model of "combinations" would require the rejection of the premise that J_D and J_C were of the same form. Assuming both models, J_C would be positively accelerating, and J_D would be linear.

However, if both models are assumed, the data violate stimulus scale convergence. To understand this, it is instructive to derive the ordinal constraints imposed by both the data and the additive model on the scale values and illustrate the systematic violations. Let $a = s_2 - s_1$, $b = s_3 - s_2$, $c = s_4 - s_3$, and $d = s_5 - s_4$ for the "combination" task. Let a^* to d^* be defined analogously for the "difference" task. The theoretical representations for the subtractive and additive models are shown in parentheses in Tables 17.3 and 17.4, together with the mean judgments.

By comparing the rank order of the "differences" with the theoretical representations in Table 17.4, it can be found that the scale for "differences" must satisfy the following: $0 < c^* < d^* < b^* < a^* < c^* + d^* < b^* + c^* < a^* + b^* < b^* + c^* + d^* < a^* + b^* + c^* < a^* + b^* + c^* + d^*$, which can be simplified, as follows:

$$0 < c^* < d^* < b^* < a^* < c^* + d^* \tag{F.6}$$

TABLE 17.3
Mean Ratings of Likeableness [a]

			Level of A		
Level of B	1	2	3	4	5
1	1.54 (0)	2.10 (a)	2.50 (a + b)	2.76 (a + b + c)	3.45 (a + b + c + d)
2	2.10 (2a)	2.92 (2a + b)	3.82 (2a + b + c)	4.44 (2a + b + c)	5.08 (2a + b + c + d)
3	2.50	3.82	5.15 (2a + 2b)	5.90 (2a + 2b + c)	6.72 (2a + 2b + c + d)
4	2.76	4.44	5.90	6 53 (2a + 2b + 2c)	7.25 (2a + 2b + 2c + d)
5	3.45	5.08	6.72	7.25	7.90 (2a + 2b + 2c + 2d)

[a] Each entry is the mean judgment of likeableness of a person described by both A and B. Each off-diagonal cell is averaged over six pairs of adjectives; 600 judgments from 300 subjects. Data from Birnbaum (1974a, Exp. 1). Algebraic symbols give additive representation, $C_{ij} = J_C[s_i + s_j]$, with $s_1 = 0$, $a = s_2 - s_1$, $b = s_3 - s_2$, $c = s_4 - s_3$, $d = s_5 - s_4$. Arrows represent inequalities showing that $a > b + c$ and $a > c + d$. Parallel-averaging model is equivalent to additive model in this case.

TABLE 17.4
Mean Ratings of "Differences" [a]

Level of B	Level of A				
	1	2	3	4	5
1	0	1.18	1.86	2.49	3.20
		(a^*)	$(a^* + b^*)$	$(a^* + b^* + c^*)$	$(a^* + b^* + c^* + d^*)$
2	-1.18	0	.92	1.64	2.43
			(b^*)	$(b^* + c^*)$	$(b^* + c^* + d^*)$
3	-1.86	$-.92$	0	.53	1.54
				(c^*)	$(c^* + d^*)$
4	-2.49	-1.64	$-.53$	0	.85
					(d^*)
5	-3.20	-2.43	-1.54	$-.85$	0

[a] Each number is the mean judgment of "difference" in likeableness, A–B. Each cell is averaged over six pairs of adjectives; 180 judgments from 90 subjects. Data from Birnbaum (1974, Exp. 3). Algebraic symbols give subtractive representation, $D_{ij} = J_D[s_j^* - s_i^*]$, with $s_1^* = 0$, $a^* = s_2^* - s_1^*$, $b^* = s_3^* - s_2^*$, $c^* = s_4^* - s_3^*$, $d^* = s_5^* - s_4^*$. Arrows represent inequalities showing that $a^* < b^* + c^*$ and $a^* < c^* + d^*$.

Notice that each difference between successive scale values is less than any two-step difference. A set of scale values satisfying Expression F.6 would be 0, 10, 18, 24, 31, where $a^* = 10$, $b^* = 8$, $c^* = 6$, and $d^* = 7$.

However, if the additive (or parallel-averaging) model is assumed, the rank order in Table 17.3 implies the following:

$$0 < c < d < b < b + c < a < b + c + d \qquad (F.7)$$

Note that $a > c + d$ and $a > b + c$, but $a^* < c^* + d^*$ and $a^* < b^* + c^*$. These contradictions in ordinal relationships for differences in scale value imply that s is nonlinearly related to s^*. In particular, Expressions F.6 and F.7 imply that the scale values for the additive model of "combinations" are concave downwards relative to the scale values estimated from the subtractive model applied to "differences." Thus, even allowing J_C and J_D to be any monotone functions, it is not possible to retain the theory expressed in Eqs. F.2 through F.5.

In summary, to conclude that the parallel-averaging model underlies impression formation and the subtractive model represents "difference" judgment would require rejection of both stimulus and response scale convergence criteria in favor of the conclusion that there are two different scales of likeableness, s^* and s, where s^* (for "differences") is positively accelerated relative to s, and two different output functions, J_C and J_D for category ratings, where J_C is positively accelerated, and J_D is nearly linear. The next subsection shows that it is possible to retain the scale convergence criterion and the subtractive model for stimulus comparison by rejecting the parallel-averaging model in favor of a configural-weight model.

Configural-Weight Model of Impression Formation

A simple configural-weight model can describe the data in the left of Fig. 17.26, using the scale values obtained from the fit of the subtractive model to "difference" judgments. The configural-weight averaging model assumes that the worst trait of a person receives extra weight. Figure 17.28 shows predictions for the configural-weight model using scale values of 0, 10, 18, 24, and 31 for the five levels of likeableness of the adjectives, assuming $s_0 = 17$. All weights were set to 1.0, but the lowest scale value in each set (which could be s_0 on some trials) was assumed to have a weight of 2.0. For example, the predicted value for cell $(1, 5)$ would be $(2 \cdot 0 + 1 \cdot 17 + 1 \cdot 31)/(2 + 1 + 1) = 12$. The predicted value for cell $(3, 3)$ would be $(2 \cdot 17 + 1 \cdot 18 + 1 \cdot 18)/(4) = 17.5$.

The predictions of the configural-weight model in Fig. 17.28 have the same rank order as the mean ratings in the left of Fig. 17.26, they show a similar pattern of divergent interaction, and they are based on the same scale values as for the subtractive model applied to "difference" judgments. The configural-weight theory differs from the parallel-averaging theory in that it postulates a

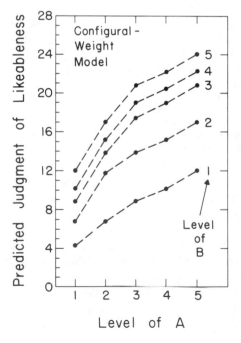

FIG. 17.28.   Predicted likeableness of combinations, based on a configural-weight model using scale values from "difference" task (Fig. 17.27). Note that rank order and shape of curves is the same as in the left of Fig. 17.26. From Birnbaum (1980b).

"real" psychological interaction between the adjectives: If a person has one bad trait, other traits will have less effect. (Configural-weight models are discussed in greater detail by Birnbaum [1974a] and Birnbaum & Stegner [1979], who also discuss a competing differential-weight averaging model, which can also predict divergence).

Thus, the following theory remains consistent with the data:

$$\mathbf{D}_{ij} = J_{\mathbf{D}}[s_j^* - s_i^*] \tag{F.8}$$

$$\mathbf{C}_{ij} = J_{\mathbf{C}}[\Psi_{ij}] \tag{F.9}$$

$$\Psi_{ij} = I[s_0, s_i, s_j] \tag{F.10}$$

$$s_i^* = s_i \tag{F.11}$$

where I is an integration rule for impression formation that contains a "real", divergent interaction. Figure 17.28 shows that a configural-weight model can reproduce the rank order of the combination data using a single set of scale values for both "differences" and "combinations" and using functions for both $J_{\mathbf{C}}$ and $J_{\mathbf{D}}$ that are nearly linear. In conclusion, by rejecting the parallelism-predicting models of impression formation, it is possible to retain scale convergence. To retain scale convergence requires rejection of the parallelism-predicting models of impression formation.

Scale-Free Tests of Impression Formation

It could be argued that the stimulus and response scale convergence criteria should be rejected, rather than the parallel-averaging model. Thus, it could be argued that there are different J functions *and* different scale values for the "difference" and "combination" tasks. Of course, such an argument is complicated, for it provides no theory to explain the change in scale values or J function beyond perhaps a vague remark that judgment proceeds in stages, so "why not insert a few more stages with internal transformations?"

In response to this possibility, Birnbaum, (1974a, Exp. 4) introduced the scale-free test. In the scale-free test of impression formation, subjects judge "differences" in likableness between pairs of hypothetical persons, each described by two adjectives. For example, how much more would you like a person described as *loyal* and *understanding* than one described as *loyal* and *malicious?*

These judgments of differences between combinations, **DC**, can be represented by the model:

$$\mathbf{DC}_{ijkl} = J[\Psi_{ij} - \Psi_{kl}] \tag{F.12}$$

where J is a monotone function and Ψ_{ij} and Ψ_{kl} are the integrated impressions of likableness.

If the parallelism-predicting model of impression formation is correct, then the following two judgments of "differences" should be equal:

1. *Loyal (L)* and *understanding (U)* vs. *loyal (L)* and *obnoxious (O)*.
2. *Malicious (M)* and *understanding (U)* vs. *malicious (M)* and *obnoxious (O)*.

According to Eq. F.12, the first "difference" can be represented $J[\Psi_{LU} - \Psi_{LO}]$, which according to the additive model can be written $J[s_L + s_U - s_L - s_O] = J[s_U - s_O]$. The second "difference" can be expressed $J[\Psi_{MU} - \Psi_{MO}] = J[s_U - s_O]$. Therefore, the judged "difference" between *loyal and understanding* compared with *loyal and obnoxious* should be *equal* to the judged "difference" between *malicious and understanding* compared with *malicious and obnoxious*. The alternative hypothesis, that the divergent interaction in the left of Fig. 17.26 is "real," predicts that the first "difference" is greater than the second "difference." This test between a null hypothesis of equality and a directional inequality assumes only that J is a strictly monotonic function. the test is termed "scale-free" because the conclusion regarding the additive model of impression formation is invariant with respect to strictly monotonic transformations of the "difference" judgments. All that matters is the rank order of the "difference" judgments.

The left side of Fig. 17.29 shows the result for a part of the scale-free test of

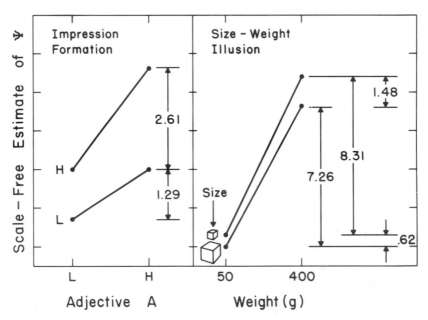

FIG. 17.29. Scale-free tests of additive (or parallel-averaging) model of impression formation and the size-weight illusion. No strictly monotonic transformation could rescale these data to parallelism. Subjects judge the "difference" between HH and HL to be 2.61, but they judge the "difference" between LH and LL to be only 1.29. Additive model requires that these two judgments be equal. From Birnbaum (1980b).

Experiment 4 of Birnbaum (1974a) for impression formation. For simplicity, only a portion of the design is presented here, and the means have been averaged over subjects and adjective replicates. (A constant has been added so that a zero "difference" is 0.) Figure 17.29 shows the divergence characteristic of ratings of likeableness in Fig. 17.26. Thus, the rank order of "difference" judgments *in this case* is predictable from differences in mean rating. It should be clear that the divergence in Fig. 17.29 would persist under any strictly monotonic transformation of the "difference" judgments.

The assumption of Eq. F.12 can be justified on the basis of Sections B and C in this chapter. However, even if Eq. F.12 were replaced with a ratio model of comparison, the conclusions regarding the additive model of impression formation would be the same (Birnbaum, 1979). Transformation to a ratio model of comparison would require exponential transformation, which would increase the divergence.

In sum, the scale-free test refutes the parallel-averaging model of impression formation.

Size-Weight Illusion

Anderson's (1972) experiment on the size-weight illusion has also been used frequently (e.g., Anderson, 1977, 1979) to illustrate his views on functional measurement and data analysis.

Anderson's (1972) data are shown in the left side of Fig. 17.30. Judgments of

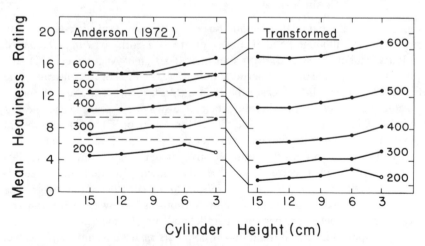

FIG. 17.30. Left panel shows mean judgments of heaviness from Anderson's (1972) study of the size-weight illusion. Dashed lines between curves show that the rank order of means does *not* constrain the scale values of heaviness. Entire curves can be shifted up or down without changing rank order of data. Points on right are monotonically related to original, and they fit the additive model equally well, yet transformed data imply scale values for heaviness that are a positively accelerated function of weight. From Birnbaum (1980b).

heaviness are plotted as a function of the size of the cylinder, with a separate curve for each level of weight. Although the interaction was statistically significant, Anderson attributed it to an experimental problem (he discarded the open point) and assumed the data were essentially parallel. If the model is additive, he reasoned, parallelism "validates" the response scale. Furthermore, he assumed that the spaces between the curves provided a scale of heaviness. Inasmuch as the spaces between the curves (representing 100 g increments) decreased as weight increased, Anderson concluded that heaviness is a negatively accelerated function of weight. Because magnitude-estimation experiments yielded exponents for heaviness greater than one, Anderson concluded that magnitude estimation must be "biased and invalid."

However, the data shown in Fig. 17.30 do not warrant such strong conclusions. Even if it were granted that the size-weight illusion is additive (which is disputed later), the data in Fig. 17.30 do not determine scale values for heaviness. To see why this is so, study the dashed lines in the left of the figure. These lines show that the data can be monotonically rescaled to many other equally additive solutions by shifting entire curves up or down. In other words, the rank order in Fig. 17.30 places virtually no constraints on the scale values for weight. For example, the right panel of the figure shows that the data can be rescaled to yield a positively accelerated psychophysical function for heaviness, in which the distances between successive curves actually *increase* with increasing weight.

Unconstrained Scale Values

Although the additive model constrains scale values to interval scale uniqueness *in principle,* and although parallelism demonstrates linearity of *J in principle* (if the additive model is assumed), the experimental design of Anderson (1972) fails to provide enough constraint either to test the linearity of *J* or to constrain scale values for heaviness. In this case, the failure to ask if the data allowed one to *refute* the possibility of a positively accelerated heaviness scale led to the unfounded conclusion that the additive model for Anderson's (1972) size-weight data was inconsistent with the heaviness scales from magnitude estimation.

If one is willing to consider multiplicative models, then even had the data been highly constrained, perfectly parallel, and shown a log-function for heaviness, the experiment could not *in principle* yield the conclusion that magnitude estimation is "biased and invalid." Suppose both the size-weight illusion and "averaging" task data were perfectly parallel and suppose the scale values were identical. Exponential transformation on both sets of data would yield perfect bilinearity, which would be deemed consistent with a multiplicative model. Furthermore, the so-called "cross-task validation" would still work. As Birnbaum and Veit (1974a, 1974b) predicted, and as Sarris and Heineken (1976) observed, when ratings fit additive (or subtractive) models, magnitude estimations tend to fit multiplying (or ratio) models. Anderson (1972) recognized the possibility of data transformation to other models but failed to point out that if magnitude estimations are exponentially related to ratings, then his conclusion regarding the validity of magnitude estimation would be an arbitrary decision rather than an empirical finding.

Scale-Free Test of Size-Weight Illusion

Birnbaum and Veit (1974b) noted that the situation with respect to the size-weight illusion is perfectly circular in scale-dependent research, such as that of Anderson (1972). If the additive model were assumed and ratings were additive, then ratings would be "validated." If the ratio model were assumed and magnitude estimations fit this model (as in Sarris & Heineken, 1976), then magnitude estimation would be "validated." Unless one model or one response scale is assumed, no conclusion can be drawn.

In order to go beyond the circular situation of scale-dependent research, Birnbaum and Veit (1974b) applied the scale-free test of Birnbaum (1974a, Exp. 4) to the size-weight illusion. Birnbaum and Veit (1974b) asked subjects to judge the "difference" in heaviness between pairs of size-weight blocks. It was assumed that "difference" ratings can be represented as follows:

$$\mathbf{D}_{ijkl} = J[\Psi_{ij} - \Psi_{kl}] \tag{F.13}$$

where Ψ_{ij} is the heaviness of weight i in block j. It follows from an additive (or parallel-averaging) model that the "difference" in heaviness between two blocks of the same weight but different sizes should be independent of that weight (t_i). If $\Psi_{ij} = t_i + s_j$, where t_i is the weight and s_j is the size, then $\mathbf{D}_{ijil} = J[t_i + s_j - t_i - s_l] = J[s_j - s_l]$. Thus, the additive model implies that the magnitude of the illusion should be independent of weight. Similarly, $\mathbf{D}_{ijkj} = J[t_i + s_j - t_k - s_j] = J[t_i - t_k]$.

On the other hand, if the divergent interaction observed by Sjöberg (1969) is real, then the magnitude of the illusion should increase as a function of weight. Similarly, if the interaction is "real," then the difference in heaviness between two different weights in blocks of the same size should depend on the common size (see Birnbaum, 1974a, Fig. 5).

Because these predictions of equality or inequality hold for any strictly monotonic function J, the test is a scale-free test. In other words, the conclusion regarding the additive model for the size-weight illusion would be invariant with respect to strictly monotonic transformation of the data.

Birnbaum and Veit (1974b) found a systematic violation: The difference in heaviness between two blocks of different sizes was larger when both blocks weighed 400 g than when both blocks weighed 50 g. Similarly, the judged difference in heaviness between two blocks of the same size that weighed 50 and 400 g was ranked larger when the block was small than when it was large. Fifteen of the 16 subjects in Experiment 2 showed these trends in the crucial rank-order test. The scale-free estimates of heaviness, derived from the subtractive model of comparison, are shown in the right of Fig. 17.29,where the numbers in the figure show the mean "difference" judgments.

Birnbaum and Veit (1974b) used a more extensive design than that just described. There were actually 21 size-weight blocks composed of seven levels of weight in blocks of three different sizes. These were factorially combined with four size-weight combinations (in the other hand) for comparison. The design was counterbalanced across the two hands, and there were two replicates, yielding a $2 \times 2 \times 4 \times (3 \times 7) = 336$-cell design. The 336 data points for each subject were rescaled to the following model:

$$J^{-1}(\mathbf{D}_{ijkl}) = \Psi_{ij} - \Psi_k + e_l \qquad\qquad (F.14)$$

where J^{-1} is a monotonic function, $\mathbf{D}_{ijkl}$ is the judged "difference" in heaviness, Ψ_{ij} is the heaviness of size-weight block of size i and weight j (with 21 levels), Ψ_k is the heaviness of the comparison block in the other hand (with four ⋅evels), and e_l is an additive effect of hand position and replication (with four levels).

The rescaled judgments were assessed by analysis of variance. Because the rescaling was based only on the subtractive model of "difference" judgment, it was neutral with respect to the size-weight illusion. Therefore, the scale-free estimates of Ψ_{ij} can be tested for additivity. Figure 17.31 shows the scale-free values of Ψ_{ij} that were derived from the rescaling. They show a similar divergent interaction to that in the simplified presentation of Fig. 17.29.

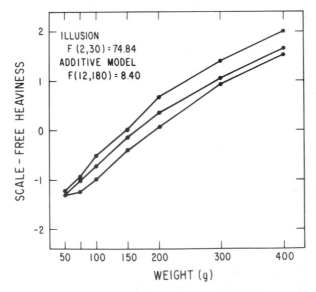

FIG. 17.31.   Estimated scale-free values of heaviness from Birnbaum and Veit's (1974b) study of the size-weight illusion. Nonparallelism (divergence) implies that the additive (or parallel-averaging) model is inconsistent with the data, and cannot be salvaged by strictly monotonic transformation.

In sum, the scale-free test refutes the additive or parallel-averaging model for the size-weight illusion and impression formation, contrary to the conclusions of Anderson (1962, 1972, 1977, 1979). These findings not only require different models for these two issues, but they also show that the methodology on which the previous conclusions were based was incomplete. Implications of the size-weight interaction for heaviness perception are discussed by Birnbaum (1975) and Birnbaum and Veit (1974b).

Scale-Free Test of Ratio-Difference Theories

The scale free test (as in Fig. 17.29) is also applicable to the ratio-difference controversy (Section C). If subjects perform differences between ratios when so instructed, the data should resemble those in the left of Fig. 17.29, that is $s_7/s_1 - s_5/s_1 > s_7/s_4 - s_5/s_4$ because:

$$\frac{1}{s_1} (s_7 - s_5) > \frac{1}{s_4} (s_7 - s_5) \tag{F.15}$$

On the other hand, if subjects judge differences between differences when instructed to judge "differences between ratios," the two judgments should be equal, for:

$$(s_7 - s_1) - (s_5 - s_1) = (s_7 - s_4) - (s_5 - s_4) \tag{F.16}$$

Thus, if observers made implicit magnitude estimations of "ratios" and then computed differences, the (divergent) inequality of Expression F.15 should hold. On the other hand, if observers judge differences between differences, the equality (F.16) should hold. For the darkness experiment described in Section C, it was found that the corresponding differences were nearly equal for both the "difference of differences" and "difference of ratios" tasks. This finding is consistent with the subtractive theory.

The ratio of differences model predicts the opposite ordering (for these pairs) from that predicted by the difference of ratios model:

$$\frac{s_7 - s_1}{s_5 - s_1} < \frac{s_7 - s_4}{s_5 - s_4} \tag{F.17}$$

The data for the "ratio of differences" task showed the rank order predicted by the ratio of differences model. Surprisingly, the "ratio of ratios" task also showed a small trend in the direction predicted by the ratio of differences model. It would be useful to see further applications of the scale-free test to the ratio-difference controversy.

On "Two-Stage" Integration

Anderson (1977, 1979) recently argued that when an experiment involves three or more variables, one can "validate" the response scale by finding nonsignificant interactions between two variables and therefore trust that significant interactions among the other variables are "real" and not attributable to nonlinearity in the judgment function.

To illustrate this idea, Anderson cited a paper by Lampel and Anderson (1968) in which college women were asked to evaluate hypothetical dates based on a photograph and two personality traits. The data are shown in Fig. 17.32, plotted as a function of the level of the first adjective with a separate curve for each level of the second. Data for low, medium, and high in attractiveness of photos are shown separately.

The constant-weight averaging model predicts that the two-by-two plots for each photo should be parallel. The interaction between adjectives was nonsignificant, averaged over levels of photos (although a divergent interaction between adjectives appears when the photo is high in attractiveness). Anderson concluded that the supposed lack of adjective-by-adjective interaction "validated" the response scale, and therefore the interaction between photos and personality traits was deemed to be "real" and not an artifact of the response scale.

However, this line of argument is not consistent. If it is to be *assumed* that adjectives do not interact, it must be shown that no transformation exists that eliminates the photo-by-personality interaction and simultaneously preserves (or produces) adjective-by-adjective parallelism. By this criterion for "validity," any transformation of the data that yields adjective-by-adjective parallelism would be deemed a "valid" rescaling. Therefore, if a transformation can be

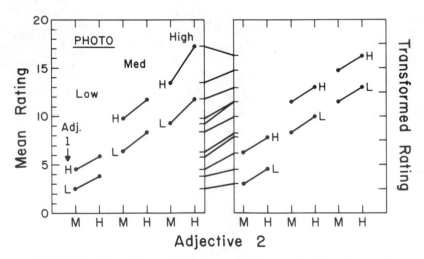

FIG. 17.32. Data of Lampel and Anderson (1968) are on the left, and rescaled data are on the right. Note that the monotonic transformation removes both the adjective-by-adjective interaction and the photo-by-adjective interaction. Therefore, these data do *not* provide convincing evidence that different operations or stages were involved. From Birnbaum (1980b).

found that eliminates the photo by adjective interactions and retains parallelism for the adjective-by-adjective interaction, one cannot use the lack of interaction between the adjectives in the raw data as evidence that the photo-by-adjective interactions are "real."

Indeed, such a monotonic transformation exists, as shown in the right of Fig. 17.32. Note that after transformation, all three adjective-by-adjective interactions are parallel (which would be deemed an "improvement" over the raw data). Furthermore, and most important, all three sets of transformed curves are congruent (differ by an additive translation), showing that the photo-by-adjective interactions have been simultaneously removed. This analysis shows that lack of significant interaction between two variables does not "validate" the "reality" of a significant interaction. The data are consistent with the hypothesis that the adjectives combine with each other by the same process as they combine with the photo. Therefore, there is no evidence for two operations in these data. (It should be mentioned that the photo-alone data, which are not presented here, would be predicted to cross the other curves according to either averaging theory under discussion and are therefore not diagnostic as to the transformation.)

These results call into serious doubt Anderson's (1974b) interpretation that the process of combining this information proceeded by "stages" in which the adjectives were first integrated by one operation and then combined with the photos by a second operation. Such a stage theory is certainly possible, but nothing in the data of Lampel and Anderson (1968) requires such an interpretation.

This discussion is not presented to argue that the divergent photo-by-adjective interaction is not "real." The assumption that adjectives do not interact is itself highly doubtful. By analogy with the results of Birnbaum (1974a), it seems likely that if a proper scale-free experiment was performed, the photo-by-adjective interaction would be confirmed. The purpose of this methodological discussion is to show that lack of significant interaction does not "validate" the response scale.

It may seem puzzling that Lampel and Anderson (1968) failed to find an adjective-by-adjective interaction. However, the dashed box in the left of Fig. 17.26 shows that the domain of their experiment was small in comparison with the domain of Birnbaum's (1974a) experiments. Apparently, the results of Birnbaum (1974a) would imply a small interaction for the small domain studied by Lampel and Anderson (1968).

A Tale of Two Ancient Philosophers

This comparison of research ranges calls to mind the tale of the two ancient Greek philosophers arguing over the shape of the earth. One of them made careful observations of plumb-bob lines separated by 100 paces. There was no evidence that the plumb-bob lines were not parallel, as they seemed to point to the same star at the same time. This parallelism was taken as evidence that the world was flat and that the star was very far away. The other scientist travelled partway across the world and discovered that plumb-bob lines do *not* point to the same stars on the same occasions. Rather, the farther apart two plumb-bob lines are, the more they appear to diverge. He concluded that the earth is spherical, that the stars are very far away, and used his measurements to estimate the size of the earth.

During the argument some passers-by provided their suggestions: "Perhaps you are both right, and the earth changes shape depending on how one does the experiment." "Perhaps you are both wrong, and the stars are not very far away." Today, we feel both flat and spherical models deserve credit—but we do not suppose that the earth changes shape or that the stars are near. The flat-earth model has proven very useful for local surveying in small regions, and the spherical model has proven useful for navigation. Both models have since given way to more refined models of the earth. More general theories encompass early approximations, rather than refute them.

To return to the problem of impression formation, it seems reasonable to suppose that Anderson's failure to detect or take seriously the divergent interaction resulted from his use of a small variation in absolute range (difference between highest and lowest scale values in a trial). For example, a 2^6 design has 64 cells, yet only two cells have a zero within-set range (111111 and 222222). All other cells in the experiment have the *same* within-set range. If within-set range is an important determinant of the interaction, it should be clear that designs employing a small number of levels are not optimal for detecting deviations. Also, Anderson may have selected response procedures that tend to produce parallel data, thereby choosing the model in advance and finding the rescaling or response scale to agree with that model. Finally, it should be mentioned that Anderson's data do show divergent interactions.

Anderson has argued that the apparent parallelism for adjectives helped validate the rating scale and thereby form part of the argument concerning the "bias" in magnitude estimation. However, it should now be apparent that the skeptic can disregard the experiment of Anderson (1962) as a nondiagnostic study that lacked power to reveal the nonparallelism. It is therefore irrelevant to the issue of the linearity of category ratings.

Manipulation of the Interaction

Birnbaum, Wong, and Wong (1976) found divergent interactions for impression formation and also for a related task in which the judge was asked to evaluate used cars. In this study, if one adjective is bad, a person receives a low rating and the other adjectives have less effect. Similarly, if one estimate of a car's value is low, the other estimates have less effect on a buyer's opinion. Birnbaum and Stegner (1979) manipulated the interaction and actually reversed it from divergent to convergent by instructing the judges to identify with either the buyer or seller of the car. When asked to take the seller's point of view (judge the lowest acceptable selling price), the *higher* estimate appeared to have greater weight. When asked to take the buyer's point of view (judge the highest price the buyer should pay), the *lower* estimate appeared to have greater weight.

A portion of the data from Birnbaum and Stegner's (1979) Experiment 5 is shown in Fig. 17.33. Judgments of the value of cars are plotted against the

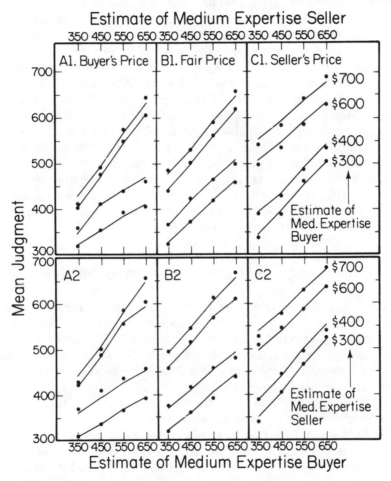

FIG. 17.33. Mean judgment of the value of used cars as a function of estimates from two mechanics who examined the cars. Panels on the left show judgments of the "highest price the buyer should pay"; panels on the right are for "lowest price seller should accept"; center panel shows judgments of "fair price." Note that curves diverge in left and center panels, and they converge in right panels. However, one cannot attribute the nonparallelism or change in shape of the curves to changes in the judgment function, for the rank order changes systematically across panels, as predicted by the configural-weight model (lines). From Birnbaum and Stegner (1979).

estimate from one source, with a separate curve for each estimate from the other source. Buyer's price and fair-price judgments show a divergent interaction, whereas seller's price judgments show a convergent interaction.

Can the results of Birnbaum and Stegner (1978, Exp. 5) be explained by assuming that the judgment function, J, depends on the judges' point of view? Recall that such an interpretation was compatible with the changing interaction in the grading on the curve experiment described in Section D (Figs. 17.19, 17.20, and 17.21). The judgment function cannot explain the change in interaction in Fig. 17.33. Note that the rank order of the points is systematically *different* in different panels. For example, from the buyer's point of view, a car with estimates of $450 and $400 is judged higher than a car with estimates of $650 and $300, whereas from the seller's point of view, the $650 and $300 car is judged about $100 higher than the $450 and $400 car. Because the rank order changes systematically, the effects of points of view *cannot* be explained in terms of a change in J. A simple configural-weight model provides a good description, using a single parameter to represent point of view, as shown by the lines representing predictions of this model (see Birnbaum & Stegner, 1979).

In order to claim understanding, one must be able to identify variables that control the effect to be explained. Thus, the ability to manipulate and even reverse the interaction by Birnbaum and Stegner (1979) goes a long way toward clarifying the process of information integration.

G.   A BRIEF DISCUSSION OF RELATED THEORIES

Throughout this chapter, an attempt has been made to compare present developments with the theories of others. Parducci's range-frequency theory, discussed in Section A, was extended and elaborated in Section D. Schneider's work on the ratio-difference question is compatible with the review of that issue in Section B. Anderson's theories of the size-weight illusion, impression formation, and functional measurement are dealt with in Section F.

Several other theoretical issues, however, deserve further discussion. This section briefly reviews theories of Rule and Curtis, Eisler, Montgomery, and Marks. Rule and Curtis have a theory of estimation of "magnitudes" and "differences" that has some points of agreement and some points of disagreement with the present theory. Eisler and Montgomery have treated the relationship between category judgment and magnitude estimation in terms of the variability of the judgments on the two scales. As Montgomery has noted, their findings can be represented in terms of a single underlying scale of sensation, in agreement with the present approach. Eisler and Marks proposed that psychophysical scales change from situation to situation, depending on the subject's task. This section shows that evidence cited to argue for changes in psychophysical scales can be explained by theories that retain the premise of scale convergence.

Magnitude-Estimation Theory of Rule and Curtis

Rule and Curtis (this volume) assume that "differences" can be represented by subtraction. The heart of their theory can be stated as follows:

$$\mathbf{M}_i = J_M(s_i) \tag{G.1}$$

$$\mathbf{MD}_{ij} = J_M(s_i - s_j) \tag{G.2}$$

where $\mathbf{M}_i$ and $\mathbf{MD}_{ij}$ are magnitude estimations of single stimuli and of "differences," and J_M is the output function for magnitude estimation. In keeping with Attneave's (1962) theory, the J_M function, which Rule and Curtis acknowledge to depend on situational factors and individual differences, is assumed to represent (on the average) the inverse of the psychophysical function for numbers.

   Their theory, in agreement with stimulus scale convergence, assumes that the psychophysical function, $s = H(\Phi)$, is independent of the task to judge "differences" or "magnitudes" and that the output function is similarly independent of these tasks. Approximating the functions H and J by power functions, Rule and Curtis represented their data as follows:

$$\mathbf{M}_i = a_M \Phi_i^{km} + b_M \tag{G.3}$$

$$\mathbf{MD}_{ij} = a_D (\Phi_i^k - \Phi_j^k)^m + b_D \tag{G.4}$$

Rule and Curtis (this volume) have estimated m from Eq. G.4 and found values between 1.1 and 2.1 with an average value of 1.47. Exponents from magnitude estimation of single stimuli are found to be close to 1.47 times larger than exponents for k derived from Eq. G.4, consistent with Eq. G.3. Furthermore, Rule and Curtis (1973) have observed that exponents for number (estimated as an input function) are close to the reciprocal of 1.47, consistent with the theory of Attneave that magnitude estimation represents cross-modality matching of numbers to stimuli and that subjective value of number is a negatively accelerated function of objective number.

   In their assumptions that "differences" can be represented by subtraction, that J_M is positively accelerated, and that H is independent of the task, Rule and Curtis are in agreement with the present approach. However, they (Rule & Curtis, 1980) challenged the conclusions of Veit (1978) that subtraction can be used to represent both "ratios" and "differences" of the darkness of papers that vary in reflectance. They noted that actual ratios and differences can be monotonically related in a small, finite factorial design with a small ratio of the largest to smallest scale values. Birnbaum (1980a) has shown however, that an extension of the Rule and Curtis theory to "ratio" and "difference" judgments could not account for the data of nine experiments, using an exponent of magnitude estimations of "ratios" in the range of values cited by Rule and Curtis (this volume).

As shown in the right of Fig. 17.4, even with $m = 1.47$, $(s_j/s_i)^m$ is not monotonically related to $s_j - s_i$ in an evenly spaced seven-by-seven design with largest "ratio" judgment of 7. Birnbaum (1980a) found that for two operations to characterize the data in Fig. 17.5, one would have to reject the assumed invariance of m and use large values of m for which the power function approximates the exponential. Further comparisons and contrasts with the views of Rule and Curtis are given by Birnbaum (1980a) and Veit (1980).

Eisler's Transformation Theories

In response to the analyses and conclusions of Birnbaum (1978), reviewed in Section C, Eisler (1978) presented two theories that would allow one to retain the ratio model for judgments of "ratios." These theories, like the stage theory of Marks (1979; this volume), assume internal transformations of scales depending on the instructions given the subject.

There are two versions of Eisler's (1978) transformation theories. In one version, the subject uses only a single operation (as in the indeterminacy theory in Table 17.1) but can apply a nonlinear transformation to the scale values after this operation for "differences." In the other version, the subject uses *two* operations and a transformation that *precedes* the "difference" operation. When the ratio model is used to represent the operation for judgments of "ratios," both theories would use the logarithmic function for the transformation (T) and would predict the following:

Task	Model	
R:	A/B	(G.5)
D:	$T(A) - T(B)$	(G.6)
RR:	A/B/C/D	(G.7)
RD:	$\dfrac{T(A) - T(B)}{T(C) - T(D)}$	(G.8)
DR:	$[T(A) - T(B)] - [T(C) - T(D)]$	(G.9)
DD:	$T\left[\dfrac{T(A) - T(B)}{T(C) - T(D)}\right]$	(G.10)

In each case, the response is assumed to be a linear function of the value listed under model.

Note that the theory predicts that **DD** and **DR** should have *different* rank orders and that **DD** and **RD** should have the *same* order, contrary to the data. To handle this problem, Eisler (1978) suggested that because $[T(A) - T(B)]/[T(C) - T(D)]$ could be negative, subjects "reinterpret" the **DD** task in order to avoid the problem of negative arguments for the log. According to Eisler (1978), evidence for such a "reinterpretation" might be found by comparing the standard deviations for the

DR and **DD** tasks. However, no systematic difference appeared for the Hagerty and Birnbaum (1978) data (Birnbaum, 1979). Furthermore, in the experiment on darkness reviewed in Section C, subjects in the **DD** and **DR** tasks were instructed to compare the darker of the (A, B) pair to the lighter. This procedure guarantees that for the experimental design used, the ratio of differences (Expression G.10) for **DD** will always be ≥ 0, thereby eliminating part of Eisler's (1978) rationale for the "reinterpretation" of **DD**.

Eisler (1978) remarked that Birnbaum's (1978) theory makes use of transformations (for the judgment function). He argues that the logarithmic internal transformation in his theory is as complex as the exponential output function for "ratios" in Birnbaum's theory. However, the judgment functions in Birnbaum's theory do not affect the rank order of the data, so at the ordinal level the judgment functions can be disregarded, whereas nonlinear internal transformations will alter rank order. Furthermore, Birnbaum and Veit's (1974a) theory of the judgment function predicts that the range of examples will affect the response range. Finally, one has to acknowledge judgment functions to account for the changes that can be induced by means of the context (Sections A and D). Additional comments on various details of Eisler's (1978) transformation theories are given in Birnbaum (1979).

In summary, the transformation theories seem unattractive, not only because of the postulated internal transformation, but also because of the "reinterpretation" argument that must be made in order to rectify an otherwise incorrect prediction of the theory, and thereby make the theory ordinally equivalent to the subtractive theory.

Stage Theory of Marks

Marks (1979) proposed a stage theory of loudness that has some similarities to Eisler's theory. The essentials of his theory can be summarized as follows:

$$\mathbf{M}_i = J_{\mathbf{M}}[L_i] \tag{G.11}$$

$$\mathbf{MT}_{ij} = J_{\mathbf{T}}[L_i + L_j] \tag{G.12}$$

$$\mathbf{MD}_{ij} = J_{\mathbf{D}}[T(L_i) - T(L_j)] \tag{G.13}$$

$$\mathbf{MDT}_{ijkl} = J_{\mathbf{D}}[T(L_i + L_j) - T(L_k + L_l)] \tag{G.14}$$

where $\mathbf{M}_i$, $\mathbf{MT}_{ij}$, $\mathbf{MD}_{ij}$, and $\mathbf{MDT}_{ijkl}$ are "magnitude estimations" of the single stimuli, magnitude estimations of "total loudness" of multicomponent (or binaurally presented) tones, magnitude estimations of "differences" between two tones, and magnitude estimations of the "difference" between two "summated" loudnesses, respectively. L_i is the subjective loudness of a tone or component, $J_{\mathbf{M}}$, $J_{\mathbf{T}}$, and $J_{\mathbf{D}}$ are monotonic output (judgment) functions for magnitude estimation in these tasks, and T represents the transformation between the so-called "L"

scale and what Marks (1979) terms the "D" scale of loudness, where $D = T(L)$. In Marks (1979) paper, T is approximated by the square-root function. (Eisler [1978] would represent T with the log function.) Marks argues that by averaging exponents across different experiments, the J_M function can be assumed to be a similarity function. However, he concludes that the J_T function is negatively accelerated (Marks approximates it by using a power function with exponent of $\frac{2}{3}$), and he presents evidence that the J_D function is positively accelerated for magnitude estimations of "differences." This agrees with Rule and Curtis (this volume), who approximate J_D by a power function with an average exponent of about 1.5.

The theory of Marks (1979) represents binaural and multicomponent summation by the arithmetic addition operation; it represents "difference" (and perhaps also "ratios") by the subtraction operation. However, in order to do this, three systematically different output transformations are required for magnitude estimations, and two different input transformations are used for loudness. (Actually, the number of transformations and output functions is still larger when one considers Marks' treatment of loudness addition within the critical band width, which is not treated here.)

Marks (1979) theory seems unduly complicated to account for the data he reviews. First, as is shown later, it is possible to retain a single scale of loudness for both "differences" and loudness "summation." Therefore, the T transformation appears unnecessary. Second, it can be shown that it is possible to explain the data using a single J.

A simpler theory that preserves scale convergence can be written as follows:

$$\mathbf{M}_i = J_M[s_i] \tag{G.15}$$

$$\mathbf{MT}_{ij} = J_T[\Psi_{ij}] \tag{G.16}$$

$$\mathbf{MD}_{ij} = J_D[s_i - s_j] \tag{G.17}$$

$$\mathbf{MDT}_{ijkl} = J_D[\Psi_{ij} - \Psi_{kl}] \tag{G.18}$$

where Ψ_{ij} is the overall loudness experience produced by s_i and s_j, and $\Psi_{ij} = C(s_i, s_j)$ represents the combination function for loudness "summation." This theory preserves scale convergence at the expense of representing combination by a *nonadditive* function, as in Birnbaum et al. (1971). It also allows one to retain the same theory for all of the J functions in Eqs. G.15 through G.18.

For simplicity and comparability with the work of others who approximate data by power functions, a rough approximation could be stated as follows:

$$\Psi_{ij} = \sqrt{s_i^2 + s_j^2} \tag{G.19}$$

where Ψ_{ij} is the "total loudness" of tones having scale values s_i and s_j. Equation G.19 is the equation for the length of the sum of two orthogonal vectors. (Equation G.19 could be generalized to include the angle between the vectors or replaced by a similar function predicting a convergent interaction to provide a more accurate representation.) Figure 17.34 shows Ψ_{ij} plotted as a function of s_i, with a separate curve for each of several values of s_j, according to Eq. G.19. Note that this theory of loudness does not predict parallelism, but predicts a convergent interaction, similar to that obtained by Marks (1979, and this volume).

It may be possible to assume that all of the output functions are governed by an exponent of about 1.5, consistent with the findings of Rule and Curtis (this volume). Note that Eqs. G.15, G.16, and G.17 become:

$$\mathbf{M}_i = as_i^{1.5} \tag{G.20}$$

$$\mathbf{MT}_{ij} = a_\mathbf{T}[(s_i^2 + s_j^2)^{.5}]^{1.5} \tag{G.21}$$

$$\mathbf{MD}_{ij} = a_\mathbf{D}[s_i - s_j]^{1.5} + b_\mathbf{D} \tag{G.22}$$

It follows that under Marks' (1979) analysis, the output function for loudness summation would be .75, so the $\frac{4}{3}$ exponent empirically obtained by Marks (1979) in his equation

$$\mathbf{MT}_{ij}^{4/3} = L_i + L_j \tag{G.23}$$

is *predicted* by this theory because Eq. G.21 becomes $\mathbf{MT}_{ij}^{4/3} = s_i^2 + s_j^2$.

Furthermore, the relationship between Marks' "L"scale and his "D" scale would also be *predicted* by this theory to be the square function in this approximation, consistent with the conclusion reached by Marks (1979). In Eq. G.21, s_i corresponds to D and s_i^2 to L. It should also be noted that the present theory handles "differences between summated loudnesses" without the postulated

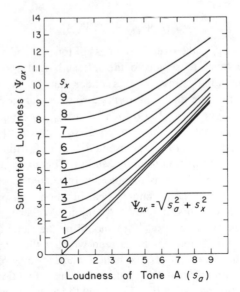

FIG. 17.34. Theoretical curves for loudness "summation" based on Pythagorean rather than arithmetic addition. Note that the difference in overall loudness due to variation of one component is less when the other component is loud than when it is soft. From Birnbaum (1980d).

internal T transformation, representing them as monotonically related to subjective differences in Ψ of Eq. G.19:

$$\mathbf{MDT}_{ijkl} = J_\mathbf{D}[\Psi_{ij} - \Psi_{kl}] \tag{G.24}$$

where $\mathbf{MDT}_{ijkl}$ is the magnitude estimation of the "difference" in loudness between two "summated" loudness experiences.

It is not seriously suggested that these power functions are the correct theoretical representation. They are used only for simplicity and comparability with the work of Marks. Any complete theory must be able to predict contextual effects on the J functions. However, the foregoing theory, oversimplified as it is, provides at least as good a representation of the data reviewed by Marks' (1979) as his theory (Eqs. G.11–G.14). Marks (1979) theory requires two scales (D and L) and three functions for magnitude estimation. It has *no theory to predict* the relationship between D and L and *no theory to explain* why $J_\mathbf{T}$ should be negatively accelerating, $J_\mathbf{D}$ should be positively accelerating, and $J_\mathbf{M}$ should be linear. The suggested theory (Eqs. G.15–G.18) uses only one scale (s_i) and one theory for the J function of magnitude estimation.

Loudness Combination

Falmagne, Iverson, and Marcovici (1979) developed a theory of loudness discrimination and combination. They presented the observer with two binaural tone pairs, (a, x) and (b, y), and asked the observer to report which pair produced the louder experience. They concluded that their data can be represented by the equations:

$$\Psi_{ax} = s_a + s_x \tag{G.25}$$

$$\mathbf{P}_{ax;by} = F[T(\Psi_{ax}) - T(\Psi_{by})] \tag{G.26}$$

where Ψ_{ax} is the overall loudness of tones a and x, s_a and s_x are the loudnesses of the tones presented to the left and right ears, $\mathbf{P}_{ax;by}$ is the proportion of responses indicating (a, x) is louder than (b, y), and F is a cumulative density function. Note that T performs a role similar to that in Marks' theory.

Falmagne et al. (1979) found that $\mathbf{P}_{ax;ay}$ decreases as a function of a, indicaing either that Ψ_{ax} does not equal $s_a + s_x$ or that T is negatively accelerated. Falmagne et al. (1979) represented T as a logarithmic function (rather than as the square-root function used by Marks). This interpretation, they noted, represents choice probabilities as monotonically related to subjective ratios rather than as differences. If the psychophysical function is also assumed to be a power function, their theory implies a "conjoint Weber's law," in which choice probabilities for (a, x) vs. (b, y) should be the same as (ta, tx) vs. (tb, ty) for any value of t. It remains to be seen whether the conjoint Weber's law will prove more than a rough approximation when tested over a wider stimulus range.

The finding that $\mathbf{P}_{ax;ay}$ decreases as a function of a is consistent with the interaction shown in Fig. 17.34 and the assumption that T is an identity function.

Such an interpretation would be hard to discriminate from the theory of Falmagne et al. (1979) on the basis of their experiments.

Therefore, it may be simpler to represent loudness summation by vector addition rather than arithmetic addition. Such a representation permits one to retain scale convergence for both input (psychophysical) and output (judgmental) functions, and seems therefore simpler and greater in explanatory power than Marks' theory, which requires two scales, three output functions, and has no theory to explain their relationship. Such a representation would also predict the major result of Falmagne et al. (1979) in terms of a single scale of sensation and a subtractive theory for stimulus comparison and discrimination.

A Transformation-Theory Account of Impression Formation

In Section F, the additive (or parallel-averaging) model of impression formation was found to be inconsistent with ratings of "combined" likeableness and "differences" in likeableness if the stimulus scale convergence criterion was assumed. It seems reasonable to ask if the transformation theories of Marks and Eisler could be extended in a consistent fashion (using the same T) to encompass impression formation.

The following transformation theory can describe the results of Birnbaum (1974a):

$$\mathbf{D}_{ij} = J_{\mathbf{D}}[T^*(s_i) - T^*(s_j)] \tag{G.27}$$

$$\mathbf{C}_{ij} = J_{\mathbf{C}}[s_i + s_j] \tag{G.28}$$

$$\mathbf{DC}_{ijkl} = J_{\mathbf{DC}}[T^*(s_i + s_j) - T^*(s_k + s_l)] \tag{G.29}$$

where $J_{\mathbf{D}}$ and $J_{\mathbf{DC}}$ are approximately linear, but $J_{\mathbf{C}}$ is positively accelerated, and T^* is positively accelerated. According to the stage theories of Marks and Eisler, however, all of the J functions should be negatively accelerating, and furthermore, T^* should be negatively accelerating. Thus, the stage theory cannot describe "differences" in terms of the *same* T^* transformation to salvage both the additive models of loudness "summation" and impression information. These results, therefore, put the transformation theory in the post hoc position of requiring different transformations for every situation. As shown in Section F, a coherent account of the data for impression formation can be given in terms of a single scale of likeableness for the adjectives and the assumption that all of the J functions are approximately linear.

Psychophysical Variability

Eisler (1963) has given an account of the relationship between category ratings and magnitude estimations in terms of the variability of the two scales. This approach is reviewed by Montgomery (this volume), who notes that the results can be given a different interpretation from Eisler's.

Eisler's interpretation can be diagrammed as follows:

$$T[H] \quad s_i^* \longrightarrow \mathbf{C}_i \longleftarrow \epsilon_i^*$$

$$\Phi_i \quad \nearrow \atop \searrow \qquad (G.30)$$

$$H \quad s_i \longrightarrow \mathbf{M}_i \longleftarrow \epsilon_i$$

where H is the psychophysical function, T is the transformation, s and s^* are the two scales of subjective value, and ϵ_i^* and ϵ_i are the error terms, representing variability. According to Eisler's early development, the variance of ϵ_i^* was assumed constant with respect to s_i^*, but the variance of ϵ_i was assumed to be linearly related to s_i. This was interpreted as a subjective Weber's law.

An alternative interpretation can be given as follows:

$$\epsilon_i$$
$$\Phi_i \xrightarrow{\quad H \quad} s_i \begin{array}{c} \overset{J_\mathbf{C}}{\nearrow} \mathbf{C}_i \\ \underset{J_\mathbf{M}}{\searrow} \mathbf{M}_i \end{array} \qquad (G.31)$$

This theory (a special case of that discussed by Birnbaum, 1979) uses only one scale of sensation and one error term, but different $J_\mathbf{C}$ and $J_\mathbf{M}$ functions for category rating and magnitude estimation in different contexts. This theory leads to the general psychophysical differential equation used by Eisler and Montgomery. It predicts that when the stimuli are scaled in accordance with Thurstone's law of categorical judgment, the estimated scale values should be independent of stimulus distribution or the task to use category ratings or magnitude estimations. Parducci (1965, 1974) has shown that Thurstone scales are nearly independent of stimulus distribution. Montgomery (this volume) has shown that although the relationship between category ratings and magnitude estimations differs for different individuals, the data can be well-approximated by the theory of one scale, assuming that the variance of ϵ_i is independent of s_i, that $J_\mathbf{C}$ is approximately linear for most subjects (for his stimulus spacing), and that $J_\mathbf{M}$ is nonlinear and varies for different individuals.

Birnbaum (1979) noted that Thurstone's simplest case (equal variances) could be applicable to matrices of both category ratings and magnitude estimations. Let $\mathbf{P}_{ij}$ and $\mathbf{Q}_{ik}$ be the cumulative proportion of responses to stimulus i less than or equal to category "j" or magnitude-estimation response "X_k," respectively. Then, one can write:

$$\mathbf{P}_{ij} = F[(s_i - t_j)/a] \qquad (G.32)$$

$$\mathbf{Q}_{ik} = F[(s_i - u_k)/b] \qquad (G.33)$$

where F is a cumulative density function (e.g., normal). If there is only a single error term, as in Expression G.31, and if the variance of ϵ_i is independent of s_i, then a can be set equal to b equal to 1.0. The relationship between t_j and j describes J_C; the relationship between u_k and X_k describes J_M. In this special case (where $a = b$), it should be possible to find a spacing of magnitude estimations (X_k) for each subject, such that $P_{ij} = Q_{ij}$. Montgomery (this volume) has shown that this prediction may be a reasonable approximation.

In conclusion, the assumption that there is a single scale of sensation with a single source of subjective variability provides a reasonable theoretical representation of the empirical relationship between means and standard deviations of category ratings and magnitude estimations. Analyses of "differences," "ratios," and "totals" may provide further insight into the loci of psychophysical and judgmental variability.

CONCLUDING COMMENTS

This chapter offers the following resolutions to the measurement controversies:

1. Overt judgments can be regarded as a monotonic function of subjective value, where the nature of the monotonic function depends lawfully on the stimulus and response distributions. The range and frequency distribution of both stimuli and responses affects the nature of this function.

2. Judgments of "ratios" and "differences" for most continua can be represented by the subtractive model using the same scale values for both tasks:

$$\mathbf{R} = J_\mathbf{R}[A - B]$$

$$\mathbf{D} = J_\mathbf{D}[A - B]$$

3. Judgments of "ratios of ratios," "differences of ratios," "ratios of differences," and "differences of differences" can be represented by the subtractive theory:

$$\mathbf{RR} = J_\mathbf{RR}[(A - B) - (C - D)]$$

$$\mathbf{DR} = J_\mathbf{DR}[(A - B) - (C - D)]$$

$$\mathbf{RD} = J_\mathbf{RD}[(A - B)/(C - D)]$$

$$\mathbf{DD} = J_\mathbf{DD}[(A - B) - (C - D)]$$

4. The judgment functions are approximately linear for category ratings and approximately exponential for magnitude estimation when the stimuli are geometrically spaced, the category-response examples are equally spaced, and the magnitude-estimation examples are geometrically spaced.

5. Scale values estimated from the subtractive theory of (within-mode) stimulus comparison appear largely independent of stimulus spacing.

6. The judgment function in information-combination experiments appears to depend on the distribution of subjective combinations.

7. Scale values estimated from cross-modality comparison and combination depend on the stimulus distribution.

8. One should neither select a standardized method for conducting experimental research on the basis of a priori considerations, nor attempt to "avoid" contextual effects by holding context fixed to some arbitrary value. Instead, it seems reasonable to manipulate procedures and contexts systematically and to base generalizations on empirically established laws of judgment.

9. The fit of a model does not simultaneously validate the response scale and model. Previous conclusions that impression formation and the size-weight illusion obey a simple averaging model (additive) were based on inappropriate conclusions from functional measurement. Methods involving scale convergence and the scale-free test should be applied to provide more strenuous tests of algebraic models.

10. Theories assuming that measurements of subjective value transcend the tasks from which they were derived should be preferred to theories assuming different scales. In particular, by representing loudness additivity with Pythagorean addition rather than arithmetic addition, it may be possible to retain scale convergence for stimulus combination and comparison. Similarly, by representing impression formation with a configural model, it is possible to retain the premise of scale convergence for combination and comparison.

Despite generations of controversy concerning the theoretical representation of subjective value and even the appropriate models and methods for measurement of subjective value, a number of empirical findings emerge that show lawful regularity. The lawfulness of stimulus comparison and combination and the regularity of contextual effects constitute results that must be explained by any viable theory. The premises just listed may provide the beginnings of a coherent solution to the controversies of psychological measurement.

ACKNOWLEDGMENTS

Preparation of this chapter was supported in part by the Research Board of the University of Illinois. Thanks are due Barbara Mellers for her valuable assistance and advice.

REFERENCES

Anderson, N. H. Application of an additive model to impression formation. *Science,* 1962, *138,* 817–818.

Anderson, N. H. Functional measurement and psychophysical judgment. *Psychological Review,* 1970, *77,* 153–170.

Anderson, N. H. Cross-task validation of functional measurement. *Perception & Psychophysics,* 1972, *12,* 389–395.

Anderson, N. H. Cross-task validation of functional measurement using judgments of total magnitude. *Journal of Experimental Psychology,* 1974, *102,* 226–233. (a)

Anderson, N. H. Information integration theory: A brief survey. In D. H. Krantz, R. C. Atkinson, R. D. Luce, & P. Suppes (Eds.), *Contemporary developments in mathematical psychology* (Vol. 2). San Francisco: Freeman, 1974. (b)

Anderson, N. H. Note on functional measurement and data analysis. *Perception & Psychophysics,* 1977, *21,* 201–215.

Anderson, N. H. Algebraic rules and psychological measurement. *American Scientist,* 1979, *67,* 555–563.

Attneave, F. Perception and related areas. In S. Koch (Ed.), *Psychology: A study of a science* (Vol. 4). New York: McGraw-Hill, 1962.

Baird, J. C. & Noma, E. *Fundamentals of scaling and psychophysics.* New York: Wiley, 1978.

Birnbaum, M. H. Morality judgments: Tests of an averaging model. *Journal of Experimental Psychology,* 1972, *93,* 35–42.

Birnbaum, M. H. The devil rides again: Correlation as an index of fit. *Psychological Bulletin,* 1973, *79,* 239–242.

Birnbaum, M. H. The nonadditivity of personality impressions. *Journal of Experimental Psychology,* 1974, *102,* 543–561. (a)

Birnbaum, M. H. Reply to the devil's advocates: Don't confound model testing and measurement. *Psychological Bulletin,* 1974, *81,* 854–859. (b)

Birnbaum, M. H. Using contextual effects to derive psychophysical scales. *Perception & Psychophysics,* 1974, *15,* 89–96. (c)

Birnbaum, M. H. Expectancy and judgment. In F. Restle, R. Shiffrin, N. J. Castellan, H. Lindman, & D. Pisoni (Eds.), *Cognitive theory* (Vol. 1). Hillsdale, N.J.: Lawrence Erlbaum Associates, 1975.

Birnbaum, M. H. Differences and ratios in psychological measurement. In N. J. Castellan & F. Restle (Eds.), *Cognitive theory* (Vol. 3). Hillsdale, N.J.: Lawrence Erlbaum Associates, 1978.

Birnbaum, M. H. Reply to Eisler: On the subtractive theory of stimulus comparison. *Perception & Psychophysics,* 1979, *25,* 150–156.

Birnbaum, M. H. A comparison of two theories of "ratio" and "difference" judgments. *Journal of Experimental Psychology: General,* 1980, *109,* 304–319. (a)

Birnbaum, M. H. *Issues in functional measurement.* Unpublished manuscript, 1980. (Available from author, Dept. of Psychology, University of Illinois, 603 E. Daniel, Champaign, IL 61820) (b)

Birnbaum, M. H. *Systextual design.* Unpublished manuscript, 1980. (Available from author) (c)

Birnbaum, M. H. *Toward a coherent theory of psychophysical judgment.* Unpublished manuscript, 1980. (Available from author) (d)

Birnbaum, M. H., & Elmasian, R. Loudness ratios and differences involve the same psychophysical operation. *Perception & Psychophysics,* 1977, *22,* 383–391.

Birnbaum, M. H., Kobernick, M., & Veit, C. T. Subjective correlation and the size-numerosity illusion. *Journal of Experimental Psychology,* 1974, *102,* 537–539.

Birnbaum, M. H., & Mellers, B. A. Measurement and the mental map. *Perception & Psychophysics,* 1978, *23,* 403–408.

Birnbaum, M. H., & Mellers, B. A. *Context effects in category rating and magnitude estimation.* Unpublished manuscript, 1980. (Available from author) (a)

Birnbaum, M. H., & Mellers, B. A. *Context effects in cross-modality comparison and combination.* Unpublished manuscript, 1980. (Available from author) (b)

Birnbaum, M. H., Parducci, A., & Gifford, R. K. Contextual effects in information integration. *Journal of Experimental Psychology,* 1971, *88,* 158–170.

Birnbaum, M. H., & Stegner, S. E. Source credibility: Expertise, bias, and the judge's point of view. *Journal of Personality and Social Psychology,* 1979, *37,* 48–74.

Birnbaum, M. H., & Veit, C. T. Judgmental illusion produced by contrast with expectancy. *Perception & Psychophysics*, 1973, *13*, 149-152.

Birnbaum, M. H., & Veit, C. T. Scale convergence as a criterion for rescaling: Information integration with difference, ratio, and averaging tasks. *Perception & Psychophysics*, 1974, *15*, 7-15. (a)

Birnbaum, M. H., & Veit, C. T. Scale-free tests of an additive model for the size-weight illusion. *Perception & Psychophysics*, 1974, *16*, 276-282. (b)

Birnbaum, M. H., Wong, R., & Wong, L. Combining information from sources that vary in credibility. *Memory & Cognition*, 1976, *4*, 330-336.

Brunswik, E. *Perception and the representative design of experiments*. Berkeley: University of California Press, 1956.

Curtis, D. W., & Rule, S. J. Judgments of average lightness and darkness: A further consideration of inverse attributes. *Perception & Psychophysics*, 1978, *24*, 343-348.

Eisler, H. On the problem of category scales in psychophysics. *Scandinavian Journal of Psychology*, 1962, *3*, 81-87.

Eisler, H. A general differential equation in psychophysics: Derivation and empirical test. *Scandinavian Journal of Psychology*, 1963, *4*, 265-272.

Eisler, H. On the ability to estimate differences: A note on Birnbaum's subtractive model. *Perception & Psychophysics*, 1978, *24*, 185-189.

Elmasian, R., & Birnbaum, M. H. *A harmonious note on pitch*. Unpublished manuscript, 1979. (Available from author)

Falmagne, J. C., Iverson, G., & Marcovici, S. Binaural "loudness" summation: Probabilistic theory and data. *Psychological Review*, 1979, *86*, 25-43.

Feldman, J., & Baird, J. C. Magnitude estimation of multidimensional stimuli. *Perception & Psychophysics*, 1971, *10*, 418-422.

Hagerty, M., & Birnbaum, M. H. Nonmetric tests of ratio vs. subtractive theories of stimulus comparison. *Perception & Psychophysics*, 1978, *24*, 121-129.

Jones, C., & Aronson, E. Attribution of fault to a rape victim as a function of the respectability of the victim. *Journal of Personality and Social Psychology*, 1973, *26*, 415-419.

Krantz, D. H. Magnitude estimations and cross-modality matching. *Journal of Mathematical Psychology*, 1972, *9*, 168-199.

Krantz, D. H., Luce, R. D., Suppes, D., & Tversky, A. *Foundations of measurement*. New York: Academic Press, 1971.

Krantz, D. H., & Tversky, A. Conjoint measurement analysis of composition rules in psychology. *Psychological Review*, 1971, *78*, 151-169.

Krumhansl, C. L. Concerning the applicability of geometric models of similarity to data: The interrelationship between similarity and density. *Psychological Review*, 1978, *85*, 445-463.

Lampel, A. K., & Anderson, N. H. Combining visual and verbal information in an impression-formation task. *Journal of Personality and Social Psychology*, 1968, *9*, 1-6.

Luce, R. D. What sort of measurement is psychophysical measurement? *American Psychologist*, 1972, *27*, 96-106.

Marks, L. E. On scales of sensation: Prolegomena to any future psychophysics that will be able to come forth as a science. *Perception & Psychophysics*, 1974, *16*, 358-376.

Marks, L. E. A theory of loudness and loudness judgments. *Psychological Review*, 1979, *86*, 256-285.

Mellers, B. A., & Birnbaum, M. H. Context effects in social judgment. Unpublished manuscript, 1980. (Available from author) (a)

Mellers, B. A., & Birnbaum, M. H. Context effects in within-mode stimulus comparison. Unpublished manuscript, 1980. (Available from author) (b)

Nihm, S. D. Polynomial law of sensation. *American Psychologist*, 1976, *31*, 808-809.

Parducci, A. Range-frequency compromise in judgment. *Psychological Monographs*, 1963, *77* (2, Whole No. 565).

Parducci, A. Category judgment: A range-frequency model. *Psychological Review*, 1965, *72*, 407-418.

Parducci, A. The relativism of absolute judgment. *Scientific American*, 1968, *219*, 84-90.

Parducci, A. Contextual effects: A range-frequency analysis. In E. C. Carterette & M. P. Friedman (Eds.), *Handbook of perception* (Vol. 2). New York: Academic Press, 1974.

Parducci, A., & Perrett, L. Category rating scales: Effects of relative spacing and frequency of stimulus values. *Journal of Experimental Psychology*, 1971, *89*, 427-452.

Parker, S., Schneider, B., & Kanow, G. Ratio scale measurement of the perceived lengths of lines. *Journal of Experimental Psychology: Human Perception and Performance*, 1975, *104*, 195-204.

Petrinovich, L. Probabilistic functionalism: A conception of research method. *American Psychologist*, 1979, *34*, 373-390.

Poulton, E. C. The new psychophysics: Six models for magnitude estimation. *Psychological Bulletin*, 1968, *69*, 1-19.

Poulton, E. C. Unwanted range effects from using within-subject experimental design. *Psychological Bulletin*, 1973, *80*, 113-121.

Poulton, E. C. Models for biases in judging sensory magnitude. *Psychological Bulletin*, 1979, *86*, 777-803.

Restle, F. A metric and an ordering on sets. *Psychometrika*, 1959, *24*, 207-220.

Robinson, G. H. Biasing power law exponents in magnitude estimation instructions. *Perception & Psychophysics*, 1976, *19*, 80-84.

Rose, B. J., & Birnbaum, M. H. Judgments of differences and ratios of numerals. *Perception & Psychophysics*, 1975, *18*, 194-200.

Rule, S. J., & Curtis, D. W. Conjoint scaling of subjective number and weight. *Journal of Experimental Psychology*, 1973, *97*, 305-309.

Rule, S. J., & Curtis, D. W. Ordinal properties of subjective ratios and differences. *Journal of Experimental Psychology: General*, 1980, *109*, 296-300.

Sarris, V., & Heineken, E. An experimental test of two mathematical models applied to the size-weight illusion. *Journal of Experimental Psychology: Perception and Performance*, 1976, *2*, 295-298.

Schneider, B., Parker, S., Kanow, G., & Farrell, G. The perceptual basis of loudness ratio judgments. *Perception & Psychophysics*, 1976, *19*, 309-320.

Shepard, R. N. On the status of "direct" psychological measurement. In C. W. Savage (Ed.), *Minnesota studies in the philosophy of science* (Vol. 9). Minneapolis: University of Minnesota Press, 1978.

Sidowski, J. B., & Anderson, N. H. Judgments of city-occupation combinations. *Psychonomic Science*, 1967, *7*, 279-280.

Sjöberg, L. Sensation scales in the size-weight illusion. *Scandinavian Journal of Psychology*, 1969, *10*, 109-112.

Stevens, S. S., & Galanter, E. H. Ratio scales and category scales for a dozen perceptual continua. *Journal of Experimental Psychology*, 1957, *54*, 337-411.

Teghtsoonian, R. On the exponents in Steven's law and the constant in Ekman's law. *Psychological Review*, 1971, *78*, 71-80.

Torgerson, W. S. Quantitative judgment scales. In H. Gulliksen & S. Messick (Eds.), *Psychological scaling: Theory and applications*. New York: Wiley, 1960.

Torgerson, W. S. Distances and ratios in psychological scaling. *Acta Psychologica*, 1961, *19*, 201-205.

Tversky, A. Features of similarity. *Psychological Review*, 1977, *84*, 327-352.

Veit, C. T. Ratio and subtractive processes in psychophysical judgment. *Journal of Experimental Psychology: General*, 1978, *107*, 81-107.

Veit, C. T. Analyzing "ratio" and "difference" judgments: A reply to Rule and Curtis. *Journal of Experimental Psychology: General*, 1980, *109*, 301-303.

Weiss, D. J. Averaging: An empirical validity criterion for magnitude estimation. *Perception & Psychophysics*, 1972, *12*, 385-388.

Author Index

Italics denote pages with bibliographic information.

A

Adams, E. W., 360, *376*
Ajzen, J., 199, *217*
Akesson, C. A., 113, *121*
Anderson, N. H., 27, 28 33, *38,* 56, *68,* 90,
    104, 123, 124, 128, 129, 130, 131, 132, 133,
    134, 135, 136, 137, 138, 139, 141, 142, 143,
    145, *147, 148,* 199, *217,* 310, *313,* 318,
    322, *335,* 348, *350,* 375, *376,* 431, 444,
    449, 451, 452, 453, 454, 455, 456, 463, 464,
    465, 467, 468, 469, 470, *482, 483, 484, 485*
Aronson, E., 212, *217,* 442, *484*
Attneave, F., 27, *38,* 107, 108, *121,* 292, *300,*
    306, *313,* 322, *335,* 341, *350,* 473, *483*
Auerbach, C., 306, *313*

B

Baird, J. C., 173, *174,* 194, *197,* 380, *397,*
    431, 438, *483, 484.*
Banks, W. P., 86, *87,* 110, 112, *121*
Beals, R., 37, *38*
Beck, J., 31, *38,* 48, 64, *68,* 308, *313*
Beck, U., 380, *397*
Berglund, U., 119, *121*
Berlin, I., 52, *68*
Bernoulli, D., 296, *300*
Bertalanffy, Ludwig Von., 80, *87*

Birnbaum, M. H., 4, 28, *38,* 64, *68,* 90, 97,
    104, 110, *121,* 328, *335,* 347, *350,* 358,
    375, *376,* 405, 406, 408, 410, 411, 412, 413,
    414, 415, 416, 417, 418, 419, 420, 421, 422,
    423, 424, 425, 426, 427, 428, 429, 430, 431,
    433, 434, 435, 436, 438, 442, 443, 444, 447,
    448, 449, 453, 454, 455, 457, 458, 459, 460,
    461, 462, 463, 464, 465, 466, 467, 468, 469,
    470, 471, 472, 473, 474, 475, 476, 477, 479,
    480, *483, 484, 485*
Blalock, H. M., 197, *198*
Block, H. D., 361, *376*
Bochner, 79, *87*
Borg, I., 221, 233, 235
Brater, M., 380, *397*
Brehm, J. W., 212, *217*
Brennan, E. M., 167, 170, 171, *174*
Brentano, F., 25, *38*
Brinker, R. P., 77, 80, *87,* 152, 153, 154, 156,
    167, *174,* 180, *198,* 317, 329, 332, *335,*
    392, *397*
Bruinsma, C., 379, *398*
Brunswik, E., 445, *484*
Bunt, A. A., 53, *69*

C

Cain, W. S., 45, 49, 50, 51, *69,* 375, *376,* 381,
    383, 392, 395, *398*

Subject Index